The Emergence of a Black Catholic Community

Morris J. MacGregor

The Emergence of a
Black Catholic Community

St. Augustine's in Washington

The Catholic University of America Press
Washington, D.C.

Copyright © 1999
The Catholic University of America Press
Manufactured in the United States of America
All rights reserved

The paper used in this publication meets the minimum requirements of American National
Standards for Information Science—Permanence of Paper for Printed Library materials.
ANSI Z39.48-1984
∞

Library of Congress Cataloging-in-Publication Data
MacGregor, Morris J., 1931–
    The emergence of a black Catholic community : St. Augustine's in Washington /
    Morris J. MacGregor.
       p.   cm.
    Includes bibliographical references and index.
    1. Afro-American Catholics—Washington (D.C.)—History.   2. St. Augustine
Catholic Church (Washington, D.C.)—History.   I. Title.
BX1407.N4BM33   1999
282'.753—dc21
98-46476
   ISBN 0-8132-0942-0 (alk. paper).
   ISBN 0-8132-0943-9 (pbk. : alk paper)

CONTENTS

ILLUSTRATIONS

The illustration used on p. 24 is courtesy of Mrs. A. P. Spivey; that on p. 112, courtesy of Mrs. Charles Stewart; those on p. 146, (a) and (b) courtesy of the Moorland-Spingarn Archives, Howard University, (c) courtesy of Father Cyprian Davis, O.S.B.; that on p. 255, courtesy of Marilyn Nickels; those on p. 304, (a) courtesy of the *Washington Afro-American*, (b) and (c) courtesy of Dr. Paul Cooke; those on pp. 343, 429, and 481, courtesy of the *Catholic Standard*, the latter a photo by Michael Hoyt; and that on p. 458, (b) courtesy of Mrs. Ruby Robertson. All other illustrations used in this work are from the archives of St. Augustine's parish.

PREFACE

This book is the history of a single parish, but it is also the history of the emergence of the black Catholic community in Washington. For more than 140 years this distinct group has borne witness to the Christian message in a way that, in the words of St. Augustine's present pastor, "liberates people, frees them from all kinds of bondage, gives them a sense of self-worth. It lifts people not only spiritually, but with the power of knowledge and self-empowerment." Yet the effort to create and foster a parish that especially serves the needs of African-American Catholics in the nation's capital has faced formidable challenges.

St. Augustine's is unique among Washington's parishes. Many of its founding members, heirs of a religious tradition stretching back to the early days of Catholicism in colonial Maryland and Virginia, were among those free black residents who had achieved a degree of prosperity and self-reliance despite the harsh climate of the pre–civil War capital. This standing allowed them to assume responsibility for establishing the city's first Catholic parish for African Americans. The parish's second generation of leaders, including a noteworthy number of Washington's so-called Aristocrats of Color, led the first battles for racial justice in the American church. During the early decades of this century, a time when Jim Crow ruled Washington, St. Augustine's imposing edifice housed the city's largest integrated congregation, many of whose members were active participants in the great civil rights movement then aborning. Recent decades have seen a renewed parish

under a series of dynamic pastors and an active parish council institute many important initiatives. St. Augustine's vibrant liturgy serves
as a model for integrating black forms of worship into the Roman rite;
its dynamic social justice programs, a beacon of hope for its inner-city
neighborhood.

Because of its uniqueness, St. Augustine's provides a useful lens
through which to view the many-faceted history of race relations both
in the nation's capital and in the American church, especially the
Archdiocese of Washington (and its predecessor, the Archdiocese of
Baltimore). In fact, every issue touching on race in the past 140 years
has resonated in a special way at St. Augustine's. Without consideration of these issues the day-to-day evolution of the parish would make
little sense. Hence, the parish history that follows also presents in considerable detail a history of race relations in church and state since
the founding of the Federal City.

Organizing this story presented special challenges. Because of the
myriad of parish activities in the last quarter century and the rich
archival resources of St. Augustine's, it was impossible to continue the
chronological account of the earlier sections of the book. The final
chapters adopt a topical approach that, at the risk of confusing the
reader about the sequence of events, tries to provide a realistic picture
of the ferment in a "parish come alive," as the slogan went, with its
multitude of religious and social programs that seemingly involved
every member of the congregation. The plethora of names in text, footnotes, and appendices recognizes this participation, but it also under-
scores the generational continuity within St. Augustine's. To an extent
unique among Washington parishes, members of today's congregation
can recall ancestors who worshipped at St. Augustine's at the turn of
the century and some even back to Civil War times. Beyond informing
the reader about the sources for the story, the footnotes are intended to
encourage those families with a long history in the parish to use these
sources when researching their own heritage in Washington.

The exceptional quality of musical performance at St. Augustine's
over the years and the special contribution made by its musicians to
the parish justify a separate history. Although the establishment of the
choir and its early activities in the 1870s and the formation of a gospel
choir a century later are discussed in the text, a comprehensive history

of music at St. Augustine's appears in an appendix. This placement seeks to elevate, not marginalize, the importance of music in the scheme of things. The early history of choral music at St. Augustine's provides some insight into the cultural interests of Washington's black middle class in the nineteenth century, a largely neglected subject. Its recent history serves as a vivid focal point for the tensions in a congregation trying to define its mission in the post-integration, post–Vatican II era.

Such a large project incurs many debts for its author. I am especially grateful to St. Augustine's pastor, Msgr. Russell L. Dillard, his former associate, Father C. Gregory Butta, and Mrs. Pauline J. Jones, the parish's historian and archivist, for their support and encouragement. With a comprehensive knowledge gained during many decades as an active parishioner, Mrs. Jones patiently answered my hundreds of questions, generously introduced me to scores of parishioners with special knowledge of parish affairs, and above all, provided me with valuable insights into parish attitudes impossible to glean from the printed record.

Many people spoke to me about their experiences at St. Augustine's, and their contribution is recorded in the footnotes and bibliography that follow. Special thanks are due to three former pastors, Msgr. Leonard F. Hurley, and Fathers Raymond B. Kemp and John J. Mudd; four associate pastors, Msgr. John D. Benson, Fathers George V. Joyce and Carl F. Dianda, and Ralph Dwan, and two Oblate Sisters of Providence, Sister Alice Chineworth and Sister Charlotte Marshall. In particular I wish to acknowledge my debt to Father Kemp, whom I have come to regard as the second founding pastor of St. Augustine's. I believe the Archdiocese of Washington is in his debt for the leadership he gave to transforming a divided, reduced congregation into a vibrant, Spirit-filled parish that serves as a model inner-city church.

Archivists and librarians are essential to the production of any historical work, and I have been fortunate in the support received from a group of specialists. As in the case of my history of St. Patrick's, Father Paul K. Thomas, archivist of the Archdiocese of Baltimore, Rev. Mr. Bernard A. Bernier, who holds a similar post in the Washington archdiocese, Father John W. Bowen, S.S., director of the Sulpician Archives of Baltimore, and Sister M. Campion Kuhn, archivist of the

Sisters of the Holy Cross, pointed me to essential holdings in their care. The St. Augustine project introduced me to several other generous archivists. Dr. Philip Ogilvie guided me through the Archives of the District of Columbia, of which he was then director. Joellen El Bashir and Donna Wells assisted me in my search of pertinent collections in the Moorland-Spingarn Archives at Howard University. Sister Reparata Clarke, archivist of the Oblate Sisters of Providence, opened that order's files to me. Dr. Mary Beth Corrigan, who initiated a professional reorganization of St. Augustine's archives, shared with me her useful guides to the collection. My colleague from past projects, Dr. Jennifer Altenhofel, again supplied me with useful information about a Washington parish. Dr. Loretta Butler shared with me her collection of materials on the Church during the integration era. Brother David Richardson, O.S.C., located several valuable documents in the archives of The Catholic University of America. Dorothy Provine was especially generous in granting access to her draft study of Washington's black residents in the Civil War era. Above all, I must thank Father Peter E. Hogan, S.S.J., and his associates Father Peter J. Kenney and Mrs. Bernice J. Jones, for giving me free rein to the documents and publications in the invaluable Josephite archives. This comprehensive collection is basic to an understanding of the black Catholic community. In addition to the scholarly tuition received in that venerable Baltimore institution, the researcher gets wonderful conversation, free copying, and free lunch. What could be better?

One again I must thank the well-informed librarians in the D.C. Public Library's Washingtonia Collection for their assistance. Both the late Carolyn Lee and her successor, Barbara Henry, in The Catholic University's Special Libraries made available to me the university's valuable Catholic newspaper collection and a group of rare documents (including the only surviving copies, it appears, of the *St. Augustine Gazette* from 1882). Andrea McGlinchey of the Arlington County, Virginia, Library solved some last-minute reference puzzles for me.

Specialized help came from a variety of scholars. Once again my cousin, Dr. Alexander P. MacGregor, translated Latin documents vital to a parish history and provided important textual criticism that illuminated the meaning of those documents. Dr. Marilyn Nickels generously allowed me to quote from her interviews with Thomas W. Turner and his associates in the Federation of Colored Catholics. Jacqueline Wilson, executive director of the Archdiocese's Office of Black Catholics provided me with useful information and access to her office's valuable interview with Msgr. Geno Baroni. Two musicians, George Dines, Jr., and Leon Roberts, led me through the complex story of St. Augustine's modern choirs. Dines's long association with the parish makes him a valuable resource when trying to understand the nuances of lay leadership. In Leon Roberts one senses the presence of an artist of the highest order and a man Spirit possessed.

As an ex-military historian still somewhat gun-shy about the intricacies of church history, I put great stock in review by experts. I thank Father Hogan, Msgr. Robert O. McMain, the archdiocesan historian, and Brother Patrick Ellis, F.S.C., president of The Catholic University, for reading and commenting on the manuscript. My old friend, Father Paul F. Liston, again generously read the complete draft. His comments were especially valuable to me because of his always balanced approach to church history. For my panel of experts I turned to Msgr. Robert F. Trisco, a member of the Catholic University faculty and editor of *The Catholic Historical Review;* Father Cyprian Davis, O.S.B., the revered expert on black Catholic history; and Dr. Philip Ogilvie, respected for his knowledge of the city's history. Any remaining errors are mine; there would be far more without the help of these generous critics.

I felt especially blessed when the Catholic University of America Press agreed to publish this work because I would again gain the help of Susan Needham, its managing editor, and Anne Theilgard, of Kachergis Book Design, who designed and typeset the book.

Finally I must mention three friends who have heard more about St. Augustine's and its trials and triumphs than they probably desired. Msgr. Michael diTeccia Farina as usual provided pointed and skillful advice, as did John Elsberg, chief editor of the U.S. Army's history program. Both he and Hiliary B. Mooney patiently counseled me on how to get my scattered ideas into coherent form and into the computer.

Morris J. MacGregor
28 August 1998

ONE 🍃 A FIRM FOUNDATION

*T*oward the end of June 1864, Father Charles I. White, pastor of Washington's St. Matthew's Church, convened a meeting to discuss a separate school and chapel for the African Americans in the congregation. A list of attendees has not survived, but certainly among those present were Edward McManus, superintendent of the parish Sunday (Sabbath) schools, and Gabriel Coakley and Mary Harrison, two black parishioners who would accept specific assignments from what an informed commentator later dubbed the committee of ways and means.[1] Members of the committee, who would come to form the nucleus of the new enterprise, probably included representatives of the Landic, Warren, and Wheeler families, along with Eliza Ann Cook, Eliza Hall, and Jane Teagle, all members of the city's black Catholic community with a special interest in education.[2]

These Catholics, proud of their status as free and productive residents of the nation's capital and increasingly frustrated in their efforts

1. Olonzo J. Olds, "Memories of Thirty-two Years," pp. 1–2, Archives of St. Augustine's Parish (hereafter SAA). This brief outline of the parish's early years was the work of a priest who began his half-century association with St. Augustine's in 1903.

2. These names were included in a list of what was called the "nucleus of the congregation," a roster that first appeared in print in the *St. Augustine's Fair Gazette*, 2 Feb 1882, the first in a seven-part history of St. Augustine's prepared by Major Edmond Mallet (copy in Rare Book and Special Collections Division, CUA Library). For a complete list of founding members, see appendix below.

to secure a permanent school for their children, had turned to Father White for help.[3] St. Matthew's pastor, a progressive administrator and acknowledged intellectual leader in the American church, was nevertheless a traditionalist when it came to race relations. His church, like most of the parishes in the Archdiocese of Baltimore of which Washington was then a part, imposed separate seating on its black parishioners. Their children were enrolled in a separate Sunday school where the rudiments of reading and writing were imparted along with the usual religious instruction, but they were not accommodated in the day schools then being organized in the parish.

Unable to ignore totally such discrimination and already under some criticism for lagging in the development of diocesan programs, White tried to ameliorate the inequity. He had come to realize that, given the size and financial resources of the black Catholic community in northwest Washington and the continuing influx of black Catholics in the wake of the recent emancipation of slaves in Maryland, African Americans might well be able to support a separate parish facility. As he no doubt made clear to this committee and, by his subsequent actions, to all black Catholics, he was willing to organize the campaign and underwrite its initial expenditures out of parish funds, but its eventual success would depend on the concerted efforts of those present and their friends across the city.

White had already taken a vital first step. On June 14 he had made a $1,200 down payment on a lot owned by St. Vincent's Orphanage just three blocks north of St. Matthew's on Fifteenth Street above L. Under the terms of purchase, two further payments totaling $2,346 would fall due within the year.[4] To raise this sum and begin to accumulate the funds required to build and maintain a combined school and chapel on

3. "History of St. Augustine's Church," a three-part series published in *The New Century*, 14, 21, and 28 Feb 1903. Although inaccurate concerning dates and the sequence of some events, this work is generally reliable and, written just thirty-nine years after the events described, contains details unavailable elsewhere.

4. Deed of Trust, Charles I. White to William W. Ward, 25 Jul 1864, D.C. Land Records, *liber* N.C.T. No. 43, folios 484–486, Office of the Recorder of Deeds. Subsequently White sold four feet along the lot's southern end to Peter Kinnehan, the owner of the adjoining property, for $166. See deed, White to Kinnehan, 3 Oct 1864, NCT 47 folios 52–54. The property was originally part of a $10,000 gift in the form of city lots Congress made to each of Washington's two major orphanages in 1832. See the author's

the property was the challenge facing the committee and the city's black Catholics. Wartime conditions in Washington had placed exceptional demands on private contributions, so the pastor wanted to postpone any major fund-raising event until conditions seemed more propitious. Consequently at this or a subsequent meeting plans were drawn up to hold a well-publicized fair in the church basement early in the new year. Meanwhile, Mary Harrison would seek pledges and contributions from black Catholics in every part of town.

To start fund raising with a burst of publicity, the committee discussed a novel idea: why not have the parish's Colored Sunday School sponsor a festival for all the city's Catholic Sunday schools on the White House lawn? Sunday schools of all denominations traditionally celebrated the Fourth of July with picnics and festivals in the city's parks, and Superintendent McManus had already ascertained that the Commissioner of Public Buildings, General B. B. French, might allow St. Matthew's group use of the White House grounds if President Abraham Lincoln agreed. With time running short, the task for winning presidential approval was assumed by a committee of three headed by Gabriel Coakley.[5]

It is no mystery why Coakley was chosen for the task. A notable member of the local black community and a man of some affluence, Coakley possessed a name personally known to the Lincoln family through his wife, Mary, an accomplished seamstress, who frequently plied her dress-making skills for the fastidious Mary Todd Lincoln.[6] What remains mysterious to modern Washingtonians is the relative ease with which an ordinary resident could approach an over-burdened and anxious Chief Executive in the darkest days of the Civil

A Parish for the Federal City, St. Patrick's in Washington, 1794–1994 (Washington: The Catholic University of America Press, 1994), p. 77.

5. Mary Harrison and William H. Wheeler assisted Coakley in this task. See The New Century, 14 Feb 1903.

6. Intv., Marilyn Nickels with William and Mary Buckner, 11 Nov 1974, copy in SAA. Mrs. Buckner learned of Mary Coakley's employment at the White House from her mother, who as a young women was taught to sew by Mrs. Coakley. The well-known dressmaker, Elizabeth Keckley, did not mention Coakley in Behind the Scenes; Thirty Years a Slave and Four Years in the White House (New York: Arno Press, 1968), but her self-aggrandizing account does admit that other seamstresses also worked for Mrs. Lincoln.

War. On June 27 Coakley strolled into the White House, where he had a brief conversation with President Lincoln. The Great Emancipator expressed interest in the project, and when Coakley concluded his request said, "Certainly you have my permission. Go over to General French's office and tell him so." [7]

A president might be accessible, but even in those times Washington's lesser bureaucrats proved exceedingly difficult to pin down. Finding it impossible to see an elusive General French, Coakley entrusted a government clerk with a message to the commissioner. In his letter Coakley reported on the president's approval and asked for a permit to use the grounds between the White House and the War Department to the west of the mansion. Such a permit might be necessary, Coakley concluded, "in order to avoid difficulty with those who might question our right to be there."

Three anxious days passed before Coakley got his answer: permission granted, "provided the assent of the President is given as stated by Mr. Coakley." Obviously French, an important leader in the local Masonic lodges and an old Washington hand, was not about to grant such an unusual permit to a group of black Catholics without written confirmation from higher authority. With less than a week to go, Coakley had little choice but to return to the White House and once again fight for a place in the milling crowd. The following Thursday found him standing in the corridor outside the cabinet room, hoping to gain the President's attention as he emerged from a meeting. When Lincoln finally appeared he was immediately surrounded by various delegations of petitioners, but, spotting Coakley on the edge of the crowd, called out "General French has not refused that permit, has he?" When assured that permission indeed had been granted but the President's signature was required, Lincoln promptly took French's permit and returned to the cabinet room, where he endorsed the document: "I assent, A. Lincoln, June 30, 1864." Passing the paper back to a grateful Coakley, he added his personal wishes for a successful festival.

The fact that Gabriel Coakley expected to be welcomed at the

7. Quoted in D. I. Murphy, "Lincoln, Foe of Bigotry," *America* (11 February 1928): 433, which reproduces letters and conversations regarding this incident. The quotations in the next paragraphs are from this source. The story of the incident, which quoted Lincoln's assent, first appeared in the *Catholic Mirror* (hereafter *CM*), 16 Jun 1883.

White House as a matter of course reflects the growing self-assurance and personal initiative exhibited by members of Washington's large community of free African Americans. Enduring unjust laws, mindless prejudices, and countless humiliations, these men and women had created a cohesive community, its members recognized by their growing prosperity and social status. About to encounter the inevitable dislocations created by general emancipation and the need to guide and assimilate thousands of newly arriving freedmen, they nevertheless faced the future confident that, out of the ferment of war, they would at last win both the civil rights due American citizens and the respect of their fellow Washingtonians.

Washington's Free Black Community, 1800–1864

Such expectations would have seemed far-fetched to the small group of free African Americans on hand to witness the arrival of the federal government in 1800.[8] Black people had lived for many decades in the ten-mile-square area selected by President George Washington and ceded by Maryland and Virginia to the central government in 1791 as the site for the new District of Columbia. Most of them were slaves living in the thriving ports of Alexandria and Georgetown or on the plantations near the confluence of the Potomac River and the Eastern Branch (the Anacostia), where the new Federal City was beginning to rise out of forest and fields. The need for workers to man the many building projects and provide services for the growing population attracted skilled artisans and common laborers, both black and white, to the area. By 1800 the District's population included 3,244 African Americans, 783 of them—almost one-quarter—free men and women. Just sixty years later on the eve of the Civil War black residents would

8. Constance M. Green, *The Secret City: A History of Race Relations in the Nation's Capital* (Princeton: Princeton University Press, 1967), pp. 53–54. Unless otherwise noted, the following essay on free blacks in Washington is based on Green's work as well as Letitia Woods Brown's *Free Negroes in the District of Columbia, 1790–1846* (New York: Oxford University Press, 1972), Frances J. Powell's "A Study of the Structure of the Freed Black Family in Washington, D.C., 1850–1880" (Doctor of Arts in History dissertation, CUA, 1980), and Melvin R. Williams's "Blacks in Washington, D.C., 1860–1870" (Ph.D. dissertation, The Johns Hopkins University, 1975).

number 14,316, free blacks accounting for nearly 80 percent of this total.[9]

This unprecedented growth in the city's short history demonstrated Washington's special attraction for free men and women of color. Along with other southern cities like St. Louis, New Orleans, and Baltimore, the capital offered job opportunities and some modicum of refuge for those of uncertain legal status. But Washington was a special case. The city's unique power structure, a mix of municipal government representing local concerns and a Congress made up of competing political and economic interests from every part of the nation, effectively frustrated any attempt to develop a monolithic strategy for governing race relations. Hence laws, customs, and traditions in the federal city remained, in Letitia Brown's phrase, "biased in favor of freedom." Despite the municipal government's efforts to curtail the freedoms of the African American by the periodic imposition of repugnant ordinances, the so-called black codes, the law recognized the free black's right to reside in the city, secure employment, own property, accumulate wealth, and organize community activities—in effect, to carry on the essentials of life. Moreover, while the white community worried about the growing number of black residents and periodically instituted regulations to discourage further immigration, it remained unconcerned over changes in the legal status of those residents, even in some cases facilitating their move from slavery to freedom.

Manumission could be achieved in a variety of ways. Some slaves were freed through the last will and testament of deceased masters or upon providing proof that they had been born of a free woman. Others gained freedom through the generosity of relatives, friends, or neighbors who would donate money for the purchase of a "brother" or "sister." Many ambitious slaves bought their own freedom. Hired out to employers, they were able to keep any money earned above an amount fixed by their masters. Alethia Tanner is often cited as an example of

9. The latter numbers do not reflect those living south and west of the Potomac. In 1846 that portion of the District of Columbia was retroceded to Virginia. Thereafter the District comprised the city of Washington, Georgetown, and Washington County, the name given to the area beyond the Anacostia and north of Florida Avenue in Washington and west of Rock Creek and outside Georgetown (*i.e.*, north of R Street and west of Foundry Creek).

this "hiring one's own time." As a slave she operated a market garden near Lafayette Square, where her customers included President Thomas Jefferson and where by 1810 she had accumulated $1,400 in excess profits, enough to purchase her freedom. During the next quarter century she used the proceeds from her business to purchase the freedom of twenty-two relatives and friends, including her nephew John Cook, who would go on to become an acclaimed educator and leader in the black community.

Several of the early members of what would later become St. Augustine's congregation shared Tanner's experience. In 1824, for example, Cecilia Ann Beans, a cook, purchased her freedom from Thomas Dashiell for $300 (and lived to amass an estate of $3,000, a considerable sum in those days, which she left for the education of her heir, John Beans). By 1837 Henry Warren, a twenty-eight-year old tinner and musician, had earned enough money to purchase his freedom from Joel Crittenden of Georgetown. In April of the same year he purchased the freedom of his wife, Maria Neal, for the nominal sum of one dollar from Amelia Sewell and celebrated the day by having their marriage officially registered. Four years later he was able to purchase the freedom of his thirteen-year-old daughter Jane (the future Jane Smallwood). In 1857 Gabriel Coakley purchased his wife and four children along with two other relatives from John Larcombe.[10]

Establishing a reputation as a free person offered yet another avenue to freedom, one that required considerable initiative on the part of the black petitioner and sometimes the sympathetic cooperation of a white citizen. A certificate of freedom would be granted to a person who could demonstrate to a court that he or she had earned wages or paid rent for an extended period of time, lived openly without challenge as a free person, or could present sworn testimony of white citizens supporting a claim of free status. Some early parishioners of St. Augustine's used this method to gain legal recognition. In 1839, for example, Charles Hamersly Johnson was issued a certificate of freedom based on the testimony of Mary Jones, a white resident, who swore that Johnson "is free in Washington." In 1841 Daniel Davidson swore in a

10. Report of the Emancipation Commissioners (M520), NARA. This valuable collection contains files on hundreds of individuals, including members of St. Augustine's early congregation. (The Coakley case, for example, is located at number 332.)

municipal court that Eliza Cook, later noted for her work educating black children but then a fifteen-year-old girl, was born free in the District of Columbia. In 1861 W. H. Upperman testified that William H. Marshall, a twenty-eight-year old cook in Washington's Billiard Saloon, had been born free.

The increasing number of free blacks and their growing economic status served to obscure the true face of race relations. Human bondage, underscored by the slave pens, chain gangs, and auction blocks—the horrific trappings of the slave trade carried on in southwest Washington—daily reminded black residents of the realities underlying society in the nation's capital. The prevailing attitude among the city's white majority was also clearly manifest in the city's efforts to restrict the size and regulate the personal conduct of its black population. As early as 1808 the council imposed a tax on the importation of slaves and declared a ten o'clock curfew on all black residents, slave and free. The 1812 charter allowed municipal officials to establish special conditions of residency on "freedmen without visible means of support." An 1821 ordinance required all free African Americans to appear in person before the mayor with proper certificates of freedom, signed by three white residents willing to vouch for their good character.

While obviously discriminatory and subject to periodic renewal, these regulations were often ignored. In fact the 1820s ushered in a period of benign neglect toward black residents, during which they were left alone to increase and prosper. It was also a period in which the city's progressive forces initiated a concerted campaign to rid the capital of slavery. The abolition movement enjoyed considerable support among Washington's leading citizens. More than 1,000 of them, including a sizable number of Catholic leaders, signed a memorial to Congress in March 1828 which not only demanded an end to the notorious trade in human chattel and abolition of runaway slave laws in the city, but also called for a ban on the importation of slaves and the gradual emancipation of all slaves in the District. A similar petition, circulated two years later by famed abolitionist Benjamin Lundy, garnered more than 3,000 signatures, nearly a quarter of all eligible voters.[11]

11. Twenty-third Congress, second sess., "Memorial of Inhabitants of the District of Columbia, Praying for the gradual abolition of slavery in the District of Columbia," 24 Mar 1828, House of Representatives, doc. no. 140. The Lundy petition, with its

Even such progressive measures were tainted by the prevailing white concern that Washington might become a haven for ever-increasing numbers of free blacks and hence, a center for rebellion. Fear of insurrection after the Nat Turner Rebellion in 1831 fueled anti-black sentiment and led to violence four years later. Following the arrest and trial of Dr. Reuben Crandell (a teacher newly arrived from New England) for distributing anti-slavery literature, and reacting to the recent attempted murder of a prominent white citizen by a black man, gangs of white men, mostly young and uneducated, roamed the streets for several days, destroying black property. Their focus appeared to be the city's few black schools. Authorities responded by organizing militia units composed of locally stationed soldiers and government clerks. These patrolled the streets and quelled what became known as the Snow Riot before it escalated into bloodshed.

Authorities were quick to condemn white lawlessness, but the riot only seemed to intensify white resentment over the continuing growth of the black population. Prodded by complaints that the black code "had resumed its old character of a dead letter," the city council passed a spate of new ordinances in 1835 that sought to discourage black enterprise and independence: one denied ownership of hotels, taverns, restaurants, and other businesses to African Americans; another resurrected the old requirement of a peace bond for resident black families, the amount now set at $1,000 with five white freeholders providing surety.

This outburst of indignation and renewed repression proved short lived. Enforcement of the black codes was again soon relaxed, and gradually an industrious, closely knit African-American community managed to overcome racist hostility and get on with the task of providing for its families and achieving some measure of prosperity. This community sought to guide and assimilate newcomers and educate its children, free of the assistance or interference of outsiders. It celebrated when the slave trade was outlawed in the city as part of the Compromise of 1850, the last great effort to avert civil war. It also took heart from the steady decline in the number of slaves and

---

many rolls of signatures, is on file in RG 233, NARA. See also, Merton L. Billon, *Benjamin Lundy and the Struggle for Negro Freedom* (Urbana: University of Illinois Press, 1966), pp. 122–24.

watched slave ownership increasingly become an economic and social liability.

If the demise of slavery in the capital could be anticipated with some assurance, an end to racial discrimination was nowhere in sight. The great compromise that ended the slave trade also produced a strong new fugitive slave law, which introduced rapacious bounty hunters to the capital. These hounded hapless runaways seeking absorption into the city's large free population, often in the process harassing and, on rare occasion, shanghaiing free men and women. Their diligence was prompted by the fact that Washington had become a major stop in the underground railroad, which was smuggling many slaves to the North and freedom. Although impossible to document, it appears certain that some of the prosperous African Americans in St. Matthew's black congregation played a role in this heroic but dangerous work.[12]

The 1850s also saw the appearance of officially sanctioned racial exclusion in Washington on a wide scale, as African Americans were suddenly denied access to places of entertainment and public accommodation. Congress had started the trend some years earlier when it barred black residents from the terrace of the Capitol, the site of the city's very popular military band concerts. Now the White House, traditionally open to all visitors, also hung out a "whites only" sign. During President Zachary Taylor's administration, black civil servants, who for generations had comprised the bulk of the mansion's domestic staff, found themselves relegated to a few menial occupations or part-time positions. Toward the end of the decade Washington's new municipal street railway began to operate separate cars for black passengers. Even this was considered progress by those who at first were excluded from all public transportation.[13]

Yet somehow the benumbing discrimination failed to discourage

12. Author's intv. with Vincent DeForest, 28 Aug 1997. DeForest, long associated with St. Augustine's, is engaged in a major study of the underground railroad.

13. An exception to the original ban on black passengers: maids accompanying white children could ride inside the cars. See Wilhelmus B. Bryan, *A History of the National Capital* (New York: Macmillan, 1914–1916), II: 529–30. See also William Seale, *The President's House: A History* (Washington: The White House Historical Association, 1986), I: 282 and 315.

the black community's pursuit of an economically secure foothold in the capital. Like the European newcomers, African Americans worked in a great variety of occupations, from tavern keepers to government clerks. The black community even boasted a few teachers, preachers, and doctors. African Americans formed a monopoly in the well-paid barbering trade, and many grew prosperous as chefs and waiters in Washington's hotels and restaurants, some of the most famous of which were black owned. In fact, black entrepreneurs repeatedly won waivers to the city's ordinances and established successful businesses in all sections of the city. Like most whites, the majority of blacks worked as low-paid laborers, but a significant number were employed in the building trades as skilled carpenters, bricklayers, and stone masons, or in the service industries as tinsmiths, shoemakers, wheelwrights, painters, cabinetmakers, and draymen—all occupations that figured prominently in any non-industrial city.[14] Black women, like their immigrant counterparts, earned their living as nurses, dressmakers, laundresses, and maids. Because its immigrant population remained small before the Civil War, Washington did not experience the sometimes violent rivalry for low-paying jobs between the European newcomers and black residents that plagued many northern cities. Instead, relatively few laborers contracted individually for relatively plentiful jobs with little inequity in hiring or pay. The notable exception was the federal government, which paid blacks less than whites.

The founding families of St. Augustine's reflected this diversity of occupations among Washington's free black residents. John West, for example, was a plasterer; Charles H. Johnson, a barber; William Wheeler, initially a waiter then a white-washer; Henry Warren, a tinner; James F. Jackson, a wheelwright; Bazil Mullen, a hack driver; Francis Backett, a teamster; William Prater, a carpenter. Alexander T. Augusta, who became associated with the parish soon after the Civil War, was a physician; James M. Toy was a tavern keeper; Henry Neale started as a waiter, then became a government messenger. The city directory listed Gabriel Coakley's occupation as "oyster," meaning one of

14. Melvin Williams estimates that 74 percent of Washington's free blacks were employed as laborers, laundresses, servants, and domestics. See "Blacks in Washington, D.C., 1860–1870," pp. 77–78.

that enterprising group who sold the popular seafood either from their own boats or from raw bars around town. In contrast, the 1860 census listed Isaac Landic, one of the congregation's most illustrious members, simply as "laborer," Francis Madison, "waiter," and William Queen, "porter." On the distaff side both Ann Coakley and Matilda M. Madison were nurses, the former earning $8 a month in the office of Dr. J. C. Riley; Eliza Cook once owned and operated a private school on Sixteenth Street. Mary Queen was a laundress, as was her daughter Catherine. Another daughter, Victoria, was a dressmaker, while son Ambrose was a cabinetmaker.[15]

Living conditions reflected this economic and occupational diversity. The majority of Washington's free blacks could be counted among the city's working poor, living in barely adequate housing, just a step above the miserable shanties that sheltered many of Washington's recent arrivals. In the matter of accommodations there was little to differentiate the treatment accorded the new black immigrants and their European counterparts. Both groups suffered the miseries of life in Foggy Bottom and the environs of Murder Bay on Tiber Island, as Southwest Washington was then called.

At the same time, by husbanding their resources and taking full advantage of a generally improving economic climate, a substantial number of black families managed to purchase homes in every neighborhood of the city.[16] Before the Civil War—in fact as late as 1880—housing in Washington was racially mixed, with none of the so-called block busting and white flight that would come to scar later decades.[17]

15. These occupations were listed in the Washington *City Directory* for 1860 and 1862.

16. Melvin Williams notes that more that 10 percent of the city's free African Americans owned property. In Wards One and Two (northwest Washington) more than 130 blacks owned property valued at above $1,000. See his "Blacks in Washington, D.C., 1860–1870," pp. 77–78.

17. Thomas R. Johnson, "The City on the Hill: Race Relations in Washington, D.C., 1865–1885" (Ph.D. dissertation, University of Maryland, 1975), p. 299. The following discussion of housing in Washington is based on Johnson's work and on Letitia W. Brown, "Residence Patterns of Negroes in the District of Columbia, 1800–1860," *Records of the Columbia Historical Society* (hereafter *RCHS*), 47 (1969–70): 66–79, and James Borchert, *Alley Life in Washington: Family, Community, Religion, and Folklife in the City, 1850–1970* (Urbana: University of Illinois Press, 1980).

Yet even in this generally integrated housing have been uncovered certain racial patterns with implications for St. Matthew's parish. In 1860 African Americans accounted for 19 percent of the city's population. Yet some 28 percent of the residents of Ward One, the populous region stretching west from Fifteenth Street to the Georgetown line, were black as were more than 20 percent of those living in Ward Two, which ran from Tenth to Fifteenth Streets. On the other hand, Ward Three, which stretched east to Tiber Creek (just west of North Capitol Street) and was home to a number of the parish's founders, was only 13 percent black. A substantial number of African Americans also lived in southeast Washington north of the Navy Yard, where a concentration of black-owned property dated back to 1824. Many of the large number of black Catholics in St. Peter's parish lived in this neighborhood. Although an early eyewitness identified a number of black residents in downtown Washington in 1800, the general tendency during the next half century was for African Americans in the northwest section of town to live north of K Street, in Foggy Bottom, or near Tiber Creek, with the whites closer to the city's business core.[18]

Pre–Civil War Washington was a city of pedestrians. In those decades before the streetcar lines made longer commutes possible, residents concentrated near the major government and commercial centers. Faced with the need to house a growing population in such a restricted area, developers began to subdivide city squares into street-front and alley-front lots. The central core formed by these alleys often contained a light industry, and the surrounding alley dwellings housed the workers associated with the industry. This profitable and acceptable response to the ever-increasing demand for low-cost housing would degenerate into slums during the next century (and remain a dolorous feature of many Washington neighborhoods even after World War II). As early as 1858 such dwellings existed in the neighborhood around St. Matthew's Church. Although the first alley residents were most often newcomers of both races to the city, more than two-

18. Christian Hines, *Early Recollections of Washington City* (Washington: 1866, repr. by the Junior League of Washington, 1981). The generally reliable Hines mentions the names and addresses of a number of black residents in the 1790s. For a modern analysis of living patterns in pre-Civil War Washington, see Melvin R. Williams, "Blueprint for Change," *RCHS*, 48 (1971–1972): 361–62.

thirds of those concentrated in St. Matthew's parish were African American.[19]

The pre–Civil War addresses of those traditionally identified among the founding members of St. Augustine's underscore the concentrated living patterns among the city's free black population. The Teagle family, for example, lived on L Street near Fourth; the Landics, two blocks away on Second; Bazil Mullen just around the block on K Street, next door to the William Wheelers.[20] The Coakleys resided near Second and H Streets. William Marshall, like Coakley an oysterman, lived near Sixth and H, while the Misses Mary and Sarah Ann Smith were a block away on Seventh Street, where their neighbor was the James F. Jackson family. In 1860 Henry Warren's family lived at 236 C Street; their next door neighbors were the William Queens.[21] The Praters lived at 525 I Street, just a block away from Eliza Hall, also on I Street. Actually, all these people resided in St. Patrick's parish, whose boundary extended to Thirteenth Street. Only a few of the familiar names can be found in the environs of St. Matthew's itself: for example, William H. Smith, a shoemaker, plied his trade and lived with his family on Fifteenth Street, across from the Treasury building, and Henry Neal lived on Sixteenth Street, south of the White House, a block from Mayor Thomas Carberry's substantial home on the site of today's DAR building. Francis and Matilda Marie Madison lived on Fourteenth Street near Pennsylvania Avenue.

All these families lived in northwest Washington in Wards One through Three, the sole identified exception being Maria Toy, who lived on D Street, Southwest, on Tiber Island. All too were financially secure enough to be included in the city directories of the day. The fact that the names and addresses of the majority of black Catholics who worshipped regularly at St. Matthew's cannot similarly be fixed

19. The population of alley dwellings in the neighborhood around St. Matthew's Church and its school and chapel for black Catholics remained relatively negligible during the Civil War. It would jump dramatically in the 1870s when more than 1,000 families lived in the alleys between 14th and 17th and K and M Streets. See Borchert, *Alley Life in Washington*, pp. 17–43.

20. This was the Landic address in 1860. By 1862 the family had settled at 498 N St, Northwest, according to the *City Directory* for that year.

21. The Warrens moved shortly after the war began to 370 Eleventh St., Northwest.

with any certainty suggests they still lived in very reduced circumstances within the parish's boundaries.

Religious organizations lay at the center of social life in the
African-American community, but even here racial distinctions governed. Following the Snow Riot some churches excluded black parishioners outright. Others, notably the Catholic and Episcopal, sought to
compromise the dictates of Christian brotherhood and southern mores
by providing for common worship, but with seating segregated and
black communicants excluded from all extra-liturgical activities.
African Americans found little spiritual comfort and social satisfaction
in such arrangements, and increasingly they sought to form their own
congregations.[22] The first of these in the District was Mt. Zion
Methodist, organized by the free blacks of Georgetown in 1814. During
the next half century the city saw the formation of eleven black
churches, representing the Methodist, Baptist, and Presbyterian denominations and boasting a combined congregation of almost 4,000,
more than one third of the free black population. Probably the most
noteworthy among these institutions were the Nineteenth Street Baptist, the Asbury Methodist, and the socially prominent Fifteenth Street
Colored Presbyterian Church. Most of these churches were served by
black pastors, some of whom, like the Reverend John Cook, occasionally preached in local white churches.

The organization of these congregations was supported by large
segments of the white community despite lingering fears, fears underscored by the black codes, that such congregations might serve as
sounding boards for agitators and insurrectionists. In fact historian
Melvin Williams sees a distinctiveness in the Christianity taught in
these churches, where traditional religious forms and doctrines were
used both to call for liberating souls from sin and bodies from
bondage.[23] A number of these black congregations were active in the
abolition movement, but with the end of the slave trade in Washington
and the perceptible decline in the number of slaves in the city, the
main emphasis in the black churches reverted to the education of chil-

22. Richard C. Wade, *Slavery in the Cities: The South, 1820–1860* (New York: Oxford University Press, 1964), pp. 271–2.

23. Williams, "Blacks in Washington, D.C., 1860–1870," p. 65.

dren and training and assimilating the mostly uneducated and impoverished newcomers.

Emphasis on education was necessitated by the fact that free African-American children were barred from public schools and most church-run private schools in pre–Civil War Washington. To compensate, free blacks and benevolent whites sponsored a large number of private schools. The period between 1807 and 1862 saw the opening of seventy-one such institutions, including fifty-two day schools (regular elementary institutions teaching the 3Rs), three night schools (with combined classes for juveniles and adults), and sixteen Sabbath schools (where pupils received basic educational skills along with religious instruction).[24] Since these schools depended on private philanthropy and the financial resources of the parents, they led a precarious existence, their average life span being just nine years. Nevertheless toward the end of the period these institutions could boast an annual student population of 1,000 to 1,200. At this time a higher percentage of black children attended school than white. In 1860, for example, 45 percent of the city's black children versus 36 percent of whites were enrolled in school. Despite an occasional advertisement that these private schools accepted "either bonded or free" students, except for literacy training provided by some of the Sunday schools operated by local churches, formal education was unavailable to slaves in the District of Columbia. One other exception: the nuns at Georgetown's Visitation Convent taught slave children in their care to read and write.

Probably the most famous of these private institutions was established in 1823 by Henry Smothers in his own schoolhouse at Fourteenth and H Streets, Northwest, and subsequently reorganized under John W. Prout. Renamed the Union Seminary in 1834, this important school, by then under John Cook, enrolled some 150 black children.

24. Lillian G. Dabney, "The History of Schools for Negroes in the District of Columbia, 1807–1947," (Ph.D. dissertation, The Catholic University of America, 1949), pp. 5 and 9–10. The following paragraphs are based on Dabney's comprehensive work and on the U.S. Office of Education, *Special Report of the Commissioner of Education on the Improvement of Public Schools in the District of Columbia, 1871* (Washington: GPO, 1871 repr. in part by Arno Press in 1969 under the title *History of Schools for the Colored Population*).

The school was badly damaged during the Snow Riot in 1835, and Cook himself was forced to flee the city. He returned a year later, however, and reopened the seminary, which would remain the largest school for African Americans in the city until it closed in 1867.

Fear of slave insurrection on the part of whites haunted by the specter of the educated Nat Turner combined with the growing financial strength of the free black community to change the management of these private schools. Before the Snow Riot in 1835 most black schools in Washington were sponsored by white organizations, principally churches and northern beneficial societies along with a number of private philanthropists. After that date, however, African Americans, already taxed for public schools from which they were barred, increasingly took full responsibility for the organization and financial support of the black schools. On the eve of the Civil War 51 of the 71 black schools in the city, including 40 of the full-time day schools where parents also bore the burden of tuition payments, were financed and controlled by black individuals and organizations.

The rebel guns that fired on Fort Sumpter in April, 1861, also shattered the cycle of repression and progress that characterized the fortunes of Washington's free black community. In April 1862 Congress ordered the emancipation of the 3,100 slaves residing in the District and compensation to their masters, an effort by the new Republican Party to still white fears by demonstrating how an orderly end to slavery would enhance the stability of black society and foster better race relations.[25] President Lincoln appointed a commission to examine petitions submitted by the District's one thousand slave owners and fix the amount of compensation. Surprisingly, among those seeking such compensation was Gabriel Coakley. Coakley had purchased his wife, four children, and two adult relatives, probably sisters, in 1858, but apparently had neglected to file certificates of freedom at the time. This meant that his relatives remained, technically, his chattel, leaving him free to file a claim. His affidavit described the various members of his family, their occupations (his wife, not so identified in the document, was simply named as the one who "does my cooking, washing, ironing, and housework"), and their estimated worth. In all, Coak-

25. Williams, "Blueprint for Change," pp. 371–3.

ley received $1,489.20 in compensation for the emancipation of his family. Attesting to Coakley's standing in the community, his affidavit was prepared by Nicholas Callan, one of the city's leading attorneys.[26]

Almost unnoticed in the general hubbub that surrounded emancipation was the repeal of Washington's black codes, which followed several weeks later. Thus quietly ended the city's fitful effort to use the law to restrict the growth and economic freedom of its black community. Gone were the hated curfews, peace bonds, and demeaning restrictions on entrepreneurship. Although the codes had been periodically ignored and frequently relaxed in response to some favored petitioner, they nevertheless had remained on the books, the most hated and visible symbol of racial repression in the capital. Their repeal added to the general feeling of hope in the local black community during the war. Close on the heels of emancipation and repeal of the codes a congressional directive called on Georgetown and Washington to establish public schools for black residents. Congress ordered those jurisdictions to set aside 10 percent of all taxes collected on black-owned property to support the schools. This amount proved woefully inadequate, and although Congress renewed its demand two years later, its continued stinginess in underwriting a project that went far beyond local resources meant that the educational needs of this rapidly growing community continued to be met mainly by private schools.

The quiet transition to a new racial order proceeded smoothly until problems arose from another source. Washington had always served as a refuge for African Americans from nearby slave states. Over the years these newcomers had been quietly assimilated into the free black community, where they received support while learning to cope with their new environment. The Civil War changed all that. Military action, principally in nearby Virginia, produced thousands of fugitive slaves seeking safety within Union lines. These so-called contrabands, strangers to urban life and unprepared to fend for themselves, began to stream across the Potomac toward the capital and freedom. By the end of 1862 some 4,200 refugees had arrived. Their numbers would increase tenfold in the next thirty months.

26. Report of the Emmancipation Commissioners. Coakley's unique claim was later noted by the famous anti-slavery editor of the *New York Tribune*, Horace Greeley. See Margaret Leech, *Reveille in Washington* (NY: 1941), p. 242.

To care for and feed this multitude was clearly beyond the slender resources of the local black community and private philanthropic societies which were already stretched to the limit. In March 1862 some of these groups formed a Freedmen's Relief Association to provide the contrabands with food, clothes, temporary housing, and employment, as well as basic schooling. By 1863 the individual Freedmen's Relief Societies were operating thirteen schools for the newcomers, staffed mainly with teachers, both black and white, supplied by the Association of Volunteer Teachers of Colored Schools. In an effort to gain popular support for this work, the *Daily Morning Chronicle* warned its Washington readers "ignorance is parent of vice and a large uneducated class is a dangerous element in any community. The only safety for all classes lies in universal education."[27] These volunteer groups struggled alone until the Freedman's Bureau, created by the federal government in 1865, undertook the education of some 8,000 newcomers in fifty-four day schools around the District.

The inevitable result of this sudden migration of impoverished thousands was massive overcrowding in shanty-filled alleys and hastily improvised government housing, often no more than flimsy military tents. Even such housing must have seemed palatial to those who had to endure Washington's winter in tarpaper shacks on Murder Bay or the swampy land along the Washington Canal (today's Constitution Avenue). Bereft of proper sanitation and without instruction in the elements of hygiene, these huddled refugees were especially susceptible to disease. The death toll began to rise. Although some were induced to escape the misery by settling in rural areas across the Anacostia and even on farmland formed out of the Lee estate in Arlington, most refused to budge from the city and a government which they believed would protect them from a forced return to their old life and sustain them in the new.

It was ironic that Washington's free African Americans would work so hard to alleviate the suffering of the contrabands. Not only did such charity place extraordinary demands on their already meager resources, but it was given despite the certain knowledge that such generosity posed a threat to their own social and economic advancement.

27. *Daily Morning Chronicle*, 8 Jul 1864. See also Melvin Williams, "Blueprint for Change," pp. 374–76.

White Washingtonians, failing to distinguish between their industrious, long-settled neighbors and the ignorant, unproductive newcomers, began to blame African Americans in general for the city's problems, forming thereby a mindset that would frustrate progress in race relations for generations.

Many white Washingtonians objected at first to the enlistment of black residents in the Union Army, despite the fact that many of these men served in place of more affluent citizens, who could buy their way out of the draft. Black recruits had been accepted for service in various state units since 1862, and in the wake of the Conscription Act of 1863 the War Department organized the Bureau for Colored Troops to enlist, train, and organize black units. By October some 2,000 black Washingtonians were in uniform. These numbers rose when a second draft law in 1864 ordered the enrollment of "all able-bodied male colored persons" and set quotas for their enlistment along with whites. Eventually some 3,300 black residents of the capital served; an initial group in the infantry and artillery of Maryland state divisions, the majority in the First and Second Regiments of U.S. Colored Troops.

Mustered into service in June 1863, a number of companies of the First Regiment received basic military training on Mason's Island (today's Roosevelt Island) where for sixty days recruits learned the manual of arms and basic infantry tactics out of sight of white critics, who still feared the idea of African Americans under arms. The First Regiment went on to serve in the defense of New Bern, North Carolina, in February 1864, and four months later at the bloody siege of Petersburg. The muster rolls of the regiment reveal several names familiar to St. Matthew's black parishioners. Serving together in Company E were George Queen, then twenty years old, Thomas Clagget, George Jackson, and Charles Butler, then age twenty-two. It is almost certain that other parishioners served in other front line units. Although not yet a member of the parish, Dr. Alexander Augusta, one of the eight black physicians who served in the Union Army, was assigned to the Seventh Regiment of U.S. Colored Troops, where he rose to the rank of brevet lieutenant colonel, the highest rank attained by a black soldier during the war.[28]

28. *OR*, series III, vol. 3, pp. 1111–13, vol. 5, pp. 600–601; and vol. 4, p. 1269. See also George Washington Williams, *A History of the Negro Troops in the War of the Re-*

Despite the overwhelming burden created by the contrabands, the African-American community saw further signs of progress in the later days of the war. The creation of the federal Freedmen's Bureau immediately began to ease conditions for the newcomers, and there was general rejoicing when in January 1865 Congress passed the Thirteenth Amendment abolishing slavery and sent it on to the states for ratification. Closer to home, Congress eliminated segregated seating on Washington's streetcars, signaling the general rejection of privately imposed racial restrictions. The same Colored Troops who were trained away from white eyes on Mason's Island in 1863 marched proudly in Lincoln's second inaugural parade in 1865.[29] Also occupying a prominent spot in that spectacle were members of the local black lodge of the Order of Odd Fellows, a group that had required police protection to march just the year before.

Black residents routinely joined with those welcoming the wounded in local rest camps and hospitals. St. Matthew's talented Henry Warren, for example, entertained hospitalized soldiers with his lively fiddle playing.[30] Black Washington no doubt took considerable satisfaction from the fact that the House of Representatives invited Henry Garnet, pastor of the Fifteenth Street Colored Presbyterian Church, to preach before Congress. Reverend Garnet used the occasion to call for emancipation, education, and enfranchisement of all American citizens. In fact, as responsibility for the care of the newly arrived freedmen was generally more widely assumed by the government after the establishment of the Freedman's Bureau, the subject of citizenship and voting rights for all African Americans, especially the long-settled, increasingly prosperous free black community in the capital, became the prime topic of debate and concern in black Washington.

---

bellion, 1861–1865 (New York: Negro University Press, 1969 [repr. of Harper Bro. ed., 1888]), pp. 137–38. The muster rolls of the First Regiment of U.S. Colored Troops, are on file in Old Military Records Branch, NARA.

29. Wilhelmus B. Bryan, A History of the National Capital: II, 535–36.

30. Intv., author with Charles Stewart, 4 Nov 1995. Mr. Stewart was Warren's great-grandson and carefully documented the life of his illustrious ancestor (and protected his Civil War fiddle).

African-American Catholics, 1784–1864

Washington's black Catholics shared the concerns and triumphs of their Protestant neighbors, but as a small minority within a minority they faced special challenges unrelated to the ongoing civil rights crusade unleashed by the war.[31] At the time of general emancipation the number of African Americans in the United States was estimated at 4.5 million of whom perhaps as many as 5 percent (225,000), but probably nearer to 150,000, were Catholic. Although such figures appear small when compared with a total Catholic population rapidly nearing the four million mark, they nevertheless represented a noteworthy increase since the birth of the republic when the number of black Catholics stood at little more than 3,000.[32]

This increase is especially significant when the barriers to evangelization among black Americans in that era are taken into account. Some of these barriers were natural and unavoidable. Until the 1860s the vast majority of African Americans lived in bondage in a region where Catholics were generally unknown and their religion feared and reviled. Notable exceptions could be found principally in Maryland,

31. Peter E. Hogan, "Catholic Missionary Efforts for the Negro Before the Coming of the Josephites," a term paper prepared for a course in church history at the Catholic University of America in 1947. Unless otherwise noted, this section on black Catholics is based on Father Hogan's essay and on Father Cyprian Davis's *The History of Black Catholics in the United States* (New York: Crossroad Pub Co., 1991), Stephen J. Ochs, *Desegregating the Altar: The Josephites and the Struggle for Black Priests, 1871–1960* (Baton Rouge: Louisiana State University Press, 1990), and Michael Francis Rouse, "A Study of the Development of Negro Education Under Catholic Auspices in Maryland and the District of Columbia," *The Johns Hopkins University Studies in Education No. 22*, Florence E. Bamberger, ed. (Baltimore: The Johns Hopkins Press, 1935).

32. "Best estimates" of black Catholic strength vary widely. For example, in *Desegregating the Altar*, p. 21, Ochs used 1860 slave figures and put the Catholic population at "approximately 100,000." On the other hand Richard A. Lamanna and Jay J. Coakley, in their "The Catholic Church and the Negro," *Contemporary Catholicism in the United States*, Philip Gleason, ed. (Notre Dame: University of Notre Dame, 1969): 149, specifically includes free blacks and more than doubles Ochs's estimate. The last figure is Bishop John Carroll's estimate in 1785 and does not include black Catholics living outside the thirteen original states. See, Report, John Carroll to Leonardo Cardinal Antonelli, 1 Mar 1785, repr. in John Tracy Ellis, ed., *Documents of American Catholic History* (Milwaukee: Bruce Publ., 1956), pp. 152–53.

along the Gulf Coast, and in some parts of South Carolina and western Kentucky, where a significant number of black slaves had adopted the faith of their white masters. But even in these strongholds many black Catholics were lost to the faith as the Church's admonition to care for the spiritual welfare of bondsmen was often ignored, victim to the woeful shortage of clergy, rural isolation, and the indifference of Catholic slave owners. These shortcomings were evident from the earliest days of the republic. In his first report to Rome in 1785, John Carroll, the newly appointed bishop of Baltimore, lamented the failure of many to educate the slaves in the tenets of their religion. He blamed this negligence on the fact that slaves, kept constantly at work, rarely received religious instruction from priests, and were, therefore, "very dull in faith and depraved in morals."[33] Such neglect also left many Catholic slaves open to the blandishments of slave preachers whose Afro-Protestant prayer meetings, with their emotional emphasis on the Word, personal conversion, and liberation, offered an alluring alternative to the structured Latin services offered by white priests closely identified with the master class.

The loyalty of free black Catholics faced other tests. They too experienced the racism exhibited by white Catholics toward the Catholic slaves. Like most African Americans they suffered from an economic rivalry with the ever-growing number of Catholic immigrants. In many cities the Irish newcomers in particular found themselves in direct competition with free blacks for scarce laboring jobs. The antagonism thus engendered, manifested on occasion in bloody disturbances launched by white thugs, led many blacks to shun a Church they identified with their economic rivals.

Despite such formidable obstacles, the number of black Catholics grew throughout the antebellum era. Some of this increase followed on the natural expansion of Catholic families bolstered by an influx of Caribbean immigrants, but a measurable amount also derived from conversions. As historian Cyprian Davis has noted, many black Catholics clung to a faith that gave them sustenance, even when it did not always make them feel welcome.[34] Ironically, in an era when the

33. Report, John Carroll to Cardinal Antonelli, 1 Mar 1785.
34. Davis, *A History of Black Catholics*, p. 259.

A PARISH FAMILY. William A. and Mary Dyson Plummer, born in Georgetown in the 1860s, attended St. Martin's School, were married at St. Augustine's in 1888, and remained parishioners there until their deaths. Pictured here with their eight children, who were all baptized and educated at St. Augustine's; Agnes Plummer Rogers (right) in 1998 continues to worship at St. Augustine's occasionally.

American church was desperately fighting the bigotry of the nativists, black Catholics were engaged in a separate battle against the prejudice and neglect of their co-religionists.

That all are spiritual brothers and sisters equal in the sight of God is a basic tenet of Catholicism, one generally practiced in the small Catholic community in colonial times. During those decades, the evidence suggests, blacks and whites of all classes worshipped together, participating in the same sacraments and listening to the same sermons, their children receiving religious instruction together. Even later, unlike many Protestant churches that began to exclude black worshippers in the wake of the Nat Turner rebellion, black Catholics continued to worship with whites. Yet while African Americans would never be excluded from a Catholic service on account of color, a marked deviation from the unity of earlier times followed the formation of regular parishes in the new republic. Bowing to social conventions, most Catholic churches segregated their black communicants, restricting them to separate sections of the church and teaching their children in separate Sunday school classes. There were exceptions; for example, the Ursuline nuns in Louisiana educated black girls in their schools, and Mother Elizabeth Ann Seton actively sought out black children for her school in Emmitsburg, Maryland. St. Mary's Church in Alexandria, Virginia, which operated a school for black girls in the 1820s, reportedly provided free pews for the poor without distinction of color. Nevertheless, at the time of the Civil War five of Washington's seven Catholic churches enforced such segregation.[35]

The moral obtuseness of the vast majority of white Catholics in the face of such manifest injustice stemmed in part from the American hierarchy's ambivalence toward slavery and race relations. In contrast to later times when the American bishops would lead the fight for social and economic justice, the pre–Civil War hierarchy limited its concerns to teaching doctrine, expounding on moral issues, and providing help to those in serious physical need.[36] Although Pope Gregory XVI con-

35. The exceptions were St. Mary's, whose parishioners were restricted to the local German community, and St. Patrick's. The celebrated 1871 *Report of the Commissioner of Education* must be discounted when it describes the integration of Catholic churches (p. 218). [For more on the accuracy of this report, see footnote 52, below.] Segregated seating prevailed at Holy Trinity, St. Peter's, St. Matthew's, St. Dominic's, and St. Aloysius. Based on eye-witness accounts by Lorenzo D. Johnson (*The Churches and Pastors of Washington, D.C.* (New York: Dodd, 1857), p. 45) and Chief Justice Roger Brooke Taney (quoted in ltr., Rev. Jacob Walter to editor, *Century Magazine*, 4 (May–Oct 1893): 958) and the work of historian Albert S. Foley ("The Catholic Church and the Washington Negro," Ph.D. dissertation, University of North Carolina, 1950), it appears safe to conclude that St. Patrick's did not have segregated seating. This policy did not, however, extend to that parish's educational institutions. See the author's *A Parish for the Federal City*, pp. 97–98.

36. Edward J. Misch, "The American Bishops and the Negro from the Civil War to the Third Plenary Council of Baltimore (1865–1884)," (Ph.D. dissertation, Pontifical Gregorian University, 1968), pp. 49–73. See also Richard R. Duncan, "Catholics and the Church in the Antebellum Upper South," *Catholics in the Old South: Essays on Church and Culture*, Randall M. Miller and Jon L. Wakelyn, eds. (Macon, GA: Mercer University Press, 1983), pp. 87–89.

demned the slave trade in 1839, slavery was never denounced as contrary to the natural law or considered a moral issue by the American hierarchy. In fact some bishops (including John Carroll himself), religious orders, and individual priests owned slaves, and eminent leaders like the bishop of Charleston, John England, publicly defended the institution.[37] The various church councils in the pre–Civil War era ignored the subject of race, concentrating instead on problems posed by the new immigrants and protecting the church from attacks by the nativists. They did this by preaching good citizenship and the avoidance of political controversy. Slavery, of course, was the greatest national controversy, one fueled by the abolitionists whose nativist instincts, if not their rhetoric, cast them in the role of enemies of the Catholic Church. In a tragic reaction to the anti-Catholicism associated with the abolitionists, many Catholics with no personal connection to slavery became pro-slavery sympathizers.

So long as slavery remained sanctioned by the government and was not morally condemned by the church, it posed no problem for the Catholic conscience. The pastoral letter issued at the conclusion of the Ninth Provincial Council of Baltimore in 1858 noted that the Church had never contested the right to own slaves and spoke with pride of the clergy's determination to stay out of the controversy, leaving the laity free to make its own judgment on the issue. This moral blindness would not only alienate the vast majority of the freedmen from Catholicism, but in historian Davis's words, "prevented the American church from playing any serious role until the middle of the twentieth century in the most tragic debate that this nation has had to face."[38]

In the face of such indifference toward slavery and the open discrimination suffered within the Church, free black Catholics, with the

37. For an example of clerical support of slavery and later modification of this support through association with black Catholics, see George M. Anderson, S.J., "The Civil War Diary of John Abell Morgan, S.J.: A Jesuit Scholastic of the Maryland Province," *Records of the American Catholic Historical Society of Philadelphia*, 101 (Fall 1990): 33–35.

38. Davis, *The History of Black Catholics*, p. 66. See also by the same author, "Black Catholics in Nineteenth Century America," *The U.S. Catholic Historian*, 5 (1986): 3. The *National Intelligencer* (28 May 1858) carried a report of the convocation of bishops and quoted extensively from the pastoral letter.

help of sympathetic clergy, increasingly sought to form separate institutions designed to meet their spiritual needs. Spearheading this activism were the refugees from the revolutionary wars in Santo Domingo, who began arriving in various parts of the United States in 1793. In the next few years some 500 of these French-speaking Haitians were added to Baltimore's Catholic population alone. For spiritual support they naturally gravitated to their fellow French-speaking immigrants, the Sulpician fathers, who operated St. Mary's Seminary on Paca Street. Here, in the lower chapel under the pastoral care of several priests including Sulpician James Herbert Joubert de la Muraille, black Catholics began to gather for mass and catechetical instruction away from whites.

Religious instruction was inhibited by the children's lack of schooling, and in 1828 Father Joubert sought the help of two Haitian women who had been conducting a free school for refugee children in their home and who were interested in religious life. Soon a third woman joined the group and, with the help of several prominent benefactors, the women opened St. Frances Academy, a school for girls. It had an initial enrollment of eleven boarders and nine day pupils. The women shared a community life as the first group of black sisters in the United States. The leader of what shortly became the Oblate Sisters of Providence was Elizabeth Lange, a Cuban of Haitian extraction who had been in the United States since 1817. Under the spiritual direction of Father Joubert, Mother Elizabeth and the other sisters professed their commitment to the religious life. Archbishop James Whitfield approved the new community, whose constitution was ratified by Pope Gregory XVI in March 1832.

The Oblates attracted members from among the American-born. When Maria Becraft, a teacher from a prominent black family in Georgetown, joined the Oblates in 1831, she was the eleventh sister to don the distinctive habit with its white bonnet and white-collared black dress and cape.[39] The sisters' reputation was enhanced by their

39. A black bonnet was substituted when the sisters went outdoors. The habit was said to resemble the clothes worn by the women of the Mennonite or Dunkard communities of western Maryland. See Sister M. Claire Warnagiris, "Maria Becraft and Black Catholic Education, 1827–1832," Research Paper, Morgan State College, 1974, cy in Josephite Archives, and Sister Frances Jerome Woods, "Congregations of Religious

heroic service as nurses during Baltimore's cholera epidemic in 1832. In 1836 they constructed a chapel on their grounds on Richmond Street, the first church structure dedicated to the exclusive use of black Catholics in the United States. For all practical purposes, this chapel became the parish church of the black immigrants and, in subsequent years, the spiritual home of an increasing number of Baltimore's black Catholics.

Joubert's death in 1843 severed the Oblates' special connection with the Sulpicians, who had decided to limit their apostolate to the training of seminarians. For five years the fledgling community endured such intense economic hardship and episcopal indifference as to threaten its very existence. At one point the Oblates were reduced to twelve members, who were forced to take in washing and mending to buy food for their few remaining pupils. Their plight became known to the superior of the nearby Redemptorist fathers, the saintly John Neumann, who obtained for them a new spiritual director, Thaddeus Anwander. Father Anwander devoted his considerable energies to putting the community on a sound footing, gaining the reluctant backing of Archbishop Samuel Eccleston, securing funds to support the sisters and their school, and personally recruiting new students. By 1849 the Oblates were again solvent, free to devote a remarkable service to the American church that continues today.

The formation of the Oblates and the Sisters of the Holy Family, a second congregation of black women founded in New Orleans in 1842, mark an important step in the evolution of the Church in the United States. The fact that so many women would respond to the call to a religious life, the vital service they performed, and the support they received from family and friends offer clear evidence of the vibrant community of faith that existed among black Catholics of that period. The existence of these groups also demonstrated that, even at that early date, black Catholics were determined to exert some measure of control over their own spiritual lives.

Further signs of this spiritual activism were appearing throughout the Archdiocese of Baltimore. In 1843 some 270 black Catholics or-

---

Women in the Old South," *Catholics in the Old South*, pp. 111 and 115. See also Grace Sherwood, *The Oblates' Hundred and One Years* (New York: MacMillan, 1932).

ganized an independent society which conducted religious devotions in the hall attached to the Baltimore cathedral. Meetings typically included hymn singing, religious instruction, and recitation of the rosary. Occasionally the Society of the Holy Family, as its members voted to call themselves, sponsored masses for the dead. Monthly dues were used to contribute to the cathedral fund and to rent and furnish their meeting rooms. Members also distributed money to the poor and contributed to the Oblates' new school. They established a lending library, which circulated books, largely on religious subjects, among members. Although short-lived, the society revealed the deeply spiritual interests of its members and their thirst for improvement. The self-governing feature of this group is also noteworthy because it occurred during an era when church authorities, fearful of the discord that often accompanied the presence of financially independent lay trustees, kept close control over all lay organizations.

The church in Washington also provided examples of a growing activism among African Americans. Schools for their children always remained the first priority of this group, and in Georgetown as elsewhere the opportunity for black children to gain a smattering of education lay mainly in the Sabbath schools operated on an erratic basis by individual parishes. Georgetown's Holy Trinity parish, for example, operated such a school between 1818 and 1830. For two hours each Sunday afternoon, children were taught reading and writing along with their lessons in Christian doctrine. To augment this meager opportunity, a group of black Catholics underwrote a day school for girls, one of the first in the city. The school, enrolling some thirty pupils annually, opened in a house on Dumbarton Street in 1820. Its proprietor was the previously mentioned Maria Becraft, a daughter of the chief steward of Georgetown's famed Union Hotel. Becraft had herself been educated in a private school for the children of the city's well-to-do and later in a school operated by Mrs. Maria Billings, the first for black children in Georgetown.

The lack of a similar opportunity for black boys must have been sorely felt, and when Father John Van Lommel, a Jesuit long associated with Holy Trinity parish, offered to sponsor such a school, black parishioners gave their support. In 1827 an academy for boys, operating under the direction of black laymen, opened in a building at the gates of Georgetown College. In that same year Van Lommel helped underwrite a major expansion of Maria Becraft's school, which became known as the Georgetown Seminary. Now a full-scale academy for boarders and day students, one of the first for females in the District, the school was housed in spacious quarters on Fayette Street across from the Visitation Convent. There, with the help of several assistant teachers including, at times, sisters from Visitation, Becraft annually educated some thirty-five pupils, whose families paid $18 per quarter for the privilege. The school continued for several years under the direction of Ellen Simonds and others after Becraft resigned in 1831 to join the Oblates in Baltimore.[40]

Both academies closed in 1833. Some historians have blamed the short life of these Catholic schools on the weakening of white support for black education after the Snow Riot.[41] Actually the Georgetown schools, which appear to have received their major support from black Catholics, closed several years before the riot, most likely victims of financial hard times. At the same time it is true that, with the exception of the short-lived St. Agnes Academy organized by Miss Arabella C. Jones in southwest Washington in 1852, a full generation would pass before another day school for black Catholics would open in the city.

Black Catholics were also active in the development of the so-called benevolent societies. Before the advent of commercial life insurance with modest weekly premiums or modern government-sponsored safety nets, like-minded citizens often banded together to provide for their burial and some modicum of support for their survivors. Typically, members of such burial societies would, after paying a modest initiation fee, meet periodically for an evening of instruction and entertainment at which dues were collected to cover funeral costs of members and provide temporary relief for their widows. Although these societies never lost sight of their declared purpose, the chance to socialize with friends and enjoy music and oratory ensured their continued popularity.

40. Warnagiris, "Maria Becraft and Black Catholic Education," pp. 8–12. See also Dabney, "History of Schools for Negroes in the District of Columbia," pp. 5–25 and Brown, *Free Negroes in the District of Columbia*, p. 133.

41. See, for example, Dabney, *The History of Schools for Negroes*, p. 12.

Sometime in the 1840s Washington's black Catholics organized the St. Tobias Society "for the decent burial of Catholic Colored persons."[42] Apparently the society initially operated as a city-wide organization under church auspices, as was clearly the case in a similarly named group in Baltimore. In any event it is reasonably certain that in subsequent years some individual parish societies were formed. (St. Matthew's Tobias Society was organized in about 1858.) The city-wide group attracted general notice in April 1851 when, following the sudden death of Archbishop Eccleston in Washington, these African Americans marched in a body along with President Millard Filmore, city and church officials, and other benevolent societies in a procession that accompanied the hearse to the railroad station.[43] In later decades benevolent societies, then organized on a more financially secure basis, tended to enlarge the scope of their interests. Thus in July 1864 a group of Washington's leading black Catholics incorporated the Colored Catholic Male Benevolent Society for the care and comfort of sick and disabled members and their families "when thought proper." Burial benefits were now of secondary importance, limited only to those members who died in "dependent circumstances." The society was authorized to buy, hold, and sell real estate and to receive gifts by will. Among its founders were such familiar names as Bazil Mullen, William Wheeler, John Warren, William Queen, John Butler, and Charles Dyson.[44]

During this same period African Americans were joining the devotional societies that were springing up in Washington parishes. They were almost certainly members of the Confraternity of the Sacred Heart begun at St. Patrick's in 1833, and a group of black parishioners was included in the first 500 sodalitists enrolled by Archbishop Eccle-

42. Helene, Estelle, and Imogene Philibert, *St. Matthew's of Washington, 1840–1940* (Baltimore: A Hoen and Co., 1940), p. 46. The Philiberts mistakenly dated the foundation of the society to the late 1850s, the date of the St. Matthew's group. The society was aptly named after the biblical hero who was persecuted because of his insistence on burying Israelite captives.

43. *CM*, 26 Apr 1851 and 25 Dec 1858.

44. Notice of incorporation was printed in the *Daily National Republican*, 8 Jul 1864, and the *Daily Morning Chronicle*, same date.

ston at St. Matthew's in December 1843. The Sodality was divided by both sex and race, each group placed under special heavenly patronage. (Black parishioners were under the patronage of the Purification of the Blessed Virgin and Saints Benedict and Philip.) By 1846 the number of black sodalists at St. Matthew's had risen to 320 men and women. A contemporary account described the "impressive and edifying" spectacle of this group receiving communion in a body on Easter Sunday: "first the men, then the women, who were robed in white with veils, a cross suspended by a white ribbon from their necks, with their rosaries around their wrists showing that they were enrolled under the banner of Mary."[45] This eyewitness account is important because its precise numbering of sodalists allows us to estimate with some accuracy the total number of black parishioners at St. Matthew's in the 1850s. By that time most Washington parishes routinely enrolled close to 90 percent of their adult members in the Sodality. Based on that percentage and a very conservative estimate of the number of married couples and family size, the congregation's black members must have numbered nearly 700.

Although it is certain that St. Matthew's segregated its parishioners by race, it is difficult to ascertain exactly where these black Christians worshipped throughout this period. Most documents refer to a segregated gallery. An eyewitness report in 1851, for example, commented on the "galleries reserved for negroes" that ran around the walls of the main church.[46] At the time of the White House lawn party thirteen years later these galleries were still being occupied by black parishioners. Their pews, like those in other parts of this and other Catholic churches, were rented for a modest annual fee to individuals, thus reserving favored seats for their exclusive use during the principal mass on Sunday. St. Matthew's gallery, reached by a stairway at the rear of the nave, accommodated up to 300 worshippers at each mass. Reporting on parish conditions to the archbishop, Pastor White remarked that when the African Americans left to worship in the new St. Martin

45. Untitled newspaper account as quoted in Philibert, *St. Matthew's of Washington*, pp. 28–29.

46. The *New Century*, 23 May 1908, quoting the reminiscences of an old parishioner who was present for a course of sermons preached in the crowded church in 1851 by the president of Georgetown College, Father James Ryder, S.J.

De Porres chapel, their pews in the gallery would be made available to the many immigrants then arriving in Washington.[47]

Yet according to an oral tradition going back for generations, African Americans worshipped in a body in the basement of St. Matthew's before the Civil War. No documentary evidence can be found to substantiate this, although the parish's financial reports of that era offer some tantalizing hints in their enumeration of collections in the "lower chapel."[48] The sole reference to race in any of these financial statements appears in the one covering 1857 to 1859 which, directly below the entry for the lower chapel, lists as "Receipts from the Colored Sodality" a sum of $30.35. Far from settling the issue of location, these reports only add to the historical puzzle. For example, during a time when a substantial number of black parishioners rented pews in the upper church's galleries and even after the opening of the little school and chapel for African Americans, religious services continued in St. Matthew's lower church. In fact sometime during the Civil War the parish spent more than $3,000 renovating and enlarging the basement chapel, although it remains unclear whether this construction was related to space for worship or exclusively concerned with the improvement of facilities for the parish's Sunday schools, whose 300 children, black and white, attended classes in the lower church. Nor is it clear how the organization of a day school for girls in the church basement during that period affected the use of the area for worship.[49]

47. Ltr, White to Spalding, 11 Oct 1864, 36-Q-5, Spalding Papers, AAB.

48. For the period November 1857–February 1859, White noted collections in the "lower chapel," including receipts from the Sunday school, totaled $591.91 while collections in the "upper church" totaled $1,252.11. Listed among expenditures for that period was $200 for the purchase of a "small organ" for the lower chapel. Statements for 1859 and 1864, the only other balance sheets surviving from those times, report proportionally similar receipts. See "Statement of Financial Condition of St. Matthew's Church, Washington D.C. for the period from November 2, 1857 to February 8, 1859," "Financial Report, St. Matthew's, February 9, 1859 to February 21, 1860," and "St. Matthew's Account current from July 1, 1864 to October 1, 1865." All in Chancery Papers, "Parishes-Washington, D.C." (a collection of documents relating to individual parishes assembled by diocesan officials, principally Bishop Owen B. Corrigan and Msgr. Joseph M. Nelligan), AAB.

49. "Financial condition of St. Matthew's Institute," n.d. (ca. December 1865), Chancery Papers, "Parishes-Washington, D.C.," AAB.

The traditional belief is that, with the black congregation growing to some 700 members, the pastor set aside a separate chapel for their exclusive use. If so, he would have adopted the course followed at St. Ignatius' Church in Baltimore, where black Catholics formed a separate congregation in the basement under the title of the "Chapel of Blessed Peter Claver."[50] But it is also logical to assume that the parish took another course. Given the limited number of priests at St. Matthew's and the growing size of the congregation at mid-century, it would have been difficult to reserve a special mass for black parishioners alone. Given the fact that all Catholics were free under Church law to attend any public mass and that blacks, like whites, would pick masses convenient to them, it seems logical to conclude that black Catholics were likely found in segregated pews at all masses in either the upper or lower church.

Attempts to sort out seating arrangements may seem like antiquarian nattering, but placement in church is instructive in tracing the evolution of an independent black Catholic community in Washington. The exact arrangement of seating may never be known, but the fact that black Catholics at St. Matthew's, as elsewhere, were segregated from their fellow worshippers during church services and that their children were relegated to a separate Sunday school was certainly enough to enhance their sense of separateness and cause them to coalesce as a separate faith community, a parish within a parish. Their treatment at St. Matthew's clearly intensified among this special group of free black Washingtonians a growing self-reliance and determination to take responsibility for their own social welfare.

Too much can be made of such attitudes in an age when all Catholics habitually deferred to their pastors as leaders and arbitrators in social affairs. Nevertheless, that a core group of African-Americans at St. Matthew's were determined to strike out on its own is clearly evident in its successful organization of a free day school in 1858. In the fall of that year black Catholics opened such an institution in the old Smothers schoolhouse. This building at the northeast corner of Fourteenth and H Streets, once burned out by the Snow rioters, was recently vacated by John Cook's Union Seminary. The new Catholic school,

50. Hogan, "Catholic Missionary Efforts for the Negro," p. 28.

whose opening roughly coincided with the opening of a day school for white girls in St. Matthew's basement, counted some 150 pupils separated in two departments: one for boys under the instruction of David Brown, the girls' classes taught by Eliza Ann Cook. The free tuition school remained in the Smothers building for two years until, funds running low, it transferred to more modest quarters in a house in the twelve-hundred block of L Street. There, a much reduced student body received instruction for one more school year before the economic dislocation that struck Washington at the outset of the Civil War forced its sponsors to suspend operations.[51]

This brief summary, little more than a tantalizing glimpse, is all that is known of this school which was a key step leading to the formation of St. Augustine's parish. The few other details provided by the frequently cited 1871 *Report of the Commissioner of Education* do not stand up to careful scrutiny.[52] Its insistence, for example, that the school was supported by the "St. Vincent de Paul Society, an association of colored Catholics," must be rejected. The first St. Vincent de Paul conference established in Washington was one organized by twenty white parishioners at St. Matthew's in July 1859, well after the opening of the school. Moreover, the conference's very detailed report of activities during its first year of operations noted that its support of education was limited to the dispersal of $24 for the purchase of textbooks and stationery for the parish day school. At the same time several members were active in soliciting funds and "hunting up poor scholars" for the day schools, which, the president of the conference clearly implies, were attended by 130 of the parish's white children.[53]

Also highly questionable is the commissioner's assertion that the free school for black Catholics "was organized under the direction of

51. *Report of the Commissioner of Education*, pp. 203 and 217.

52. The report's highly laudatory account of Catholic efforts on behalf of black Washingtonians is wrong in a number of respects, no doubt as a result of its generalizing from the slightly more progressive attitude apparent at St. Patrick's. See Foley, "The Catholic Church and the Washington Negro," pp. 131–34. These errors are particularly puzzling because the report was prepared in 1871, roughly contemporaneous with the incidents cited and certainly at a time when many eye-witnesses were still available to correct mistakes.

53. Ltr., Richard H. Clarke to Members of the St. Vincent de Paul Conference of St. Matthew's, 22 Apr 1860, repr. in *CM*, 5 May 1860.

Father Walter." Jacob Walter did not arrive in Washington until April 1860 after his appointment as pastor of St. Patrick's. At that time he was not yet associated with the St. Vincent de Paul Society and had little connection with St. Matthew's black parishioners. In fact, St. Matthew's pastor was one of Father Walter's bitterest critics and would surely have blocked what would have been seen as interference from his fellow priest.[54]

Discounting notions of the school's sponsorship by St. Patrick's pastor and a bogus St. Vincent de Paul society actually serves to enhance the achievement of this resourceful group of black Catholics. Lacking any notable encouragement from their co-religionists, economically pressed by the need to provide assistance for increasing numbers of newly arriving relatives and friends, and inhibited in their organizational efforts by the city's repressive black codes, these free men and women nevertheless established and sustained for three years a full-fledged educational institution. The sacrifice involved in renting space for 150 pupils and supporting teachers must have sorely tried the resources of what was only then becoming a financially viable group. Many black Catholics, like many other free African Americans in the city, were still operating on the edge. It is precisely because of the sacrifices made by its unheralded sponsors, determined despite considerable opposition to provide for their children's education, that this school marks such a special achievement.

The White House Lawn, July 4, 1864

One unanticipated byproduct of the free school was the practical experience gained by a group of black Catholics in organizing and sustaining a major fund-raising activity. Thus the ways and means committee that met with Father White in the summer of 1864 to discuss the organization of a school and chapel were well aware of potential donors and the efficacy of various fund-raising methods. Naturally

54. See the author's *A Parish for the Federal City*, p. 167. What might have confused the author of the commissioner's report was that, at the time of its publication, Father Walter was a strong supporter of Blessed Martin de Porres chapel and of its pastor, Father Felix Barotti, and a major contributor to the finances of the new parish. See chapter 2, below.

enough Mary Harrison opened her pledge list with those near at hand. Willis Young, the first to contribute, donated $18 (approximately $165 at today's values), a considerable amount coming from a plasterer with a family of four to support. Young's gift was quickly followed by donations from John West and Isaac Landic and others. In the first day of the drive, Harrison collected $85.[55] With the help of the Turner sisters (Elizabeth, Anna, and Mary), John West, and William H. Wheeler, Harrison also organized a fund-raising festival at Washington's Asbury Hall which would raise another $250.[56] Meanwhile, with the necessary permissions secured, Coakley's group organized the White House affair. Invitations went out to the city's parishes, prizes were selected, and a band secured.

It was a gloomy time to be planning a festive July Fourth. The war had entered its climactic months, and the press was reporting unparalleled casualty figures and property losses. Balanced against General Sherman's victories in Georgia were the costly stalemates in the recent Battles of the Wilderness and Spotsylvania in nearby Virginia. General Grant's siege of Petersburg, with elements of the First U.S. Colored Regiment and a number of St. Matthew's parishioners in the lines, was underway, and most ominous of all, Confederate General Jubal Early had crossed into Maryland on July 2, headed toward Washington. The press added to the tension by publishing sketchy accounts showing Confederate raiders daily drawing closer to the capital. A hastily gathered Union force would finally halt the rebels at Ft. Stevens out on the Seventh Street Road (now Georgia Avenue), less than five miles from the White House, but not before Early's troops had thoroughly frightened and further demoralized the wartime capital.

Still, Independence Day had always been a major event in Washington, and despite the burdens of war, the citizens seemed determined to mark the day in high spirits. Several papers mentioned the

55. To clarify the church's finances over the years, equivalent values in 1992 dollars will be mentioned from time to time. These translations are based on a formula developed by the U.S. Bureau of Labor Statistics and published in its annual *Handbook of Labor Statistics*.

56. Charles Whitby, Jr., et al., *Monsignor Alonzo J. Olds: Golden Jubilee of the Priesthood, 1903–1953, With a History of St. Augustine's Church* (Washington, 1953), p. 12.

large gatherings sponsored by the various Sunday schools, singling out
for special notice those of the Colored Sabbath School Union and the
"Catholic Schools (colored)," whose affair at the White House was, according to the *National Intelligencer*, the first such event ever seen in
that place. The *Daily Morning Chronicle* commented favorably, if
somewhat patronizingly, on the fashionable styles worn by "this class
of citizen," approving of their deportment, which it found "orderly,
deferential, and unexceptional."[57]

The Catholics were probably too busy enjoying themselves to take
umbrage. In "cool and pleasant weather without oppressive warmth,"
church organizations and individual parishioners from six parishes
flocked to the White House grounds. Pupils with their teachers from
the Sunday schools appeared en masse, the *Evening Star* counting
"100 scholars" in St. Matthew's contingent alone. John H. Butler, a St.
Matthew's parishioner, served as chief marshal of the event assisted by
Isaiah Bolden. Along with the music, students entertained by offering
recitations, both patriotic and romantic, delivered by the likes of Andrew and Richmond Queen, Mary Teagle, and members of the Gray,
Mullen, Bowie, Pleasants, and Frazier families, all familiar names in
the early history of St. Augustine's.[58] President Lincoln and members
of his cabinet likely made a brief appearance, and, the *Star* reported,
"the day was passed apparently very much to the satisfaction of the
immense crowd of colored people."[59] Based on gate receipts, it has

57. *Daily National Republican*, 6 Jul 1864 (first quote) and *Daily Morning Chronicle*, 6 Jul 1864 (second quote). See also *The Evening Star*, 5 Jul 1864, and the *National
Intelligencer*, 6 Jul 1864.

58. Examples of the patriotic and sentimental recitations included: "A Soldier's
Dream" by Jerome Malloy; "The Declaration of Independence" by Andrew Queen;
"The Little Child Who Loves to See" by Miss Frazier; and "Sweet Sixteen" by Misses
Adams and Gray. All these participants and their offerings are detailed in the *Evening
Star*, 5 Jul 1864.

59. *The Evening Star*, 5 Jul 1864. Curiously, Coakley's account (published in Murphy, "Lincoln, Foe of Bigotry") is the only one to mention a visit by the Lincolns and
members of the cabinet. At least three local papers covered the event, but failed to note
a presidential appearance. Also to be considered, the Lincoln's had taken up residence
in the summer White House at Old Soldier's Home the previous Saturday (see the *National Intelligencer*, 4 Jul 1864). Still, the President made the four-mile trip to the Executive Mansion every day accompanied by a military guard. Given his administration's policies, it is possible that the First Family would show its support of Washing-

been estimated that some 1,500 people were present for the food, music, and performances.

Obviously a social success, the party was also a major fund raiser. The press reported that $1,200 was collected in one afternoon, $785 of that sum in gate receipts. The *Daily National Republican* issued the group a public "well done," mentioning that the money would be appropriated for the erection of a schoolhouse. A grateful organization committee voted a resolution of thanks to the President and Secretary of War Edwin M. Stanton for use of the White House grounds.[60]

The success of the White House event and the favorable publicity in the city's newspapers further demonstrated the progress that this small but resourceful group of black citizens had achieved in the nation's capital. They and their non-Catholic neighbors had taken a leadership role, increasingly assuming responsibility not only for their own future but for the instruction and care of the recently arrived freedmen. They formed a middle class that supported the schools and churches, which had become the life-blood of the emerging black community. The experiences and initiatives of this elite group—for so they were considered by blacks and whites alike—would shape black society for decades to come.[61] The willingness of the Catholics in this group to support the separate parish community that was about to begin would also play an important role in shaping race relations in the American church during the next century.

---

ton's free black community with such an appearance. Although Murphy's account was not published until 1928, it is based on the observations of an eye-witness and is probably accurate.

60. The resolution was mentioned in a history of the parish in *The New* Century, 14 Feb 1903. See also Daily *National Republican*, 8 Jul 1864, the *National Intelligencer*, 9 Jul 1864, and the *Daily Morning Chronicle*, 8 Jul 1864.

61. Ira Berlin, *Slaves Without Masters: The Free Negro in the Antebellum South* (New York: Vintage, 1976), pp. xv–xvi.

TWO ❧ FOR EVERYONE A
PREORDAINED PLACE

*W*ork on the combined school and chapel for African-American Catholics on Fifteenth above L Street began in October 1864. Pressed to keep expenses at a minimum, Father White and his ways and means committee developed plans for a modest two-story brick structure measuring 25 by 45 feet. The first floor, a single large room, would serve as the chapel, while the upstairs would be divided into two classrooms 22 by 25 feet. The building was to be placed near the southeast corner of the lot, providing space for later additions, and even, should future finances allow, a separate church building of modest size.

Archbishop Spalding approved the plans and agreed to Father White's placing $3,000 in trust for initial building expenses.[1] To save money, members of the congregation pitched in with the actual building, digging the foundations themselves. Nearly contemporaneous accounts tell how the men would return home at the end of their long work day, only to lay aside their lunch pails and grab a quick meal before setting off in the evening gloom to dig footings for their new building.[2] Others worked on the interior. John West, a plasterer, personally

1. "Baltimore Journal of Martin John Spalding," 21 Oct 1864, Spalding Papers, AAB.

2. This story, a treasured part of the parish's rich oral tradition, most recently appeared in print in Sandra Fitzpatrick and Maria R. Goodwin's *The Guide to Black Washington* (New York: Hippocrene Books, 1990), p. 224. On size and location of Saint

finished the building's walls.[3] Further evidence of the financial constraints plaguing the committee: erecting the simple building was
drawn out over an inordinately lengthy period. As late as December
1865 Father White was still awaiting delivery of the keys from the contractors.[4] The little chapel was finally opened for mass on February 11,
1866, fifteen months after the first shovel of dirt was turned.

The opening ceremony was a simple affair. Father White, not the
bishop, blessed the chapel, not according to the rites for a new church,
but "simply as a place or building." A visiting priest from Georgetown
College then sang a high mass at which White preached. In succeeding weeks Father Dominic Young, O.P., the pastor of St. Dominic's,
served the congregation. Clearly the task of conducting services in two
churches was too much for the elderly White and his single assistant,
so he applied to the Jesuits at Georgetown for help. Father Edmund J.
Young, S.J., was the first of a succession of priests who for more than a
year would make the long trip across the Rock Creek bridge every
Sunday to manage activities in the chapel. These included Sunday
school classes both before mass and at three o'clock in the afternoon,
as well as confessions and catechetical instructions for interested
adults. After Young's departure, Jesuits William Cleary and Stephen
Kelly served the little congregation.[5]

The chapel and school were placed under the spiritual protection
of Blessed Martin de Porres. It is likely that Father White and his
building committee selected the name, an especially appropriate
choice. Martin de Porres, beatified less than thirty years before, was a
Dominican lay brother of African-Spanish ancestry famous for his ex-

---

Martin's, see ltr., Barotti to Spalding, 13 May 1868, 33-C-8, Spalding Papers, AAB. See
also ltr., White to Spalding, 11 Oct 1864, 36-O-5, same source.

3. Intv., Marilyn Nichols with William and Mary Buckner. An example of St. Augustine's strong oral tradition, Mrs. Buckner's account of West's involvement was based
on her conversation with Aaron Russell, a fellow parishioner and the grandson of John
West.

4. Ltr., White to Spalding, 15 Dec 1865, 36-P-14, Spalding Papers, AAB.

5. For an account of the new chapel's services, see ltr., White to Spalding, 4 Mar
1866, Chancery Papers, "Parishes-Washington, D.C.," AAB. The *Catholic Directory,
1867* (p. 59), notes that the chapel "also in St. Matthew's parish," was "attended from
Georgetown College." See also, Edward Reynolds, *Jesuits for the Negro* (New York: The
America Press, 1949), pp. 52–53.

ceptional works of charity among the poor of sixteenth-century Lima, Peru. In more recent times, his native country has designated Martin the patron of social justice in recognition of his efforts on behalf of downtrodden minorities. Everyone involved seemed aware that church law allowed the dedication of a simply blessed chapel to a beatus. A full-fledged church was a different matter then, but by the time black Catholics needed a church, White told Spalding, perhaps Martin would have been declared a saint. Having said that, Father White and most Washingtonians proceeded to call the new institution *St.* Martin's Church and *St.* Martin's School. (Finally canonized in May 1962, St. Martin is now evoked as the patron of interracial justice in the United States.)[6]

The final accounting for the new facilities must have been gratifying to even the most fiscally conservative. Added to the $3,615 spent for the lot was $7,133 for construction and $576 for furnishings for chapel and school rooms—a grand total of $11,324. At the time of the formal dedication almost half this debt had been discharged, a testament to the skill of the organizers and the generosity of Washington's black Catholics and their benefactors.[7] In addition to the sums realized from the White House festival and the fund raiser in Asbury Hall in 1864, the parish fair, finally held in St. Matthew's basement on Easter Monday 1865, raised another $1,730.[8] These grand events aside,

6. Ltr., White to Spalding, 4 Mar 1866, Chancery Papers, "Parishes-Washington, D.C.," AAB. On Blessed Martin, see the *Catholic Standard* (hereinafter *CS*), 20 Apr 1962. The relative obscurity of this holy man well into recent times is evident in the work of two American scholars. John Cromwell, (in his "First Negro Churches of Washington," *Journal of Negro History* 3 (Jan 1922): 103) described Martin as Father White's assistant "who officiated at most services." W. E. B. DuBois (as quoted in *The Colored Harvest*, 29 (Oct–Nov 1941): 6) described Martin, in reality a Dominican, a brother, and a blessed, as a Franciscan, a priest, and a saint. This volume will follow White's example (and the 1870 *City Directory*) and use the familiar "St." Martin.

7. Ltr., White to Spalding, 4 Mar 1866, Chancery Papers, "Parishes-Washington, D.C.," AAB. Included among these benefactors was St. Matthew's parish itself. The $1,200 down payment on the property was paid out of parish funds and subsequently included as part of the discharged debt. See ltr., White to Spalding, 11 Oct 1864, 36-O-5, Spalding Papers, same source.

8. Receipts for the church fair were reported in *The Fair Gazette*, 23 Feb 1882, cy in Rare Book and Special Collections, CUA Library. *The New Century*, 14 Feb 1903, describes a choir concert under the direction of W. T. Benjamin and accompanied by

some $1,500 (ten times that amount in today's values) was raised in just twenty months through pledges and private contributions from members of this financially hard-pressed group of Catholics at a time of great social and fiscal uncertainty. Elated by such generosity, Father White predicted that the little congregation would be able to pay between $1,000 and $1,500 annually on the debt. He even entertained hope of assistance from the Freedmen's Bureau toward the cost of the school, although nothing seems to have come of this appeal.[9]

Estimates of the size of the new congregation vary. Several later sources reported a total of 200 adults with 50 children in the Sunday school and another 50 to 60 pupils in the new day school. Others reported the adult congregation numbered less than 100.[10] Such very modest figures may well have been invented by reporters who sought thereby to dramatize the amazing growth of the parish during its first decade. These numbers were certainly belied by White's report that pew rents for 1866 would total $550 with expectations of earning as much as $750 from this source in the near future. Based on typical pew fees of that time, it seems likely that St. Martin's initial congregation numbered at least 200 families. Even this slightly larger figure serves to underscore the sense of pioneer spirit that infused the new enterprise.

Obviously a separate place of worship with all its attendant responsibilities and hard work was not for everyone. The majority of Washington's black Catholics elected to remain, at least for the time being, in their old parishes. As late as 1875 a visiting European ecclesiastic reported that one of St. Matthew's galleries continued to be occupied by black communicants. During these same years the records at St. Patrick's and St. Aloysius showed that considerable numbers of

---

"Madame Jenkins, pianist," which collected another $432. No documentation corroborating this account has been located.

9. Ltr., White to Spalding, 4 Mar 1866, Chancery Papers, "Parishes-Washington, D.C.," AAB.

10. In his "Memoirs of Thirty Years," Father Olds's estimate of 200 adults repeats the figure first reported in the *CM* on 17 June 1876. Unfortunately, the *Mirror* was inconsistent. On 20 May 1876 it reported an initial congregation of less than 100, a number used by William B. Webb and J. Wooldridge in their *Centennial History of the City of Washington, D.C.* (Dayton, OH: United Brethren Pub. House, 1892), p. 538.

black Catholics continued to be baptized and married in those churches. The latter church also may have operated a large school for black
girls during the decade after the Civil War.[11] For whatever reason,
many black Catholics within walking distance of the new chapel elected to stay, even as segregated communicants, in other churches.

The Church's Racial Policy in the Post–Civil War Era

Those who stayed away from St. Martin's might be forgiven if they
dismissed the new congregation as merely an afterthought, probably
no more than a temporary adjunct, to the school that had won the enthusiastic support of all the city's black Catholics. In fact it is difficult
to generalize with any certainty about the attitude of African-Americans at the end of the Civil War toward racially separate houses of worship. Although their widespread backing and financial sacrifice clearly indicated the universal support these laymen and women gave to a
school for their children, church statistics make it clear that, whether
for reasons of convenience, habit, or conviction, a significant number
living in northwest Washington did not attend the new chapel. Some
scholars attribute this to the fact that, with all their failures, Washington's Catholic churches made African Americans feel more welcome
than their Protestant counterparts—hence the reluctance to abandon
old parishes. In particular they appreciated the advantages that had
accrued to their children in the Sunday schools that by then were being sponsored by every parish in the city. Moreover, despite second-
class treatment, many black Catholics, like white Catholics, had developed a strong loyalty and affection for their old parishes, feelings
that transcended the undercurrent of racism that permeated most aspects of the city's spiritual life.[12]

11. Canon Peter L. Benoit, "Diary of a Trip to America, 6 January–8 June 1875,"
25 Jan 1875, CB6-33, ASSJ. The existence of such a school at St. Aloysius, first mentioned in *Report of the Commissioner of Education* (p. 218), has been recently questioned by a Jesuit scholar. See Reynolds, *Jesuits for the Negro*, p. 53.

12. This thesis, first advanced in the *Report of the Commissioner of Education*, pp.
217–18, has been put forward by Cromwell in his "First Negro Churches of Washington," pp. 108–9, and Williams in his dissertation, "Blacks in Washington, D.C.," pp.
51–52.

On the other hand, those who supported a separate parish represented a Catholic version of a movement already underway among
black Protestants to form independent churches. Just as the freedmen
were striving for economic and political independence in the post–
Civil War period, they were also establishing their own churches in
record numbers. In many parts of the South, black Catholics, seeking
to escape from the humiliation of segregated parishes but stymied by
the Church's rejection of independently organized congregations, simply abandoned the Church and joined their Protestant friends. Such an
avenue was unacceptable to most of Washington's black Catholics,
whose strong faith could be traced over several centuries to colonial
Maryland and Virginia. But if their faith was firm, they nevertheless
could not help but envy much that other black Christians enjoyed. Independent black churches, with their many extra-liturgical activities,
served as community news centers, employment agencies, and social
clubs for their members.[13] Small wonder that a group of Washington's
long-settled and economically secure African Americans strongly supported a separate parish where they might experience more of the social accoutrements of church membership and also the chance to assume direction over some aspects of parish affairs.

Nor was there any indication that a separate parish for black
Catholics had much support among the clergy. Despite his role in the
building of St. Martin's, Father White certainly never thought of the
chapel as a first step toward a separate parish. He was a jealous
guardian of St. Matthew's size and wealth, as is indicated by his forceful, if finally unsuccessful, campaign against the establishment of the
new St. Stephen's in the western region of his parish. His superiors
would later jokingly speculate about the angry reaction of the "little
Doctor" (their nickname for the diminutive scholar-pastor) when the
creation of an independent black parish was announced.[14] White
seemed content to accept as a permanent arrangement a substantial

13. The lure of the independent churches is discussed in Randall M. Miller, "The
Failed Mission: The Catholic Church and Black Catholics in the Old South," in
Catholics in the Old South: Essays on Church and Culture, pp. 167–68, and William Os-
borne, "Slavery's Sequel: A Freeman's Odyssey," *Jubilee* 3 (Sep 1955): 17.

14. Ltr., Thomas Foley [vicar-general of the archdiocese] to Archbishop Spalding,
16 Jul 1867, 36A-I-10, Spalding Papers, AAB.

number of black families continuing to worship in a separate gallery of the main church while another group attended the chapel attached to the new school.

The exact attitude of Archbishop Spalding toward separate parishes for African Americans at the time of the opening of the new chapel is more difficult to discern. While he included St. Martin's in his list of new "houses of worship" abuilding in Washington in December 1864, he seemed to make a significant distinction in his journal between the school and chapel for black Catholics and the chapels-of-ease dedicated to St. Stephen and the Immaculate Conception. The latter two proto-parishes were being developed in keeping with Spalding's exacting plan whereby settled parishes (in this case St. Matthew's and St. Patrick's) were assigned the task of providing an all-purpose building that could serve as a church until Catholics in the neighborhood were able to build a proper church and then turn the initial building into a school. At St. Martin's on the other hand, a school, not a church, was the paramount incentive, and the parishioners were responsible for most of the project funds. The so-called "church for Negroes," was offhandedly defined by Spalding as a project being "taken care of by Dr. White."[15] Nevertheless in the end it was Spalding who decided in favor of racially separate parishes, a decision that would profoundly influence the future course of race relations in the Archdiocese of Baltimore. Just as the Civil War had challenged the nation's treatment of African Americans, it also altered Spalding's attitudes. In addition to a conservative political outlook and desire to preserve unity at all costs shared by all the bishops, Spalding projected a strong paternal attitude toward slaves, which reflected his Kentucky background and led to his support of the pro-slavery faction before the Civil War.[16] He tended to identify the abolition movement with the nation's anti-

15. "Baltimore Journal of Martin John Spalding," 20 Dec 1864 (pp. 8–9), Spalding Papers, AAB. The first quote is taken from an account of Spalding's visit to Washington provided by the *CM*, 24 Dec 1864.

16. The following paragraphs on Spalding and the formation of separate black churches are based largely on Thomas W. Spalding, *Martin John Spalding: American Churchman* (Washington: The Catholic University of America Press, 1973), esp. chaps VI and VII; Misch's "The American Bishops and the Negro from the Civil War to the Third Plenary Council"; and Ochs's *Desegregation of the Altar*, pp. 32–43.

Catholic elements and condemned the Emancipation Proclamation. Concerned that the four million slaves, suddenly freed, would face untold misery and brutal treatment, especially from those locked in economic competition with them, Spalding had favored some form of gradual emancipation.

Yet, as his biographer points out, when he became archbishop of the Premier See, Spalding developed the ability to look beyond the Church's immediate problems to consider its long-term needs. Primary among these needs in his mind was providing for the spiritual care of the largely unchurched freedmen. "I think it is precisely the most *urgent* duty of all," he told a fellow bishop, "to discuss the future status of the *negro*." These men and women "are thrown upon our Charity, & they silently but eloquently appeal to us for help. It is," he concluded, "a golden opportunity for reaping a harvest of souls, which neglected may not return."[17] Closer to home, the archbishop also feared that, through neglect, many black Catholics would be lost to the Church. Clearly if this rich deposit of faith was to be sustained, special efforts by the hierarchy were needed to counteract the prejudices these Catholics endured both in the Church and in the larger black community, which generally shared the anti-Catholic feelings of many Protestants. This was especially true of the Catholic freedmen, who had lost even the modicum of religious stability offered under Catholic masters. Spalding was no doubt aware that many of the new freedmen from Southern Maryland were being lured away from the Church after their first contact with Washington's black Protestant establishment.

The religious condition of African Americans was one of the chief topics Spalding wanted the bishops to discuss at the Second Plenary Council scheduled for October 1866. With Rome's backing he specified that the council consider the question of separate black churches, missionary efforts among the newly emancipated, ordination of black priests, and creation of a national administrator to coordinate and supervise evangelization efforts among the freedmen. The bishops, ever jealous of their prerogatives and resentful of any outside interference, objected strongly to the latter proposal. As for the rest, discussion of

17. Ltr., Spalding to [Abp. Of New York] McClosky, 9 Oct 1865, quoted in Thomas W. Spalding, *Premier See: A History of the Archdiocese of Baltimore, 1785–1989* (Baltimore: The Johns Hopkins University press, 1989), pp. 189–90.

the "Negro problem," hurriedly squeezed in during the council's last session on October 22, revealed a hierarchy unable to agree on any specific course of action.

The bishops forthrightly affirmed the need for greater pastoral care of African Americans, appealed for foreign missionaries to work with the freedmen, and condemned any priest who "forgetful of his office," would turn African Americans away from the sacraments. Bishops from northern dioceses clearly assumed that ministry to the freedmen and women was the sole concern of their brothers in southern dioceses and that they should not interfere. So they settled for the status quo, leaving it to individual bishops to devise a policy appropriate for their separate jurisdictions. Thus was abandoned any hope of concerted, forceful action on behalf of black Catholics and evangelization of the freedmen.

The bishops' failure to address aggressively the spiritual needs of the millions of unchurched freedmen can be laid to their preoccupation with the needs of the millions of Catholic immigrants then arriving in their dioceses. The demands these newcomers imposed on the manpower and material resources of the American church overwhelmed all other concerns. Even some of the more caring pastors persisted in regarding the African Americans streaming into the cities merely as rivals to Catholic immigrants for scarce jobs.[18] In such a rivalry for attention, the largely non-Catholic black population was fated to be ignored.

No such justification can be advanced for the council's failure to attack the injustices visited on black Catholics. As in most other American institutions, the Church harbored many who retained a strong sense of racial superiority which, at best, manifested itself in a form of paternalism that assumed black Catholics were somehow outsiders to be cared for rather than co-heirs of the Kingdom.[19] In some areas of the country outright racism prompted many white Catholics to

18. See, for example, ltr., Jacob Walter to Gibbons, 28 Oct 1878, 74-B-3, Gibbons Papers, AAB. Walter claimed that "the negro element here has driven away nearly all of our Catholic laboring men. For every white man employed on the streets there [are] at least 20 negroes."

19. Martin E. Marty, *Pilgrims in Their Own Land; 500 Years of Religion in America* (Boston: Little Brown, 1984), p. 238.

refuse to worship with blacks; even in the more enlightened Archdiocese of Baltimore, segregation in church and exclusion from Catholic institutions and organizations only offered a benign aspect of the same racism. Reacting to this treatment, some black Catholics and their sympathizers in the clergy began calling for the establishment of separate parishes for African Americans, echoing the demands of the various immigrant groups for the formation of so-called "national" parishes to meet their particular needs.

In such an atmosphere it is not surprising to find Archbishop Spalding and his progressive allies turning to the idea of separate churches and schools as the only practical way of addressing the prejudices of whites and of insuring that black Catholics were not ignored. By no means an ideal solution to the church's race problems, separate facilities were actually a pragmatic accommodation to growing demands for segregation in white America. They also suited the hierarchy's hands-off policy toward social questions (the bishops' boast: "We disclaim all right to interfere with your judgment in the political affairs of our common country, and . . . control you in the constitutional exercise of your freedom").[20] Separate churches would also help ameliorate the indignation and humiliation felt by self-confident black Catholics who, reacting to racism and neglect, were in danger of succumbing to the allure of Protestantism. Spalding and his fellow bishops in the Baltimore Province discussed the issue during their Tenth Provincial Council in April 1869. Their decision, published in the form of a pastoral letter, was quite specific:

We therefore desire that separate schools and churches be established for the blacks, wherever, in the judgment of the Ordinary, they may be deemed practicable and expedient. Where special schools and churches are not erected for them, every facility should be afforded their religious and moral training, as far as circumstances will permit.[21]

Among the facilities for religious and moral training the bishops included separate religious education in Sunday schools and adult instruction classes, separate religious devotions like missions and re-

20. Statement issued by Fourth Provincial Council of Baltimore, May 1840, quoted in Misch "The American Bishops and the Negro," p. 69.

21. Tenth Provincial Council statement, repr. in *CM*, 15 May 1869.

treats, and separate religious confraternities, such as sodalities and benevolent societies. Spalding and his allies also called on the religious orders, with a special appeal to foreign missionaries, to aid in the work of evangelization.

The bishops' solution had its obvious drawbacks. Even as these separate parishes would come to represent a dynamic expression of African-American identity, achievement, and vitality, they also came to personify the American church's failure to confront the evil of racism. Designed to offer better spiritual care for black Catholic families, separate churches and schools also discouraged white acceptance of blacks as neighbors and fellow worshippers and widened the gulf between the races, a gulf which, over the next century, would become a rigid separation that famed historian John Tracy Ellis condemned as "the single greatest failure of the American church." [22]

Spalding was no doubt aware of the negative aspects of the scheme, but he approached the future with confidence. In November 1870 he invited all the church societies and organizations in Baltimore to the laying of the cornerstone of the new headquarters for the Oblate Sisters of Providence. "I rejoice to see Germans, Irish, and Americans here today, carrying out the true spirit of the Church," he told the mixed gathering before going on to summarize his personal philosophy: "There are no parties in heaven. I want all my children—Irish, German, American, African—I want them all to go to heaven." [23]

A Separate Parish

In fact Spalding had not waited for the formal meeting of the bishops of his province to act on behalf of his African-American children. Prior to his departure for an extended European visit in May 1867, he issued a pastoral letter in which he reflected on the concerns of "our colored brethren," including the need for separate schools and mis-

---

22. Intv., author with John Tracy Ellis, 17 Jun 1991. See also Peter Hogan, "Archbishop Curley and the Blacks," *The Catholic Historical Society of Washington Newsletter* 4, no. 1 (Jan–Mar 1996): 12, and John P. Marchall, "Patrick Francis Kenrick, 1851–1863: The Baltimore Years" (Ph.D. dissertation, The Catholic University of America, 1965): 32off.

23. As quoted in Spalding, *Premier See*, p. 196.

sions, as parishes were often called in those days. From Rome two months later he followed up with specific instructions to his vicar general, Thomas Foley, to appoint a pastor for a separate St. Martin's. The man selected for the job, the founding father of what would soon become St. Augustine's parish, was Felix Barotti.

Barotti was a recent newcomer to America. Born in 1838 in Bibiana in the Piedmont region of northern Italy, he had always dreamed of becoming a missionary. He prepared for the priesthood under the aegis of the Vatican's Congregation de Propaganda Fide, and at the time of his ordination in 1865 was awaiting assignment to the China missions.[24] But service in the Orient was not to be. The rector of Barotti's seminary, aware of Spalding's need for more priests, informed the archbishop that he could spare two men, and with Propaganda's permission Barotti and a companion were sent to America.

It is not clear if the archbishop had Barotti in mind for St. Martin's from the beginning. In requesting the priests, Spalding had mentioned to Cardinal Barnabo, the head of Propaganda, the need to work among the Protestants, freed African Americans, and immigrants.[25] After spending four months at St. Charles College where they underwent intensive tutoring in the English language, the young Italians received assignments with no discernible connection to black Catholics. Spalding responded to Bishop William Henry Elder's urgent pleas for help in his Diocese of Natchez by sending Barotti's fellow missionary to Mississippi, but Barotti himself was assigned to St. Peter's on Capitol Hill, where he spent eleven months learning the operations of an American parish.[26] Finally, on 23 July 1867, the news arrived from Baltimore:

I appoint you the Pastor of the Chapel of Blessed Martin de Porres, in the city of Washington. You will have the same control in the affairs of this Chapel, in accordance with the Statutes of our Diocesan Synods, which other Pastors

24. A comprehensive summary of Barotti's career appeared in a series of articles by M. B. Johnston in *The Fair Gazette* 4–10 February 1882. Propaganda Fide directed the universal Church's world-wide missionary effort. Throughout the nineteenth century, dioceses in the United States reported to the pope through this body.

25. Spalding, *Martin John Spalding*, p. 174.

26. Ltrs., Elder to Spalding, 5 Feb 1867, 33-V-3, and Spalding to Elder, 18 Feb 1867, and Letterpress Book, p. 273. All in Spalding Papers, AAB.

have in their churches for the benefit of religion and the care of the colored people attending the said chapel.

Foley went on to authorize the new pastor's receiving from White a statement of the financial affairs of the chapel, prudently adding that Barotti might prefer living nearer to his new church rather than sharing St. Matthew's rectory with White.[27]

There is little doubt that the separation caught Father White by surprise. Vicar-General Foley predicted that the news of creating two new parishes within St. Matthew's boundaries, Blessed Martin's and St. Stephen's, would "bring a hornet's nest on my head, but the weather is very cool and pleasant, and I shall meet the tea-pot tempest with becoming severity." What particularly concerned Foley was the news that the Jesuits could no longer supply priests for St. Martin's and that for several weeks in the summer of 1867 the congregation had been forced to attend mass elsewhere. "The work has been retarded too much already," he complained, clearly unconcerned with how the "little doctor" might react to the news. "This is not an age of waiting for old people," he told Spalding; "we must jump on the car of progress, or we will be left behind." To that end he announced that Barotti's appointment would be effective on the first day of August.[28] Foley's comments may have been designed in part to impress his absent superior with his no-nonsense administration of the archdiocese, but undoubtedly Father White's nonchalant direction of the little congregation at St. Martin's had retarded the enterprise begun with so much enthusiasm just nineteen months before. Although their statistics might disagree, all accounts of the congregation's early months concur that little progress had been made in attracting black Catholics to the new chapel and school.

The special chemistry that quickly developed between the young, enthusiastic Italian priest and what must have been at that point a somewhat skeptical congregation brought about an immediate transformation in the fortunes of St. Martin's. The tiny community celebrated its first mass with its new pastor on August 1, 1867, and Barotti,

27. Ltr., Foley to Barotti, 23 Jul 1867, cy in SAA.

28. Ltr., Foley to Spalding, 16 Jul 1867, 36A-I-10, Spalding Papers, AAB. The first quote is from ltr., Foley to Spalding, 23 Jul 1867, 36A-I-11, same source.

FELIX BAROTTI, founding pastor of St. Augustine's parish.

heeding the vicar general's warning, moved into a small frame house next door, which the parish rented for $30 a month. In succeeding months Barotti showed himself a resourceful leader possessed of a simple, inspiring faith, an infectious optimism, and a fierce loyalty that won everyone's allegiance and forged a team that would, in the next decade, create a vital urban parish. The adults especially appreciated the open, unaffected way he approached everyone, from the humblest new convert to the princely archbishop. The children in particular loved him. Contemporary accounts report the mutual enjoyment priest and students received from the many excursions and picnics he organized for them. His attention to these matters surely exceeded anything expected of a busy pastor. Parishioners could not stand back, one observer concluded, when they saw "this cultured priest, the associate of the highest in the land, laboring so incessantly and unweariedly for the interests of themselves and children."[29] More important, Barotti inspired the congregation to action.

From the beginning pastor and people focused on the school, but until the establishment of a separate parish, the school in its quarters on the second floor of the new building lacked the finances and personnel to organize on a professional basis. Classes were at first under the direction of Mary T. Smith (later the wife of William T. Benjamin, the well-known singer), Ambrose Queen, and Lewis Brown, all dedicated amateurs without any special training for their jobs.[30] The situation changed dramatically when in late 1867 an experienced teacher, Sister Mary Seraphine Noel, O.S.P., succeeded as principal of the girl's school. This remarkable woman was the daughter of John Noel, a prosperous Haitian-American with businesses in Baltimore and Wilmington, Delaware.[31] Born in Santo Domingo and educated in France before joining the Oblate Sisters of Providence in 1851, she served for several years as principal of St. Benedict's school for boys in the Fells Point section of Baltimore. Her mother's death, the closure of St. Benedict's, and the need to care for her enfeebled father prompted her to leave her community in 1860. During the Civil War the pair moved to Washington, where Sister Seraphine likely operated a small school for children of St. Matthew's parish in the parlor of her home at Vermont Avenue and L Street.[32] Sometime in late 1867 she succeeded Miss

29. Quoted in *The Fair Gazette*, 6 Feb 1882. For an example of the children's reaction to one such excursion, see *CM*, 31 August 1873.

30. *The Fair Gazette*, 20 Feb 1882. Queen, listed among the parish's founders, died in 1894. Brown's name was listed in the history of the parish serialized in *The New Century*, 21 Feb 1903.

31. The Noels were related to Pierre Toussant, the saintly Haitian immigrant whose cause for canonization is now under investigation.

32. Sherwood, *The Oblates' One Hundred and One Years*, p. 136. See also, "The Origin of Saint Augustine's School, Washington, D.C.," prepared by the Oblates Sisters Archives, 23 Apr 1983, cy in SAA. Surveys of Catholic institutions and city schools in the *National Intelligencer* (12 Apr and 16 Dec 1865) both list "a Catholic colored school" operating under the auspices of St. Matthew's Church. The *Catholic Directory* for 1866, listed on page 62 a "school for colored children in St. Matthew's parish," all lending support to the idea that Sister Seraphine was operating some kind of parish school as early as the fall of 1864.

Smith as director of the girls' division of the new St. Martin's School. At the same time, a veteran teacher of Washington's black children, Eliza Ann Cook, enlisted as her assistant. Although no longer a member of the Oblates, Sister Seraphine retained her religious name, continued to wear the habit of her beloved congregation, and was universally recognized as a religious, thus connecting the Oblates to the very foundation of a school they have served into recent days.

Sister Seraphine herself was trained as a musician and, in addition to the usual academic subjects, provided her young charges with a grounding in church music. On February 16, 1868, her pupils were signaled out for notice when they substituted for the parish choir at Sunday mass and vespers. Their rendition of the intricate Latin chant prompted a reporter to marvel at how children could master the difficult music after so brief a period of training, all thanks to the diminutive nun directing them from the chapel's tiny pump organ.[33]

In a certain sense the singing that day celebrated the real beginning of St. Martin's School, for it marked the birth of a parish association that would provide the means for developing a full-fledged educational institution. At the urging of Father Barotti, members of the congregation organized the Blessed Martin's Educational Society. Modeled on the Young Catholic Friend's Society, which for a generation had helped send needy white boys to religious schools, the new group used the monthly contributions of its members to meet the tuition costs of the parish's poor children. Parish support was especially necessary at this time because St. Martin's School, unlike some of the other private institutions in town, received no assistance from the Freedmen's Bureau or any other government source. Indicative of the solid support always given educational initiatives by black Catholics, the society quickly enrolled several hundred members and became the major underwriter of what for many of its pupils was a free school.[34] As was typical of Catholic schools of that era, more affluent parents at St. Martin's were expected to pay a modest tuition fee. In many Catholic parishes paying pupils were enrolled in an academy separate from the parochial (free) school. Although St. Martin's did have separate academy and parochial school departments, the records

33. *CM*, 7 Mar 1868.
34. *CM*, 7 Mar 1868 and 13 Mar and 24 Apr 1869.

fail to indicate whether the distinction between the two was based on ability to pay.

Assured a steady source of income, the school expanded rapidly. Commencement exercises in July 1869 featured a procession through the neighborhood of the 93 girls and 47 boys who constituted the student body. A local reporter was on hand to describe the exercise in the little church hall, where distinguished guests and proud parents listened to student recitations and a musical recital before watching the distribution of awards and prizes. That year William H. Ross and Evangeline Tidball won the gold medals.[35]

When classes opened for the 1869–70 academic year the school had acquired two new professional teachers. Sister Seraphine now had Julia Smith, a graduate of the Oblates' St. Frances Academy in Baltimore, to assist her in training the 85 pupils enrolled in both the female academy and the girls' division of the parochial school, while John McCosker, a graduate of Georgetown College, taught the 60 similarly divided male students. McCosker was the first of three white male teachers to hold this post in the next six years. St. Martin's also operated a night school where 15 older students otherwise employed during the day received academic training. Then as now teacher's wages were modest: McCosker received $150 annually; the combined salary for Sister Seraphine and her assistant was $205. A student body of 160 overwhelmed the capacity of the second-floor classrooms, and for the next five years the girls' division was quartered in a building on Vermont Avenue.[36] In succeeding years enrollment steadily grew so that by 1877 the pastor could report 286 full-time students, 91 boys and 195 girls, in attendance. To help defray rising costs, the education society periodically sponsored fund raisers like the parish festival held each night during Christmas week in 1871 when suppers and entertainments were provided for parishioners and their friends who donated to the cause.[37]

35. *CM*, 24 Jul 1869.

36. *Report of the Commissioner of Education*, pp. 240 and 262.

37. *CM*, 23 Dec 1871. Enrollment figures are from the *Notitiae*, various years. Those annual reports contradict the assertion made by Dabney (*History of Schools for Negroes in the District*, pp. 189–90) that the school was closed for several years before the coming of the Holy Cross sisters in 1875.

The parish also sponsored a Sunday school for those children not enrolled in its day school. By 1874 some 200 students were attending catechism classes taught mainly by members of the congregation. This Sunday school was also a source of community building. In August 1873, for example, Father Barotti and 150 teachers and adult parishioners escorted some 400 children, including the entire Sunday school, on a steamboat excursion to Marshall Hall. Apparently little notice was given to the strictures of the increasingly austere Archbishop Spalding, who in 1868 had banned parish-sponsored dances and excursions. Certainly Spalding's pastoral letter was ignored when Barotti marched with 700 children and adults to the city wharf before setting off on a river excursion to Giesboro, Maryland.[38]

Like the parish school, music has always been a unifying force in the community of Washington's black Catholics. Blessed with unusually gifted singers, little St. Martin's lost no time in organizing and training a choir that quickly earned notice as one of the finest in the city. During the period of transition under the Jesuit fathers the community had made do with the musical efforts of a small group, led by parishioners William Benjamin and later Henry A. Jackson, singing the familiar hymns and simple chant responses at the occasional high masses. Yet within months of St. Martin's becoming an independent parish, a regular choir was performing at various church functions.[39]

It is uncertain when a full-time director was selected, but the choice of John Esputa demonstrated that Father Barotti was not one to stint on quality when it came to supplying his parish with things he deemed essential. Esputa's services could not have come cheaply. A member of a distinguished family of artists, he had founded a successful music conservatory on Eighth Street, Southeast, near the Marine Corps barracks, where for years he and his son trained many of Washington's professional musicians. The most famous of these was the great American composer-conductor John Philip Sousa, who studied with Esputa for four years and would later arrange music sung at parish vespers services. No stranger to church music, Esputa had also directed the choirs of St. Peter's and St. Dominic's before accepting responsibil-

38. *CM*, 30 Aug 1873, and *The Fair Gazette*, 6 Feb 1882. On Spalding's prohibition, see Spalding, *Premier See*, p. 193.

39. Notice of the choir's work appeared in the *CM* as early as 7 Mar 1868.

ity for the new group at St. Martin's. Esputa individually coached the choir's twenty members, selecting seven soloists, including the especially talented Mrs. Jane Smallwood, daughter of the fiddle-playing Henry Warren, Mary Coakley, and the noted basso William T. Benjamin, who, like the bass in Rossini's famous opera, was also a barber by trade. In succeeding years the group won a city-wide audience for its rendition of some of the major religious works. On Easter Sunday 1873, for example, it performed Haydn's *Second Mass* accompanied by a full orchestra "with fine effect," as one critic put it.[40] Even taking into account a roomy annex that had by then doubled the chapel's seating capacity, the presence of so many musicians must have caused much squeezing and shoving in a congregation dressed in its Easter finery.

In those early years the choir also frequently performed concerts of popular music for large paying audiences. In February 1872, for example, it gave what was dubbed "a concert of sweet sounds" for the benefit of the church.[41] The notion of using the choir to raise money obviously appealed to a group of artists who naturally sought a wider audience for their music-making. In 1873 Esputa and bass soloist Benjamin teamed up with local entrepreneur T. Harry Donahue to organize the Colored American Opera Company composed principally of members of St. Martin's choir. With considerable fanfare they launched the company with a performance on February 3, 1873, of Julius Eichberg's *The Doctor of Alcantara*, a "chaste and beautiful opera," according to the advertisements, before a racially mixed audience of 1,500 Washingtonians in Lincoln Hall.[42] Encouraged by the public's response, the company gave a series of performances in the larger Wells Opera House before launching a tour of selected northern cities. The uniformly favorable reviews, which singled out the company's skilled chorus, always identified the opera troop with St. Martin's, further enhancing the reputation of the new parish just as the large audiences provided the church with much-needed revenue.[43] In 1874 the pastor reported

40. *CM*, 19 Apr (source of quote) and 12 Jul 1873. For a full account of the choir, see Appendix 1, below.

41. *CM*, 24 Feb 1872.

42. *The Republican*, Jan 1873, as quoted in *CM*, 1 Feb 1873. See also *CM*, 4 Jan and 15 Feb (source of quote) 1873.

43. *The Evening Star*, 10, 11, and 13 May 1873, and *CM*, 10 May 1873.

that musical performances had earned some $1,400 for the parish in that year alone. Most important, the choir and its accomplishments served to encourage a strong sense of community, which was attracting converts to the faith and new parishioners to the little parish.

The sense of community was also enhanced by the rapid growth of parish societies during those early years. In addition to the education society and an association of Sunday School teachers, the parish boasted a Sodality of some 155 members, some no doubt transfers from the Sodality organized among black Catholics at St. Matthew's before the Civil War. The parish's Rosary Society, 200 members strong, encouraged daily recitation of the Marian devotion that had recently become so popular in the American church.[44] The amazing proliferation of mutual aid societies at St. Martin's during its first years—and indeed throughout Washington's churches—could be attributed to the practicality of such insurance organizations and the social benefits derived from membership.[45] Their formation was actively encouraged by the American bishops, who considered them a responsible method of alleviating some of the economic hardship of sickness and accidents in the work place and a wholesome alternative to labor unions and secret societies. These parish groups, which first appeared before the Civil War and reached peak membership during the late 1870s, often used nationality or race as a unifying theme. Hence the popularity of the various Hibernian societies, the German Catholic Central Verein, and the Colored Catholic Male Benevolent Society.

This latter group, founded by a group of black residents in 1864, immediately associated itself with the new parish, where it continued to address the financial needs of sick members and, when necessary, provided them a "decent Christian burial."[46] With similar ends in mind for female parishioners, Mary Wheeler, Eliza Dodson, and Eliza-

44. So reported by Father Barotti in the 1874 and 1875 *Notitiae*. By 1877 membership in the Sodality had reached 230, in the Rosary Society, 300.

45. Although St. Augustine's *Notitiae* reported eight benevolent societies operating in the parish in 1874 (ten societies by 1877), records survive for only the six discussed below. The following account is based principally on a history of parish societies printed in *The Fair Gazette*, 18 and 20 Feb 1882.

46. On the organization of this group, see chapter 1, above. The society's incorporators were: Charles Hurbert, John Warren, William H. Wheeler, Charles Dyson, James M. Terrell, David Atkins, William Queen, John H. Butler, and William Ford.

beth, Anna, and Mary C. Turner organized the Ladies' Mutual Relief Association in 1867. Membership was limited to Catholic women between fifteen and thirty years of age. All officers were female, but, bowing to the realities of Victorian society, the bylaws also provided for the admission of "not more than twelve gentlemen . . . five of whom constitute a Board of Trustees for the transaction of outside business." A year later some female parishioners, including Cornelia Butler, Louisa Howard, and Elizabeth Turner, formed the Ladies' Tobias Society, which concentrated on enrolling the parish's older women. Despite the traditional linking of Tobias societies to funerals, this organization, like all such mutual aid groups, emphasized the care and financial support of sick members. Unlike their sisters in the Mutual Relief Association, however, these women forthrightly barred males altogether. It also charged a hefty $10 initiation fee, which may have explained the organization of the rival United Aid Association in 1871. With only a $4 membership fee, this group did admit males, but limited their number at any time to sixteen.

By far the most popular of these mutual aid societies was the Catholic Beneficial Society organized in 1870 by William Wheeler, Francis Hawkins, Lewis Brown, Francis Stewart, William Marshall, and Robert Magruder.[47] The society quickly grew to 400 members with a capitalization of $3,000. Although it limited membership to Catholics "in good health capable of supporting themselves," the society's progressive constitution made no distinctions between the sexes, and in fact two women, Charlotte Luckett and Ruth Diggs, served as president during the group's formative years. The bylaws also stipulated that benefits would be denied to those dying "outside the Catholic faith." Members donned distinctive uniforms for all society functions. The large membership necessitated an elaborate organization of eight subcommittees to carry on the group's insurance business throughout the city. One last distinctive feature: at a time when local parish priests serving as society chaplains often tended to run such groups, the Catholic Benevolent Society's bylaws stipulated that the services

47. In addition to these men, officers in the early years included Daniel Spriggs, Anna E. Nelson, Thomas Ennis, Calop Smith, Francis Madison, Charles Johnson, and Stephen Smallwood, See *CM*, 30 Oct 1880.

of its chaplain would be limited to leading the opening and closing prayer.

Nor were the youngsters overlooked. The Children of Mary was organized in 1875 for parishioners fifteen years and younger. Adult trustees (including Annie Gillem, Nellie Freeman, George Thomas, Horace Dyer, and Kate Simms) collected a small monthly fee from the young members which was used to support children during illnesses or to assist in their burials, an all-too-common occurrence in nineteenth-century Washington. Like the popular Catholic Benevolent Society, the 200 children in the Children of Mary wore uniforms to their functions: gray suits, black hats, and white gloves for the boys; blue dresses and capes, white ruffles and hats for the girls.

Uniforms played a major role in the longest lived of these mutual aid groups, the Knights of St. Augustine. A quasi-military organization, the Knights were formed in 1872 in St. Peter's parish by a group of black Catholics from all parts of the city. Gabriel Coakley served as one of the first commanders. The instant popularity of the Knights not only answered the need for social services around town, but also reflected the American male's infatuation with colorful costumes and military exercises. Within two years membership had increased to the point where an independent branch, the so-called Commandery Number 2, was organized at St. Martin's by a dozen of the city's prominent African Americans.[48] The Knights cared for the sick and sponsored programs to "further Christian principles and encourage civic virtues." They also attended all funerals in the parish in full uniform, which consisted of a black frock coat and trousers, purple sash, a chapeau with gold braid, and a belt with military sword. The Knights and their close order drill in military regalia were a familiar sight at parish functions, and they frequently represented the parish at city parades, including the very popular annual festivities marking Emancipation Day.

48. The original officers included: commander, W. H. Smith; first deputy, W. H. Burgess; second deputy, Eugene R. Lewis; financial scribe, Isaac Landic; chaplain, Father Barotti; recording scribe, Lewis B. Brown; deputy recorder, William H. Smallwood; herald, William E. Brooks; warden, Horace Dyer, drill master, John Mitchell; standard bearer, Francis Hurbert; board of governors: James F. Jackson, William T. Benjamin, Daniel Clark, John Middleton, James S. Butler, and Thomas H. Smith.

The society's officers imposed strict military order on members, who were fined for any absence from weekly drill or failure to sit up with a sick fellow Knight. In time the Knights created a ladies' auxiliary whose presence may have helped soften the rigor of the military discipline.[49]

The Catholic knighthoods were wildly popular during the postwar decades, and before long a rival group to the Knights of St. Augustine surfaced at St. Martin's. In 1879 thirty-three members of the parish organized the Knights of St. Benedict. This group sported a uniform of blue serge with silver lining, and like the other knighthoods cheerfully bore the considerable cost of distinctive hats, badges, sashes, and swords that proclaimed their membership in their special club. Like many honorary armies, the Knights of St. Benedict had more officers than troops. Almost half of its initial members held special office.[50]

In discussing the number and robust health of parish organizations with a reporter, Father Barotti admitted with obvious pride that St. Martin's lacked one group that figured so prominently in the life of other parishes in the diocese. For the "very satisfactory and gratifying reason that there is not a person of intemperate habits in the congregation," as the *Catholic Mirror* put it, Barotti's congregation saw no need to sponsor branches of the temperance societies that thrived at St. Patrick's, St. Aloysius, and elsewhere because of the scourge of alcoholism that bedeviled so many families in the nineteenth century.[51]

The various religious and beneficial societies often appeared in city-wide events. For example, St. Martin's organized one of the divisions of the parade staged in December 1870 to welcome Archbishop Spalding back from the first Vatican Council and to protest the Italian Army's capture of the Papal States. Dubbed the largest civilian procession in the history of the city, the line of march contained more than 20,000 Catholics and was reviewed by the archbishop and President

49. *CM*, 2 May 1884 and *CS*, 31 Oct 1952.

50. *CM*, 6 Dec 1879. Officers included: commander, William Smallwood; first deputy, Joseph Simms; second deputy, George Jackson; recorder, Francis X. Beckett; financial officer, John Young; almoner, William Lofton; chaplain, Father Tarro; captain general, Jacob Reader; Herald, James Wood; standard bearer, Vincent Marshall; board of governors: James Butler, James T. Norris, James W. Harris, Robert Coates, and Lewis B. Brown. On the Catholic knighthoods, see Spalding, *Premier See*, p. 218.

51. *CM*, 12 Jul 1873. See also the *Fair Gazette*, 17 Feb 1882.

Ulysses S. Grant. It was a spectacular event that demonstrated the increasing prominence of the Church in the life of the nation's capital and incidentally underscored the growing strength of black Catholics within the archdiocese. With William T. Smith serving as grand marshal, the African-American division included among its nine units St. Martin's band, its Sodality, Education Society, and Benevolent Society, along with similar groups from other parishes. After singling out the parade's black division with its usual patronizing observations about the neatness and admirable order exhibited by the marchers, the *Catholic Mirror's* local reporter went on to admit that the imposing number of marchers, their handsome banners and fine band, made this division "a very attractive feature of the immense procession" which "will not soon be forgotten by the multitudes who witnessed that magnificent pageant." Nor was the significance of the division's size lost on the city's anti-Catholic bigots, some of whom publicly expressed their dismay that so many African Americans had embraced the Roman church and openly demonstrated their solidarity with their white co-religionists.[52] Six months later St. Martin's societies participated in a torch-light parade celebrating Pope Pius IX's silver anniversary. This time Richard Wells served as marshal in an event that saw the St. Martin's contingent march past all the city's Catholic churches before participating in an extravaganza of sound and light at Gonzaga's new parade grounds.[53]

The proliferation of confraternities and social organizations, evidence of the parish's robust health, must have finally convinced skeptical black Catholics, who began flocking to St. Martin's from all over northwest Washington. By 1873 the congregation had grown to an estimated 1,500 members. In December of that year the church sponsored a week-long mission by the Lazarist fathers, which attracted some 1,000 from all parts of the city.[54] Especially noteworthy was the number of converts. Typically one third of St. Martin's annual confirmation

52. For an account of anti-Catholic sentiment and analysis of the parade's importance, see *Americana Supplement to St. Jospeh's Foreign Missionary Advocate* 3, no. 4 (1885): 21–22. The quotations are from *CM*, 3 Dec 1870 and 23 Sep 1871. See also "Baltimore Journal of John Martin Spalding," n.d. (ca. 3 Dec 1870), p. 54, Spalding Papers, AAB, in which he estimated the parade's strength at 30,000.

53. *CM*, 24 Jun 1871.

54. *CM*, 8 and 13 Dec 1873. The Lazarist fathers are now more commonly referred to as the Vincentians.

class was composed of adult converts, a statistic unprecedented in Catholic Washington. It was not unusual to see as many as forty new Catholics kneeling to receive the archbishop's anointing and tap on the cheek.[55] This large congregation was augmented at every service by numbers of white visitors—harbingers of the crowds to come—attracted to the church by its convenient location and, above all, by the exceptional beauty of its music.[56]

Before long the little chapel was bursting at the seams. Soon after Barotti's arrival the parish built a frame addition to serve both as a parish hall and during church services as an extension that would expand seating capacity to 600. An exact description of the interior has not survived, but over the years improvements were made to add to its beauty and comfort. Contemporary accounts remark on a series of lamps fixed along the walls of the chapel to spread a warm, soft glow over a large, rectangularly shaped room. A painting by a European master depicting the scourging of Christ at the pillar, a gift of noted Washington banker William W. Corcoran, decorated the sanctuary, which was dominated by a wooden altar surmounted by banks of candelabra that, as described by one reporter, made the sanctuary a blaze of light. Fire was a constant worry in such a situation. Father Barotti was badly burned in a quickly extinguished blaze that broke out on the altar during services on Holy Thursday in 1870. On two other occasions, in what were dubbed "singular incidents," the veil and drapery surrounding the statue of the Blessed Virgin in the sanctuary were consumed by fires of unknown origin while the rest of the chapel remained untouched.[57]

All the work associated with the spiritual care of this growing congregation devolved on one man whose health was never especially strong. In addition to celebrating mass, vespers, and popular devo-

55. St. Martin's was growing so fast that in 1869 two confirmation ceremonies were required in one year. On the number of converts, see *CM*, 13 Mar 1869, 29 Apr 1871, and 21 May 1873.

56. See, for example, *CM*, 13 Mar 1869 and 23 Sep 1871. A busy pastor, Father Barotti was a poor statistician. His *Notitiae* were often incomplete and misleading. Strength figures during this period are at best informed guesses. The *Mirror*, for example, estimated the congregation's size on 19 Nov 1870 at 2,000, only to revise that figure downward (to 1,100) in its issue of 12 Jul 1873.

57. *CM*, 23 Apr 1870 and 17 Aug 1872.

tions, Barotti baptized, married, and buried black Catholics from all sections of the city. He also found time to prepare adult converts while staging an elaborate annual Forty Hours Devotion, Lenten and Holy Week services, and all the other ceremonies associated with the great Christian feasts. To supplement parish funds, he had agreed to say daily mass for the Little Sisters of the Poor at Third and H Streets, Northeast, at 6:00 A.M. In September 1871 a worried congregation surprised him with a gift of a handsome horse and buggy with a silver-mounted harness, which must have eased the burden of his sunrise trek across town and his visits to far-flung parishioners.[58] Finally in 1872 the parish received its first assistant pastor, Bartolomeo Sanmartino. The archbishop had arranged for the services of this graduate from the same Italian seminary that trained Barotti, but the congregation was forced to foot the bill for his journey.[59] Sanmartino quickly proved his worth, rapidly adapting to his new country and plunging wholeheartedly into the busy life of the parish.

Race Relations in Church and State, 1865–1875

The formation of a separate parish for black Catholics took place during a turbulent period in the history of race relations in the nation's capital. It was a decade in which powerful congressional forces, the so-called Radical Republicans, with the enthusiastic support of Washington's old free-black establishment tried to transform the promise of emancipation into a guarantee of social and political rights for all African-American residents. Congressional leaders in particular hoped to use the federal city, which they controlled, as a testing ground for civil rights legislation that could later be applied across the country. These efforts were resisted by the local power structure that viewed the unprecedented growth of the city's black population as a threat to the established social order. Convinced that more civil rights measures would only attract more impoverished freedmen, they increasingly opposed change in the social or political status of black Washingtonians.[60]

58. *CM*, 23 Sep 1871.

59. Barotti tartly informed the archbishop in his 1874 *Notitiae* that the archdiocese owed St. Augustine's $200 for Sanmartino's travel expenses.

60. Unless otherwise noted, the following paragraphs are based on Williams,

In fact the growth in the number of African-American newcomers after the Civil War was spectacular, rivaling in percentage the influx of European immigrants to the great cities of the North. By 1870 the black population of the District stood at 43,422, more than a 300 percent increase in a decade. By 1880 that figure would swell to 59,596, the majority, as before, recent immigrants from rural areas of Maryland and Virginia. By then and for many decades to come black residents would account for one third of Washington's population.[61]

Unlike the European immigrants, who quickly found work in the expanding industries of the great northern cities, the untrained newcomers to Washington were forced to compete for a limited number of laboring and service jobs in a city whose main industry was government. The need to help these unfortunates continued to overwhelm the social welfare agencies of the government, private philanthropies, and the city's churches after the Civil War. The Freedmen's Bureau remained the major benefactor, finding employment, most often as servants, for hundreds of newcomers. It provided housing for many of the impoverished—building, for example, eighty-six modest homes on Delaware Avenue at the foot of Capitol Hill. Only in the early 1870s would conditions start to improve a little. Meanwhile assimilation of the freedmen remained a slow, often agonizing process. Unlike the free blacks of earlier decades, very few of these newcomers were able to break into the skilled job categories. Barred from most unions (the hackers' union was a notable exception), they were denied the chance to apply for the higher paying jobs that had been the avenue of advancement to earlier generations. Nevertheless they took what work was available, and while many remained desperately poor and all would face great trials in the decade of economic depression ahead, they managed to make some headway. By 1870 more than 80 percent of all black Washingtonians were living in traditional households with a male head of family providing the major source of income. Two years

---

"Blacks in Washington, D.C., 1860–1870," Johnson, "The City on the Hill: Race Relations in Washington, D.C., 1865–1885," and Powell, "A Study of the Structure of the Freed Black Family in Washington."

61. These figures include the sizable black populations of Georgetown, Anacostia, and the area north of Florida Avenue. In 1870 the black population of Washington City alone stood at 35,392, representing 32.4 percent of its total.

later the government, judging the worst past, closed the Freedmen's Bureau.

There were other signs of progress. The Freedmen's Aid societies and the Freedmen's Bureau concentrated on education, organizing free schools in all parts of town that trained thousands of the new residents. Although illiteracy remained high, progress was astonishing among a hard-pressed group only recently arrived from areas where schooling was expressly forbidden to them. Despite protracted resistance on the part of local authorities, both Georgetown and Washington agreed in 1868 to pay the sums due the woefully under-financed black public schools. By 1869 some 2,500 students were attending twelve such schools; another 2,400 were in private schools and night classes such as those sponsored by St. Martin's.[62] The crowning glory of this revitalized system was Howard University. Chartered by Congress in 1867 at the request of General O. O. Howard of the Freedmen's Bureau and fellow members of the Congregational Church and dedicated to the ideal of biracial education, the new private institution opened with three separate departments, including a normal school for the training of teachers. In 1868 the university's prestigious schools of law and medicine were added. In succeeding years several members of the Howard faculty would become parishioners at St. Augustine's, thus establishing a relationship between these two institutions that has continued into recent times.

In January 1867 Congress passed, over President Andrew Johnson's veto, a bill guaranteeing unrestricted manhood suffrage in the District of Columbia. A congressional petition signed by 2,500 black citizens supporting the bill provided some counterweight to the determined opposition of the city government. Some 8,200 black men (along with 9,200 white men) registered to vote in the 1867 election. No African Americans ran for office that year, but in the election the following year John F. Cook, one of Washington's best-known black citizens, won a seat on the fourteen-man board of aldermen, and Stewart Carter, a black barber, was elected to the city council.

While black Washington used its newly won political power judiciously, its representatives did not hesitate to push for civil rights

62. *Report of the Commissioner of Education*, p. 262.

measures. Some of their work was done for them by a sympathetic Congress. In 1868, following the adoption of the Fourteenth Amendment, which guaranteed equal protection of the laws to all citizens, Congress removed all racial distinctions in the charters and ordinances of the District of Columbia and specified that African-American men were eligible for jury duty. Influenced by the strength of the black vote, Washington's city council passed strong civil rights measures in 1869 and 1870. These barred discrimination in hotels, restaurants, saloons, and other places of public entertainment.

African Americans might well have concluded in 1871 that their civic ambitions were nearing fulfillment. They were well represented in the city government and supported a mayor sympathetic to the needs of the struggling newcomers. They watched with pride as black senators and congressmen, representatives of several of the reconstructed southern states, deliberated in the halls of the Capitol. Hundreds of black citizens were winning positions in the junior grades of the federal bureaucracy, others in the city government, including the police department.[63] These white-collar workers united with an increasing number of small businessmen to create a sturdy black middle class. As more and more black-owned businesses sprang up, many African Americans, including some of the city's working poor, regularly deposited money in the Freedmen's Savings and Trust Company, a black-owned bank that occupied imposing quarters on Lafayette Square. Only congressional ineptitude in 1870 frustrated a generally accepted plan to integrate the city's economically threatened public schools. Most welcome to the average black resident, the series of increasingly explicit anti-discrimination laws and regulations had passed the city council without opposition and were generally obeyed.

Although the social color line common in all Southern cities generally prevailed in Washington, the emerging black middle class was winning the respect of both the black and white aristocracies, and considerable integration at public events was common. It was readily apparent that in the give and take of home rule, the races were coming to accept each other as partners in the necessary task of transforming a sleepy urban backwater into a modern capital. Yet even in those heady

63. On the extent of this government employment, see ltr., Michael Walsh to Benoit, 27 Feb 1882, 24-MHT-10, ASSJ.

times the seeds of future bitterness could be discerned. As historian Thomas Johnson has observed, Washington's experience demonstrated the futility of laws and well-meant efforts on all sides for the improvement of the black community when those in power successfully oppose real change in the social structure.[64] White opposition to black demands for civil rights had faded, only to be replaced by a paternalistic reaction to black achievements at best and at worst a rigid social exclusion that presaged the reign of Jim Crow that was soon to come. For its part the rising black middle class responded by developing a separate social system, a secret city, historian Constance Green called it, which would exist distinct from, but a part of, Washington for more than a century.

Adding further stress to race relations was Washington's increasingly precarious economic position. The city was going broke while Congress continued to rail against the unpaved streets and open sewers, the multitude of homeless beggars, and the rise in crime and municipal debt. Overlooking its own culpability as the town's largest landlord, it blamed the hapless citizenry. Surprisingly, few objected in February 1871 when Congress finally modified home rule by creating a form of territorial government in the District. Although citizens retained considerable authority, including control of the city's purse in a popularly elected house of delegates and a non-voting representative in Congress, the concept of home rule was set back with the introduction of a presidentially appointed governor and eleven-member upper chamber of the territorial legislature. Together these various units would preside over a city government that finally united Georgetown, Washington, and the rest of the District into one political unit. Some historians consider the Territorial Act an effort by Congress to disenfranchise African Americans. If any congressmen were so motivated, they must have been disappointed when blacks continued to vote, electing five of their number to the new territorial legislature. President Ulysses S. Grant appointed three prominent African Americans, included the universally venerated Frederick Douglass, to the new municipal council.[65]

64. Johnson, "The City on the Hill," pp. 150–51.

65. For a critical interpretation of the Territorial Act, see Marvin Williams, "A Blueprint for Change," *RCHS* 48 (1971–72): 392–93.

The new territorial government would survive only three years. The seeds of its destruction and the fiscal chaos it brought to Washington could be found in the financial panic that struck the nation in 1873, but the unbridled extravagance of the new government's board of public works and its buccaneer director, Alexander "Boss" Shepherd, was the proximate cause of its demise. Free of any form of local control, Shepherd single-handedly transformed the city overnight, providing residents with modern urban amenities and finally fulfilling Pierre L'Enfant's monumental vision of a capital filled with beauty and delight. Miles of gas mains, sewers, streets, and sidewalks were laid, trees were planted, avenues lit, and parks created. Shepherd was a skilled politician. His public works provided employment for black and white laborers in exchange for their vote for bond issues. For a while jobs remained plentiful, even for the city's poorest black residents, and Shepherd remained a popular figure among the city's job seekers.

Desperate for money to continue their extravagance, Shepherd and his subordinates assessed local property at confiscatory rates, forcing many residents, including some new black homeowners, into foreclosure. Unfortunately, Washington's fiscal disaster coincided with the onset of one of the nation's most severe depressions. While payment of back wages to those laborers working on the public improvement projects initially staved off the worst, by 1874 salaries were down to a dollar a day, the Navy Yard and other major employers had laid off most of their workers, and the number of federal clerks and messengers had shrunk. Soon Washington was sharing with the rest of the country the worst of hard times. The relief rolls grew, as did public begging and homelessness. When workers' wages plummeted to fifty cents a day, Congress intervened, underwriting a continuation of the public works projects and thereby allowing many of the poor to survive. But the depression had other consequences. Schools were overcrowded, and many black children were not accommodated. Public health assistance collapsed; petty crime and arbitrary arrests rose. The failure of the Freedmen's Bank in 1874 wiped out the savings of a large segment of the black middle class. Everywhere there was unemployment, depression, and despair.

Congress reacted in 1874 by abolishing the territorial government, temporarily placing the city under control of three commissioners appointed by the President. This arrangement was made permanent by the Organic Act of 1878. In exchange for a system of taxation without representation, the city won the federal government's pledge to underwrite one-half of its annual budget. Without complaint the electorate quietly surrendered the franchise, and the three commissioners, appointed by the president, assumed their century-long control of Washington. Most Washingtonians seemed to consider the abolition of home rule a small price to pay for some financial relief and the creation of an orderly municipality largely controlled by prominent citizens instead of the political opportunists associated with the Radical Republicans. Race also played a part. The new territorial government effectively blunted the growing political power of black citizens, a fact no doubt welcomed by those fearful of further change in race relations. Virtually unnoticed at the time, disenfranchisement effectively cut off the useful and wholesome contacts that had been developing between the races in the free-for-all of local politics. Under the new regime there was little reason for blacks and whites to seek each other out for mutual benefit, and they soon began to go their separate ways.

The story of race relations in postwar secular Washington had its parallel in the local Catholic church. Not that the basic religious needs of African-American Catholics were ever neglected. In addition to the robust religious life at St. Martin's, significant numbers of black Catholics attended Holy Trinity in Georgetown. There Father Stonestreet had also established a free school for their children, which by 1873 boasted some seventy pupils.[66] And although the existence of a similar school for black girls in St. Aloysius parish has been questioned in recent times, there is no doubting the large contingent of black Catholics who worshipped at the Jesuit church on North Capitol Street, albeit from segregated pews in its upper balcony.

With over a thousand African-American parishioners, St. Peter's on Capitol Hill rivaled St. Martin's itself in organizations and societies for black Catholics. Every Sunday evening the church was reserved for these groups, which attended vespers and conducted their business and social meetings.[67] In 1871 the pastor, Father Francis E. Boyle, con-

66. *CM*, 14 Jun 1873.
67. *CM*, 3 May 1873.

ducted a series of religious conferences, along the lines of the popular parish missions, for African Americans in southeast Washington. Their popularity led to further missions at St. Peter's and eventually prompted Boyle to give a series of missions for black Catholics in twelve parishes across the southern Maryland counties. Such an assignment had been proposed by Archbishop Spalding in 1867, and the aging prelate must have been gratified to hear of Boyle's enthusiastic reception by these faithful laymen and women in the cradle of American Catholicism. Reporting on one such mission, Boyle told Spalding: "Eight lectures and three sermons aroused an enthusiastic spirit, spinning new sentiments of gratitude and devotion in that poor Colored race, who are at once, the most forgiving of past injuries & the most responsive to present kindness." [68]

Fighting the indifference of many priests and lay people in his diocese, Archbishop Spalding threw his considerable influence behind two organizations that would have a tremendous influence on the American church and Washington's black parish. He supported the fledgling Oblate Sisters of Providence and outlined for them a mission that encompassed all parts of the United States beginning with the construction of a combined headquarters, school, and orphanage in Baltimore. Spalding, however, does not deserve the credit for finding a group of priests to work with African Americans. It was his friend and agent in Rome, Bishop Michael O'Connor, who convinced the future English cardinal, Herbert Vaughan, to expand the operations of his recently formed missionary society, St. Joseph's Society of the Sacred Heart for Foreign Mission, to include the newly emancipated slaves in America. In 1871 Spalding welcomed the first missionaries from their motherhouse at Mill Hill near London to Baltimore where they established their American headquarters and received from him their first parish in America. At first referred to as the Mill Hill fathers, the priests of the American province of the society were popularly called the Josephites, a name formally adopted when the American province was dissolved in 1893 and an independent American society

68. Ltr., Boyle to Spalding, 23 May 1871, 33-F-9, Spalding Papers, AAB, and Spalding, *Martin John Spalding*, p. 371. Although some of the Jesuit pastors in the region looked askance at Boyle's venture into their territory, the missions were warmly applauded in the Catholic press. See, for example, *CM*, 13 May 1871.

with a similar mission and some of the same personnel was established.[69]

Spalding addressed the subject of race one final time in September 1871. Just months before his death he convened a special conference of the clergy to promulgate the papally approved decrees of his provincial council. He exhorted the assembled pastors to renew their efforts in behalf of the newly freed slaves, "that they might be instructed in the truths of the Christian religion."[70] His actions in the last years of his life mark the high point in the effort to draw the races together in the nineteenth-century American church. After 1872, anti-black sentiment increased, and exclusion, long apparent in Washington's parishes, won official sanction.

Reporting to the bishops on the national picture in 1874, Jesuit missionary Francis X. Weninger branded the position of black Catholics "intolerable." Their children were now excluded from every parochial school operated by whites and therefore must attend public schools, where their faith was endangered. As for the parents, Weninger reported that even when the clergy occasionally invited them "they found no ready welcome among English-speaking Catholics." Just how bleak the situation was becoming in Washington was spelled out by Canon Peter Benoit, a special emissary of the Josephite superior in England, during his 1875 visit. "The antipathy against the Negro is here [in Washington] what we found in Baltimore," he reported. Using St. Matthew's to exemplify the difficulty priests faced in ministering to both races, Benoit passed on the comments of one of the parish assistants. He could not even "sit down side by side with a Negro so strongly is everybody carried away by the general dislike."[71]

Archbishop James Roosevelt Bayley, Spalding's successor, gave up the struggle early on. Calling the antipathy of whites "ineradicable,"

69. On the reorganization of the missionary society in America and the foundation of the American Josephites, see chapter 5, below. This volume will follow the popular custom and refer to these earlier English missionaries as Josephites.

70. Quoted in the *CM*, 9 Sep 1871.

71. Ltr., Rev. F. X. Weninger to the American Bishops, 19 Mar 1874, cy in appendix to Misch, "The American Bishops and the Negro"; Benoit, "Diary of a Trip to America," CB6-32-34, cy in ASSJ.

he told Benoit that he had but little hope of any substantial good being done among the general African-American population. He concentrated instead on ministering to black Catholics in separate facilities such as St. Francis Xavier in Baltimore and St. Martin's, and in the black-dominated missions in the Upper Marlboro region of Prince George's County. Although the Josephites had come to America expecting to work among the freed slaves throughout the South, the practical-minded Bayley sought to limit their service to the care of black Catholics in regular parishes. Bayley's fellow bishops subscribed to his view that evangelization of the African American was hopeless, and thus abandoned the dream of Spalding and his Vatican allies that the unchurched freedmen would be won to the faith.[72]

What began as an effort by Archbishop Spalding and his allies to provide a special ministry for black Catholics became an excuse for the separatists. After the formation of St. Martin's, the task of separating black and white Catholics continued apace. As early as 1868 Father Barotti was complaining that some of his fellow pastors, taking advantage of St. Martin's efforts to work with the needy, were referring all welfare cases involving black residents to St. Martin's. Spalding, seeking as he put it, to comfort Barotti "in his adversity," had further refined his racial policy: "I wish the colored people not in your immediate bounds to be free to go to any priest or church they may prefer, and the priest called on should hear them."[73]

While eager to wash their hands of any responsibility for needy African Americans, some of these same pastors were jealous of St. Martin's ability to attract white Catholics to its services. In 1873, for example, Father White took exception to his parishioners' being invited to attend a mission at St. Martin's. "I will frankly say," the doughty old pastor lectured the new archbishop, "that I do not think it is in order for him [Barotti] to encourage our white people to receive the sacraments at his place." The priests of St. Martin's had enough to do in ministering to black Catholics, whose spiritual interests would

72. Misch, "The American Bishops and the Negro," pp. 385–87.

73. Unfortunately, these vital letters are lost. The above is based on extracts from and a summary of Spalding's ltr. to Barotti, 22 Aug 1868, in Spalding's *Litterarum Registrataurm*, 1868, Spalding Papers, AAB, and in an untitled summary, SAA.

suffer, White added, "if whites are allowed to trespass upon their space."[74]

Archbishop Bayley addressed these complaints during his synod in 1875. At that time he carefully drew up regulations for the administration of the sacraments in those churches dedicated to the service of German-speaking and black Catholics. These regulations were noticeably at variance with those of his predecessor. Where just seven years before Spalding had explicitly ordered that black Catholics be accepted in any church and enjoined any priest they called upon to attend their needs, Bayley's synod now decreed that black Catholics, like their German-speaking counterparts, would receive the sacraments of baptism and marriage only in churches designated specially for them, churches in which reception of these sacraments would be banned to all others.[75] If this was actually meant, it clearly contradicted church law and was universally ignored. Bayley also limited the responsibility of pastors of white churches when it came to administering the last rites for African Americans. These priests must be available "for those requesting this sacred ministry" when "*it is to be feared that their [own] pastors cannot be summoned at the needful moment [opportune time]*."[76]

Bayley was quick to remind Barotti of his infraction of the new regulations. In 1876 he told the pastor that complaints about white Catholics being married and baptized at St. Martin's continued and warned that Barotti "must not interfere in any manner with the white Catholics of Washington. These are not in any way subject to your jurisdiction."[77] Yet the archbishop was noticeably less strict when it came to enforcing his regulation among the other pastors. Black Catholics living on Capitol Hill complained both to him and to his suc-

74. Ltr., White to Bayley, 25 Nov 1873, 44-W-3, Bayley Papers, AAB.

75. Bayley, *Synodus Dicecesana Baltimorensis Octava*, 27 Aug 1875 (Baltimore: Murphy and Co., 1876), pp. 23–25, cy in ASSJ.

76. *Synodus Dicecesana;* emphasis added. It is curious to note that, while these synod paragraphs attempt to draw a parallel between the German-speaking and black parishes, in the vital case of calling on a priest for the sick, the provisions applied to the German-speaking are considerably less restrictive. See analysis of the synod statement by Professor Alexander P. MacGregor, cy in SAA.

77. Ltr., Bayley to Barotti, 10 May 1876, SAA.

cessor about the hardship they suffered when they were ignored by local pastors, who directed them to St. Martin's some four miles away. They reported cases where Catholics had died without spiritual ministration because local priests refused to come.[78]

It was obvious that many had come to accept Bayley's regulation as justification for a complete separation of the races. In 1879 Barotti pleaded with the archbishop to modify what he now called "the law concerning the colored people." Addressing himself to the obligation of Washington's Catholics to care for the poor, he charged that this "law" had disadvantaged black Catholics. Some pastors, he reported, had gone so far as *"to positively forbid"* their St. Vincent de Paul societies attending to black Catholics in their parishes, referring all such cases instead to the financially hard-pressed black parish.[79] These pleas went unanswered, and increasingly black Catholics began to create a separate Catholic society. Only the obtuse would view the development of the black beneficial societies and knighthoods as simply a desire for independence. When African Americans were excluded as a matter of course from the Young Catholic Friend's Society, they formed their own educational society. When the prestigious Carroll Institute organized by Washington's Catholics in 1873 ignored members of the black middle class, they responded by forming their own literary society and debating clubs. When the city's Catholic benevolent societies united in a loose confederation in 1873, the various black societies were not included.[80]

Meanwhile, the *Catholic Mirror,* an official publication of the archdiocese, continued to reflect the prejudice of many white Catholics on the matter of civil rights and race. Considerable space was devoted to criticism of the "idle, indolent and unworthy portion of the colored population," even as the paper's Washington correspondent complained about industrious freedmen pushing Irish immigrants out of jobs. Reports from Washington also burlesqued those local Protestant churches that supported the Fifteenth Amendment and those con-

78. Ltr., A. Harthman *et al.* to Gibbons, 22 Apr 1878, 73-R-4, Gibbons Papers, AAB.

79. Note, Barotti to Bayley, 1 Jan 1879, included in *Notitiae*, 1878, AAW.

80. On the organization and membership of the District Catholic Benevolent Union, see *CM*, 16 Nov 1782 and 18 Jan 1873.

gressmen who tried to integrate the capital's schools. At the same time the paper heaped praise on the archdiocese for what it called the exceptional care the Church lavished on the freedmen, arguing that when black Washingtonians wanted help, even the Protestants among them turned to the Catholic church. As for black Catholics, the paper reminded readers of how well treated they were "in their places," in the churches. The paper rebutted a priest-critic who claimed that African Americans felt unwanted in the archbishop's own church, arguing that "they [black Catholics] still have their place in the Cathedral" adding that "if they leave it, it is by their own choice." Commenting on the opening of a new church for African Americans in Baltimore, the editors concluded, "In buying and resorting to a church of their own it would appear that instead of whites not wanting them in their churches, . . . they do not want the whites." [81]

Although no doubt reflecting the attitudes of many local Catholics, the *Mirror's* views must be understood as those of one of the most unreconstructed groups left in the region. It should be remembered that the paper's extreme pro-Southern position during the war had caused the Lincoln government to jail its editors. Now back in control, they seemed oblivious to recent changes in civil rights. Certainly their widely aired opinions did not reflect the views of all Washington Catholics. Despite the widening social separation of the races in the capital, a substantial number of white Catholics worshipped at St. Martin's, where they always received a warm welcome. Influential members of the white community demonstrated their support by actively engaging in parish celebrations and participated in the many parish fundraisers. During the 1870s local Catholics of all hues took obvious pride in the achievements of the dynamic new parish on Fifteenth Street, a pride that, it must be admitted, sometimes did find reflection in the *Mirror*.

Of manifest concern to black Catholics, the abrupt end to the postwar thaw in race relations hardly came as a surprise. Certainly no African American, even one who had been a part of prewar Washington's generally prosperous free black society, was a stranger to dis-

81. *CM*, 22 Feb 1868 (first series of quotes) and 28 Oct 1868 (last quote). Out of scores of articles and editorials, see in particular 2 Feb 1867, 18 Sep 1869, 20 Nov 1869, 16 Apr 1870, and 18 Feb 1871.

crimination. As before, black Washingtonians listened to demands from both church and state that they accept the racial status quo, that they restrict themselves to a pre-ordained place in society. As they had in past decades, however, African Americans in the capital responded with renewed expressions of hope in a better future and a dogged determination to achieve it on their own. Typical of this reaction was the determination of the people of St. Martin's to build a mighty religious temple, equal to any in the city.

THREE ✠ COMING OF AGE

*F*rom the very beginning, pastor and parishioners were united in their determination to build a large and imposing church. The congregation had fast outgrown its little chapel, even after a frame annex, built in 1867, doubled the seating capacity to 600. At the same time the school had become so crowded that half its pupils were forced to study in make-shift classrooms in quarters rented nearby. Beyond these pragmatic reasons for embarking on such an expensive project, however, lay an unspoken, more compelling motive. These Catholics, so often ignored or patronized by their co-religionists, yearned not only to create a suitable center for parish worship, but to raise a conspicuous monument to their accomplishments and aspirations.

Building a New Church

Their pastor had laid the groundwork for the project within months of his arrival. In early 1868 Father Barotti consulted Baltimore architect E. Francis Baldwin about requirements for a new church. It was obvious that the present property was too small to accommodate building on the scale envisioned by the parish. The first priority, then, was to secure a parcel of land ample enough for a large church building and a future school and rectory. Such a lot would cost $20,000 in postwar Washington, Barotti estimated, a prohibitive amount for the struggling congregation.

What must have seemed a heaven-sent opportunity arose that May, when four lots immediately behind the chapel, along with the one adjoining on Fifteenth Street, the site of Barotti's rented quarters, came on the market. Their purchase, Barotti pointed out to Archbishop Spalding, would both save the parish the expense of leasing a rectory and include at no extra cost a private alley that would add another thousand square feet to the parish's holdings. The total price was $10,000; Barotti assured a clearly nervous Spalding that one-third of that sum could be raised immediately, adding that, before the second installment fell due, "I hope I could make out prety [sic] well." Employing a familiar selling technique, Barotti warned Spalding that a decision was needed immediately because one of the lots was scheduled for auction. Its loss would also mean loss of the alley, which was vital to the architect's plans for the proper placement of a new church. Spalding responded promptly, "consenting that a new foundation be built for Blessed Martin's contiguous [to the property already owned], after consulting experts."[1]

The next five years were busy ones for pastor and congregation. Some misgivings must have been expressed when the architect submitted his proposal for a modified gothic edifice of brick and stone measuring 135 by 65 feet with seating for 1,200. While this would mean possession of one of the city's largest churches, even in those optimistic postwar times the estimated $100,000 price tag had to be daunting. Still, to an eternal optimist like Barotti, the project was doable. As predicted, the parish met the second installment on the new property during 1869 and even raised some additional thousands to purchase a lot around the corner on L Street. This would serve as the site for a temporary church and school when the chapel was razed to make way for the new building. Meanwhile, the enterprising Barotti promised the congregation and the bishop that the architect's estimated costs could be substantially pared down. The parish would postpone building the expensive church tower called for in the plans. It could also obtain much of the building materials from surplus and second-hand sources.

1. Ltr., Barotti to Spalding, 13 May 1868, 33-C-8, and Spalding Letterpress Book, 14 May 1868. Both in Spalding Papers, AAB.

Building under the direction of general contractor John Chapman began in the summer of 1873. To reduce costs, men of the parish excavated the foundations by hand. Reminiscent of earlier times, they gathered at the site every evening, many from a considerable distance, digging up mountains of dirt and hauling it by wheelbarrow to horse-drawn carts waiting in the street.[2] By October 1873 the *Mirror* could report that, notwithstanding financial pressures, work was progressing satisfactorily and that Barotti hoped to sing Christmas Mass in the new church basement. Fortunately, wiser heads prevailed, and when the old chapel, which had been carefully shored up with girders while the digging went on all around it, was finally razed in April 1874, the congregation moved instead to a simple 26 by 120 foot frame building hastily erected on the recently purchased L Street lot. When the basement of the new church was finally occupied in September 1875, it was the parish schools, not a temporary sanctuary, that occupied the rooms especially furnished for their use.[3]

The financial pressures alluded to in the *Mirror* were real enough. The heady optimism enjoyed by workers and businessmen who had prospered thanks to Boss Shepherd's building spree was waning in 1873 as the chill of depression began to grip Washington. Yet even as harsh times approached, some start-up money was found for the new church. Barotti canvassed Washington Catholics for personal loans. One of the first to respond with $3,000 was Father John J. Keane, who while at St. Patrick's and later as bishop of Richmond and first rector of Catholic University was always a stalwart supporter of black Catholic causes. Several of the parish's own mutual benefit societies also loaned substantial sums. In all, $29,000 was raised from private sources in less than a year.[4] At the same time there were some outright gifts. In addition to several small legacies and donations, the parish

2. Whitby, *SS. Paul and Augustine, Two Hundred Years*, p. 18.

3. Ltr., Barotti to Bayley, 19 Nov 1875, att to *Notitiae*, 1875, submitted 1 Jan 1876, AAW. Barotti also reported that the new church basement was being used by the 300 pupils of the Sunday school. See also *CM*, 11 Oct 1873.

4. Ltr., Barotti to Bayley, 19 Nov 1875, att to *Notitiae*, 1875, AAW. A James Jackson loaned the parish $4,000 in 1875. Unfortunately, parish records do not indicate if this is the same James Jackson who ran a prosperous wheelwright business and is listed among the parish founders.

received more than $5,000 from the choir and the Colored Opera Company, receipts of their many performances in Washington and neighboring cities. Records indicate that nearly one-third of the initial building costs of the new church were met by the choir, supporting the claim that the walls of St. Augustine's were purchased for a song.

Even before the new church was completed, its new name, St. Augustine's, had come into common use. The change grew out of the requirement that all churches be placed under the patronage of a saint. Father White's prediction that Martin de Porres would be canonized before black Catholics built a church in Washington proved wrong. The parish proposed the new patron, a choice the archbishop called "appropriate and in every way excellent."[5] It is not difficult to see why. A native of North Africa, Augustine was the son of a Roman official and the saintly Monica, an African woman universally venerated as a model of Christian motherhood. One of the most celebrated intellectuals of the Western world, Augustine was baptized in early manhood through the ceaseless importuning of his mother. He served for many years as bishop of the African city of Hippo, and his powerful literary output, especially his *Confessions* and *The City of God*, have had a deep and lasting influence on Christian thought.

Laying the church's cornerstone was scheduled for Sunday, June 14, 1874. Representatives of all the city's Catholic organizations met several times to plan what was expected to be the mightiest public display of Catholicism in the capital's history. In the end some two thousand Catholics, many colorfully bedecked in the uniforms of the Irish, German, and African beneficial societies and bearing the banners and flags of their groups, formed a line of march more than a mile in length. The press reported on the surge of people crowding every sidewalk and balcony as the parade made its way from city hall down Third Street to Pennsylvania Avenue and up Fifteenth Street to the church. Archbishop Bayley's well-known aversion to martial music provided the only damper on the festivities.[6] Denied the company of the local bands that were a great source of pride to the city, the marchers wended their way in silence, surely a pious if not particular-

5. Ltr., Bayley to Barotti, 20 Jun 1874, quoted in *The Fair Gazette*, 26 Nov 1894.

6. Bayley's ban on marching bands in religious parades spoiled many church celebrations in Washington. See the author's *A Parish for the Federal City*, pp. 193–4.

ly pleasurable event. An estimated ten thousand people were on hand to watch the archbishop bless the foundations and cornerstone, a large piece of Carrara marble donated by Father Barotti's old seminary and personally blessed by Pope Pius IX.[7] Bayley confided that night in his diary his satisfaction with the "immense" crowd and the sermon preached by the eloquent Francis Boyle, but he also hinted at the toll exacted by such pomp and circumstance: "I came home on the ten o'clock train—more dead than alive."[8]

The work went rapidly forward. By August the walls were well advanced, and the builder predicted he would have the whole under roof by October. Nevertheless the *Mirror* was wildly inaccurate when it predicted that the church, like those being built for St. Dominic and Immaculate Conception parishes, would open later that winter.[9] In fact another eighteen months would pass before the first mass was celebrated in the new building. Part of the delay could be blamed on the usual difficulties encountered in so large a project, but the chronic shortage of funds during the deepening financial depression was also a major deterrent. As promised, Barotti had been able to scale down costs considerably. A surprising source of help came from the city's frequently criticized office of public works. St. Augustine's was able to obtain much useful and costly material at no charge from the stocks considered surplus by Boss Shepherd from his extravagant building projects. Reports circulated of the diminutive Barotti touring the city in the parish's horse-drawn cart, picking up materials from the various construction sites.[10] By far the most important contribution, however, came in July 1874 when Jacob Walter, the pastor of St. Patrick's and a generous patron of St. Augustine's, arranged for the transfer of 74,000 bricks salvaged from the razing of the old church on F Street. An exacting manager, Walter initially demanded that most of the bricks be considered a loan, but soon thereafter canceled this provision and made an outright gift of the valuable material. At the same time he turned a substantial personal loan to the parish into a gift. Walter's

7. The parade and cornerstone laying were fully reported in the *CM*, 30 May, 6 Jun, 13 Jun, and 20 Jun 1874. See also, *CM*, 17 Jun 1876.

8. Diary of James Roosevelt Bayley, 14 Jun 1874, Bayley Papers, AAB.

9. *CM*, 15 Aug 1874.

10. *CM*, 17 Jun 1876.

generosity was particularly remarkable because it occurred at a time when work on his own new church had been suspended because of the lack of funds.[11]

Whereas St. Patrick's pastor adamantly refused to go into debt for a new church, the ebullient Barotti suffered no such qualms. In October 1875 he bluntly informed the archbishop that he needed a $20,000 loan to pay off notes coming due and to finish the building. The deepening financial depression seemed only to reinforce his optimism. Admitting that many parishioners were left without financial resources, especially since the failure of the Freedmen's Bank, he claimed that they were "not afraid of the responsibility of the debt which they understand and are eager for." They could be depended on for steady contributions, he assured Bayley, "which will gradually wear away indebtedness." Warming to the subject, he pointed out that those critics who constantly carped about the cost of building so large and beautiful a structure actually stimulated the congregation's "honest pride" which was "the surest guarantee of the success of the work." News of the grand new church had in fact stimulated so much interest that some "prominent protestant colored people" had been led to apply for pews.[12]

Perhaps unsure that his arguments would sway the fiscally conservative archbishop, Barotti asked his fellow pastor Jacob Walter, known throughout the archdiocese for his business acumen, to endorse his request. Walter's response was a mixed blessing. He noted the congregation's ability to raise $10,000 annually during depressed times and concluded that Bayley "can safely allow him to go on" despite the fact that current interest rates were running at a brutal 8 percent. After looking over the books, however, Walter concluded that the parish needed only $15,000 to finish. Given that sum, Walter predicted, the congregation could be in its new church by summer.[13] Whether Barotti's confidence or Walter's hard-nosed estimate carried the day, Arch-

11. Walter even paid the $115.50 drayage charge for hauling the bricks across town. See ltrs., Walter to Gibbons, 21 Sep 1874, 72-S-2, and 27 Aug 1881, 76-C-8. Both in Gibbons Papers, AAB. See also Signed Agreement, F. Barotti and J. Walter, 3 Jul 1874, cy in SAA.

12. Ltr., Barotti to Spalding, 25 Oct 1875, cy in *Notitiae*, AAW.

13. Ltr., Walter to Bailey, 13 Dec 1875, att to *Notitiae*, 1875, AAW.

bishop Bayley agreed to underwrite a $15,000 loan from a New York bank. He had done this without consulting his lawyer, he pointed out, and was frankly worried because the parish debt was now "as heavy as you will be able to manage." Aware that the Sunday collections and pew rents would remain reduced during the depression, he urged Barotti to postpone everything not absolutely necessary. "I beg of you," he concluded, "not to increase the debt in anyway."[14] For once Barotti must have taken Bayley's admonition literally, because two months later the archbishop had to intervene in the case of the plasterer who was pleading for long overdue wages. Noting that workmen were especially pressed "in these hard times," Bayley urged Barotti to do all he could to meet this particular obligation. "You know I do not like to be troubled about these things," he added, "I have troubles enough without them."[15]

The parish responded as it had in the past, by staging a grand concert for what it called its most pressing debt: the wages of the workmen. All Washington was invited to hear the parish choir and popular musicians from around the city perform under the direction of Professor Schreider of the Marine Band. With tickets going at the premium price of a dollar, enough was raised to pay the most pressing bills. Testifying to Barotti's successful foraging for supplies and the generous work of a determined congregation, particularly its choir, the cost of the new church, nearly $75,000, was almost one-quarter less than originally estimated. When its doors opened, nearly one half of that total had been collected.[16]

The object of all this sacrifice was a building of pressed brick trimmed in Seneca and Ohio freestone. Its 65-foot-wide facade was dominated by three high gothic portals surmounted by a rose window sixteen feet in diameter. The steep roof was topped by four carved pinnacles and, over all, a great Celtic cross. To enter the church, a visitor passed along elegant iron railings up a flight of granite steps. Each door opened into a large vestibule, which in turn emptied through folding doors under a broad organ loft into three aisles that stretched toward the sanctuary more than 100 feet away. The ceiling, arching 54

14. Ltr, Bayley to Barotti, 4 Jan 1876, cy in SAA.
15. Ltr., Bayley to Barotti, 13 Mar 1876, cy in SAA.
16. *CM*, 22 Apr and 17 Jun 1876.

feet above polished wood floors, was supported by two rows of clustered pillars each decorated with gilded bosses and capitals. Pews of
carved ash and walnut trim were furnished with covered seat cushions
whose brilliant hues added warmth to the interior.

The walls of the church, elaborately frescoed by Neapolitan artist
Lorenzo Seataglia, were pierced by a series of fourteen large stained-
glass windows, designed by the nationally known artist H. T. Gem-
hardt. They were aligned under a corresponding set of smaller arched
windows admitting sunlight from high above in the clerestory. Light
was also supplied by clusters of ornate gas lamps grouped on each pillar. One reporter marveled at the "scientific adjustments" that produced a "bright but soft light," supplied by a circlet of twelve burners
forming a "halo" around each column. The effect was no doubt beautiful, but 120 open gas jets burning at one time must have caused more
than one parishioner to cast an anxious glance for the nearest fire exit.

An altar rail of turned walnut separated nave from sanctuary. Bowing to the archbishop's request that expensive items be postponed to
better times, the parish temporarily made do with the simple wooden
altar from the old chapel. The sanctuary did, however, include new
side altars, dedicated to the Sacred Heart and Blessed Virgin. These
were made of wood painted to resemble marble. Dominating the interi-
or of the building were three life-size paintings mounted high above
the main altar. Works by the renowned Roman artist Filippo Costaggini, who had recently completed a series of paintings in the U.S. Capitol rotunda, they represented three Christian heroes especially venerated by the congregation: St. Augustine in his bishop's robes flanked
on his right by Blessed Peter Claver in the black cassock of the Jesuits
and on his left by Blessed Martin in the distinctive black and white
habit of the Dominicans.[17]

Then as now St. Augustine's placed special emphasis on its baptis-
tery, which occupied a separate recessed chapel near the south entrance. There, light from three stained-glass windows streamed down
on marble floors and a marble font that, 120 years later, continues to
dispense the saving waters on St. Augustine's new Christians. The

17. For a description of Costaggini's work, see ltr., deRuyter to Lesson, 16 May
1890, 3-G-3, ASSJ. Costaggini would later design ornamental scroll decorations for the
walls of the nave.

INTERIOR, ST. AUGUSTINE'S CHURCH, 1891, showing marble altar designed by E. F. Baldwin and paintings of Sts. Augustine, Peter Claver, and Martin de Porres by Italian artist Costaggini.

church also contained a spacious, high-ceilinged basement with finished rooms large enough to accommodate the parish's many social functions and Sunday school along with supplementary classroom space for the free school.[18]

Formal dedication of St. Augustine's took place on Trinity Sunday, June 11, 1876, the year of the nation's centennial. A throng of distinguished guests joined the congregation to fill the large church to overflowing. The uniformed Knights of St. Augustine escorted the guests. In addition to some 100 representatives of the city's various Catholic societies, these included two senators and four congressmen, the first African Americans in the U.S. Congress, along with officers of flag rank representing the army and navy, former mayors, the chief of police, and various dignitaries of the city's business community. A procession of local clergy and representatives of the religious orders in the archdiocese escorted the archbishop as he blessed the church's exterior and interior walls before proceeding to his throne in a sanctuary ablaze in candlelight. In keeping with the realities of those times, the only African Americans evident in the crowded sanctuary built by black Catholics and dedicated to their use were the ranks of altar boys whose violet cassocks, white surpluses, and flowing red ties rivaled the archbishop's robes in splendor.[19] A grateful parish had invited the generous Father Walter to sing the Solemn High Mass. Music was supplied by an eighteen-piece orchestra and chorus of sixty voices led by Professor Esputa. Reporters spent reams of paper describing the event, but Archbishop Bayley's diary entry summed up the religious, artistic, and social aspects of the day most succinctly: "At 10 o.c. dedicated St. Augustine's beautiful new ch. for the coloured people.

18. Numerous reports survive describing the church at the time of its dedication. See especially, the *CM*, 20 May and 17 Jun 1876, and the *Fair Gazette*, 17 Feb 1882. See also the *Evening Star*, 12 Jun 1876.

19. One further exception: among the clergy in attendance on Archbishop Bayley was Father Patrick Healy, the president of Georgetown College. Healy had been born a slave in Georgia. Two of his brothers were also priests, one eventually serving as bishop of Portland, Maine, the first bishop of mixed black-white parentage in the country. This remarkable family also produced a son who became the father of the U.S. Coast Guard, Captain Michael "Iron Mike" Healy. None of the Healy brothers saw fit to publicize their black heritage, however, and the fact that such a priest participated in the dedication went unnoted.

Preached an hour. Ch. filled with many members of Congress, etc. [Had] a very nice dinner."[20] No doubt the congregation's satisfaction was great when it read about its achievements in the *Evening Star*, one of Washington's leading newspapers. Concluding its lengthy description of the day's events, the *Star* added that the beautiful church "is a credit to the colored people, who have alone built it, and to Rev. Mr. Barotti, whose kind pastorate incited a love for their religion in his flock."[21]

Parish Responsibilities

Proud custodians of one of Washington's largest and most striking churches, the pastor and parishioners immediately launched into a multifaceted program of activities in keeping with the responsibilities of a major city parish. Their first order of business was not, as demanded by the archbishop, to inaugurate an austere budget plan to discharge the parish debt, but, on the contrary, to order suitable and costly furnishings for the new church. The parish would receive many valuable gifts in the next decade, including a hand-carved pulpit designed by the church's architect to harmonize with the gothic interior. The pulpit was donated by James Wormley, proprietor of the famed Wormley's Hotel and a leading black entrepreneur.[22] It also received a valuable chasuble, originally a gift of Pope Pius IX to Washington's Tabernacle Society. The chasuble was the second major papal item possessed by the parish.[23] Other expensive additions were not donations, however, and their cost added appreciably to the parish debt.

20. Bayley Diary, 11 Jun 1876, Bayley Papers, AAB. See also, *CM*, 3, 10, and 17 Jun 1876, and *Evening Star*, 12 Jun 1876.

21. *Evening Star*, 12 Jun 1876.

22. *CM*, 8 Dec 1883. Wormley's hotel, at nearby Fifteenth and H Streets, was a gathering place for many of the nation's major politicians. It was the site of the so-called Wormley conference, which resolved the stalemate following the election of 1876 by giving the presidency to Republican Rutherford B. Hayes in return for restoring Democratic control in the old Confederacy. For a description of the hotel, see Fitzpatrick and Goodwin, *Guide to Black Washington*, pp. 246–47.

23. *CM*, 5 Jan 1878. The chasuble was sold by the ladies of the society to raise money. Its wealthy purchaser donated it to St. Augustine's. It must be counted among the parish's lost treasures.

Easily the most expensive item in the new church was a grand two-manual pipe organ with thirty-eight stops. The elaborately painted ornamental pipes and oak furnishings raised its cost to $14,000, an obligation assumed by the congregation even before the new church opened. The organ was dedicated and played for the first time during high mass in September 1876, when the first of many special collections was taken up to help pay for it.[24] The second major item, the gothic high altar, was consecrated by Archbishop James Gibbons, Bayley's successor, on February 10, 1879. Also designed by the church's architect E. Francis Baldwin, the altar was fabricated by John P. Mullen of Baltimore out of multicolored Tennessee and Italian marble. It rested on a marble platform reached by a flight of white marble steps, the only church in Washington, the *Mirror* boasted, where the entire altar and approaches were of marble.[25] Prior to the dedication of the new main altar, the parish had completed the side chapels with the purchase of marble statues of the Sacred Heart and the Blessed Virgin.[26] These purchases, along with additions and improvements to the church exterior and grounds, substantially—perhaps even irresponsibly, in view of the continuing depression that had seriously hampered contributions—raised the debt.

Other pressing needs vied for part of the parish's meager resources. Since the razing of the old chapel, part of the school had been housed in space on the second floor of the temporary church on L Street while the primary grades occupied the new church's basement. Although Father Barotti had told the archbishop that the property on L Street could be sold after the new church opened, it was obvious that the parish would need a separate school building. The property carried a $1,900 mortgage, but with student enrollment rising, the pastor saw no way out. Arguing that the parish had "a desirable property in the best part of the city," he asked his superior to approve an additional $2,000 to convert the hastily-erected but commodious structure into a modern schoolhouse. The remodeling inspired the *Mirror's* reporter to one of his frequent rhetorical flights: "All that the art of the builder and

24. *CM*, 2 and 9 Sep 1876. In contrast, the church's stained windows, including the rose window, cost $1,455 and the 180 pews just $2,400.

25. *CM*, 8 Feb 1879. See also, *CM*, 15 Feb 1879.

26. *CM*, 7 Oct 1876 and 17 Nov 1877.

painter could do to make it perfect was done." He declared the school-house superior to the "pretentious" buildings in the neighborhood and predicted that with the "splendid sisters" in charge, the school "will be an honor to the church and the colored Catholics of Washington."[27]

The sisters referred to were members of the Congregation of the Holy Cross. By 1875 Sister Seraphine had given up supervision of the school to prepare for new responsibilities associated with the parish, and Father Barotti, especially concerned with the constant turnover of teachers in the boy's division, used the occasion to place the school in the hands of a teaching order that would provide stability and expertise for a growing institution. The Holy Cross sisters agreed to staff the school, and Sisters Angelica (Holton) and Octavia (McConnery) arrived in September, the first contingent of a staff that would operate the school during the next twenty years. The agreement called for an annual salary of $400 for each sister. Although these wages were slightly higher than normal in the area, the sisters agreed to lodge at the Academy of the Holy Cross on nearby Massachusetts Avenue, thus sparing the parish the expense of providing a convent.[28] During their first year at St. Augustine's, the sisters taught 56 boys and 70 girls, as well as the 30 pupils in the night school. They also joined members of the congregation in teaching the 350 pupils in the parish's Sunday school.

Commencement exercises in 1876, which honored Laura Dey, Annie Wells, Robert Randolph, and Mary Spriggs with medals for achievement, also revealed a reorganization of the school into primary and senior departments. Further alterations in the building would allow in succeeding years for additional classrooms and the introduction of a wider variety of subjects in the senior department. In time what

27. *CM*, 8 Sep 1883.

28. Annals of the Holy Cross at St. Matthew's, pp. 14–16, Archives of the Holy Cross Academy, Washington, D.C. See also *Our Provinces. Centenary Chronicles of the Sisters of the Holy Cross, 1841–1941* (Notre Dame: St. Mary's of the Immaculate Conception, 1941), 56–58, and Sister M. Campion Kuhn, "The Sisters Go East—and Stay," a paper delivered at the Congregation of the Sisters of the Holy Cross Annual Historical Conference, 1983, p. 68. Indicative of the popularity of at least one of these teachers was the large number of girls in the parish christened Euphemia in tribute to a sister who served at St. Augustine's for fifteen years. See Sister Mary Angels, C.S.C., "Report on the Holy Cross Sisters at St. Augustine's" (ca. 1970), SAA.

was in effect a junior high school curriculum was added, which provided instruction in rhetoric, algebra, bookkeeping, plain sewing, and drawing.[29] Those who successfully completed these advanced courses were specially honored. In 1883, for example, Mary Middleton was awarded the gold medal at graduation.

The dramatic increase in teachers' salaries and the cost of remodeling the schoolhouse added significantly to the congregation's ongoing financial problems. Although the parish frequently failed to pay the teachers their full salaries, the cost of operating the school rose 300 percent in just four years.[30] Nor could relief be sought in the form of raised tuition payments. The truth was, St. Augustine's was beginning to find itself competing with the public schools, which, though not yet able to provide for all the city's African-American children, were free and provided an attractive alternative to private schools. Father Barotti and his assistant, seemingly unconcerned with the strong Protestant influence in public schools, asserted that Catholic children could "frequent the common schools without harm" so long as they regularly attended Sunday school. This opinion was disputed by some of their fellow priests and by many parents in the congregation, who remained strongly committed to the concept of parochial education.[31] They took considerable pride in the fact that their school was judged highly by archdiocesan officials, who had concluded that its students "are apt and make a far better showing than the colored pupils in the public schools in the studies of grammar, rhetoric, algebra, bookkeeping, besides the elementary branches of an English education."[32]

29. The school were frequently noted in the *CM*. See esp. issues of 30 Jan 1875, 15 Jul and 9 Sep 1876, 2 Feb 1878, and 16 Jun 1883. See also Rouse, "A Study of the Development of Negro Education Under Catholic Auspices," p. 61.

30. Teacher salaries that totaled $260 in 1874 had, by 1878, risen to $900. See various *Notitiae*.

31. Canon Benoit, emissary from Josephite headquarters, was specially critical of Father Sanmartino's argument that public schools posed no danger to the faith of Catholic children because many of the teachers in the public schools were Catholic. Benoit's tart conclusion: "I fear that the priests [at St. Augustine's] . . . seem not to have any accurate knowledge of their Catholic population." Benoit, "Diary of Trip to America," 25 Jan 1875, CB6-34, ASSJ.

32. From an 1883 article in the *CM*, as quoted in *American Supplement to St. Joseph's Foreign Missionary Advocate* 1, no. 3 (Jul 1883): 15.

Despite the obvious financial burden, the congregation agreed that the school should remain free to students unable to meet the modest tuition charges.

Also competing for parish funds, at least for a brief period, was a short-lived home for aged women in northwest Washington. The home was a brainchild of Matilda Madison, a prominent member of the parish who proposed that St. Augustine's sponsor such an institution. Father Barotti, convinced that only a religious order possessed the dedication and expertise to make a success of such an enterprise, refused to pursue the matter. Undeterred, Madison turned to Father White at St. Matthew's for help. He agreed to sponsor the home, and in November 1874 Washington Catholics were invited to a festival, the first in a series of fund raisers at St. Matthew's to underwrite the Madison project. These activities provided White with enough money by August 1875 to make a substantial down payment on two lots, one containing a modest frame house, near Nineteenth and R Streets.[33] White planned to build a large home, but settled initially on spending $800 to enlarge and remodel the existing structure, making it suitable for twenty residents. Responsibility for what was called the Home for Aged Colored People was entrusted to a corporation whose board, in addition to White, included two other priests and two prominent laymen, the noted philanthropist Thomas E. Waggaman, and St. Augustine's Isaac Landic.[34]

As Barotti predicted, these busy men were unqualified to supervise the day-to-day operation of an old-age home. Following Father White's death in 1878 they repeatedly appealed to the Little Sisters of the Poor to assume control, only to be refused. Nor were the sisters, fearful of white Washington's racial attitudes and aware of the archdiocese's policy toward racially separate institutions, ready yet to take the aged black women into their new home on H Street. In desperation the trustees turned to Father Barotti. Waggaman pointed out that the financial burden would be light. Although the parish would need to underwrite day-to-day operations, it would be able to pay off the home's modest debt with funds on hand along with a small legacy left for that

33. *CM*, 21 Nov 1874, 21 Aug 1875, and 29 Jan 1876.

34. Certificate of Incorporation of the Home of Aged Colored People, 26 Feb 1876, *Liber* Acts of Incorporation D.C. No. 2, folio 77, cy in 72-V-2, Gibbons Papers, AAB.

purpose by White. A practical businessman, Waggaman put the choice in stark terms: without St. Augustine's support the home would close and the property sold at a great loss; should the parish assume responsibility "until some future time" when the Little Sisters could be persuaded to take control, the aged would live in peace and the property increase in value. The home's future was up to St. Augustine's and Archbishop Gibbons.[35]

Barotti was left unswayed by such arguments. He remained convinced that no good purpose was served in assuming responsibility for a charity doomed to fail without the support of a congregation of religious women. He was, however, sensitive to popular opinion, and when he urged the archbishop to close the home, he also asked that the unpopular decision be seen as one taken by the trustees. Barotti confessed that to link him to the closing "will bring on me an ill feeling from the col. people both cath. & protestant." They would say, he predicted, that "I opposed their interests and that this was done to divert the funds of the poor into the church."[36] This was the only recorded instance of the much-loved pastor opposing the wishes of his congregation or of showing any concern about public opinion. Whatever the merits of his position, Barotti lost the argument. Archbishop Gibbons ordered St. Augustine's to assume control of the home.[37] For over five years the parish kept the institution open, met its expenses, and managed its operation.

The need for such an institution finally ceased after 1885 when the Little Sisters added a new wing to their building that provided separate departments for black men and women. In fact as early as 1880 the Little Sisters had approached Archbishop Gibbons about admitting aged African Americans. Gibbons agreed, but demanded that the races be separated. The sisters petitioned Congress for assistance, explaining that "we are urged to make no color distinction, but we are already crowded and have no money to buy another house; and you are well aware that it is impossible to have the Negroes together with the

35. Ltr., Waggaman to Barotti, 10 Feb 1879, 74-I-12, Gibbons Papers, AAB. See also *CM*, 13 Apr 1878.

36. Ltr., Barotti to Gibbons, n.d. (ca. Feb 1879), 74-J-12, Gibbons Papers, AAB.

37. Ltr., Barotti to Gibbons, 14 Mar 1879, 74-L-1, Gibbons Papers, AAB.

whites."[38] Congress voted them $5,000, enough to purchase a small house and refurbish it as a shelter for thirty residents until the new facilities were opened in 1885.[39] Surviving records fail to indicate whether the sisters or St. Augustine's received the proceeds from the sale of the Home for Aged Colored People after its residents transferred to the new quarters.

That a struggling parish could overcome many obstacles to build an imposing church, a symbol to all Washington of the achievements of black Catholics, spoke volumes about its pastor's dynamic leadership and social vision. Its subsequent slide into a level of debt that threatened its significant achievement revealed a pastor with little aptitude for fiscal discipline. Father Barotti's sunny optimism, expressed so persuasively when he was seeking the archbishop's permission to borrow money in 1875, proved of little avail when the bills came due. Barotti was right in predicting that pride in their beautiful church would stimulate the congregation to even greater generosity. Unfortunately, he failed to understand how a maturing congregation would also naturally be forced to assume ever greater financial obligations, such as the more fully staffed and better equipped school appropriate to a major city parish. Further, it took more money to operate a large church, especially when the pastor and people found it impossible to resist the impulse to add expensive furnishings. For them the archbishop's exhortation to postpone all but the most essential things meant putting off for a matter of weeks or months rather than years or decades.

Their spending spree took place just as unemployment and economic distress spread across all classes of citizens in the capital. As the effects of the depression worsened, demands on the parish's purse intensified. Only the charity of its beneficial societies saved some of the poorest families from total ruin. The more the congregation gave, the higher the debt became. At the end of 1879, the parish debt, consisting of the bank mortgage arranged by Bayley and the many private

38. Quoted in Louis G. Weitzman, *One Hundred Years of Catholic Charities in the District of Columbia* (Washington: The Catholic University of America Press, 1931), p. 81.

39. *CM*, 7 Apr 1883.

loans negotiated by Barotti over the years, was conservatively estimated at $58,090. The $3,800 interest due on this debt amounted to nearly 70 percent of the parish's receipts that year. Through circumstances largely beyond its control, the parish faced a genuine financial crisis, one that would require a generation of hard work and sacrifice to bring under control.

In fairness to the beleaguered pastor, the few options left open produced amazing results. Reflecting the growth in membership and the enthusiasm all felt about the new church, collections rose dramatically, although sometimes visitors needed a stern reminder. With collections at the crowded Sunday vespers service averaging a mere $5.00 despite attendance by many well-heeled Washingtonians, the pastor announced in October 1878 that the choir would be discontinued unless contributions increased. He outlined the expenses involved in maintaining Professor Esputa's renowned group and added that so many guests actually only served to inconvenience parishioners. Since people of all denominations gathered to hear the music, he reasoned, all should contribute. To that end he had a collection box positioned at the main door. Money thus collected, and he expected it to be a considerable amount, would be used to cover choir expenses.[40]

Echoing successful fund raisers at other parishes, St. Augustine's sponsored cultural lectures such as the one given at Ford's Opera House in April 1878 by "Dr." J. Web Rogers on "Relations between the Colored Race and the Catholic Church" and popular entertainments such as a stereopticon show on Germany and castles on the Rhine by "Professor" Edward Turner.[41] And then there were the parish picnics, where parishioners and their guests would gather at popular spots like White's Lot (today's Ellipse) or at the Van Ness mansion to enjoy barbecues and games. One held at Tivoli Park in September 1880, for example, raised a large sum from more than one thousand attendees. On this occasion, however, the newspaper reported that a massive thunderstorm in the early evening "ended all joy."[42]

Parish fairs, held with ever-increasing frequency after 1877, pro-

40. *CM*, 26 Oct and 2 Nov 1878.

41. *CM*, 6 Apr 1878 and 12 Mar 1887.

42. *CM*, 18 Sep 1880. See also among many accounts, *CM*, 14 and 28 Jun and 9 Aug 1879.

vided a steady source of income. The $1,981 realized from the 1880 fair, for example, represented more than a third of all receipts in a year when pew rents and collections had hit a new high of $3,200. These sums were especially impressive considering that St. Augustine's fair was but one of many held by churches throughout the city, all competing for the city's scarce entertainment and charitable dollars. St. Augustine's was especially notable for the fact that, in a capital that was leaning toward racial isolation, its fairs were racially integrated, with social doyennes of both races presiding over the various booths and confection tables sponsored by the parish and other Catholic organizations.[43] The fairs were attended by thousands during their usual two-week length. The 1878 fair, interrupted by the death of Pope Pius IX, promptly added a further week to its schedule. Typifying the generous amount of free publicity afforded these events, the *Catholic Mirror* informed its Washington readers that the fair was now "back in business," noting that the Knights of St. Augustine had visited in a body and "sensibly emptied many tables" of all sale items. *The Bee*, the city's major black newspaper, reported on the schedule of events, prizes, and names of those in charge of the various tables at the 1883 fair.[44] Later fairs boasted publication of a daily newspaper sponsored by the Carroll Institute and the Tabernacle Society, which contained scores of advertisements, letters, and reports on a variety of religious and historical subjects, along with pertinent information concerning what was being sold at the various booths. The papers, written in a lively style, featured articles on the day-to-day success of the event and news about the participants.

The fairs offered entertainment in the form of choral recitals and band concerts, dramatic readings, and martial arts exhibits. Illuminati of church and state regularly attended. The archbishop not only actively encouraged Washington's Catholics to support the hard-pressed parish in these fund raisers, but frequently participated himself, in lat-

43. The names of Washington aristocracy of both races sponsoring and attending the fairs were regularly reported in the press. See, for example, *CM*, 18 Feb and 18 Mar 1882.

44. *The* [Washington] *Bee*, 17 Nov and 8 Dec 1883, and *CM*, 23 Feb 1878. See also *CM*, 5 Feb 1881 and various issues of the *Fair Gazette*, Feb 1882, cy in Rare Books and Special Collections, CUA Library.

er years accompanied by the new apostolic delegate.[45] They and scores of congressional figures, city officials, and military officers of note would purchase objects donated by local craftsmen, judge the military contests, browse the white elephant tables, buy chances on door prizes, and enjoy the food. News of prize winners appeared in the press—for example, the city was informed that Felix Barotti Benjamin, the newborn son of the well-known musician, won the baby shoe contest at the 1882 fair. That same evening fairgoers were entertained by the Capitol City Guards, Washington's best-known black militia organization recently returned from participating in the celebration of the Baltimore Orioles victory in the newfangled baseball playoffs.[46] The fairs were a social highlight of the parish year, patronized to a surprising degree by the congregation's Protestant friends and neighbors. Their importance in the development of parish cohesion, fostering better race relations, and raising money during the last quarter of the century can not be overestimated.

The End of the Beginning

Both pastor and parishioners might be forgiven for not dwelling overlong on gloomy financial matters at a time when their new church was becoming a spiritual and cultural center in the capital. In 1878 the *Mirror* boasted about the number of diplomats, congressmen, and "the aristocracy" frequently seen at St. Augustine's. These "elite and upperclass citizens," the reporter asserted, considered it their special privilege to be present, especially during Sunday vespers, when the choir "which cannot be surpassed" sang the beautiful motets and responses appropriate to that ancient service. The nationally read journalist Frank Carpenter noted that the music at St. Augustine's was so famous "that many strangers include a service on their sight-seeing program." One of these visitors marveled at the unusual sight of large

45. Gibbons routinely published letters encouraging attendance at the St. Augustine fairs. See, for example, ltr., Gibbons to Walsh, 28 Oct 1881, repr. in *CM*, 12 Nov 1881. For a description of activities at a typical fair, see *CM*, 18 Feb 1882.

46. *CM*, 18 Feb 1881. For examples of the extensive coverage of the fairs replete with names of donors, winners, and organizers, see *CM*, 25 Feb 1881, 11 Feb 1882, and 15 Dec 1883.

numbers of Protestants of both races gathered with their Catholic neighbors in the church.[47]

Especially prominent among these guests were President and Mrs. Rutherford B. Hayes, who frequently made the five-block journey from the White House to attend Sunday afternoon vespers. Equally welcomed was the pre-eminent black leader, Frederick Douglass. Appointed by Hayes as U.S. Marshal for the District, the eloquent Douglass commented after one of his visits:

It is perfectly delightful to go to that Saint Augustine Catholic church and see the perfect freedom which prevails between white and colored. It is so in all the Catholic churches of the District, but Saint Augustine's is the colored people's pride. The Catholics set a very fine example to their Protestant brethren in that respect.[48]

Just how many Catholics claimed membership in St. Augustine's parish remains a mystery. Actually the exact size of any congregation in Washington during this period can only be estimated. The evidence suggests that by 1880 nearly 2,000 black Catholics belonged to the parish, by no means the largest Catholic congregation in the city, but one standing on the threshold of phenomenal growth.[49] Amid the welter of visitors, parishioners devotedly counted the seasons with appropriate liturgical celebration. Then as now Trinity Sunday and the feast of St. Augustine were given special notice when visiting preachers and ecclesiastical dignitaries presided over ceremonies that employed the parish's formidable musical forces.[50] Lenten and May devotions were

47. *CM*, 2 Feb 1878 (1st quote) and 29 Jul 1878 (2d quote); Frank Carpenter, ed., *Carp's Washington* (New York: McGraw-Hill Book Co., 1960), p. 239 (3d quote); and Jane W. Gemmill, *Notes on Washington, or Six Years at the National Capital* (Washington: Brentano Bros., 1883), pp. 108–09.

48. Extract from intv. with J. H. Beadle printed in the *Yenowine's Illustrated News* [Milwaukee, WI], 10 May 1894, repr. in *St. Joseph's Advocate* 3, no. 1 (July 1894): 601–02.

49. Figure derived from reports of the number of parishioners making their Easter duty, little more than an educated guess by Father Barotti, as well as figures for Sunday school attendance and baptismal and burial records—all included in the annual *Notitiae*.

50. These ceremonies were always given detailed coverage in the *Catholic Mirror*. See, for example, 2 Sep 1876, 15 Feb 1879, and 8 Sep 1888.

crowded affairs, as were the archbishop's visits for confirmation, which always included an impressive number of adult converts kneeling to receive the sacrament. A sober reminder of nineteenth-century urban life, the large number of adult and infant baptisms was in some years offset by an equal number of children and infant burials.

The affairs of the busy city parish were managed by two priests. Father Barotti's first assistant, Father Sanmartino, remained to see the new church consecrated before being replaced by yet another Italian immigrant, Peter B. Torro. A well-educated man, Torro proved a popular figure at St. Augustine's, where he was particularly appreciated as advisor to several of the beneficial societies. He was especially attracted to the martial trappings of the Knights of St. Benedict, whom he served as chaplain. Despite lengthy and debilitating bouts with malaria, Father Torro was often on hand to cheer the Knights as they performed their military drills and marches.[51]

Still, many special responsibilities attached to the operation of a church with parishioners scattered across the city fell to the pastor. Barotti could be seen in all parts of town visiting the sick and consoling the afflicted. The constant search for funds occupied an inordinate amount of his time and drained his flagging energies. His daily visit to the Little Sisters of the Poor only added to his burdens. The parish's gift horse and buggy proved indispensable in carrying out his many duties. It was more than a minor inconvenience when the horse bolted one summer day in 1875, throwing Barotti and damaging the buggy. The priest seemed far more worried about the buggy's injury than his own, and he quickly raised the $25 needed for repairs.[52] In 1879 he went out of his way to defend the expense of maintaining a private vehicle, pointing out to any busybodies in the chancery that the horse was fed and stabled at his personal expense out of the money paid him by the Little Sisters.[53] In an age that set great store on flights of oratorical brilliance, the charismatic Barotti adopted an entirely different method. His sermons, straightforward, matter-of-fact instructions on matters of faith and doctrine, were delivered in a simple, conversation-

51. Father Torro's re-occurring illness was the subject of numerous newspaper reports. See, for example, *CM*, 12 Apr 1879 and 31 Jul 1880.

52. *CM*, 21 Aug 1875.

53. Postscript to *Notitiae*, 1878 (submitted 1 Jan 1879), AAW.

al tone that both charmed and animated his audience. The congregation was proud of their gifted, academically honored pastor. The unaffected love of the diminutive Italian priest cast its spell, uniting pastor and people to an extent that excited the interest of African Americans across the city. One commentator remembered that Barotti's name was a household word in Washington and his devotion to the interests of his flock a major cause for its increase.[54]

In 1879 Barotti suffered what was then called a serious bilious attack while on a sick call. Although he recovered, a worried congregation urged him to take a restorative popular in those times: a sea voyage. Leaving the Dominican Father John Albert Bokel in charge, Barotti made a whirlwind trip to Europe, visiting his aged father, reporting personally to the newly elected Pope Leo XIII, and stopping at the shrine at Lourdes.[55] The trip seemed to restore him, but ceaseless concern about the debt and the increasing round of pastoral duties had taken their toll. In January 1881 he developed pneumonia after being exposed to a winter storm returning from a sick call to the dying Mrs. Isaac Landic.[56] Two months later Barotti attended the inauguration of President James Garfield with his brother, a visitor from Baltimore. Afterward he accompanied his brother to the railroad station on the Mall, where the two sat on the waiting train saying their goodbyes. Engrossed in conversation, the pair failed to notice the train's departure, and Barotti was forced to jump off at the first stop in Ivy City. From there he had to trudge miles home through the snow. Despite his obvious weak state, he refused to slow down, telling a friend, "I don't have time to be sick." Nevertheless on May 2, after a full day of parish duties and while watching parish children playing outside his window, Barotti suffered a fatal heart attack. He was just forty-three years old.

54. M. B. Johnson, "Father Barotti, First Pastor of St. Augustine's Church; A Memoir of his Life and Services," serialized in *The Fair Gazette* (Feb 1882). This lengthy account was written one year after the pastor's death and contains much information that is unavailable elsewhere. The following description of Barotti's last months is based on this report.

55. *CM*, 17 Mar 1879. Barotti's fellow pastor, St. Patrick's Jacob Walter, was treated to two transatlantic voyages by his congregation. Unlike Barotti, Walter's trips restored his health.

56. *CM*, 19 Mar 1881.

The death of the young pastor produced an outpouring of grief. The funeral saw the streets around St. Augustine's jammed with those unable to squeeze into the large church. A mile-long cortege followed the hearse to Mt. Olivet, where Isaac Landic, William Wheeler, Alexander Thomas, William Smith, Willis J. Smith, and James E. Jackson carried the coffin to a temporary resting place.[57] A Barotti Memorial Association was formed to devise some tangible expression of the congregation's regard for their late pastor, and in September a crowd of 3,000 mourners witnessed the erection of the impressive monument that still graces Barotti's resting place on a gentle hill in Mt. Olivet surrounded by several members of his flock.[58] Buried adjacent to Barotti in what in those days was a cemetery whose sections were rigidly segregated by race were parishioners Cecilia Beans, the rectory's first cook, Sister Seraphine and her father, Mary Harrison, the parish's first fund raiser, William H. Queen, Isaac and Elizabeth Landic, and Romaelus and Cecilia Warren. Barotti must have planned all along to break Mt. Olivet's color barrier when in 1872 he purchased so large a plot in its white section for $150. The first to be buried there was John Noel, the patriarch of the Haitian immigrant family, in 1881; the last was Cecilia Warren in 1899. They all rested near the graves of Thomas Waggaman, Denis J. Stafford, and other prominent white Catholics.[59]

Even as he grieved over the sudden death of the popular pastor, Archbishop Gibbons was busy planning the future of Washington's black congregation. A protege of Archbishop Spalding, Gibbons fully subscribed to his predecessor's belief that black Catholics should worship in parishes established especially for them and that their spiritual care was best left, not to diocesan clergy, but to specially dedicated

57. For a detailed description of Barotti's death and burial, see *CM*, 7 and 14 May 1891.

58. *CM*, 17 Sep 1881. Officers of the Memorial Association were: Isaac Landic, Charles A. Butler, Willis J. Smith, William H Wheeler (who died before the memorial was completed), William Smallwood, Mary A. Harrison, Mary C. James, Louisa Bowie, Isaiah Hatton, Ananias Herbert, Benjamin Waters, and Gracie Dyson. The monument, a massive 15-foot marble cross, was designed by Charles Roussent and carved at the Rousseau marble works. Its cost, $500, was subscribed in five days. In addition to books and furnishings, Barotti's estate totaled $200, which he willed to the parish housekeeper, Mildred Dodson. See *CM*, 6 and 27 Aug 1881.

59. Interment and Owner's Cards, Mt. Olivet Cemetery.

missionaries.[60] It was not surprising, therefore, that when mourners gathered back at the rectory after the funeral, Gibbons asked the American provincial of the Josephites, John R. Slattery, to join him in a stroll around the garden. There Gibbons came straight to the point: he wanted the Josephites to assume responsibility for St. Augustine's parish.[61]

Demonstrating remarkable temerity for a young priest, Slattery adamantly refused the archbishop's request. Referring to the parish's huge debt and the persistent rumors that anxious creditors were already calling for payment, the Josephite argued that assuming such a burden would endanger the very existence of his fledgling community. A surprised Gibbons called in reinforcements in the person of the persuasive Bishop John Keane of Richmond. Keane renewed the assault, yet even when confronted by the two men on whose patronage the Josephites most depended, the stubborn Slattery held his ground. Only after separate negotiations with the archbishop and the provincial did Keane come up with a workable compromise: Slattery would agree to assume responsibility for the parish, subject to the approval of his superior, Bishop Vaughan, in London; in return, Gibbons would agree to accept *in writing* full responsibility for the parish debt and its annual interest payments.

Slattery's reluctance must be seen, not as an attempt to evade service with Washington's black Catholics, but solely as a pragmatic reaction to a potential financial disaster for his tiny community. As revealed in subsequent years, this often contentious man would fight with a missionary's zeal for the spiritual and social welfare of African Americans. His superiors especially admired his priestly dedication as well as his sound business management and flair for public relations. His defects were also readily apparent. Impatient and arrogant, the brash young American was always quick to point out the defects of his subordinates, micromanage their work, and openly cast doubt on their ability, all which made him singularly unsuited for the task of di-

60. Evidenced in countless official documents, Spalding's views were even discussed in contemporary journals. See, for example, *American Supplement to St. Joseph's Foreign Missionary Advocate* 3, no. 4 (1885): 21–22.

61. A detailed account of this conversation is contained in ltr., Slattery to Canon Benoit, 6 May 1881, 22-MHT-22, ASSJ. (Emphasis in the original.)

recting a religious community of priests recently arrived from Europe.[62]

Full of misgivings about St. Augustine's, Slattery spent a month in Washington, where he served as interim pastor (Father Tarro remained temporarily as his assistant) and tried to bring some order to the parish's tangled financial affairs. A survey of what passed for Barotti's accounts—in reality a mass of scattered bank notes, unpaid bills, and unverifiable loans—quickly revealed the true extent of the parish's precarious position. To Slattery's chagrin, the debt actually totaled over $74,000 with interest rates on sixty-four separate private loans averaging an almost usurious 9 percent. Calling the accounts "a perfect mess," a despondent Slattery predicted to his superiors in London that the parish "cannot be maintained."[63] But Gibbons remained adamant: St. Augustine's would survive backed by the full faith and credit of the archdiocese. Unable to escape the responsibility, Slattery set about paying off the most pressing creditors with $10,000 borrowed from the archbishop; for the rest he sought to renegotiate the loans at lower rates. In succeeding weeks Slattery's optimism returned. With the archbishop's backing, he decided, the parish could endure. He even thought it possible to fulfill Gibbons's hope that the parishioners could somehow reduce the debt by $5,000 a year. As for the struggling Josephites themselves, he told his worried superior in London, "I believe we are safe." He had prevailed on Gibbons to sign every outstanding loan, thus making any written guarantee unnecessary because, as he put it, "when the notes mature, the holders will naturally look to the drawer."[64]

As American provincial, Slattery was also entitled to select the parish's new pastor. His inclination was to appoint William Hooman

62. Ltr., Benoit to Vaughan, n.d. (ca. Feb 1884), 29 MHT 14, ASSJ. See also, Peter F. Hogan, *The Josephites; A Century of Evangelization in the African American Community* (Baltimore: The Josephites, 1993), pp. 15–16.

63. Ltr., Slattery to Benoit, 19 May 1881, 22-MHT-18, ASSJ. For a full account of the debt, see ltr., Slattery to Gibbons, 25 May 1881, 75-V-5, Gibbons Papers, AAB. Evidence of Barotti's informally contracted loans was continually popping up. See ltr., Slattery to Gibbons, 23 Jul 1881, 76-A-10, same source, explaining the tortured route one $900 loan took through a succession of creditors before coming to the worried Slattery's attention.

64. Ltr., Slattery to Vaughan, 15 Jun 1881, 22-MHT-21, ASSJ.

because of the young Englishman's financial acumen, but on June 1, 1881, Michael F. Walsh succeeded Father Barotti as St. Augustine's second pastor, and Hooman was assigned as his assistant.[65] The thirty-year-old Walsh had been born in Ireland's County Cork. Brought as a child to America, he entered the seminary following an aborted business career. As a seminarian he developed a strong interest in the spiritual welfare of African Americans, and in 1872 he went to London to be professed as a Josephite. He served as an assistant at St. Francis Xavier's, Baltimore's venerable black church, before moving to Washington. Although relations between the two priests would soon sour, Slattery was at first full of praise for the jovial Irishman. Reflecting the congregation's assessment of Walsh as one who showed an unusual affection for his flock, Slattery described the new pastor as "an out and out black priest"—high praise from an outspoken champion of black causes.[66]

In uneasy tandem Walsh and Slattery set out to attack the debt problem. They had some outside help. The archbishop authorized a special collection for the parish throughout the diocese. The results were gratifying; the affluent parishioners of the Baltimore cathedral, for example, donated $530. One of Walsh's major chores in those years was the "collections," the name given to his periodic visits to Washington parishes where he made a special plea for help. This consisted for the most part in soliciting members for the St. Augustine's Debt Association. A brainchild of Slattery, the association promised special spiritual benefits, including a plenary indulgence granted by Pope Leo XIII, to any who contributed at least $3 annually (or twenty-five cents a month) to the cause. Archbishop Gibbons kicked off the drive with a well-publicized pledge of $100 a year.[67]

65. Hooman was ordained in 1874 and later served in the Josephite missions in Upper Marlboro and other regions of Prince George's County.

66. Ltr., Slattery to Benoit, 17 Jun 1881, 23-MHT-1, ASSJ. The congregation's assessment is described in *Tenth/Two Hundredth Anniversary of the Church of SS. Paul and Augustine* (Washington, 1971), p. 20. For a flattering assessment of Walsh as pastor, see *The Bee*, 19 Jul 1884.

67. *CM*, 28 Oct 1882. Walsh laid out the details of membership in the debt association in letter to Canon Benoit, 1 Mar 1882, 24-MHT-11, ASSJ. For details of money collected, see "Rev. John Slattery Account Money deposited in Metropolitan Savings Bank for St. Augustine's Ch.," 23 Dec 1881, Chancery Papers, "Parishes-Washington,

As usual, Slattery instructed Walsh on every step of the operation. He exhorted the pastor to divide the association into parts, separating those making an annual pledge from the less affluent who were expected to donate by the month. He wanted the spiritual benefits increased. They should promise three masses for deceased members of the association rather than a single requiem mass. As for solicitation among the city's white Catholics, Slattery wanted Walsh to publicize the parish's frightening annual interest costs as well as the large annual payment demanded by the archbishop. If anything, Slattery advised, overemphasize the fiscal dangers, for "the higher the bow is aimed, the higher the arrow will hit."[68] Walsh was clearly uncomfortable with this assignment, and after a few months effort, he simply ignored Slattery's demands and ceased active solicitations outside the parish.[69] Slattery grumbled to his superiors in London that Walsh "silently but surely ignores your Servant, who as the result, is put in a very bad light before the Archbishop."[70] But in truth, while collections around the archdiocese helped, the major portion of the money raised to reduce the debt came through the efforts of St. Augustine's own parishioners, and here, Walsh's warm rapport with the congregation, not Slattery's financial acumen, was of paramount importance. In 1882 the parish hired a special organizer, Lt. Edward Sturdy of the U.S. Navy, to manage what would be its best publicized and certainly most profitable fair to date. The choir's concert at Lincoln Hall in December netted $800 in one night, more than the debt association contributed in one year.[71]

D.C.," AAB. The parish's financial statements, 1882–1884 (collected in Chancery Papers, AAB) provide a detailed account of all the parish loans, amounts due, and interest rates.

68. Ltr., Slattery to Walsh, 21 Dec 1881, CBI, p. 189, ASSJ.

69. The debt association would remain in business, collecting donations, for almost a decade. Although Walsh once threatened a door-to-door canvas of the city for funds, he actually continued to resist Slattery's demands for continued solicitations. See, for example, ltrs., Slattery to Walsh, 25 Nov 81, CBI, p. 187, ASSJ, and Walsh to Gibbons, 9 Jan 1883, 77-A-5, Gibbons Papers, AAB.

70. Ltr., Slattery to Benoit, 11 May 1882, 24-MHT-19, ASSJ.

71. The 1882 fair raised over $3,300, considerably more than the diocesan collections. See CM, 4 May 1882. On organizing the 1882 fair, see ltr., Walsh to Gibbons, 18 Dec 1881, 76-K-6, Gibbons Papers, AAB. On other money raised by choir, see CM, 14 Jan 1882 and 16 Jun 1883.

Other elements converged to ease the emergency. Loan consolidation in 1882 reduced the crushing interest burden by one third.[72] A change in the District's laws now exempted churches from paying property taxes on all but rectories and vacant land. The city's gradual recovery from the depression was being reflected in increased Sunday collections. Pew rents in 1882 more than doubled those of previous years and, along with the increased Sunday collections, brought in $3,500 in 1882. With the loan on the reconstructed schoolhouse paid off, the parish school with its large student body, most now paying tuition, became, for the first time, self-supporting.[73] A rather smug pastor could report to the archbishop in January 1883 that the parish had met all its current expenses and fulfilled the archbishop's imposed goal with $5,005.50 deposited in Riggs Bank to be used toward discharge of the parish debt. The pastor also took the occasion to remind Gibbons that the second annual payment on his pledge to the debt association was due, and Walsh was looking forward to the archbishop's $100 check.[74]

Growing Pains

The parish's success in controlling its debt did nothing to alleviate the tension between Slattery and Walsh. Slattery once complained that St. Augustine's was "a source of endless crosses. Humanly speaking, I should be glad if we were rid of it."[75] Like many impatient supervisors, he failed to see that some of these crosses were self-imposed. In fairness to the busy provincial, his imperious manner underscored a longstanding and still unsettled dispute among Josephites over lines of authority. Slattery firmly subscribed to the proposition that the Josephite society, not the appointed pastor, was responsible for any parish as-

72. Slattery reported that the annual interest on the debt in 1882 would be $3,000, a $1,700 reduction over the previous year. See ltr., Slattery to Benoit, 5 Jan 1882, 24-MHT-2, ASSJ.

73. On the school debt, see ltrs., Benoit to Vaughan, n.d. (ca. Feb 1884), 29-MHT-14, ASSJ, and Walsh to Gibbons, 1-P-2, Gibbons Papers, AAB. On relief from city taxes, see ltr., William Tuidall to John Hanna [St. Augustine's lawyer], 8 Apr 1882, L.R. 84110, Office of the Commissioners, D.C., cy in SAA.

74. Ltr., Walsh to Gibbons, 9 Jan 1883, 77-A-5, Gibbons Papers, AAB.

75. Ltr., Slattery to Benoit, 8 Feb 1882, 24-MHT-7, ASSJ.

signed to it by the archbishop, and therefore the provincial, not the pastor, was in charge. Moreover, he was convinced that Archbishop Gibbons had no faith in Walsh's abilities and held Slattery personally responsible for St. Augustine's finances. Naturally enough, Walsh just as firmly held the opposite view.

Born into a prominent American business family, Slattery had shown considerable skill in bringing order to the parish's tangled finances, setting it on the road to solvency. He sincerely considered Walsh and his assistant priests incapable of dealing adequately with the situation and subjected them to an endless drumbeat of criticism.[76] Blind to a pastor's legitimate desire to assume responsibility for his parish, Slattery took satisfaction in reporting to his superiors that he had "a long talk with W[alsh]—telling him my fears, & his weaknesses etc."[77] In the midst of one of his lengthy and condescending recitals of the pastor's supposed shortcomings, Slattery magnanimously added that Walsh was not entirely to blame, since financial mismanagement "is as natural to you as water to the duck." To correct these deficiencies, he promised to visit St. Augustine's every fortnight to review the parish records.

A livid Walsh, who had trained as a bookkeeper in his youth, reacted predictably. He reminded Slattery of the Josephite rule that provincials must not "meddle unnecessarily" in the activities of their pastors but "show them confidence and treat them with every consideration and encouragement." He believed Slattery ignored this directive. "As far as I can see it appears to me that fighting is the only way you have to get along." Slattery could come to Washington as often as he liked, Walsh warned, but he was not prepared to go over the accounts with the provincial. His patience tried to the limit, the frustrated pastor added, "I heartily hate your ways and manners as you do mine. . . . I am willing to work for the St. Jos. Soc. and for the col'd, but I will not be made a mere convenience of—cornered & crushed."[78]

76. Ltr., Slattery to Walsh, 25 Nov 1881, CBI, p. 187, ASSJ.

77. Ltr., Slattery to Benoit, 26 Sep 1883, 28-MHT-19. For an earlier example of Slattery's harsh criticism, this time over Walsh's handling of a loan dispute with Father Walter of St. Patrick's, see ltrs., Slattery to Walsh, 10 Oct 1881, and to Walter, same date, CBI, pp. 179–80. All in ASSJ.

78. Ltrs, Slattery to Walsh, 9 May 1882, and Walsh to Slattery, 20 May 1882, both encl. to ltr., Slattery to Vaughan, 22 May 1882, 24-MHT-20. On Slattery's concern over

Slattery appeared taken aback by the rejoinder. Even though an appeal to Josephite headquarters in London resulted in Walsh's being admonished to obey Slattery, the provincial went out of his way to calm the troubled waters. In February 1883 he admitted to Bishop Vaughan, the society's superior-general in London, that Walsh had succeeded in reducing the debt, "for which he deserves most credit, since he raised the finances which your servant manipulated."[79] But it was too late for fence mending. That same month the American Josephites voted Slattery out of office, replacing him with Alfred Leeson. Not one to give up easily, Slattery, who claimed that the archbishop "has no confidence in either Walsh or Leeson in regard to the debt at Washington," protested his assignment to far-off Richmond, Virginia. A sympathetic Bishop Vaughan, who recognized Slattery's outstanding abilities, had pressed the new American provincial to allow Slattery's special relationship with St. Augustine's to continue. Lesson, however, took a firm stand and, with Gibbons's consent, placed Walsh in sole charge of parish finances, subject to a quarterly report to the chancery.[80]

Walsh used the first of these special reports in May 1883 to give the archbishop a general state-of-the-parish summary. He included the news that the current indebtedness of $63,000 represented nearly a 10 percent reduction in less than two years. With regular income on the rise and more than $1,000 a year coming in from the Debt Association, the parish could meet its expenses while steadily reducing the debt through its frequent fairs and other fundraising activities. The good news about the debt aside, Walsh had more important information to impart: "At last we enjoy the confidence & good will of our congregation." This was especially gratifying to those Josephites serving in a parish still mourning the passing of the beloved Barotti. "They are good to us," he concluded simply.[81] One of Father Walsh's first assistants, Gerard Weirsma, was so moved by his own experiences at St.

his responsibilities under Gibbons, see "IV Annual Report St. Joseph's Society of the Sacred Heart American Province," encl. to ltr., Slattery to Vaughan, n.d. (ca. Jan 1883), 26-MHT-21. On Walsh's background in finance, see his ltr. to Rev. Alfred Leeson, 23 Apr 1883, 1-N-1. All in ASSJ.

79. Ltr., Slattery to Vaughan, 7 Feb 1883, 27-MHT-6, ASSJ.

80. Ltrs., Vaughan to Leeson, 23 Apr 1883, 1-E-4; Leeson to Vaughan, 14 May 1883, 27-MHT-27; and Slattery to Vaughan, 12 Feb 1884, 29-MHT-12. All in ASSJ.

81. Ltr., Walsh to Gibbons, 8 May 1883, 77-G-4, Gibbons Papers, AAB.

Augustine's that he reported them to the Josephite community in London. When news that he had been reassigned circulated in Washington, just when he was beginning to know his parishioners, he added, Wiersma was overwhelmed by expressions of their regard. The rectory was crowded with well wishers, and, he reported, one of his converts, an elderly women with a practical eye for life's necessities, not only brought the priests their New Year's Day dinner, but gave Wiersma a huge basket of eatables for his long journey to Kentucky.[82]

While consideration of debts and the place of the new church in the scheme of things preoccupied church leaders and parish dignitaries, only the service of dedicated priests could win the hearts of the ordinary people in the pews. There was plenty of such work to be done, as another of Walsh's young assistants, Father Francis P. Kerwick, reported about his first two months in the parish. Since arriving, Kerwick had instructed 13 converts, conducted 16 funerals, and married 10 couples. His sick calls took him daily to all parts of eastern Washington, his assigned area, and to several hospitals five miles from the church. Some parishioners had little money for or understanding of good nutrition. Kerwick reported visiting one man who was being fed pickles and lemonade to nourish him through a malarial attack. The priest took it upon himself to cook the hapless patient a meal of oatmeal broth, a nourishing if not particularly appetizing concoction. Although he was amused by the liturgical mistakes made by some of the less sophisticated parishioners, Kerwick's unpretentious account of bringing the sacraments to scores of those dying in poverty and neglect still possesses the power to move the reader as it must have moved those who witnessed it a century ago.[83]

As rapport developed between priests and people, the parish finally came to assume the characteristics of a mature urban faith community. The large church now needed four masses on Sunday to accommodate the crowds. With two daily masses, Sunday vespers, and frequent novenas and special devotions, the church was a busy and prayer-filled place. Special events, like the annual Forty Hours devotion, brought people from all over town. The annual parish mission

82. Ltr., Wiersma to Benoit, n.d. (ca. Mar 1883), 26-MHT-18, ASSJ.

83. Ltr., Kerwick to Benoit, 5 Jan 1882, 24-MHT-1, ASSJ.

also drew great crowds. Typically lasting two weeks, the mission segregated parishioners by sex and provided guest preachers who railed against sin and exhorted them to penance in the vivid and gruesome detail so enjoyed by Victorian audiences.

The richness of the parish's liturgical life was frequently described in the press. By the mid-1880s the "intelligent and sober, reverent conduct" of the altar boys, the "exquisite" decorations designed by the altar society, and the "talent" displayed by St. Augustine's Excelsior Band during special church ceremonies, began to vie with the parish choir for notice in the press.[84] The *Mirror* also frankly described the dilapidated condition of the altar furnishings in an era when the parish debt and support of the poor took precedence. As a result, various organizations around town, principally the Tabernacle Society, donated sacred vessels, altar linens, and new outfits for the altar boys.[85]

Parish fund-raisers, especially the picnics, fairs, and concerts, remained at the center of the congregation's social life. As Walsh once said of the picnics, "the people want these outdoor sports and I shall let them have plenty of them. Then they will then be in good humor for the big Fair in the Fall."[86] Judging by the huge numbers of participants, every parishioner, it seemed, was somehow involved in organizing, supplying, or performing on these special occasions. Meanwhile, guest lectures, stereopticon shows, and dramatic readings provided the intellectual and cultural uplift considered essential in any large urban parish of the day. The meetings of the parish's many devotional and beneficial societies kept the church basement alight every night of the week. The Knights of St. Augustine were especially active during

84. The quotidian events of parish life were the stuff of local news in the two Catholic papers and the *Advocate* during the last quarter of the century. See, for example, *CM*, 6 Sep 1884 (first quote); 20 Oct 1883 (2d quote), 2 Dec 1882 (on band) and 29 May 1886. The *Advocate* (Jan 1886) discussed the two-week mission conducted in October 1885 that produced 20 converts and 20 others reconciled to the Church after many years away. The advent of the *Church News* (hereinafter *CN*), a weekly Catholic paper first published in Washington in Oct 1886, opened an important source of information on St. Augustine's liturgical life. See, for example, the detailed breakdown of baptisms, confirmations, and first communions in the 2 Dec 1888 issue.

85. *CM*, 8 Mar and 22 Nov 1884 and 6 May 1893.

86. Ltr., Walsh to Gibbons, 8 May 1883, 77-G-4, Gibbons Papers, AAB.

A PARISH FAMILY. Charles E. and Anna May Stewart with nine of their children. Mr. Stewart was a great-grandson of Henry Warren and great-nephew of Jane Smallwood, both founding members of the parish. He and all his forebears worshipped at St. Augustine's. His widow and children, like so many descendants of early parishioners, have scattered to other parishes, but return occasionally to worship at the mother church.

this period, not only lending their colorful presence to many church functions, but representing the parish in city celebrations. The *Bee* singled them out for their participation in the 1885 Emancipation Day parade, the largest ever held in Washington.[87]

Early on, the Josephites assigned three priests to serve the rapidly growing congregation, but the shortage of personnel in their American province caused a retrenchment in June 1882.[88] Many other parishes made do with two priests, but St. Augustine's special city-wide responsibilities and the onerous work involved in reducing the debt made the shortage of personnel keenly felt. Despite pleas from all sides, the Josephite superiors in London failed to assign additional priests to a rectory that was undermanned and showing the effects of the internal dissension that would lead in a few years to the collapse of the Josephite's American province.[89] Walsh continually juggled the parish schedules, finding temporary help where he could. In desperation he appealed directly to London in early 1884: "I honestly & truly believe before God that there is a very great loss of souls caused here by want of another priest."[90] This dramatic plea failed to move his superiors, but Walsh's own serious illness in 1885—a lung inflammation that required a long sea voyage to cure—underscored the seriousness of the problem. The pastor of nearby St. Matthew's was prevailed upon to

87. *The Bee*, 11 Apr 1885. The *Bee*, the *Catholic Mirror*, and later the *Church News* were especially generous in their coverage of the many functions sponsored by the parish. See, for example, *The Bee's* notice (19 Jan 1884) of the lecture in Lincoln Hall and the monster 4th of July picnic sponsored by the Knights in Van Ness Park in 1884 (26 Jul 1884 issue), the latter article including a warm portrait of the parish's new assistant pastor, John deRuyter. See also the *CM's* lengthy reports (12 and 26 Jan 1884) on the parish-sponsored lectures by Msgr. Placide L. Chappelle, a friend of St. Augustine's and later archbishop of Santa Fe and New Orleans.

88. Ltr., Walsh to Benoit, 14 Sep 1883, 28-MHT-18, ASSJ.

89. On dissolution of the English Josephites in America, see chapter 5, below. Signs of the breakup were evident quite early at St. Augustine's. See, for example, ltrs., Slattery to Benoit, 11 May 1882, 24-MHT-19, and 30 Dec 1883, 28-MHT-25; deRuyter to Benoit, 19 Apr 1883, 27-MHT-23; and John [deRuyter] to same, n.d. (ca. Jun 1883), 1-P-20a. All in ASSJ.

90. Ltr., Walsh to Benoit, 17 Jan 1884, 29-MHT-7, ASSJ. For examples of Walsh's efforts to secure priests to help on special occasions, see, for example, ltrs., Walsh to Leeson, n.d. (ca. Aug 1883), 1-P-20, and Leeson to Vaughan, 29 Aug 1883, 28-MHT-14. Both in ASSJ.

help out temporarily, and later that year St. Augustine's was once again provided a full complement of four priests.[91]

The struggles of the Josephites in restoring the material well-being of the parish and their own considerable problems as a missionary community trying to make its way in America should not mask their very real accomplishments in Washington. Sacramental statistics in their new parish favorably compared with those of the city's most venerable institutions. During their first five years in control, St. Augustine's baptized 922 (including 153 adults), prepared 410 children and adults for First Communion, instructed 519 Catholics (including 191 adults) for Confirmation, dispensed the last rites and buried 575, and married 165 couples.[92] The congregation had every right to take pride in its accomplishments, and great labor went into preparing for the celebration of the new church's tenth anniversary. Sexagesima Sunday, February 28, 1886, was selected for the milestone, a bit premature but planned to coincide with a visit by the archbishop. A jubilant Walsh, once again in good health, noted that Gibbons, who had visited the church on three previous occasions, always enjoyed his stay at St. Augustine's. The parish even loosened the purse strings enough to buy a new carpet to gussy up the prelate's bedroom. The choir pulled out all the stops for the anniversary mass, which featured Gibbons presiding from a purple throne erected in a sanctuary crowded with clergy and twenty-two altar boys. Everyone reassembled in the afternoon to watch the archbishop confirm 93 children and 35 adults. Isaac Landic and Alexander Thomas served as sponsors for the men and boys and Louise Hamilton and Lavinia Dey for the women and girls.[93]

Once asked to comment on the increasingly prosperous condition of "this very magnificent church" despite its heavy debt, Father Walsh

91. Walsh's trip, which included a long visit to his native Ireland and to London and Rome, ended in November 1885 when he returned, carrying with him a special papal benediction for the congregation. See ltrs., Walsh to Leeson, 17 Jul (1-N-7) and 23 Jul (1-N-8) 1885; Leeson to Benoit, 30 Jul 1885, 31-MHT-27, and to Vaughan, 9 Oct 1885, 32-MHT-14, and Walsh to Benoit, 30 Nov 1885, 32-MHT-28. All in ASSJ.

92. Statistics as reprinted in *St. Joseph's Advocate* 4, no. 2 (Apr 1886): 150.

93. Ltr., Walsh to Benoit, 11 Jan 1886, 33-MHT-4, ASSJ. A full description of the anniversary ceremony with the text of the archbishop's sermon appeared in the *CM*, 6 Mar 1886.

pointed out that "our capital is the good will of the people."[94] An expected response perhaps, and easily dismissed as pious cant, it nevertheless contained a large kernel of truth in the case of St. Augustine's. The phenomenal growth of the parish in the 1880s, especially the numbers of converts revealed in sacramental statistics, gave special witness to its spiritual vitality. While the labors of Josephite missionaries and workings of Divine grace cannot be discounted, the dogged determination of the congregation to spread the Good News and its continued generosity despite frequent denigration by fellow citizens and co-religionists were certainly signs of a mature Christian community. Like any mature group it was also determined to have its views heard. Church and state were about to get an earful.

94. *CN*, 3 Oct 1886.

FOUR ❧ A NEW IMAGE

*M*any of the parish's founding members were still on hand to attend the mass celebrating the tenth anniversary of the new church in 1886. Kneeling shoulder to shoulder with them were representatives of a new generation of parish leaders about to make their presence felt, not only at St. Augustine's but across the American church. Through sacrifice and sheer determination, the older group, part of the free black society of antebellum Washington, had overcome major social and financial obstacles to create a flourishing urban parish. The new generation was prone to accept this achievement—the imposing church, progressive school, and lively parish organizations—as a given. Increasingly their gaze was trained outward. Less concerned with the day-to-day struggle of the debt-ridden parish, they were determined to protest injustice and demand the recognition due black Catholics, who were becoming a distinct minority in the Church.

These groups did not act alone, for there were white Catholics who provided important support, first in the formation of the parish and later in the larger struggle for racial justice. The affection shown by a discerning congregation made it obvious that Felix Barotti had transcended the prejudice that plagued so many Catholics to become the catalyst that transformed a tiny community into a major parish. As Father Walsh would ruefully admit months after the Josephites arrived at St. Augustine's, "Our society has not yet done anything like the work of the individual Father Barotti."[1] Viewed in the context of those times, men like Martin Spalding and John Slattery also acted honorably and sympathetically, and in succeeding years the cause of racial justice would find outspoken champions in John Ireland, the fearless archbishop of St. Paul and friend of St. Augustine's, and a few lay leaders like John Boyle O'Reilly, the widely-read journalist and critic.

Yet despite important help from some of their co-religionists, it remained for black Catholics to shoulder the major burden. While the cooperation and goodwill of the congregation are essential to a church's survival, even in a hierarchical religion, more was required in the case of Washington's first black parish. Here in a special way, it was the congregation, not its bishops and priests, who created a burgeoning faith community and fought prejudice. The older generation had succeeded in making St. Augustine's the center of a vibrant black Catholicism in the capital; it would fall to the new generation to thrust the parish into the forefront of the first battle for racial justice in the American church.

A Social Profile, 1880–1900

These new parish leaders with their markedly militant attitude did not spring out of a social vacuum. Their interests and well-being closely mirrored elements in the local African-American community of which they were a part. That community was undergoing dramatic change during the last decades of the nineteenth century. With the failure of home rule in the 1870s, the first, hesitant steps toward a socially integrated city had faltered. The general toleration and even friendliness that characterized the immediate post–Civil War era, when political cooperation between the races had produced some notably progressive ordinances aimed at righting ancient wrongs, gradually faded, to be replaced by a period of deteriorating race relations. By the turn of the century, rigid separation—enforced by custom and sanctioned by the courts—had destroyed any short-term hope for a just and tolerant society in the nation's capital.

1. Ltr., Walsh to Benoit, 27 Feb 1882, 24-MHT-10, ASSJ.

The cause for the change in direction was easy to perceive. Lacking meaningful social contact with blacks, white Washington drifted along in its myopic way, free to indulge long-cherished prejudices about a homogeneous black community in which crime, ignorance, and "shiftlessness" prevailed. Serious discussion of race relations ceased. In the words of one authority, "white people . . . in the course of twenty-odd years resolved the problem of race relations by tacitly denying its existence."[2] Segregation spread apace. The color line in social affairs, breached in the postwar period, was once again rigidly drawn. Increasingly all but the elite of the African-American community were barred from restaurants (but not saloons) and places of entertainment. Upscale businesses (including some owned by black entrepreneurs) refused what was called the Colored Trade. Housing, even for the wealthiest and most distinguished black families, was becoming unavailable in the most desirable neighborhoods, and inexorably the move to segregated neighborhoods began. By 1900 some 75 percent of black Washingtonians lived in separate enclaves such as those near the southwest waterfront, in Foggy Bottom, and in the area around Florida Avenue and North Capitol Street and along Eleventh Street, Northeast. Also by 1900 more than 90 percent of those living in Washington's alley dwellings were working-class African Americans. Although integrated neighborhoods would continue to exist well into the new century, the exodus of black families from core residential areas, such as the fashionable K Street and Sixteenth Street corridors, was almost complete by 1900.

Most of the city's unions had refused to accept African Americans, thereby closing off most employment in the lucrative building trades. Although jobs were available for teachers in the city's nationally praised black public schools, other city agencies, including the police department, provided few openings for black residents. Even the First Separate Colored Battalion of the District's National Guard, which traced its lineage back to the militia battalions organized for Civil War

2. Green, *Secret City*, p. 120. Except where noted, this summary of race relations is based on Green and Borchert, *Alley Life in Washington*; Johnson, "The City on the Hill"; Willard B. Gatewood, *Aristocrats of Color: The Black Elite, 1880–1920* (Bloomington: Indiana University Press, 1990), and the very useful introduction by Adele Logan Alexander to Fitzpatrick and Goodwin's *The Guide to Black Washington*.

veterans, had survived repeated efforts to disband it, only to be denied service in the regiment Washington sent to Cuba during the War with Spain.

Attempts to restore civil rights through legislation or the courts proved fruitless. Congress repeatedly dismissed pleas for new laws, and in 1883 the Supreme Court declared the Civil Rights Act of 1875 unconstitutional when applied to the states. While still binding in Washington and the territories, the law was practically ignored in District courts where plaintiffs received little relief from unsympathetic judges. Finally in its landmark 1896 decision in the case of Plessy *vs.* Ferguson, the Supreme Court declared that separate but equal accommodations satisfied the requirements of the Fourteenth Amendment, thus laying the legal foundations for the reign of Jim Crow. Ironically, the great influx of newly freed slaves, which had dismayed white Washington and caused so much hardship for black residents, was over. By 1885 the black population stood at 65,000, more than half of whom were former slaves from Maryland and Virginia. In the next quarter century, however, the number of African Americans would increase by only 1,050 annually, while the black percentage of the total population began to slide.

Contrary to popular white perception, Washington's African Americans did not constitute a homogeneous society. In fact black Washington was a complex mix of distinct social classes whose structure had grown increasingly rigid as segregation strengthened its grip on the city. Where once a more outwardly focused Civil War generation had used financial success and political power as measures of social status, a new generation tended to measure everything in terms of class and color. Of course wealth would always be a factor, but increasingly as black society was forced by segregation to focus inwardly, major emphasis was placed on education, professional status, ancestry (with preference given to those connected to pre–Civil War free black society) and skin color (dark skin was never a barrier to advancement, but light skin was always an asset).[3] Such emphasis introduced an inflexibility that not only made it more difficult for the less fortunate to rise,

3. Mary Buckner, a noted Washingtonian and parishioner of St. Augustine's, commented on the usual habit of concealing any family connection to slavery. Only late in life did she learn that her grandmother was born free in Washington in 1826, because

but, when added to the discrimination that all African Americans suffered, subjected the black community to new social and economic tensions. Where the Civil War generation had accepted responsibility for helping needy newcomers and advancing racial causes, the new generation, disillusioned by the unrelenting discrimination, tended to concentrate less on mutual help and more on individual advancement and the interests of one's particular group.

At the top of the social pyramid were the so-called aristocrats of color, the small group of first families whose achievements, intellectual interests, and fashionable lifestyles made them most interested in advancing the cause of integration. As segregation became more widespread, these "old cits," as they like to be called to differentiate themselves from recently emancipated citizens, generally divorced themselves from the interests and concerns of humbler folk. Their attention centered on the affairs of Howard University and a small group of socially distinguished churches, chiefly St. Luke's Episcopal, St. Augustine's, and Fifteenth Street Presbyterian. They were also strong champions of the Washington Board of Trade (the powerful alliance of local business leaders) and the Oldest Inhabitants Association, a fraternal group seeking to foster civic pride among leading African Americans. These aristocrats were not totally oblivious to the hardships of the less fortunate, as attested by the several relief committees and institutions for the care of widows and orphans they sponsored. In general, however, charity was not their main concern; rather, they concentrated on winning full civil rights and social recognition for the so-called talented tenth of the African-American population. Such a victory, so the theory ran, would eventually produce greater opportunity for those less fortunate.

The upper class carefully separated themselves from other folk. They entertained in exclusive clubs like the venerable Lotus Club and societies like the Bethel Literary and Historical Association; they shunned the more exuberant celebrations popular with the masses, such as the annual District Emancipation Day parade and the mammoth church picnics. Countless news stories described their exotic vacations, elaborate weddings, and fashionable receptions for out-of-

---

such matters were never discussed in polite society. See intv. Marilyn W. Nickels with William and Mary Buckner, 11 Nov 1974, cy in SAA.

town guests. More acerbic reporters and comedians gained fame poking fun at their pretensions and social ambitions. For example, Washington's aristocracy was a favorite target of the well-known black journalist John E. Bruce. The celebrated "Bruce Grit" satirized the "furst families" who possessed "more family pride to the square inch . . . than there are fleas on a dog's back."[4] Some papers like the *Bee* would print a gushing report of a Newport vacation or European trip of some Washington "cit" on one page and denounce the foibles of the "bon ton" on another.

Membership in this aristocracy was obviously exclusive, but it was also amorphous. Some were included because of outstanding educational or professional achievements, others because of important government or church positions, and still others, like Frederick Douglass, because of their national fame. Alongside familiar names like Cook, Grimke, Terrell, and Bruce were several well known at St. Augustine's. Congressman James E. O'Hara was a parishioner during his years in Washington in the 1880s. Widely recognized as leaders of black society, the New York–born O'Hara and his aristocratic wife were noted for their cultured interests and lavish entertainments. Like politicians before and since, O'Hara learned too late that identification with Washington's gentry did not sit well with the folks back home. His failure to send his children to black schools and his aloofness from the voters were said to have cost him re-election to a third term. Another parishioner, William Henry Smith, was also recognized as one of Washington's social leaders. A man of considerable wealth, Smith was for years the librarian of the House of Representatives, and, as one wag put it, the only Washingtonian "who has made money by politics pure and simple—that is, has saved it from his salary." For many years Smith was an active member of St. Augustine's congregation, where he helped organize the Knights of St. Augustine. His name often appeared in the local society columns; the *Bee* even saw fit to report when his son passed the civil service examination in 1884.[5]

4. As quoted in Gatewood, *Aristocrats of Color*, p. 55. See also Williams, "Blacks in Washington, D.C., 1860–1870," pp. 229–30.

5. *The Bee*, n.d. (ca. Jul) 1884. The quote is from an article by J. H. Beadle in *Yenowine's Illustrated News* [Milwaukee, WI] as reprinted in *St. Joseph's Advocate* 3, no. 1 (Jul 1894): 601.

Also included among Washington's first black families was the relative newcomer Alexander T. Augusta. Retiring from the Army Medical Corps with the rank of lieutenant colonel, Augusta became first superintendent of Freedmen's Hospital, which he guided through its formative years.[6] In 1869 he joined the faculty of Howard University, the first black professor at any American medical school. The distinguished Augustas, active members of the Howard University community, found time to participate in parish activities. At the doctor's death in 1890 it was discovered that he had bequeathed large sums to both St. Augustine's and the Oblate Sisters on condition that his wife pre-deceased him. Unfortunately for those charities, a hale and hearty Mrs. Dr. Augusta, as she was always called, lived to enjoy the money herself.[7]

Just below these so-called aristocrats, but still considered members of Washington's "black 400," was a prosperous group of professionals, government clerks (a title in those early Civil Service days used to denote the federal government's mid-level staff), and businessmen who shared many of the interests and ambitions, if not the exclusiveness, of the "cits." In today's lexicon this would be the upper middle class, a group especially threatened by the growing chill in race relations in the capital. Barred from professional associations and otherwise inhibited by new social and legal barriers, these gifted and enterprising residents struggled mightily for success. Those in government managed to retain their positions even when the Cleveland administration began to curtail mid-level positions opened to African Americans.[8] Those in business slowly built up clienteles despite the fickle habits of the many black and as well as white customers who preferred the eclat of white-owned establishments. Against great odds,

6. Augusta was educated at the University of Toronto after being turned down because of color by the University of Pennsylvania. The Augustas lived at 1319 L St., two blocks from St. Augustine's.

7. Provisions of the Augusta will can be found in Dorothy S. Provine, compl. and ed., *District of Columbia Free Negro Registrars, 1821–1861* (Bowie, MD: Heritage Books, 1996).

8. In 1891 African Americans filled 2,400 of the 23,144 civil servant positions in the federal government. Although many of these were classed as messengers and other minor positions, a substantial number were more responsible posts. For example, among the Interior Department's 337 black employees (5 percent of its work force), 127 were ranked as clerks, copyists, and transcribers.

others managed to amass substantial wealth in the city's thriving real estate, insurance, and catering trades.

Members of this upper middle class also devoted considerable energy to seeking recognition for their achievements. As will be seen, it was members of this group who formed the backbone of the first protest movement in the Catholic Church against racial discrimination. The noted African-American spokesman Archibald Grimke commented on the interests and loyalties of these Catholics:

Among the Colored Catholics of Washington are numbered some of the best and most intelligent members of the race here: doctors, dentists, educators and business men. But while they are loyal to their church, they are loyal also to their race, which speaks volumes of praise for the Catholic church, for no church can long command the loyalty of its Colored members if that church in time were to prove in practice wanting in loyalty to the full manhood rights and citizenship of the Colored race.[9]

This social group provided St. Augustine's with some of its most influential parishioners. They included Charles H. Butler and Willis J. Smith, who for many years filled responsible positions in the U.S. Treasury Department, Butler in the Division of Appointments. One of the youngest of this group, William S. Lofton, was born in Arkansas in 1862 and became a Catholic shortly after his arrival in Washington as a teenager. Lofton was one of the first to graduate from Howard University's school of dentistry. He established what would be a prosperous practice on M Street. A financial trustee of St. Augustine's, Lofton would further strengthen his ties to the parish when he married Livinia Dey, a prominent choir soloist, opera performer, and later director of the children's choir.[10] P. A. Dickson, formerly a well-known Methodist minister, was a successful businessman and later served as diocesan auditor of St. Augustine's finances. John F. Hamilton was a supervisor in the Post Office Department. His home, described as "one of the most comfortable" in the city, was the scene of a lavish reception on the occasion of the marriage of his daughter, Louise, to William Prater

9. Archibald Grimke, "Colored Catholics of Washington, D.C.," *Alexander's Magazine* (Jun 1907): 110.

10. The Lofton-Dey wedding in 1889 was a major social event in black society that year and received much press coverage.

in 1890. John F. Robinson was the proprietor of the "Woodmont," a fashionable hostelry from which he also ran one of the city's lucrative catering businesses. Ananias Herbert served for many years in the largely ceremonial position of doorkeeper of the Supreme Court. His funeral at St. Augustine's in 1892, the largest seen in the church since that of Father Barotti, was attended by a number of Supreme Court justices and leaders of the legal profession.

There is little doubt of the social standing of a major portion of St. Augustine's congregation which, as Father Walsh reported in 1882, was "awfully high-toned. You could hardly touch it with a forty foot pole." The noted chronicler of Washington society Frank Carpenter also had something to say about the congregation. Reporting in 1885 on what he called the "Catholic Church in the fashionable part of town . . . whose Negro choir is famous," Carpenter asserted that the congregation was made up of the aristocracy: the men arrived for mass dressed in plug hats and kid gloves and the ladies "wearing dresses that would not disgrace a White House reception." The ubiquitous but circumspect reporter Canon Benoit simply noted that "a number of the attendants at S. Augustine's are in good circumstances."[11]

The 1880s also saw the emergence of a strong black middle class in Washington. These were the small shopkeepers, government messengers, and artisans who, less financially secure than the aristocrats, concentrated on making ends meet rather than trying to reform society. Historians have noted a sharp division between this group and the leaders of black society.[12] They have also found that the middle class displayed far more sympathy for the poor than their aristocratic brothers. In both Protestant and Catholic congregations, the struggling middle class was the driving force behind the beneficial societies and charitable enterprises. Increasingly toward the end of the century this group found its principal form of entertainment in church meetings, parish socials, choir concerts, picnics, and fairs.

11. Ltrs., Walsh to Benoit, 27 Feb 1882, 24-MHT-10 (first quote), and Benoit to Vaughan, n.d. (ca. Feb 1884) (third quote). Both in ASSJ. Carpenter, *Carp's Washington*, p. 239 (second quote). The oral tradition of the parish supports these assessments. See Nickels intv. with William and Mary Buckner.

12. Cultural historian Willard B. Gatewood offers a useful summary of the conclusions of these historians. See his *Aristocrats of Color*, esp. chapters I–IV.

Among the many hard-working members of this social class active at St. Augustine's was Anna Fluger, who for years operated a dress-making shop on New York Avenue near the White House. Advertisements for Fluger's services were frequently found in the parish journals and fair gazettes. John I. Jackson, a Canadian immigrant, operated an upholstery and cabinet-making business on Fifteenth Street. (Jackson, a shopkeeper, went on to become an influential member of the Oldest Inhabitants Association so favored by the "cits," showing that perhaps too much can be made of the social distinctions drawn by the experts.) Washington-born William J. Jackson served for forty years on the police force. His funeral at St. Augustine's in 1919 was reported in the press and attended by many of the city's finest. Daniel Spriggs held one of the positions on the White House domestic staff traditionally reserved for African Americans. His family was one of the most active in the congregation; Spriggs himself was especially interested in the Knights of St. Augustine's, which he commanded for more than forty years.

The substantial economic gains made by so many African Americans since the Civil War could not mask the very different fate suffered by the working poor and the nearly 16,000 black unemployed in Washington in the 1880s. With work in the building trades and other traditional avenues of advancement barred by postwar discrimination, these poor and uneducated newcomers were forced to rely on uncertain employment as domestic servants, porters, street hucksters, and other menial, part-time work. For the most part they struggled along with little help from the city government or their more fortunate neighbors. The rigid class structure, exaggerated by deteriorating race relations, found them shunned by the more prosperous African Americans and mercilessly criticized by the whites. Even their gaudy, noisy entertainments—periodic attempts to break out of their harsh and dreary daily lot—were ridiculed by their "betters" in both races. Largely out of sight in tenements and noisome alley dwellings, they formed an invisible society. St. Augustine's is generally classed by the experts as a parish of the socially prominent, but it also obviously counted some of the struggling poor in its congregation. They made their presence known in several ways. Throughout the 1880s the priests reported that a large group of families could not afford to contribute. During 1888, for example, the church's expenses were shouldered by just 100 families.[13] Like the great majority of their counterparts in the public schools, the children of St. Augustine's poor rarely finished their studies. Despairing parents, who saw no advantage in continuing their children's education, withdrew them as soon as they had learned to read and write, expecting them to find work to help their needy families. The extent of the problem was obvious from the fact that in a whole decade of operation, just eight children remained in the parochial school long enough to graduate.[14]

Obviously at least some members of the congregation lived in dire poverty during those hard years, while others struggled mightily for a bare subsistence, but all accounts agree that the social and economic level of the majority of parishioners exceeded that of any other group of black Catholics in the area and was equal to that of the most prominent black Protestant congregation. This fact has been the subject of much speculation.[15] Some of the reasons for this are readily apparent. For many in the congregation Catholicism was the faith of their fathers and St. Augustine's the church their parents had built. They were directly descended from Washington's pre–Civil War free black society, a group that had endured the hard times and taken advantage of the good to become well established in the capital. They had also assisted their less fortunate relatives who streamed into the city from Maryland and Virginia after emancipation. With this help and because of the schooling they received in the parish, many of these newcomers had achieved a foothold on the long climb to prosperity.

But what of the hundreds of adult converts, many of them prosperous residents, some well-educated, distinguished newcomers to Washington? What attracted them to Catholicism and specifically to St. Augustine's? In the end, what made many of Washington's prominent black Catholics endure the snubs and often supercilious treatment of

13. Comment of the pastor as reported in the *CM*, 21 Jan 1888.

14. *St. Joseph's Advocate* 3, no. 3 (Jul 1885): 108–09. The Sunday school, on the other hand, had 500 children enrolled in 1885.

15. In addition to the contemporary accounts of Carpenter, Grimke, Beadle, and others already cited, see Gatewood, *Aristocrats of Color*, pp. 295–98, and John Muffler, "This Far by Faith: A History of St. Augustine's, The Mother Church for Black Catholics in the Nation's Capital," (Columbia University Teachers College, D.Ed., 1989), pp. 60–65 and 172–75. The following paragraphs are based on these sources.

their fellow Catholics? Without denigrating the power of the Holy Spirit to evangelize and faith to endure, some complex human factors relating to race relations in Washington seem to have played a part.

In general, African Americans of the upper classes eschewed the emotional fever found in many Protestant denominations and were attracted to Catholicism by its liturgy. It must be remembered that the attraction of St. Augustine's choir was based on its performance of Latin motets and masterpieces of European music. It would be many decades before the exhilarating sound of Negro spirituals and gospel music would gain an audience in the church. Like so many before and after them, these Catholics were attracted to the soul-satisfying spectacle of the centuries-old Roman ritual accompanied by stirring music and performed with dignity in a beautiful church.

Of special importance to St. Augustine's immediate future, many of the socially prominent were assimilists, whose aspirations centered on a racially integrated society. Even as segregation gained strength in the capital, these assimilists were encouraged by the fact that St. Augustine's attracted so many white worshippers. Almost unique in Washington, a typical service at the church on Fifteenth Street would find the two races fully integrated in the pews and at the altar rail. The lack of black priests, although noticed, was not yet a matter of tension. The frequent visits by national political leaders and by leading members of the hierarchy and other distinguished clerics seemed to underscore the parish's importance in the scheme of things. To discerning outsiders this racial amity pointed toward the eventual integration of society, which they ardently desired. Like their contemporaries among the more prosperous European immigrants, these prosperous black Washingtonians longed to join the American mainstream and saw in a parish like St. Augustine's an entree into that society.

Prominent black leaders like Archibald Grimke and Frederick Douglass lent weight to such assumptions by stressing the positive aspects of race relations in the Catholic Church. Many black Catholics were not so easily beguiled by such skimpy evidence. Nevertheless, the continuing discrimination they received from their fellow Catholics did not turn them away, but merely made them more determined to fight for recognition and to assume their rightful place in the City of God.

The First Protest Movement, 1889–1895

The loss of home rule especially affected Washington's black aristocracy and upper middle class, which had looked on the democratic
give and take in the political arena as a prelude to an integrated city.
After that avenue of advance closed, they slowly relinquished their
public leadership role, generally retreating into a somewhat bitter and
certainly unproductive isolation. This was less true of Catholic members of the group, who instead focused their attention on the plight of
African Americans in the Church. These black professionals, whose
numbers made them especially prominent in the Archdiocese of Baltimore, were becoming increasingly restive under the restraints imposed
by some pastors and congregations and endorsed by timid bishops. Far
from joining their neighbors in dignified isolation, they began to voice
their dissatisfaction.

Although members of St. Augustine's congregation would figure
prominently in this protest, the movement actually started in Ohio with
the work of a charismatic journalist, Daniel A. Rudd. Judged by any
standard Rudd was a remarkable Catholic. Born in 1854, one of twelve
children in a slave family in Bardstown, Kentucky, he moved shortly
after the Civil War to Springfield, Ohio, where with a brother's help he
obtained a secondary education. In the process Rudd discovered a talent for journalism and public speaking and an uncanny knack for what
is today called public relations. After a decade as a journeyman reporter, Rudd launched his own newspaper, the *Ohio State Tribune*, at
the age of thirty.

Local journalism quickly paled on the vigorous Rudd, who went on
to cultivate a broader audience for his talents among the small elite of
educated black Catholics scattered throughout the country, especially
in the large cities of the East and the Midwest. Typified by the leaders
of St. Augustine's congregation, this group was prosperous, confident
of advancing in their professions, concerned about the education and
welfare of African Americans in general, and especially anxious to
learn more about the condition of their fellow black Catholics around
the country. They were also eager to assert themselves as full-fledged
members of the Church. Rudd could identify with these aspirations,
and with the backing of an Ohio physician, Thomas Whitson, and the

assistance of his nephew, John R. Rudd, he changed the name and the character of his paper. In 1886 the *American Catholic Tribune* published its first edition, clearly stating its purpose: "To give the great Catholic Church a hearing and show that it is worthy of at least a fair consideration at the hands of our race."[16] The paper boasted that it was endorsed by a group in the hierarchy, including Cardinal Gibbons.[17] There seems to have been some truth in this, for publisher Rudd found himself frequently invited to appear before large Catholic organizations around the country. To enhance the pages of the *Tribune* Rudd selected well-known African Americans to double as local reporters and sales agents. Like other Catholic weeklies, the *Tribune* passed on news of individual parishes of note, the latest items from the Holy See (the paper boasted a Roman correspondent, a young black seminarian at the Urban College), and columns of fiction and jokes providing light but edifying entertainment. Readership grew quickly. By 1892 the weekly (usually four pages in length, but sometimes expanded to eight pages when the news justified it) was selling 10,000 copies.

The *Tribune* was unique among Catholic papers in its outspoken emphasis on civil rights. It remained firmly opposed to segregation. Its readers were kept informed of the growing horror of lynchings and the multiplication of Jim Crow laws and were treated to a generous selection of articles by the leading civil rights activists of the day, including Frederick Douglass and T. Thomas Fortune. On the condition of African Americans in the Church, Rudd took an entirely different approach, preferring to emphasize an upbeat message about the glowing future for black Catholics.

Rudd's sunny optimism could not mask the continuing neglect suffered by black Catholics as underscored by the performance of the American hierarchy during the recent Third Plenary Council of Baltimore. This council, unlike its predecessor, was convened at the insistence of Roman authorities. Propaganda Fide, the Roman congrega-

16. Little scholarly attention has been given to this important Catholic. This brief sketch is based on Davis, *The History of Black Catholics*, pp. 164–70; Joseph Lackner, "Dan A. Rudd, Editor of the *American Catholic Tribune*, from Bardstown to Cincinnati," *Catholic Historical Review* 80 (1994): 258–81; and Hennessey, *American Catholics*, pp. 190–92. The quotations cited are from the Davis work.

17. Gibbons had been elevated to the College of Cardinals in 1886.

tion responsible for what was still considered the missionary church in the United States, was concerned with several issues including the evangelization of African Americans. In May 1883 Cardinal Giovanni Simeoni, the prefect of the congregation, invited the American archbishops to Rome, where he presented them a list of topics to be discussed in plenary council. Roman officials were clearly disappointed with the failure of the American bishops to organize a unified approach to the conversion and education of African Americans. While recognizing the work of the tiny band of Josephites, they demanded a concerted effort to break down the barriers existing between the races "in order to bring about, by means of the charity of the gospel, the realization both in theory and practice that they [African Americans] are brothers in Christ Jesus."[18]

Admittedly the bishops had many important subjects to consider in their council, and the question of race relations appeared to most to lack the urgency of other problems facing a largely immigrant church. Still, the demands of Roman authorities could not be ignored, and some positive action was proposed on evangelization of African Americans. The council called on seminaries to encourage young priests to take up such work and religious orders to assign personnel to the task. At the same time it agreed to study Bishop Keane's proposal that a special seminary be established to train priests for work with African and Native Americans. The bishops discussed the training of black lay catechists to aid these missionaries, although responsibility for finding volunteers and raising money to support them was left to the individual dioceses. Most important, the council decreed that an annual collection be taken up in all churches to support this missionary effort. The bishops organized an episcopal commission under Cardinal Gibbons to distribute the money and to receive periodic reports on the work. The first collection in 1887 netted $86,000, providing for the disbursement of about $2,000, mostly for support of schools for black children, to each of some twenty southern dioceses.[19]

18. Rpt. of Cardinal Franzelin to Propaganda, as quoted in Misch, "The American Bishops and the Negro from the Civil War to the Third Plenary Council," p. 502. This summary of the council's work is based on Misch's dissertation.

19. Only 20 of the 76 American dioceses had any significant black population in the 1880s. For a comprehensive review of the collection from an individual mission-

This flurry of councilar activity aimed at the conversion of African Americans allowed the bishops to take the moral high road, ignoring the sometimes blatant discrimination suffered by those already in the Church. The Church now counted thousands of black communicants, many educated assimilists eagerly awaiting a clear declaration on racial justice from the bishops. Instead they were treated to a muddled call for separate black parishes with priests "whose sole duty" was the pastoral care of African Americans as an antidote to the discrimination of white Catholics. Typical of the attitude of some in the hierarchy was Bishop William H. Gross's well-publicized sermon to the council fathers on "The Mission for the Colored People," in which the leader of the church in Savannah described the "low moral standing" of black Americans, the "travesty of religion" being offered by black preachers, and the changes that could be realized only "through Catholic dogma and the sacraments."[20] Educated and successful black Catholics were growing increasingly restive with such talk, but like many reformers at the beginning of a campaign, publisher Rudd preferred to accentuate the positive, making of any modest gain in the treatment of black Catholics a headline event. Little note was made in his paper of segregated church galleries, barriers faced by black children seeking a Catholic education or refuge in Catholic orphanages, and the impediments confronting those seeking entry to seminaries or convents. Instead, claiming that criticism of the Church's racial policies was based on misinformation, the *Tribune* reiterated a clear and optimistic message: "The Catholic Church alone can break the color line. Our people should help her to do it."

In an age replete with national conventions and unions, Rudd conceived the idea of a national gathering of black Catholics, and he used the pages of the *Tribune* and his own frequent lectures around the country to organize and promote the first National Congress of Colored Catholics. He moved prudently, submitting his proposed agenda to

ary's experience, see ltr., Slattery to Benoit, March 1884, 29-MHT-4, ASSJ. The collections, inadequately publicized, produced a disappointing amount in the early years. The first five collections raised $351,000, a minuscule amount (less than one cent per year per Catholic) when compared with the sums donated by Protestant congregations during the same period.

20. As quoted in Misch, "The American Bishops and the Negro," pp. 543–44.

Archbishop William Elder of Cincinnati for approval and consulting every step of the way with Father John Slattery, soon to be superior of the newly independent American Josephites, who suggested the date and place for the convention. Also appealed to for support, Cardinal Gibbons added his endorsement with his customary call for caution in matters of race relations: "I hope that your deliberations will be marked by wisdom and discretion, and will be free from every senti- ment which would compromise you as Catholics or as citizens. I trust the convention will redound to the honor and welfare of the race."[21] After considerable discussion among interested parties, the congress, its delegates chosen by individual black parishes and societies, was scheduled to open at St. Augustine's in January 1889.[22]

St. Augustine's was a natural choice. Not only the largest black Catholic Church in the nation, it was located in the capital and includ- ed among its members some of the most enthusiastic endorsers of Rudd's idea of black unity. In the months preceding the meeting, parish societies sponsored fund raisers and organized hospitality com- mittees, while men like Charles H. Butler and William J. Smith helped devise the program.[23] The congress opened on New Year's Day 1889 with a Solemn High Mass presided over by Cardinal Gibbons and cel- ebrated by Father Augustus Tolton, the nation's only black priest. The mass was attended by many parishioners as well as the leaders of sev- eral national Protestant denominations and representatives of Wash- ington's black aristocracy. Following mass eighty-four delegates from around the country assembled in the parish hall to hear Butler and Smith give welcoming addresses.[24] From the beginning Rudd had

21. As quoted in the *CN*, 28 Oct 1888.

22. The extent of the Rudd's "networking" in preparation for the first congress, es- pecially his dealings with Elder and his own program committee, can be seen in his correspondence with Slattery during the period. See, for example, ltrs., Rudd to Slat- tery, 8 May 1888, 9-K-8, 2 Jul 1888, 9-K-10, 2 Aug 1888, 9-K-11, and 30 Oct 188, 9-K- 13. All in ASSJ.

23. The preparations were carefully covered in the local press; see, for example, *CM*, 17 Nov and 16 and 22 Dec 1888. Father Walsh outlined the purpose of the congress and the reason St. Augustine's was hosting the event in an interview published in the *Evening Star*, 30 Oct 1888.

24. Fourteen states and the District of Columbia were represented with three-quar- ters of the delegates coming from parishes and societies in the District, Maryland, and

THE FIRST COLORED CATHOLIC CONGRESS, 1899. Delegates pose for group picture on the steps of St. Augustine's Church, site of their historic meeting.

made his purpose clear: "Colored Catholics ought to unite." To that end he wanted delegates "under the blessing of Holy Mother Church," to come together "to get to know one another and take up the cause of the race."[25] The convention's temporary chairman, William Smith of St. Augustine's, expanded on this concept, reminding delegates that they had assembled, not to discuss doctrine or theology, but to "talk

Pennsylvania. A useful resume of the meetings of the first three congress, *Three Catholic Afro-American Congresses*, was published by the *American Catholic Tribune* in 1893 and reprinted by Arno Press in 1978. For a scholarly account, see Spalding, "The Negro Catholic Congresses, 1889–1894," *Catholic Historical Review* 55, no. 3 (Oct 1969): 337–57. The following paragraphs are based on these works.

25. Quoted in Cyprian Davis, "The Holy See and American Black Catholics," *U.S. Catholic Historian* 7 (1988): 158.

about our needs as a people, and by conference and consultation to try and devise ways and means of bettering our condition, religious and socially." The many addresses that followed tended to reflect the cautionary advice of Cardinal Gibbons rather than Smith's appeal for open discussion.

The two ceremonial highlights of the congress indicated the seriousness with which both Washington and Rome took the occasion. The first occurred when the delegates were invited to the White House to meet President Cleveland; the second when they received a special blessing from Pope Leo XIII for the success of the congress. More important as indicating the future course of events was the debate that was generated on the closing day of the Congress by a draft "Address to the Colored People" prepared by the resolutions committee. This draft, a bland recital of Catholic accomplishments and condemnation of secret societies, intemperance, and other dangers discussed in recent Church councils, was rejected by some, including Willis J. Smith and Father Walsh, who deemed it "unworthy" of the true sentiments of the congress. Walsh reminded the delegates that the chief work of the congress had been "to put forth strongly and with due moderation, your sufferings, your wants, and your aspirations."

The dissenters won, and the draft was returned to the committee, where laymen like William S. Lofton and William Smith rewrote it, producing a more realistic assessment of the needs of black Catholics addressed to the whole American church. Lamenting that "the sacred rights of justice and humanity are still sadly wounded and immeasurably obstructed," the congress expressed confidence that the Church would dispel the prejudices of misguided people and promised the cooperation of black Catholics in organizing parochial schools and industrial schools for black youth, literary societies and other cultural organizations for adults, as well as orphanages and other charitable institutions. It also called for an end to discrimination in labor unions, housing, and employment and called on all Catholics to help "by their sympathy and fellowship in the great and noble work which we have thus inaugurated for the welfare—social, moral, and intellectual—of our entire people."[26]

26. Quoted in *Three Catholic Afro-American Congresses*, p. 72.

The participants had good cause for the optimism that bathed the closing banquet in St. Augustine's parish hall. Exulting in their newly discovered unity and determined to continue the work of the convention, delegates were already mapping out plans for further committee work and future meetings. They had been greeted by a uniformly supportive press. Washington's widely read *Bee* reported with approval on the ability and influence of the delegates, singling out "our esteemed' friend" Daniel Rudd for praise for the management of the convention. The *Catholic World* predicted that the congress "opened a new era which few could foresee" in racial progress. Meanwhile, the sixteenth convention of the Catholic Young Men's National Union passed a resolution approving the work of the congress, especially the resolution to establish agricultural and industrial schools, and invited black groups around the country to join its organization.[27] Indeed, the congress seemed to stimulate a flurry of interracial activity, including the participation of black delegates in the first congress of lay Catholics that met in Baltimore in May 1889. Of special significance to Rudd and his colleagues, the black congresses also seemed to energize a major champion of social justice in the church, the outspoken archbishop of St. Paul, John Ireland.

Known for his fiery eloquence as the "Consecrated Blizzard of the West," the leader of the progressive wing of the American hierarchy entered the fray with a memorable sermon on racial justice delivered from the altar of St. Augustine's on May 4, 1890. Speaking before a congregation that included numerous congressmen and other prominent government officials, Ireland dismissed the pious rhetoric of his colleagues, noting that "no church is a worthy temple of God where a place is marked off for colored people. It is a shame and a scandal in a temple of God when a man, because of his color, is driven to an obscure corner or to a loft."[28] Ireland himself had served as a chaplain in the Union Army during the Civil War, and he spoke with pride about the long and successful fight against slavery. Now discrimination was the enemy, he declared, and he condemned segregation. "I know no

27. *The Bee*, 5 Jan 1889; *Catholic World* 49 (April 1889): 94–103; and Catholic Young Men's National Union, *Proceedings of the Sixteenth Annual Convention . . . 1890*, p. 99.

28. The speech was quoted, practically in whole, in the *CM*, 10 May 1890.

color line. I will acknowledge none." He admitted that his views would sound rash and untimely to some, but he demanded that the doors of all Catholic institutions be opened immediately to all, regardless of color. Despite the fiery words, Ireland was no revolutionary. He demanded fair play, but no special treatment. He asked his black listeners to work patiently for educational opportunities and economic independence, and he urged them to state their grievances and seek redress where it should be given "in a proper spirit."

That was precisely what Butler, Lofton, and the other progressive leaders of the black congress movement planned to do. While Ireland's speech "set the heathen on fire," as one commentator put it, these black laymen quietly began a united assault against injustice in the Church.[29] The first fruit of their work was another congress, which convened in Cincinnati in July 1890. Here in the wake of the euphoria caused by Ireland's declaration, delegates led by Lofton and Butler focused on specific problems and proposed specific solutions. In a militant address Lofton reminded delegates of the plight of black children who, despite the Church's demand that Catholics attend Catholic schools, were denied admittance to all but a handful of parochial schools. He sarcastically referred to leaders who failed to support their own teachings when they allowed Catholic schools and colleges to exclude qualified African Americans. While supporting the need for all sorts of schools, Lofton stressed the importance of agricultural and vocational training for economically disadvantaged youth. Such sentiments might have seemed at odds with the distinguished academic backgrounds of Lofton and his friend, but they and most of the delegates to the congress sympathized with Booker T. Washington's focus on vocational and agricultural training. At Lofton's urging, the congress petitioned the federal government to underwrite an industrial school for black Catholics in Washington. Charles Butler also emphasized what he called polytechnical education, reminding delegates that black children were forced into the public schools for secondary

29. Ltr, L. W. Reilly to Slattery, 24 May 1890, 9-N-6, ASSJ. For a brief survey of the national reaction to Ireland's speech, see *St. Joseph's Advocate* 2, no. 3 (July 1890): 150–51 and 166–69; *CM*, 10 May 1890; and ltr. Slattery to Vaughan, 5 May 1890, 39-MHT-15, ASSJ. The sermon evoked a flurry of editorials, articles, and letters in the local Catholic paper—see, for example, *CM*, 17 and 24 May, 7 Jun, and 30 Sep 1890.

instruction, "possibly at the loss of their religion." He called on the congress to sponsor a national Catholic high school in Washington.[30]

With no encouragement from the hierarchy, little came of these proposals or of similar demands enunciated at a third congress in Philadelphia in January 1892. By then, however, the major theme of this protest movement had emerged. At the instigation of aggressive reformers like Lofton, Butler, and a few others, a unified and energized group had defined several concrete proposals to improve the position of black Catholics and to end discrimination. Their agenda far surpassed the timid goals suggested by Daniel Rudd just five years before.

These national meetings prompted a flurry of activity in local black parishes and organizations. In June 1890, for example, St. Augustine's had selected delegates to represent the parish at the second congress and hosted a picnic to collect funds to pay their way to Cincinnati.[31] The *Catholic Mirror* spoke approvingly of the second congress's call for an industrial school, reminding readers of a recent aborted effort among Washington Catholics to found such an institution.[32] Meanwhile, Charles Butler, who had been appointed by the second congress to chair a committee to seek help in organizing a school in Washington, had to report a general lack of interest among the nation's bishops and federal authorities. He took some consolation, however, from the fact that Mother Katharine Drexel, the saintly supporter of many African and Native American causes, planned to open such a school in Pennsylvania. Her decision, he was convinced, was influenced by the work of the second congress.[33] On the eve of the third congress, Archbishop Ireland responded to an invitation to attend a parish fair by spending a day at St. Augustine's. While there he urged the congre-

30. The remarks of Lofton and Butler were considered newsworthy enough to gain detailed coverage in *CN*, 20 Jul 1890.

31. The parish delegates, in addition to speakers Lofton and Butler, included both William T. and Willis H. Smith and Father Walsh. See *CM*, 5 Jul 1890 and *CN*, 29 Jun 1890.

32. *CM*, 20 Jul 1890. On the aborted effort to start a school and orphanage in Washington, see below and chapter 5.

33. Rpt., Chm., Industrial School Cmte, 23 May 1891, repr. in Minutes of the Meeting of the Exec Cmte of the Colored Catholic Congress, 23 May 1891, cy in 7-N-9a, ASSJ. On the efforts of Mother Katharine, see chapter 5, below.

gation to send a strong delegation to Philadelphia and exhorted his wildly cheering audience to demand its rights firmly and in charity.[34]

Yet another congress was held in conjunction with the Columbian Catholic Congress in Chicago in September 1893. While it was largely overshadowed by activities associated with the Chicago World's Fair and Exposition, it nevertheless provided black Catholics with a far larger stage on which to air their grievances. A delegation from the black congress was invited to participate in the meeting of the national Catholic Congress where they heard, among others, two significant addresses on race relations in the Church. Father Slattery spoke on evangelization; the important task of addressing the vast assembly on discrimination was undertaken by St. Augustine's Charles Butler.[35] Butler's eloquent address "The Future of the Negro Race" showed just how far the black laity had come in these years of meetings and association in defining its demands. He began by suggesting that the future of race relations in the United States depended on whether the proud Anglo-Saxon meant to rid himself of race prejudice and accord his black brother simple justice. He was particularly critical of segregation and other forms of discrimination, rhetorically asking, "How long, oh Lord, are we to endure this hardship in the house of our friends?" He reminded his largely white audience that the centuries of toil by African Americans, in concert with the labor of others, had made the great Columbian Exposition possible, and he appealed to white America, especially white Catholics, to help abolish prejudice. This was not a plea for charity, he concluded, but a demand for "a right that has been dearly paid for."[36]

34. A report of Ireland's sermon and his visit to the fair appeared in the *CN*, 13 Dec 1891.

35. Butler's selection was the result of considerable negotiation. Congress officers considered Rudd unequal to the task, and they outright rejected Lofton. All agreed with Slattery that Butler would make an eloquent and effective spokesman. See ltr., Lofton to William H. Onahan (secy., Columbian Catholic Congress), 2 Jun 1893, CUA Archives; Butler to Slattery, 5 Feb, 16 Mar, 3 and 31 May, and 30 Aug 1893, 4-K-7 through 4-K-11, all in ASSJ; and ltr., Slattery to Butler, 10 Apr 1893, LPB-1-115, same source.

36. Butler's speech was reprinted in whole in *Program of the Catholic Church in America and the Great Columbian Catholic Congress of 1893* (Chicago: J. S. Hyland & Co., 1897), pp. 122–24.

Before the fourth congress adjourned the delegates approved the establishment of the St. Peter Claver's Catholic Union, a permanent organization designed to represent the 200 various black parishes and societies in the country. Dr. Lofton was elected president, and in October he invited all Catholic societies, white as well as black, to join the Union's campaign to promote black churches, schools, and orphanages. At the same time, Lofton explained to Cardinal Gibbons, the group had no intention of making such institutions a permanent feature of the American church. Its ultimate aim, rather, was to secure free access for black Catholics to all institutions "on common and equal grounds."[37]

On its last day the fourth congress also appointed a committee on grievances to prepare for the next national meeting by documenting Butler's charges of discrimination in local churches. In an unprecedented move the committee sent a questionnaire to every American bishop, requesting data on racial practices in his diocese. Specifically, the prelates were quizzed on segregated seating in churches, admittance to their schools, hospitals, and orphanages, and treatment of black candidates for seminaries and convents. The few bishops who did respond tended to deny discrimination or blamed any instances of such behavior on individual pastors and parishes acting against diocesan policy. The most widely publicized example of such buck-passing was Cardinal Gibbons's response to charges that in his own cathedral black Catholics were restricted to seating on backless benches in the rear of the church. Gibbons, whose generous support of St. Augustine's and the Josephite Fathers as well as his qualified endorsement of the Colored Congress movement had won the respect of black Catholics and ranked him among the progressive bishops on racial matters, was nevertheless reluctant to challenge long-held social attitudes of Maryland's white Catholics. He begged the question of discrimination, blaming the cathedral's lay trustees for the segregated seating. He went on to caution his black audience that it must be patient and wait for a change in public opinion. Some of the more assertive black spokesmen were beginning to question Gibbons' habit of seeking refuge from difficult questions by citing the power of public opinion, but on the whole the delegates remained loyal to the cardinal, seeking

37. Ltr., Lofton to Gibbons, 31 Oct 1893, 92A-E-13, Gibbons Papers, AAB.

his approval for a fifth congress to be held in his city in October 1894. Gibbons blessed the congress, but called on delegates to exercise "wisdom, forbearance, prudence, and discretion."[38]

The fifth, and last, congress demonstrated both the increasing outspokenness of some key leaders and a corresponding erosion of support among those who favored a more cautious approach. Dr. Lofton's fiery presidential address set the tone for the activists. He called on the bishops to banish distinctions based on caste or color. He wanted American business interests to turn from their effort to attract new immigrants to fill their jobs and remember instead the millions of loyal and law-abiding black citizens. He looked for the day, he concluded, when bishops and laity would join in stamping out prejudice, which, he declared, "is today destroying the life blood of the country." Warmed by his rhetoric, an enthusiastic audience in an unprecedented move agreed to send a delegation to Philadelphia to present to the bishops assembled there for their annual meeting a list of complaints based on the findings of their recent national survey.

In contrast to Lofton's uncompromising demand for assimilation, Father John Slattery called on the delegates to accommodate to the political and social realities of the times. During his years as the American provincial of the English Josephite Fathers, Slattery had developed a reputation as a forceful enemy of discrimination and a vocal champion of several causes important to black Catholics.[39] His demand for what he called competitive equality—the right for African Americans to earn a living at fair wages and to enter the professions—was well publicized, and men like Daniel Rudd and Charles Butler regarded him as their close ally.[40] Slattery also played a significant role in the

38. Quoted in Spalding, "The Catholic Negro Congresses," pp. 351–52. The Baltimore cathedral controversy was reported in a letter to the New York *Sun* from Robert Wood, chairman of the grievance committee, 29 Jun 1894. On Gibbons's answer, see Misch, "The American Bishops and the Negro," p. 571. For a more favorable interpretation of Gibbons's attitude, see John Tracy Ellis, *The Life of James Cardinal Gibbons, Archbishop of Baltimore 1834–1921* (Milwaukee: Bruce Publ., 1952), vol. II, pp. 396–99.

39. For a carefully nuanced survey of Slattery's role in the evolving demands for racial justice, see Ochs's *Desegregating the Altar*, particularly pp. 58–89.

40. Slattery's views on competitive equality were discussed in his speech to Sixteenth Convention of the Catholic Young Men's National Union. See *Proceedings*, pp.

congress movement, not only because of his useful advice on organization and suggestions for topics for discussion, but also as a source of financial support. In addition to his many articles and speeches on racial justice, Slattery once found time to use his considerable gift for sarcasm to defend the economically pressed St. Augustine's against a bigot's charge that the beautiful church was built by an indefatigable priest with money from generous whites. Slattery pointed out that the church cost $76,000 to construct and at the time of the "reverend builder's death" carried a debt of $72,000, which the parishioners were slowly reducing. Where, then, was all this fabled white generosity, Slattery asked?[41]

Slattery had worked tenaciously for the establishment of a seminary dedicated especially to the training of priests for the evangelization of African Americans. He was also one of the first to call for the ordination of black priests. As early as 1886 he bluntly warned that white men would never convert black America.[42] This view had permeated his celebrated speech before the first congress, in which he dismissed the oft-repeated charge that black Catholics did not want black priests, pointing to the reception tendered Father Tolton by the delegates. He predicted that the Church would never succeed in evangelizing African Americans "until we have hundreds and thousands of colored priests."[43] Slattery worked hard to place black candidates in American and European seminaries and paid for their support. He was a close friend and supporter of Father Tolton and rejoiced when one of his own proteges, Charles Uncles, was ordained by Cardinal Gibbons in 1891, the first black American ordained in the United States. Although Slattery would always remain an ardent proponent of a black clergy and a broad evangelization effort, his support for the movement's activists had certainly cooled by the time of the fifth congress. Some historians have identified a strongly paternalistic attitude in Slattery's championship of black causes, and while labeling so com-

34–35. For examples of Butler's special affection for the Josephite, see ltrs., Butler to Slattery, 23 Dec 1891, 4-K-1, and 25 Apr 1892, 4-K-2. Both in ASSJ.

41. *CM*, 23 Jan 1892.

42. Ltr., Slattery to Benoit, 4 Mar 1886, 33-MHT-15, ASSJ.

43. As quoted in Ochs, *Desegregating the Altar*, p. 77. See also *Three Catholic Afro-American Congresses*, pp. 45–47.

plex a thinker is difficult, it is clear that Slattery embraced Booker T. Washington's idea of self-help and accommodation to segregation. Slattery's speech at the fifth congress reflected this philosophy: he cautioned delegates to practice forbearance and to leave agitation for civil and political rights to others. The contrasting approaches of Lofton and Slattery foreshadowed the great debate that would begin in earnest a decade later when W. E. B. DuBois and his followers in the new National Association for the Advancement of Colored People would begin to challenge those who, like Booker T. Washington, urged an accommodation with segregated society. It was a debate that would also resonate in St. Augustine's congregation and the Church in Washington in later generations.

The Baltimore congress in 1894 marked the end of the black congress movement and with it a temporary suspension of any nationally organized effort by the black laity to push for racial reform. Sporadic attempts by Lofton and Fredrick McGhee on behalf of the St. Peter Claver Union to revive the movement at the turn of the century failed. In an uncharacteristic move Lofton expressed regret for "certain mistakes" made at the fifth congress and asked Father Slattery to "bury the past" and seek to organize yet another meeting because the Church was losing the chance to convert many of the brightest African Americans.[44] Nothing came of this bid for renewal, and although important local initiatives would continue at St. Augustine's and elsewhere, it would take a new generation of lay activists after World War I to revive the national effort.

The movement's demise has been blamed on a concerned hierarchy's reaction to the increasingly strident demands of leaders like Lofton, culminating in the questionnaire seeking to document discrimination and the presentation of grievances at their meeting in 1894. In truth, the bishops of that era, even those who shared the progressive ideas of the congress leaders, tended to recoil from any sign of lay autonomy, and the black congress movement fell victim to the indifference or active opposition of bishops just as did other national lay organizations of the day. Moreover, the lay activists were beginning to encounter opposition to their tactics in their rank and file. Slattery's

44. Ltr., Lofton and McGhee to Slattery, 20 Jan 1900, 14-M-25, ASSJ.

approach was popular with many black Catholics around the country, and support for Lofton's more confrontational strategy had waned considerably by the time of the fifth congress in 1894—which, despite much pleading by organizers, attracted only thirty-eight delegates. Yet while short-lived, this protest movement, so closely identified with St. Augustine's and its lay leaders, was important in the development of the racial history of the American church. It marked the first time the black laity demonstrated before a national audience their sense of identity, pride, and confidence as African Americans and as Catholics. This first concerted effort to fight discrimination in the Church and to lay out the aspirations of an often neglected segment of Catholic society had revealed a people, in historian Davis's words, "conscious of its responsibility and devoted to a common ideal."[45]

Efforts at the Local Level

An underlying theme of the deliberations at the five black congresses was the need for reform at the local level. It was only appropriate, therefore, that the dynamic group which represented St. Augustine's at these meetings also worked at the parish level to broaden educational opportunities and gain wider recognition for parish organizations. Frustrated by their failure to obtain a secondary school for black Catholics in Washington, Lofton, Henry Hall, and others in the parish organized the Toussaint L'Ouverture Institute in February 1892.[46] A literary society named in honor of the slave who liberated San Domingo, the institute was designed to further the advancement of young men by means of organized lectures and night classes. It was modeled after the Carroll Institute, which since 1873 had been preparing white youth lacking a high school education for positions in the federal government and the city's rapidly growing business community.

Typical of the times, both organizations were restricted to male stu-

45. Cyprian Davis, "Black Catholics in the Nineteenth Century," *U.S. Catholic Historian* 5 (1986): 17.

46. Officers included Lofton, president, B. Aloysius Lemon, vice president, Harry Bell, secretary, and T. W. Short, treasurer. All were members of St. Augustine's congregation. For organization of the institute, see *CN*, 8 May 1892 and 10 Mar 1894.

dents. The L'Ouverture Institute met for several years in the hall of the Catholic Benevolent Association before opening its own clubhouse, first at 1624 O Street and later at 1213 Seventeenth Street. Classes for young men were conducted twice weekly by a professional teacher, A. J. Lopez, who prepared his students for the civil service examination and offered lessons in bookkeeping and office skills. The indefatigable Charles Butler supervised the night school. The young men paid no tuition since the cost of the teacher, library, and meeting rooms was underwritten by the officers and board of directors.[47] Students were also invited to attend the institute's frequent lectures and testimonials featuring prominent black educators, politicians, and professionals. In May 1895, for example, the institute sponsored a gathering at which many noted visitors discussed the contribution of the recently deceased Frederick Douglass to the nation.[48]

Although many of its members and students were St. Augustine parishioners, the L'Overture Institute was not sponsored by the parish, which already supported both a literary society and a debating club. Part of the era's general fascination with popular culture and general uplift, the Barotti Literary Society had been a flourishing parish organization since 1888. Such groups provided urban populations with wholesome entertainment as well as cultural improvement. The society in St. Augustine's parish, whose Sunday school teachers participated practically en masse, boasted a large membership.[49] Most of those who figured in the black congress movement were also members: Charles Butler, for example, served as the society's first president. Similar to societies in other large parishes, the St. Augustine group sponsored literary evenings, where books were analyzed, topics debated, and works of famous authors quoted. Musical recitals were often part of these literary evenings. Frequently there were lectures on cul-

47. In 1895 the board of directors consisted of Robert Coates, W. J. Smith, Henry W. Duckett, Joseph Miles, J. D. Woodland, Matthew Butler, Donald Spriggs, William Marshall, and Charles Butler. New officers included Thomas Spriggs, Richard Wells, and J. W. Queen. See *CN*, 16 Mar 1895.

48. *CN*, 18 and 25 May 1895. The meeting adopted a resolution honoring Washington's most famous black citizen as a model for Negro youth.

49. *CN*, 14 Apr 1894.

tural subjects. In June 1888, for example, a large audience heard Major Edmund Mallet, a prominent Washington Catholic and government official, speak on African-American progress in the arts and education.[50]

An altogether more serious intellectual pursuit, the St. Augustine's Acme Debating Association, was also organized in 1888. Here young men were encouraged to study and argue controversial topics of the day.[51] Some of the debaters attended a night school opened in 1893 by the Knights of St. Augustine for their young members. Charles Butler was the major promoter of this venture in adult education, which was definitely an outgrowth of the black congress movement. He organized the classes along the lines of the larger L'Ouverture Institute, but the training sponsored by the Knights, Butler informed Father Slattery, would include religious subjects so that those "who are not quite as fortunate as others" might benefit from the latest information available.[52]

This flurry of educational initiatives at the local level never diverted the lay activists at St. Augustine's from their effort to obtain a vocational school in the Washington area. Throughout the last decade of the old century Charles Butler and the others maintained a constant drumbeat of speeches before lay Catholic groups, letters to influential friends, and strategy meetings with allies in their continuing effort to win support for the school. In seeking wider backing for their cause, they took advantage of the recent affiliation of several of the parish's lay organizations with various national Catholic unions. The Knights of St. Augustine, for example, had led the way when in 1887 they joined the Knights of St. John, a 10,000-man national union of uniformed beneficial societies. When the organization descended on the capital for its tenth national convention in 1889, the 500 members of the three local commandaries of the Knights marched in the grand parade reviewed by President Benjamin Harrison, and their representa-

50. *CN*, 17 Jun 1888.

51. The founding officers of the association included Eugene Curtis, president, Joseph Brown, vice president, Edward Gorden, secretary, Louis Brown, treasurer, and Charles H. Dorsey, marshal. See *CN*, 23 Sep 1888.

52. Ltr., Butler to Slattery, 16 May 1893, 4-K-10, ASSJ.

CRUSADERS. Leaders of the
black Catholic lay congress
movement and St. Augustine
parishioners (clockwise from
above): Dr. William S. Lofton,
an early graduate of Howard
University's School of Dentistry;
William Henry Smith, librarian
of the House of Representatives
Library; and Charles Butler of
the U.S. Treasury Department.

tives participated in the convention's deliberations at Carroll Hall. St. Augustine's Ananias Herbert and Gabriel Coakley, by then a parishioner of St. Peter's on Capitol Hill, both served on the arrangements committee.[53] Butler and the rest used the camaraderie that evolved during these meetings to enlist support for the school.

Encouraged by their friendly reception in the Knights of St. John, St. Augustine's Knights, along with the parish's Barotti Literary Society, decided to accept the invitation to join the Catholic Young Men's National Union, and they elected delegates to yet another convention in Washington in 1890. This time Dr. Lofton served on the arrangements committee, which accepted the thankless task of finding accommodations for visiting black delegates, who were banned from staying with other delegates at Washington's segregated Arlington Hotel.[54] He and several other black delegates addressed the convention, concentrating on the educational needs of black Catholics. As the result of their efforts, the convention passed a resolution approving the work of the black congress and its proposal to establish agricultural and industrial schools.[55] In successive years, delegations from St. Augustine's congregation attended subsequent national meetings.[56] In 1892, for example, Butler was invited to address the delegates of the Young Men's National Union in Albany, New York. He used the occasion to remind his audience about the struggle for secondary education among black Catholics, and in July he dashed off a line to Father Slattery seeking his latest thoughts on the subject.[57]

53. A description of the proceedings, along with a list of delegates, appeared in the *Evening Star*, 24 Jun 1889. The Knights of St. John included three Washington branches: the Knights of St. Columbkille, a largely Irish-American group, the Knights of St. Peter, and the 500-man Knights of St. Augustine. See *CM*, 22 Jun 1889. For a brief history of the Knights of St. John, see Foley, "The Catholic Church and the Washington Negro," pp. 299–301.

54. Ltr., N. T. Taylor, secy., Catholic Young Men's National Union, to Slattery, 8 Oct 1890, 5-C-1, ASSJ. See also *CN*, 28 Sep 1890, and *CM*, 20 Sep and 11 Oct 1890.

55. *Proceedings of the Sixteenth Annual Convention of the Catholic Young Men's National Union*, p. 99.

56. In addition to Butler and Lofton, delegates from the Knights of St. Augustine to the Catholic Young Men's convention in 1891 included Robert Coates, Ananias Herbert, and Alexander Thomas. See *CN*, 13 Sep 1891.

57. Ltr., Butler to Slattery, 14 Jul 1892, 4-K-5, ASSJ.

As attested by their frequent meetings and correspondence, a close friendship had developed between the dynamic Josephite and Butler. In contrast to the fiery Lofton, Butler adopted a less confrontational approach to race relations. In his many speeches and letters on the subject he concentrated on the practical danger of continued discrimination: the loss of thousands of Catholic youth to the Church. He stood shoulder to shoulder with his Protestant friends in everything he did "for the uplifting of my race," he once told Slattery, but he was concerned that in neglecting the needs of African Americans the Church was losing ground to other religions.[58] Butler supported Slattery's efforts to get a group of young black educators in Baltimore to start a vocational school in the archdiocese, along the lines of the Josephite school in Wilmington, Delaware, and the Christian Brothers school at Rock Castle in central Virginia.[59] Although his effort did not bear immediate fruit, Butler continued to struggle against the overwhelming indifference of the vast majority of American Catholics in that sad era.

Unfortunately, the danger of losing thousands of young Catholics because of the lack of church-sponsored schools seemed lost on many church leaders, who continued to think of African Americans as non-Catholics to be converted rather than as an increasingly large group of the faithful to be nourished. Butler's warning, ignored in the United States, would find a sympathetic audience in the Vatican.

A Powerful Ally

The fight against discrimination in the Church acquired a new and powerful ally in 1904 in Cardinal Girolamo Gotti, head of Propaganda Fide. Gotti bluntly told the new apostolic delegate to the United States, Archbishop Diomede Falconio, that "it has been referred to this Sacred Congregation that in some of the dioceses of the United States the condition of the Catholic negroes, not only in respect to the

58. Ltr., Butler to Slattery, 30 Nov 1899, 11-N-10, ASSJ.

59. Ltr., Slattery to Butler, 2 Dec 1896, LPB-2-438-9, ASSJ. See also ltr., Butler to Slattery, 11 Dec 1896, 11-N-9, ASSJ. The Wilmington school was established by Father John deRuyter, a former assistant pastor at St. Augustine's.

other faithful but also in respect to their pastors and bishops, is very humiliating and entirely different from that of the whites."[60] Ignoring the polite circumlocutions usually employed by Vatican officials, Gotti curtly told Falconio to bring this matter to the attention of Cardinal Gibbons, who should take steps to lessen and gradually eliminate such discrimination.

Gibbons acted promptly, presenting Gotti's comments to his fellow archbishops. Although these leaders reacted predictably, complaining that Rome was meddling in an extremely sensitive area about which it knew little, they did circulate Gotti's demand among all the bishops, calling for the correction of any such abuses. The Vatican kept up the pressure. The pope's principal spokesman, Cardinal Merry del Val, publicly reassured the editor of an African-American newspaper of the pope's special regard and urged all Catholics "to be friendly to Negroes, who are called no less than other men to share in all the great benefits of the Redemption."[61] Cardinal Gibbons understood that more was expected of the American hierarchy, and in May he appointed a committee of three archbishops to review the American church's treatment of African Americans.

What immediately prompted this and later Vatican interventions on behalf of black Catholics has not yet been fully determined by historians, but it seems clear that private initiatives, including the work of the grievance committee in the last two black Catholic congresses, played a role. The proximate cause for Gotti's outburst was most likely the scathing denunciation of discrimination in the American church prepared by the Josephite priest, Joseph Anciaux. All the charges aired at the black congresses were reinforced by his recitation of specific, shocking examples of the humiliation suffered at the hands of shortsighted and prejudiced Catholics, including some priests and

60. Ltr., Gotti to Falconio, 18 Jan 1904, as quoted in "The Holy See and American Blacks in the Files of the Apostolic Delegation 1904–1914," a paper by Cyprian Davis, cy in 80-T-10, ASSJ. The following paragraphs are based on that paper and Davis' *The History of Black Catholics in the United States*, pp. 195–96; his "The Holy See and American Black Catholics," pp. 170–72; Ochs's *Desegregating the Altar*, pp. 137–43; and Misch's "The American Bishops and the Negro," pp. 569–74.

61. As quoted in Ochs, *Desegregating the Altar*, p. 141.

bishops. The well-connected Anciaux saw his report circulated among the highest officials of the Church.

It is likely that some of Ancioux's information was already known to Vatican officials through the reports of the first apostolic delegate, Archbishop Francesco Satolli. Satolli's appointment to the new post in January 1893 did not sit well with most of the hierarchy, which feared that the presence of a papal representative would only provide the bigots in the American Protective Association and the Ku Klux Klan with more ammunition. In fact, many bishops considered such an appointment as an unnecessary intrusion into American affairs. Nevertheless, Satolli proved a resourceful diplomat and a popular figure among American Catholics. From the first he displayed a strong interest in the welfare of African Americans. His home on Washington's Belmont Street was not far from St. Augustine's, and the tall Italian prelate could often be seen presiding at masses and special church services in the black parish. His approachable manner when he attended the parish's various social functions made him a popular visitor. At the 1894 fair, for example, he spent Thanksgiving evening talking to the fairgoers, listening to the music, touring the exhibits, and taking chances on the door prizes.[62]

In August 1893 Satolli received a copy of the questionnaire later sent to the bishops by the fourth black congress, along with a request for an audience from Robert Wood, the New York politician and chairman of the grievance committee. It seems likely that the two men met and discussed racial discrimination in Catholic institutions. Dr. Lofton then invited Satolli to address the fifth congress. Although the apostolic delegate did not appear at any of the sessions in Baltimore, he composed a carefully designed letter which was read to the delegates. If Satolli's remarks revealed many gaps in his understanding of the situation, it also showed his strong sympathy for the plight of black Catholics. Especially significant was the fact that Satolli would eventually return as a cardinal to assume a high position in the Roman curia, where his growing awareness of racial conditions in the American church, nurtured in part by his association with St. Augustine's congregation, would help influence later Vatican interventions.

62. *Fair Gazette*, 26 Nov and 3 Dec 1894.

It also appears that the Vatican heard directly from the black laity. In June 1894 Robert Wood published an open letter in the New York *Sun* inviting black Catholics to write to him if they wanted their grievances carried to Rome for delivery to the pope. Whether Pope Leo XIII was ever made aware of this lay initiative is not yet known, but it seems likely that Wood's material found its way to the Vatican, either through the reports of the apostolic delegate or by means of sympathetic friends in Rome.

In the short run this Vatican intervention effected little change in the treatment of black Catholics. The deliberations of the committee organized by Cardinal Gibbons did nothing to end segregation in churches or exclusion of black Catholics from schools and charitable institutions. Instead, the bishops established in 1907 a new national agency, the Catholic Board for Mission Work Among the Colored People. Like previous initiatives, the board's charter expressed the bishops' lofty ambition of converting black Americans and ignored the problem of discrimination against those already in the Church.[63] In the end the new board proved to be yet one more vehicle for fiddling with the collection and dispersal of money, largely duplicating the work of the commission formed in 1888 for supporting African and Native American missions. Despite the hard work of its director, Father John Burke, the board took many years to get on its feet, constantly impaired by the parsimony and indifference of many bishops.

The creation of the new collection agency ended the first campaign in what would be a long war for justice in the American church. This black-organized, national protest was a remarkable event in that war. In an era when congregations were expected to pray, pay, and obey— as the old saying went—a group of articulate African-American laymen, representatives of a largely overlooked minority in the church, organized on a national level, defined their needs, and addressed their demands to the bishops and to Rome itself. Their achievement is all the more remarkable when considered in the context of the times. The first black congress took place just a quarter-century after the Emancipation Proclamation and just as Jim Crow was beginning his dolorous

63. Rouse, "A Study of the Development of Negro Education under Catholic Auspices," pp. 73–74.

reign. Although some of the protest leaders, like Daniel Rudd, were ex-slaves who bore the burden of their deprived past, many were descendants of a long line of free black citizens, well educated, and financially secure. Those identified as St. Augustine's parishioners were in this latter group, and their active work on behalf of their less fortunate co-religionists placed them in a special category among Washington's "black 400," a fact that would become even more obvious when they turned their considerable energies to the internal affairs of their parish.

FIVE 🕮 CHALLENGES FOR

A NEW CENTURY

*I*n view of the obstacles already surmounted, St. Augustine's congregation could approach century's end with considerable optimism. Parishioners now numbered 3,000, many of them recent converts. They and a large group of visitors of both races routinely packed one of Washington's largest and most beautiful churches for a crowded schedule of services, testifying to a vibrant faith frequently noted in the press. Although a continuing financial crisis tended to monopolize the energies of both priests and laity, the era of uncontrolled spending was past and the debt under control. Reacting to their routine exclusion from most diocesan institutions and organizations because of race, parish leaders, assimilists all, stood in the forefront of those who were defining the special grievances of black Catholics.

Much remained to be done, and none could discount the challenges that lay ahead. Concentration on debt reduction had diverted attention from other pressing obligations. Consequently relief of parish poor had lagged seriously, and even the school was showing signs of neglect. Evolving residential patterns in the capital had begun to shift the center of black population to the extent that church authorities were seriously questioning the need for a separate black parish on Fifteenth Street. Nor could such speculation remain academic for long. The dissolution of the American province of the English missionary society entrusted with management of St. Augustine's had begun. The departure of these priests would force Cardinal Gibbons to reconsider

diocesan policy on racially separate parishes. Sure to figure in his deliberations was the large number of white Catholics, many of them
parishioners of nearby St. Matthew's, who had become regulars at St.
Augustine's. Their presence tended to nullify the rationale for racially
separate churches and posed yet another threat to the continued existence of the parish.

In the end, all parish decisions would be influenced to some extent
by the challenge confronting every black resident as racial discrimination began to increase in Washington. Tragically, this renewed racism
was gathering strength just as the black community was at its most
fragmented. Artificial divisions between its social and economic classes, noticeable since the 1870s, had so increased that discrimination
within the African-American community itself and indifference of
many of its leaders to the needs of the least fortunate precluded development of a unified response to this fresh assault on civil rights. Instead, the various social elements that made up the black community
each sought to protect their particular interests by making separate accommodation with the new order. A renewed sense of racial unity and
an effective fight against discrimination were still a generation away.
Until then life would go on with little hope for justice and little for individuals to do but endure in silence.

Charity At Home

Some of the tension among the social classes may have figured in
the failed effort in the late 1880s to establish a Catholic orphanage for
Washington's black children. Father John deRuyter, an assistant priest
at St. Augustine's and an early sponsor of the project, talked about
"the great interest taken by both whites and colored" in the success of
St. Monica's Orphanage and Industrial Home for Colored Children; in
fact, with the notable exception of Sister Seraphine Noel, no prominent
black Catholic seems to have been associated with the enterprise.[1]
Such indifference could not be blamed on a lack of need. With the exception of St. Ann's Infant Asylum, which at that time cared for
foundlings and indigent mothers of both races, Catholic orphanages

---

1. Ltr., deRuyter to Leeson, n.d. (ca. Oct 1886), 3-E-4, ASSJ.

excluded African Americans.[2] Both St. Vincent's, the girls' home operated by the Sisters of Charity, and St. Joseph's, supervised by the Holy Cross Sisters for boys, were founded in St. Patrick's parish earlier in the century to serve Washington's Catholics. Although both received some government support, they thrived on private charity, mostly in the form of countless fund-raising affairs. Organized diocesan support only began in 1885 when a special collection was taken up in all the city's churches for the boys' orphanage. As might be expected, St. Augustine's contributed very little to this racially exclusive institution.[3]

Although such patent discrimination failed to move church officials, the need to provide for black orphans stimulated the charitable impulse of a number of prominent white Catholics. Father deRuyter's experiences as chaplain at Children's Hospital made him especially sensitive to the problem, and he broached the idea of an orphanage to a group of wealthy friends, including lawyer John F. Hanna, Washington socialite Alice Riggs, and financiers E. Francis Riggs and William W. Corcoran. In March 1885 the group set in motion plans to incorporate an orphanage, which they hoped would be staffed by the Holy Cross Sisters and financed in part by the federal government. The pastor, Father Walsh, put deRuyter in charge of the effort, but warned that in no way could the financially pressed St. Augustine's accept monetary responsibility for the charity.[4] Although little came of this in succeeding months, deRuyter's friends did provide enough startup money for him to begin placing a few needy children in foster homes in Washington and Baltimore.

Translating these good intentions into reality was mainly the work of Marie E. Patterson, a wealthy St. Louis heiress recently settled in Washington. Patterson had from the time of her arrival interested her-

2. Founded by Father White during the Civil War and operated by the Sisters of Charity, St. Ann's remained integrated until the eve of World War I. Although a reduction in federal support and the dramatic jump in the number of illegitimate white children have been suggested as reasons for excluding black infants after that date, the strengthening of Jim Crow attitudes in the capital obviously played a part. See Foley's "The Catholic Church and the Washington Negro," pp. 227–30.

3. Louis G. Weitzman, *One Hundred Years of Catholic Charities in the District of Columbia*, pp. 5–13.

4. Ltrs., deRuyter to Leeson, 5 June 1885, 3-E-2, and 17 Nov 1886, 3-E-7. Both in ASSJ.

self in the children of St. Augustine's. She organized a sewing school for the parish's girls before going on to address the plight of the orphans.[5] In June 1885 she rented a three-story brick house at 1411 L Street, which she turned over to Father deRuyter, who cheerfully donned overalls to paint and otherwise ready the house to serve as a temporary orphanage. Patterson also announced her intention of purchasing land near St. Augustine's and building an institution large enough to house the children and their caregivers, as well as the Holy Cross Sisters teaching at St. Augustine's school. Until Hanna and his friends could win the Holy Cross congregation's agreement to operate the new institution, Patterson arranged for Sister Seraphine to supervise the temporary home on L Street. By July, Sister Seraphine and a small group of children were in residence.[6]

This ordered progress was interrupted by the sudden loss of two of the orphanage's principal supporters. In November 1885 John Hanna was killed in a carriage accident. The removal of this skilled lawyer-lobbyist and old Washington hand greatly reduced chances of negotiating some kind of federal support. Less than a year later Sister Seraphine, for over a generation closely identified with the care and instruction of Washington's black children, died suddenly, leaving the day-to-day operation of the new home in disarray.[7] At first things seemed to continue as planned. The Holy Cross Sisters reached a preliminary agreement with the asylum's organizers to replace Sister Seraphine: they sent Sister Euphemia, for many years a teacher in St. Augustine's parochial school, and Sister Scholastica, a young novice recently assigned to St. Augustine's, to care for the children. Cardinal Gibbons formally approved the new institution, and a board of trustees was organized to assume legal responsibility and draw up papers of in-

5. Described as an industrial school, the sewing class had 70 pupils who met weekly in the parish school. Patterson provided all supplies, and the articles made were given to the children. See *CN*, 23 Jan 1887.

6. Ltrs., Walsh to Benoit, 20 Oct 1866, 34-MHT-10, and to Leeson, 17 Oct 1886, 1-N-14. Both in ASSJ. See also *CM*, 24 Jul 1886.

7. Sister Serphine's funeral and burial next to her father and Father Barotti in Mt. Olivet were major events at St. Augustine's, where the priests and people had a special devotion to the former member of the Oblate Sisters of Providence. See *CM*, 16 Oct 1866, and *CN*, 10 Oct 1866. On Hanna's importance to plans for gaining federal support of the orphanage, see ltr., deRuyter to Benoit, 4 Nov 1885, 32-MHT-18, ASSJ.

corporation. True to its name, St. Monica's Orphan and Industrial School was dedicated to the care of needy children and to their training "in practical duties of life, so that they can go out into the world and make an honorable living."[8]

Even as the Catholic press was publicizing a series of open houses, pound parties, stereopticon shows, and choir concerts to raise money for the new orphanage, the enterprise experienced a fatal series of blows.[9] In a surprise move coinciding with the trustees' application for incorporation, the Holy Cross Sisters announced that they could not assume responsibility for St. Monica's. Their refusal may well have had a financial basis connected with the burden imposed on the religious order by the parish's frequent failure to pay the sisters teaching in the parish school, but an angered Father Walsh believed otherwise. Only two sisters ever showed any interest in living with black children, he claimed, concluding that "as the Holy Cross sisters will not come and live with colored children they can hardly be said to be devoted to our work." Consequently, he and the other priests proposed to invite the Sisters of St. Francis from Mill Hill, the order of English nuns associated with the Josephites, to assume control of both the parish school and the orphanage. Assuming approval could be obtained from both Cardinal Gibbons and his provincial, Walsh hoped to have the Mill Hill Sisters in place by September 1887.[10]

Nothing came of this scheme, and the Holy Cross Sisters remained in charge of St. Augustine's school while the orphans came under the care of lay women hired by the trustees. In succeeding months Cardi-

8. Membership of the board read like a page from *Who's Who*: in addition to Riggs and Patterson, it included Madam Bonaparte, Mrs. Thomas Waggaman, Mrs. John Kenna (wife of the senator from West Virginia), Mrs. Florence Vance (wife of the senator from North Carolina), Harriet Loring, Heloise McCue, Eliza Redfern, M. F. Morris, and P. E. Sands. See *St. Joseph's Advocate* 5, no. 1 (Jan 1887): 204–5, and *CM*, 20 Nov 1886 and 19 Feb 1887. The charter was printed in the *CN*, 21 Nov 1886. See also, same source, 24 Oct and 7 Nov 1866, and *CM*, 23 Oct 1866.

9. *CM*, 6 Nov 1886 and 29 Jan 1887, and *CN*, 3 Apr 1887. St. Monica's hosted a profitable pound party in December 1886. See *CM*, 4 Dec 1886. The so-called pound party was derived from the old custom of charging a pound of food or goods as admission for a charitable entertainment. By the 1880s most attendees at such parties gave cash in lieu of food or goods.

10. Ltr., Walsh to Leeson, 15 Nov 1886, 1-N-15, ASSJ.

nal Gibbons agreed to appear at a benefit lecture for St. Monica's, and the trustees appealed for a contribution from the new commission established by the bishops to raise and distribute money to the Negro and Indian Missions. Despite these efforts and a series of well-publicized fund raisers, the little asylum's finances remained precarious. The trustees, apparently retaining some hope that the Mill Hill Sisters might still agree to serve, considered it prudent to postpone the formal opening until September 1887.[11] But that date came and went with no sign of the sisters. When Marie Patterson, still the principal financial sponsor, withdrew her support following a dispute with the priests of St. Augustine's over the project's long-range future and Father deRuyter was transferred, St. Monica's quietly closed its doors.[12] By December 1888 the *Catholic Mirror* was again lamenting the lack of a home "for thousands of neglected and abandoned foundlings and orphans." It reported that Cardinal Gibbons had directed the priests at St. Augustine's to leave nothing undone to diminish the debt "so that all that can be done be accomplished to the speedy bringing into existence of asylums and houses of industry so much needed."[13]

Certainly the withdrawal of the Holy Cross Sisters and the orphanage's principal sponsor were serious setbacks, but that it should have proved fatal to a project of such vital concern demonstrated several obvious truths. Despite some support from St. Augustine's choir and Sister Seraphine's brief participation, St. Monica's was from its inception the handiwork of a small group of wealthy white Catholics. The tepid response of parish organizations to appeals for the orphanage stood in marked contrast to their enthusiastic participation in the fairs and picnics which raised thousands of dollars for the parish debt. In fact, as should have been obvious to any perceptive observer in the late 1880s, the day had arrived when any enterprise, no matter how

11. *CN*, 27 Feb 1887. On application for funds from the Colored and Indian Missions collection, see ltr., Walsh to Leeson, 2 Feb 1887, 1-N-17, ASSJ.

12. Ltr., Lady Mary E. Herbert to Father Slattery, 19 Nov 1888, 6-5-5, ASSJ.

13. As quoted in *CM*, 8 Dec 1888. Four months later Father Slattery, commenting on the situation, listed a home for boys as the primary need of black Catholics in the region (a home for girls already existed in Baltimore). See ltr., Slattery to Rev. John Anler, 16 Apr 1889, 4-D-16, ASSJ.

worthy, that expected support from African Americans must also expect to share direction of its affairs with African Americans.

Actually, without the sustained commitment of a group of religious caregivers, any nineteenth-century orphanage was likely to fail. The refusal of the Holy Cross Sisters to assume responsibility and the failure to obtain the services of the Mill Hill Sisters may have had many causes, but it served to underscore the ineffectiveness of the bishops' exhortations in plenary council for religious congregations to become involved in the black apostolate. Even without the sisters, the orphanage should have been able to continue, at least on a limited scale for a limited time, with contributions from wealthy Catholics, including those well-off parishioners of St. Augustine's who belonged to Washington's black elite. That the orphanage closed so quickly supports the charge that Washington's aristocrats of both races had a limited view of their obligation toward the less fortunate.

The plight of the city's orphans and the need for industrial training, though pressing, was only beginning to capture the attention of St. Augustine's lay leaders as demonstrated at the sessions of the Catholic congresses. For the present, concern centered on the more traditional responsibilities of caring for the poor and educating the young. By 1888 it had become obvious that St. Augustine's charities needed better organization. The beneficial societies continued to provide relief for widows and orphans and even some limited assistance in times of sickness and unemployment. They had prospered over the years, routinely posting healthy budget surpluses. The Male Benevolent Society, for example, listed a $2,000 surplus in 1887.[14] The Catholic Beneficial Society had enough funds to build a new headquarters on Eighteenth Street between L and M, which served it and many other parish groups as a meeting place and recreational center. But these societies were not expected to minister to the needs of Washington's poor. Strictly speaking, they were insurance companies, and most of their funds were used to support members and their survivors.

Generally, parishioners looked to the priests to do what they could in visiting the sick and providing emergency relief for the desperate

14. *CN*, 27 Feb 1887.

out of parish funds. The spectacle of Father Richard Burke, speeding across town on his trusty tricycle to visit Catholics in Freedmen's and other hospitals, had become a familiar sight in the capital.[15] Yet there was a limit to what the priests could accomplish in a city where their mission extended to residents of color in every quarter of town. Catholic inmates at the city's reform school and jail needed visiting and counseling. The parish poor, those lacking the safety net enjoyed by members of the beneficial societies, needed to be identified and cared for, and the collection and distribution of food and clothing and money for rent and fuel needed to be organized. This was work for laymen and women.

In recent years members of the particular (city-wide) council of the St. Vincent de Paul Society had provided assistance to some black Catholics, but in publicly thanking this white group, especially for its work at Freedmen's Hospital, Father Walsh declared that it was time for St. Augustine's to share the burden.[16] On April 22, 1888, the president of the city-wide council participated in a ceremony at St. Augustine's marking the organization of the parish's St. Vincent de Paul conference and the election of its first officers, including Willis J. Smith, vice-president, and Charles Butler, secretary.[17] In an unusual reversal of procedure, the president, Isaac Landic, was not elected until the second meeting. (After Landic's death in 1900, Ignatius Jackson became president, a post he would hold until 1928.) In July the new St. Augustine's conference was introduced at the city-wide meeting of the society at St. Patrick's and "cordially received by the assemblage,"

15. Burke's colorful but practical mode of transport was described in the *CM*, 29 Oct 1887.

16. *CN*, 15 and 22 Apr 1888. The report of the St. Vincent de Paul Society for 1886 showed numerous visits to patients at Freedmen's Hospital and the city's reform school, which included 7 African Americans among its 25 Catholic inmates. The society also drew attention to the fact that its members "visit and take relief to the houses of the poor without regard to race, color, or religion." See *CM*, 12 Feb 1887.

17. The society's other officers, including Isaac Landic, president, Alexander B. Thomas, treasurer, Paul A. Dixon, librarian, and William H. Lewis, keeper of the wardrobe, were elected at a subsequent meeting. See *CN*, 29 Apr and 6 May 1888, and ltr., John F. Cole to H. Pellen, secy. of St. Vincent de Paul of Washington, 28 Feb 1935, Natalie Cole Johnson Papers, Moorland-Spingarn Archives, Howard University (hereinafter HUA).

which pledged its assistance to those now beginning work in the black parish. From the first, the quarterly meetings of the city-wide council, along with its Sunday masses and communion breakfasts, were racially integrated. When the society would meet in a white church that traditionally segregated its congregation, the black Vincentians took their seats among their white confreres.[18] What should have been commonplace received extraordinary attention, prompting the international headquarters of the St. Vincent de Paul in Paris to welcome the news of the harmonious reception of St. Augustine's Vincentians as "contributing in a small way to effacing these race prejudices so contrary to the spirit of the Gospel."[19]

The new conference lost no time in getting to work. In its first year the men canvassed the needy of the parish and collected and distributed $161 for fuel and rent. During its first Christmas season it began a tradition of preparing food packages for many of the local poor. Charles Butler recruited young teachers from the Sunday school whose members were especially effective in visiting the young inmates of the reform school and jail, teaching them their catechism and distributing tobacco and newspapers. They also visited with residents of the poorhouse and local hospitals. John F. Cole, a long-time official of the St. Vincent de Paul, later recalled his early days in the junior branch when the needs of the poor greatly outstripped the society's resources. Facing weekly grocery bills often exceeding $50, the society rarely had more than $10 in the till. It was thus forced to appeal to the pastor for supplements from regular parish funds.[20] In time the St. Vincent de Paul Society improved its financial position by sponsoring musicals and theatrical events. In 1893, for example, it produced two benefit performances of *The Elks Reception*, a popular musical farce, which realized a handsome amount for the society's charity coffers.[21] Al-

18. Foley, "The Catholic Church and the Washington Negro," pp. 275–76.

19. Ltr., A. Amreau Pangin, vice-president general, Society of St. Vincent de Paul, to Milton E. Smith, 29 Jul 1889, reprinted in *St. Joseph's Advocate* 2, no. 2 (Apr 1890): 73. (The *Advocate's* volumes were renumbered, beginning in 1889.) The St. Augustine conference was aggregated with the world-wide society in Paris in April 1890. See *CN*, 20 Apr 1890. St. Augustine's was the ninth parish in the District of Columbia to be so aggregated.

20. Ltr., Cole to H. Pellen, 28 Feb 1935, Natalie Cole Johnson Papers, HUA.

21. *CN*, 9 Dec 1893.

though the St. Vincent de Paul would remain the mainstay of the parish's work with the poor for many years, other special groups formed from time to time to supplement its efforts. Both the St. Monica's Relief Society, organized in 1889, and the St. Augustine's Relief Society, organized in 1891, were examples of these smaller groups providing much-needed, specific help for the poor of the parish.[22]

The growing number of poor parishioners also placed an extraordinary burden on the parish school. Traditionally free for those who could not afford its modest tuition, the school had included enough paying students to keep it self-supporting over the years, although during some periods that meant short-changing the sisters by severely reducing their salaries. It also meant neglecting repairs to a building that remained—despite the remodeling in 1876—a flimsy wooden structure.[23] When by 1883 the sisters' salary had fallen $1,200 in arrears, they referred the matter to the cardinal for relief, only to learn that he had told the pastor that he need not pay what was owed.[24] Even so, by 1888 the precarious balance was tipped, and the school fell into debt. Pleading for a $500 donation from the bishops' commission for the Negro and Indian Missions, Father Walsh cited the surprising increase in the number of poor students and the parish's ongoing struggle with its debt as reasons for the request.[25] Walsh's application, like many such requests for support, expressed the need in dire terms. Or so it must have seemed to Father Edward R. Dyer, the secretary of the

22. *CN*, 2 Feb 1890 and 15 Feb 1891. The first officers of the St. Augustine's Relief Society were: Eugene Curtis, president; Charles W. Gordon, vice-president; W. T. Brown, recording secretary; James L. Wood, treasurer; Charles W. Owens, chief marshal; Peter J. Brooks, assistant marshal; Edward Gordon, financial secy.

23. Ltr., Benoit to Vaughan, n.d. (ca. Feb 1884), 29-MHT-14, ASSJ.

24. "Archives Narrative for Academy of the Holy Cross, Washington, D.C.," vol. 1, pp. 14–16, Archives of the Sisters of the Holy Cross.

25. Ltr., Walsh to Rev. Edward Dyer (secy., Commission for the Catholic Missions Among the Colored People and the Indians), 25 Jun 1888, 117-DY-13, ASSJ. The episcopal commission was organized at the direction of the Third Plenary Council. Cardinal Gibbons served as chairman and Father Dyer of St. Mary's Seminary secretary. Dyer, with the approval of the commission, distributed the funds collected nationally during Lent. Walsh was appealing to Dyer for a share of the first collection in 1887. See Misch, "The American Bishops and the Negro," pp. 556–60.

bishops' commission, who sent St. Augustine's only $200. Undaunted, Walsh was back the next year asking again for $500 plus an additional $300 to make up for the money denied the year before. In his lengthy justification, Walsh added that "ours is the only Catholic school for colored children in this city and from all parts we have poor children; indeed, the poorest of the poor." He also told Dyer about the allure of Washington's fine public schools and the need to provide tuition-free education to keep Catholic children in church schools. In proof of the school's effectiveness, Walsh pointed to the large number of first communicants, which he attributed to the training received in the school.

This latest plea for assistance inadvertently revealed why the parish, despite its debt, could not meet the school deficit by itself. It was, it turned out, busy raising money for a new rectory. Displaying considerable chutzpah, Walsh appended an appeal for help in financing this new house for the priests to his request for school aid. He explained that Father Barotti's old home had been condemned by the doctors who claimed it had caused much illness among the clergy. Warming to his subject, Walsh admitted that he was trying to raise $4,000 for the project in the city and hoped to get an equal amount from the bishops' commission! In later asking Cardinal Gibbons to endorse his request for school aid, Walsh conveniently omitted any mention of the new rectory drive, merely warning the archbishop that the sisters "may throw up our schools if not paid." [26]

The bishops' commission ignored Walsh's request for help with the new rectory, but it did send $400, enough money to keep the school going.[27] August 1890 found the pastor back once more, hat in hand. This time he explained that the sisters had submitted a bill for $654.50 owed on their salaries above what they had managed to collect from the paying students. He went on to describe the school, which was educating 300 children, as "the stronghold of our Catholic life." Ironically, this remarkable fact had not prevented the parish from relying on the generosity of the Negro and Indian Mission fund to

26. Ltrs., Walsh to Dyer, 13 Mar 1889, 119-DY-14, ASSJ, and to Gibbons, 15 May 1889, 86-A-4, Gibbons Papers, AAB.

27. Ltr., Walsh to Leeson, 17 Aug 1889, 1-N-22, ASSJ.

keep its school afloat while it went about raising nearly $5,000 for a new rectory.[28]

In response the commission sent St. Augustine's $600 for its school but not a cent for the rectory. Whether it was convinced by Walsh's lengthy explanation of the pressing need or by his not-so-subtle hint that Cardinal Gibbons was personally interested in the school, the commission also saw fit to donate another $600 for teacher salaries and repairs the following year.[29] Actually, the congregation was probably unaware of the growing financial crisis facing the school. Those parents who could, paid tuition fees which, when supplemented by donations from the bishops' commission, allowed the school to remain open so long as the sisters were willing to teach at reduced pay. Meanwhile, the pastor, with the archbishop's blessing, continued to channel all financial support into debt reduction and the fund for a new rectory.

Although uninvolved in the school's financial problems, leaders of the congregation were quick to defend it against other threats. They had been concerned for some time with the number of saloons in the neighborhood. Thanks to the District Commissioners' indiscriminate granting of liquor licenses, gin mills had become a growth industry in the capital. By 1890 the popular downtown neighborhood contained six saloons, four of them sharing the square block with the church and school. The foul language and drunken antics of their patrons had become a sore trial for the sisters and their charges. Equally worrying, the parish's long immunity to the lure of demon rum once bragged about by Father Barotti had ended, and some of St. Augustine's young men could be found frequenting these local bars. In June 1890 the parish organized a committee consisting of Charles Butler, James I. Jackson, Willis J. Smith, Dr. Lofton, and Father Walsh to collect signatures petitioning the Commissioners to rescind the licenses. Nor were these newly militant leaders shy about expressing their feelings on the subject. "Colored Catholics have done so much for themselves in this city," they reminded the city's appointed executives, "that it seems almost beyond belief that they should now have to suffer the curse of

28. Ltr., Walsh to Dyer, 16 Aug 1890, 119-DY-15, ASSJ. For more on the new rectory, see below.

29. Ltr., Walsh to Dyer, 10 Jul 1891, 119-DY-16. See also ltrs., Walsh to Leeson, 17 Sep 1890, 1-N-27, 3 Jul 1891, 1-P-6, and 18 Jan 1892, 1-P-14. All in ASSJ.

having white men plant gin mills to steal away the dollars of their young men."[30] Whether their action helped reduce the number of saloons in the neighborhood, it clearly showed that this large group of citizens did not intend to be taken for granted.

The parish's extraordinary debt not only curtailed its support for free schooling, but colored its approach to all financial matters. Gone were the old days when unrestricted spending and borrowing preceded fund-raising. For example, when a house and lot directly behind the church, which provided vital access to the rear of the property, was sold under court order in 1887, Father Walsh bought it for $1,000, but only after a special envelope collection was scheduled to provide the necessary funds.[31] In announcing the collection, Walsh made clear that, if the money could not be raised in this manner, the parish would forgo the purchase rather than add to the debt. At first this pragmatic approach extended to the building of the new rectory. In May 1889 Cardinal Gibbons authorized Walsh to collect the estimated $8,000 needed for construction, but not to begin building until the money was raised. When it became clear to him that aid from the bishops' fund would not be forthcoming, the energetic pastor devised a succession of money-making schemes. He organized a lecture series (prices: 25 cents per ticket; $1.00 per series), which attracted hundreds of Catholics from around the city to hear prominent orators speak on crowd-pleasing subjects like "Fabiola—Story of the Martyrs" and "Popular Religious Errors." A special parish fair was held in early 1890 and a subscription fund launched with great fanfare when Cardinal Gibbons donated the first $2,000.[32]

Walsh was particularly skilled in what today would be called public relations. Announcements of the subscription drive were always accompanied by stories about hard-working priests who had forgone their salaries and were forced to live in a dangerous building so damp that the wallpaper was falling off the second story walls. One news article reported that the bedrooms were so small (seven feet across) that one priest found it necessary to sit down in order to put on his coat.

30. As quoted in the *CM*, 21 Jun 1890.

31. *CN*, 9 Oct 1889.

32. Ltrs., Walsh to Leeson, 17 Aug 1889, 1-N-22, and to Vaughan, 10 May 1889. Both in ASSJ. See also *CM*, 7 Dec 1889, and *CN*, 27 Oct 1889.

Another missionary claimed that a Washington summer in his little room on the second floor was more debilitating than his years in the tropics.[33] Walsh even intervened when his superior in Baltimore composed a last-minute appeal for donations to be issued over Gibbons's signature. It was too long, Walsh claimed, and must be shortened so that it could be "taken in at a glance." Even more objectionable: the draft "looks like a put up job—not being in the handwriting of his Eminence."[34]

Parties, concerts, steamboat excursions, and other fund raisers followed one after another in early 1890. In March the hard-strapped congregation, which continued to bear the burden of regular church expenses and payments on the debt, was able to scrape together a $700 donation for the rectory fund. Acknowledging this special sacrifice, Walsh published the names of the donors. Their gifts, which ranged from $5 to $100, were evidence, Walsh claimed, "that members were doing much to help themselves and are not entirely dependent upon help from other parishes as has been charged in some quarters."[35]

With almost half the necessary funds in hand by May 1890 the cardinal relented and allowed work to begin. The old rectory was razed, and a commodious brick building, designed by the church's architect, E. Francis Baldwin, begun. "The house is going up like grass," Father Walsh reported toward the end of the month, adding with no little trepidation: "Collections must be pushed."[36] To spur contributions, he undertook a door-to-door canvas of potential donors, but even this effort failed to raise the full amount in time, necessitating a carry-over loan. Reverting to old habits, the archdiocese borrowed $5,900 in March 1891, using the rectory property as collateral. But unlike earlier splurges, this debt was paid in full in just forty-eight months.[37] The final cost of the rectory was $10,000, of which the congregation donat-

33. *CN*, 27 Oct and 29 Dec 1889. See also ltr., Walsh to Leeson, 17 Aug 1889, 1-N-22, ASSJ.

34. Ltr., Walsh to Leeson, 25 Feb 1891, 1-P-4, ASSJ.

35. As quoted in the *CM*, 8 Mar 1890.

36. Ltr., Walsh to Leeson, 22 May 1890, 1-N-24, ASSJ.

37. Ltr., Walsh to Leeson, 23 Feb 1891, 1-P-3, ASSJ. See also Deed of Trust on Lot 49, square 197, 2 Mar 1891, liber R.L.H. folio 124 and liber 1558, folio 424, D. C. Land Records, cys in SAA.

ed $2,000, a sum matched by the cardinal. The rest came from pledges made by friends around the city, principally those who frequented services at St. Augustine's.[38]

Special donations from visitors and parishioners also allowed for the purchase of numerous church furnishings. In late 1886, for example, Mrs. John Ryan, a wealthy New Yorker and frequent parish visitor, donated a new set of carved Stations of the Cross. The pastor personally selected the statues, fabricated at L'Union Internationale Artistique in Paris and admitted into the country duty free through the good offices of the Secretary of the Treasury. Costing $1,100, the stations featured *alto relievo* figures, measuring two by five feet, carved in the Gothic style. These were installed on Ash Wednesday in 1887. The old stations were donated by the parish to a small mission for African-American Catholics near Charleston, South Carolina, the first of several such donations by St. Augustine's.[39] Meanwhile, Washington's Tabernacle Society donated vestments, chalices, and altar furnishings, while other patrons arranged for the private printing of a biography of Blessed Martin and the acquisition of a large gold ciborium.[40] Donations specifically earmarked for church decorations enabled the parish to complete the trio of Costaggini paintings over the main altar and install a memorial plaque honoring Father Barotti on the tenth anniversary of his death in 1891. The marble tablet, an elaborate structure carved in the gothic style, was inscribed to the "founder and first pastor."[41] During this period the parish also added marble flooring to the sanctuary and renovated the church interior, including the first repainting and cleaning of the high ceilings.

38. *CN*, 31 Jan 1892, which also corrected earlier, erroneous reports about the new rectory. The parish did not, for example, purchase land for the rectory, but built on the site of the old. The priests temporarily rented quarters nearby.

39. Ltr., Walsh to Benoit, 20 Oct 1886, 34-MHT-10, ASSJ. See also *CN*, 17 Oct 1886, *CM*, 26 Feb and 5 Mar 1887, and *St. Joseph's Advocate* 5, no. 1 (Jan 1887): 204.

40. *CM*, 17 Nov 1888 and 6 May 1893. The life of Blessed Martin was translated from the Italian original by Lady Mary Herbert, a major patron of Cardinal Vaughan and the Mill Hill Fathers.

41. Designed by Mullen and Sons of Baltimore, the tablet measured five by three feet and cost $250. See *CN*, 26 Apr and 6 May 1891. The Costaggini painting was installed on the thirteenth anniversary of the canonization of St. Peter Claver. See *CN*, 3 May 1890, 25 Jan, 24 May, and 1 Aug 1891.

MEN OF ST. AUGUSTINE'S, CIRCA 1890. James "Bernard" Maynard (seated at left), parish sexton who would die in 1924 at the foot of the altar he had served for forty-six years, pictured here with usher Theodore Matthews and an unidentified (standing) parishioner.

Contributions for church furnishings were placed on a more organized basis in March 1890 when Mary Dorcas and fifteen women in the parish formed the Donation Club. Using their modest initiation fee and monthly dues, members were able to purchase needed items for the beautification of the church and rectory, such as a large statue of St. Anthony erected on a sanctuary pillar in 1899.[42] Within three years membership had grown to over 300, including among the "industrious, hard-working women," as the *Mirror* described the majority, many prominent society figures of both races who served as honorary members.[43] The ladies hosted teas and strawberry festivals, the genteel fund-raising socials appropriate to Washington at the end of the century. At their Friday night meetings, the members, all skilled seamstresses, prepared articles for the church, such as a complete set of cassocks and surplices for the altar boys, and other items for sale at the church fairs. As their organization grew, the women began to assume the general fundraising efforts of the now-defunct Barotti League.

As for the debt itself, the pastor continued to consolidate loans, sometimes at a low 3 percent interest rate, which allowed the parish to pay off other, more expensive indebtedness. From time to time some unrecorded obligation from Father Barotti's chaotic bookkeeping days would suddenly pop up. For the most part these old loans went unclaimed, but the ever-vigilant Father Slattery from far-off Richmond continued to nag Walsh about such details.[44] Perhaps Slattery was

42. The five-foot statue, carved in Germany, was designed to match a similar likeness of St. Joseph previously installed on the opposite side of the sanctuary. See *CN*, 19 Aug 1899.

43. *CN*, 18 Nov 1893, and *CM*, 15 Nov 1893. Original officers included Dorcas, president, Josephine Harris, vice-president; Clara Wheeler, secretary; Regina Taylor, assistant secretary; and Mary L. Brown, treasurer. One source (Charles Whitby, ed., *Msgr Alonzo J. Olds: Golden Jubilee of the Priesthood*, p. 47) lists Mary Davis as organizer of the club, but all other accounts give that recognition to Miss Dorcas. For later works by this group, see *CN*, 7 Dec 1895 and 25 Jul 1896.

44. Details about these loans were the subject of much correspondence between pastor and archbishop. See, for example, ltrs., Walsh to Gibbons, 4 Jun 1884, 78-F-5, and 15 May 1889, 86-A-4. Both in Gibbons Papers, AAB. On Slattery's continued interference, see, for example, ltrs., Walsh to Slattery, 17 Aug 1886, 10-R-2, and 16 Sep 1886, 10-R-3; Slattery to Leeson, 17 Sep 1886, 3-H-7; and Leeson to Slattery, 1 Nov 1886, 10-K-3. All in ASSJ.

right to be concerned about Walsh's management techniques. On at least one occasion the impetuous pastor was forced to apologize to Cardinal Gibbons for an unauthorized expenditure. In his report on parish finances in 1886 Walsh had included the welcome news that the debt had been reduced by another $1,500, adding that it would have been more but for the necessity of spending $2,000 on special improvements to the school and a repointing of the church front "ordered" by the architect. Walsh's acting on such "orders" from the architect upset Gibbons, who let the pastor know by return mail of his displeasure. Ruefully thanking the cardinal for his prompt reply, Walsh apologized for acting without permission and promised "to make it a study to avoid making unnecessary expenses."[45] This exchange seemed to settle matters, but it may well have planted a doubt in Gibbons's mind that would grow in succeeding years.

Despite such setbacks, the debt was slowly going down, even though the number of parishioners with the means to contribute significantly year after year remained small. In 1888, for example, just 114 pew holders could be counted in a congregation numbering 3,000. The annual report was typical of the period: $1,800 in pew rents, $3,000 in collections; $1,464 from parish entertainments. In addition the church reported its usual annual $500 contribution from the cardinal, $300 from the sisters at Visitation Convent for the services of the parish priests, and $700 in stole fees. Interestingly, a majority of those spending money at the parish's popular fairs were non-Catholics, just as a majority of those in hospitals and other institutions who were receiving assistance from the parish were non-Catholic.[46]

45. Ltrs., Walsh to Gibbons, 6 Jan 1886, 80-B-2 (first quote) and 7 Jan 1886, 80-B-2 (second quote). Both in Gibbons Papers, AAB.

46. The parish financial statements and *notitiae* for this period (cys in SAA) provide a generally reliable record, although statistics on parish population appear at best to be estimates. The parish reports, audited by parishioners designated by the archbishop, were regularly published in the Catholic press. See, for example, *CN*, 10 Jan 1888, and *CM*, 19 Jan 1889. The Josephites provided an even more detailed account in their *St. Joseph's Advocate*. See, for example, 6, no. 2 (Apr 1888): 369.

A Change in Leadership

The cardinal's reprimand for Walsh's spendthrift ways did not seem to upset St. Augustine's pastor. In fact, as Walsh reminded a Josephite superior in June 1887, he had been in Washington for six years and had found St. Augustine's so "delightful for soul and body" that the time had sped by. As for the debt that sparked Gibbons's criticism, "the good Lord has never allowed that to press too heavily on my mind."[47] Just the year before he had spelled out for his superiors in England those priestly delights found in the large African-American parish. The spectacle of so many being attracted to the Faith, the steady increase in the number of adult baptisms, and the couples making their marriage vows was a special consolation to the four priests. Walsh explained how he and Father Cornelius Hurley conducted regular convert classes at the church, while the younger Father Richard Burke "is hunting all over the city," giving instructions to those unable to travel to Fifteenth Street. Adult baptisms were commonplace, and the huge confirmation classes were the marvel of the diocese. He described a long weekend spent by the archbishop in the parish, a stay that featured a Solemn High Mass and concluded with 128 parishioners being confirmed. Typical of congregations of that day, the crowd listened with pleasure to an hour-long sermon delivered by Bishop Joseph Dwenger of Fort Wayne, Indiana, in language "so plain and simple," Walsh added, that even the very young and elderly could grasp its meaning.[48]

Walsh also sought to explain the consolation he derived from a well-ordered communal life. The busy priests rose early for prayer and private devotion followed by public masses. They met for meals followed by brief periods when, together, "the mail is read, a pipe smoked, and a few words chatted." Evenings were usually full, each attending parish affairs, giving instructions, and conducting business with those otherwise occupied during the day. For the rest, it was a quiet life "visiting the widow and orphan we keep ourselves unspotted

47. Ltr., Walsh to Benoit, 24 Jun 1887, 34-MHT-27, ASSJ.

48. Ltrs., Walsh to Benoit, 11 Feb and 2 Mar 1886. Both in 33-MHT-9, ASSJ. The sermon was covered in both the secular and the religious press.

from this world."[49] This idyllic missionary's life, if it ever existed, proved remarkably ephemeral. True, the debt never unduly alarmed Walsh, and the spirituality, enthusiasm, and affection of his large congregation undoubtedly provided much consolation, but disagreements with his fellow priests—indeed, the increasingly tenuous position of the missionary society to which he belonged—filled his days with distraction and rancor. Less than three years after he had painted his glowing description of life at St. Augustine's, he was confessing to the head of his society that "I have had more trouble with the house than with the church the nine years that I am here."[50]

In part his troubles were externally driven, the result of the growing numbers of white Catholics in evidence in the parish and the conflict in the Josephite community on how to respond to their demands for attention. So great had the number of white attendees become that *The Bee*, the city's major black paper, took notice of it in a poem published on its front page in August 1886. Lyrically describing the sunlight falling on the "faces dark and faces fair," the poet obviously approved the racial mixing in a congregation composed of "Ethiop's sons and daughters meek and Norman, Celt, and Saxon maidens mild." In one of its many references to the same phenomenon, the *Catholic Mirror* described the "very general sprinkling of whites" at St. Augustine's Forty Hours Devotion in 1887. The African-American ushers and pew holders "were extremely courteous in providing seats for their paler-faced brethren, who were sandwiched among them in such a brotherly way as would have made glad the heart of the most ardent advocate of 'liberty, equality, and fraternity.'"[51]

What seemed like examples of improved race relations were, for different reasons, criticized by the Josephites and some of their fellow priests in Washington. As for the latter group, they continued to resent the fact that many of their parishioners regularly attended St. Augustine's. Canon Benoit bluntly diagnosed the cause of what he called "the jealousy of neighboring priests." But for the Eucharist, Benoit explained, whites were barred from all the sacraments at St. Augustine's

49. Ltrs., Walsh to Benoit, 11 Feb and 2 Mar 1886, 33-MHT-9, and 31 May 1886, 33-MT-24 (last quote). Both in ASSJ.

50. Ltr., Walsh to Vaughan, 10 Mar 1890, 39-MHT-5, ASSJ.

51. *The Bee*, 21 Aug 1886 (first quote), and *CM*, 5 Nov 1887 (second quote).

(a disappointment to those white brides who dreamt of marching down the beautiful church's long middle aisle). Nevertheless, neighboring pastors resented the loss of income when so many affluent members of their congregations attended and contributed to the black parish.[52] Obviously sympathetic with these pastors, the *Catholic Mirror* frequently reminded its readers that St. Augustine's was "a colored church *only* for colored," on one occasion justifying the distinction by explaining that, while African Americans were free to attend any church, they preferred St. Augustine's, "which is distinctly their own."[53]

The presence of so many whites and the need to provide hospitality for some white organizations also troubled some Josephites, because it flew in the face of the special promise taken by the missionaries to work exclusively among African Americans. From their earliest days in America, some members of the society ignored the orders of their founder, Bishop Vaughan, and offered mass and dispensed the sacraments to whites—sometimes, as in the case of their missions in Prince George's County, because they were the closest Catholic presence, elsewhere because the more affluent white Catholics could support them when their impoverished black congregations could not.[54] Some of the more idealistic missionaries condemned such relaxation of the rule. Father William Hooman, for example, reported to Vaughan that when he served briefly at St. Augustine's in 1881 he had found Father Slattery hearing confessions of white Catholics, something he himself had refused to do even when so ordered by the archbishop.[55] More pragmatic leaders like Walsh sought a middle ground. During his pastorate, whites were barred from the confessional. Moreover, the priests rarely socialized with white Washingtonians. At the same time whites were encouraged to attend mass and other services and to patronize parish entertainments, which were regularly publicized in both the secular and the religious press.[56]

More troubling to some of Walsh's critical assistants and a source of tension in the Josephite community, St. Augustine's priests served

52. Ltr., Benoit to Vaughan, n.d. (ca. Feb 1884), 29-MHT-14, ASSJ.

53. *CM*, 8 Dec 1888 (first quote), and 28 Jul 1883 (second quote).

54. Ochs, *Desegregating the Altar*, pp. 44–46.

55. Ltr., Hooman to Vaughan, 2 Jan 1883, 26-MHT-22, ASSJ.

56. These matters were candidly discussed in the *CN*, 31 Jan 1892.

as chaplains for several white organizations. In January 1882 Walsh had accepted appointment as spiritual director of the Tabernacle Society, an organization of socially prominent white women dedicated to making vestments and altar linens and providing expensive altar furnishings for poor churches. Before they had alienated its pastor, the ladies had met at St. Patrick's, but in recent years no priest in the city would agree to serve them. Walsh volunteered, assuming correctly that such service would provide St. Augustine's with a steady source of income and incline the group to favor the parish and other Josephite missions in the distribution of vestments and furnishings. Although Father Slattery, then still the American provincial of the missionary society, pointed out that such a position "on the surface appears a little diverting from the black work," the matter was referred to his superiors, who agreed to the appointment.[57]

Initially, Walsh's duties were limited to offering a monthly mass, which the women attended at St. Augustine's in a body, and to lead Benediction when appropriate. Just as critics feared, however, this proved only an opening wedge. Within months, the president of the society, Mrs. General William T. Sherman, apparently with Walsh's approval, sought permission for the women to have their confessions heard at St. Augustine's. An aroused Slattery warned Bishop Vaughan that such a concession would provide other Josephite missionaries the excuse for hearing white confessions. "If we begin to yield," he added, "then good-by to the black Missions." Slattery was especially concerned that the frequent and publicized attendance of these white women at St. Augustine's would distract the priests from their avowed purpose.[58] Despite Walsh's angry protests, permission to hear the ladies' confessions was denied, although he retained his post as chaplain, a continuing source of controversy and friction in the rectory and in his missionary society.[59]

57. Ltrs., Slattery to Vaughan, 7 Nov 1881, CBI, p. 184 (source of quote) and Third Annual report of the American Provincial, 1881, CBI, p. 197. Both in ASSJ. See also *CM*, 21 Jan 1882.

58. Ltrs., Slattery to Vaughan, 17 Mar 1882, CBI, p. 207, and to Walsh, 5 Apr 1882, CBI, p. 211. Both in ASSJ.

59. Ltrs., Walsh to Vaughan, 12 Oct 1882, 26-MHT-14, and 20 Dec 1882, 26-MHT-13. Both in ASSJ. Slattery later charged that Walsh was causing much discord among

Perhaps the mercurial Irishman learned from this exchange or from the continued protests of his assistant priests, because he took an entirely different tack when it came to St. Augustine's providing chaplains for the nearby Visitation Convent. Canon Benoit once remarked that Walsh was unsteady in his opinions, "harshly condemning at one time what he approved of at another."[60] In fact this case was quite different from that of the Tabernacle Society. Many priests in the diocese were routinely drafted by the archbishop to serve as chaplains at convents, and providing such services for the Visitation nuns would not have been considered by diocesan authorities a violation of the Josephite vow against serving white Catholics. But it appeared so to the likes of Father Cornelius Hurley, who took very seriously his vow, as he put it "to do nothing that will tend to the neglect or desertion of the coloured [sic] people." Hurley charged that nearly every Josephite mission was forced to attend convents of white nuns "to the prejudice of the coloured people." At St. Augustine's, he told Vaughan, he was frequently forced to leave penitents in the confessional to go for some duty at the convent and often lost much time in such visits, time "which should be given to our own people." His co-worker, Father deRuyter, joined the protest, pointing out that St. Augustine's could probably make do with a smaller staff if relieved of this duty.[61] For years Walsh pleaded with his superiors to be rid of the convent, objecting not so much in principle, but for the practical reason that St. Augustine's parish was too large and the number of priests too small to serve both the convent and the congregation.[62] Cardinal Gibbons remained unmoved, and the parish priests retained their duties at Visitation Convent.

Another source of tension regarding white presence at St. Augustine's rose during the last years of the Josephite tenure in the parish.

---

the Tabernacle Society members. See ltr., Slattery to Vaughan, 14 Dec 1882, 26-MHT-9, same source.

60. Ltr., Benoit to Vaughan, n.d. (ca. Feb 1884), 29-MHT-14, ASSJ. The convent was located on today's DeSalles Place, near the Mayflower Hotel.

61. Ltrs., Hurley to Vaughan, 12 Feb 1883, 27-MHT-7, and deRuyter to Leeson, 3 Aug 1885, 1-N-31. Both in ASSJ.

62. Ltrs., Walsh to Leeson, 9 Jul 1893, 1-N-3, 8 Aug 1883, 1-N-4, and 13 Dec 1886, 1-N-16. All in ASSJ.

Sometime after the death of Cecilia Beans, Father Barotti's much-loved cook, and Eliza Dodson, the housekeeper, two maiden sisters of Father Richard Burke moved in to take over those chores. In this case the objection centered not only on the race of the newcomers, but also on the fact that they were relatives of one of the priests. In voicing his strenuous protest, Father Hooman emphasized the appropriateness of employing African Americans in jobs in a black parish, a view he claimed to share with all his fellow Josephites with the exception of Fathers Walsh and Burke. He went on to brand as prejudiced those clergymen who questioned the honesty of black servants, even as he raised questions about his own attitude when he added, "colored servants do *more* work and are less expensive to poor Missions such as ours than white ones."[63] Vaughan acted quickly, and an obviously irritated Walsh was forced to give the Burke sisters notice. When the new rectory opened, it was under the care and management of Maria Fair Young and later Mildred Brooks and Victoria Brooks, all African Americans and parishioners.[64]

These arguments over principles occurred during a period rife with petty quarrels and personality clashes in the rectory. In February 1890 an ill Walsh reported wearily to his superior about one fractious assistant; "having undertaken (and I thank God with success) to care for one poor crank—you, without a word of notice, sent me another."[65] In fact, Walsh and several of his assistants, good priests and very successful ministers to Washington's African Americans, proved to be highly individualistic men poorly suited to communal life. Their difficulties with each other reflected the general malaise affecting all members of the American province of an English missionary society frustrated with the indifference of white Catholics to the needs of their black brethren. Each priest, it seemed, held firm ideas on how he and each of his fellow missionaries should conduct themselves. The evidence provided in the scores of letters circulating among colleagues and superiors shows that none was reluctant to criticize or to demand

63. Ltr., Hooman to Vaughan, 8 Feb 1890, 34-MHT-27, ASSJ.

64. Ltrs., Vaughan to Walsh, 21 Feb 1890, 39-MHT-2, and Walsh to Vaughan, 10 · Mar 1890, 39-MHT-5, and to Leeson, 11 Mar 1890, 1-N-23. All in ASSJ.

65. Ltr., Walsh to Leeson, 1 Feb 1890, 38-MHT-24, ASSJ.

special consideration.[66] Much of the busy pastor's day must have been filled with these extra-parish concerns. Ironically, the bitter differences that colored Walsh's relations with Fathers Hooman and deRuyter in particular never seemed to affect the exceptional rapport each enjoyed with the parishioners, who openly demonstrated their special respect and affection for the priests.

Walsh himself was frequently ill—"damaged bellows," he labeled his pulmonary problems. The European vacation in 1885 seemed to restore his health, but three years later he was experiencing prolonged bouts of fever, which would confine him to bed for weeks at a time. He made the most of his indispositions. Every report of illness was accompanied by requests for transfers to healthier climes, mountain rest, or a renewed call for more assistants. In June 1891 his worried doctor packed him off to the mountains of western Maryland, and Walsh warned his provincial that his health was such that he could not remain in Washington much longer.[67]

Adding to the pastor's anxiety were his continuing difficulties with the debt. At times he lashed out at his provincial for what he considered Father Leeson's failure to act. "It seems like an eternity to me to wait for you to move," he told Leeson in 1890, warning the provincial that he intended to take him to court over his failure to absolve Walsh of responsibility for one of the liens on the parish.[68] In February 1891 Cardinal Gibbons finally lost his patience when Walsh came, hat in hand, seeking yet another loan to satisfy some anxious creditors and to pay off the balance due on the new rectory. He "suggested and invited" Walsh to resign.[69] Obviously shaken by this surprise request, Walsh refused to respond. He explained to his provincial that since the

66. For examples of this correspondence, often providing opposing viewpoints on issues of the day, frequently searching in scope and sometimes humorous in expression, see especially ltrs. in the 1-E and 1-N series, ASSJ.

67. See, for example, ltrs., Walsh to Leeson, 26 Mar 1886, 1-N-9, 21 Jun 1888, 1-N-19, and n.d. (ca. Jun 1891), 1-P-8. All in ASSJ. See also *CN*, 15 Feb 1891. Among the many reports on Walsh's European vacation in 1885, see *St. Joseph's Advocate* 4 no. 3 (Jul 1886): 166, and *CM*, 12 Dec 1885.

68. Ltr., Walsh to Leeson, 31 May 1890, 1-N-25, ASSJ.

69. As quoted in ltr., Walsh to Leeson, 15 February 1891, 1-P-2, ASSJ.

missionary society, not Gibbons, had appointed him to St. Augustine's, the society, not the cardinal, must decide when Walsh would leave Washington. But, clearly, Walsh knew his days were limited. He had asked to be relieved the year before, he reminded Leeson, and now, given the cardinal's attitude, he hoped that his departure could be soon arranged. Actually, Walsh would remain at St. Augustine's for almost another full year, and except for a brief meeting in the rectory at Christmas time, the two apparently never met again. All business between the cardinal and pastor was conducted through the offices of Walsh's provincial.[70]

While these events were unfolding in Washington, the American province of the Mill Hill missionary society was undergoing dissolution. With a strong push from John Slattery and in consultation with Cardinal Gibbons, who agreed to place the new Josephite foundation within his jurisdiction, Archbishop Vaughan recognized the formation of an independent community in the United States in November 1891.[71] Each missionary was left with three options: remain with the English society, join Slattery and the new American Josephites, or enlist in an American diocese as a regular diocesan priest. Walsh and both his assistants elected to leave; Walsh and Burke applied for incardination in the Diocese of Harrisburg. Walsh was anxious to get away, and he waited impatiently for Vaughan to arrange the necessary dispensation.[72] With only four Josephites agreeing to join Slattery in the new American society, it was obvious that many of the Josephite parishes and missions must be abandoned. One of these was St. Augustine's. Finally, in early 1892, Gibbons formally relieved the Josephite Fathers of their responsibility for the Washington parish, effective St. Valentine's Day.[73]

70. See, for example, ltr., Walsh to Leeson, 29 Jul 1891, 1-P-5. On the last meeting between Gibbons and Walsh, see ltr., Walsh to Leeson, 22 Dec 1891, 1-P-9. Both in ASSJ.

71. On the breakup of the Mill Hill missionaries, see Hogan, *The Josephites: A Century of Evangelization in the African American* Community, pp. 20–22; Ochs, *Desegregating the Altar*, pp. 83–85; and Robert O'Neil, *Cardinal Herbert Vaughan* (Tunbridge Wells: Burns & Oates, 1995), pp. 318–21.

72. Ltrs., Vaughan to Leeson, 4 Nov 1891, 1-G-6, and Walsh to Leeson, 28 Dec 1891, 1-P-10; 1 Jan 1892, 1-P-11; and 15 Jan 1892, 1-P-13. All in ASSJ.

73. Ltr., Gibbons to Leeson, 14 Jan 1892, 2-P-17, ASSJ.

News of the imminent departure of the Josephites and Walsh's decision to leave the missionary society swept through the congregation and prompted a group of leading parishioners to petition Gibbons to retain the well-liked pastor in his post. Their delegation was informed that Walsh's continuing ill health necessitated his transfer to a more bracing climate.[74] Walsh's health was not the only reason for his departure, but no other explanation was ever publicized. Finally on January 20 the secular press reported the cardinal's choice of a replacement: Father Thomas Sim Lee, pastor of neighboring St. Matthew's, would also serve as pastor of St. Augustine's and would be assigned two extra assistants to help with the task. All the priests were to live at St. Matthew's.[75]

The *Catholic Mirror* assured Washington readers that "the more cool-headed and conservative element among the pew-holders soon put a stop to any demonstration"; the *Evening Star* for its part reported that news that the independent African-American parish was once again to be a mission of St. Matthew's had generated "a spirit of rebellion in the breast of the congregation."[76] The *Star* went on to quote Dr. Lofton, who had agreed to serve as chairman of a hastily formed committee which planned to meet with Father Lee in an effort to sort out the facts in the situation. All of the members of his committee—Willis Smith, Charles Butler, John Jackson, William Benjamin, and A. B. Thomas—were involved in the Colored Catholic Congress movement. All were laymen adept at presenting carefully framed petitions to Church authorities and at publicizing their demands. Lofton claimed that these men represented the conservative element in the parish, which did not want "to add fuel to the already fierce fire of indignation that is blazing." They had not yet lodged any protests, he added, but if they failed to receive proper assurances from Father Lee, they would prepare a "decisive protest" and present it to the cardinal in person.[77]

Although Gibbons had yet to express himself publicly on the parish's fate, his discussions with Father Slattery a decade earlier had convinced the Josephite provincial that the archbishop considered St. Augustine's poorly situated to serve Washington's black Catholics.

74. *CN*, 31 Jan 1892.
75. *Evening Star*, 20 Jan 1892.
76. *CM*, 30 Jan 1892, and *Evening Star*, 22 Jan 1892.
77. As quoted in the *New York Age*, 30 Jan 1892.

They were beginning to concentrate in the southeast section of the city, Gibbons believed, and his long-range plan, Slattery reported, was to turn St. Augustine's over to the white Catholics in the area and, after building a church for white Catholics on Capitol Hill, make St. Peter's the city's church for African Americans. That Slattery was convinced this would eventually happen was one reason he had fought to make Gibbons legally responsible for the parish's debts. Not an admirer of the archbishop, Slattery also admitted that nothing should be taken for granted, because, he claimed, Gibbons suffered from two major defects: "shortness of memory & changeableness of purpose."[78]

The fact that thousands of African Americans remained in northwest Washington and that the faith and toil of several generations of black Catholics had built St. Augustine's just may have dampened Gibbons's enthusiasm for such a scheme. At any rate, nothing was heard of these plans in the ensuing decade, during which the archbishop time and again came to the aid of the financially pressed parish with loans and donations. Nevertheless, when reports of Lee's new assignment were published, an agitated congregation immediately jumped to a similar, sinister conclusion. An unusually restrained Lofton explained to the press that the parish was fighting "in a cool, deliberate, manly way" for its independence. He pointed to what he called the "evident ultimate designs of some officials" to secure the property of St. Augustine's for St. Matthew's. Many, he claimed, believed that, should St. Matthew's pastor gain control of the black church, pew rents would gradually rise, driving out the present occupants and thereby allowing St. Matthew's to inherit a large, beautiful church and sell off the valuable property occupied by its aging and dilapidated church at Fifteenth and H Streets.[79]

The meeting with Father Lee on Friday, January 22, only served to strengthen these suspicions. Lee sought to assure Lofton's committee that the cardinal had no intention of degrading St. Augustine's. He explained that, with only a limited number of priests to care for a very large number of parishes, Gibbons was merely trying to save manpower by combining the staffs of two nearby churches. The parishes were

78. Ltrs., Slattery to Vaughan, 15 Jun 1881, 22-MHT-21 (source of quote), and to Benoit, 17 Jun 1881, 23-MHT-1. Both in ASSJ.

79. Lofton's remarks are quoted extensively in both the *Evening Star*, 22 Jan 1892, and the *New York Age*, 30 Jan 1892.

ST. AUGUSTINE'S CHURCH, 1876–1947.

not to be merged, Lee emphasized; he would serve equally as pastor of an independent St. Matthew's and St. Augustine's. Henceforth, the two new assistants, Paul K. Griffith and George A. Dougherty, as well as the two assistants already at St. Matthew's would be available for parishioners of both parishes.[80] The necessity of such a radical step was highly dubious and could only raise eyebrows in a congregation that had often been forced to make do with the services of just two priests. Press reports noted the agitation that prevailed among the 2,000 Catholics of both races who gathered in St. Augustine's basement on January 24 to hear the committee's account of the Lee interview. Presided over by Willis Smith, the mass meeting listened to numerous speakers recommend that Gibbons be asked to reconsider his decision and appoint an independent pastor who would reside in the parish rectory. After some debate, an eight-man committee was appointed, and two days later its members went to Baltimore for a meeting with their spiritual leader.[81]

It must be assumed that this spontaneous yet united and well-publicized protest from Washington's black Catholics took Gibbons by surprise. Although the cardinal's concern for the welfare of African Americans was genuine, it is also obvious that he was an eminently practical politician, anxious to accommodate whenever possible to the prevailing social customs of his day. Comfortable with the segregation practiced in predominantly white parishes, he supported the concept of separate churches for African Americans and considered it appropriate that special missionaries serve these parishes. Surprisingly, his cautious approach had earned him both the continuing respect of the segregationists and the gratitude of black Catholics. But now the sudden departure of the Josephites forced him to involve regular diocesan priests, a turn of events that would end the special isolation that in the past comfortably differentiated a parish controlled by foreign missionaries. Subordinating St. Augustine's to St. Matthew's by placing Lee in charge of both would perpetuate the special status of the black congregation outside the ecclesiastical mainstream. But before he could implement this plan Gibbons had to face these articulate laymen repre-

80. *CN*, 24 Jan 1892.

81. In addition to those in the earlier committee, this group included Paul A. Dickson and John Green. For a description of the committee's work, see *CM*, 30 Jan 1892.

senting an agitated and united congregation, which was demanding its own independent pastor and, by inference, equal status with other parishes in the diocese. Gibbons had had first-hand experience with this group during his attendance at the first Colored Catholic Congress and was aware of the increasing stridency of that lay movement's demands. In the end, St. Augustine's would get what it wanted.

At the meeting on January 26, Gibbons assured the committee from St. Augustine's that the parish would retain its independence and that he would shortly appoint a new pastor, who would reside in the parish rectory. Reporting back to the congregation during another mass meeting the next night, the committee added that "as evidence of his interest in the welfare of the parish," the cardinal would visit St. Augustine's and preach on the first Sunday of March. Within days the chancery announced that Father Griffith would be the new pastor and Father Dougherty his assistant. On February 21 Griffith celebrated his first mass at St. Augustine's and attended a reception after vespers, where he was introduced to the congregation. The press quoted the reaction of one parishioner to the occasion: "We feel that a new era was dawning in the history of St. Augustine's."[82]

As proved by subsequent events, the appointment of a dynamic diocesan pastor, anxious to work with his congregation, did institute a new era in the history of St. Augustine's. Little noted at the time, however, was the key role played by the black laity in charting an alternative course for black parishes in America, parishes in the diocesan mainstream. In a period when the laity rarely questioned the decisions of the hierarchy and when the use of mass protest was rare and the means of publicizing such protest scarce, an articulate group within St. Augustine's congregation had aroused the parish and formulated what amounted to a demand that they be treated as equals.

A New Approach to Old Problems

Paul Griffith was well suited to his new assignment. Like so many diocesan priests of that time, he was born in Ireland. He arrived in

82. As quoted in *CN*, 31 Jan 1892 (first quote), and *CM*, 27 Feb 1892 (second quote).

America in 1850 at the age of four. The family with its fourteen children settled in Illinois, where the father became a successful farmer. On the eve of the Civil War young Paul used the occasion of a visit to his brother, a Washington physician, to drop out of school and begin an apprenticeship in the capital's dry goods trade. Eventually he became senior partner in the firm of Griffith and Anderson, a locally prosperous clothing store. Called late to the priesthood, the thirty-year-old businessman entered the diocesan seminary in 1876 and was ordained ten years later by Cardinal Gibbons. Following assignments in Howard County, Maryland, Griffith returned to his adopted city in 1892. He would remain at St. Augustine's for the rest of his life.

Griffith was on hand to welcome the cardinal during his promised visit to the parish in March, when, amid general rejoicing, the prelate reiterated his promise that St. Augustine's "would not be interfered with, but would always remain as it now is, a church for colored people."[83] The new pastor wasted no time in focusing on the greatest threat to that independence—the debt. An experienced businessman, he was obviously disappointed with his predecessor's failure to reduce the financial burden more expeditiously. In fact he was openly critical of what he considered the extravagance of the Josephites. While privately demanding that the missionary society repay the parish for household expenses incurred during its last months in residence, he compared the large amount charged to the parish by his predecessor for rectory expenses with what he and his assistant were living on. What particularly irritated him was one item in the Josephite accounts listing the purchase of oysters at the outlandish price of fifty cents a dozen! How, he asked the American provincial, could such luxurious living be reconciled with their profession of poverty? If the restitution demanded appeared too great, he added threateningly, the Josephites should take it up with the cardinal. On another occasion he went after his predecessors for the loss of two chalices once part of St. Augustine's inventory and now gone. Receiving no satisfaction, Griffith appealed to the chancery, explaining that one of these chalices was of considerable value, a gift of silver, gold, and precious jewels from the parishioners.[84]

83. As quoted in *CM*, 12 Mar 1892.

84. Ltrs., Griffith to Leeson, 15 Mar 1892, 3-N-20 (source of quote) and to Slattery, 9 May 1892, 6-E-7. Griffith's complaints to Gibbons about the missing chalices were at-

Clearly Griffith, like Father Slattery a decade earlier, believed that an aggressive program could eliminate the debt, which now stood near $56,000.[85] The *Catholic Mirror* superciliously pointed out the difficulty in raising such a sum among Washington's black Catholics, who rarely remain in one parish "for colored shift about, from necessity, no doubt." Further betraying the paper's bias, the article added sarcastically that "opulent friends of the colored people at the North might help these brethren pay their church debt and construct a suitable school and hall."[86]

Griffith ignored the bigots and during the next decade concentrated on a debt reduction campaign. New life was pumped into old fundraising techniques. Benefits and collections became a constant. As one event occurred, another was in preparation. Slide shows, lawn parties, minstrel performances, strawberry festivals, monster picnics, and, above all, parish fairs—attended by the cardinal and the apostolic delegate featuring marching bands and military societies—not only raised significant sums of money, but provided welcome diversion for a congregation barred from many amusements offered in a southern city.[87] For example, parishioners and their friends flocked to the week-long lawn party sponsored by the ladies of the Sacred Heart League in 1895, and 1,600 paid to hear noted orator Father Denis Stafford's lecture, "Dickens—His Power and Pathos." The Donation Club ladies realized a modest amount from their Martha Washington Tea Party in 1896.[88] None of these groups, however, matched the social eclat of the Barotti League, an organization of prominent parishioners dedicated to

tached to the *Notitiae*, 1893 and 1894. In 1893 the Baltimore chancery asked the provincial to turn over to Griffith all books and papers belonging to St. Augustine's that remained in the possession of the Josephites. See ltr., C. F. Thomas (chancellor) to Leeson, 26 Mar 1893, 1-A-10. All in ASSJ.

85. "List of Creditors, St. Augustine's Church, January, 1892," 1-P-12, ASSJ. The major creditors were the Metropolitan Bank of Baltimore ($33,150 at 6 percent) and Cardinal Gibbons ($10,000 at no interest).

86. *CM*, 1 Aug 1891.

87. The fairs, bigger than ever, were discussed for weeks on end in the Catholic press. See, for example, *CN*, 9 Dec 1899. Gibbons's appearances were carefully orchestrated. See ltr., Griffith to Gibbons, 11 Nov 1896, 94-B-H2, Gibbons Papers, AAB.

88. For press coverage of some of these events, see *CN*, 22 Aug 1892, 8 Dec 1894, 5 Jan and 15 Jun 1895, and 2 Oct, 21 Nov, and 19 Dec 1896.

fund raising for the church. Its Fete Champetre and Lawn Party, a three-evening affair in August 1893, attracted some 700 people nightly. They strolled through rectory grounds decorated with Japanese lanterns while enjoying music performed by the U.S. Marine Band and a "grand open air vocal concert." Door prizes amounting to a then-exceptional $150 only added to the excitement. These carefully staged affairs (the Champetre was repeated in following summers) not only earned money for the church, but also quickly became the place to be seen. The parish's *bon ton* flocked to join the league.[89]

Griffith did not rely on entertainments alone. Like Slattery before him, he believed in the efficacy of pledges that committed parishioners to regular contributions to a sinking fund as he called it. Soon after his arrival he inaugurated the St. Augustine's Union, an association of contributors pledged to pay off the debt. The names of all members, and the amount they pledged, were published and their intentions remembered in masses offered in the parish every Wednesday and Sunday. A group of twenty-six parishioners was authorized to solicit new members for the Union and collect pledges. To make their job easier, the pastor forbade any other parish society from soliciting cash contributions. These societies were a blessing to the parish, Griffith explained, "but at the same time they should be self-supporting and an assistance, not an added burden." Henceforth the various choirs, donation groups, and the rest were on their own; the pastor was brooking no competition for his Union.[90]

Like most of Washington's middle class and its working poor, St. Augustine's congregation was hard hit by the great panic of 1893, which caused many banks to fail and sent the nation's businesses into severe depression. Many contributors were forced to adjust their pledges to meet the new financial realities, but still the money accumulated. In 1894, for example, the Union collected $2,396. In suc-

89. On the purpose of the league and a surviving program from one of its festivals, see items in Natalie Cole Johnson Papers, HUA. See also *CM*, 26 Aug 1893 and 18 Aug and 1 Sep 1894. The rectory lawn was enlarged in 1900 so that bigger events might be staged *al fresco*. See *CN*, 30 Jun and 1 Aug 1900.

90. The purpose of the Union, the names of the collectors, and a list of members were published in the "Financial Statement of St. Augustine's Church for the Year 1894," copy in SAA.

ceeding years its received a boost when Cardinal Gibbons, pleased with the parish's determination, offered to cancel repayment of his $10,000 loan on condition that the congregation raise an extra $2,500. Griffith immediately called on "all those employed" to rent a pew or contribute to the Union so that the cardinal's challenge might be met.[91]

All this effort paid off. In 1899 Griffith disbanded the St. Augustine's Union and its small army of fund raisers (although he would resurrect the successful money-collecting organization, under a different name, eight years later to raise funds for a new school).[92] As 1901 drew to a close, a jubilant pastor could report to his generous congregation that they had reduced the debt to a manageable $6,000 and that the parish was now free to contemplate other worthy objectives so long held in abeyance. Already $1,000 had been collected toward the cost of a new pipe organ and a drive was contemplated for the purchase of a new schoolhouse. In fact, despite the calculated curtailment of expenditures during the 1890s, money had been spent on other things. In 1896, for example, the parish had paid $1,000 for an addition to the new rectory to provide rooms for the housekeeping staff. Three years later, $2,000 went for repairs to the church roof and chimney. Like any smart landlord, Griffith looked for help from the government. In 1897 he successfully petitioned the District of Columbia to plant trees and repair the sidewalks in front of the church and rectory. Adding to the ambiance, Griffith had the rectory grounds replanted and enlarged to provide a pleasing site for parish lawn parties, another source of fundraising.[93]

Nor were the poor, and those temporarily out of work because of the depression, neglected. Receipts from the poor box and other charities like the Jubilee Alms and St. Anthony's Bread rose steadily during the decade. Periodically the parish instituted special collections for the poor at all masses. This charity sometimes transcended parish bound-

91. For a complete picture of the debt reduction drive and the contribution of the various parish societies, see "Financial Statements of St. Augustine's Church" for the years 1892–1902. All in SAA.

92. The Union was discontinued in early 1899. See *CN*, 7 Jan 1899.

93. These lawn parties were usually hosted by the choir or some other parish organization. See *CN*, 12 and 19 May and 30 Jun 1900. On the District's contribution, see Public Works Index, #2484, 23 Apr 1897, and #2872, 6 May 1897, DC Archives.

aries, as when a special collection was earmarked for the suffering poor of India and Puerto Rico or for survivors of the Galveston Hurricane of 1900. To supplement the traditional work of the St. Vincent de Paul, a group of parish men organized the St. Augustine's Relief Society to assist the temporarily unemployed. A group of parish women under the leadership of Annie Jackson formed the St. Augustine's Sewing Circle to repair and help distribute the used clothing collected by the Vincentians for the needy.[94]

Inexplicably, St. Augustine's school, a focus of interest since the parish's foundation, fell victim to the debt eradication campaign. In June 1892 Griffith had presided over the annual commencement that saw only fourteen students (out of a student body numbering 146) graduate. It reminded him of the cruel dilemma he faced: the school placed a severe financial burden on the parish and was suffering from decreasing enrollment because of competition from the public schools. At the same time he was convinced that without a Catholic education many children would lose their faith. He decided to gamble. Beginning in September 1893, the school would be free to all. Meanwhile, the parish would ask for a major increase in the annual contribution of the Commission for Negro and Indian Missions. Its usual donation was not enough to keep the school open half the academic year, Griffith reported to the Commission, so he was making a "strong appeal" for $1,000.[95]

His plan was only partially successful. While canceling tuition brought about an instant and dramatic increase in enrollment, the necessary outside help was not forthcoming. The bishops' commission again made a $500 contribution ("the drop in the tub," as Father Dougherty put it) and ignored Griffith's special request, as it did the following year when he submitted an impassioned plea for a one-time emergency contribution of $25,000 to replace the old schoolhouse.[96]

94. This work for the poor was publicized in the Catholic press. See, for example, *CN*, 7 Dec 1895, 2 Oct 1896, and 15 May 1897.

95. *Notitiae*, 1893.

96. Ltrs., Griffith to Dyer, 12 Jul 1892, 45-DY-21; 20 Sep 1893, 45-DY-22; 3 Aug 1893, 45-DY-23. All in ASSJ. The quote is from ltr., Dougherty to Dyer, 24 Oct 1894, 21-DY-46, same source. See also "Programme of the Closing Exercises of St. Augustine's School, Washington, D.C., June 15, 1892," SAA.

The end came suddenly. In August 1895 the city's board of health condemned the old structure. With no money to rebuild and without funds to pay the sisters' salaries, which were in arrears for over a year, Griffith had no choice but to close down.[97] Some of the students enrolled in the new St. Cyprian's School on Capitol Hill, but most were left to enter the public schools.

In later years the pastor would say that parochial education had merely been "suspended" at St. Augustine's, but actually almost a full generation of young parishioners would go without a Catholic education in what appears to have been a major shift in priorities.[98] In a decade when the congregation was reducing the debt by an average $5,000 annually despite a major depression, it was unable, or unwilling, to save a school that actually predated the parish and had been a major impetus in the foundation of St. Augustine's. Whether Griffith ever openly involved parishioners in his decision is unknown, but certainly there was no criticism of the closure in a congregation that had made its opinions forcefully known on more than one occasion.

One explanation for the parish's failure to protest the school closing was the excellent reputation of its flourishing Sunday school. There, hundreds of students who attended Washington's generally fine public schools received careful instruction in religion under the supervision of Father Dougherty and a large staff of lay teachers headed by Matilda Wheeler, Ella Toy, and Fannie Grimes. The enthusiasm and dedication of these volunteers were stimulated by their frequent social events and fund raisers. Amateur theatricals had become the rage in Washington at the turn of the century, and as in many other parishes, Sunday school teachers led the way. In 1892, for example, the St. Augustine group sponsored a series of performances of the popular operetta *The Noble Revenge*, and in 1894 soprano Lavinia Dey Lofton directed the parish's would-be actors and musicians in a production of *The New Year*, which played to large, paying audiences. The teachers also organized parish reunions, awarded prizes to the best students, and gave special recognition to the best teachers. A lively

97. "Archives Narrative for Academy of the Holy Cross, Washington, D.C.," vol. I, pp. 14–16, Archives of the Sisters of the Holy Cross.

98. Ltrs., Griffith to Dyer, 9 Jul 1895, 45-DY-24, and 19 Oct 1895, 45-DY-25, and James R. Matthews [pastor of St. Cyprian's], to Dyer, 7 Sep 1895, 83-DY-6. All in ASSJ.

and fun-loving group, they also went about the serious business of training the children in the principles of their faith in a way that eased the concern over the loss of the parochial school.[99]

Under the dynamic new pastor and his assistants, St. Augustine's began to resemble more closely the typical American parish of the turn of the century.[100] These men proved especially adept at channeling the energies released by a new sense of spiritual and social community, as could be seen in the revitalization of the older parish organizations and the formation of new ones. The Sodality, for example, which traced its roots back to the free black sodalists of pre–Civil War times, was reorganized in 1892, when the parish group became affiliated with the Sodality's Vatican headquarters, the *Prima Primaria*, and when a slate of lay officers was installed with suitable ceremony. Romulus Smothers and Frances Frelinghuysen were elected prefect and vice-prefect. Membership grew rapidly. In May 1896 more than 500 sodalists were on hand for the annual reception of new members. For some reason the group amended its constitution in 1895 to limit officers to two consecutive terms, and in 1897 Thomas Stewart, who would remain a mainstay of the Sodality for many decades, replaced Smothers as prefect.[101] The recruitment of male members was facilitated by the formation in 1895 of a cadet branch. In addition to their spiritual duties, this group of teenagers staged minstrel shows, declamation performances, and plays, all for male audiences only. The presence of so many men in what in recent decades has become a largely female organization would characterize St. Augustine's sodality until the World War I era.[102]

As in other parishes, the League of the Sacred Heart, now inter-

99. The Catholic press, especially the *Church News*, was generous in its coverage of the Sunday school. The names of scores of students and teachers appeared each year. See, for example, *CN*, 17 Sep 1892, 7 Oct 1893, and 6 Jan and 10 Mar 1894.

100. The parish acquired a third priest in 1894 with the arrival of the newly ordained southwest Washington native, Francis X. Bischoff.

101. Miss Carrie Bloise also served as prefect for many terms. The activities of the parish Sodality were frequently reported in the Catholic papers. See, for example, *CN*, 6 Apr and 22 Jun 1895, 11 May 1896, and 15 and 22 Jun 1898.

102. Ltr., George W. Johnson to Pauline J. Jones, 23 Sep 1958, SAA. By 1916 only sixteen male members remained in the Sodality, including Johnson, Charles Inloes, John Butler, and Horace Dyer.

nationally organized in an Apostleship of Prayer, vied with the Sodality as the most popular devotion. In June 1894 some 450 parishioners received their scapulars, signifying membership and pledging them to a regime of daily prayer, monthly masses, and frequent league meetings. The following year the group welcomed 150 new members and ten promoters, officers who helped organize the spiritual work of the league.[103]

The parish also organized a branch of the Father Theobald Matthew Total Abstinence Society in 1892. Named after the Irish apostle of temperance, the society sought to conquer the scourge of alcohol, an especially popular cause in large city parishes with predominantly Irish populations. As seen in St. Augustine's efforts to curb the growth of saloons in the neighborhood, the parish's enviable immunity from this disease had ended, and in fact the temperance society emerged as one of the parish's most popular organizations. Its Sunday evening meetings often found the church hall overflowing, as the audience listened to spirited denunciations of demon rum, sang temperance hymns along with its specially formed choir, and enjoyed recitations and other uplifting entertainments. In February 1893 eighteen parishioners took the pledge at a well-advertised meeting; a year later another thirty-six men pledged life-long abstinence. At a time when men were the target of the reformers, several women served as officers of the group. In 1894, for example, Mary A. Wheeler was elected president, Annie Saunders, secretary, and Fannie Grimes, treasurer.[104] Although Cardinal Gibbons adopted a notably moderate approach toward drinking and even earned the enmity of the more radical temperance leaders by insisting that failure to keep the pledge did not constitute a sin, he too encouraged abstinence, especially among the young. As a regular part of each confirmation ceremony he asked the boys to take the pledge. Unlike some fanatics, he did not expect these children to make a lifetime commitment, but to abstain until their majority and thereafter practice moderation. His practical approach was evident in his warning after administering the pledge to St. Augustine's confirmandi in

103. *CN*, 16 and 30 Jun 1894 and 22 Jun 1895.

104. The activities of the society and its leaders were the stuff of parish columns in the Catholic press. See, for example, *CN*, 9 Jun 1894, 19 Oct 1895, 17 Mar 1900, and *CM*, 17 Feb 1893.

1898: "I don't want you to understand that I mean that when you become twenty-one you must go out and get awfully drunk in order to make up for lost time. You should try to abstain for all times."[105]

To provide a wholesome outlet for many of these young people, the parish underwrote a company of military cadets. Beginning in 1894 the unit drilled weekly under a veteran of the Washington Fencibles, one of the city's spit and polish militia units. In subsequent years officers were selected on the basis of military competition, a drum and bugle corps was organized, and close-order drills were conducted twice weekly during the school year.[106] Soon the smartly uniformed teenagers were participating in many parish ceremonies.

These ceremonies were both numerous and immensely popular, serving to draw the parish together into a self-conscious community of believers. In October 1892, for example, the parish participated in the celebration of the four-hundredth anniversary of Columbus's voyage. It was a grand display of Catholic strength featuring the men of every parish, who marched in a torchlight procession with bands and bugles and richly caparisoned horses and carriages through the city's streets to a rally in Gonzaga's stadium. In January 1894 in an act strangely prophetic, various parish organizations participated in the cornerstone laying for the beautiful church at Fifteenth and V Streets dedicated to St. Paul, which seventy-seven years later would become St. Augustine's home. In 1895 the parish priests inaugurated an annual New Year's reception, at which speakers reviewed the previous year's progress and singled out individuals for their special achievements. In 1896 Charles Butler, representing the parish, welcomed Cardinal Gibbons to the celebration of St. Augustine's thirtieth anniversary, which included a parade through central Washington with the Knights of St. Augustine serving as honor guard. In July 1898 the congregation filled the church to pray for peace and for the victims of the fighting during the war with Spain. Later that year another ceremony marked the ar-

105. Quoted in *CN*, 2 Apr 1898.
106. The activities of the cadets were followed in the *Church News*. See, for examples, 21 Apr 1894, 20 Jul and 7 Sep 1895, and 25 Jul 1896. The first officers of the corps were: Randolph Henson, captain; Washington Brooks, 1st lieutenant; Aloysius Adams, 2d lieutenant; James Butler, 1st sergeant; William Johnson, 2d sergeant. In later years the group was trained by Sgt. Coughlin of the U.S. Fourth Artillery.

rival of a first-class relic of the parish's patron saint. In an era that set much store on veneration of the saints, the possession of a piece of St. Augustine's finger, mounted in a gold filigreed reliquary, a gift of the Vatican, was a source of pride and reverence for the congregation.

These special occasions served as benchmarks in the quotidian round of ecclesiastical ceremonies that filled the church. The annual missions, Forty Hours observences, Marian devotions, and Trinity Sunday anniversaries—all expressed in age-old liturgies that employed brilliant vestments, masses of candles, clouds of incense, and a choir performing to the highest standards—added resonance and old-world color to church attendance in Washington. Such ceremonies, frequently underscored by the presence of the apostolic delegate, visiting members of the hierarchy, and distinguished African-American leaders, served to reinforce a sense of pride and accomplishment in a parish largely isolated from other Catholics by racial barriers growing ever more rigid in the nation's capital. Ironically, even as the Church and its leaders continued to deny people of color full fellowship in the communion of believers, the strong Catholic faith and sense of Catholic community possessed by these African Americans were strengthening them for the trials ahead.

SIX ⚜ JIM CROW WASHINGTON

*T*he first decades of the twentieth century marked the triumphant conclusion of an effort across the South to disenfranchise African Americans and to establish by law and custom their uniformly inferior position in society. Unlike the Black Codes of pre–Civil War days, which were more often honored in the breech, the so-called Jim Crow laws introduced a rigid system of segregation. Racial separation now intruded into every area of life and was enforced by officials employing intimidation and fear and, with increasing frequency, by vigilantes using the whip and noose. The Supreme Court's decision in 1896 in the case of Plessy *v* Ferguson, which sanctioned segregation, also marked the end of any progressive efforts by the federal government to protect the civil rights of black citizens.

Although spared many of the regressive ordinances enacted elsewhere, Washington was nevertheless a southern city and used legally sanctioned covenants and regulations enacted with the cooperation of its federal masters to subject black citizens to much of the same segregation imposed elsewhere in the South. No matter that the city was generally recognized as home to the largest concentration of prosperous and educated African Americans, no black resident, whatever his class, escaped the discrimination imposed on many aspects of life. As a result, separation of the races, more nearly complete than in any other city in the Union, some claimed, now existed in a capital where just a few decades before the first tentative steps toward mutual recognition and understanding had taken place.

This breakdown in interracial understanding was particularly painful for black Catholics, whose church, echoing secular society, continued to ignore generally the commandment of universal brotherhood. Ironically, the American church, including the church in Washington, was itself suffering a renewal of discrimination at the hands of nativist bigots. As a result, a change in attitude could be detected. In contrast to earlier times when Catholics of both races demonstrated a confident, outward-looking attitude toward their fellow citizens, the local church in recent decades had begun to develop a largely self-absorbed interest in parochial concerns. Echoing a trend evident throughout the country, Washington's Catholics adopted a habit of introspection that emphasized to a far greater extent than ever before how they differed from their neighbors. This so-called ghettoization is commonly associated with the great wave of European immigrants and their wary reaction to the native bigots. In the case of St. Augustine's, religious ghettoization was exacerbated by race. Not only were its parishioners conscious of their isolation from other African Americans, who shared in the general anti-Catholicism of the day, but they were also forced to endure the mindless racism of many of their own co-religionists. Only recently they had watched the Church's leaders turn a deaf ear to the legitimate complaints raised by the Congresses of Colored Catholics. As a result, the congregation of the new century, more than ever before, tended to seek spiritual and social fulfillment in its own exclusive company.

The erection of an imposing church, largely paid for by St. Augustine's parishioners, might symbolize to the rest of the African-American community the permanence and importance of an often derided religion, even as it allowed a black congregation to feel a certain sense of superiority over many nearby white parishes. But these motives clearly took second place in a group that had come to look to the parish to fulfill its social needs. As important as were the charitable and educational ends that motivated them, the myriad of societies and clubs with their eternal round of festivals, fairs, picnics, parades, excursions, balls, and lectures added to a growing sense of community and provided a safe, comfortable center for social intercourse that sustained black Catholics throughout the Jim Crow era.

Discrimination in the Capital

The opening decades of the new century witnessed a concerted campaign to limit the civil rights of Washington's black citizens. In discrimination in public accommodation, the capital eerily began to resemble its pre–Civil War past. Despite a federal civil rights law, proprietors fearlessly barred African Americans from their places of business. Anyone who bothered to protest received scant redress from the courts, finally losing all hope when in 1913 the Supreme Court declared this last protection against segregation unconstitutional. By then only public transportation, libraries, a few churches, and the ball games at Griffith Stadium remained unsegregated.[1]

The federal government led the way in job discrimination. Hopes raised by President Theodore Roosevelt's symbolic gesture of inviting Booker T. Washington to dine at the White House were quickly dashed when the hero of San Juan Hill, who had witnessed (only later to disparage) the heroic performance of black troops during the War with Spain, approved the dishonorable discharge of a whole battalion of black soldiers.[2] A few high-profile positions traditionally filled by African Americans retained black incumbents, but Roosevelt failed to appoint Washingtonians to any of these jobs. Black society might still dance the night away at the annual Chandelier Ball honoring employees of color in the White House, but the number of celebrants steadily decreased and none could be blind to the ominous trend.[3] Even more

1. This summary of discrimination in early twentieth-century Washington is based mainly on Green's *The Secret City*, Fitzpatrick and Goodwin's *The Guide to Black Washington*, and Borchert's *Alley Life in Washington*.

2. The men of the first battalion of the 25th Infantry refused to name those involved in a disturbance in Brownsville, Texas, in August 1906. The unit had been subjected to severe abuse at the hands of local citizens, and some members likely played a part in a shoot-out that took the life of a civilian. The discrimination in the regular army, the questionable proceedings at Brownsville, and Roosevelt's attitude toward black soldiers are discussed in Bernard Nalty's *Strength for the Fight* (New York: The Free Press, 1986), pp. 68–97.

3. Seale, *President's House*, vol. 2, pp. 792–93.

disturbing, minority representation in the regular civil service began to drop, and those remaining found themselves regularly passed over for advancement. Conditions deteriorated further when the Democrats under Woodrow Wilson came to power in 1913. Not only was the curtailment of black employment accelerated, but segregation in federal offices grew apace. The sight of blacks and whites eating together so offended the sensibilities of Mrs. Wilson, a southern lady of the old school, that the White House openly abetted efforts by cabinet officers to assign African Americans to separate offices, restrooms, and lunch tables. The president explicitly approved the imposition of these Jim Crow regulations.

The city government followed suit. Only the rare municipal position remained available to black office seekers and always ones at the lowest level. Even the small number of black police and firemen shrank, although after World War I Commissioner Louis Brownlow did establish an all-black platoon in the fire department that gave a small group of men employment and chance for promotion. Black teachers discovered plum assignments in the city's black schools going to white teachers. With the building trades largely closed to black applicants and most businesses segregated, craftsmen lacked the opportunity to keep up their skills, and soon many trained artisans were reduced to the precarious life of the common laborer. Domestic service was all that was available to the vast majority of women. The lucky few found work cleaning government offices or in laundries; most were relegated to the confining life of live-in maids. (The transition from live-in to day work that began around World War I would prove a great boon to these women, allowing them more freedom to attend church services and contribute their time to church organizations, which greatly prospered from this new class of volunteer.)[4]

As segregation became entrenched, distinguished African Americans found themselves no longer welcome in civic organizations that previously supported interracial cooperation. Groups like the Board of

4. Elizabeth Clark-Lewis, "From Servant to 'Day Worker': A Study of Selected Household Service Workers in Washington, D.C., 1900–1926" (University of Maryland: Ph.D. Dissertation, 1983), pp. 93, 121–23. See also her *Living In, Living Out: African American Domestics in Washington, D.C., 1910–1940* (Washington: Smithsonian Institution Press, 1994).

Trade and the Women's Christian Temperance Union, once shining examples of progressivism, dropped black members or organized segregated branches. Prominent Protestant divines spoke openly of black inferiority. Such pronouncements by men of their ilk, abetted by numerous pseudo-scientific studies claiming to prove racial disparities, provided strong support for the caste system rapidly developing in a capital where even prosperous and well-educated African Americans of impeccable demeanor, if noticed at all, were denied the most elementary signs of respect and forced to endure a suffocating patronization.

Loss of job opportunity and renewed discrimination resulted in a precipitate drop in the percentage of black residents.[5] Nevertheless by 1920 the city would be home to almost 110,000 African Americans. With no new housing and with the development of informal agreements between sellers and buyers to enforce residential color lines, the city began to develop the largely segregated neighborhoods that would come to characterize Washington throughout most of the century. Although the number of alley homes had begun to decline, some 16,000 Washingtonians, almost all of them poor blacks, still crowded into these by then miserable dwellings, which posed a serious threat to public health. Large concentrations of black residents lived in southeast and southwest and in Foggy Bottom. At the same time, most of the middle class, driven out of favored neighborhoods along K Street and Massachusetts Avenue by whites escaping business developers in the inner city, tended to follow the streetcar routes along the North Capitol, Seventh, and Fourteenth Street corridors. They especially favored areas along Florida Avenue and U Streets that had had substantial black populations since the Civil War. The black elite now tended to concentrate in comfortable homes in LeDroit Park near Howard University and in the western Shaw area south of U Street (especially in the comfortable row houses on T Street and the blocks above Logan Circle). Another region especially favored was the so-called Strivers' Section, between Fifteenth and Eighteenth Streets south of Florida Avenue.

5. The black percentage of the population, which had leveled off soon after the Civil War at about 33 percent, had dropped to 25 percent by 1920.

A random sampling suggests that St. Augustine's congregation followed the general movement of black families north of the old K Street line. Many familiar names could be found in the handsome townhouses that lined the streets of the Shaw section. The widow Frances Frelinghuysen, for example, lived on Vermont Avenue, while the families of James Toy and John Prater, both men with good jobs in the post office, now lived on Church Street, as did Aloysius Lemmon, who was categorized in the city directory as a *skilled* laborer. Others in this comfortable neighborhood included the families of Daniel Spriggs, Thomas Short, and Sylvester Reeder, all in the civil service. John F. Cole, a leader of the congregation, lived at 1426 S Street. Even some more humbly employed, like Benjamin Butler and Washington Thomas, porter and janitor respectively, lived on Corcoran Place off Fourteenth Street. An upscale group of parishioners now resided in the neighborhood centered on the Strivers' Section. These included Charles Dyson, who worked in the State Department, on N Street; the William Wheelers on Mintwood Place; and the Edward Gordons on S Street. The Bowser family, on the other hand, resided in LeDroit Park, close to Howard University where their son, Russell, was a student.

Some parishioners resisted the trend. At least a few, like James B. Maynard, the church sexton, Regina Taylor, a housekeeper, and Birch Edelin remained in the blocks surrounding the church, while Dr. Lofton continued to see his patients at his home on M Street. Annie DeVaul, a hairdresser, William H. Robinson, a carpenter, and Horace Dyer and Henry Coates, all active church workers, lived at some distance from the church in the once-popular neighborhood west of the now-enclosed Tiber Creek. Presumably some less affluent members such as Henry W. DuKette and Stephen Ennis, both listed as laborers, lived with their families on Virginia Avenue in Foggy Bottom. The former included among his children the first priest produced at St. Augustine's.[6] The formidable Mary Ann Cooke also lived in Foggy Bottom with her husband, William Washington Cooke, and their children. They had moved from the southwest "island" in the late 1870s, disgusted with their treatment at St. Dominic's. Mary Cooke in particular

6. The name is variously spelled Duckett, Du Kette (the spelling of Father Norman A. DuKette's name in the official *Kennedy Directory*), Duckette, and Dukett. In later years the family would move to Ninth St., N.W.

had grown tired, she later explained, of watching her children wait patiently week after week for the white children to receive their *Sunday Messenger* in church before they could claim the leftovers. She had not worked herself up from slavery to put up with such nonsense, she decided, and her family moved to Twentieth Street, where they made the trip each week to St. Augustine's and equality.[7]

The appearance of a virulent racism took one segment of Washington society by surprise. The aristocrats of color, who had evaded most forms of discrimination in the past by distancing themselves from their less fortunate neighbors, now found their immunity from persecution evaporating. As late as 1902, for example, the *Washington Post* was still praising the city's black upper class for its academic achievements, business successes, and contribution to the arts in the capital. The prosperous members of St. Augustine's congregation came in for their share of praise when the *Post* published a lengthy profile of the parish in 1905, in particular extolling the work of the parish's charitable and musical organizations. Remarkable in a period when segregation was becoming the norm, the paper went on to report with obvious satisfaction the mixing of the races at mass, declaring that St. Augustine's put into practice "the broad theory of the Catholic church that it is a place for all mankind."[8]

At first the press continued to emphasize the class distinctions that had so fragmented black society. In the early years of the new century, for example, the *Bee,* still the city's leading African-American paper, kept up a drumbeat of criticism against the disadvantaged, condemning their immorality and satirizing their ostentatious behavior.[9] But as Jim Crow tightened his grip on the city and as the *Star* and the rest of white press moved from compliments to criticism and finally to outright hostility toward black residents, the usually supercilious *Bee* changed its tune. It became a leader in documenting the ceaseless attacks on civil rights and in advocating a united response to what was becoming an intolerable situation. Various churches and organizations followed

7. Intv., author with Dr. Paul P. Cooke, 3 Jan 1997.

8. Unmarked copy of article, attributed to the *Washington Post*, n.d. (ca. Aug 1905) (source of quote), SAA. See also *Post,* 20 May 1905 and 3 Aug 1910.

9. See, for example, *The Bee,* various issues, May–July 1901. For an especially virulent attack on black preachers, see 14 Dec 1904.

suit. The result was a growing cohesion in the black community, one that found all classes interested in boycotting segregated establishments and promoting black businesses like the famed Howard Theater, which opened in 1910. The Twelfth Street branch of the YMCA was another important product of this new-found black unity and self-awareness. Its opening in 1912 in turn stimulated further cooperation among the city's black congregations and scores of black organizations, civic, charitable, and professional. For the first time since the Civil War, Washington's African Americans began to act like a unified community.

One significant manifestation of this new unity was the organization of the Washington branch of the National Association for the Advancement of Colored People. The new civil rights group grew out of the ferment that followed a meeting of progressives headed by W. E. B. Dubois at Niagara Falls in 1906. These dynamic young activists rejected the passive philosophy of Booker T. Washington and the prevailing notion that African Americans must earn recognition in American society by hard work and calm acceptance of their role as second-class citizens. They produced a manifesto of rights and goals that set the civil rights agenda for more than a half century. Although the NAACP represented a union of black and white progressives, its Washington branch, organized in 1912, was predominantly African American from its inception. Within four years, membership had climbed to 1,164, the largest in the country and one that included a number of St. Augustine's parishioners. Among these Dr. Daniel Williams, the surgeon-in-chief at Freedmen's Hospital, and Mr. and Mrs. John F. Cole were early members, as were William Miner and Thomas Wyatt Turner, leaders in the on-going fight against discrimination in the Church. Peter Quander and William Prater, representatives of families long associated with St. Augustine's, were active members as was the elderly but still feisty dressmaker Anna Fluger, who proudly included her occupation and New York Avenue dress shop in the NAACP's membership list.[10] From the first these hard-working activists played a useful role

10. These names were culled from incomplete membership lists for the period 1914–19 contained in the NAACP correspondence files, 1913–29, in the Archibald Grimke Collection, HUA. This review also found partially identified members of the Savoy, Shorter, and Saunders families, all St. Augustine names. A check of complete membership lists, if they still exist, would most likely reveal others.

in the fight against the segregationists in the Wilson administration. They won continued congressional support for Howard University, forestalled legislation promoting residential segregation, and succeeded in getting reinstated a number of unfairly dismissed civil servants. Above all, members served as watchdogs for the national organization, scrutinizing the activities of the central government while carrying the torch for civil rights in Washington.

Civil rights agitation took a back seat when America went to war in 1917. Catholics of all classes and colors, spurred on by Cardinal Gibbons and other church leaders anxious to confront Protestant bigots with a strong demonstration of patriotism, plunged into the war effort. St. Augustine's representatives joined laymen from every parish in town in organizing a Memorial Day Mass and mammoth rally. The theme of the demonstrations as well as the patriotic sermons ordered in all the churches was Catholic determination to "Stand by the President" during the war. In October a Solemn High Mass was celebrated in each parish in accordance with the president's proclamation to pray for the success of the army and navy.[11]

St. Augustine's sons donned the uniform of a segregated army to fight for their country. A church full of relatives and friends joined the pastor in a prayerful send-off for a large group of new soldiers in October 1917. At least eighty men served with the American Expeditionary Forces in France, many in the highly decorated 93d Division under the command of French officers, others in the first battalion of the National Guard's 372d Infantry. Among those of note were Captain Clarence C. Davis, who commanded a unit of the 372d, Dr. Albert Ridgely, who served in a battlefield hospital, and Father William McVeigh, an assistant pastor who volunteered to serve as a chaplain in France. A proud congregation sent Father McVeigh off with a purse of $300. One family saw three of its young men, Augustus, Frank, and Lewis Garner, leave to fight in France. Another young soldier off for France was Llewellyn Scott, who would later become famous for his exceptional work among Washington's destitute. Scott had been received into the

11. *Evening Star*, 13 May 1917, and *Baltimore Catholic Review* (hereafter *BCR*), 27 Oct 1917.

Church at St. Augustine's and worked hard to overcome a severe case of rickets before passing the army physical.[12]

Meanwhile on the home front parishioners supported the sale of war bonds, the so-called liberty loans, and along with most churches suffered various wartime shortages. The particularly cold weather of January 1918 left thousands of homes, including the many poorly constructed dwellings of impecunious blacks, without heat and the city with one day's supply of coal. St. Augustine's was one of many churches scheduled to be closed to conserve fuel. The archdiocese offered to hold services in unheated churches, but city officials remained adamant that they be shut down "for the war effort." Finally a compromise was reached, and enough fuel was distributed to allow all churches to remain open six hours a week. No such compromise was allowed when the Spanish influenza epidemic struck the city late in the summer of 1918. More than 3,500 died in six weeks, and thousands of sick filled the hospitals. City services were disrupted, and troops had to be called in to help bury the dead. St. Augustine's priests visited scores of sick in Providence and Freedmen's hospitals, at times making as many as twenty sick calls a day throughout northwest Washington. Finally in September the District Commissioners ordered all churches closed, and St. Augustine's, like the rest, canceled all public masses, funerals, and outdoor services. Miraculously, only one parishioner died during the epidemic.[13]

The lack of welfare services for soldiers segregated in camps around the country stimulated a small group of parishioners to demand help from the Church. In the early days of the war the needs of white Catholic soldiers were met by the National Catholic War Council, a group formed at Catholic University in 1917 to coordinate volunteer work performed by Catholic organizations in support of the war effort.

---

12. Among the many who served, the following were members of the Holy Name Society and later celebrated by the Holy Name Guild: Eugene T. Butler, Andrew R. Edelen, Leon A. Eskridge, Lewis W. Garner, Clarence R. Gilmore, Charles W. Gordon, DeReef Holton, Leo S. Holton, Bernard I. Jackson, George W. Johnson, James T. Johnson, Teagle King, Joseph E. Lee, Anthony Lucas, John A. Miles, Charles B. Plummer, Dr. Ridgely, Aloysius Wharton, and John H. Wilson. Source: SAA.

13. St. Augustine's *Parish Review*, Dec 1933, cy in SAA.

Although the YMCA had set up faculties to help needy black soldiers, no such provision had been made by the NCWC. When this anomaly was brought to the attention of Thomas W. Turner, a biology professor and acting dean at Howard University, he moved quickly. Together with a small group of fellow parishioners he outlined the problem for the priests at St. Augustine's, who recommended that they approach Cardinal Gibbons on the matter. A sympathetic Gibbons in turn sent them to the NCWC, where they convinced Colonel P. H. Callahan, director of the NCWC's welfare department, that action must be taken. Callahan hired a group of African-American social workers and assigned them to duty in cantonments in military camps around the country, where they provided help for soldiers until the end of the war.[14] This wartime incident launched Turner's remarkable career as a church activist, one with important consequences for the parish and the American church.

Parishioners were intensely interested in the performance of black units. Many gathered to hear Lieutenant Cru of the French High Command discuss the role of African-American soldiers in France in a lecture sponsored by the Holy Name Society. Shortly after the armistice that brought an end to the fighting in November 1918, the parish heard Lieutenant Peter Seamon, a veteran of trench warfare, speak on his experiences in the famed Buffalo Division and demonstrate weapons used in combat. In November 1919 the Holy Name Society sponsored a grand reception to welcome back to the parish seventy-nine of her sons who had served overseas. The parish's welcome was spoken by Professor Turner and Judge Robert H. Terrell.[15]

The return of peace only heightened racial tension in the capital.

14. Marilyn W. Nickels, "The Federated Colored Catholics: A Study of Three Variant Perspectives on Racial Justice as Presented by John LaFarge, William Markoe, and Thomas Turner" (Ph.D. dissertation, The Catholic University of America, 1975), p. 31. This dissertation was later published as *Black Catholic Protest and the Federated Colored Catholics, 1917–1933: Three Perspectives on Racial Justice* (New York: Garland Publ., 1988). Nickels' account is based on conversations with Turner. Nickels (or Turner's failing memory) incorrectly identified Father James J. O'Connor, an assistant, as pastor.

15. The program for this homecoming reception survives in the Thomas W. Turner Papers, HUA. James Dent was chairman of the event. The Donation Club also sponsored a welcome home party in October. The *BCR* provided detailed coverage of sever-

On one side, economic distress reappeared in the black community when the brief but welcome increase in wartime employment dried up. In addition to chronic racial slights, the community especially resented the denigration of returning black combat veterans. White residents, on the other hand, were agitated by the so-called Red Scare, which imagined a dangerous communist behind all social unrest and accepted without question inflammatory headlines that associated black residents with the subversives and the rest of the ills affecting the city. Tension reached a flash point on July 19, 1919, when roaming bands of white servicemen on furlough combined with local toughs in an indiscriminate assault on black citizens. The melee continued to escalate on succeeding nights when armed African Americans retaliated. Some of the worst fighting centered in southwest Washington and along Seventh Street in the eastern Shaw area. Only the presence of eight hundred soldiers and marines supporting local police kept the rioting bands from joining forces in the downtown business area. Peace was restored, but only after five days of mayhem that saw a number of citizens killed.

For the most part during the decade that followed, white Washington ignored the warning, and Jim Crow continued to reign supreme. Two events might be used to symbolize this nadir in race relations in the city: the first occurred in 1922 at the dedication of the memorial on the Mall to the Great Emancipator when distinguished black guests were unceremoniously herded into a far-off, segregated seating section. The other occurred in 1925, when massed ranks of white-clad Klansmen staged a parade on Constitution Avenue that ended in a rally on the Washington Monument grounds. No white official saw fit to object to either event, and a frustrated black community, its prewar unity now largely forgotten as its leaders became engrossed in internecine squabbles, seemed to lose the collective will to fight the mounting injustices. By the mid-1920s an increasingly isolated and fragmented black community had appeared, surrounded by white suspicion and neglect and rigidly segregated with a color line carefully

---

al of these activities. See, for example, 20 Oct 1917, 25 May 1918, 8 Jun 1918, 3 Aug 1918, 15 Feb 1919, 22 Mar 1919, and 25 Oct 1919.

drawn through all the old neighborhoods to denote the boundaries of what had become a separate, secret city within the capital.

The Zenith of Power and Influence

Ironically, World War I and the following decade that marked the nadir of race relations in the nation's capital also witnessed the apotheosis of St. Augustine's as the nation's premier black parish. In the size and importance of its congregation, the scope and influence of its many parish organizations, its material achievements, and its influence on the gathering campaign for racial justice in the Church, St. Augustine's became an acknowledged center of African-American Catholicism. If for a variety of reasons this ascendancy would prove short-lived, the parish nevertheless achieved a preeminence probably exceeding the wildest dreams of that small band of free blacks who had begun the work just a half-century before.

It is difficult to measure the exact size of a downtown parish with its many unregistered transients, but a national church census after the war reported that, based on an actual head count, some 3,000 Catholics regularly attended St. Augustine's.[16] Sometime during this period the parish rearranged its basement facilities to create a crypt church, which in a pinch could nearly double its seating capacity to 2,000. The racial composition of this large congregation rapidly changed in the new century. As previously noted, some white Catholics, attracted in the main by the beauty of the church and its extraordinary choir, had been attending St. Augustine's since the 1870s, making its services the largest regularly integrated events in the city. White attendance would rapidly increase after 1909, when St. Matthew's moved into its new church on Rhode Island Avenue, which, although less than a mile away, seemed a very distant and far-off place to many insular Washingtonians. Consequently, St. Augustine's inherited many of those who lived in the old Fifteenth Street area as well as those who worked or frequented the shopping, business, hotel, and banking centers. Another significant group of white attendees includ-

16. The results were published in the *BCR*, 1 Dec 1923. See also Foley's "The Catholic Church and the Washington Negro," pp. 146–50, which is the basis of this and the following paragraphs on the composition of St. Augustine's congregation.

ed many Irish servant girls, telephone operators, and others obliged to work on Sunday who took advantage of the parish's very early mass scheduled for the convenience of black domestics. Overnight, St. Augustine's became *the* downtown parish for what was now the city's major commercial area. In 1907 the respected black journal *Alexander's Magazine* estimated that almost as many whites as blacks could be counted among those thousands gathered at St. Augustine's. Although this statistic was no doubt exaggerated, it is certain that a significant minority of the regular churchgoers were white and that over the next two decades their numbers would threaten to overwhelm the black congregation, whose size would begin to diminish after the war as the number of other black parishes in the city increased.

Archbishop Bayley's rules governing membership in a black parish may have remained on the books, but to accommodate this influx of white attendees, diocesan regulations were certainly modified. For example, the stricture concerning baptisms and marriages continued, but whites in increasing numbers began to rent pews in the church. Renting a pew represented a symbolic transfer of membership between parishes, in this case between St. Matthew's and St. Augustine's, which was not a territorial parish but retained city-wide responsibilities for black Catholics. Numbered among those white Catholics who routinely attended St. Augustine's and rented their pews were some of the city's most prominent citizens, including the chief justice of the U.S. Supreme Court, Edward Douglas White, and Frank Riggs and his sons, the proprietors of Riggs Bank. Attracted by the prestige of these distinguished individuals and the aristocrats of color who occupied the front pews was a substantial sprinkling of diplomats, including members of the staffs of the Haitian and Japanese embassies as well as representatives of the Philippine Islands.

The pastor of St. Matthew's frequently objected to this transfer of parishioners from his parish by means of renting pews, but he was overruled on appeal to the apostolic delegate, who confirmed the right of Catholics to rent pews in any church in the city. Their informal membership in the parish thereby granted quasi-recognition, these white Catholics began to participate more fully in other phases of parish life. Now they joined the lines of those waiting to confess their sins, just as some of them called on priests of the parish to give them

the last rites and to be buried from St. Augustine's—another right recognized in canon law and confirmed by the archbishop over the objections of jealous pastors. At least a few of these newcomers expressed
their devotion to the parish by working at the parish fairs and picnics
and joining its societies, but for the most part those organizations remained exclusively African American.

The welcome these white newcomers received at St. Augustine's
testifies to the remarkable ability of black Catholics, themselves victims of innumerable racial slights, to exercise Christian forbearance.
All were made to feel welcome, although no African American could
have missed the point of one parishioner's experience. After being refused access to the confessional at nearby St. Paul's because of her
color, she was forced to join the long lines of white penitents waiting
before the confessionals at St. Augustine's. Yet only once did Father
Griffith find it necessary to intervene, when early on a small group of
whites tried to avoid mingling with parishioners by seating themselves
in one area of the church. He tartly reminded them that if they were
reluctant to rub shoulders with black Catholics they could take themselves off to one of the all-white churches nearby.[17]

Actually there were very few all-white Catholic churches in a city
where an estimated one out of every five Catholics was black. Of the estimated 10,000 black Catholics in Washington at the turn of the century, only half could be accommodated at St. Augustine's and St. Cyprian's, the city's second black church opened on Capitol Hill in 1893.
Most others worshipped at St. Dominic's, in the populous southwest
section, or at St. Aloysius, the Jesuit church that served the North
Capitol Street area. That still left a significant number of black parishioners, particularly at St. Teresa's in Anacostia, Holy Name in what was
then considered the far northeast, St. Stephen's in Foggy Bottom, and
Holy Trinity in Georgetown. At all but St. Augustine's and St. Cyprian's,
black Catholics endured what the sociologists called "minimum partic-

17. Both incidents are recounted in Foley's work. For another instance of being denied access to the confessional at St. Paul's, see Marilyn Nickel's intv. with William
and Mary Buckner, 11 Nov 1974. An account of the self-segregating white worshippers
was later published by E. Franklin Frazier in his *Negro Youth at the Crossways: Their
Personality Development in the Middle States* (New York: Schocken Books, 1967), p.
125.

ipation," that is, they were admitted to mass and reception of the sacraments, but on a segregated basis when possible and usually in segregated seating. At St. Aloysius, for example, black baptisms were scheduled on a different day and the 1,500 black parishioners were expected to participate in all church services from a segregated balcony high overhead. Segregation at St. Dominic's was denoted by a ten-foot wide aisle that stretched across the nave and divided the rear pews occupied by African Americans from the rest. In larger parishes like St. Aloysius and St. Domonic's, black parishioners joined spiritual societies like the Sodality, but attendance at their functions was segregated. In all cases the rule of minimum participation meant rigid exclusion from full participation in parish social organizations as a matter of course.

The variety and vitality of parish organizations at St. Augustine's offered a sharp contrast to the treatment of black communicants in other parishes. Actually, these groups served a dual purpose. In pursuit of their stated spiritual or social ends, they also required laymen and women to devise parish programs and direct the dispersal of large sums of money, still a relatively rare phenomenon in the Church at that time. This stewardship was particularly helpful to ordinary black citizens, affording them the chance to develop leadership and management skills in a city largely bereft of such opportunities. In overwhelming numbers, members participated in the spiritual organizations common to every parish. The Sodality, League of the Sacred Heart, and St. Vincent de Paul Society all maintained their schedules of special monthly masses with communion breakfasts and weekly devotions and holy hours in addition to prescribed corporal works of mercy. For example, the Sodality supplemented its devotions with regularly scheduled visits to the old folks' home at Blue Plains, while the League of the Sacred Heart maintained a roster for visits to the sick at Freedmen's Hospital.[18] Many parishioners were enrolled in more than one of these organizations whose strict rules of attendance committed them to many busy hours of prayer and good works throughout the year.

The quartet of popular spiritual organizations had been completed in 1911 when St. Augustine's formed its own Holy Name Society. Origi-

18. Muffler's "This Far By Faith," pp. 83–93, provides a useful summary of these organizations during this period and their influence on the life of the parish.

nally established to promote frequent reception of the Eucharist and to fight profanity, the Holy Name quickly became the major spiritual organization for Catholic men in the nation. It proved no less popular at St. Augustine's, where within two years it could count 400 adult members and 200 boys enrolled in a junior branch. Some of the most prominent civil rights activists in the American church served as presidents of St. Augustine's Holy Name, including John I. Jackson, Thomas W. Turner, Dr. Eugene Clark, and John F. Cole.[19]

The individual parish units formed a diocesan union to which St. Augustine's sent representatives. Although these men participated in the union's business meetings, that city-wide body all too often reflected the racial prejudices of the day. Unlike the St. Vincent de Paul, whose integrated gatherings in the city's churches were followed by integrated communion breakfasts (for many years at the cafeteria operated by the admirable Evan Scholls), the Holy Name Union callously insisted on following the custom of the host parish by segregating African Americans. Blatant racism of this type was particularly galling to these distinguished Catholic leaders, as an angry Thomas W. Turner informed Bishop Owen B. Corrigan, Gibbons's auxiliary, following an incident at Corpus Christi Church in Baltimore in 1915. While their white brothers marched up the center aisle to their reserved seats for a Holy Name Mass, black representatives were unceremoniously directed off to a segregated corner of the church. Many simply walked out, but the St. Augustine's unit, with no other chance to hear mass that Sunday, endured the insult which Turner condemned in unsparing detail. Such conduct was especially outrageous, he pointed out to Corrigan, when it occurred in a church dedicated to the Body of Christ, and he warned that black Catholics would not "put up" with such treatment. Corrigan seemed genuinely amazed by such criticism, branding Turner's complaint "unwarranted." All he was trying to do, he explained, was to "reserve good seats for colored men, who would be arriving from out of town."[20] Given obtuseness of this sort on the part of

19. Other leaders included: Leo Holton, Edgar L. Kenney, T. R. Sheppard, Alfred H. Selby, Andrew R. Edelen, Jr., Joseph P. Quander, George W. Johnson, Bradshaw Vowels, John Wilson, Walter A. Jones, Charles Whitby, Lawrence C. Hill, and Randolph Brooks.

20. Ltrs., Turner to Corrigan, 2 May 1916 (first quote), and Corrigan to Griffith, n.d.

church officials, it was not surprising that such treatment continued, and when the Sodality formed a similar union in 1918, it excluded outright any representation from black parishes.[21]

A colorful dividend of membership in the Holy Name Society was the chance to participate in the grand parades sponsored by the group in Washington. The first parade, in 1910, saw some 6,000 marchers, representing almost every parish in the region, swing up Pennsylvania Avenue past the White House where President William Howard Taft reviewed the various contingents as their bands blared out "Hail to the Chief." In 1912, St. Augustine's men were among the 12,000 marchers and 20,000 spectators who knelt together near the Washington Monument for the concluding devotions. In succeeding years the annual event assumed a pattern familiar to coming generations of area Catholics. Contingents from parishes throughout the region, many with excellent parish bands, joined massed ranks of male religious from the houses of study associated with Catholic University garbed in their distinguishing habits to march in divisions down Constitution Avenue. The line of march for the parishes was arranged alphabetically, with St. Augustine's large contingent near the head of the parade.[22] Yet even in these public demonstrations of Catholic unity lay the specter of racial insensitivity that would lead to later division. The president of St. Augustine's Holy Name Society protested to the union's spiritual director about newspaper accounts of the 1915 parade, which referred to young blacks in the line of march as "pickininnies," a word they had copied from the Church's own *Baltimore Catholic Review*."[23] The frequently stated purpose of these outdoor events, which would contin-

---

(ca. May 1916), cy encl. to ltr., Turner to Griffith, 13 May 1916 (second quote). Cys. of both in Turner Papers, HUA.

21. Foley, "The Catholic Church and the Washington Negro," p. 283. The Sodality Union would continue to bar black sodalists until 1946.

22. Foley, "The Catholic Church and the Washington Negro," pp. 273–74. In some years the parish of the reigning president of the Holy Name Union headed the parade.

23. Ltr., Turner to Corrigan, 4 Feb 1916, Turner Papers, as quoted in Nickels, "The Federated Colored Catholics," p. 28. The *Review*'s account of the parade referred to stated: "A feature of the demonstration was a huge American flag carried by twelve little pickininnies from Washington. One hundred little colored boys from St. Augustine's parish, dressed in white sailor suits, elicited much applause along the line of march." *BCR*, 16 Oct 1915.

ue to grow in size and complexity in the next decades, was to demonstrate the God-centeredness of Catholic organizations and to attract
non-Catholics to the Church. The parades would also provide Cardinal
Gibbons's successor, a forceful advocate of what would later be called
"muscular Christianity" with a bully pulpit to condemn the weak-
kneed backsliders and to extol Catholic manhood. "No mollycoddles
here," Archbishop Michael J. Curley would tell the crowd in 1922.[24]
Unfortunately the usually forthright and outspoken Curley never saw
fit to comment on the discrimination frequently practiced by the religious society he was addressing.

The treatment received by St. Augustine's representatives in city-
wide meetings of both the spiritual and beneficial societies added to
the sense of isolation that characterized black parishes in the Jim Crow
era and reinforced the congregation's concentration on parish affairs.
As elsewhere, the beneficial societies were a major component of the
congregation's social life, and two new groups appeared during this
time to augment the work of those that had survived over the decades.
St. Monica's Auxiliary of the Knights of St. John, established in 1913
through the efforts of Jane Wade and Mary Willis, offered women of the
congregation the chance to invest in some form of health and life insurance while providing the parish with a new arena for social activities.[25]
It happened that the St. Augustine auxiliary was organized before the
national women's group amended its constitution in 1922 to exclude
African Americans. Thus St. Monica's Auxiliary constituted the only
black presence in this racist group, continuing down the years to participate in the organization's national activities while being studiously
ignored by the city's other auxiliaries. To their credit, the Knights, always an integrated society, consistently opposed the women's effort to
exclude blacks, but to no avail.[26]

Over the years the Knights of St. John increased their presence in

24. See, for example, accounts in *BCR*, 14 Oct 1922 (source of quote), and 9 Jan
and 20 Feb 1931.

25. The first officers of the Auxiliary included Annie J. Webster, president; Mary
E. Beckley and Annie DeVaul, vice-presidents; Genevieve L. Burke and Fannie Turner, secretaries; Lulu Prater, treasurer; Julia Hicks, messenger; Mary Willis, sentinel;
and Ida Newton, guard.

26. Foley, "The Catholic Church and the Washington Negro," p. 301.

the parish with the formation of a second commandery and a cadet branch in 1919. So did the Catholic Beneficial Society, the parish's oldest fraternal insurance organization, when it formed a juvenile division. Meanwhile the smaller but more disciplined Knights of St. Augustine and the more narrowly focused St. Augustine's Relief Society continued to attract new members. Their prosperity testified not only to the prudent financial investments of their members, but to the popularity of their social activities, which entertained the congregation in high style. Nor were these groups limited to practical business and entertainment. Their corporate contributions to various parish fund drives, frequently noted in the church's annual financial statements, increased the donation of their members, who usually also made an additional contribution in their own names. In 1914, for example, a number of young members individually donated to the parish's debt association in addition to their Juvenile Beneficial Society's $100 contribution.[27]

Conspicuously absent from this list of Catholic fraternal and beneficial societies was the nation's largest and most influential, the Knights of Columbus. Although not organized along parish lines, by 1899 the Knights had enrolled large numbers of men from all of Washington's white parishes into five local councils. The organization's bylaws restricted membership to practicing Catholic men, but the District councils also insisted on barring African Americans. This exclusion was especially resented by black lay leaders because, as the popularity of the Knights increased, they came to be accepted as a kind of semi-official representative of laity, practicing a brand of loyalty to the Church and ostentatious patriotism particularly admired by the hierarchy. Colorfully decked out in their ceremonial regalia and flashing swords, they began to form a conspicuous part of almost every ecclesiastical function.

A group of civil rights activists from St. Augustine's headed by Thomas Turner publicly protested the color bar in 1916. He addressed his complaint to one of the parish priests because, he claimed, "most such organizations are established by priests . . . whom we look to lead

27. Many of these annual statements have survived in the parish archives. Filled with the names of hundreds of parishioners of the period, they provide a useful source for those researching their family's history.

us into the larger field of temporal and spiritual graces." If whites needed such an organization to protect their interests, Turner reasoned, the need for such protection was doubly true for blacks.[28] Nothing came of this appeal, so Turner and his friends took their case to higher authority. They were applying for admission to the Knights, they told Cardinal Gibbons, because, as they put it, "the needs of our people can only be known through the expression of the colored man himself." They believed that representatives of black Catholics "should have a voice in all societies and in every activity connected with Mother Church," and to that end they asked Gibbons to use his influence to break the color ban. Again they were frustrated. Gibbons, never a crusader, ignored their arguments and instead counseled them to form their own society, since, he declared out of hand, separate societies "served the interests of the Colored Man best."[29]

Discrimination in extra-parochial organizations and the failure of the hierarchy to condemn such activity would strengthen the resolve of the activists to fight for justice in the Church. They also added to the feeling of isolation among the ordinary man and woman in the pew, who more than ever before turned inward to the parish community for fellowship and entertainment. As in the past this ability to enjoy their own company was greatly enhanced by activities of the Sunday School teachers, the ladies of the Donation Club, and the young adults in St. Augustine's Lyceum. While the lay Sunday School teachers conscientiously guided their 500 young charges through the Baltimore Catechism, they also had fun at their socials and fundraising events. The whole parish enjoyed their musicals, dances, and picnics. The serious young students of the Lyceum also added to the parish's social life. Successor to the Toussaint L'Ouverture Society organized by the lay activists in 1894, the Lyceum retained the literary aims of the older group, but with less emphasis on formal classes and more on social pastimes popular with the young. In addition to its literary and musical events, the Lyceum sponsored lawn parties, carnivals, and dinners to help reduce the parish debt.

Six women of the congregation began a new form of social work in

28. Ltr., Turner to Rev. James J. O'Connor, 8 Jan 1916, Turner Papers, HUA.

29. Ltrs., Turner et al., to Gibbons, with handwritten annotation, 23 Dec 1918, 124-C-4, and Gibbons to Turner, 7 Jan 1919, 124-G-4. Both in Gibbons Papers, AAB.

1913 when they organized the "colored auxiliary" of Washington's Christ Child Society. Founded in 1883 by Mary Virginia Merrick to provide Christmas presents for poor children, the society had expanded over the decades to bring many necessary social services to children of the working poor, including day care, food supplements, and convalescent care and fresh air vacations. In later years it would operate settlement houses and become a national society with units in thirty-three states.[30] The parish group, organized by Anna Greenfield, Clara Wheeler, Addie Spriggs, Sophia Hawkins, and Mrs. Francis Fletcher, who served as first president, expanded in a similar manner. At first it supported its work by the substantial dues collected from each member, but as the need increased the women supplemented their income by the sale of Christmas seals and the collection of toys and goods from local retailers. Soon they were sponsoring a broad program of works, including visiting children in Freedmen's Hospital, caring for the children of ill or working mothers, and supporting the chronically sick. In 1928 they purchased a small farm near Bel Alton, Maryland, to serve as a fresh air camp. Lack of funds forced them to operate this venture on a small scale with only fifteen children being accommodated at a time—a far cry from the society's spacious camps for white children at the shore. The St. Augustine's auxiliary had from the first protested against the need for a separate facility and went this route only when it became apparent that there would be no relaxation in the racial bar at the white camps. In fact the Christ Child Society, later a model of racial justice, practiced a rigid form of racial separation throughout the Jim Crow era. It refused full membership to the auxiliary at St. Augustine's, whose interests were represented in the parent organization by a white member of the society's board of governors. This official was also expected to attend the meetings of the parish group and supervise the dispersal of its funds. Despite such callous treatment, the Colored Auxiliary continued its important work for many years under the direction of Addie Spriggs, with the assistance of Elizabeth Holton, Mary Johnson, and Mabel Baker.

In addition to these groups the parish during the World War I era

30. The following paragraphs are based on Foley's "The Catholic Church and the Washington Negro," pp. 305–8, and Weitzmann, *One Hundred Years of Catholic Charities in the District of Columbia*, pp. 154–55.

supported its renowned choir and recruited and trained the large band of young men who, as servers and masters of ceremony, still constituted the only regular presence of African Americans in the sanctuary. The Donation Club, which had provided so many needed items for the church and rectory over the years, would continue as one of the congregation's most popular organizations until its dissolution in 1934 when its activities, by then almost exclusively focused on the school, were assumed by the School Club. In the post–World War I era Rosa Colbert, Matilda Eskridge, and Mary Graham led this generous group of women.

The Coming of the Oblates and a New Pastor

The major focus of both priests and people of St. Augustine's during this period was restoration of the parish school. After more than thirty years' struggle the congregation had managed to erase the debt on the church, but at the cost of seeing its venerable school close. Father Griffith, for one, believed a school essential to the parish's wellbeing. After praising the piety of the congregation, he had reported to the diocesan chancellor as early as 1906 on a worrying lack of initiative among many of the less educated, the prevalence of mixed marriages, and the large numbers who eventually drifted away from the Church. A good measure of the blame, he believed, lay in the lack of Catholic schooling and the failure of the public schools to instill a sense of morality and industriousness in their pupils.[31] Many evidently agreed, for everyone seemed eager to take on the challenge of a new school, even though all recognized that the rapid rise in real estate values in the Fifteenth Street area would make it a costly enterprise. Hoping to duplicate the successful fund-raising effort that had wiped out the church debt, Griffith organized a St. Augustine's Association in 1907 that enlisted scores of volunteers to raise money for a school and other needed improvements. Their efforts received a boost from the noted benefactress Mother Katharine M. Drexel, who donated $2,000 toward the purchase of a school property.[32] Within a few months the as-

31. Ltr., Griffith to P. C. Gavan [chancellor], 24 Sep 1906, 45-DY-26, cy in ASSJ.

32. Agreement signed by Cardinal Gibbons, Mother Katharine Drexel, and Father Griffith, December 9, 1907, original in SAA. The agreement stipulated that, should the

sociation had enlisted 115 patrons, prominent Washingtonians and hard-working parishioners alike, who donated an additional $1,000.[33]

Emboldened by this generosity, Griffith purchased the Allen property, which consisted of two lots with a brick house directly across from the church, for $34,600 with a 10 percent down payment. At the same time he leased a large house at 1127 Fifteenth Street to serve as a temporary school and convent.[34] At Cardinal Gibbons' instruction he signed an agreement with the Oblate Sisters of Providence to staff the school. Specifically, Griffith promised to pay each teacher $225 with an additional $100 to the convent in return for the sisters' performing incidental chores, including teaching in the Sunday school, preparing altar breads, and caring for the church altars. The parish would also supply coal for heating the building. In turn, Mother Magdalen, the Oblate superior, agreed to supply four sisters (and more when needed) who would also visit the children in their homes "when absent or sick," and prepare the pupils for reception of the sacraments.[35]

The new school opened on September 21, 1908, with 130 pupils in kindergarten through fourth grade in addition to a Sunday School with 300 students. Plans called for the addition of a grade (and sister) in each succeeding year. The first teachers included Sister Juliana (Meakins), who served as superior of the new convent, along with Sisters Luke (Russell), principal, and Sisters Eusebius, Johanna, and Ignatius. They were prepared to follow the curriculum designed by the archdiocesan school board and aimed, as Father Griffith put it, "to have as high a standard as that of any other school of the same grade in the city." The new free parochial school was filled to capacity from its

---

school not be built, the money be turned over to Gibbons for the education of black children in the Baltimore archdiocese. In 1922 Mother Katharine would also give $2,000 to Holy Redeemer Church to begin a school (see agreement, dated February 1922, in Chancery Papers, "Parishes-Washington, D.C.," File, AAB). In 1988 Mother Katharine was declared blessed, an important step toward canonization, by Pope John Paul II.

33. Annual Statement of St. Augustine's Church, 1908, cy in SAA.

34. Statements, Paul Griffith to J.L. Kolb, Real Estate and Insurance Agent, 15 Jul and 18 Nov 1908, sub: Purchase of Lots 76 and 77 in Square 214, cys in SAA. See also *Notitiae*, 1909.

35. Articles of Agreement, signed by Rev. Paul Griffith, pastor, and Mother Magdalen, O.S.P., and Mother James, O.S.P., 18 Sep 1908, O.S.P. Archives.

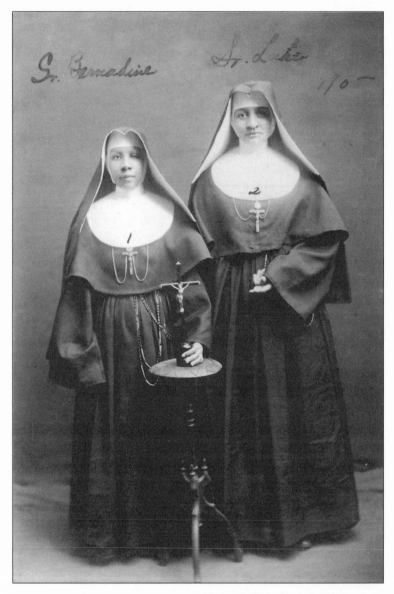

OBLATE SISTERS OF PROVIDENCE. Mother M. Luke Russell (right), principal of St. Augustine's school for eleven years, with fellow teacher Sister M. Bernadine Ruiz.

ST. AUGUSTINE STUDENTS, 1914.

opening, new applications coming in daily. Although the pastor confessed that the temporary school was "far short of what it should be,"
he nevertheless thanked those who had made it possible to furnish the
leased building and promised that when the new debt was sufficiently
reduced, the parish would erect a new schoolhouse and hall.[36]

Financial realities dictated that, despite keen interest in the
school, the pastor's planned expansion would be longtime in coming.
The newly acquired property across from the church allowed the
school to transfer quickly into a parish-owned building, but the continuing need to house the convent and school in the same structure left
no room for adding to the number of grades or the size of the faculty.

36. Paul Griffith, "St. Augustine's School, Opened Sept. 21, 1908," n.d. SAA. See
also Sister Mary Petra, "Blossoms Gathered From the Lower Branches or A Little Work
of an Oblate Sister of Province" (privately published by the Oblate Sisters of Providence in 1915), pp. 50–51.

By 1914 the student body stood at 155, a mere 25-pupil increase in seven years. During that same period the number of sisters had actually dwindled to four.[37] But some relief was in sight. In October 1914 a property immediately adjacent to the school at 1121 Fifteenth Street was forced into an emergency sale, and the parish was able to acquire the roomy building for a mere $7,500.[38] The necessary renovations completed, the smaller building was transformed into a convent, while the new purchase was fitted out with eight small classrooms. The transfer took place in September 1915, and a month later the parish was applying for a free water permit for 1121 Fifteenth Street under the city's agreement to provide such services to all accredited schools.[39] Enrollment immediately began to rise. The *Baltimore Catholic Review* reported in 1917 that the school comprised some 200 pupils and that "all classrooms were taxed to capacity." Somehow the sisters were able to make room for a few more. By 1923—a statistical high point for the old school building—235 students were in attendance, many of them going on after graduation to one of the city's fine public high schools.[40] Although the Knights of St. Augustine donated $300 to outfit a small playground in the area between the convent and school, realization of the pastor's hope for a large school building, playground, and parish hall still appeared far in the future.

As in the past, teachers salaries rarely matched the amounts promised. The convent's meticulously kept annual financial statements not only show how the sisters managed in reduced circumstances, but offer a glimpse of their work-filled days.[41] In 1917, for example, the sis-

37. *BCR*, 12 Dec 1914. In 1914 Sister Luke was still principal and taught with Sisters Loretto, Conception, and Leonarda. See undated "Article D," St. Augustine's file, O.S.P. Archives.

38. Contract, dated 16 Apr 1914, for purchase of parts of lots 10 and 11, square 214 containing 2,679 square feet, cy in SAA. See also ltrs., Daniel W. O'Donoghue to Griffith, 8 Oct and 14 Nov 1914. See also, *BCR*, 21 Nov 1914 and Property Agreement #20037, D.C. Superior Court in Equity, cy in SAA.

39. Dept. of Public Works Index #128805, 7 Oct 1915, D.C. Archives. The meager documentary record concerning the old school was supplemented by the author's intv. with Alma Plummer Rogers, a student in that institution.

40. *BCR*, 20 Oct 1917 (source of quote) and 1 Dec 1923. School population as reported in *Notitiae*.

41. See annual financial report, various years, St. Augustine's file, O.S.P. Archives.

ters received just $960 in salary, a sum they supplemented by laun-
dering church linens ($60.10), teaching music and tutoring in Spanish
($123.40), providing lodging for a boarding student ($90), sewing and
selling needlework and collecting and selling scrap iron and newspapers ($69.70). When added to a number of modest donations, receipts
reached a grand total of $1,420.80, exactly $34.13 over expenses! Donations and gifts from grateful parishioners figured in most year's receipts. The School Club contributed a modest sum annually, and private donors were frequently heard from. Among the latter were two familiar names: Father Griffith bequeathed the teachers $200 in his will,
and Leo Olds, director of the youth choir, once presented the sisters
$12 to buy material for new habits. Convent expense accounts revealed
the Oblates' frugal life style. In addition to food and medical expenses
(trips to Georgetown Hospital and to the dentist and eye doctor all
scrupulously detailed in their annual summary), the sisters always had
enough left over to subscribe to various scholarly and religious journals and to contribute a bit most years to worthy charities. Busy, dedicated women, they quickly captured the respect and affection of the
whole parish.

It is difficult to reconcile the realities of the parish's financial situation in this period with the heightened anxiety exhibited by the pastor
over indebtedness. In June 1917 he apologized to the chancellor for his
inability to contribute to diocesan collections because, he explained,
after paying off a $4,000 bill for school renovations, the parish was left
with just $443 in the till. A year later he was confessing to the cardinal
that for the last twenty-five years he had hidden the true extent of the
parish's financial difficulties because "God knows I do not want to
worry you." Now a $10,000 note on the school property was coming
due and he was prepared to launch a new subscription campaign.
Would the cardinal head the list of donors?[42]

Actually, both the financial difficulties and the cardinal's ignorance
were highly exaggerated. Griffith had certainly shown no such overwhelming concern in earlier years. In 1913 he had launched a costly
renovation of the church, apparently without a qualm. The old gas

---

42. Ltrs., Griffith to Louis R. Stickney, 18 Jan 1917, and to Gibbons 1 Jan 1918
(source of quote), cys of both in SAA.

fixtures were replaced by electric lights, and the church was repainted and extensive frescoing added. The paintings that had dominated the sanctuary were replaced with costly stained glass windows imported from Germany.[43] True, some of the new fixtures were donated, but most were purchased by the congregation through special collections. For example, the window depicting the Blessed Virgin was the gift of Belle Robinson, a parishioner; the new marble altar for the Virgin's chapel was given by the Sodality while the oriental rug in the sanctuary was paid for by the Donation Club. The other windows, however, and the electrification were all supplied out of regular parish funds.[44] In fact considerable money was spent in the parish during those years when Griffith claimed he was sparing the cardinal worry over parish finances.

Nor should the debt have been all that daunting. By 1917 the parish's total obligation (mostly on school property) was $31,800, a relatively modest sum considering the congregation's repeatedly demonstrated willingness to support the parish and the relative prosperity of wartime Washington. With the exception of a small annual grant from the Bishops' Committee for the Catholic Missions Among Colored People and Indians for the free parochial school, the parish had been self-supporting for years.[45] Cardinal Gibbons was obviously referring to the distant past when, trying to convince the pope in 1914 that Washington was financially unable to support an independent diocese, he described how two of its major parishes, St. Augustine's and St. Matthew's, depended on him to save them from bankruptcy.[46] In fact the cardinal's $100 donation for the new school in 1908 marked his only gift to the parish in the new century.

43. *BCR*, 29 Nov 1913 and 14 Mar 1914. The central window featured scenes from the life of SS. Augustine and Monica; to the left a depiction of the Immaculate Conception and St. Ann; to the right, St. Joseph in his carpenter's shop. The windows replaced the paintings by Costaggini, whose disposition is unknown, but whose value today would be considerable. They constitutes another of the parish's lost treasures.

44. The *BCR* during this period frequently reported on improvements to the church and sanctuary. See, for example, issues of 20 Feb 1915, 10 Feb 1917, and 27 Nov 1920.

45. St. Augustine's was one of ten churches in the diocese that applied for support from the committee. Available records suggest that the annual subsidy averaged $500. See, for example, ltr., Griffith to Gavan, 9 Jan 1911, 109-A-10, Gibbons Papers, AAB.

46. Ltr., Gibbons to the Pope, 1 May 1914, 113-Q-1, Gibbons Papers, AAB.

Griffith's sudden concern over money was fueled by an ongoing feud with the board of governors of Mt. Olivet Cemetery. The parish had borrowed $10,000 from that well-off institution in 1908 to pay off a bank loan on the school property at a low interest rate and with the agreement that so long as interest payments were kept up the note would not become due.[47] In a sudden change in policy, the board's president (and pastor of St. Matthew's), Father Lee, announced that the price of graves in the poorly cared for black section of the cemetery would, like the price of white graves, be almost doubled and that the interest on St. Augustine's loan would be raised. When Griffith protested, the board sold St. Augustine's note to a private lender, who indicated that full payment would be expected in the near future. At the time it was announcing these changes, the board also declared a hefty dividend for its investors, six of Washington's parishes.[48]

A furious Griffith openly branded the haughty, aristocratic Lee a "Shylock for enacting such a contemptible piece of business." While the parish could continue its interest payments, he explained to Gibbons, it could not liquidate the debt at that time, and he warned the cardinal of the scandal that would ensue should the mortgage holder take the parish to court. He wanted the cardinal to force the board to buy back the note and allow St. Augustine's to continue paying interest at the old rate until it was able to pay off the loan. His anxiety over the matter, he added, had caused heart problems that had driven him into the hospital for two weeks. Gibbons was unmoved. He was convinced, he claimed, that the cemetery board was within its legal rights. Ignoring Griffith's dire predictions, he ordered the parish to continue paying the higher interest rate.[49] No mention was made of the possibility of default, but perhaps Gibbons understood the situation better than appears from this distance. His directive seems to have spurred Griffith into a well-publicized subscription drive, which in the early months of

47. Ltr., James Hood, secy., American Security and Trust Co., to J. Leo Kolb [attorney], 22 Dec 1901, SAA. The bank loan, in the form of a deed of trust, was entered into on 14 Jul 1908.

48. Ltrs., Griffith to P. J. Walsh, treasurer, Mt. Olivet Cemetery Company, n.d. (ca. 20 Jan 1915), cy in SAA, and to Gibbons, 11 Jan 1917, 119-J-4, Gibbons Papers, AAB.

49. Ltr., Edward Connelly [chancellor] to Griffith, 18 Jun 1918, 119-L-3, Gibbons Papers, AAB.

1918 easily raised the needed $10,000. The fact that contributions never lagged below $800 in any week of the campaign obviously meant that many prosperous parishioners opened their purses wide. In expressing his gratitude for their generosity, Griffith emphasized as well the number of small contributions which, he pointed out, underscored the continued generosity of the city's struggling working-class Catholics.[50]

The parish celebrated Griffith's silver anniversary as pastor with great pomp in December 1917, just as the latest fund-raising campaign got underway. But in truth the old Irishman, now seventy-two, had begun to fail. Within the year he had entered Georgetown Hospital, where he died on January 22, 1919. As the first pastor had done, Griffith divided most of his few worldly possessions among parish friends.[51]

Ten priests served as assistants during Father Griffith's long pastorate. Probably most notable among them were George A. Dougherty, who was principal assistant for twelve years before transferring to Catholic University, where he would eventually become vice rector, and Peter L. Ireton, who would later be consecrated bishop of Richmond, Virginia. Both men remained staunch friends and supporters of the parish throughout their long careers and close friends of one of their fellow assistants, Alonzo J. Olds, who would become St. Augustine's fourth pastor. Unlike his immigrant predecessors, Olds was descended from an old Yankee family, which traced its roots to the seventeenth-century founders of Massachusetts. In 1892 at the age of sixteen he was accepted as a candidate for the priesthood in the Baltimore Archdiocese, eventually graduating from St. Charles College and St. Mary's Seminary. A talented singer and baseball player, the seminarian with the broad New England accent quickly earned a special prominence among his classmates. He was ordained by Cardinal Gibbons in December 1903 and began his priestly duties at St. Augustine's the fol-

50. *BCR*, 23 Feb and 4 May 1918. The $10,000 deed of trust on the school property was released to Gibbons on 7 Sep 1918 (see cy in SAA), just eight years after the parish assumed the obligation.

51. Griffith's funeral, attended by the cardinal, the apostolic delegate, and many priests, is described in full in the *BCR*, 1 Feb 1919. Among those mentioned in his will were Martina Irving, the choir soloist, and John I. Jackson and Daniel Spriggs, parish leaders.

lowing month. He would remain in the parish until his death fifty-three years later, a record of service unsurpassed in Washington to this day.

The young curate quickly exhibited those characteristics that would endear him to the congregation and earn its loyalty despite the painful trials and disappointments in the years to come. In the increasingly impersonal world of a large city parish he was anxious to learn all about the people in his congregation. As one observer later noted about Olds, "in a world . . . where individual wishes and hopes and ambitions are very little regarded, and people are considered by group or community, there is nothing people value more in a priest than this faculty of knowing them for who and what they are, this interest in them as persons, this gracious gift of being polite to their souls."[52] The always approachable Olds was obviously interested in individuals. As an old man he would recall his first meeting with some of the parishioners he came to know so well. Within days of his arrival he had witnessed the marriage of Daniel and Addie Marshall Spriggs, baptized Anna Louise Green, and made his first sick call to the bedside of Henrietta Crawford.[53] Many fellow priests envied his preaching style—as one of them put it, "his witty and pointed talks, which were unconventional, original, but never undignified."[54] His conscientiousness, obvious interest in the ambitions and well-being of young parishioners, and unabashed championship of racial justice earned the congregation's trust, just as his open and frank nature won their affection.

Approval of the new pastor would not be immediately universal, however. His relaxed management style and failure to address promptly the need for a bigger school clearly irritated at least a few older parishioners, who, used to the hard-driving, fiscally demanding Griffith, found it difficult to accept the new regime. They held fire for three years before complaining to the new archbishop in mind-numbing detail about their pastor's supposed shortcomings.[55] They charged that

52. Remarks of Msgr. John K. Cartwright, 4 Jan 1957, quoted in CS, 11 Jan 1957.

53. Actually, Mrs. Crawford, an ex-slave and widow of a Methodist preacher, would outlive Olds. In 1959 she received congratulations from Cardinal Patrick A. O'Boyle on her 107th birthday, which made her at the time the oldest Catholic in the archdiocese.

54. Quoted in CS, 11 Jan 1957.

55. Ltr., "Old Members of St. Augustine's" to Curley, 10 Jan 1922, Chancery Papers, "Parishes-Washington, D.C.," AAB.

the parochial school, pressed for space, routinely turned away hundreds of applicants each year, many of them Protestants who wanted a Catholic education for their children, while the sisters remained "packed like sardines" in an inadequate convent. They dismissed arguments that a new combined school, parish hall, and convent would be too costly and require more space than was available on Fifteenth Street. A parish hall was an expensive and unnecessary diversion, they claimed, urging that the new school be started at once. As for cost, take care of the school, they demanded, and forget about adding yet more marble altars to the church. Particularly irritating to them was the fact that the donation made by the Knights of St. Augustine to equip the school yard had yet to be spent. Vaguely reminiscent of the abstemious Father Griffith's criticism of the Josephites who preceded him, these self-righteous laymen condemned Olds and his assistants for driving around town in a newfangled Model T and frequenting the city's race track. In particular they lamented the transfer of Father Andrew H. Mihm, who, they claimed, was responsible for the remarkable growth of the Holy Name Society and the return of so many lapsed Catholics to the sacraments.

These accusations, undoubtedly heartfelt but highly debatable or downright inaccurate, clearly lacked any support from the parish's lay leaders and the great majority of their fellow parishioners. Archbishop Curley wisely dismissed them without comment. Nevertheless, the criticism of this small and unrepresentative group serves to underscore the importance of maintaining a proper balance between spiritual inspiration and the more prosaic physical stewardship when leading a shrinking congregation during an era of heightened racial animosity. Despite his many striking qualities, Olds would in time lose that sense of balance, to the detriment of the parish's well-being.[56]

Such problems appeared remote during the roaring twenties when the relative prosperity of a large congregation and its visitors made it easy to be an effective caretaker of St. Augustine's patrimony. In terms of size and wealth, the congregation reached its apex. The debt, which

56. Although admired for his pastoral compassion, Olds gained a reputation in the diocese over the years as a poor administrator. See intv., author with Msgr. E. Robert Arthur, 20 Jun 1995, cy in SAA. Arthur is a close observer of the administration of the archdiocese and was a friend and colleague of Msgr. Olds.

totaled $19,620 at Father Griffith's death in 1919, was liquidated with-in two years. The parish routinely met all its obligations despite the considerable extra burden imposed by caring for needy African Amer-icans across a wide swath of northwest Washington. In forwarding St. Augustine's modest contribution to the annual Indian and Colored Mission collection, Olds grumbled that the parish was taxed for so many things that it was "well nigh broke." Pointing out to the chancel-lor that the parish's assessment for the diocesan charity appeal was over $1,000, the same amount asked of larger, far wealthier parishes, Olds added: "I'll guarantee that we gave more to the poor last year than any church in the city."[57] The obvious point of these comments aside, St. Augustine's for once had few material concerns, and in fact the first tentative discussions were taking place concerning the possi-bility of abandoning the old Fifteenth Street neighborhood in favor of a new site where modern parish facilities—a larger church, school, rec-tory, and convent—might be constructed. Meanwhile, the need to pro-vide spiritual assistance to a congregation of nearly 3,800 and to par-ticipate in the work of the many parish organizations severely taxed the staff, which was often augmented by visiting priests from the Catholic University and elsewhere. In 1923 the archbishop sent St. Augustine's a third regular assistant, but in less than a year the parish was back to three priests.[58]

A Grid of Segregated Parishes

Most Washington Catholics seemed oblivious to the effects of dis-crimination on their black neighbors and tended to blame the victim for the crime. As early as 1906, for example, *The Patrician,* a widely

57. Ltr., Olds to Gene [Connelly], 21 Mar 1922, cy in SAA.

58. Ltrs., Olds to Curley, 22 Mar 1923, O-948, Curley Papers, and Rev. Joseph J. Deppe [assistant pastor, St. Augustine's] to Connally, 13 Jul 1922, Chancery Papers, "Parishes-Washington, D.C." Both in AAB. Father James J. O'Connor, the senior assis-tant, would not be replaced when he was transferred at the end of 1923, leaving Fathers Deppe and Robert J. Froehlich to serve a congregation that was beginning to dwindle with the opening of the new black parishes. The congregation's exact size during this era remains a puzzle. The habit of rounding off all official counts at 3,000 raises suspi-cion about the accuracy of such statistics. The figure used here is an extrapolation based on the more accurate baptism and burial figures.

read local Catholic monthly, called the Washington press to task for its frequent discussion of racial problems, warning journalists against constant agitation of the "Negro question."[59] Although all wished the black man well, the author piously concluded, he will soon believe "that he owns the country and can prevent free speech and intimidate the President." Encouraging this attitude was "clearly doing the Negro a great wrong." Cardinal Gibbons sounded a similar note in 1913 when asked to appeal to President Wilson on behalf of racial justice in government employment. After defending his own racial record, he rejected any such activist role as "impolitic," since he was unacquainted with the President and any such request would imply criticism of the new administration.[60] In 1915 *The Patrician* was back again with more advice on racial matters. This time Msgr. William Russell, the pastor of St. Patrick's, lectured the faithful on the social and political mores of the day, bemoaning the fact that "the Negro is pampered."[61]

No such moral obtuseness inhibited the Roman Curia. Convinced that black Catholics were being abandoned and efforts to evangelize black Americans were at a standstill, the Vatican set out to investigate race relations in the United States. The main points of interest included the need for an independent bishop to take responsibility for black Catholics, discrimination in Church institutions (in particular at the Catholic University) and the ordination of black priests.[62] In June 1912 Cardinal Gaetano DeLai had sent the apostolic delegate, Archbishop Giovanni Bonzano, information received by his Consistorial Congregation criticizing racial conditions in the American church. The congregation was preparing to discuss the matter, and to that end the cardinal ordered Bonzano to supply Rome with facts and, after consultation with local observers, to submit proposals. Two American priests with considerable experience in the black apostolate, Paulist John E. Burke, head of the new Catholic Board for Negro Missions, and Josephite John Albert, both submitted remarkably accurate data and

59. *The Patrician* (Dec 1906), pp. 6–7.

60. Ltr., Gibbons to Thomas W. Turner, 17 Sep 1913, Turner Papers, HUA.

61. *The Patrician* (Nov 1915), pp. 1–14.

62. The following discussion is based on Father Cyprian Davis's study of these documents best summarized in his *The History of Black Catholics*, pp. 198–220, and Stephen Ochs's *Desegregating the Altar*, pp. 226–40.

progressive proposals, among other things stressing the need for black clergy, a seminary for their training, and a bishop appointed especially to supervise them. Bonzano, however, ignored their advice when answering DeLai, adopting instead an unreconstructed stance. Although he admitted that the key to evangelization of black America was an increase in the number of priests dedicated to that mission, he dismissed the idea of a black clergy. African Americans, he insisted, preferred white priests, whom they perceived to be "from a superior race and hence had greater trust placed in them."[63] He offered little hope for developing black priests. Despite his personal acquaintance with the educated and highly articulate spokesmen of St. Augustine's congregation, models of moral probity and solid citizens, he questioned the lax morals of black Americans in general, pointing out what he called their "proclivity to material pleasures." He also dismissed the notion of creating special administrative machinery in the American church to encourage black converts and protect their interests.

In marked contrast to Bonzano's hostile and tactless comments, the always diplomatic Cardinal Gibbons sought to placate Rome's concerns by reporting at length on the hierarchy's efforts since the Third Plenary Council to address the subject of a black apostolate. He admitted that African Americans wanted black priests and professed himself anxious to develop a black clergy. In the end, however, Gibbons offered no more hope than Bonzano. Surveying the effects of Jim Crow on America, conditions, he stressed, over which the Church had no control, he claimed that the obstacles to an African-American clergy "are seemingly unique and the problem would require delicate handling." Yet the need was evident, "and never lost sight of by those who have the evangelization of the colored race at heart."[64] Such nobly expressed sentiments betrayed the cardinal's ability to simultaneously appear masterful but remain inactive. Once more Gibbons carried the day. Although his report had largely ignored the treatment of black Catholics, especially the lack of educational opportunities beyond elementary school, it was enough to convince Vatican authorities that at least some progress had been made and no new directives were called

63. As quoted in Davis, *The History of Black Catholics*, pp. 206–7.

64. Ltrs., Gibbons to De Lai, 28 Mar 1914, 113-G-1, Gibbons Papers, and Olds to Curley, 22 Mar 1923, O-948, Curley Papers, AAB.

for. Actually all Bonzano and Gibbons had done was to buy the hierarchy a little time. DeLai's response was really a thinly veiled criticism of the American bishops, and further agitation on the race question was sure to provoke further scrutiny from Rome.

Such agitation began with a group of activist laymen at St. Augustine's. Washington's black Catholics were never indifferent to the paternalism and segregation encountered in every area of religious life, but the catalyst who transformed their concern into an organized response was Thomas W. Turner. By any measure Turner, a staunch layman, was a relentless crusader for justice in the American church. Born into a Catholic family in Charles County, Maryland, in 1877, he managed, despite formidable economic handicaps, to acquire a basic education and graduate from Howard University. A gifted biologist, Turner enrolled in Catholic University's graduate school in 1901, where he studied until forced to find work to support his family. With some help from Fathers Griffith and Slattery, he joined the faculty of the Tuskegee Institute and later Baltimore High and Training School.[65] Turner returned to Howard in 1913 to teach biology. There he was active in the NAACP, leading its hugely successful local membership drive. He also retained a lively interest in Catholic Action. Once he pleaded with Cardinal Gibbons to donate a copy of the *Catholic Encyclopedia* to Howard University, which had "little money but many Catholic students." Not only would this be a charitable act, he added, "but it would be extending the faith in ways which we know not."[66] During his years as a leader in the fight for racial justice in the Church, a fight that began at St. Augustine's, the scholarly Turner remained a dedicated educator and scientist. In 1921 he earned a doctorate from Cornell University before going on to serve for many years as chairman of the science department at Hampton Institute.

After their success in obtaining social welfare support from the bishops for black servicemen, Turner and his small group of fellow

65. Ltrs., Griffith to Slattery, 6 Dec 1901, 13-P-5, and Slattery to Griffith, 7 Dec 1901, 13-P-6. Both in ASSJ. For a summary of Turner's career, see Marilyn Nickels, "A Tribute to Thomas Turner," *Impact* 6, no. 3 (Apr–May 1976).

66. Ltr., Turner to Gibbons, 9 May 1919, 126-G-6, Gibbons Papers, AAB. Howard got its encyclopedia, but the donor most likely was St. Augustine's parish, not the cardinal.

parishioners continued the habit of meeting at his home to discuss racial conditions in the Church. This group, which became known as the Committee of Fifteen, concluded that the key to the evangelization of black Americans and the nurturing of black Catholics was the formation of a black clergy. It followed that seminaries must begin to accept black candidates and that, transcending the demands of simple justice, Catholic education must be made available to black students for the very pragmatic reason of inspiring and fostering vocations. These laymen also believed that the needs of black Catholics would be known only when their representatives had a voice in all Catholic societies and activities. Dubbing themselves The Committee Against the Extension of Race Prejudice in the Church, they announced their aims to Cardinal Gibbons and other members of the hierarchy.[67]

The committee decided to take advantage of the meeting of the country's bishops in September 1919 to air their specific grievances. In the wake of the bloody race riots that had renewed Vatican interest in the plight of African Americans, these laymen, all St. Augustine parishioners, presented a lengthy brief describing in considerable detail the all-pervasive racism in the Church.[68] Declaring that the Catholic church would be truly Catholic only when African Americans were made welcome, the committee promised to work for "better feeling and closer union among all Catholics" and to remove all barriers that kept black men and women from the "temporal and spiritual graces" of the Church. But it added a warning. Its members would continue to investigate discrimination and present evidence of such injustices to the proper ecclesiastical authorities.

Despite international interest in America's bloody race relations,

67. Ltr., Turner, et al., to Gibbons, 23 Dec 1918, 124-C-4, Gibbons Papers, AAB. Signing with Turner were J. Arthur Stenson, Eugene Clark, Joseph Wade, and Thomas W. Short. Although Turner later claimed that the committee was organized in 1915 (see ltr., Turner to Gibbons, 7 Jan 1919, 124-G-4, Gibbons Papers, AAB), it seems likely that he was dating it from the first informal meetings of his friends. It appears certain that the committee was formally created in late 1918.

68. For a detailed account of the committee's charges, see Davis, *The History of Black Catholics*, pp. 216–20. The following quotes are taken from this source. This first annual meeting marked the birth of a national organization of the American bishops that eventually evolved into today's National Conference of Catholic Bishops and the U.S. Catholic Conference.

the bishops once again satisfied themselves with issuing a vague declaration against racial hatred, concluding with the insensitive and patronizing exhortation that black Catholics should learn "from their
teachers the lesson of Christian virtue."[69] Turner and his group ignored this unctuous advice and, true to their promises, continued to
publicize examples of racism. In November Turner sent a copy of the
committee's brief to the apostolic delegate and solicited his help in
fighting discrimination. He focused on two charges: the Josephites
refused to admit black candidates to their seminary, and the Catholic University now barred black students, a special hardship for
black teaching sisters, who, denied the opportunity to attend summer
courses in education, were finding it difficult to obtain state certi-
fication.

At the same time Turner commenced a debate with the president of
St. Mary's Seminary about the failure of that institution to admit black
candidates. After some hedging, Father Edward R. Dyer admitted that
to accept African Americans would make it impossible to serve a great
many bishops "who would be unwilling to commit their subjects to us
if we received colored students." Professing his personal desire for
black priests, Dyer quoted President Grover Cleveland to justify St.
Mary's policy: "It is a condition, not a thing that confronts us."[70] Turner, a devout Catholic, was not above scoring a moral point when he
could. He questioned Dyer's assertion that the bishops would object to
admitting black candidates and asked Dyer to have them canvassed on
the subject, reminding him that "colored people are frequently denied
justice and equity simply because one white man bumptiously objects." As for Cleveland, Turner remarked, he was a politician, a Cae-
sar, not a bishop and a representative of Christ.[71]

Having painted himself into a corner, Dyer hastily amended his argument. Actually it was the seminarians, not the bishops, he explained, who objected to integration, going on to note what was surely
a first: the bishops were merely bowing to the seminarians' wishes and

69. "Pastoral Letter of the Archbishops and Bishops of the United States, 1919," as
quoted in Davis, *The History of Black Catholics*, p. 217.

70. Ltrs. Turner to Dyer, 11 Oct 1919, TWT-26, and Dyer to Turner, 14 Oct 1919,
TWT-27. Both in Sulpician Archives, Baltimore (hereinafter SAB).

71. Ltr., Turner to Dyer, 18 Oct 1919, TWT-28, SAB.

not imposing on them "a condition which would be exceedingly difficult for a very large number of them to accept." Dyer also dismissed
Turner's demand that the Church take a stand against discrimination,
declaring it unnecessary for the religious and social development of a
people "that they mix and commingle indiscriminately with a distinct
people." He professed opposition to segregating black Catholics in a
corner of a church. His solution: create a separate portion of the
church from front to back for African Americans.[72] Apparently to this
notable director of priest formation, discrimination was primarily a
matter of horizontal geography. Unfortunately, Dyer's level of racial
sensitivity was typical of many Catholics in the 1920s.

Turner's committee received no more satisfaction from Cardinal
Gibbons when it renewed its complaints against discrimination in the
Josephite seminary. Gibbons denied that qualified African Americans
were turned away; he claimed that admission was based on fitness, not
race. He asked Turner to use his influence to assure "your people" that
much was being done and that "there is not a Bishop in the United
States but what is concerned with the spiritual progress of the Colored
Race and doing all in his power along that line."[73] As the future would
clearly demonstrate, Gibbons's dubious assumptions were rejected by
black Catholic leaders and his exhortation fell on deaf ears.

As Jim Crow's hold on Washington strengthened after World War I,
Cardinal Gibbons and his successor sought to make segregation more
palatable by making it more efficient. This period saw the formation of
five new parishes (a sixth and last, St. Benedict the Moor, would be organized during World War II) which, when added to St. Augustine's
and St. Cyprian's, would constitute a separate system meant to serve
black Washington. These eight parishes formed a separate grid imposed on the map of city parishes. Their boundaries, thus extending to
the District's borders, overlapped the boundaries of several white
parishes in the process. In time each of them (with the notable exception of St. Augustine's) would be given into the care of the Josephites,
whose status as a missionary society added to the isolation of these
congregations from the rest of the diocese and its diocesan clergy. This

72. Ltr., Dyer to Turner, 23 Oct 1919, TWT-29, SAB.

73. Ltrs., Turner, et al., to Gibbons, 1 Mar 1920, 131-P, and Gibbons to Turner, 15
Mar 1920, 131-P2. Both in Gibbons Papers, AAB.

isolation would be strengthened over the years by the racially separate branches of diocesan organizations in these parishes such as the Holy Name and Sodality. It was made even more explicit when Archbishop Michael J. Curley, Gibbons's successor, decided to centralize the reception of confirmation in the city, and along racial lines. Beginning in 1923, all white confirmations would be held at St. Patrick's; the sacrament would be dispensed to black Catholics at St. Cyprian's.[74]

Since its founding in 1893—an event marked by a parade of 10,000 Catholics, including a large contingent from St. Augustine's— St. Cyprian's had grown to rival the mother church in size and wealth. By 1913 it enrolled 340 children in its free school (also conducted by the Oblates), supported a home for the aged, and had almost paid off the debt on its large church.[75] In 1914 a third parish (begun as a mission dedicated to the Incarnation) was founded in Deanwood, a small black community in the far northeast section of the District. The congregation grew slowly, numbering just 570 by 1930, but it was destined for a steady rise as that neighborhood grew during World War II.

In 1920 two more black parishes were added to the roster. As early as 1910 black Catholics at St. Dominic's had petitioned the archbishop for a separate church in Southwest. Gibbons agreed and asked the Josephites to assume responsibility. Finally in 1919 a temporary home was fitted out for what was then called Good Shepherd, but this enterprise was abandoned less than a year later when St. Vincent de Paul Church on South Capitol Street was turned over to the black congregation as white parishioners left that neighborhood. The recently refitted building was converted into a parish school. That same year Our Lady of Perpetual Help was organized across the Anacostia River for the black Catholics of St. Teresa's, who for several years had been holding separate services in the basement in anticipation of forming a separate parish. Beginning in 1918 a large group of St. Aloysius's black parishioners had attended separate services in the basement of the church on North Capitol Street. Four years later this group, under the direction of a Josephite father and with the help of the Jesuits, organized a new parish, Holy Redeemer, on New York Avenue. Another part of the

74. *BCR*, 23 May 1923. In later times the combined confirmations would prove unsatisfactory, and the sacrament was again administered in individual parishes.

75. *CM*, 30 Sep 1893, and *BCR*, 6 Dec 1913.

city map was filled in when Epiphany parish formed in 1925 to serve black Catholics in Georgetown.

It must be stressed that the creation of these parishes was actively sought and gratefully accepted by most black Catholics of those times. Weary of being merely tolerated in the neighborhood church, they envied the status of African Americans at St. Augustine's and St. Cyprian's and their active participation in the full panoply of parish associations. Overlooked in the general euphoria, however, was the ominous direction such separatism was leading to in Washington. Beginning with St. Augustine's establishment as a so-called national parish a half-century before, the dual system of parishes had produced the notion, contrary to canon law and the decrees of the Council of Trent, that black Catholics should be limited to attendance at black parishes. Catholics quickly began to think in terms of "your" church and "our" church, making it easier for racist congregations and their racist or complacent pastors to "refer" any African American entering "their" church to the nearest "black" church with a clear conscience. By 1930 the Catholic Church in Washington, which had resisted the trend for more than a century, finally joined its Protestant brothers and sisters in dividing its congregations racially.

Still, some ignored the trend. Through nostalgia or stubborn loyalty, but mostly because of sheer geographical convenience, some African Americans, especially among the elderly, elected to remain in their old parishes, albeit in segregated seating, where they continued to participate in the liturgy and some of the parish's religious associations. Particularly notable for the continuing large number of African Americans in their congregations were Holy Name and later St. Anthony's parishes, whose boundaries included large black neighborhoods far removed from any of the new black churches. But here also the inevitable result of continued second-class treatment could be seen, especially among the young, upwardly mobile. They refused to submit to such discrimination. While a few made the special effort to travel the long distances to St. Cyprian's or Holy Redeemer, many, rationalizing that such distances excused them from attending mass, quietly drifted away.[76]

76. Foley, "The Catholic Church and the Washington Negro," p. 152, notes the case of some 800 fallen-away black Catholics living within the confines of Holy Name Parish in the 1930s.

The development of the black parish system would have a profound effect on the fortunes of St. Augustine's. In 1922 the parish boundaries were officially set for the first time. Henceforth St. Augustine's was responsible for black Catholics living between Eighth Street, Northwest, and Rock Creek and from the Mall to Gerard Street. The men of the parish attempted to take a census of the congregation that year, but typical of any large downtown church, the results were inconclusive.[77] What was obvious to all, however, was the loss of many from the parish's eastern sections to the new Holy Redeemer congregation. Also apparent was how quickly black Catholics in other sections of town were developing new loyalties. The pull of the old mother church was weakening. St. Augustine's was now but one of eight black parishes, about to face the severe trials produced by a great depression with its loyal black and white parishioners slowly diminishing in number and affluence.

77. *BCR*, 29 Mar 1922.

SEVEN 🕮 TRIUMPH AND

ITS AFTERMATH

*T*he rapid organization of additional parishes for the city's
African Americans would soon challenge St. Augustine's primacy, but during the 1920s at least, the mother church of Washington's
black Catholics continued to lead the way both in terms of material
prosperity and of influence. Despite Jim Crow's persistent hold on the
Church and its institutions, the sight of the integrated congregation at
St. Augustine's and its active lay leaders spurred on the progressives
in their fight for a future where segregation, either forced or self-imposed, would give way to a unified community of believers.

No one during that decade could predict the massive challenge
that would confront the black community during the years of depression and world war that followed. Nor was St. Augustine's prepared for
the sudden change in its fortunes during the 1930s. Bold plans made
in the years of prosperity would have to be shelved while the embat-
tled congregation struggled to save its patrimony. If the triumph over
similar trials in the past gave confidence, the slow reduction in membership and the growing demands on increasingly meager resources
made the outcome this time far less certain. Of necessity, the congregation's focus during the Great Depression was inward looking. Ironically, this concentration on material things occurred just when the first
glimmer of racial reform appeared in the American church. Although
so often in the lead in the past, St. Augustine's parishioners might be
forgiven their failure to detect the coming changes, given their arch-

bishop's quixotic treatment of prominent black lay leaders and the racist stance of pastors and congregations in their immediate neighborhood. Nevertheless, new forces for reform were beginning to gather, forces that would radically transform the Church in Washington and St. Augustine's in particular during the coming decades.

A Decade of Triumph

Thanks to Thomas Turner and other activist members of the congregation, St. Augustine's remained in the vanguard of the fight for racial justice in the 1920s. Their Committee for the Advancement of Colored Catholics persevered despite the continuing indifference of the hierarchy and a noticeable cooling in Vatican interest. Their efforts were both encouraged and hampered by Cardinal Gibbons's successor, Michael J. Curley, who arrived in Baltimore in November 1921. For the Irish-born Curley, Baltimore represented a promotion from his post as bishop of St. Augustine, Florida, where he had shown a pastoral concern for black Catholics and an interest in evangelization of African Americans. There too he had earned headlines for his forthright defense of sisters arrested for teaching black children. These experiences, however, had not prepared him for dealing with the articulate black laymen in his new diocese, especially the educated members of Turner's group, professionally successful and politically adept activists.[1]

Curley seemed genuinely shocked when Turner and Eugene Clark confronted him on his first trip to Washington in January 1922 with their specific complaints about the failure of seminaries and the Catholic University to admit African Americans. After consulting with the head of his own seminary and the rector of the university, Curley dismissed the complaint, exhibiting what historian Peter Hogan called a pragmatic hesitancy to achieve social change by confrontation. Attempting to justify his position, the archbishop went so far as to report to the apostolic delegate that black Catholics preferred white priests. As for segregation, Curley concluded that the Church should "leave

1. See Hogan's "Archbishop Curley and the Blacks," pp. 2–16 (especially regarding Curley's defense of the teachers, pp. 2–3), and Stephen Ochs's summary in his *Desegregating the Altar*, pp. 242–45.

well enough alone," explaining that "it would be the height of impudence" to suggest that blacks and whites mingle in churches in the South.[2]

In keeping with these views Curley sponsored the formation of new black parishes and actively supported the Cardinal Gibbons Institute, a school for African Americans at Ridge, in St. Mary's County. Organized by Father John LaFarge, S.J., with seed money left for that purpose by the late cardinal, the institute followed the Tuskegee pattern, combining basic academic subjects with practical training in agricultural, industrial, and mechanical sciences. It also boasted an extension program aimed at improving the homemaking and agricultural skills of people in the area. Turner was offered the position of principal, which he rejected, but both he and Washington's Judge Robert Terrell served on its board of trustees.[3] The school opened with twelve students in 1924 in a handsome building paid for by a substantial grant from the Knights of Columbus and a $10,000 contribution from the black Catholics of Baltimore and Washington. Lacking regular diocesan support, the school was forced to close in 1933. At Archbishop Curley's prompting it reopened five years later under Jesuit management, but its finances always remained precarious. Over the years it remained a favored charity of St. Augustine's congregation.[4]

Like his predecessor, the new archbishop approached the idea of organized black protest warily, and his early relations with the committee of St. Augustine's activists were stormy. In 1922, for example, members of the committee met with others interested in raising funds for the Cardinal Gibbons Institute then forming. Their host for the occasion, Josephite Father Francis Tobin of Holy Redeemer parish, took exception to their comments on the proper role of black Catholics in devising policy for black schools. His abusive behavior prompted a complaint to the archbishop, in which the committee raised the stakes

2. As quoted in Ochs, *Desegregating the Altar*, p. 242.

3. Material on the school can be found among Turner's papers, HUA. See also John LaFarge, *The Manner Is Ordinary* (New York: Harcourt, Brace, 1954), pp. 208–16.

4. St. Augustine's William Prater was president of the institute's board of trustees, which pledged to raise the money for the buildings. The kick-off drive in January 1924 opened with a parade of the city's Colored Catholic Auxiliaries and a Mass at St. Augustine's. See *BCR*, 12 Jan 1924.

by questioning what they considered the Josephite Society's paternalistic attitude toward African Americans and demanding its removal
from Washington's churches. Curley, in response, scolded the group
for provoking what he termed useless agitation. An unrepentant Turner
shot back at length, reiterating his group's criticism of the Josephites
and conditions at Holy Redeemer.[5]

Turner had been hearing similar complaints from representatives of
various black Catholic organizations around the country during their
visits to the capital to coordinate support for the new black high school.
Following a series of meetings with these new allies beginning in early
1924, he decided to form a national organization to discuss and publicize their complaints. From the first he was determined that his Federation of Colored Catholics, as he called it, would avoid the mistakes of
the old Colored Congresses, which, he believed, were dominated by
priests who thought they could speak for black men. As Turner later
explained, he wanted "an organization of Catholic men, not a Catholic
organization." In this he took Father Olds's advice. There would be no
meetings presided over by clergymen. Black Catholics were going to
run the show. The meetings would remain true to Church doctrine, but
they would be directed by "the sort of folks that Black people could be
sure were safe."[6] To act independently yet win clerical support required the group to walk an exceedingly fine line. The new federation,
Turner explained to Mother Katharine Drexel, was designed "to provide Negro Catholics the opportunity to confer among themselves and
with their white friends as to the best means of providing the welfare of
the colored." Turner had no doubt about what such means were. His
group wanted "to integrate the Negro minority into the corporate life of
the whole church rather than to seek how we might segregate ourselves
further as a means of escape from our present handicaps."[7]

5. Ltrs., J. Arthur Henson [secy. of Turner's committee] to Curley, 30 Dec 1922, H-
792, and Curley to Henson, 5 Jan 1923, H-791, and Turner to Curley, 18 May 1923, T-
790. All in Curley Papers, AAB.

6. Intv., Turner with Marilyn Nickels, 24 Mar 1973. See also Nickels's intv. with
William and Mary Buckner. Cys in SAA.

7. Ltr., Turner to Mother Katharine, 22 Aug 1924 (first quote), and Turner, "Essay
Prepared on the Origins of the F.C.C. [n.d.] (second quote). See also, ltr., Turner to Fellow Catholics, 15 Oct 1925. All in Turner Papers, HUA.

The new federation's first convention was held at St. Augustine's in December 1925. Archbishop Curley, who had agreed to serve as spiritual director, addressed the gathering, which, in addition to spokesmen for black Catholic groups from around the country, included representatives of the orders and societies in the Church devoted to the black apostolate. The success of the meetings allowed Turner to practice a little diplomatic fence mending. Thanking Curley for his participation and his "wholesome and sane advice," the new federation's president continued: "We feel highly grateful that the activities which we have set for ourselves fall so completely within the scope of those laid down by Your Grace."[8]

St. Augustine's pastor played an active role at the convention, and even more so at the second gathering, also hosted by the parish, the following year. At that time Olds addressed the delegates on the struggle to found St. Augustine's, a story largely unknown to this new generation of black Catholics. He also stressed the need to drop individual differences and develop a unified approach to race problems. A highlight of the second convention was the opening mass celebrated by Father Norman DuKette, one of the country's first black priests and a son of St. Augustine's. DuKette also led a delegation of conferees to visit the new apostolic delegate, Archbishop Pietro Fumasoni-Biondi, and outline for him the needs of African-American Catholics. (Father Olds, reflecting a political daring rare among parish priests, had recommended that the federation involve the apostolic delegate as a counterweight to some of the more resistant members of the hierarchy.)[9]

Although decidedly uneasy about it, Archbishop Curley continued to support the federation throughout the 1920s. He personally welcomed delegates to the fourth convention in Baltimore in 1928 and, following their meeting in Detroit in 1930, agreed to put their request for financial support before the Negro and Indian Mission Board. He was not sanguine about this move. Even if the federation received fifty

8. Ltr., Turner to Curley, 9 Dec 1925, cy in Turner Papers, HUA.

9. Intv., Nickels with William and Mary Buckner. See also, Report of the Convention of the Federation of Colored Catholics, December 5 and 6, 1926, cy in Turner Papers, HUA. Senator David I. Walsh of Massachusetts was the principal speaker at the second convention.

times the amount they requested, he noted, that sum would only meet 5 percent of their need.[10]

Thus the decade ended on a high note for the reformers. Their organization had grown rapidly in size and notice and, more to the point, some of their demands were beginning to be heeded. Foremost among these was the issue of black priests. Although little progress was yet to be registered among the Josephite or secular seminaries, the opening of a seminary by the Society of the Divine Word at Bay St. Louis, Mississippi, promised to begin filling the need. This institution had received encouraging support from the Holy See and some progressive American bishops who, in turn, had been bombarded with demands by the federation. If the tactics adopted by Turner and his allies would be fiercely debated in the decade to come, their goal—an integrated Church with its many societies and organizations opened to all people of faith—remained clear and would be adopted by all church reformers in the days to follow. In reflecting on this important reform movement, it is well to remember that many of its first leaders were parishioners of St. Augustine's, whose wholehearted support sustained the reformers in their crusade.

Even as it participated in these significant events, St. Augustine's was developing plans for an ambitious building program that reflected the status and needs of a major Washington parish. Only partially executed in succeeding years, this program produced a financial crisis that would endure for decades, ending only when the congregation moved into its present location almost a half century later. The pastor's plan made sense at the time. The parish desperately needed a modern, spacious schoolhouse but found it prohibitively expensive to build in what was now the center of Washington's professional and business district. Truth be told, even the church itself, revered by parishioners as a symbol of the struggle and accomplishments of their forebears, was increasingly inconvenient for the majority of worshippers, most of whom lived a considerable distance to the north. It was one thing to cater to the needs of transients and those working in the neighborhood,

10. Ltrs., Curley to Federation, 5 Oct 1928, T-795, and to Turner, 3 Oct 1930, T-797, and 12 Dec 1930, T-798; Turner to Curley, 29 Sep 1930, T-796. All in Curley Papers, AAB.

but, given the value of the property, why not build a new parish plant elsewhere, letting the proceeds from the sale of the old property pay the costs?

Archbishop Curley had made Catholic education the cornerstone of his strategy for the diocese, and Olds skillfully played to that interest when he broached the subject of a move in October 1924.[11] He had found property, he told Curley, just seven blocks from the church, which, at twice the size of the present school and convent grounds, would be ideal for the much-needed school and hall. The cost of about $40,000 was easily affordable, he added, because sale of the old school and convent would bring in an estimated $100,000. Olds had already obtained a city permit to build a school and auditorium on the property, which was located on Thirteenth Street between R and S Streets, then headquarters of the Women's Christian Association.[12]

Although the archbishop's response was quick and to the point— "Go ahead and purchase the new site"—the deal was never consummated.[13] Three years would pass before another property was found, this time seven blocks north on Fifteenth above R Street. The site of the Washington Home for Foundlings, this property was considerably larger than the Thirteenth Street plot and, with the addition of two neighboring lots, also available, would easily accommodate not only the school complex, but a large church and rectory as well. Its location on broad Fifteenth Street adjacent to the prestigious Fifteenth Street Presbyterian Church added to its desirability, but it also affected the price. After lengthy negotiations, the parish agreed in February 1928 to pay $93,000, including two initial payments of $10,000, the second of which would be due in June. (An additional $33,000 was added to

11. Ltr., Olds to Curley, 2 Oct 1924, O-949, Curley Papers, AAB. On Curley's well-known championship of Catholic schools see, for example, account of his "Address to Washington's Catholics," *Evening Star*, 14 Mar 1922.

12. Ltr., John W. Oehmann [D.C. Inspector of Buildings], to Olds, 18 Sep 1924, SAA. The city permit carried a condition: since the property was in a residential zone, any entertainments held in the proposed auditorium must be directly restricted to school or church activities.

13. Ltr., Curley to Olds, 3 Oct 1924, O-950, Curley Papers, AAB. Surviving records are silent on the reason the deal fell through.

the debt in April 1929 when the parish purchased the two adjoining lots with houses at 1717 and 1719 Fifteenth Street.)[14] At a mass meeting in the church basement on February 24 the congregation heard their pastor promise to build "the finest parochial school in the city" and a parish hall that could seat 1,000. The latter would serve as a gathering place for teenagers of all faiths—not a dance hall, the pastor added, but a center "for evenings of clean and wholesome pleasure." Other speakers, including the District's school superintendent and Senator David I. Walsh of Massachusetts, praised the plans, and the parishioners showed their approval by pledging $12,000 on the spot to meet the second payment.[15]

At first everything went according to plan. The pastor hired an architect, Maurice F. Moore, to design a complete parish complex and a builder to carry out the first phase of the project. In December the old school and convent were sold for $133,900. Unfortunately, as later events would demonstrate, the contract specified only a small down payment with the parish holding a $100,000 note due over a three-year period.[16] Completion of the new school building was scheduled for October 1929; the new convent and auditorium to follow shortly thereafter. The three-story, state-of-the-art building, designed in the Tudor style, contained twelve classrooms built above a large basement for playrooms and support facilities. It was situated on the northeast corner of the site behind the convent, itself a handsome, two-story stone-faced Tudor building with pitched slate roof. The Oblates, unaccustomed to such luxurious surroundings, immediately dubbed their new home "the castle."[17] The auditorium, rising south of the convent, also faced Fifteenth Street. As revealed in the architect's plans, drawings of which appeared in the press in the summer of 1929, this auditorium was designed to serve in time as the crypt or basement of a large Tudor-Gothic church in dressed limestone with carved buttresses along its lengthy sides separated by stained-glass windows. The church's

14. Property Purchase Contracts (signed by Father Olds for Archbishop Curley), 6 Feb 1928 and 20 Apr 1929, SAA.

15. A lengthy account of the parish meeting was carried in the *Washington Tribune*, 2 Mar 1928.

16. Deed of Sale, 21 Dec 1928, SAA.

17. Intv., author with Sister Mary Alice Chineworth, O.S.P., 18 Dec 1996.

west front was to be dominated by a carved stone canopy and rose window adjoining a ninety-foot bell tower. The tower base would provide a separate entry both to the church narthex and to the auditorium below. In those last heady days of the roaring 1920s, the generally prosperous congregation confidently expected the sale of the old church property and the completion of the new complex to be a simple, ongoing process that would find them in their new church in the near future. In the meantime the auditorium, utilitarian in aspect, would serve as a center for parish functions.[18]

Unfortunately, state-of-the art schools and Gothic churches carried outsized price tags, even in the 1920s. The pastor had estimated the total expense of all parish buildings at around half a million dollars, but when the cost of the school-convent-auditorium complex alone was added to the mortgage on the property, the parish suddenly found itself facing a $375,000 debt. True, it held a $100,000 note from the purchaser of the old school, and as late as October 1929 Father Olds was still confident that the sale of the church and rectory would take place "at an early date." According to his calculations these assets would allow the parish to move into its new buildings "comparatively free of debt."[19] Olds's confidence was not shared by the archbishop, who had been taking a close look at the parish books and as a consequence was becoming decidedly cool to the idea of moving ahead with the new church and rectory. Comparing parish statistics for 1921 and 1928, he pointed out that the size of the congregation had fallen 15 percent in seven years, with the number of infant baptisms and converts dropping by almost 50 percent. Even the school population had fallen from 236 to 171 pupils. Although income had risen slightly, the parish carried a huge debt in 1928. The trend was unmistakable, and, he pointed out to Olds, "it would be well to keep these figures before you with an eye to the future."[20]

18. *Washington Post*, 27 Oct 1929. Detailed descriptions of the new parish complex and architect's drawings were published in several papers, including the *Washington Times*, 27 Sep 1930. All on file in SAA.

19. As quoted in the *Washington Post*, 27 Oct 1929.

20. Ltr., Curley to Olds, 23 Feb 1929, O-953, Curley Papers, AAB. The archbishop would repeated his warning a year later. See ltr., Curley to Olds, 25 Feb 1930, O-957, same source.

Typically, the builder failed to complete the school on schedule. Dedication was postponed until December, and the school opening delayed until January. By then many parents deemed it practical to leave their children in the public schools, where they were temporarily enrolled, for the rest of the school year. But this setback did not diminish the satisfaction of the crowd that flocked to the dedication ceremony. They listened to Bishop John McNamara read a message from the archbishop in which the plain-spoken prelate complimented them "for setting a pace in the matter of progressive achievement for every colored congregation in the Country."[21] The ceremony concluded with a march led by the uniformed Knights of St. John and other parish organizations up Fifteenth Street to the new building, where the congregation gingerly stepped around the unfinished convent walls and the footings of an auditorium which everybody by then was confidently calling "the church basement."[22]

A Decade of Trial

Little noted during the festivities surrounding the dedication of the new school was the stock market crash in October, which ushered in the greatest depression in the nation's history. As the economic situation worsened in succeeding months, Washington watched local businesses fold, banks fail, and government salaries be cut. Construction of the Federal Triangle and projects in the District's own public works department helped stave off the worst, but the racial practices of Washington's trades unions meant that little of this work was opened to black residents. A new president, Franklin D. Roosevelt, brought some hope to the jobless, not so much because of his New Deal programs, which did little to improve the lot of black Americans, but because the administration of the many new government programs added significantly to the government payroll, thereby promising an upturn in

21. Curley could not attend, but he specifically asked that his remarks be included in the program. See ltr., Curley to Olds, 14 Nov 1929, O-955, Curley Papers, AAB. See also, ltr., Olds to Curley, 12 Nov 1929, O-955, same source.

22. The dedication was described in the *BCR*, 6 Dec 1929. Organizers of the ceremony included William J. Smith, chairman, Genevieve Burke, and Dr. Eugene Clark.

local business. Hope went largely unfulfilled when whites won most of the jobs and black entrepreneurs failed to share in the renewed commerce. Economic hardship visited all classes and colors, but poor blacks were the hardest hit. And their numbers were rising dramatically with the arrival of thousands of newcomers desperately fleeing the abject poverty of a depressed, rural South. Without public work or safety net, these unfortunates crowded into the city's alleys and slums, looking to their neighbors for help and competing with them for any menial work that came available.

Like everyone else in those dark times, St. Augustine's parishioners had no money to spare, not even enough to attend the always popular parish dances—a sure sign, the pastor reported, that they were broke.[23] Still, Olds remained optimistic. Once the convent and auditorium were completed, he explained to Curley in February 1930, a large loan would become available. With that and the expected payment of what was owed on the old school and convent, the parish could make do until the church was sold. Then, he concluded, "You will not have much cause to worry, and an immense load will be lifted from my shoulders."[24] As it turned out such optimism was ill-founded. As economic conditions worsened in the capital, the parish's precarious financial status imploded. The purchaser of the school property, equally hard-pressed, could not meet his obligation, and the parish had to sell his note at discount.[25] With payments due on the parish's loans, Olds was forced to take out short-term, high-interest notes just to avoid foreclosure. As a result, indebtedness rose out of control. Adding to the woe, architect Moore began dunning the parish for money he claimed was owed him on the uncompleted parts of the project. The dispute, including Moore's threatened lawsuit, was suspended at least temporarily when the hard-pressed parish paid the architect a hefty settlement.[26] A

23. Ltr., Olds to Curley, 2 Mar 1933, O-967, Curley Papers, AAB.

24. Ltr., Olds to Curley, 20 February 1930, O-956, Curley Papers, AAB.

25. Ltr., Claude Warren [real estate manager] to Curley, 30 Jun 1932, Chancery File, "Parishes-Washington," AAB.

26. Agreement between Abp. of Baltimore and Maurice F. Moore, 19 Nov 1932, Chancery File, "Parishes-Washington," AAB. Many documents relating to the lengthy feud are located in SAA.

chastened pastor, harried by creditors and with no place to turn for relief, confessed to the archbishop in 1933 that he firmly believed "it is
the Grace of God, only, that has kept me from losing my mind."[27]

Curley stepped in. He refused to sign any more loan extensions.
Instead, he gave Olds $10,000 and arranged for several better-off
parishes to loan $20,000 more to keep the creditors at bay for another
year. Meanwhile he canvassed Baltimore's financial circles to find
some institution willing to consolidate St. Augustine's many debts into
a single loan at a lower interest rate. But with the debt rising monthly,
he admitted that little could be done to ease the situation until the
church was sold.[28] The sale of the church and rectory was also the pastor's fervent hope. In March 1933 he had reported that the District government was expressing interest in the site. "If they will only buy it, he
added, "we will not have to worry much about paying for our new
buildings."[29] But like previous rumors, this too proved false. Finally in
October 1935 a serious offer was negotiated by the prominent real estate broker, John Saul. Lest this happy prospect raise false hopes in
the pastor and congregation, Archbishop Curley issued a clear warning:

Whatever money is acquired, if a sale is made, must go to part payment of
your debt, minus the amount that might be necessary to put your new Rectory
into fairly decent living condition.

There can be no question whatsoever of doing anything with the upper
church until such time as we are in a position where we shall have no debt
and plenty of money ahead. I do not think that you and I are going to live to
see that time.

27. Ltr., Olds to Curley, 2 Mar 1933, O-967, Curley Papers, AAB. For a detailed
account of the efforts between 1930 and 1936 to rescue St. Augustine's from its financial problems, see ltrs. and rpts., O-956 through O-978, Curley Papers and the St. Augustine documents in the Chancery File, "Parishes-Washington," AAB.

28. Ltrs., Curley to Olds, 14 Mar (O-968), 10 Jun (O-973), and 4 Nov (O-974) 1933,
and 10 Jan 1934, O-975. All in Curley Papers, AAB. Olds borrowed from four pastors.
Holy Name's Father John W. Dowling refused until, ordered by Curley, Olds repeated
the request (see ltr., Curley to Olds, 4 Apr 1933, O-972, same source). In the end several of the parishes turned the loans into gifts (see, for example, ltr., Charles R. O'Hara
[pastor, Holy Comforter], to Lonnie [Olds], 11 Jul 1946, SAA).

29. Ltr., Olds to Curley, 31 Mar 1933, O-970, Curley Papers, AAB.

The rectory to which Curley referred was two structures included in the 1929 purchase situated on the south end of the property near the new auditorium. These, he believed, could be combined and converted into a suitable home for the priests. He was putting all this in writing, he added, to counter any moves by "that famous Architect"—his name for the litigious Moore—who, he suspected, would be back with fresh demands when he heard about the sale of the old church.[30]

Curley's letter is important because it clearly indicates that, as early as 1935, the archdiocese had given up all idea of building the new church. If the old church sold, St. Augustine's congregation must be content to worship, for the foreseeable future, in the suitable but hardly salubrious setting of their new auditorium. No doubt a prudent resolution, the decision to cancel plans for the new church was made without reference to the wishes of the congregation and without seeking the advice of its leaders. That such practices were the norm in pre–Vatican II times did not allay the pain it would cause parishioners when it finally came about or counter their belief that somehow a black parish was once again being dealt with in an exceptional manner.

This latest effort to sell the church failed at the last minute, but some financial relief was realized when the archbishop obtained a loan consolidating the parish debt, which by January 1936 amounted to more than half a million dollars. Through a special arrangement backed by the principal of a large bequest given the archdiocese, the Safety Deposit and Trust Company of Baltimore also agreed to apply part of the parish's monthly interest payments to the principal, thereby reducing the debt incrementally.[31] Even to meet this reduced payment proved a challenge. Contributions from the hard-pressed congregation remained exceedingly modest throughout the decade. In January 1932, for example, only 357 parishioners were able to make any regular contribution, and their donation averaged just 60 cents each per week. Despite periodic claims that the Depression was over, succeeding years were hardly better. By the first quarter of 1937 some 540 families

30. Ltr., Curley to Olds, 5 Oct 1935, O-977, Curley Papers, AAB.

31. Minutes of the Archdiocesan Board of Consultors Mtg., 10 Jan 1936, AAB. The peculiar arrangement, made possible by the company's management of the O'Neill bequest, was spelled out at a Consultors meeting on 3 Oct 1944, AAB.

contributed to the Sunday collection, but by then the average per family had dropped to half the earlier total.

The constant search for money led to some innovative schemes. To attract some of Washington's wealthy Catholics and visitors to the city, Olds scheduled noon masses during Lent (where collections brought in $50 per week) and a 12:30 high mass on Sundays. The beauty of the choir and the appeal of the fashionably late hour succeeded in attracting a large contingent of the well-to-do. Reasoning that more might come if the hour were further advanced, Olds gradually inched up the time toward the unheard of hour of 1:00 P.M. The result was an overflow crowd of 2,500 at the last mass, not only a money maker, but an outstanding exhibition of interracial amity.[32] In February 1936 a disconcerted archbishop finally put an end to what he considered the exceedingly unorthodox state of affairs. "After very careful consideration," his office announced, "the best interests of Religion require the canceling of the very late masses."[33] If the beautiful choir and the late hour of services was going to attract rich, slug-a-bed Catholics, they would have to do with a mass beginning no later than 12:15.

As in the past, parish organizations worked hard at fund raising. In March 1937, for example, the Holy Name Society sponsored a Grand Easter Social that attracted a large, money-spending crowd with good food and a popular dance band. That same month the Junior Club, a young adult group organized in 1934 by Mrs. Katherine Dean, also sponsored an Easter entertainment as well as a father-daughter dance. Not to be outdone, the Sodality donated $210 to the debt fund, the receipts from several of its recent card parties and other social events, while the young people organized a Sacrifice Club that raised money through pancake parties and dances and theatricals.[34] In fact by this time the worst of the crisis had passed. Under the consolidated loan the parish was meeting its monthly obligation without help. In the late 1930s payments on the debt were averaging more than $15,000 annu-

32. Foley, "The Catholic Church and the Washington Negro," p. 147.

33. Ltrs., Rev Joseph M. Nelligan to Olds, 16 Feb and 1 Mar 1938, Chancery File, "Parishes-Washington," AAB. See also ltr., Olds to Curley, 19 Feb 1934, O-976, Curley Papers, AAB.

34. The *St. Augustine's Parish Review* described many of these events during the 1930s. Those noted are from the April 1937 edition, cy in SAA.

ally.[35] Although most of this was used to meet the interest payments on a debt that now totaled over $600,000, the parish's income had finally started to rise (the $54,800 realized in 1941 more than doubled the 1933 figure), and the debt slowly began to recede. After examining the books in September 1941, an obviously relieved archbishop reported to his consultors that St. Augustine's financial problems were "gradually being solved."[36]

Such relief might be expected from one who bore the ultimate financial responsibility for the parish, but finances were just one element of the crisis facing St. Augustine's parishioners in a city where racial discrimination remained the rule. Ironically, considering the terrible economic hardship it produced, the Depression saw the first signs of improvement in the status of Washington's people of color. In part these first small victories in the long battle just beginning over Jim Crow's hold on the capital occurred because the black community itself rediscovered the power of united action. The hard times that affected everyone were also attacking the stultifying class divisions that had inhibited Washington's progressive black leaders from action in past decades and had caused many of the city's best and brightest to flee to New York where a healthy openness was transforming Harlem into a mecca for black culture. An effort to unite Washington's black society could be seen in the organization of the New Negro Alliance led by William H. Hastie, dean of Howard's law school, James Nabritt, later president of the university, John Aubrey Davis, and others. These determined activists reasoned that the best weapon against economic discrimination was the boycott. They began by picketing businesses in the U Street area that refused to employ black workers. Early successes spurred them on to fight discrimination in the city's major department stores and grocery chains. In 1938 the Supreme Court recognized their constitutional right to exert consumer pressure on businesses that discriminated, paving the way for Martin Luther King, Jr., and the rest of the civil rights heroes of later generations.

If the promises of equal treatment implied in the New Deal, espe-

35. Ltrs., Olds to Nelligan, n.d., and Nelligan to Olds, 14 Oct 1936, Chancery File, "Parishes-Washington," AAB.

36. Minutes of Consultors Mtg, 30 Sep 1941, AAB. See also "Compilation of Income and Debt of Sts. Augustine and Paul's Churches, 1911–1961," n.d., cy in SAA.

cially in such agencies as the Works Progress Administration, the Civilian Conservation Corps, and local public housing agencies, proved largely illusory, other signs of change were not long in coming. The Community Chest, which since its founding in 1928 had drawn the city's charities together in an integrated organization, prepared the way for the interracial cooperation that others soon followed. In 1935 the Washington Federation of Churches invited black churches to join, and three years later the National Council of Christians and Jews followed suit. The split in the union movement in 1937 saw the progressive Congress of Industrial Organizations (C.I.O.) begin to challenge the racial discrimination of the older trade unions in the capital, not only on the job but in all its social activities. All these groups were influential because, by forcing the races to interact, they began to break down the barriers that sustained the two, separate societies.

The following year, 1938, saw the formation of a local branch of the Urban League dedicated to the idea that interracial progress and economic justice were attainable through mutual understanding and persuasion. This more conservative approach achieved few successes before World War II, and black Washington's attention continued to focus on the NAACP, which sought to safeguard the rights of African Americans in the Federal government in its evolving relief and recovery programs. In 1939 one of its demands was answered when the attorney general organized the civil rights section in the Department of Justice, which after a slow start would figure so prominently in the civil rights revolution soon to begin. Meanwhile, labor leader A. Phillip Randolph's credible threat to organize a mass march on Washington in 1941 prompted President Roosevelt to create a Fair Employment Practices Committee to investigate discrimination in wartime industry.[37]

All these organizations and movements were portents of a better future, but in Washington, as elsewhere, the overwhelming strength of the forces of discrimination that had developed unchecked over the decades remained largely undiminished. Nothing better symbolized the state of racial affairs in Washington than the DAR's refusal in 1939

37. A useful summary of these activities can be found in *Freedom to the Free; Century of Emancipation, A Report to the President by the U.S. Civil Rights Commission* (Washington: GPO, 1963), pp. 107–17.

to allow Marian Anderson to sing in Constitution Hall. Secretary of the Interior Harold Ickes, who had already made significant improvements in the way his department treated black employees, immediately arranged for the contralto to perform on the steps of the Lincoln Memorial. The fact that this supremely gifted artist was denied equal treatment on account of race received national notice and provided thoughtful Americans more convincing proof of the inherent injustice of segregation.

Catholic activists were yet another group that found the 1930s a time of trial. For Thomas Turner and his allies in the Federation of Colored Catholics especially, the division that arose among Catholic progressives early in the decade marked the end of their control of the fight for racial justice in the Church. A pragmatic leader, Turner had always welcomed support from white Catholics; in particular he welcomed two Jesuit priests, the charismatic William Markoe and the intellectual leader in the American church's fight for social justice, John LaFarge.

Markoe was a dynamic champion of racial causes in St. Louis, where he had worked successfully to attract hundreds of black converts to the Church. But where Turner saw in the almost exclusively black federation a vehicle for the empowerment of the black laity, Markoe found the group with which he became affiliated in 1931 too narrowly focused on blatant forms of discrimination and ignoring the larger objective of evangelization of all black Americans.[38] Both agreed that changing white attitudes was essential, but they strongly disagreed over the role of white Catholics in this evolution. Turner, recalling the failure of the old Colored Congress movement, which had degenerated into a discussion group dominated by the clergy, insisted that a sustained, aggressive fight against discrimination in the church demanded black leadership in a black-dominated organization. Only black Catholics, he argued, truly understood the problem and were willing to confront it directly by demanding the redress of specific grievances from the hierarchy, who could enforce reforms. He wanted an organization similar to the Hibernians, which would provide a unit-

38. The dissolution of the federation is discussed in Nickels' comprehensive study, "The Federated Colored Catholics." Davis provides a useful summary in *The History of Black Catholics*, pp. 221–29.

ed voice for black concerns.[39] In this Turner was borrowing a technique developed in the NAACP, an organization in which he also played a leading role. Markoe, on the other hand, argued that the organization's first objective should be the transformation of white attitudes. To that end it must teach whites to understand that segregation, like other forms of discrimination, was evil. Their consciences thus appealed to, they would be led to join in an effective fight for racial justice. It was essential, therefore, that the federation be interracial in character, and whites share in its leadership.

Although Father LaFarge was not directly involved in the clash that followed, he too was a strong proponent of the interracial approach. The fight against discrimination was not an end in itself, but just part of this great thinker's philosophical construct that looked to a reform of the whole social order based on faith and providing hope and justice to the disaffected. First he sought an intellectual change. Get leaders of both races to talk to each other and come to understand their Christian calling by serving as witnesses to racial justice. These lofty principles would come to animate his Catholic Interracial Council, which would figure so prominently in the great changes to come in succeeding decades.[40]

The dispute over whether the federation should be racially exclusive led to a split in the organization in 1932. By then many members, principally from western and northern states, had become frustrated with the repeated failures of Turner's confrontational approach. In particular they were disappointed with the leadership's effort to lobby the bishops to lift the racial bar at Catholic University. Although Cardinal William O'Connell was sympathetic to their demands, he accepted the judgment of university authorities as expressed by Rector James H. Ryan to Dr. Eugene Clark, the president of Miner's Teachers College and Turner's loyal lieutenant, "that, without prejudice to the case, the time is not ripe to admit colored students to the University."[41] A major-

39. Ltr., Turner to Curley, 3 Apr 1933, T-807, Curley Papers, AAB.

40. The debates in the Federation as well as the ultimate consequence of the ideas put forth by Markoe and LaFarge are explored by John T. McGreevy in his *Parish Boundaries: The Catholic Encounter with Race in the Twentieth-Century Urban North* (Chicago: University of Chicago Press, 1996), especially chapter 2.

41. Ltr., Ryan to Clark, 27 May 1932, Turner Papers, HUA.

THOMAS WYATT TURNER, organizer of the Federation of Colored
Catholics and a leading crusader for racial justice in the American
church.

ity of delegates to the federation's 1932 convention agreed with Markoe
and his allies that the word *interracial* should be added to the organization's title, signifying a change in philosophy. Eventually Turner and
the delegates from the Washington region accepted a compromise,
agreeing to the unwieldy name, National Catholic Federation for the
Promotion of Better Race Relations. The wary truce that followed was
shattered when Markoe arbitrarily changed the name of the federation's journal to the *Interracial Review*.

Through months of intermittent squabbling, members of St. Augustine's congregation steadfastly supported Turner and his method of fighting discrimination. In particular Dr. Clark defended the original concept of the federation as set out in its constitution. In this he was supported by St. Augutine's William Prater. Prater served as the federation's agent/organizer. He traveled widely to recruit new members and report on conditions in local churches. His insistence on confronting local authorities led him into a dispute with the Markoe faction. Both St. Augustine's Marcellus Smith, who served as the federation's secretary, and William Miner actively supported Turner. Along with Father Olds they were among the older federation members present in November 1932 when Clark, in an effort to mediate the dispute, invited both Turner and Markoe to meet in his home. This summit meeting failed, and Turner was subsequently removed from the presidency during an executive meeting of the federation. The lines of battle were drawn. Speaking to a gathering of 300 delegates from various organizations representing Washington's black Catholics in February 1933, Father Olds reiterated his support for Turner and the aims of his organization.[42] Following a series of similar meetings around the country, seventy-five of Turner's loyal supporters, including the members from St. Augustine's, gathered in the Holy Name Guild Hall in Washington in June to condemn his ouster in what Clark and others derisively termed a "rump session."

In the end Turner and his friends resigned from the renamed organization, and in August they convened what they called the Ninth Annual convention of the Federation of Colored Catholics at St. Augustine's. Following mass in the old church, the delegates, all from Pennsylvania, Virginia, Maryland, and the District, retreated to the auditorium at Fifteenth and R Streets for their business session. Turner was installed as president of the greatly reduced group, and the delegates agreed, among other things, to resubmit his most recent list of demands to the next meeting of the American bishops.[43] All of Wash-

---

42. *Baltimore Afro-American*, 25 Feb 1933. The controversy received exhaustive coverage in this leading black newspaper. See, for example, issues of 24 and 31 Dec 1932 and 14 and 21 Jan 1933.

43. The proceedings of the ninth convention, along with the resolutions adopted, are summarized in *The Voice* 1, no. 1 (1934), cy in ASSJ.

ington's black parishes sent delegates to this and subsequent conventions, several of which were held in the city. (The eleventh convention, for example, met for three days at Holy Redeemer Hall and closed with a reception and ball at the Odd Fellows Hall at Ninth and T Streets.) Following in Archbishop Curley's footsteps, his auxiliary Bishop John M. McNamara addressed the 1935 convention, which was also attended by the superior general of the Josephites, Father Louis B. Pastorelli.[44] St. Augustine's Holy Name, its Catholic Beneficial society, and the St. Monica's Auxiliary all publicly pledged their support.[45] Nor did their enthusiasm seem to wane when Turner, pleading illness, stepped down from the presidency. He was succeeded by George A. Henderson of Pittsburgh, and later by Eugene Clark.

The division among the reformers proved tragic for both factions. The larger group allied to Father Markoe survived for only a few years while the reconstructed federation continued to meet until 1954. Its members always retained a touching faith in the idea that Rome and the hierarchy would correct racial wrongs. For their pains they were generally treated by the bishops they approached as troublemakers.[46] Although to the end the federation retained a small group of local loyalists, they found themselves increasingly marginalized as most progressives gravitated toward the more energetic Catholic Interracial Council during the 1940s. Ironically, the argument over method proved irrelevant. Effective reform, when it came, proved to depend not only on the authoritative voice of individual bishops, but also on the conscience-driven reformation of an informed laity.

For one usually so forthright and strong-willed, Archbishop Curley remained uncharacteristically remote from the federation's internecine battle. Declaring himself unwilling "to get mixed up in this very unpleasant affair," he removed himself from contact with both Turner's and Markoe's groups, although both continued to claim him their spir-

44. *Evening Star*, 30 Aug and 1 Sep 1935. See also illustrated account of McNamara's presence at the convention in the *Baltimore Afro-American*, 4 Feb 1933.

45. See ltrs. to the Federation from W. A. Prater (HNS); Sadie Primus (Catholic Beneficial Society) and M. G. Eskridge (St. Monica's Auxiliary). All reproduced in *The Voice* 2, no. 1 (1935), cy in ASSJ.

46. Mary Buckner clearly expressed this idea in her intv. with Marilyn Nickels.

itual director.[47] The evidence suggests that Curley was influenced to a great extent by his close advisor on racial matters, the Josephite Father John Gillard. Gillard himself was highly critical of what he considered the radical and presumptuous actions of black laymen, but it certainly took no urging from any advisor for the always publicity-shy archbishop to bridle at the news generated by the lay group. Curley was particularly irritated at accounts of discrimination in his diocese that had appeared in the NAACP's *Crisis* and the *Baltimore Afro-American*—stories, he was convinced, that emanated from Turner's friends in Washington and the Cardinal Gibbons Institute.

Actually, like many prelates of that era, Curley is difficult to classify when it comes to race questions. Throughout the rest of the decade and on into the war years the often-ailing archbishop continued to exhibit a frustrating dichotomy when considering the concerns and needs of black Catholics. On the one hand, some genuinely progressive steps occurred during these years, if not on his initiative then certainly with his approval and sometimes with his determined support. At the same time, much of the mindless racism that had infected his diocese since the worst days of Jim Crow was allowed to continue unabated. Without clear and forceful direction from the top, church officials fluctuated widely in their reaction toward the progressive impulses that were beginning to breach the walls of segregation in the Washington church.

The first sign of progress during these years was the lifting of the color ban at Catholic University. At the urging of some members of the faculty and university officials, the once-open school had begun to close its doors to black students before World War I and until 1933 had successfully resisted the demands of reformers and the Vatican to reintegrate its student body. At that time Archbishop Curley, the university's chancellor, reacting to complaints from the superior of the

47. Ltr., Curley to Turner, 30 Mar 1933, T-806, Curley Papers, AAB. Curley's stand-off attitude is revealed in his increasingly acerbic exchanges with Turner during 1932–33. See, for example, ltrs., T-802 through 807, same source, and unnumbered ltrs., same period, Turner Papers, HUA. The discussion of this colorful and energetic archbishop that follows is based on the perceptive and balanced summaries by Peter Hogan in "Archbishop Curley and the Blacks," and Thomas Spalding in his *The Premier See*, chap. 13.

Oblates, insisted that black sisters who needed university training to win their teaching certificates be admitted to the Sisters' College. Dismissing critics, Curley noted that "the few white nuns who will object are unworthy of their calling."[48] Sisters Mary Consolata and Mary of Good Counsel, names familiar to students at St. Augustine's, were the first two sisters of color to matriculate, soon to be joined by increasing numbers of black teachers from around the country who attended the regular summer course of study. Still, Rector Ryan and other bishops on a board of trustees that included Curley continued to resist further change, telling the apostolic delegate in 1934 that no other exceptions to the school's segregation policy would be forthcoming "due to the peculiar conditions existing in Washington."[49] Finally in 1936 a new rector, Bishop Joseph M. Corrigan, was finagled by the dean of the graduate school, Roy J. Deferrari, into admitting black students in all branches of the university. Although Corrigan, influenced by the progressive priests in the recently formed Clergy Conference on Negro Welfare, increasingly warmed to the idea of an integrated school and supported it against the traditionalists on the faculty, he nevertheless tried to impose some restrictions. Black students would continue to be barred from the residential halls and from participation in many extracurricular activities. Such demeaning treatment would endure until a new archbishop and university chancellor succeeded Curley in 1948.

Paralleling many of Washington's secular institutions, some Catholic agencies began to experiment with integration during Curley's reign. Catholic Charities, organized as a semi-autonomous diocesan agency in Washington to oversee the difficult task of centralizing the local church's charitable operations, had been an integrated and interracial organization from its beginning in 1922. Under its dynamic second director, Father Lawrence J. Shehan of St. Patrick's, Catholic Charities was linked to the Community Chest and its operations modernized by a trained staff that included a number of black social workers. Under Shehan too, St. Augustine's Dr. Clark and Daniel Spriggs

48. As quoted in Foley, "The Catholic Church and the Washington Negro," p. 195. For a brief summary on the integration of the university, see Foley, pp. 192–98, and refinements to the story by Conley, "All One in Christ," pp. 39–45.

49. Quoted in C. Joseph Nuesse, *The Catholic University of America Centennial History* (Washington: The Catholic University of America Press, 1990), p. 321.

began their long years of service on the board of directors of this vital diocesan agency.[50]

Leading the way as models of racial equality were the new so-called settlement houses. In 1935 members of Catholic University's Department of Sociology and School of Social Work under Msgr. Paul H. Furfey opened Il Poverello, a settlement house in a slum area in the eastern Shaw region. Interracial in staff, activities, and clientele, the institution emphasized individual casework and first aid for victims of economic and social poverty in Washington's alley dwellings. Il Poverello's staff of university students and part-time volunteers successfully fed and offered remedial training to a generation of Washington's desperately poor. A similar institution was established in 1940 at the instigation of Dr. Mary Elizabeth Walsh. Supported by an interracial board of directors consisting of members of the faculties of Howard and Catholic Universities, government workers, and public school teachers (including St. Augustine's William Buckner), Fides House on New Jersey Avenue was able to engage many of the city's large charitable organizations in its work. Its wide-ranging programs involved many volunteers of both races from all parts of the city.

Another important element in this first period of renewed interracial cooperation was the opening in 1935 of Blessed Martin de Porres Hospice, a Catholic Worker House of Hospitality on I Street. Inspired by its founders, the saintly radical Dorothy Day and Peter Maurin, the Catholic Worker Movement had stirred the social consciousness of a generation of Catholic progressives, including the convert Llewellyn Scott. After his wartime service as a soldier in France, Scott had returned to Washington (but not, because of his changed residence, to St. Augustine's, where he had been received into the Church) and to his modest-paying job in the federal government. Strained economic circumstances did not, however, deter him from purchasing two houses and converting them into a hospice that managed to feed and shelter nightly as many as seventy-five derelicts of both races in Swampoodle's slums. For years the university-trained Scott would return after a day's work to his little shelter, where he would spend his nights pro-

---

50. Foley, "The Catholic Church and the Washington Negro," pp. 224–25. The following summary of integrated institutions in Washington is based on Foley's comprehensive study, pp. 224–322.

viding for his derelicts. Although Scott ceased operations in 1942, this remarkable apostle to the down and out later opened a new hospice during hard times after the war.

In contrast to the many Catholic organizations that steadfastly maintained the color barrier, three groups stand out as exemplars of the interracial ideal. The Franciscan Tertiaries, or Third Order, a lay auxiliary that followed a modified form of St. Francis' religious rule, began enrolling black members in 1925. During the war an African American was elected vice prefect of the men's section and would go on to become director of the group. The women and junior sections also included many Catholics of color, who participated in all the spiritual and charitable work of the Third Order. Unlike these Franciscans, who tended to avoid group social affairs, the many black nurses in the Archdiocesan Council of Catholic Nurses, mostly graduates of Freedmen's Hospital School of Nursing, had participated fully in all the spiritual, cultural, and social activities of their group since its foundation in 1940. The no-nonsense professionals in the council arranged their meetings and activities in places that would accept racially mixed audiences, a difficult task in a still-segregated capital. They enjoyed the dubious honor of seeing their reservation to use the clubhouse of the Catholic Daughters of America canceled when, reminiscent of their sisters in the DAR, that haughty group balked at hosting black healthcare workers.

A third organization that bore witness to the ideal of an integrated Church was the Catholic Evidence Guild. This intrepid band of street preachers organized a Washington branch in 1932 when a small group of black and white laymen and women began to explain Church doctrine to people gathered in open air forums like Franklin and Judiciary Squares and in largely black neighborhoods in the South Capitol Street, Anacostia, and Lincoln Park areas. Alien to modern taste, sidewalk preaching was a popular pastime in Washington before and during World War II, and scores of black Catholics were prompted to participate. Some found achieving the guild's license difficult, but large interracial classes learned from instructors, delivered practice "pitches" before critical audiences, and shared in the guild's days of spiritual recollection.

Overshadowing all these commendable efforts was the work of the

Catholic Interracial Council of Washington. Organized in 1944 by thirty-six black and white laymen distinguished by their positions in government and academe, the council was inspired by Father LaFarge's influential New York group and reflected his approach to race relations—that is, merging black and white activists in a common effort to change attitudes and to influence Catholic institutions through education, dialogue, and witness. The Washington council began through a series of meetings, the first organized by Mrs. W. E. Gannon and the Jesuit Father Wilfrid Parsons at Georgetown University, and a second held at the home of Justine B. Ward on November 24, where officers were elected and an application for recognition by Archbishop Curley composed. The council was first led by G. Howland Shaw, a former assistant secretary of state, but the charismatic John J. O'Connor, a native Washingtonian and professor at Georgetown University, was its guiding father for many years.[51] St. Augustine's Dr. Paul Cooke, professor of English at Miner's and later president of the District's Teacher College, was a charter member and secretary of the organization. Others in this influential group from St. Augustine's included William N. and Mary Cooke Buckner, Gertrude Blackistone, Louise Briscoe, and Pauline J. Jones.

Archbishop Curley was aware of all these interracial initiatives in Washington, and if his intervention on their behalf lacked the vigor with which he approached other areas of Catholic concern, his undeniable concern for black Catholics was demonstrated on numerous occasions. For example, although no great fan of Newman Clubs, he appointed a Benedictine priest to serve as chaplain for the Catholic student group organized at Howard University in 1931. After the war he saw that a Josephite was assigned to care for the students at Morgan State. Despite his indifference to the development of a black clergy, Curley willingly appointed a black Josephite pastor of St. Joseph's mission in Glenarden, Maryland.[52] He also established a large number of black parishes throughout the diocese. Obviously counter to the interracial ideals of the progressives, these churches were ardently desired by the vast majority of black Catholics who, frustrated by the dis-

51. For a description of the council's work, see Chapter 8, below.

52. Evidence of Curley's antipathy toward the ordination of black priests is presented in Ochs's, *Desegregating the Altar*, pp. 313–14.

crimination visited on them in most parishes, yearned for a place where they could practice their faith without artificial barriers and enjoy the fellowship that so enriches parish life.[53] Over the years Curley quietly sought to ameliorate the discrimination evident in so many parishes in his diocese, admonishing pastors to ignore complaints from bigots and treat African Americans in the "kindness and gentleness of Christ."[54] Unfortunately, as will be seen in the neighborhood surrounding St. Augustine's, such quiet exhortations were steadfastly ignored by some pastors.

In the last year of his life, the old, almost totally blind lion of Baltimore roared out his strongest challenge to the bigots. Since its formation in 1918 Washington's Sodality Union had refused to admit the sodalities from the black parishes. In 1946 the prefect of Holy Redeemer's Sodality raised the point with the national director, Father Daniel Lord, who assured her that sodalists of color had a right to belong. At this point Curley stepped in, ordering his chancellor to inform the president of the union that black parishioners were to be admitted immediately. No need to put the question to a vote, he added, because exclusion on the basis of color was contrary to the gospel and Church teaching. The matter was beyond debate.[55] Curley's intervention produced an immediate change. Sodalities from black parishes were quickly affiliated with the inter-parish union. Individual members from St. Augustine's and the rest began to participate in the annual public demonstrations sponsored by the group, their delegates attending union meetings and, as the months passed, sharing in its social activities.[56]

Yet if the integration of the Sodality demonstrated the validity of Turner's thesis that bishops could produce needed reforms by fiat, the continued discrimination practiced in some local parishes also indicated the boundaries of that approach. The limits to episcopal power were underscored in the case of the notorious treatment of black Catholics at St. Paul's, St. Augustine's immediate neighbor at Fifteenth

53. Mary Buckner speaks from personal experience about this desire for socialization at the parish level. See intv. with Marilyn Nickels.

54. Quoted in Spalding, *The Premier See*, p. 346.

55. Spalding, *The Premier See*, p. 380.

56. Foley, "The Catholic Church and the Washington Negro," pp. 283–84.

and V Streets. St. Paul's had been established in 1885 to serve the rapidly growing white population in the northern reaches of St. Matthew's parish. By 1930, however, a marked ecological change had occurred in the neighborhood. The southern section of the parish, always a racially mixed area with whites traditionally living on the main streets and avenues and generally prosperous black families occupying the row houses on the side streets, had, with the exception of Sixteenth Street, become a completely black neighborhood with U Street the center of commercial and theatrical life for black Washington. During the same period the socially elegant northern section of the parish, dominated by the embassies and mansions surrounding Meridian Hill Park and the middle-class Kalorama area, remained white. By 1930 this neighborhood had been reduced to an island of white-only blocks, which fought to keep black residents moving up Fourteenth and Eighteenth Streets at bay by the use of restrictive real estate covenants.

This civic resistance had its parallel in the parish, where a pattern of minimum participation of black worshippers—to borrow the jargon of the sociologists—was rigidly enforced. In contrast to the Christian treatment afforded black parishioners by St. Paul's founding pastor, Msgr. James F. Mackin, the long pastorship of Father Cornelius Dacey, himself a native of Washington's Swampoodle area, was marked by rank discrimination. Dacey instructed ushers to restrict African Americans to the last four pews of the church. On numerous occasions he informed black visitors from the pulpit that he did not want to see them in St. Paul's. He even refused to distribute communion to black worshippers. Instances were reported of the pastor's passing over a black nun kneeling at the communion rail. Only after distributing communion to all the whites did he return to give the sister, clad in her holy habit, communion. When bad weather kept Father Olds from offering weekday mass for the sisters in their convent, the Oblates would attend nearby St. Paul's, well aware of the humiliation they were in for.[57]

Dacey's antipathy toward African Americans was well known in the city. Archbishop Phillip M. Hannan, himself a native of nearby St. Matthew's parish, later recalled the bigotry:

57. Intv., author with Sister Mary Alice Chineworth, O.S.P. Dacey's behavior is recounted in Foley's "The Catholic Church and the Washington Negro," pp. 114–19 and 139–41. Unless otherwise noted, this summary is based on Foley's work.

Father Dacey was the pastor of St. Paul's, and he was against blacks. Now part of that was that he was against everybody. I mean, he had an unfortunate temperament. All of his ushers knew it by the way—my first cousins lived in the parish, in St. Paul's, and they told me about it. I know if a black would come into St. Paul's the ushers would let them in and put them someplace where Dacey couldn't see them. But Dacey had that unfortunate attitude which was accepted by some people as the prevailing attitude of the Church. It wasn't, it was Dacey's attitude.[58]

Others at the time were unwilling to accept such behavior. Dacey's bigotry earned his parish headlines in the local black press and shocked many of St. Paul's laymen, themselves no angels when it came to racial restrictions. At one point they formed a special committee, which visited Archbishop Curley and asked him to intervene. In a lengthy exchange, Thomas Turner, once again president of the Federation of Colored Catholics, joined the fray. He provided Curley with specific instances of Dacey's treatment and demanded that the archbishop take steps both at St. Paul's and at St. Martin's, another hot spot, "to appease the disturbing situations which are continually arising." Noting that Dacey's actions were only the most extreme in a city where discrimination was common in Catholic churches, Turner repeated his conclusion that "the major portion of the difficulty is inherent in the attitude of many of the clergy." It was this attitude that was driving so many black Catholics out of the Church, he claimed. If something could be done to change such attitudes during a man's seminary days, he reasoned, "it would go far toward helping to create a better bi-racial relationship in the Church."[59]

The archbishop, unsurprisingly, viewed the situation at St. Paul's somewhat differently. In some instances, he charged, the confrontation was deliberately provoked to gain headlines in the local press. But Curley was too honest to deny the facts reported by Turner and, uncharacteristically of the old warrior, he confessed his impotence in the matter. The racial encounters at St. Paul's, for which he had "nothing but the saddest kind of regrets," were not, he pointed out, of his making. "What am I going to do to solve this Race problem?" he asked. He

58. Intv., author with Archbishop Hannan.

59. Ltrs., Turner to Curley, 21 Mar 1939, T-808 (1st quote) and 8 May 1939, T-810 (2d quote). Both in Curley Papers, AAB.

would convey the facts to St. Paul's pastor, but concerning the animosity that caused the confrontations, that would cease, he was convinced, only when both sides began to exercise good will. In the end he ducked his responsibility, advising Turner and his associates to avoid the problem. "There are several Churches for the colored in the city," he concluded, adding that if he were in their shoes "I certainly would attend one of the Churches for my own race rather than expose myself to insult."[60]

Actually, any decisive move on Curley's part would expose his diocese to a lengthy public scandal. Father Dacey was one of a small number of irremovable pastors, a position established by the Third Plenary Council to insure stability in the local diocese by giving some senior priests a lifetime assignment to a parish. These men could be removed only for the most serious offenses and then only after a full canonical trial. Curley clearly had no stomach for such a confrontation, and besides, Dacey was not the only Washington pastor exhibiting a callous bias against black Catholics. The pastors of St. Mary's and St. Martin's also tried to bar African Americans from their churches, arguing that they should be served at St. Augustine's or Holy Redeemer. When challenged by the head of the Catholic Interracial Council, Msgr. Edward L. Buckey, pastor of St. Matthew's, blandly admitted that, while all persons belonged to the Mystical Body of Christ, black Catholics "ought to go to their own parish and support their own pastor."[61]

Although it is easy to sympathize with the progressives who longed for Curley to fire one of his famous thunderbolts at these clerical miscreants, one must recognize the inhibitions that governed a man of his background when faced with so many members of his diocese, lay and cleric alike, still in thrall to Jim Crow. To generate a spirit of good will was a valid aim, and in December 1946, just weeks before his final illness began, the archbishop assembled a group of lay leaders at his residence to advise him on race relations.[62] Curley's desire to evangelize the African-American community, evident since his days in Florida, was undoubtedly sincere and undiminished. Unfortunately, to the

60. Ltr., Curley to Turner, 22 Mar 1939, T-809, Curley Papers, AAB.
61. Quoted in author's intv. with Abp. Hannan.
62. Hogan, "Archbishop Curley and the Blacks," p. 11.

end of his long career he failed to appreciate the strength of the demands for racial justice and to harness the ferment in the black Catholic community to the good of the Church.

The Good Fight

St. Augustine's parishioners, secure in their bustling downtown church, were immune to much of the blatant discrimination suffered by Catholics of color elsewhere. The hundreds of white worshippers who routinely joined them at all regular services helped form an integrated congregation that approached the ideals championed by the Interracial Council and the other progressive forces slowly gathering. These quasi-parishioners provided substantial assistance to the debt-ridden church; more importantly, their presence, as well as their cordial reception, clearly contradicted their cautious archbishop's contention that times were not ripe for integration. Nevertheless, except for the fulminations of the increasingly marginalized Federation of Colored Catholics, there was little agitation for change. The self-imposed ghetto that served to isolate all American Catholics from fellow citizens was especially apparent in the case of black Catholics. Increasingly between the wars they too came to belong to separate parishes that offered a full panoply of religious and social organizations which isolated them from the hurt and indignity suffered in congregations that insisted on segregation. While sympathetic to the aims of the activists, the average black Catholic nevertheless enjoyed and supported racially separate churches which, while isolating him from his fellow Catholics, also provided a welcome harbor from the storms of discrimination suffered elsewhere.

A danger to the health of these parish organizations was the obvious trend in population figures. Throughout the inter-war years St. Augustine's steadily lost members, as Holy Redeemer and the other new parishes began to enlist the loyalty of those black Catholics living at a distance from Fifteenth Street. By 1939 the parish rolls were down to just 1,683 names, nearly a 50 percent drop in two decades. Faithful attendance by so many white Catholics and transients tended to obscure the seriousness of the loss, but, despite a temporary upsurge occasioned by the great growth of the city during the war, the size of the

parish seemed likely to become even smaller, given the changing social composition of the population living within its reduced boundaries.[63]

The harmony within St. Augustine's only seemed to intensify the
shock parishioners felt when the ugly world of racial injustice occasionally intruded. They were especially disturbed, for example, to see
their beloved Oblates callously forced to sit in the rear of the bus when
boarding at Federal Triangle for the long trip to their mission school in
Alexandria. Sister Mary Alice Chineworth, O.S.P., herself a mid-west-
erner and newcomer to segregation, recalled years later how young
GI's, also unfamiliar with Jim Crow, would offer the standing sisters
their seats, which were prudently declined.[64] Closer to home, parishioners heard tales of their young parochial students who dropped in at
the beautiful chapel of the Sisters of the Perpetual Adoration (at 1419
V Street) to "make a visit" as thousands of pious children were encouraged to do, only to be turned away by the cloistered nuns who
wanted no part of their African-American guests.[65] More ominously,
reports circulated that a dying Catholic alley dweller, whose home was
just paces away from the walls of St. Matthew's new, cathedral-like
church on Rhode Island Avenue, was denied ministration by the nearby priests while the pastor, Msgr. Buckey, called for a priest from St.
Augustine's, a half mile away, to administer the last sacraments. Even
after Archbishop Curley's death, St. Matthew's ushers routinely enforced their pastor's policy of segregating black worshippers in the
rear pews. All requests by black Catholics for assistance were met
with a formal statement issued in the pastor's name: "We do not serve
colored."[66] Similar treatment was meted out at St. Mary's and Immaculate Conception. At the latter church especially, the frequent presence
of idealistic young students from nearby Howard and Catholic Universities resulted in several clashes with that parish's rapidly dwindling

63. *Notitiae*, various years. At the end of the war the parish census registered
2,500 members, a temporary gain of almost 800.

64. Intv., author with Sister Mary Alice Chineworth, O.S.P.

65. Intv., author with Pauline J. Jones.

66. These often-reported incidents are repeated in Foley's "The Catholic Church
and the Washington Negro," pp. 156ff, where he presents a comprehensive survey of
discrimination in the downtown parishes prior to Archbishop O'Boyle's arrival.

white congregation. Catholic chaplains at Howard estimated that many dozens of their students drifted away from the Church as a result of their treatment at Immaculate Conception.

Yet all was not doom and gloom. St. Augustine's found much to celebrate in the interwar years. All concerns were laid aside, for example, when the chance presented itself to welcome a black priest to the city. The presence of priests of color was always a source of pride and joy for Washington's black Catholics, especially when one of their own was raised to the altar. Since the days of Father Tolton, practically all of those serving in the American church found their way to the ornate sanctuary on Fifteenth Street. Father Joseph A. John, a member of the Society for the African Missions, was a guest of the parish soon after his ordination in 1923. Standing with him at the altar were Fathers John Dorsey and Charles Uncles, the first black Josephites. Father Norman Dukette's first mass in February 1926 was a cause of special celebration. Here was a young man, a member of one of the parish's large families raised on nearby Ninth Street. So great were the crowds straining to attend the event that fifteen policemen were needed to manage the press of traffic at the corner of Fifteenth and L Streets. Two hundred alumni from Dukette's alma mater (today's Loras College) were on hand to honor their classmate and thoroughly integrate the proceedings. Unfortunately, given current diocesan policy and despite Father Olds's strong urging, Dukette had been denied entrance to the local seminary and had trained for the Archdiocese of Detroit instead.

The parish's Wade family led the celebration when their son Francis sang his first mass in the old church in May 1934. Father Wade had been an altar boy in the parish, making the long trek from the family's home at Eighteenth and T Streets every morning to serve mass before attending classes at the old parish school across the street. Barred from the diocesan seminary, Wade first became a Franciscan lay brother, later joining the Divine Word Fathers at their new seminary in Mississippi. On the eve of World War II, the Josephites ordained one of St. Augustine's own, Father Chester Ball. A graduate of the parochial school, Dunbar High, and Miner's Teachers college, "Chet" Ball was a pacesetter. He attended the Catholic University a year before that school officially desegregated. He was the first black priest assigned a mission of his own in the diocese (St. Joseph's in Glenarden) and the

A PARISH FAMILY. Caroline Duckett Wade, daughter of the Duckett/DuKette family, which had worshipped at St. Augustine's since the 1870s and produced one of the nation's first black priests, is seated among her children, all baptized and educated at St. Augustine's, including Father Francis G. Wade, S.V.D., and Mothers M. Angela and M. Pius, both Oblate Sisters of Providence.

first appointed a pastor by Archbishop O'Boyle (Georgetown's Epiphany in 1952). He served as O'Boyle's personal chaplain during the 1950 Holy Year celebration in Rome. Perhaps most significantly, as historian Albert Foley pointed out, Ball's easy adjustment to the role of pastor in Washington's racially charged atmosphere helped O'Boyle open the ranks of the diocesan clergy to black candidates.[67]

The parish school proved a rich source of vocations. In addition to the priests, at least seven students went on to don the habit of the Oblate Sisters of Providence during the interwar years. Of special note, the Wade family saw two of its daughters join their brother in the service of the Church. On the eve of World War II, Mother Angela was

67. Albert S. Foley, S.J., *God's Men of Color: The Colored Catholic Priests of the United States 1854–1954* (New York: Farrar, Straus & Co., 1955), pp. 233–34. Foley provides useful sketches of many of the country's first 72 black priests.

supervisor of St. Cyprian's School while her sister, Sister Pius, was teaching in a high school operated by the Oblates in Charleston, South Carolina.[68]

The interwar years also saw another generation of parishioners making their mark in the professions. Among the many teachers in the congregation, the distinguished educators Eugene Clark, Paul Cooke, and their colleague at Miner's Teachers College, mathematician Juanita Smackum, occupied a special niche. Equally vital to the development of the upcoming generation were those who dedicated their lives to Washington's excellent public schools, including Mary Cooke Buckner, Katie Dean, Agnes and Anne Tillman, and Georgina Blackistone. The medical profession was represented by the likes of Drs. Annie E. Green, Ethel Sutton (whose non-medical attainments included service as the parish May Queen in 1913), Mary L. Gardner, and Albert Ridgely, who was remembered fondly for his stylish treatment of a large brood of daughters whom he brought to church every Sunday from their home near Ninth and S Streets in the family's gleaming Buick. The parish also boasted a professional musician, violinist Louis von Jones, who would later become the first musician of color to join the National Symphony Orchestra. In an altogether separate category was the multitalented Dr. John Edwin Washington, dentist, public school teacher, author of a well-regarded study of Abraham Lincoln, and organizer of the District's school athlete program.

Given the accomplishments of these and many other achievers in the congregation, it was small wonder that emphasis continued to center on education. No doubt stimulated by the new, well-equipped building, enrollment at St. Augustine's, which shrank in the 1920s, revived. In 1939 the school had 348 students registered; by 1945, a statistical high point, some 475 pupils were attending classes conducted by fourteen sisters. Since the days of the old Colored Catholic Congresses, parish leaders had been in the forefront of those demanding Catholic high schools for black children. They may well have been taken aback when St. Cyprian's, exchanging action for words, added a ninth and tenth grade to its school. Not to be outdone, Father Olds, ig-

68. Other parishioners joining the Oblates in that era included Harriet Robinson (Sr. Jane Francis), Elaine Dean (Sr. Monica), Helen Suydon (Sr. Cabrina), Elaine Johnson, (Sr. Celeste), and Regina Jackson (Sr. Paschal).

noring the parish's precarious financial position, followed suit in 1931. The school formed a ninth grade and Olds announced plans to establish the three remaining grades "as soon as possible."[69]

Meanwhile some of St. Augustine's alumni were making a name for themselves in the city's public high schools. The same publication that announced the beginning of a high school also noted with pride that one of the parish's former students had recently been named most outstanding scholar and athlete of the prestigious Dunbar High School and another had served as valedictorian at Armstrong High. The alumni proved loyal. To provide extra support for their alma mater they organized an association in 1932 to promote companionship and stimulate interest in ongoing school programs. Under their first president, Matilda Eskridge, they drew up a constitution which committed them to sponsoring school functions based on their substantial dues.[70] Serious support also came from the Parental School Club, which in addition to financial aid also sponsored the parish's first Negro History Week in February 1934.[71] Another group of parishioners organized a vacation school in 1936, which for a number of years in affiliation with the Confraternity of Christian Doctrine allowed local children to participate in a intensified course of religious education. The teachers, all professional educators in the public schools and college students under the direction of Gertrude Blackistone and Katie Dean, volunteered a month of their vacation time to the cause. In 1937, for example, some 140 children, including 40 non-Catholics from the neighborhood, enrolled, and the best of their work projects were sent on for exhibit in a national contest in St. Louis.[72]

Although most of the parish's mainline organizations continued life as usual in the years leading up to World War II, those focused on alleviating the hardships created by the Great Depression worked extra hard to cope with the crisis. With just twelve active members under the

69. Announced in St. Augustine's Parish Review (Dec 1931): 13. The rest of the high school was never completed, and the ninth grade was phased out early in the war.

70. The original board of officers included Marie Wade, vice-president; Octavia Tillman, Lewis Meredith, and George Dines, Sr., secretaries; and Martina Irving, treasurer. See St. Augustine's Parish Review (March 1932): 10.

71. Washington Post, 12 Feb 1934.

72. Washington Tribune, 31 Jul 1937.

direction of William A. Prater, the St. Vincent de Paul Society remained the center of charity in the parish. In 1933, for example, the Vincentians collected $1,087, monies from the church's poor boxes and private donations from a few more fortunate at St. Augustine's and neighboring parishes, which they used to buy and distribute some three tons of flour, blankets, shoes, and clothing. Nearly $400 was distributed for fuel and even for carfare for school children. The Vincentians were also able to save a number of hard-pressed families from eviction, and most important, through their connections in the community find work for scores of jobless men and women.[73] Members of the parish group participated in the integrated affairs of the city-wide St. Vincent de Paul, sometimes held in such grand settings as the Willard and Raleigh hotels, but more often in simple parish halls. In 1944 St. Augustine's hosted the particular council's annual meeting, which was dedicated to the memory of John F. Cole, a mainstay of the parish's Vincentian work for a half century and a charter member of its Holy Name Society.[74]

At the request of Archbishop Curley, who sought to include more women in the diocese's charity work, a group established a branch of the Ladies of Charity in the parish in March 1933. One of eighteen such parish units in the city, the new organization was expected to complement the work of the local Vincentians, especially in coordinating inter-parish activities at large city agencies like the home for the aged at Blue Plains and the District Receiving Home. Actually, St. Augustine's had organized a women's charitable group, the Big Sisters, more than a decade before to dispense specialized assistance to needy women and girls and prepare Christmas baskets for the poor. When the interrelated needs of family members became more apparent during the Depression, these women expanded their mission. By the time of the archbishop's request, their experiences had prepared them to assume the duties as an affiliate of the worldwide Vincentian program. Like their male counterparts, their delegates participated in the organization's diocesan meetings, which were always integrated. In fact,

73. The society's work received considerable publicity. See, for example, *The Voice* (April 1934) and various issues of *St. Augustine's Parish Review*, 1931–1937, cys in SAA.

74. Copy of remarks by Harry J. Kirk and an undated (ca. 1944) article in the *Evening Star*, Natalie Cole Johnson Papers, HUA.

MEN OF ST. AUGUSTINE'S. Members of the Holy Name Society attend the Union First Friday luncheon. Clockwise from bottom left: Mr. Hamilton, Bradshaw Vowels, Father George Joyce, Joseph Slye, Charles Whitby, Jr., Joseph Johnson, Dr. Eugene Clark, Dr. Pinyon Cornish, and Robert Murray, III.

the Ladies of Charity sometimes elected to dispense with their annual functions in years when the city's segregation laws made finding a suitable restaurant or hotel impossible. Although few in number, the parish group under its longtime leaders Mary Johnson and Addie Spriggs was closely identified with St. Augustine's efforts to cope with the Depression.[75] Armed with their collection baskets, they were a familiar sight on the steps of the church after Sunday mass and a constant reminder of the parish's continuing mission to the poor.

The work of these organizations is even more remarkable when considered in the context of the other special pleas directed at the congregation. With the strain of the enormous debt hanging over all, the parish did what it could. When a struggling group of Catholics in far out Takoma Park sought to begin a church in 1930, St. Augustine's responded by donating an altar.[76] In the mid-1930s the Christ Child Society, desperate for money to match a potential Community Chest grant for its struggling summer camp, turned to the hard-pressed congregation for support. The Cardinal Gibbons Institute was constantly pleading for help. In 1942 its students made the long trip from their rural home to present a program at St. Augustine's at which the pastor and parishioners dug deep for yet another donation.[77]

Not everything was focused on charity. The Knights of St. John and the St. Monica's Auxiliary continued their active social program during the inter-war years. In the early 1930s St. Augustine's Daniel Spriggs was appointed district deputy of the popular national organization and went on to play a key role in the drive for new members during the Depression. He was also instrumental in forming in 1940 St. Augustine's Cadet Commandery No. 8, a branch of the Knights for sixty boys from St. Augustine's and St. Cyprian's. Their smartly trained units, which featured a fife and drum corps of forty-five pieces, became featured performers in all subsequent Holy Name parades,

75. Whitby, *Golden Jubilee of the Priesthood*, p. 50; Foley, "The Catholic Church and the Washington Negro," pp. 287–89. On the Big Sisters, see *St. Augustine's Parish Review* (Dec 1931): 5.

76. *CS*, 5 Jan 1995.

77. *BCR*, 11 Dec 1942. On the Christ Child Society, see *St. Augustine's Parish Review* (Mar 1932).

which, under Archbishop Curley, remained colorful and grandiose excursions in Christian witness. Like other parishes in an age when amateur entertainment was the rage, St. Augustine's supported the efforts of its young thespians. With access to Washington's theatrical life severely restricted by Depression budgets and Jim Crow rules, large audiences flocked to the new auditorium to watch the teenagers in the Junior Club stage musical comedies and operettas. On a more serious note, the school's ninth graders also staged an annual Passion Play for a large local audience.[78]

The constant busyness involved in all these social and charitable activities did not diminish the rich spiritual life of the congregation. Despite pastoral grumbling about the sometimes sparse attendance at Holy Name functions, by any measurement the spiritual societies of the parish remained healthy, and in 1937 they were joined by yet another group, the Blessed Martin de Porres Retreat League. Organized by black Catholics from around the city, the league promoted regularly scheduled days of prayer, study, and spiritual reflection led by prominent theologians. The league also sought to increase devotion to Blessed Martin, whose heroic life was just then being discovered by a new generation of black Catholics. In fact the league's initial program for its promoters was held in a chapel in the basement of St. Augustine's dedicated to the saintly Dominican and the parish's first patron.[79] Many area Catholics would participate in the league's spiritual exercises over the decades. Included among the first twenty-two who organized the branch at St. Augustine's were Lucinda C. Dyer, Margaret A. Mahoney, Sadie E. Johnson, and Flossie Baxton and her daughter Florence.[80]

78. The musicals were given much coverage in various issues of *St. Augustine's Parish Review*. The stars of the Passion Plays, Jacqueline Biays, Constance Thomas, and Ann Nelson, were especially featured in the *Review* of April 1937. For more on the musicals, see Appendix I, below.

79. The statue of Blessed Martin that graced the old church crypt still stands in today's St. Augustine's.

80. *BCR*, 12 Nov 1937, 22 Oct 1943, and 5 Dec 1947. Other early members of the league's general committee included Ethel Briscoe, Robie Dines, Emma Jackson, Laura Ward, Ida Duvall, Marie Wade, Maria Coates, and Annie Taylor.

Like other area Catholics, parishioners coped as best they could when Washington was transformed into a wartime capital in 1942. As in the past many of the parish's sons went off to serve, this time in far-flung parts of the globe. Men like William Taylor made the supreme sacrifice while fighting in the 92d (Buffalo) Division in Italy. His brother John, who rose to the rank of warrant officer, and fellow altar boy Sgt. Carlisle Marshall, both served with the 95th Engineers during the construction of the Alcan Highway, an engineering miracle that traversed the Alaskan wilderness during the darkest days of the war. Paul Cooke served in the Army Air Corps. Carlton Smith was an Army sergeant even before war was declared, and Joseph Curtis, who with his father had sung in the Sanctuary Choir, was drafted in August 1941. Commissioned as a 2d lieutenant, he served in an engineer unit in France during the fighting. Curtis eventually rose to the rank of major in the Army Reserves. The Moore family saw six sons don uniform. William Moore served in the U.S. Navy while his brother Charles saw duty with the 92d Division in Italy. On the distaff side, Esther H. Jackson, only later a parishioner at St. Augustine's, joined the WAFEs, the women's auxiliary in the Army Air Corps, where she served with the famed Tuskeegee Airmen under then Col. Benjamin O. Davis, Jr.

Lights Out

The war was entering its last, climatic months when the parish received the gratifying news that the pope had raised their pastor to the rank of right reverend monsignor. Far rarer then than now, such an honor not only attested to the prominence of the parish and Olds's long service to the diocese, but, when bestowed on a priest long identified with the cause of racial justice, also underscored the increasing importance the apostolic delegate and Vatican officials placed on racial matters. A group of parishioners made the trip to Baltimore's cathedral on June 11, 1945, to see Archbishop Curley invest their old friend in his new purple robes. But even this heart-warming honor could not shield the aging pastor from the severe blow that would befall him less than six months later. On January 17, 1946, William L. Galvin, an attorney representing the archbishop of Baltimore, announced the sale of St. Augustine's Church and rectory for $300,000 to two Washington attorneys acting for an unnamed principal. Under terms of the agreement the parish was allowed to occupy the buildings for another year, during which time it could remove any church furnishings or other possessions it desired. The year's grace was considered sufficient time in which to renovate the auditorium at Fifteenth and S Streets into a permanent church and to prepare appropriate housing for the clergy. In fact for the past twelve years St. Augustine's had been holding regularly scheduled Sunday masses in the auditorium for the convenience of those in the neighborhood and to relieve overcrowding in the old church. Now temporary altars and folding chairs were to give way to marble furnishings and pews.[81]

Although Msgr. Joseph M. Nelligan, the chancellor, professed at the time that the archdiocese was unaware of the name of the purchaser, news quickly circulated that the *Washington Post* was the new owner. The secrecy and speed that surrounded the transaction and most of all the callous disregard, unusual even in those days, shown by diocesan officials for the opinions of the pastor and people left parishioners deeply embittered. If all were aware that no new church would be built in the foreseeable future, none, including Msgr. Olds, seemed ready for the news that they would also lose their old church. Still, for some time rumors had circulated in the parish concerning attempts by St. Matthew's influential pastor to have St. Augustine's removed from its strategic location in the downtown area. It was no secret that the African-American church had for years succeeded in attracting some of St. Matthew's most famous and generous parishioners to its services, much to the consternation of its clergy. Although it appears unlikely that such considerations figured in the sale of the church, the sense of powerlessness shared by so many black Catholics made it easy for them to believe that Archbishop Curley had betrayed them. This feel-

81. *Evening Star*, 21 Jan 1946, *Times-Herald*, 22 Jan 1946, and Washington *Afro-American*, 26 Jan 1946. The sale attracted coverage on at least one national newspaper. See *The Pittsburgh Courier*, 2 Feb 1946. The considerable problems associated with the move will be discussed in chapter 8, below.

ing translated into a general distrust of Church authorities that would last for many years.[82]

Actually the old warrior archbishop was innocent of the callous treatment carried out in his name. By now blind and often confined to his hospital bed, Curley had left the running of the archdiocese to his chancellor.[83] That bureaucrat considered the sale of St. Augustine's a simple, straightforward matter. The church, long in need of major repair, had recently been condemned by the city as unsafe when one of its walls was found badly out of line and the floor under the nave so dangerously weakened by termites that it was seen to sag under the weight of an overflow congregation. Something had to be done immediately, but the parish's precarious financial position precluded the complete rebuilding called for. Actually, Baltimore was rarely generous with its Washington parishes. As one observer put it, "they [the archdiocese] didn't have a lot, but still "they really were very very difficult about St. Augustine's."[84] It must also be remembered that the parish had been trying to sell the church and rectory since 1929. In fact in 1935 a more financially attractive offer was seriously considered only to fall through on technical grounds.[85] The effort may have been somewhat dampened but never abandoned after Archbishop Curley made it clear at that time that in case of any sale the money must be applied to the huge debt and not to a new church. In effect the decision to relocate St. Augustine's to the auditorium at Fifteenth

82. Both Foley, in "The Catholic Church and the Washington Negro" (pp. 150–51), and Muffler, in "This Far By Faith" (pp. 138–39), discuss this thesis; Mary C. Buckner gives additional details in her intv. with Marilyn Nickels.

83. Although St. Patrick's Msgr. Lawrence J. Shehan had recently been named Curley's auxiliary bishop, there is no indication that he or Bishop McNamara, the auxiliary in Washington, were consulted in the sale of St. Augustine's.

84. Intv. Rev. Rory Conley with Msgr. Louis Quinn, 31 Oct 1991, cy in AAW. There is little in archival sources about the condemnation of the old church. Archbishop Curley warned Olds in 1935 that money was unavailable to complete the renovations demanded by city officials. Mary Buckner also reports on her conversation with Olds about the need to tear down the old church in intv. with Marilyn Nickels. Foley's sympathetic account in his "The Catholic Church and the Washington Negro," (p. 150), composed just three years after the sale, offers the most information.

85. Intv., author with Father George V. Joyce, 18 Nov 1996.

and R Streets was made in 1935; it was not a secret and sudden deal in 1946.

The Solemn High Midnight Mass on Christmas 1946 marked the last celebration in the old church. His priestly career intimately tied to the building for forty-two years, an emotional pastor refused to participate. Instead he quietly offered mass for the sisters in their little convent chapel where he had been saying weekday mass for sixteen years. On the Sunday following Christmas the regularly scheduled masses took place in the basement auditorium that had now become St. Augustine's home.

EIGHT ✠ EXILE

*O*nly seven city blocks separated St. Augustine's old gothic church and the converted auditorium on Fifteenth Street, but to many parishioners the psychological distance between the two was vast. Somehow a broken, dispirited pastor and a bitter and greatly diminished congregation had to cope with the most severe social dislocation in the parish's history.[1]

In practical terms the challenge appeared overwhelming. As a result of the move the parish lost a third of its members overnight; by 1949 average Sunday attendance had slid to 1,400, a little over half the number counted in the wartime crowds worshipping in the old church.[2] Included in this loss were important elements of the congregation. Many of the articulate, activist members, disgusted with what they considered their callous treatment by Archbishop Curley and preoccupied with the interracial initiatives of Washington's progressive Catholics, simply drifted away from St. Augustine's or disassociat-

1. This introduction is based on information elicited in the author's interviews with Father George V. Joyce and Msgr. John D. Benson, both assistant pastors during the period, and Paul Cooke and Pauline J. Jones, both parishioners closely identified with many of the parish's organizations at that time. Also consulted was Marilyn Nickels's intv. with William N. and Mary C. Buckner, members of the congregation and leading Washington Catholics. Cys of all in SAA.

2. Ltr., Rev. George L. Gingras to Archbishop Patrick A. O'Boyle, 27 Oct 1959, cy in SAA.

ed themselves from its affairs. As the parish population dwindled the congregation of Holy Redeemer, the nearest black church, rose to a record-breaking 5,508 active members. White Catholics who had crowded into the old church also went elsewhere for the beauty and convenience they sought. In the parish's last years downtown the congregation for many services had numbered nearly 50 percent white. Now this generally well-heeled group gravitated to St. Matthew's or St. Patrick's, when those churches began to provide masses at the popular late hour. A third group of parishioners—African Americans, many of them converts, who flocked to Washington for jobs during the war—never developed emotional ties to St. Augustine's. Loyalty based on old family associations did not apply to them, and many simply opted for closer churches after the move.[3] All these groups had made a significant financial contribution to the parish, and their defection and the fact of the formidable debt meant that, should the churches of the archdiocese be racially integrated, St. Augustine's might well be dissolved.

Despite seemingly intractable barriers, it was becoming increasingly obvious that integration of the city's Catholic churches was in the foreseeable future. Shortly after his arrival in January 1948, Archbishop Curley's successor in Washington, Patrick A. O'Boyle, made it clear that racial justice was one of his primary aims, beginning with an ordered but progressive integration of the archdiocese. St. Augustine's, which for generations had welcomed increasingly large crowds of white worshippers, represented the one truly integrated house of worship in the capital.[4] Although the move abruptly ended this model association, the parish's lay leaders remained ardent advocates of integration. At the same time, past experience, especially the frustrations encountered by the Federation of Colored Catholics, had convinced

3. Foley, "The Catholic Church and the Washington Negro," Table 6, p. 74. Foley notes that by 1949 St. Cyprian's, Incarnation, St. Vincent de Paul, and St. Benedict's all exceeded St. Augustine's in the number of parishioners.

4. Foley (in "The Catholic Church and the Washington Negro," p. 150) estimated that "over fifty percent" of the congregation was white before the move; this figure dropped to less than 5 percent in the following three years. His figures, unsubstantiated and probably exaggerated, nevertheless describe a phenomenon recognized by others. See, for example, author's intv. with Archbishop Philip M. Hannan.

them that only African Americans could serve as authentic spokesmen for black Catholics and therefore must demand an active role in any changes taking place. Just how a greatly reduced congregation, marginalized by its necessary concern with surviving as a parish, would participate in the momentous changes about to come to its city and church remained a question.

New Challenges

Such important concerns were temporarily eclipsed by the need to adapt the auditorium for its new role and provide a home for the priests before the year of grace guaranteed by the purchaser expired. A chaotic situation developed when architect Maurice Moore insisted on his contractual right to supervise the design and execution of the work. Following a lengthy dispute with Archbishop Curley, who through his chancellor, Joseph Nelligan, managed the negotiations from far-off Baltimore, Moore's rights were recognized and a general contractor, Charles E. Wire, was hired. Another six months would pass while other locations were considered for the new rectory and for Moore to win his argument that the two little houses next to the convent should be completely remodeled in the luxurious style planned back in 1929.[5] Work finally began in mid-December 1946, just weeks before the deadline set for evacuating the old buildings.

Confirming the minor role he now occupied in these administrative matters, the pastor was forced to ask Chancellor Nelligan to request an extension of the parish's deadline for leaving the old rectory. Unmoved, the new owners stood firm on the agreed-upon date, claiming that the delay had already cost their clients thousands of dollars.[6] Nelligan seemed embarrassed by the need to ask for an extension and anxious to distance himself from the decisions that caused it. In October he had reminded Olds that the long delay in starting the new rectory "was not occasioned by this Office [the chancery] but by the decision of the Most Reverend Archbishop to do nothing until the transaction having to do with the sale of the old property was entirely

5. Muffler's "This Far By Faith," pp. 139–46, offers a useful guide through the mass of documents in SAA covering these disputes.

6. Ltrs., Nelligan to Olds, 9 Nov 1946, and Gavin to Nelligan, 7 Nov 1946, SAA.

completed."[7] No doubt Olds's reputation as a poor money manager was well earned (it would be enhanced by the cost overruns associated with his new rectory), but the blame for the fiasco that produced missed deadlines and severely disrupted parish life must also be directed at his superiors in Baltimore, who seemed bent on teaching subordinates in sleepy Washington how things should be done.[8]

With little time to spare, Olds arranged for the transfer of the altars, statues, communion rail, and other furnishings, including the sanctuary's marble flooring, to the auditorium.[9] At a later date a separate agreement was reached to remove the three stained glass windows in the apse of the old church. These and the pipe organ could not be accommodated at the new location and were donated to a needy parish.[10] Olds was also able to find temporary quarters for the priests at a considerable distance on Cathedral Avenue. From there they commuted daily to their duties at the church, a procedure hardly conducive to an image of an involved clergy or to restoring hope to a badly demoralized parish.

Boxed in by agreements his superiors in Baltimore had reached with architect and contractor, Olds was left to plead with perfectionist Moore about deadlines. The lease on his temporary quarters was due to expire in June, and he wanted Moore to fulfill his promise to have the rectory completed at that time. The absence of the priests, he pointed out, "will only further accentuate our present parish dis-organization." He was also anxious about cost overruns. He had already paid out $45,000, and he wanted an exact estimate of further expenses. As for the "auditorium," he agreed with his superiors that the cost of renovating the entrance and adding a choir loft must not exceed $25,000. No fancy adornments were called for, he added, just enough

7. Ltr., Nelligan to Olds, 7 Oct 1946, SAA.

8. On Olds's reputation as a poor money manager and the chancery's habit of mir-co-management, see author's intvs. with Abp. Hannan and Msgr. E. Robert Arthur, and ltr., Father George V. Joyce to author, 18 Nov 1996. Cys of all in SAA.

9. Agreement, St. Augustine's Church with George Reed, Municipal Decorating Co., 26 Nov 1946, SAA. Included in the items moved were the baptismal font, pulpit, and memorial tablet honoring Father Barotti. The fate of the latter is unknown.

10. Ltr., Andrew I. Hickey [parish lawyer] to Olds, 6 Feb 1947. See also Whitby, "Msgr. Olds: Golden Jubilee of the Priesthood," p. 34, The recipient of the windows and organ is unknown.

change to make the building suitable for weddings and funerals and for meeting the building code.[11] His pleas were in vain. In mid June the parish's attorney warned the chancery in Baltimore that the work would not be finished that month. Further, there was little chance of dismissing Moore from the project, since he had already applied for a District permit and was going ahead with the renovations to the auditorium.[12] The situation was exacerbated by a labor dispute involving a subcontractor who had hired a few non-union workers, actually unemployed parishioners, to help with the work.[13]

Adding to the confusion, the house the priests were using was sold out from under them. Father Olds was able to borrow a two-bedroom apartment across from Sacred Heart Church, but that meant one assistant sleeping in the living room while Father John D. Benson, the new curate, was left to camp out with friends at nearby rectories. The pastor finally took the unusual step of sending Benson home to his family in Massachusetts. This situation continued until September 1947, when Olds entered the hospital for a long stay following a serious fall, and Benson returned to inherit the couch. Olds's absence meant that Benson and Fathers Joseph Scannell and George V. Joyce were left with the formidable task of sustaining a dispirited congregation through its darkest hour and coping with the seemingly immovable architect and project director.[14]

None of the assistants had been apprised of the financial aspects of the move, but it quickly became apparent that Father Olds's poor business sense had not improved with time. During these months the Sunday collection averaged $154. Yet for all his stern warnings, Olds was apparently unable to rein in the builders' determination to make

11. Ltr., Olds to Moore, n.d. (ca. May 1947), cy in SAA. The choir loft was never constructed.

12. Ltrs., Andrew I. Hickey to Nelligan, 10 May and 11 Jun 1947, cys in SAA. See also Dept. of Public Works, case #258210, 2 Jun 1947, sub: Proposal for entrance for 1715–6 Fifteenth Street, D.C. Archives.

13. Little is known about this dispute beyond the affidavit signed by George Reed on 25 April 1947, cy in SAA. See also Muffler, "This Far By Faith," pp. 143–45. Reed was the sub-contractor charged with tile work in the auditorium interior; despite his claims, the incident appears to have been more a labor than a racial dispute.

14. Unless otherwise noted, these paragraphs on the parish in the late 1940s are based on the author's intvs. with Benson and Joyce.

ST. AUGUSTINE'S, 1947–1961. The converted auditorium on Fifteenth Street
above R beside the newly constructed rectory (far left) and convent built in 1929.

everything absolutely first class. Marble and air conditioning were lux-
uries in 1947, and they came with a luxurious price tag. In the end the
remodeled rectory cost $109,000, an overrun of nearly 100 percent.[15]
When this total and the sums needed for furnishings and alterations in
the church auditorium were subtracted from the amount realized on
the sale of the old church, only $133,000 was left to apply to the debt.
By the time all accounts were settled in 1948, including a final payment to the architect of $5,600, the parish debt once more stood well
over a half-million dollars.[16]

With their pastor still hospitalized, and they themselves about to

15. Ltr., Hickey to Nelligan, 13 May 1947, attached to draft of 1948 *Notitiae* (never
submitted to the chancery), SAA.

16. Maurice Moore, Receipt and Release, 31 Dec 1948. See also "Comparative list
of receipts and debts of St. Paul and St. Augustine Parishes, 1911–1961," n.d. (ca. Dec
1961), SAA.

be evicted from their second temporary quarters, the three assistants took matters into their own hands. They decided to move into the unfinished rectory; Father Benson, the junior man, was elected to inform the contractor. He finally got the architect and contractor to agree to a release date on the rectory and even received a donation from them in the form of kitchen appliances and $2,000 cash. To supplement the scraps of furniture rescued from the old rectory, he approached the P. J. Nee Furniture Company on nearby Fourteenth Street. It provided beds, desks, and the rest at a generous discount. Meanwhile, illness forced Father James Scannell, the first assistant, to return to Baltimore permanently.[17] Joyce and Benson carried on, and soon the cook and housekeeper were back on duty as the parish returned to some semblance of order. Once more, sick parishioners all over town were visited by priests, converts in ever-increasing numbers received instructions, and parish organizations resumed their schedule of meetings and functions. A measure of slowly improving conditions: some old worshippers considered lost to the parish reappeared. Even a few white Catholics, residents of the nearby Chastleton and other posh apartments on Sixteenth Street, began coming to the church auditorium for Sunday mass. Both Joyce and Benson were now conducting day and evening instruction classes, one following quickly on the last. Toward the end of the decade they averaged 150 converts a year, an amazing record that stemmed from the undiminished interest in the Catholic religion showed by African Americans in those times.[18] Although annual attendance figures remained shockingly low when compared to the wartime crowds in the old church, by late 1948 the new building would sometimes fill with worshippers, as it did when the celebrated orator Msgr. Fulton J. Sheen came to speak at the funeral of a friend and long-time parishioner.

The gradual return to normalcy testified to both the resilient faith

17. Scannell was later hospitalized in Baltimore, where he died of a brain tumor. His transfer immediately before the split between Baltimore and Washington further imbalanced the allotment of personnel and added to the friction between the two jurisdictions.

18. *Ebony* (in volume 1, no. 5, (Mar 1946): 28–32) summarized the results of evangelization among African Americans at the end of the war, which included 20,000 converts in 1945 alone.

of black Catholics, and an awareness in the core congregation of its heritage, a nearly century-long struggle to gain its rightful place in the Church. As their priests were well aware, they remained angry with their archbishop. Their leaders, educated and accomplished citizens, were at one with their pastor in seeing the prelate's decisions about St. Augustine's informed by a subtle racism. They would not easily be taken in again by pious exhortations and promises. Gone forever was that naive trust with which they greeted Cardinal Gibbons's triumphal visits and welcomed his promises of a better future. Nor were they deluded about the implications of the large debt. The grand gothic church planned with such joy twenty years before was never going to be. As long as segregation ruled the Church in Washington, their parish could expect no great change.

Given such attitudes, the continued progress of parish institutions seemed even more remarkable. The school remained a central focus of what was always a family-oriented parish. These mostly middle-class black Washingtonians were determined to provide their children a disciplined, Christian education. An average of 455 students were enrolled in classes under the supervision of Mother Mary Angela Wade (herself a daughter of the parish) and eleven sisters. A highlight of these postwar years—and indicative of the attainments of some pupils—was the school's performance on WTOP's "Quizdown," a weekly contest in which teams from various city schools vied for prizes in a program that tested their knowledge in a broad range of subjects. The school also won notice from the archdiocesan education office in that period for its efficient administration and accomplished pupils.[19] Since black children were still barred from the city's Catholic high schools, the parish secured the services of seminarians from the Augustinian College to conduct religious instruction classes. Every Friday night teenagers from around the city gathered for a session of religion classes followed by dancing and ping pong.

Recreation under Catholic auspices was of special concern to those involved with the parish students. Willis Thomas was in charge of the altar boys in 1946, and he and George Dines, Sr., in particular

19. Some of these attainments are summarized in a report prepared by the Oblate Sisters of Providence in 1984 entitled "The Palace," cy in SAA.

wanted to see the boys enjoying the wholesome competition of team sports. The logical answer was participation in the Catholic league then being formed by Father Thomas B. Dade, which was modeled on the Catholic Youth Organization originated by Bishop Bernard Sheil in Chicago.[20] Dade had already enlisted a board of directors headed by Leo Rover, the U.S. Attorney for the District of Columbia, to sponsor the program and drafted a group of priest-athletes to manage the games and tournaments. He also insisted on paid referees and umpires to ensure a professional operation and shield officials from the partisan demands of over-enthusiastic parents and parish priests. The idea of participating in this city-wide league and competing for team recognition would obviously appeal to young players and raise morale, so Thomas and Dines asked Father Joyce to arrange for St. Augustine's enrollment in the CYO.

CYO tradition, if not simple justice, demanded that the Washington organization defy local custom and integrate its games. Dade won agreement from a few pastors, but his board of directors threatened to resign over the issue, and most pastors, citing local attitudes, refused to cooperate. Bowing to the inevitable, Father Joyce called a meeting of representatives of six parishes and Fides Settlement House in October 1946 to form a separate league for the black basketball teams. Dade agreed to pay for the referees and supply the trophies; J. H. Cole, an official of the D.C. Recreation Department, promised to supply the necessary officials and arrange for the use of public school gyms. St. Augustine's George Dines was elected director of the separate CYO division, which sponsored two leagues, one for juniors (ages 15 to 17) and a so-called midgets league for the 12- to 14-year olds. Dines and his colleagues agreed to postpone consideration of a girls' league until the boys' league was more firmly established.

20. Intvs., author with Willis Thomas, 28 Jan 1997, and Father Joyce. Unless otherwise noted this account of the CYO is based on these interviews; a memo, George Dines, Sr., to Father Joyce, n.d. (ca. 1948), sub: Report of the Athletic Committee C.Y.O., SAA; Foley's, "The Catholic Church and the Washington Negro," pp. 270–71; and an unsigned article in the *Interracial Review* 21 (May 1948): 14. The name CYO was not adopted by the Washington group until 1948 when Archbishop O'Boyle overruled an earlier decision by the Baltimore chancellor, who hoped to avoid association with the organization founded by the progressive Bishop Sheil.

Like its white counterpart, Dines's group experienced many problems in getting parishes enrolled, organizing teams, covering extra expenses, and assuring that sufficient players appeared at the appointed time at assigned gyms.[21] The African-American league was further hampered by having to schedule its games at those odd times when the public schools were not using their facilities. For its part St. Augustine's team practiced outdoors on its own playground. Willis Thomas also arranged with Father Thomas Lyons, then connected with nearby Mackin High School and later a popular auxiliary bishop of Washington, to use the Mackin gym for practice. Despite these shortcomings, the first year proved successful. Several more parishes joined the league, and boys from across the city were on hand to attend the banquet and awards ceremony hosted by St. Cyprian's at the end of the season. Encouraged by these early efforts, the group organized a softball league and scheduled a number of social events to introduce boys to their counterparts in other parishes. From time to time during the next two years, Father Benson was able to organize games between black teams and white teams. St. Augustine's, for example, played basketball with Nativity, and its softball squad traveled to Mt. Rainier to meet St. James's team.

The league continued for two seasons before the limited number of rivals and the constant problem of scheduling games in places and times convenient to the teams and their cheering followers began to deflate morale. Dines and the other committee members discussed these problems with Father Joyce, who arranged a meeting with Dade. Left unspoken at first was the practical and fair solution. Archbishop O'Boyle's determination to integrate the diocese was by then well known, and the injustice of the current situation so struck Joyce that during the course of the meeting he abruptly recommended that Dade integrate his organization. A flustered Dade had to admit that his board of directors remained adamantly opposed to the racial policy of the national organization. For his pains, Joyce was called on the carpet by Archbishop O'Boyle the next day, not because O'Boyle disagreed with Joyce's intentions, but because the timing of his demand threatened the orderly execution of the archbishop's long-range plan for the

21. These details are covered in a series of league minutes, 19 Jan–2 Nov 1947, on file in SAA.

complete but peaceful integration of his diocese. Nevertheless several weeks later Joyce learned that the CYO director had arranged for a game between the first-place teams of the black and white leagues. (St. Augustine's, that year's champion of the black league, lost to St. Dominic's in a very public crossing of Washington's color line.) He also invited the league to renew its request for integrated games "at a later date." Instead the black parishes quietly withdrew from the CYO in 1949. The Catholic Interracial Council was not so quiet. In February 1950 both the *Post* and the *Evening Star* published letters from the council's director, John J. O'Connor, protesting the then-current $25,000 fund drive for the CYO, charging that its segregation made it impossible for many Catholics to support the organization.[22]

Such contention did not fit in with the archbishop's plans for a quiet, permanent change in racial policy. The following year he appointed three prominent African-American Catholics to the board of directors of the CYO and urged the black parishes to rejoin. Although no timetable was demanded, he made clear to the board that negotiations were to begin to produce an integrated sports organization. Eventually St. Augustine's, St. Cyprian's, and Holy Redeemer accepted O'Boyle's invitation and organized teams for the CYO, which in the more enlightened spirit of the 1950s would slowly begin to integrate youth activities in the diocese.

Finding places to stage parish events in a still-segregated city occupied much of Father Benson's time. The search for hotels that would provide communion breakfasts for parish organizations was a difficult and often frustrating experience. In some instances the parish actually helped to break down some of the city's carefully guarded barriers. In sports, for example, it won the right to play games in parks operated by the National Park Service, a first for the area. For the most part parish organizations simply avoided the problem by sticking close to home. The two assistant pastors created a usable gathering space by the simple expedient of tearing down several walls in the school. There Benson, also in charge of youth activities, ran the Friday night dance for the teenagers. With television still in its infancy, the men of the parish would gather in the rectory basement where the priests served beer and sodas while everybody enjoyed the Saturday Night Fights on the

22. *Evening Star* and *Washington Post*, 15 Feb 1950.

newly acquired, 8-inch set. As chaplain of the Sodality, Benson often found himself invited to the homes of people like Mrs. Erma B. Cornish, the prefect, and some of her long-time associates. Raised in modest circumstances himself, Benson could recall even a half-century later the gleaming silver services and other paraphernalia that graced the drawing rooms of these aristocrats of color.[23] Their teas raised $5,000 yearly for the strapped parish. Benson also arranged the first Sodality union prayer breakfast at the Franciscan Monastery, the only place he could find where two hundred black women and white women could eat together.

Another organization was added to the parish roster in these years when St. Augustine's men formed a post of the Catholic War Veterans. Post 1593 also included veterans from Holy Redeemer, and it and a similar group formed at St. Cyprian's were united with veterans from thirteen white parishes in a District of Columbia department.[24] Representatives from all these posts met monthly to promote projects and inter-post activities. Among these were a softball league (St. Cyprian's took home the championship in 1949) and the communion breakfasts and annual dinner dances. Again, the city's racial barriers interfered. The games had to be played on federally owned lots, and the black posts could not participate in the bowling league, because no alley could be found that admitted black citizens. Much time was spent finding hotels willing to host interracial groups.

One organization popular with African Americans, the Knights of St. Peter Claver, never gained a foothold in Washington. Archbishop O'Boyle was frankly skeptical when a Josephite pastor asked to form a commandary in 1949, reasoning that the presence of two such groups in town—the Knights of St. John was already firmly established in all the black parishes—would lead to rivalries and weaken both organizations.[25] With the Knights of St. Peter Claver denied admission and the

23. St. Augustine's Sodality, canonically established on 10 March 1950 by the Archbishop of Washington to conform with the new rules of the Sodality Union, was affiliated with the Primary Sodality in Rome on 6 April 1950. See ltr., General of the Society of Jesus to Archbishop O'Boyle, 6 April 1960, cy in SAA.

24. Foley, "The Catholic Church and the Washington Negro," pp. 296–97.

25. Ltrs., O'Boyle to Gingras, 13 Dec 1949, and to P. Neary [the layman proposing the new group], 13 Dec 1949, and Gingras to O'Boyle, 29 Sep 1950. All in SAA.

predominant Knights of Columbus still barring African Americans, the Knights of St. John continued to increase in popularity in the postwar period. Commanderies and cadet units were formed in six of the city's black parishes. These energized units began to dominate the Baltimore Grand Commandery of the national organization. Reflecting old attitudes, the white units responded by withdrawing from both the diocesan and the national organizations. At the national level, where a strict nondiscriminatory policy prevailed, African Americans, including representatives from St. Augustine's, played an increasingly important role in gaining equal treatment and opportunity for black knights. This progressive stance did not, however, extend to social issues arising in the church and the city at large. Dominated by an older and more conservative leadership, the Knights concentrated on their own affairs. Agitation for racial justice was restricted to their still unsuccessful effort to persuade the women's auxiliary to drop the color bar inserted in its constitution in 1922.[26]

Social problems attendant on Washington's postwar transformation into a major metropolis were slow to appear in the western Shaw region. The area surrounding the parish complex remained a relatively quiet neighborhood of modest homes dominated by apartments for more substantial residents on Sixteenth Street and the bustling commercial corridors on Fourteenth and U Streets, the latter also featuring a theater district rivaling the still-segregated downtown entertainment centers. It was a region where neighbors knew each other and boys from all over the area met for pickup games in St. Augustine's schoolyard. The almost village-like atmosphere was typified by an incident that occurred at St. Augustine's in 1949. One day the two young assistants and some parishioners were interrupted in their effort to beautify the lawn in front of the church auditorium when a large government limousine drew up nearby. Laying down their rakes and shovels, they were surprised to find themselves playing host to President Harry S. Truman. The president, it seemed, had recognized Father Benson from chance encounters during his early morning walks around town, and he had stopped for a few minutes on his ride down Fifteenth Street to say hello. Before the meeting ended the city slickers had received a

26. Foley, "The Catholic Church and the Washington Negro," pp. 298–301.

lengthy lecture in lawn care from an old Missouri farmer who also happened to be the city's first resident.

This postwar calm was not destined to last. By the end of the decade the social problems that accompanied the host of poor newcomers streaming into the crowded city had begun to intrude on the neighborhood. Petty street crime and brawls involving teenagers became more frequent; by 1950 drug use, harbinger of the scourge to come, made its first appearance in the neighborhood. So even while FBI agents sought applicants from among St. Augustine's young parishioners for a position on director J. Edgar Hoover's personal staff, Father Benson was visiting friends of parish teenagers in the D.C. lockup. The gradual neighborhood transformation would induce many of the area's middle-class black families to move away, posing yet another challenge to the parish's impulse for social action, much less its existence.

During this transformation the parish essentially operated without a pastor. Monsignor Olds had returned from his long hospital stay only to retire to his rooms. There he would visit with old parish friends and follow the fortunes of his beloved Washington Senators. In January 1948 he made one of his rare public appearances during Archbishop O'Boyle's installation. As one of the senior representatives of the city's clergy he publicly pledged his obedience to the new Ordinary. Obviously in a weakened state, he made his way across the sanctuary of St. Matthew's Cathedral on the arm of Father Chester Ball, S.S.J.[27] Later that same year the new archbishop joined St. Augustine's parishioners in celebrating the pastor's forty-fifth anniversary as a priest. A highlight of the solemn ceremony was the participation of the three priests, Fathers Dukette, Wade, and Ball, who had grown up in the parish and whose vocations had been nourished by their old pastor. The day-long festivities ended when parishioners crowded into the school library to greet Olds and watch one of their leaders, Edgar L. Kenney, present him with a substantial purse.[28]

27. For Olds's part in the installation and the subsequent celebration of his 45th anniversary, see Whitby, "Monsignor Alonzo J. Olds: Golden Jubilee of the Priesthood," pp. 33–34.

28. Kenney, an active member of several parish organizations, was at that time serving as secretary of the archdiocesan Union of Holy Name Societies.

PRIESTS FROM THE PARISH. Msgr. Alonzo J. Olds celebrates the forty-fifth anniversary of his priesthood with three sons of the parish (from left): Fathers Norman Dukette, Chester Ball, S.S.J., and Francis Wade, S.V.D.

In a certain sense Alonzo Olds was the ultimate victim of the decision to sell the old church. Although not particularly elderly even if in indifferent health, Olds was left a bitter, discouraged, and resigned man, willing to cede his responsibilities to those around him. To the end he remained accessible to old friends, who loved him for the brave battle he had waged for racial justice. They knew that over the years he had endured the taunts of bigoted colleagues who viewed long service in a black parish as a sign of mediocrity. (The same colleagues who on occasion failed to include him in diocesan functions lest he insist on bringing some of his parishioners with him.) Somehow the loss of the old church, and his failure to secure for his hard-working friends their long-anticipated new church, broke his resolve. The old crusader suddenly grew indifferent to the cause on the very eve of great change in the Church and the city. In the months following his anniversary he asked Archbishop O'Boyle to allow him to retire, citing poor health. O'Boyle agreed, and in March 1949 appointed George L. Gingras, a thirty-seven-year-old assistant at St. Francis de Sales recently returned from service in the U.S. Army chaplains, as administrator of St. Augustine's.

It is intriguing to speculate on just why the new archbishop, himself committed to a carefully nuanced strategy of racial change, would select a relatively young man whose fewer than eight years in the priesthood were devoid of any contact with the minority community or the concerns of an inner-city parish.[29] Doubtless central to O'Boyle's decision was the no-nonsense approach to parish administration that Gingras had exhibited during his years at St. Francis. Furthermore, Gingras was a close friend of Father John Roeder, one of the archbishop's principal advisors, who likewise appreciated his fellow Washingtonian's disciplined, hard-charging management style. Overriding all other considerations: at a time when many eligible priests shunned assignment to black parishes, Gingras was both available and willing to do the job.

Such willingness, however, did not indicate a progressive racial philosophy. Although born in New Jersey, George Gingras had lived most of his life in Washington, where he attended St. Peter's School on Capitol Hill before going on to Gonzaga and Georgetown University. During those years he had absorbed the racial outlook typical of white Washington of that era. He had no particular love for African Americans. As one of his associates put it, the new administrator "was born in a world of prejudice and grew up in a world of prejudice."[30] Such an attitude stood in stark contrast to that of Father Olds, who was loved and admired, not only for his championship of racial causes, but because of the obvious pleasure he received from friendships formed in

29. The following paragraphs on Gingras's philosophy are based on author's intvs. with Msgrs. Benson, Arthur, Michael T. Farina, and Leonard F. Hurley, and Father Joyce, Dr. Paul Cooke, and Pauline Jones. Copies of all in SAA. For a brief summary of Gingras's life, see *CS*, 17 Nov 1977.

30. Intv., author with Father Joyce.

the parish. His genuine interest in the welfare of the congregation was underscored by the friendly attitude of his family, especially his brother and sister, who were frequent visitors and closely associated with all sorts of parish activities. In Gingras the congregation had a distant, if correct, leader whose relatives, though living nearby, shunned the family-oriented parish for many years.

If Gingras's racial attitudes were fairly typical for a white Washingtonian of his day, they were, his associates quickly learned, not so set as to defy transformation. They found their superior ready to learn and willing to be corrected. Actually Gingras was a racial moderate, but a man who had yet to learn that black Catholics, particularly the accomplished professionals who formed the core of the congregation's leadership, had been involved in the fight for racial justice for decades and rejected the paternalistic treatment of the past.[31] Determined to have an effective pastor who would react forthrightly to the needs and aspirations of his congregation, Fathers Joyce and Benson subjected him to what in later times would be called sensitivity training. Countless hours were spent over dinner or in easy chairs discussing the nuances of race relations and arguing specific cases. Slowly Gingras grew to understand what should have been obvious: black Catholics had legitimate grievances that needed to be addressed; to be an effective pastor of one of the nation's leading black churches, one must take up its causes and earn its congregation's affection. This transformation would in time produce a new leader for the archdiocese's fight for racial justice.

Signs of Change in Church and State

The war on segregation—the fight to eliminate all the legal, administrative, and social barriers that prevented African Americans from enjoying full participation in national life—began in earnest as World War II came to an end. Nearly one million black men and women had served in the armed forces during that conflict. They used as their well-publicized rallying slogan the "Double V" sign, indicating their

31. For a highly critical assessment of Gingras at that time by one of these parish leaders, see Marilyn Nickels' intv. with William N. and Mary C. Buckner, cy in SAA.

determination to fight simultaneously for victory over totalitarian forces abroad and victory over discrimination at home. These veterans injected new life into the struggle for civil rights. In the nation's capital in particular, young black professionals were joined by increasing numbers of white neighbors to form a multitude of progressive organizations that launched a systematic assault on restrictions in public accommodation, education, jobs, and housing. Groups such as the NAACP and the Urban League, the American Veterans Committee, the Congress of Racial Equality (CORE), the Catholic Interracial Council, and the Jewish Community Council employed a wide array of techniques in a new biracial show of unity. Although the forces of reaction stubbornly resisted, the power of the Federal executive and the courts, spurred on by the continued demands of an enlightened minority, prevailed. It took eight years to accomplish, but the integration of the city's schools and public recreational facilities in 1954, following the Brown v. Board of Education decision, nearly completed a process that had already seen the opening of theaters, restaurants, and public housing and the enactment of presidential orders that effectively ended discriminatory employment in the federal government. As historian Constance Green noted, "Manifestly, a social revolution further-reaching than that of the Reconstruction era was in the making."[32]

Resistance to integration did not disappear with these victories. The rapid growth of the black population and the continued flight of the white middle class to the suburbs had convinced many of those whites remaining that the integrity of their neighborhoods and their economic well being were threatened.[33] They became desperate to maintain a firm color line by enforcing restrictive housing covenants and otherwise maintaining a wall of separation between the races in daily life. Racial tension increased during the 1950s as an increasingly secure black middle class, itself under pressure from the inner-city poor, began to spread further into formerly white bastions. Block bust-

32. Green, *The Secret City*, p. 311. This brief survey of postwar Washington is based on Green, 275–312, and Rory Conley, "'All One in Christ' Patrick Cardinal O'Boyle, the Church of Washington and the Struggle for Racial Justice 1948–1973," Master of Arts Thesis, The Catholic University of America, 1992.

33. During the war years, Washington's black population increased by half. In 1950 it stood at 280,000, more than one-third of all residents.

ing, the effort of unscrupulous realtors to prey on these fears and tensions, became the order of the day. Clearly, despite impressive progress, the civil rights revolution had just begun.

A similar rearguard action was played out in a number of local Catholic parishes and organizations even as the campaign for racial justice got underway. Actually, as historian Rory Conley has pointed out, the integration of Washington parishes affected only those traditionally white churches situated in black neighborhoods or along the ever-changing lines that divided the city racially.[34] Yet in this small group of parishes resistance was often ugly and public. For example, Washington was treated to reports during the war that the pastor of St. Martin's on North Capitol Street had bought two properties near the church to keep the neighborhood from "going colored."[35] St. Mary's on Fifth Street, Northwest, was the scene of a racial incident with international implications when one of its ushers delivered a note to a visitor, a Panamanian diplomat no less, which directed the dark-skinned man to the nearest "Negro Catholic Church." The National Committee on Segregation in the Nation's Capital used this incident in its influential 1948 publication, *Segregation in Washington*, to illustrate racism in the Church.[36] Far more serious were reports of black Catholics who, like many other government and business employees in the region, wished to attend St. Mary's popular midday novena service but were harassed by ushers. Such ill treatment culminated in a series of confrontations that eventually led some to abandon the Church in anger.

Another hot spot was Immaculate Conception, a white enclave in a largely black neighborhood at Eighth and N Streets, Northwest. There

34. Conley lists 11 parishes in the integration conflict but names only 7 in his "'All One in Christ'," p. 85: St. Dominic, St. Aloysius, St. Mary's, Immaculate Conception, St. Paul's, St. Stephen's, and St. Martin's. Four others could be mentioned: Nativity, Holy Comforter, Holy Name, and St. Matthew's. Unless otherwise noted, the following paragraphs are based on Conley's survey and Foley's "The Catholic Church and the Washington Negro," pp. 134–45.

35. In an effort to exonerate himself, the pastor later explained that church funds had not been used in the purchase, which was merely a private investment. See untitled, undated survey (ca. 1948) by the Washington Interracial Council, cy in SAA.

36. In her *Secret City*, pp. 286–88, Green pointed out the important contribution made by this publication to changing attitudes in Washington. Unfortunately, the incident at St. Mary's is the only mention of the Catholic Church.

a series of pastors fought well into the postwar period to maintain a rigidly segregated church. African-American Catholics were huddled into a few pews in a back corner. Any overflow stood while, during most masses, a tiny white congregation rattled around in the rest of the commodious building. Complaints from distinguished visitors from nearby Howard University were routinely dismissed by the pastor, who defended the rudeness of the ushers against the "troublemakers." Similar treatment at St. Paul's received national attention when *Ebony*, noted for its complimentary coverage of the Catholic church, published an illustrated article noting the parish's rigid segregation of parishioners in 1949. Despite urgent denials from apologists and the claim of one correspondent that the article was Communist inspired, the magazine's account, based on personal visits by one of its editors, was generally accurate.[37] Especially troubling in these incidents was the complicity of senior members of the local clergy. Although he once hosted a delegation from the Catholic Interracial Council in his church, the resident auxiliary bishop and pastor of St. Gabriel's, John M. McNamara, generally deplored what he considered the excessive zeal of those seeking integrated churches. He must be included among those who fought to retain the status quo.[38] Also well known were the efforts of the rectors of St. Matthew's to maintain segregated seating in the cathedral.[39] These were only the most prominent among many older priests and sisters who continued to display antipathy toward their

37. *Ebony* 4, no. 7 (May 1949): 13–18. A series of letters to the editor (vol. 4, no. 11 [Sep 1949]) included a lengthy document written by then-Bishop Philip M. Hannan in which he boasted about St. Augustine's integration but did little to contradict the magazine's charges about St. Paul's. Among the most impassioned apologists, see ltr., Margaret Garrity, Catholic Conference on Industrial Problems, to John Johnson, ed. of *Ebony*, n.d., encl. to ltr., Margaret Cox to Father Fontaine (pastor of St. Paul's), n.d. (ca. May 1949), cy in SAA. On charge of possible Communist involvement, see ltr., Frank H. Kunkel to Pastor of St. Augustine Roman Catholic Church, 20 Apr 1949, SAA.

38. On McNamara's attitudes toward Thomas Turner and others, see Marilyn Nickels' intv. with Horace McKenna, S.J., 24 Oct 1974, and author's intv. with Msgr. Benson.

39. Author's intv. with Archbishop Hannan. Msgr. Edward L. Buckey's habit of relegating black Catholics to the backs pews of St. Matthew's and referring black Catholics to St. Augustine's was continued by his successor, Msgr. John K. Cartwright, until Archbishop O'Boyle put a stop to it in 1948.

fellow Catholics. Their attitude would provide a provocative challenge to a new archbishop bent on the complete and peaceful integration of the Church in his care.

Counterbalancing the traditionalists' opposition to integration was the rich mix of reform organizations that were attracting both clergy and laity in increasing numbers. Efforts by students from the area's Catholic colleges and Howard University's Newman Club and progressive newcomers from among those flocking to Washington during the war had caused the city's Friendship houses and hospices to flourish. In 1948 a third Friendship House opened at 1513 U Street where it served many of St. Augustine's neighbors in the western Shaw region. The new archbishop appointed Father Joyce spiritual moderator of the St. Peter Claver Center, which boasted a permanent staff of three under the committed Christian social worker Mary Houston.[40] Influenced by these examples and goaded by their national leadership, a number of city-wide Catholic organizations re-patterned their racial relationships. The result was a notable increase in interracial activities in a still officially segregated city.

A primary catalyst for this increased cooperation was the local Catholic Interracial Council, which reached the peak of its influence in the early postwar years. The council had quickly outgrown the living rooms of its first sponsors and accepted the invitation of Msgr. Lawrence J. Shehan, pastor of St. Patrick's and always a firm supporter, to hold its gatherings at Carroll Hall.[41] Notable among those joining an already active council while retaining their membership in Turner's largely quiescent Federation of Colored Catholics were St. Augustine parishioners Dr. and Mrs. Eugene A. Clark, Walter A. Jones, Mrs. Mercer Cook, Harriet Gillem Dixon, Mrs. James Quander, and Theresa Braxton Posey. Surprising for those pre–Vatican II days, several of the Oblates teaching at St. Augustine's also joined the council. To devise strategies and coordinate initiatives, the council formed a steering

40. *Interracial Review* 22 (Feb 1949): 30.

41. The group received similar support from Msgr. John Russell, Shehan's successor. Both men would eventually assume important posts in the Church—Shehan as Baltimore's cardinal and Russell as bishop of Richmond—where they pressed for racial justice.

committee which included two physicians, Paul F. Cornely and Lena Edwards, and the noted educator Euphemia Haynes, all associated with St. Augustine's.[42] The committee concluded that the first requirement of any practical program was a careful survey of racial policies then in effect in the city's Catholic institutions. Subsequently, they formed teams that studied admission policies at local Catholic hospitals and high schools and colleges as well as the many parish-related organizations such as the Holy Name, Sodality, and fraternal orders.

Most attention centered on the practices in the inner-city churches, and in March 1947 the steering committee organized a survey of six parishes, including St. Matthew's Cathedral, St. Peter's, Sacred Heart, and St. Stephen's. On a single Sunday bi-racial teams entered each of these churches before the principal mass, walked down the main aisle and seated themselves in the center section. Although Professor O'Connor reported in the *Interracial Review* that most churches accepted the visitors, thereby demonstrating that the majority of Washington's Catholics were "ready to accept blacks equally," in fact only half the churches surveyed allowed the teams to sit undisturbed. Follow-up surveys by smaller groups at parishes like Nativity and St. Joseph's produced similar mixed results.[43] Other surveys surfaced some curious anomalies. For example, Providence Hospital began admitting black students to its nursing school in 1947, and shortly thereafter Georgetown accepted black doctors on its staff, but both institutions continued the rigid segregation of patients. As late as 1957 sisters at Providence were resisting any attempt to change their policy of segregated semi-private rooms, inflicting discomfort on patients and concern to their doctors. Responding to complaints from a professor of surgery at

42. Dr. Cornely later served as president of the city's prestigious John Carroll Society. See author's intv. with Paul F. Cornely, 15 Mar 1997. Unless otherwise noted, the following section on the council is based on this source and the author's intvs. with Dr. Paul P. Cooke, Pauline J. Jones, and Father George V. Joyce. See also, Marilyn Nickels's intv. with William and Mary Buckner, and John J. O'Connor, "A Man's A Man For A'That," *Interracial Review* 20 (Jun 1947): 86–89.

43. The survey was described in the *Interracial Review* 20 (Mar 1947): 44, and in a brief history of the council published on its 50th anniversary in December 1994, cy in SAA.

Howard's School of Medicine, Archbishop O'Boyle visited the hospital, vowing "to take the cross off its roof" if it did not change.[44] The mixed reports of success and failure produced many ironies. Once the council reported with some astonishment the practice of sisters teaching at Sacred Heart school (which barred black students) of helping every Saturday at Fides House, a bastion of interracial activities. This curious anomaly prompted Professor O'Connor to observe that African Americans wanted justice from the Church, not charity.[45]

The council participated in a number of interfaith initiatives in the late 1940s. It sponsored a student survey that tested the feasibility of interracial seating at downtown restaurants. It joined CORE and others in an unsuccessful campaign to integrate the YMCA and the Greyhound bus terminal. Its junior members joined those picketing the National Theater. Meanwhile their seniors sponsored a forum on lynching, which featured first-hand reports from NAACP field workers, and joined the legal fight against the District's restrictive real estate covenants.[46]

From the first the council was determined to be heard by Washington's new resident archbishop. Its members had been disappointed by his predecessor, whom they politely dismissed as "not an outstanding champion of interracial justice." On the other hand, they had always enjoyed a warm relationship with the apostolic delegate. Archbishop Ameleto Cicognani had celebrated mass for them at his home and on occasion hosted their social receptions. The council was heartened by advance word on Patrick O'Boyle.[47] Although a native of Scranton, Pennsylvania, he had spent his entire priestly career in New York City where his work in Catholic Charities especially had given him an inti-

44. Ltr., Dr. Mitchell W. Spellman to Gingras, 2 Jul 1957, with encls., SAA. The quotation is from an intv. with Msgr. Geno Baroni conducted by the Office of Black Catholics, 29 Sep 1983.

45. *Interracial Review* 22 (December 1949): 188.

46. These various activities were chronicled in the "Washington Reporter" article that appeared monthly in the *Interracial Review*. See, for example, 19 (Nov 1946): 173; 20 (Feb 1947): 29; 20 (Oct 1947): 158; and 22 (Dec 1949): 189–90.

47. *Interracial Review*, 20 (Jun 1947): 94 (source of quote) and 21 (Feb 1948): 28–29.

CRUSADERS. Leaders of the
Catholic protest movement and St.
Augustine parishioners (clockwise
from above): Dr. Eugene Clark, president of Miner's Teachers College
and leader of the Federation of Colored Catholics; Dr. Paul Cooke,
president of D.C. Teacher's College,
and his aunt, Mary Cooke Buckner,
both leaders of Washington's
Catholic Interracial Council.

mate knowledge of the needs and aspirations of that metropolis's various ethnic and racial minorities. Through their connections with their colleagues in New York the Washington group was no doubt aware of O'Boyle's precedent-making integration of New York's orphanages, and even before his arrival they pledged him their cooperation. True to his word, O'Boyle met with a small group of council leaders at his new home in St. Patrick's rectory just two weeks after his arrival in January 1948. He listened to the results of their surveys and to their special plea that the diocesan school then in the planning stage (Carroll High School) should shatter local practice and admit black students. Finally Father Parsons pressed the issue: "When does a decision come?" he asked O'Boyle, adding, "We have had so many studies and nothing really has been done."[48]

O'Boyle made no immediate commitment to the council's leaders, but his intentions soon became clear. In mid-March he informed his consultors that he was going to eliminate the city's dual parish system, a decision he reiterated before a general gathering of the clergy two weeks later. Although documentation is sparse, it seems clear that O'Boyle also responded quickly to some of the most egregious discrimination reported in the Interracial Council's surveys. Reports circulated that he had called in the pastors of St. Mary's and Immaculate Conception, warning them that they faced "official action" if their offensive treatment of black Catholics was not halted.[49] Declaring that behavior of this kind was contrary to church teaching, O'Boyle publicly stated that "the doors of every Catholic Church in Washington are wide open to all who wish to come in to pray and to worship Almighty God."[50] Meanwhile he continued to show in various ways his support for the reformers. He used the purse presented to him on his arrival to

48. Quoted in "O'Boyle Memoir Notes," 11 Jun 1979, AAW. These notes were dictated by Cardinal O'Boyle in preparation for a never-completed autobiography. For a detailed survey of the development of O'Boyle's racial policy for the city's parishes, see Conley's "'All One in Christ,'" pp. 81–87.

49. As reported in Foley's "The Catholic Church and the Washington Negro," p. 139. Conley (in "'All One in Christ,'" pp. 86–87) confirms that both pastors had back-to-back meetings with the new archbishop. See also William S. Abel, ed., *Patrick Cardinal O'Boyle As His Friends Knew Him* (Washington, 1986), pp. 9–10.

50. Quoted in *America* 80 (25 Dec 1948): 308.

purchase a new home for Howard University's Newman Club. In May 1948 he attended a well-publicized reception sponsored by the Interracial Council in his honor at the elegant Catholic Daughters of America clubhouse (much to the dismay of some of the matrons, who learned belatedly that they were playing host to a racially mixed group). He also presided at a mass marking the beginning of the council's fall season of activities.[51] For these actions and his many strong pronouncements on racial justice in his first year in the city, the NAACP presented O'Boyle a special award in March 1949.

The testimony of Archbishop O'Boyle and fellow leaders like Archbishop Joseph Ritter of St. Louis as well as the efforts of key lay leaders in the fight for racial justice won the Catholic church a reputation among African Americans for fairness—a reputation, historian Cyprian Davis observed, that was often compromised at the local level, as was apparent in Washington.[52] Nevertheless, the open fight against discrimination within the Church led many African Americans to a heightened awareness of Catholicism. In 1949 alone some 8,000 black adults to join the Church, a phenomenon attributable in part to the witness of the reformers.[53] The stand taken by leaders like O'Boyle also encouraged articulate African Americans to defend the Church when it was unfairly attacked. For example, when the *Pittsburgh Courier*, a black paper that enjoyed national circulation, published a series of articles criticizing what it inaccurately defined as the Church's racial policy, Henry Minton Francis, a senior Department of Defense official (Francis would eventually become deputy assistant secretary) and parishioner of St. Augustine's, wrote a detailed rebuttal. Like other such apologists, Francis did not ignore the failures of the bigots, but pointed to the Church's unequivocal teachings and the efforts of many Catholics to live up to these teachings.[54]

Even such a forceful personality as Patrick O'Boyle must have found the opposition so clearly expressed by leaders of what one ob-

51. See intvs., Conley with Archbishop Philip M. Hannan, 1991, AAW, and Marilyn Nickels with William and Mary Buckner. See also *Interracial Review* 21 (May 1948): 77–79, and (Nov 1948): 174.

52. Davis, *The History of Black Catholics*, pp. 252–53.

53. See "Other Faiths, Please Copy," *The Cleveland Herald*, 1 Apr 1949.

54. Ltr., Francis to Stanley Roberts, ed., *Pittsburgh Courier*, 3 Feb 1950, cy in SAA.

server called the "native clergy of the old Archdiocese of Baltimore and Washington" somewhat intimidating.[55] At that initial discussion of racial policy with his consultors, O'Boyle found himself challenged by the usually diffident Bishop McNamara, who warned of the many difficulties that would attend the decision to integrate. Adding insult to injury, McNamara went on to ask if the apostolic delegate was not really the author of what clearly to him seemed a distasteful move. Nor did O'Boyle find any strong support from the white laity in general. Despite the efforts of the racial progressives, a significant percentage of local Catholics would continue to oppose integration for years.[56] Obviously, the episcopal lightning bolt demanded by the reformers would only succeed in hardening such opposition. Instead O'Boyle decided to exert quiet but steady pressure, looking to achieve incrementally the integration of the churches, with the schools to follow—first those in the metropolitan area, then those in the more volatile southern Maryland counties. To the traditionalists he promised flexibility, not demanding wrenching change overnight. To the reformers he promised progress, but warned that "charity cannot be legislated." As he put it to Dr. Paul Cooke, when that St. Augustine parishioner reported continued discrimination in one of the southern suburbs, "I'll do what I can, but I can't achieve it [integration] all at once."[57]

This prudent approach helps explain O'Boyle's decision in 1949 to renew the old boundary decrees that organized the city into the dual system of black and white parishes. In the inner northwest section of the city, for example, the new decrees continued to superimpose on a grid that carefully divided the region among six white parishes a separate map that gerrymandered the same territory between St. Augustine's and Holy Redeemer.[58] Bolstering the decision to retain the old

55. Author's intv. with Father Joyce.

56. A survey sponsored by the *Catholic Digest* found as late as 1955 that 42 percent of the nation's Catholics remained opposed to integration. See *Evening Star*, 19 May 1956.

57. Remarks made during the mass to mark the Interracial Council's 1948 fall season as quoted in *Interracial Review* 21 (Nov 48): 174. (first quote). Author's intv. with Dr. Paul Cooke (second quote).

58. See, for example, Boundary Decrees, St. Paul's Parish, 9 Feb 1949, and Holy Redeemer Parish, 3 Oct 1949. Both in AAW. Holy Redeemer's boundaries would not be changed to conform to the territorial division until 3 February 1968.

boundaries was the fact that, given the fast-changing demographics of the region, parishes like St. Augustine's would not be able to support themselves if forced to rely on congregations restricted to their immediate neighborhood. The boundary decrees would allow pastors of black churches to continue serving people from all over town, but as O'Boyle's subsequent actions made clear, the decrees were only a stopgap measure.

In the case of Immaculate Conception, the renewed boundary decree lasted less than two years. The plan O'Boyle approved for the integration of this parish demonstrated his low-keyed approach to reform. As designed by St. Augustine's pastor, the change was based on two fundamental suppositions. First, integration would take place in a firm but quiet manner while it was made clear to all that racially separate parishes would never again be established in the archdiocese. Second, Catholics would be firmly encouraged to attend the church nearest their home, where they would make themselves known, contribute to the parish, and be made welcome. In outlining the proposed plan for O'Boyle, Gingras warned that integrating Immaculate Conception and the other problem parishes would cause some hardship for St. Augustine's and Holy Redeemer, who depended on attracting members from across northwest Washington. St. Augustine's, he reported, had already lost at least a dozen families to the now-integrated St. Martin's and stood to lose many more as time passed.

The plan for Immaculate Conception presupposed installation of a new pastor. The incumbent's views were well known, Gingras added, and a new face "would give a big boost to the whole plan." Although boundary adjustments would be delayed, administrative agreements with neighboring parishes over finances and other prickly subjects would be entered into immediately. In this, Gingras promised the full support of St. Augustine's. He also provided a checklist for the new pastor: conduct a complete census, no matter the hardship, to identify all black and white Catholics in the region; issue envelopes to all and publish lists of contributors so all might feel they belong; begin a convert class immediately, with a particular welcome to African Americans; admit all Catholic children to the schools and open the grammar school to non-Catholics, provided their parents agreed to attend orientation classes; immediately integrate the choir, ushers, altar boys, and all parish organizations; and finally, establish a strong St. Vincent de Paul Society to tend to the many poor in the neighborhood.[59] O'Boyle followed Gingras's proposals at Immaculate Conception. Ironically Gingras would have occasion to dust his plan off and apply it with slight variation in his own parish a decade later.

A New Home

Even during those early years at St. Augustine's, Gingras was kept busy with numerous extra-parish responsibilities. Time-consuming yet surely among the most satisfying of these tasks was his work for Camp St. Florence, a summer holiday program for underprivileged city children. Founded by Father James Caufield in 1948, the camp was located first on the grounds of the Cardinal Gibbons Institute at Ridge, Maryland, and later at campgrounds donated by Msgr. Joseph Denges and his brothers at Canoe Creek, Maryland. Unlike the Christ Child camp for girls and the Merrick camp for boys, Camp St. Florence was not segregated, although most of the poor children involved came from the black community. The camp provided free vacations for 600 boys and girls each season under the direction of Bernard C. Johnson, an officer in the D.C. Police Department (today the permanent deacon at St. Mary's in Washington). Johnson was provided special leave privileges by the Catholic chief of police in order to supervise the long summer sessions. Women were hired to supervise the girls; the boys were cared for by councilors recruited from among archdiocesan seminarians like Raymond B. Kemp and members of several religious orders.[60] In appointing Father Gingras director in October 1950, the always cautious Archbishop O'Boyle, who for many years had worked in child-care institutions, added: "I know that you will exercise prudence and good judgment."[61] Actually, Gingras had little direct contact with the camp itself, but along with his board of directors he faced the daunting task of raising funds to operate and improve the facilities.

59. Ltr., Gingras to O'Boyle, 20 Dec 1951, cy in SAA.

60. Intv., author with Rev. Mr. Bernard C. Johnson, 20 Mar 1997, cy in SAA, also the source for the following paragraphs. See also *CS*, 7 and 14 May 1954. Two of those councilors, Joaquin Bazan and Patrick McCaffrey, are now Washington pastors.

61. Ltr., O'Boyle to Gingras, 7 Oct 1950, SAA.

The board's longtime president, George W. Johnson, a senior official in the city's St. Vincent de Paul Society and parishioner at St. Augustine's, organized the first city-wide raffle, whose promise of fabulous prizes produced large sums for the camp. Gingras hosted a posh banquet annually to honor the major benefactors he so assiduously courted year round. These principal sources were augmented by diocesan charities and frequent private donations from the archbishop himself, who demonstrated by his close oversight and personal visits to the camp his interest in the welfare of underprivileged children.[62]

During the 1950s Gingras also served as spiritual director of the Sodality Union, moderator of the Archdiocesan Council of Catholic Women, executive secretary of the Good Friday Observance Committee, and director of the Office of Motion Pictures. Yet despite his many responsibilities, operations in his own parish were not neglected. The size of the congregation had stabilized with Sunday attendance throughout the 1950s hovering around 1,400. Attendance at St. Augustine's school actually increased 20 percent during the decade. By 1960 nine Oblate Sisters of Providence (their wages now raised to $50 a month) were teaching 483 children. Perhaps related to this increase was a corresponding drop in the number of children attending the twice-weekly CCD (Sunday school) program. Participation in parish societies remained strong. In 1956 the Sodality claimed 532 members; the Holy Name 250. Volunteers in gratifying numbers continued the work of the Ladies of Charity and St. Vincent de Paul while 100 children were enrolled in the parish-sponsored boy and girl scout troops and 75 teenagers belonged to the CYO.[63] An especially noteworthy innovation during these years was the Sodality's introduction of the so-called block rosary program, in which the popular devotion was publicly conducted in parishioners' homes throughout the neighborhood. To inform interested non-Catholics, Gingras instituted a public inquiry forum during the mid-1950s, where he lectured on the teachings of the Church and encouraged questions from the audience. In one year

62. See, for example, ltrs., O'Boyle to Gingras, 2 Apr 1952, 28 Oct 1955, 22 Oct 1956, and Gingras to O'Boyle, 5 Oct 1959. All in SAA.

63. For a complete statistical breakdown, see ltr., Gingras to O'Boyle, 27 Oct 1959, cy in SAA, and various *Notitiae*. See also Marguerite E. Parker, "A History of St. Augustine's Sodality," a report prepared in 1990, SAA.

this program resulted in eleven adults joining the Church; one, Jerry Mason, a student at Howard, later went on to become a Holy Cross brother.[64]

A parish organization established during this period would play an important part in St. Augustine's later efforts to revitalize its deteriorating neighborhood. In early 1951 Mary Houston, director of the St. Peter Claver Center, suggested to Father Gingras through friends that he organize a credit union. A federally recognized, parish-based credit union was a truly revolutionary idea in those times, but Gingras immediately grasped the usefulness of such an institution to St. Augustine's peculiar circumstances. It would provide a source of credit for all sorts of short-term needs for those in the congregation whose financial status made them ineligible to borrow from regular commercial lenders. At the same time, engaging the parish's more affluent members in this new form of capital venture would induce them to help the needy with a handup rather than the usual handout. It would also dissipate some of the snobbishness and indifference to the plight of the needy that lingered among some of the aristocrats of color. He asked Houston to draw up a specific plan.[65]

With the help of Charles Whitby, Willis Thomas, George Dines, Sr., and other parishioners, the proper applications were completed, and St. Augustine's Federal Credit Union received its charter in January 1952. Limited to parishioners and their immediate families, the credit union began with just eight charter subscribers and $156.50 in capital. It grew quickly, and within eight years some 675 members had invested assets totaling $150,000 on which they regularly earned 4 percent interest. Loans were limited to $4,000, and during its first fourteen years, nearly 3,500 loans totaling $1,500,000 were negotiated with only negligible losses. The credit union maintained an office in a church building, where its credit committee processed loan applications and its supervisory committee audited the books. This work, all

64. John A. O'Brien, "Sharing Our Treasure," a National Catholic News feature dated 26 June 1961, cy in SAA.

65. Intv., author with Pauline Jones. Jones was the parishioner who arranged the exchange of views between the pastor and Houston. On sensitizing the affluent members of the congregation to the need for a credit union, see author's intv. With Msgr. Leonard Hurley, cy in SAA.

FIRST COMMUNION CLASS. The large class, typical of St. Augustine's school in the 1950s, poses with parish administrator, later pastor, Msgr. George L. Gingras, in the church-auditorium.

volunteer, was carried out by some of the congregation's most distinguished members, including Bernard A. Cole, principal of Merritt School, William N. Buckner, retired principal of Armstrong High School, Juanita S. Tolson, a public school teacher, and Angela B. Bishop, retired principal of Douglas Simmons School.[66]

The postwar financial progress of Washington's middle class was reflected in the way St. Augustine's indebtedness was brought under control. With receipts approaching $70,000 annually, Gingras was able to meet the interest on the debt and gradually nibble away at the principal. Some support from diocesan sources helped the congregation reduced its obligation to $396,000 by 1952, a feat that earned the

66. Also included among these volunteers were Marion T. Cunningham, Irene S. Powell, Annie E. Tillman, Mary C. Buckner, Julia M. Sayles, Lawrence C. Hill, Mary C. Walton, and many other retired teachers and federal employees. See *Evening Star*, 4 Mar 1961. For further details on the credit union, see *CS*, 3 Mar 1966 and the *Washington Afro-American*, 19 Feb 1977.

congratulations of its fiscally conservative archbishop.[67] During the next seven years the congregation had, in addition to shouldering the annual $7,000 interest payment, been able to reduce the debt by another $45,000. By 1959 enough money was coming in to justify the expenditure of a significant amount to redecorate the church auditorium. Fire doors were installed and green velvet curtains added to the altar-stage area. There was enough in the till to allow for a substantial contribution to the archbishop's charity appeal, for which an amazed O'Boyle sent special thanks.[68]

It was during this period of increased financial comfort that Gingras, always the resourceful administrator, prepared a detailed statistical profile of the parish. This document is important because it offers a clear picture of a congregation that, despite the momentous changes since the war, had retained much of its historic, middle-class character. The survey listed a membership of 1,800, including 54 white parishioners. One-third of the congregation was over 55 years old; 22 percent were children. Fully one-half lived in the Shaw neighborhood (the survey dubbed it "the urban renewal area"); 46 percent scattered throughout the District and 4 percent in the suburbs. One half the adults were employed in white collar jobs, 3 percent in the professions, and 5 percent were self-employed in private businesses. Ten percent worked in skilled manual labor positions, 20 percent as unskilled laborers. Reflecting the aging population, 12 percent of the congregation was retired.[69] Adding to the picture of a middle-class parish in a rapidly changing neighborhood, the *Afro-American*'s society columnist, Pearlie Cox Harrison, published gushing accounts of the tours taken by the St. Augustine's Travel Club.[70] Such trips were still a

67. Ltr., O'Boyle to Gingras, 23 Dec 1952, SAA. The large reduction in the debt was caused in part by a $100,000 contribution, probably the initial payment of a settlement reached with the archbishop of Baltimore concerning the division of assets and personnel, for which more see below.

68. Ltr., O'Boyle to Gingras, 8 Jan 1959. News of the decorations added to the church was published in a Sodality News Sheet, March 1959, cy in SAA. During this period the parish published an annual statement that detailed all debt and interest payments.

69. Gingras, "St. Augustine, 1717 15th Street, NW, Square No. 207, Lot No. 803, 805, and 815," no date [ca. 1959], cy in SAA.

70. See, for example, *Washington Afro-American*, 14 Sep 1957.

novelty in the days before bargain jets, and the names of the tourists and the cities visited across the country were all dutifully chronicled. The club was yet another indication of the social and economic status of large numbers of parishioners.

Also during this period several members of the congregation received special recognition for their service to the Church. In March 1959 Archbishop O'Boyle installed Eugene Clark as a Knight of St. Gregory, the highest papal honor granted to laymen, for his contribution to the betterment of race relations in Washington. At the same time George Johnson was awarded the rank of a Knight of St. Sylvester for his work with the St. Vincent de Paul, especially his efforts on behalf of the summer camp program. Later that month Pope John XXIII conferred the *Pro Ecclesia et Pontifice* medal on five present and former parishioners as a sign of his "special esteem for their efforts on behalf of the Church and the Holy Father." The recipients included Erma Cornish, the longtime prefect of the Sodality, Mary Johnson, a stalwart in the Ladies of Charity, and Grayson McGuire, Jr., active in several parish organizations along with Dr. Euphemia Haynes and Lewellyn Scott for their labors in the Interracial Council. The parish also celebrated two other events: one of its sons, Matthias DeWitt Ward, was ordained a Fransican priest in 1955 and in 1959 Archbishop O'Boyle helped celebrate the 107th birthday of Henrietta Crawford, the oldest Catholic in the diocese. Mrs. Crawford, the widow of a Methodist minister and mother of eight, was born a slave in Charles County, Maryland, and had been a member of St. Augustine's parish for many years.[71]

Meanwhile Gingras's work had not gone unrecognized. In December 1955 he was made a monsignor. His letter of thanks revealed a growing sensitivity to racial matters. In obvious sincerity he told the archbishop that he understood the honor was for the people of St. Augustine's and was a token of O'Boyle's "deep interest" in their welfare. He hoped other priests would so view it, so that it might serve as an incentive to them to work for the betterment of race relations.[72] In the

71. Ltrs., Gingras to O'Boyle, 11 Apr 1958, and O'Boyle to Crawford, 14 Apr 1959. Both in SAA. See also *CS*, 3 Jun 1955.

72. Ltr., Gingras to O'Boyle, 28 Dec 1955, cy in SAA. Three years later Gingras was elevated to the rank of right reverend monsignor, an honor, he told the archbishop,

midst of these happy events, the retired Msgr. Olds continued to live quietly in his rooms in the rectory whose construction had caused him so much heartache. Sensing his end near, he drew up a list of his worldly goods on the last page of the parish ledger in 1956. After detailing his books, a few pieces of furniture, and his 1938 Dodge sedan, he mentioned his dearest possession, "the very best friend a man could have—my dog, Lady." With some echo of the trouble that had haunted him so long he added: "These are all mine, and I owe the church not *one cent* for any."[73] His death on New Year's Day, 1957, left the congregation to mourn the man who had lived among them and fought for them through good times and bad for fifty-three years. A week later George Gingras was named St. Augustine's fifth pastor.

Indicating just how far Gingras had progressed in his transformation into a racial progressive, news of his appointment elicited strong approval from key parishioners. The school principal, Sister Mary Consolata congratulated the new pastor, telling him, "You were our choice." Charles Whitby, the secretary of the Holy Name Society, thanked the archbishop for the appointment, adding that it brought solace and encouragement to the congregation, because Gingras's seven years among them had "endeared him to his people and the community."[74] In thanking the archbishop for this latest sign of confidence Gingras added, "I know the St. Paul's problem and the St. Augustine's debt worries you, but in good time you will have an answer. In the meantime I will wait your future decisions, and do what I can here to help them."[75] In fact for some years Gingras had been aware that O'Boyle was thinking about merging the two parishes.

The desegregation of the archdiocese had been accomplished quickly and quietly. By the mid-1950s even the schools in southern Maryland had neared full integration with only a minimum of tension. Similar progress was registered in local Catholic colleges, professional

---

that would make the parish happy. See ltr., Gingras to O'Boyle, 29 Dec 1958, cy in SAA.

73. Olds, undated notation on last page of the Parish Ledger, 1956, SAA.

74. Ltrs., Sister M. Consolata (Gibson) to Gingras, 12 Jan 1957, and Whitby to O'Boyle, 21 Jan 1957. Copies of both in SAA.

75. Ltr., Gingras to O'Boyle, 15 Jan 1957, cy in SAA. Note that this letter was written four years before the Archdiocese of Baltimore discharged St. Augustine's debt.

societies, and social institutions. Nevertheless, problems continued because of the changing demographics of the city, over which Archbishop O'Boyle had no control. Although 131,000 black newcomers took up residence in the city during the 1950s, their numbers failed to match the strength of the white flight to the suburbs. Washington's population actually decreased in the 1950s. By decade's end African Americans for the first time formed a majority of the city's residents. Largely neglected in the census story was the equally significant flight of the black middle class, not yet to the suburbs, but away from the increasingly poor housing and attendant social problems of the inner city to the far-flung reaches of northeast and northwest Washington. Also significant to the Church, the great majority of the black newcomers—unlike their predecessors who came from Catholic Maryland or nearby Virginia—hailed from the deep South where Catholicism was largely unknown.

These shifts in population, especially the drop in the percentage of Catholics among the new inner-city residents, posed a serious challenge to an archbishop determined to foster integration. In fact along a wide swath that arced across many of the neighborhoods from the Anacostia to Rock Creek there was a considerable drop in the number of Catholics of both races. Nowhere was the problem more starkly illustrated than in the western Shaw region. By 1956 St. Paul's parish claimed a congregation of 1,242, including 42 children. (Admittedly estimates, these and later statistics clearly inflated the actual number of people who worshipped in the church during the late 1950s.)[76] Only a small minority, perhaps as few as 500 Catholics, still lived in the Meridan Hill neighborhood. In contrast St. Augustine's, just four blocks away, enjoyed a relatively stable congregation, although significantly reduced from the past with fully half its parishioners living outside the Shaw area.[77] Without enough black and white Catholics in the area to maintain two integrated parishes, and with St. Augustine's

76. These figures, all prefaced with the word "about," are taken from the *Notitiae*. Casting further doubt on the reliability of these figures, the *Notitiae* for the following year claimed a population of 1,500 (including 100 children).

77. On the eve of the merger, St. Augustine's population, more likely an accurate figure because of Gingras's careful record keeping, stood at 1,575, including 650 children.

forced to make do with a church/auditorium, the logical solution was to merge the two. But strict logic does not always rule when dealing with change in the Church. Even the most forceful bishops approach mergers and church closings with trepidation. Loyalty to individual parishes built up over decades of family attendance creates such opposition that, in some American dioceses, bishops have faced boycotts, lawsuits, and mass demonstrations. Every step becomes the subject of controversy. The case of St. Augustine's and St. Paul's was especially complicated by racial considerations. Small wonder that Archbishop O'Boyle took so long to make a move.

On October 26, 1959 he convened a working group, in which Gingras and key chancery officials studied the practical questions involved in a merger. Given the delicate nature of the discussions, knowledge of O'Boyle's intentions was a closely guarded secret. No member of either congregation was informed, and, as far as can be determined, Father Edmund Fontaine, the elderly pastor of St. Paul's, was never involved in the discussions. To refresh his personal impressions, O'Boyle used a scheduled visit to St. Augustine's the following week to inspect the plant and spend time with the parishioners. He declared himself "delighted" with what he learned and congratulated Gingras on the job he was doing. His only suggestion: install a cover on the pyx in the tabernacle. The always liturgically proper and keen-eyed O'Boyle had spotted this minuscule infraction.[78]

A full complement of clergy was on hand for O'Boyle's visit. At the archbishop's request, Father Benson had reluctantly left the parish in 1950 to represent the diocese in the US Army's Chaplain Corps. Several priests had served briefly in his place until Father Charles Wilk arrived in 1954. But Wilk's help was limited by his collateral appointment as a teacher in a diocesan school. When the very popular Father Joyce was transferred in 1957, Gingras made a special plea for more assistance. O'Boyle had no one to spare, but promised changes soon, and in short order Fathers Roger P. Gallagher and the newly ordained Leonard F. Hurley took up their duties at St. Augustine's.[79]

78. Ltr., O'Boyle to Gingras, 22 Oct 1959, SAA.

79. Ltrs., O'Boyle to Gingras, 6 Jun and 4 Sep 1957, SAA. Other priests provided some temporary assistance during those years, including the Benedictine, Father Bernardine Patterson.

Looking to a conclusion to the discussions about the parish's future, Gingras prepared for the archbishop a summary of the problems involved and made a host of recommendations. He tackled the question of parish boundaries first. St. Augustine's, reflecting recent changes in the old dual racial system, now extended from far-out Shepherd Street on the north to the southwest waterfront, and he wanted the merged parish to be restricted to the present boundaries of St. Paul's. Parishioners living close to St. Stephen's, St. Gabriel's, Sacred Heart, Immaculate Conception, St. Mary's, St. Matthew's, and St. Patrick's should henceforth be served by those parishes while those loyal few who might insist on returning to St. Augustine's from other parts of town "could be cared for intelligently." Such a reconfiguration, he concluded, could be used as a model for future mergers, "and create the needed atmosphere and climate for such arrangements for other parishes."

On the question of the proposed name for the newly merged parish, the pastor's conclusion was logical and canonically correct, but widely missed the psychological point. He agreed that the simplest solution was to rename the parish SS. Paul and Augustine, with the apostle awarded primacy over the doctor of the Church.[80] This solution completely overlooked the unwieldiness of the title and the inclination of people to shorten such names, the long-troubled relations between the two congregations, and the proud tradition of the mother church of African Americans that stretched back nearly a century. Even in so sophisticated a congregation, such a solution was bound to smack of yet another demand that they step to the back of the bus. Although there was no public outcry at the time, the new name caused resentment among some elements of the congregation. Gingras's agreement with this proposal showed that his sensitivity training still had a way to go.

In matters pertaining to integrating the congregations, Gingras followed the plan devised earlier for Immaculate Conception. He proposed an immediate conversion to a single Sodality, Holy Name, and all other parish organizations. He wanted to abolish pew rents, because they represented a possible source of division. He insisted that

80. In his intv. with the author, Msgr. Leonard Hurley asserted that Gingras did not propose the name. Nor did any parishioners make their objections to the name known at the time.

all masses be celebrated in the church at Fifteenth and V Streets while St. Augustine's immediately be reconfigured as the parish auditorium and social hall. The latter changes were important, he explained, so that there be no misunderstanding on the part of either congregation that the V Street church "is the only parish Church for both groups." He also wanted a specific place reserved for the credit union, which he considered of prime importance to the parish's future. Further, he analyzed the financial records of both parishes in numbing detail, no doubt in an attempt to convince his fiscally conservative superior that, despite St. Augustine's then still sizable debt, the combined parish faced a substantially better financial future than either of its predecessors.[81]

His reassurances apparently failed to convince his cautious archbishop, who sat on the problem until 1961 when the parish received an unexpected windfall. For some time Archbishop O'Boyle had been negotiating with his counterpart in Baltimore over a fair division of assets as prescribed by Rome when the Archdiocese of Baltimore and Washington divided in 1948. No moneys were received by Washington at that time, and, given the pressing need for the expansion of church facilities after the war, Archbishop Francis P. Keough of Baltimore had been reluctant to act in the intervening years. Finally in 1961 Keough offered and O'Boyle accepted what O'Boyle's chancellor later described as a bad deal. As final settlement of the ordered division of assets between the two sees, Baltimore agreed to pay St. Augustine's debt, which had been contracted with the Safety Deposit and Trust Company of Baltimore in 1936 by Archbishop Curley and was the largest debt in the new archdiocese.[82] In early 1961 an obviously elated pastor drew a slashing line across the space allocated for debt information in the annual *Notitiae* (the official parish report to the archbishop) and wrote $00.00.

Only after Baltimore had agreed to pay St. Augustine's debt and when the aged Father Fontaine was preparing to retire, did Archbishop O'Boyle act. On September 19th the chancery published a decree that, citing the decrease in the size of the Catholic population of the

81. Ltr., Gingras to O'Boyle, 27 Oct 1959, cy in SAA.

82. Intv., author with Archbishop Hannan. Hannan was O'Boyle's chancellor at the time of the settlement.

area, united the two neighboring parishes under the title of SS. Paul and Augustine. The parish boundaries, conforming with slight differences to the old boundaries of St. Paul's, extended from Q Street on the south to Girard on the north and roughly between Sherman Avenue and Ninth Street on the east to Connecticut Avenue on the west.[83] The congregations of both parishes had finally been informed at all masses on the previous Sunday. Msgr. Gingras was appointed pastor of the combined parish and, along with Father Hurley, would join Father Vincent P. Cieri, who had been serving at St. Paul's, in the old rectory on V Street. Father Fontaine, now pastor emeritus, would live at St. Augustine's rectory with Fathers Roger Gallagher and Geno Baroni, a newcomer who would soon be known throughout the city.[84]

The church that would serve the new parish, while not quite as commodious as the original St. Augustine's, was considered one of Washington's most beautiful. It was built in 1894 in the English Gothic style after designs prepared by the Alexandria, Virginia, architect, Phillip N. Dwyer.[85] As to be expected in a church attended by distinguished diplomats and leaders of Washington society whose embassies and homes lined Sixteenth Street and Meridan Hill, no expense had been spared in its construction. Superimposed over a Potomac bluestone base, the walls of soft white Baltimore County marble extended 85 feet across the front and more than 150 feet in depth. The 80-foot

83. O'Boyle, Decree (in conformity with the prescriptions of Canon 1423) 19 Sep 1961 (countersigned by Philip M. Hannan, chancellor). The boundaries were confirmed in ltr., Msgr. Edward J. Herrmann to Gingras, 21 Sep 1961, St. Augustine file, AAW. See also ltr., Hannan to Vincent P. Cieri, 12 Sep 1961, cy in SAA.

84. Father Fontaine would continue to live quietly in the comfortable rectory until his death in November, 1968. Gingras's appointment as pastor was ordered by O'Boyle in ltr., O'Boyle to Gingras, 13 Sep 1961, SAA.

85. Dwyer studied architecture in Baltimore and once served as an official in the Treasury Department. He designed St. Joseph's on Capitol Hill and in 1881–83 he completely remodeled St. Mary's in Alexandria, which the V Street church closely resembles. See The Plaque (A quarterly publication of the Historic Alexandria Foundation) Dec 1984, pp. 1–3. Although St. Paul's was dedicated on 30 December 1894, much of the work on both interior and exterior was left for later completion. The following descriptions are based on articles appearing in the Evening Star, 31 Dec 1894, and CM, 6 Jan 1895.

towers, massive 24-foot square structures with tall lancet window openings and Gothic arches, were surmounted by stone spires topped with crosses rising 176 feet from the ground. (Unfortunately, the spires were dismantled after the 1957 hurricane because it was erroneously assumed that they were structurally unsound.) A unique feature, the main entrance was reached through triple stone arches under a carved railing and triangular pediment rising over 14 feet tall under the church's imposing rose window. Around the church's gleaming white exterior were stone cornices and moldings ornamented by Gothic scrolls and carvings.

The interior, which rose 56 feet in the open nave and 31 feet at the side aisles, originally seated some 1,000 in quartered oak and ash pews arranged along five aisles. The roof was supported by ten clustered steel Corinthian columns resting on massive brick pillars. The sanctuary, over 32 feet wide, was dominated by a magnificently fashioned Gothic altar flanked by more simply carved altars in the 16-foot semi-circular wings of the apse.[86] At the other end of the church rose a choir gallery with the ranked pipes of a three-manual Moeller organ, an important example of that American company's uniquely-designed instruments. The heavily carved Gothic ribs in the walls and ceiling served as settings for the stained glass windows designed in Munich, Germany. Of particular note were the seven finely crafted windows, each 12 feet high, spaced along the apse above the main altar and the ten windows in the clerestory. Those running along the nave, although not matching the others in quality, nevertheless offered a good example of what is known as Gothic story art in their depiction of scenes from the life of Christ and the Virgin and saints. Although many treasures were lost during St. Augustine's move from downtown, several important relics, principally the high pulpit and baptistry, survived the

86. This exceptionally fine example of American-designed gothic work, was created by the Gorham Company of New York and commissioned by Therese Droz, a French maid in the employee of Mrs. Marshall Field, the Washington socialite who lived in the Venetian-styled palace at Sixteenth and Euclid Streets. The altar cost $10,000 in 1916. It seems likely that Mrs. Field contributed part of that sum as a memorial to Droz, who died before its completion. See ltr., L. Hiedinger, to Msgr. James F. Mackin, 17 Jun 1916, and associated documents in Deed File, SAA.

two moves up Fifteenth Street. (The altars were not brought to V Street, but one of them found a new home as the centerpiece of the Oblates' convent chapel.)[87]

Even the prospect of gaining so beautiful a structure did not immediately overcome the surprise and anger that rose from people who, for the second time in a generation, had been presented with a *fait accompli*. True, some of the parish leaders like Beatrice Holton Stewart, many of the newcomers and converts, and especially the young families determined to give their children a structured education under the Oblates professed satisfaction with the merger. As Stewart put it, many refused to "get sad about the past." In fact she and some of the others looked forward to the move. To many of the stalwarts who had already endured one preemptory move in 1947, however, the change represented yet one more bitter pill to swallow. They could remember back over a lifetime of slights endured at the hands of their fellow Catholics at St. Paul's, and linking St. Augustine's to that group somehow seemed a betrayal of all the sacrifices they and their forebears had made.[88] As Gingras had projected, many began to worship at parishes in their new neighborhoods while almost all the whites who had been attending St. Paul's, also out of old loyalties, began to drift away. In short, integration, so ardently desired, came with a price tag. As the so-called national parishes and parishes based on race were transformed into geographical parishes, old ties began to weaken. Sentimental attachments endured, but many of the most active members of the congregation could be expected to turn their attention elsewhere.

No doubt Archbishop O'Boyle had a presentiment of this trend. Two months after the merger he expressed his satisfaction with the smooth financial and physical transition. "I know that you will do everything possible," he counseled Gingras, "to keep the united

87. At a cost of $1,250. See ltrs., Gingras to O'Boyle, 21 Oct 1961 and 8 Jan 1962. Both in SAA. The cost for moving the pulpit was $560. The total cost of changing the church-auditorium back into a meeting room with stage, kitchens, basketball courts, etc., was $9,500.

88. Mrs. Stewart's views were cited in the *Washington Post*, 16 Jul 1984. For the contrary position, see Marilyn Nickels' intv. with William and Mary Buckner, and author's intv. with Pauline J. Jones and Father Joyce. See also Muffler's "This Far By Faith," pp. 151–56.

parishes on an even keel."[89] Closer to the scene, Gingras and his assistants better understood the challenge ahead. To address the immediate problem of lingering animosities in the two congregations, the sermons harped on "Christian, Christian, Christian," one former assistant recalled.[90] But in the longer term some way needed to be found to shift the congregation's focus outward from its preoccupation with old hurts, perhaps by revitalizing St. Augustine's historic interest in the social needs of its neighbors. Time was short. Although none could foretell, the clock was rapidly ticking toward a day when fires of frustration and hate would literally transform the city and the parish neighborhood forever.

89. Ltr., O'Boyle to Gingras, 21 Nov 1961, SAA.
90. Author's intv. with Msgr. Hurley.

NINE ⚜ THE CHALLENGE OF

SOCIAL ACTIVISM

*F*or nearly a century St. Augustine's had provided a focal point in Washington for the special spiritual gifts of African Americans while at the same time serving as an effective instrument of gospel-based social activism. Over the decades this activism had encompassed not only the charitable impulse of a group of Christians, themselves often hard pressed, to care for the less fortunate, but also, through the efforts of articulate lay leaders, to champion civil rights and racial justice both in the Church and in society at large. Although the parish's spiritual focus never wavered, reduced circumstances and preoccupation with parochial cares after the closing of its grand old church and years of exile tended to inhibit the congregation's involvement in the physical welfare of its neighbors. Moreover, the integration of the archdiocese had caused the loss of many dynamic members to far-flung parishes just as other, more impersonal, institutions in the Church and city came to bear the brunt of old social obligations. Having lost both the responsibility and resources, the congregation remained in the postwar years largely uninvolved with its western Shaw neighborhood, where discrimination in housing and an influx of impoverished newcomers were radically changing the social climate.

It would have been understandable if the newly united congregation of SS. Paul and Augustine, its members distanced from many of the cares of their neighbors and somewhat secure in their middle-class respectability, had opted after 1961 to concentrate on spiritual concerns. Instead it joined in the ferment that characterized the decade just beginning. Urged on by a priest of remarkable social vision, the parish began to identify with its immediate neighborhood and its myriad social problems, supporting a number of innovative programs that anticipated those used by churches and government agencies in the ensuing war on poverty. Unfortunately a reputation as a caring people would not spare the parish the desolation visited on the region in the late 1960s. Nevertheless, the spirit of renewal that accompanied the return to social concerns served to re-energize important elements of the congregation, preparing them in a unique way to accept the responsibilities and opportunities defined for the people of God by the Fathers of the Vatican council.

Into the Neighborhood

In order to dramatize the social initiatives that would finally transform the parish in the 1970s and 1980s it became the habit of reporters to portray SS. Paul and Augustine as a desperately poor church where "only a few dollars came in each week in the collection basket," a parish that often had to borrow to pay its heating bills and numbered in its congregation "some of the poorest black people of Washington." Further demonstrating that truth is often the first victim of the polemicist, numerous accounts also described the parish as "the dumping ground for the 'problem' priests of the diocese." [1] In fact, as carefully compiled parish profiles made clear, throughout the 1960s the predominantly middle-class congregation provided generous support, serving as the principal source of funds for a school growing more expensive every year with the increased number of lay teachers and needy children and for a parish center that served as a principal resource for neighborhood social programs. While it was true that ignorance and prejudice made some priests reluctant to serve in the inner city, the parish, far from a dumping ground in the postwar decades, enjoyed the services of a number of extraordinarily dedicated clergymen, some of whom played a major role in the fight for racial justice in Washington.

1. See, for example, Lawrence M. O'Rourke, *Geno, The Life and Mission of Geno Baroni* (New York: The Paulist Press, 1991), p. 8 (1st and 2d quotes), and Gerald R. McMurray, "Remembering Geno Baroni," *America*, 151, no. 7 (22 Sep 1984): 146 (3d quote).

Giving them the benefit of the doubt, it could be concluded that such commentators were confusing the parish with the neighborhood that surrounded it.

Ironically, by 1961 the parish had finally emerged from its postwar travail only to find its western Shaw neighborhood assuming many of the characteristics of the poorest regions of the inner city. Changes in the past decade had been startling. Rapidly disappearing were the majority of predominantly middle-class residents of both races who were fleeing their comfortable old apartments and town houses that lined the shaded streets between Q and Girard Streets. In their place were appearing great numbers of impoverished tenants, some recently arrived in Washington, others victims of redevelopment schemes of previous decades that were transforming squalid old neighborhoods into gleaming new cityscapes at the expense of the black poor who were summarily evicted. The restrictive covenants and block busting begun in the late 1940s had inflated the cost of available housing, which in turn led to an overcrowding and general deterioration that rapidly enveloped the Clifton-Cardozo neighborhood. Often lost in such displacements were those traditional social restraints provided by extended families, caring neighbors, and church communities. Instead, frustration, especially among the young, deepened as these neglected and untrained residents were constantly bombarded by alluring advertisements for the good life while lacking the resources to participate. Overnight, it seemed, overcrowding and unemployment spawned, as one witness described it, "a violence of life which stifles the development of human beings."[2]

It was but a short step from such physical conditions to the breakup of families, drugs, and crime. Well into the postwar period the commercial and entertainment establishments on U Street had offered a vital and attractive alternative to downtown Washington. By the early 1960s, Fourteenth and U marked one of the city's major open drug markets. The Thirteenth Precinct, which had long guarded the placid neighborhood from its headquarters at Twelfth and U, now participated in an expanding war against the city's highest crime rate with orders to

2. Geno Baroni, Homily Delivered at the Labor Day Mass, 5 Sep 1983, repr. in *Restorations* (Oct. 1984), p. 6.

shoot to kill. Desperate street people became commonplace. Considering the unmet needs and frustrations of the new residents, one commentator accurately observed about the neighborhood in 1966 that "all the elements that produced riots in Harlem and Watts wait for a spark to touch off a similar explosion here."[3]

Less than 2 percent of the estimated 45,000 residents of this troubled neighborhood were Catholic, yet during the turbulent 1960s SS. Paul and Augustine ranked among the busiest churches in the city in terms of community outlook and the delivery of social services. To a great extent this activity could be traced to the inspiration of two men. In Msgr. Gingras the parish had a pastor who had over the years become sensitized to the special needs of this community, a priest willing to shed old ways of doing things and support new approaches to newly discovered parish responsibilities. Equally important, Gingras had by 1961 become a key player in the government of the diocese. He had just been appointed a consultor, a member of the group designated by Church law as the Ordinary's senior advisory body. Moreover, the archbishop had come to place great trust in this gifted administrator's judgment, increasingly turning to him to act as the diocese's point man in racial matters. Gingras would represent the archbishop on public commissions and speak in O'Boyle's name to the press on racial matters. In short, as a powerful insider, Gingras could play a key role by providing a cloak of legitimacy for any initiatives involving community projects that might otherwise rouse the always numerous ecclesiastical critics. Nor were such initiatives lacking after Father Geno Baroni appeared on the scene.

In Baroni the parish had in its midst one of a small group of Catholics who were radically changing the way the American church viewed its mission to the poor and dispossessed. These apostles of social activism had concluded that the traditional treatment of the poor— through the St. Vincent de Paul societies and even the more sophisticated resources of Catholic Charities organizations—was no longer sufficient in view of the intransigent system that was locking them into a permanent underclass. It was not enough, Baroni once bluntly put it,

3. Arthur McNally, "Green Pastures in a Black Ghetto," *Sign* 45, no. 6 (Jan 66): 19.

"for the Church to be the ambulance service that goes about picking up the broken pieces of humanity for American society."[4] For Baroni the need was clear: government, business, and the churches must forge new public policies to end the exploitation. Personal attitudes must change. Those committed to equal rights and a war on poverty must begin to see the poor as equals in the struggle, not objects of some missionary impulse. In the end this one priest would lead a campaign to reshape the social objectives of the American church.

Such a philosophy did not spring full blown, and Baroni frequently pointed to the influence of his family background and his early experiences at SS. Paul and Augustine as essential to his development as a social activist.[5] Born in a miner's camp in the Pennsylvania coal country, Baroni was the son of struggling, illiterate immigrants—his father a union organizer, his mother a domestic who would remain in service even after her son gained national prominence. His first-hand experience of the harsh life of the poor outsider led to an uneasy period as a curate in the Diocese of Altoona-Johnstown and eventually to a nervous breakdown. Seeking medical help and a change in service, Baroni, by then a part-time student at the Catholic University, volunteered in October 1960 to join the staff at SS. Paul and Augustine. Although he would remain one of Gingras's curates for just five years before the archbishop assigned him to broader responsibilities, he continued to reside in the parish throughout the decade, and his influence over many parish and community projects he had inspired remained strong.

In the later, more political phase of his career, Baroni's efforts centered on an effort to convince America's blue-collar ethnic groups and its African and Hispanic minorities of their similar problems, urging them to unite in a common campaign for economic justice. Vaguely reminiscent of the great nineteenth-century Populist leaders, his efforts, like theirs, failed to bear fruit as the specter of racial animosity and economic jealousy continued to frustrate any united effort. Nevertheless, closer to home, he continued to urge parishioners at SS. Paul and Augustine to see the Hispanics of the Adams-Morgan area as al-

4. From Baroni's Labor Day Homily, 5 Sep 1983.

5. O'Rourke's *Geno* (pp. 1–70) provides a detailed account of the evolution of Baroni's social philosophy and the influence his experiences at SS. Paul and Augustine had on that philosophy.

GENO BARONI. The famed reformer characteristically moving quickly from one task (the parish's presentation of a station wagon to its Oblate sisters) toward another. Note the usually rumpled Baroni's spiffy black fedora, which won special notice from Archbishop O'Boyle.

lies, explaining that power politics was nothing more than group politics and cultural politics.[6] Meanwhile some influential critics in the Church were unsettled by the overtly political aspects of his career especially when he was appointed assistant secretary of Health, Education, and Welfare by President Jimmy Carter. Nor was Baroni always particularly easy to work with. Possessed of a mercurial temperament, he suffered from bouts of depression that forced him into therapy. He was a brilliant innovator, but when criticized would confuse both friend and foe by abandoning his plan of action to attack the problem from an entirely different perspective. He was the first to admit to a lack of steadfastness. No sooner had he launched a program and se-

6. *Washington Post*, 29 Aug 1984.

cured a loyal staff than he would leave them to take up another cause. A human dynamo with unbounded interests and enthusiasms, Baroni would often tie up all three of the rectory's phone lines as he struggled through his estimated 200 daily calls.[7]

Such quirks never bothered those closest to him, including his colleagues in the rectory, his allies in the Protestant and Jewish clergy, and the hundreds of friends he touched in the congregation and in the neighborhood.[8] He was among the first to form strong alliances with activists like his close friends Episcopal priest William Wendt and Presbyterian minister Philip Newell. The poor African Americans in particular recognized in the immigrant's son a fellow outcast, and they enjoyed his easy association with them and his obvious concern for their welfare. A poor sleeper, the naturally gregarious Baroni would roam the neighborhood during the night, often the first customer at the Park Road newsstand where he could be seen drinking coffee or cadging a piece of fruit. (He was a compulsive fruit eater, strewing his bed with peach pits and cherry stones.) Thus the soft-spoken curate with the common touch was a familiar sight roaming the rough and troubled streets of the largely non-Catholic neighborhood, moved by the suffering he saw and learning first hand the connection between economic oppression and crime and misery in the inner city.

At the same time Baroni saw much reason for hope among those who had maintained their sense of values despite grinding poverty. He strongly criticized the famous report by Daniel P. Moynihan, then a deputy secretary of Labor, for reaching conclusions about poverty and the African-American family that Baroni's own experiences in the Shaw-Cardozo region simply did not support.[9]

Baroni himself considered his experiences in the neighborhood

7. McNally's portrait in "Green Pastures in a Black Ghetto" provides many interesting details of Baroni's peripatetic life at SS. Paul and Augustine. For an eyewitness view of Baroni's whirlwind activities in the rectory, see author's intv. with Msgr. Leonard F. Hurley, 12 Mar 1997, SAA.

8. In 1968 Baroni received enough votes to capture third place in the *Washington Afro-American's* Favorite Ministers Contest. See *Washington Afro-American*, 25 May 1968.

9. Baroni's criticisms were widely reported. See, for example, *Mississippi Register*, 12 Mar 1965.

basic to his evolving understanding of Christian charity. Nowhere was this connection better articulated than in the last homily he preached before his death:

In my own experience, the two examples of family and parish are critically important. My mother and father could not read or write any language, but they were the first voices of justice in my life . . . The second most important voice of justice was the parish experience of St. Augustine where I was honored to serve between 1960 and 1970. At St. Augustine's, black people of great faith taught me by their life and their history of racial discrimination, in and out of the Church. And yet, even today, we can walk but a block from this church and see and hear and learn what I learned from 14th Street and St. Augustine's parish. Can we not see the overcrowding? Can we not see the bad housing? Can we not see unemployed men and women and youth? Can we not sense the violence of life in this marvelous achievement of mankind called the 'capital city'?[10]

At his arrival Baroni found a neighborhood ripe for a new form of Christian charity, a charity that had shed the paternalistic ways that characterized even the best of past programs by uniting the expertise of black and white volunteers with the needs of the neighborhood as articulated by the poor themselves. All would share in the direction and responsibility for what would be undertaken. He was confident that he could attract volunteer help and involve the needy in the programs, but what at first presented a major obstacle to a parish of limited resources was a building that could both house all this planned activity and serve as a material symbol of the parish's determination to involve itself in neighborhood causes.

For some time the object of his attention had been the old convent of the Perpetual Adoration Sisters at 1419 V Street. With the few cloistered nuns now gone, the grand old Victorian pile had become a pawn in several schemes involving the future of Mackin High, the diocesan school that occupied the well-maintained building next door. Shortly after the parish merger, Gingras had proposed that the diocese purchase the convent from the nuns for $100,000 as part of a complicated deal that would bring the parish school and convent to V Street in exchange for Mackin's moving into the parish's buildings on Fifteenth

10. Excerpt from Baroni's Labor Day Homily, 5 Sept 1983.

Street.[11] Although the diocese acquired the convent, the high cost of moving Mackin (estimated at $600,000) killed Gingras's plan, and by March 1962 diocesan officials were seriously discussing other proposals for the building, including the idea of refurbishing it as a residence for the Salvatorian Fathers then teaching at Mackin.[12]

By this time Baroni had convinced Gingras of the need for a parish center, even as the pastor had come to realize that giving 1419 V Street to the Salvatorians would only insure that Mackin remain indefinitely on V Street, a permanent bar to a united parish plant. He summarized the arguments against such a decision for O'Boyle, adding the recommendation that the convent be used instead to serve neighborhood needs along the lines of a St. Vincent de Paul hospice or a Fides house. It must have been obvious to O'Boyle, as it was to everyone else, that there were not enough Catholics in the neighborhood to justify a traditional parish center. Prudence dictated therefore that Gingras scale down the full scope of Baroni's intentions, so he simply informed O'Boyle that the neighborhood needed the help, the convent was perfectly located to provide such help, and the priests and people of the parish, he promised, would lend their complete cooperation to such a project. Either Gingras's skillful exposition of the practical problems connected with expanding Mackin or his argument for the new charitable enterprise won the day, for later in 1962 Archbishop O'Boyle turned the convent, debt free, over to the parish to be used as a center for its charitable activities.[13]

In short order the new Parish Center, as it was called, became a

11. Gingras, "Summary of Points Involved with the Complete Removal of Mackin H.S. to the old St. Augustine Property," n.d. (ca. 1961), cy in SAA.

12. "Various High School Proposals," 16 Mar 1962, unsigned memo composed in the chancery, cy in SAA. The Salvatorians would be replaced by the Holy Cross Brothers in later years.

13. Documentation on the purchase of the convent and its transfer to parish control is incomplete. The original donor, New York philanthropist Ida M. Ryan, bequeathed it to the archdiocese with the stipulation that, should the sisters leave the country, the property would be given to Georgetown College (see ltrs. Gibbons to James Mackin [pastor of St. Paul's], 25 Apr and "Ascension Day" 1902; Mackin to Gibbons [with att ltrs. and notes from Ida M. Ryan to Gibbons], 29 Apr 1902; and Ryan to Gibbons, 2 May 1902. All in SAA). It can be assumed that, however the disposition of the property

lively hub. The parish's credit union, its St. Vincent de Paul Society, and the city's Catholic Interracial Council all transferred their operations to the old convent, and Baroni persuaded Mary Houston, now working in a government welfare agency but still closely connected to Washington's Friendship houses, to become director of the Center's activities. Soon Houston and a group of young women, all activists who combined the spirit of Dorothy Day's Catholic Worker Movement with the volunteerism popularized by America's own Peace Corps, were living in the nuns' old quarters on the building's upper floors. They constituted the early core participants in the parish's new community projects while continuing to earn their living in various jobs throughout the city.

Baroni had always envisioned the parish in Parish Center to mean all the residents living within its boundaries, not just its tiny Catholic minority. It was necessary, he realized, to dispel some old notions before such an idea was accepted. "The new role of the church in the city," he declared on more than one occasion, was "not just concerned with taking care of its own."[14] Full of new arguments and new ideas, he led a sometimes baffled and hesitant pastor deeper and deeper into the neighborhood's problems, defining the new enterprise as a vital center of service to the whole community. Symbolizing his intentions, Baroni had the fearsome jagged glass tops of the old convent walls and its iron gate removed, a gesture of welcome to the parish's non-Catholic neighbors.

The first neighborhood group to accept the invitation to participate was the local Alcoholics Anonymous group, which began to hold meetings in the building on Sunday nights. It was quickly followed by TOPS (Take Off Pounds Sensibly), whose overweight members began to use the building's large meeting room for their regular nondenominational exercises. Aided by her fellow Center residents, aroused parishioners, and volunteers from around town, Houston quickly launched an educational program for neighborhood children. Within months the parish was operating tutorial classes, a small day care cen-

---

worked out, the cost of the building to the diocese was less than the estimated $100,000 price tag.

14. As quoted in *Washington Post*, 20 Jul 1965.

ter, and a literacy training program, which involved some of the seniors from the nearby Roosevelt Hotel as teachers.[15]

Another group affiliated with the Center from its first months was the Young At Hearts Club, an organization for senior citizens. Anticipating the interest in organizing these once-neglected Americans into a social and political force, Baroni hoped to enlist the services of the seniors in his community activities. With Mary Houston's help, he got Beatrice Holton Stewart, a retired school teacher and one of the parish's most prominent lay leaders, along with parishioners Gertrude Smith and Lucinda Dyer, to organized a club affiliated with the National Council of Senior Citizens. Baroni served as the club's spiritual director. Beginning in 1963 with eight women from the parish, the Young At Hearts quickly succeeded in enrolling a hundred members from the community, and by 1965 had a long waiting list of applicants. Members met in the Center, where they organized trips, planned square dances, and arranged for guest speakers. Seniors also collected clothes for the needy, prepared gifts for distribution at D.C. General Hospital, and provided volunteers for many Center programs. These dedicated women, who would remain associated with the Center for many years, celebrated their second anniversary with a big party attended by Archbishop O'Boyle and friends from the neighborhood.[16]

The Center's summer day camp was the first large-scale community project. Begun in 1963 with 200 neighborhood children, the camp was directed by Belford Fisher, a teacher of slow learners in the D.C. school system, with twenty-five local teenagers specially trained as councilors. Thanks to a $6,675 grant from the Junior League of Washington (who gave an even larger amount the following year), the three-week program was expanded to seven weeks in 1964. The children, all safely off the streets through much of their summer vacation, attended Montessori classes and received instructions in music, dance, drama, and arts and crafts. Nor was their day all serious learning. The sched-

15. For a survey of the various programs operating in the Center, see McNally's "Green Pastures in a Black Ghetto," Russell Shaw's "Mary Etheredge is Dead," *The National Catholic Reporter* (2 Jun 1965), and a survey reported by David Gordon in the *Washington Post*, 4 Aug 1964.

16. The work of the club was detailed in the *CS*, 12 Mar 1965. See also *Washington Post*, 21 Apr 1963, and author's intv. with Pauline J. Jones.

ule also called for frequent field trips using school buses loaned by Our Lady of Mercy school in Potomac. Picnics, swimming parties, and dances for the teenagers filled out a program that would enroll increasing numbers of local children in each succeeding year.[17]

A prudent pastor was careful to keep the archbishop informed about the growing summer school program. O'Boyle, who had made a personal $100 contribution to the Center in 1963, was concerned about financing so large a project, which soon required the services of at least seven qualified teachers and child specialists to operate its remedial classes. Gingras's reports and news of the Junior League's grant seemed to calm his fears, for by August 1964 the archbishop was congratulating the parish for its summer camp, nominating Father Baroni for special thanks.[18] Actually, as might be expected with so careful an administrator in charge, financial support for the Center, a mix of grants and contributions from parish funds, proved not too difficult to obtain. Baroni successfully solicited support from his growing number of contacts while various organizations in addition to the Junior League—including the Sodality Union, the United Planning Organization, and the National Institutes of Health—all provided money for various elements of the program. By 1966 such groups had contributed over $42,000 to the Center during a period when costs to the parish averaged another $16,000 a year.[19]

Father Baroni worked hard at convincing members of the local community that what might appear a denominational effort was actually intended to engage the whole neighborhood. He began by organizing an advisory council to serve as a bridge to the community, a mechanism for getting neighbors involved.[20] The council, which worked with director Houston and her associates in devising the Center's expanding programs, was dominated by parishioners at first, but in short order

17. *CS*, 31 Jul 1964. The camp would have over 300 children enrolled by 1965 with an operating budget in excess of $8,000.

18. Ltrs., O'Boyle to Gingras, 26 Mar 1963 and 17 Aug 1964, and Hannan to Gingras, 6 May 1964. All in SAA.

19. Ltr., Gingras to O'Boyle, 29 Jul 1966, cy in SAA, and *Notitiae*, various years.

20. For a useful discussion of the Parish Center at mid-decade, see author's intv. with Ralph Dwan, 28 May 1997, cy in SAA. In the mid-1960s Dwan was an assistant pastor at SS. Paul and Augustine and Baroni's successor in the Center.

non-Catholic neighbors began to play a major role. The group sponsored social affairs that sought to attract people from all over the
neighborhood. It also worked closely with the V and W Streets Neighborhood Council, a local group organized with Baroni's encouragement
in 1963 to sponsor block club projects. The two groups in particular
collaborated on the Center's summer day camp and a local campaign
that enlisted citizens in a neighborhood clean-up program.

Probably the most obvious sign of the parish's intention to welcome
the neighborhood was the construction of the V Street Commons, a
transformation of the old convent's yard into a city park designed by
landscape technician Karl Linn. Meant as an inviting place especially
for the community's seniors and children to gather, the commons
boasted a basketball court and, for community gatherings and amateur
theatricals, a small amphitheater situated under shading trees. Soon
neighbors were assembling for outdoor barbecues and other organized
socials. Building the commons typified Baroni's approach to community affairs. First he recruited volunteers to plan the work under Vincent
DeForest, then formed a nonprofit corporation to wheedle a federal
grant under the Manpower Development and Training Act to pay for it,
and finally arranged for hiring sixty high school drop-outs to do the
work, providing them with both job experience and spending money.
Spurred on by the presence of the new commons, the Center became a
true center of community activities, busy from morning to night with
children streaming through to play in the yard, work in the crafts room,
or rehearse their amateur plays. Some 100 parents met every Thursday
evening to discuss neighborhood concerns, while credit union in-
vestors, members of the Interracial Council, and senior citizens added
to the constant flow. One active participant in these happenings was
Freda Barbarika, an artist and social worker especially interested in
cultural enrichment programs. In 1964 Barbarika succeeded Houston
as the Center's director.

Baroni's community initiatives did not go unnoticed by Lyndon
Johnson's administration as it launched its war on poverty. For example, Baroni's innovative ideas about neighborhood credit unions and
the extraordinary success of SS. Paul and Augustine's own credit
union helped persuade federal officials that credit unions should be
incorporated into their landmark social measures in the mid-1960s. It

seemed only fair, therefore, that a parish which influenced the war on poverty should also benefit from these government programs. And so it was that SS. Paul and Augustine was among the first to apply for and receive a grant for a Head Start program. Designed by the Johnson administration to provide special pre-school training for culturally handicapped children, Head Start is still considered among the most successful government efforts on behalf of the needy. At Baroni's insistence, the program at the Center, alone among all those in the Washington area, boasted teachers trained in the Montessori method. They were supported by a small army of volunteers, including doctors, psychologists, social workers, and a child-development specialist. Using the need for assistants in the Head Start classes, Baroni tapped another federal program, the Neighborhood Youth Corps, to hire local teenagers to gain work experience and special training while earning a government salary.

These innovative programs, which united the efforts of parishioners, community volunteers, and neighborhood activists, particularly appealed to Archbishop O'Boyle, who wanted to duplicate them at the diocesan level. At a clergy conference in September 1965, after pointedly congratulating Father Baroni "for fighting on the front lines for a long time" and leading his somewhat hesitant colleagues in a round of applause for the tireless defender of the city's downtrodden, O'Boyle announced the formation of the Archbishop's Committee for Community Relations and Baroni's appointment as its full-time executive director. To replace Baroni at SS. Paul and Augustine, O'Boyle named Ralph Dwan, a young priest who had been running a summer program for children near St. Joseph's on Capitol Hill designed on the SS. Paul and Augustine model.[21]

Dwan's first task was to find a replacement for Freda Barbarika, who had left the Center to work in Puerto Rico designing audio-visual aids for illiterate children. He chose Kate Trainor, a social worker and community organizer. They agreed that Trainor would concentrate on the Center's after-school programs and serve as principal liaison with the growing number of community activities springing up in the neigh-

21. Ltr., O'Boyle to Gingras, 1 Sep 1965, SAA. The account of the clergy conference and the O'Boyle quotation are taken from McNally's "Green Pastures in a Black Ghetto," p. 27.

borhood. Trainor emphasized the Center's tutorial program and within two years had over 200 volunteers from all over the city assigned to individual children, not only teaching reading, but planning weekend activities together, developing a close relationship between tutor and friend (what in later times would be called mentoring). Trainor also devised more recreational programs for the neighborhood teenagers. The Department of Recreation's Roving Leader program was using the Center as a base for all kinds of projects under the direction of its local leader, Harold Bell, a former professional football player, who came up with many new ideas for keeping the young people off the streets. Soon the click of cue sticks on pool balls could be heard in the old convent as the kids gathered for tournaments.

Trainor's work with the Center's advisory board led to even greater involvement in community projects and the parish's identification as a resource center for neighborhood change. What started with potluck suppers and neighborhood barbecues to open the Center to the community now took on a more serious mission involving the neighborhood in identifying local problems and learning how to confront them together. One of the early participants in these get-togethers was Robert Smith, a Presbyterian minister and community organizer, who later returned to the Center to conduct training sessions to develop community leaders in projects involving local housing, employment, and youth programs. Meanwhile, Dwan concentrated on the Center's summer school program, which was growing in both the scope of its activities and the number of participants. By 1966 the Center served as sponsor for TEAM-UP (Training and Enrichment for All for the Maximum Use of Their Potential). The special educational project was directed by Holy Cross Sister Melathon, former head of St. Joseph's Home for Boys. With Marguerite Seldon, principal of nearby Harrison elementary school, Dwan administered the Harrison Co-op program, which used both the Center and the school to house its summer program. This latter, in addition to the usual array of activities, now included classes for mothers and a home visit program.[22] The community school coordinator at Harrison School, Gladys Harris, built the project into a fifteen-hour-a-day program funded by major public grants. In

22. For a discussion of these expanded programs, see *CS*, 9 Jun 1966.

1966 parishioners from nearby Augustana Lutheran Church joined SS. Paul and Augustine's PTA and Harrison personnel in what had by then become a major ecumenical effort.

Although a few parishioners always remained involved in the Center's tutoring program, the summer schools and day camps depended mainly on local teenagers paid out of government grants, VISTA volunteers, seminarians from local houses of study, and volunteers from literally all parts of the world. Many of these volunteers would come to stay for weeks or months at the Center. Thanks to their help and generous donors the cost to the parish remained constant. Father Dwan had been trained as a lawyer before ordination, and he enlisted the help of some of his attorney friends in forming Community Assistance, Inc., an organization of interested laymen who paid the modest salaries of the Center staff, including its team of community relations workers. The expanded Harrison Co-op program was a joint venture with the D.C. government: D.C. paid the salaries and the parish contributed use of its buildings. Other grants from government and private groups also helped support the programs. Although the parish's $16,000 annual supplement was relatively modest, it nevertheless represented approximately 10 percent of its annual revenues.[23]

The Center and the Civil Rights Movement

To Geno Baroni the alleviation of poverty was inextricably linked to the fight for civil rights. Overcoming impoverishment and racism in the inner city, he declared, represented the greatest challenge for American Christians.[24] As he delved into the rich history of SS. Paul and Augustine he came to understand how deeply the curse of racism had afflicted the Church and how difficult was the task facing those dedicated to overcoming the indifference or hostility still prevalent among clergy and laity alike. In this his beliefs squared with the explicit teachings of the American bishops. At the urging of a dying Pope Pius XII, but only after a concerted fight led by Archbishop

23. Ltr., Gingras to O'Boyle, 29 Jul 1966, and Gingras, "Report of SS. Paul & Augustine Parish," Jan 1967. Copies of both in SAA.

24. As quoted in O'Rourke, *Geno*, p. 40. Except where otherwise noted, the following paragraphs on Baroni's role in the civil rights movement are based on this source.

O'Boyle, the American bishops dared to take an unequivocal stand, declaring in November 1958 that racial discrimination was immoral and unjust and could not be reconciled with the truth that God created all with equal rights and equal dignity.[25] Obviously apprehensive about the civil rights revolution gathering strength around them, the bishops called for a decisive plan of action that avoided both the gradualist approach that had allowed inaction in the past and what they saw as the "rash" approach of radicals that would stymie future progress. From his vantage point in the inner city, Baroni knew that the hour had passed for any kind of carefully designed and paced plans of action.

The modern civil rights revolution has many antecedents, but probably the most dramatic unveiling came on that day in 1955 when a weary Rosa Parks refused to move to the back of a public bus in Montgomery, Alabama. Her act of civil disobedience sparked a wildfire of protest that propelled the charismatic Martin Luther King, Jr., then a young Baptist preacher, into the leadership of a dynamic movement that galvanized the African-American community and its white allies into an unrelenting struggle for equality. Few Catholics appeared in the vanguard of this struggle, but in Washington Baroni found himself working with a select group of white clergyman in alliance with the movement's local black leadership, especially Walter Fauntroy, Channing Phillips, and Ernest Gibson. To his surprise, Baroni also found a strong ally for his activism in Patrick O'Boyle.

O'Boyle's single-minded dedication to racial justice had long been recognized, but so too was his aversion to priests or sisters engaging in public demonstrations. Baroni, therefore, expected the worst when his picture appeared in a local paper marching before the White House in the front ranks of a demonstration in support of the southern freedom fighters. Answering the expected summons to the archbishop's office, Baroni nervously explained what he, Fauntroy, and the others were doing. Instead of a tongue lashing, the surprised priest heard his bishop

25. Conley, "'All One in Christ'," pp. 113–15. Conley's work, Richard A. Lamamma and Jay J. Coakley's "The Catholic Church and the Negro," in *Contemporary Catholicism in the United States*, Philip Gleason, ed. (Notre Dame: University of Notre Dame Press, 1969), and Davis's *The History of Black Catholics in the United States* all provide useful surveys of the Church during the civil rights revolution.

mildly respond, "All right, Father. By the way, I was pleased to see in this picture you had your hat on. That's the way I like my priests to appear in public. You can go now." For once the usually sartorially sloppy Baroni had met the always correct O'Boyle's standard for clerical attire.[26] On a more serious level, the conversation convinced Baroni that his method of bearing witness in the fight for civil rights had his boss's backing.

O'Boyle lent the weight of his office to the cause in other ways. In a series of sermons and statements in the early 1960s he outlined a strategy for convincing Americans that social justice was a religious and moral issue. Reflecting the ecumenical spirit stimulated by the Vatican Council, he also suggested to an Urban League audience in May 1963 that Washington's churches launch a common effort to fight racism.[27] This led to the creation of Washington's Interreligious Committee on Race Relations. Chaired by O'Boyle, the committee included forty-two church leaders, who served as advocates for equal opportunity in training, employment, and fair housing. From offices in the Parish Center on V Street, the committee's staff prepared testimony, arranged lobbying efforts before local governments, and organized the committee's pledge to favor contractors and suppliers who developed equal opportunity employment programs. As chairman, O'Boyle testified frequently before the D.C. Commissioners and other governmental bodies on behalf of proposed ordinances to ban discrimination in housing and to encourage fair employment. He even testified in opposition to a proposed extension of the inner loop of the freeway until suitable provisions were made for the those evicted.[28] The committee also announced its support for the March on Washington, a mass rally organized by national civil rights groups under the leadership of A. Phillip Randolph. In succeeding years O'Boyle stepped up the pace of his appearances.

26. As quoted in O'Rourke's *Geno*, p. 37. The conversations in O'Rourke's book are based on a series of interviews with Baroni. O'Boyle's obsession with seeing all his priests wear hats finally ended when he was visited by a hatless apostolic delegate, who explained that "nobody in Rome wears hats anymore."

27. Conley, "'All One In Christ'," pp. 130–31. O'Boyle consistently supported the work of the Urban League. See *CS*, 7 May 1954.

28. *Washington Star*, 17 Sep 1963. The freeway was eventually halted at the New York Avenue line.

Although clearly uncomfortable walking the shadowy line that separated church and state, he nevertheless served as spokesman for the Interreligious Committee at various White House meetings called in support of the federal civil rights acts.

The March on Washington for Jobs and Freedom, until then the largest civil rights demonstration ever held in the nation's capital, was scheduled for August 28, 1963, coincidentally the feast of St. Augustine. Although participation by identifiable Catholic groups was assured because of the Interreligious Committee's sponsorship, the personal participation by the archbishop in the form of an invocation directly preceding Dr. King's address was not. O'Boyle balked at what he considered inflammatory remarks planned for delivery by the spokesman of the Student Non-Violent Coordinating Committee, John Lewis. Only after last-minute negotiations conducted by the venerable civil rights activist Bayard Rustin, Dr. King's assistant and future U.N. Ambassador Andrew Young, and Father Baroni was a compromise reached in the wording of Lewis' speech that paved the way for O'Boyle's leading the great throng in prayer just minutes before King told the world about his dream. During the brief interval between the two talks, Ralph Bunche, the distinguished United Nations official, leaned over to O'Boyle and said, "Now you're going to feel just a little like you are in a black Southern Baptist Church."[29] It was a moment of high purpose and exciting theater to savor, especially for the doughty prelate, who had fought hard for racial justice in Washington.

Catholic Washington's participation was organized by the local Catholic Interracial Council from its office in the Parish Center. Reflecting the lingering fear in government quarters that the march might turn violent, O'Boyle frowned on the idea of women religious participating. Essentially an old-fashioned prelate, he admonished them to stay in their convents and pray for the success of the enterprise while welcoming all the male religious in the diocese to the event. O'Boyle asked that a parish priest accompany any parish group attending and even encouraged them to carry banners identifying their parish. A special mass was scheduled in six area churches, and several parishes of-

29. As quoted by Archbishop Hannan in his intv. with the author. For an extended survey of O'Boyle's role in the march, see Conley's "'All One in Christ'," pp. 134–40. See also Baroni intv., 29 Sep 1983, Office of Black Catholics, AAW.

THE MARCH ON WASHINGTON, 1963. Archbishop Patrick A. O'Boyle offers
a prayer as Whitney Young and Walter Reuther flank Dr. Martin Luther King, Jr.,
just before the latter delivered his "I Have a Dream" address.

fered to provide food and accommodation for those attending the demonstration from a distance.[30]

Given its decades of dedication to civil rights, it was not surprising
that SS. Paul and Augustine proved especially hospitable. While Gingras and Baroni concentrated on the broader aspects of diocesan participation, parishioners Pauline J. Jones and Lozzie York set about organizing logistical support for visiting demonstrators. They arranged

30. Memo O'Boyle to All Pastors and Superiors of Religious Orders of Men and
Women, 19 Aug 1963, and Memo, Joseph Nichols, Chm, CIC Committee, to All Reli-
gious of the Archdiocese of Washington, n.d. (ca. 20 Aug 1963). Copies of both in SAA.
In an attempt to correct what he believed were exaggerations in the Nichols memo,
O'Boyle reiterated his "official position." See memo, Msgr. John B. Roeder [chancel-
lor], to all Pastors and Superiors, 22 Aug 1963, cy in SAA.

sleeping accommodations and meals in the Center for more than a score of guests. Mass on the morning of the march had special meaning for parishioners used to celebrating every August 28 in a special way. Although many parishioners chose to attend the demonstration with their colleagues in various civic and religious societies, a group of stalwarts, including Gertrude Blackistone, Anna Steen, and Rita Sylvester joined Jones and York as they accompanied their pastor in the long walk to the Lincoln Memorial. A disappointed Father Hurley, as junior assistant, was left home to mind the parish. Apparently overlooked by both pastor and sister superior in the excitement of the moment was the archbishop's ban on participation by women religious. The black habits of the Oblates could be seen mingled among the marchers in the parish contingent.[31]

The partnership between patrician insider Gingras and his streetwise assistant, Baroni, grew even more effective in the years following the March on Washington, and through their efforts the parish became closely identified with the civil rights struggle in the capital. Msgr. Gingras continued to work the system. He acted for the archbishop in promoting the integration of the CYO and the Sodality Union. In one of his proudest moments as pastor he watched parishioner Eula Trigg elected first African-American president of the union. In 1964 he accepted appointment to the D.C. Commissioners' Human Relations Council, a quasi-governmental body charged with advising the commissioners on equal employment opportunity and ensuring compliance with the nondiscrimination-in-employment clause now written into all government contracts. He joined the governing body of the Interreligious Committee on Race Relations, where he represented the diocese when the archbishop was in attendance at the various sessions of the Vatican Council.[32] Gingras also served on the Interreligious Committee's executive board when that body sponsored the capital's first National Home Visit Day in 1964, an event planned to encourage black and white Washingtonians to visit each other in an attempt to

31. Author's intvs. with Pauline J. Jones and Msgr. Leonard Hurley. See also *CS*, 27 Feb 1986.

32. Ltr., O'Boyle to Gingras, 27 Aug 1964, SAA. See also *Washington Post*, 13 Nov 1977.

further racial understanding. The visits were coordinated by the committee's staff in the Parish Center. To manage the practical aspects of an operation that involved thousands of individuals in the congregations of many denominations throughout the city, the committee recruited the experienced Mary Houston, who in turn was assisted by a number of SS. Paul and Augustine parishioners and members of the Catholic Interracial Council.[33]

Meanwhile Father Baroni continued to work the streets, involving the neighborhood more closely in the activities of the Parish Center and attracting ever larger crowds of volunteers from around Washington to help out. It was during these productive years that the Center came to serve as a true center of neighborhood activism and that faces familiar in Washington's civil rights campaign could be seen moving through its halls. Stokely Carmichael, then a student at Howard, came to tutor children and discuss politics and theology. H. Rap Brown, the militant spokesman, put in an occasional appearance. Another visitor to V Street during those years was a youthful civil rights activists soon to gain national prominence, Marion Barry.

The most dramatic moment in the partnership between SS. Paul and Augustine's pastor and assistant occurred in March 1965 following Martin Luther King's call to the nation's clergy to join him in a demonstration at Selma, Alabama. The event was planned as a continuation of a voting rights march brutally suppressed on March 7th by the Alabama highway patrol. King in effect was daring the nation's clergy to risk their own security by personally facing the police batons, carrying out in a practical way the principles they had been espousing from their pulpits. Baroni immediately grasped the importance of a Catholic presence at Selma, but his pastor at first demurred. Like O'Boyle, Gingras was reluctant to involve priests in public demonstrations, but his years in the parish, and exposure to priests like Joyce and Baroni had sensitized him to the true nature of the civil rights struggle. Beyond these influences, Gingras was a man of immense integrity, and by the time of the Selma incident that integrity had come to demand that he

33. During the first year the home visit program attracted 2,000 participants, a number doubled in the following year. On the diocese's involvement in this initiative, see Conley's "'All One in Christ'," pp. 142–43.

act.[34] He not only changed his position, but once committed, threw his considerable weight behind gaining O'Boyle's approval for four priests to join the contingent of Washington clergymen scheduled to fly to Selma on a chartered jet.

The only hitch in their plan was O'Boyle's requirement that they obtain the approval of the bishop of Mobile-Birmingham, whose diocese included Selma, for their public appearance in his diocese. In a day filled with comic intrigue, Baroni, with special help from Floyd H. Agostinelli, one of O'Boyle's lay advisors, engineered the four priests' successful failure to find Bishop Toolen, whose aversion to demonstrators was well known. At the same time they faced the more daunting task of evading the fervid efforts of busybodies and obstructionists in the chancery to abort the mission. Meanwhile, news that Archbishop O'Boyle had granted his priests permission to march swept through the Catholic Interracial network, and priests and religious from many dioceses used that fact to pressure their bishops for permission. Others simply pretended that O'Boyle's action applied to all and took off for Selma.

The parade marshals recommended that the four hundred frightened clergymen stuff rolled newspapers in their hats to ward off the worst effects of the police batons.[35] Gingras and Baroni instead used their breviaries, those thick prayer books then carried by all priests. With the weight of the Divine Office resting lightly on their brows, Washington's representatives set off, two-by-two on Alabama's Jeff Davis Highway. The march itself proved somewhat anti-climatic. Dr. King halted his colleagues at the Edmund Pettis Bridge, where they knelt in prayer. With that the troopers stepped aside, leaving open the route to the capitol in Montgomery. King ordered the demonstrators to return to their starting point in Brown's Chapel, thus bringing the first phase of the demonstration to a peaceful end. The Selma March, a

34. The image of an outwardly austere, correct pastor filled with a newly discovered conviction of racial justice runs through the author's interviews with five of Gingras's close associates—Fathers Joyce, Benson, Hurley, Kemp, and Dwan. "A sweetheart of a man," Ralph Dwan concluded his observations.

35. For a colorful account of the Selma march and the activities in Washington that preceded it, see O'Rourke, *Geno*, chap. 5. See also, Conley's "'All One in Christ'," pp. 146–49.

milestone in the civil rights revolution, also marked a watershed in
Catholic attitudes toward the struggle. The sight of priests and sisters
participating in an act of civil disobedience before armed troopers was
a vivid sign of a new-style Christian witness, a harbinger of later phases of the struggle for racial justice, which would enlist thousands of
Catholics, especially religious and young students, in the cause. It was
an especially important moment in the history of St. Augustine's. The
presence of priests and sisters at Selma could in considerable measure
be attributed to the determination of Geno Baroni, a man who publicly
admitted that his own introduction to the civil rights movement sprang
in good part from his understanding of St. Augustine's century-old
struggle for racial justice.

The Selma march seemed to push Gingras and Baroni deeper into
the civil rights struggle. Both were asked to join a group which met to
discuss with President Johnson the status of civil rights programs in
the wake of the Alabama demonstration. Both testified before the U.S.
Civil Rights Commission: Gingras, representing the diocese, to explain the principles behind the Church's stand on fair employment;
Baroni to report on his experiences with job-opportunity workshops at
the Parish Center.[36] It was during this period that Gingras and Baroni
found themselves being used increasingly by the archbishop to investigate conditions at inner city parishes. Gingras advised O'Boyle and
the various pastors on managing parish programs while Baroni followed up with community action plans appropriate for the various
neighborhoods.[37] Gingras also played a leading role in the organization
of the archbishop's Poverty Program Committee and was later appointed one of his three vicars for urban affairs. In September 1965 the
team was broken up when O'Boyle relieved Baroni of his parish assignment and appointed him executive secretary of the new Committee
for Community Relations.[38] (Before assuming appointment in the
Carter administration, Baroni would also work for the National Confer-

36. McNally, "Green Pastures in a Black Ghetto," p. 26.

37. Examples of parishes receiving such visitations included Our Lady of Perpetu-
al Help, Immaculate Conception, Our Lady of Victory, St. Peter's on Capitol Hill, and
Epiphany. See, for example concerning Our Lady of Perpetual Help, ltr., Gingras to
O'Boyle, 8 Sep 1965, cy in SAA.

38. Ltr., O'Boyle to Gingras, 1 Sep 1965, SAA.

ence of Catholic Bishops where he was instrumental, among other things, in establishing the Campaign for Human Development, a national program begun by the bishops in 1970 to fight poverty.)

Parish Affairs

In fact Baroni's departure was but one of a series of personnel changes that occurred in the mid-1960s. With Fathers Hurley and Roger P. Gallagher also leaving for other assignments, three newcomers appeared: Carl F. Dianda, Andre Bouchard, and Ralph H. Dwan. As first on the scene, Father Dianda, a Washington native, became first assistant, a term in Gingras's lexicon, Dianda jokingly recalled, that meant first to be blamed for anything going wrong around the parish.[39] Actually things went smoothly. Gingras, who had experienced first hand life in a strife-torn rectory at St. Francis de Sales, was determined to preside over a happy household, so he assigned subordinates responsibilities and let them work without interference. Thus Dianda supervised the school, served as chaplain at nearby Children's Hospital, maintained the parish buildings, and managed the big rectory on Fifteenth Street. Bouchard, who had helped out in the parish during his diaconate, arrived as a new priest, an outgoing man who immediately developed a wide acquaintance among parishioners and neighbors alike. Bouchard projected a flamboyant style typified by his flashy automobile (which he let parish youngsters drive) and an earthy casualness that attracted and entertained rather than offended sensibilities. He quickly became a force for change in the neighborhood. With an altogether different approach Dwan, a University of Michigan law school graduate, quietly demonstrated his own special skill as a community activist in his structured direction of the Parish Center. Each of these three young priests exhibited a lively understanding of the rapidly changing state of race relations in the city and the Church, changes that would affect in profound ways the parish's subtly nuanced social structure in the decades to come.

Reflecting in part the important programs sponsored by the Center

---

39. Author's intv. with Father Dianda. Much of the following information about life in the parish, 1965–67, is based on this interview.

during that period, the parish frequently played host to noted activists of the day, guests who provided a heady atmosphere for young, socially aware priests. For example, Saul Alinsky, the famous community organizer and front-line fighter in the war on poverty, used SS. Paul and Augustine as his headquarters in Washington to discuss the feasibility of beginning a campaign similar to his successful operation in Chicago. Ivan Illich, the Jesuit father who was publicly questioning the Church's traditional teachings on charity and social change, practiced his arguments in the rectory. Some of the Church's leading experts on social questions, men like Msgr. George Higgins, the famed labor theorist, frequently took a break from their duties at the National Catholic Welfare Conference headquarters to visit Msgr. Gingras and friends in the parish. Among the many interested men in their audience were two young residents completing their studies in Washington, John F. Donahogue, now the archbishop of Atlanta, and Brian Davis Usanga, now the bishop of Calabar in Nigeria.

Nor were the new assistants reluctant to protest diocesan decisions, as, for example, their publicized reaction to local seminary guidelines. For many decades the parish school had nurtured vocations, proud of the number of its students to enter religious life. As recently as 1962, for example, it had witnessed the ordination of one of its own, Father James B. Joy, Jr.[40] In keeping with that tradition, Father Dianda encouraged three interested eighth graders to apply for admission to Cathedral Latin School, the diocese's new preparatory seminary, only to see them rejected for academic reasons. The fact that all three were accepted in other Catholic high schools led to the obvious conclusion about lingering race problems within Archbishop O'Boyle's own jurisdiction. Dianda and Bouchard let it be known that they would no longer encourage young African Americans to pursue a religious vocation in the archdiocese. (In subsequent years the seminary welcomed black students, and St. Augustine's first African-American pastor would be a graduate of Cathedral Latin.)

Another incident found the intrepid three standing up to their formidable archbishop. In 1966 O'Boyle's chancery notified their pastor

40. Msgr. Joy followed his mentor, Msgr. Benson, into the military, where he recently completed thirty years of service as an Army chaplain.

that he was about to be transferred to a suburban parish. Although saddened by the news, Gingras, always the loyal lieutenant, quietly readied himself for the change, but not so his assistants. In a no-holds-barred letter they outlined for the archbishop why such a move was ill-advised. They reminded O'Boyle how closely Gingras had become identified with racial causes. As the highest-ranking Catholic to participate in the Selma march, he now operated in the national spotlight, speaking for the Church on matters of racial justice. His removal, and the substitution of a man with no special affiliation with the black community, would obscure the racial image the Church hoped to project. These objections led O'Boyle's to intervene. In answer to the point-blank question, Gingras admitted that he did not want to leave his parish. The order was rescinded immediately.[41] For their pains the three assistants were called on the carpet. O'Boyle forcefully informed them that personnel decisions were his to make and that their action had no part in his determination to keep Gingras in the parish. To those who knew O'Boyle well, however, this meeting most likely served as the wily prelate's way of admitting just the opposite.

Why O'Boyle proposed to move Gingras in the first place is unknown, but he may well have been concerned by a new, pessimistic tone in the pastor's reports on the parish's future. For some years annual statements to the parishioners as well as reports to the chancery had stressed the fact that the parish was beginning to lose members and income at a time of increased expenses and responsibilities. Gingras summarized these concerns for the archbishop in July 1966. Attendance had dropped 20 percent in three years, and it was evident, Gingras added, that "stable persons of both races are seeking better housing, better neighborhood environment, with less inclination to encounter the vast social problems of the inner city."[42] Some three-quarters of the members of his congregation were now over fifty years of age, the vast majority on limited, fixed incomes in a period when expenses in the school and the seven buildings in his care were rising. Recently announced tuition increases should tide the school over for a few years, but the church was in need of extensive repair and the old

41. In its effort to reach Gingras, who was vacationing at sea, the chancery had to resort to ship-to-shore phones. See author's intv. with Father Dianda.

42. Ltr., Gingras to O'Boyle, 29 Jul 1966, cy in SAA.

rectory should be replaced. Before sound plans could be drawn up, Gingras warned, decisions must be made on the future of the many buildings the parish supported.

Six months later he was back with further concerns. Renewed efforts to transfer Mackin High School to the larger school building down Fifteenth Street had again failed. With his hope of consolidating the parish on V Street dashed, Gingras now focused on the Parish Center and the unavoidable and expensive repairs needed to meet the District's building code. He proposed that the building be remodeled and its upper floors transformed into a temporary rectory. Tearing down the old one, he argued, would realize considerable savings. He also wanted to be rid of the big rectory on Fifteenth Street, although he admitted that, since the parish was located in the Shaw Renewal area, any changes must be studied with the possibility in mind that the parish's community programs might make it eligible for matching funds.[43]

Gingras always defended the work of the Parish Center, but by 1967 this too was beginning to cause him concern. He had in earlier years gone along with Baroni's increasingly bold plans, not however, without much tugging and pulling. One assistant recalled sometimes waking at 2 A.M. to what sounded like someone being killed out on the street, only to realize that Gingras and Baroni were at it again over some course of action. He and the other priests quickly came to understand that these fights were not serious. All Gingras desired was to be kept informed, so he would be able to defend the parish against its critics.[44] Although Gingras continued to defend the Center's programs in the months after Baroni's departure, it became obvious that he was increasingly concerned over the extent to which Father Dwan and the director, Kate Trainor, were involving the Center in the community. As he explained to O'Boyle, certain areas like legal aid, consumer purchasing training, job training, and community organizing were best addressed by the United Planning Organization or other governmental agencies. The cost of duplicating their work or developing meaningful new programs required a larger budget than the parish could supply,

43. "Report of SS. Paul & Augustine Parish, January, 1967," cy in SAA.
44. The assistant is quoted in McNally, "Green Pastures in a Black Ghetto," p. 26.

YOUNG AT HEARTS CLUB pictured here with its leader, Beatrice Holton Stewart, and Msgr. Gingras in a parish center meeting room. The organization of seniors was one of the many groups that enlivened 1419 V Street during the 1960s.

even with help from such charitable groups as Community Assistance, Inc.[45]

Where the earthy Baroni would have responded to such concerns with passionate arguments and loud threats, the scholarly Dwan quietly pursued his agenda in the community, but he never succeeded in communicating his vision to his worried boss.[46] Finally his plan to organize a project to rehabilitate slum housing in the neighborhood and elsewhere in the city proved too much for Gingras, who feared that his young assistant and his idealistic friends would be swindled. As Dwan, who admired Gingras, later put it, "the group thought it a good plan, but Gingras worried that these do-gooders were his people and

45. Ltr., Gingras to O'Boyle, 29 Jul 1966, cy in SAA. See also author's intv. with Ralph Dwan.

46. In his interview with the author, Father Raymond Kemp, who deeply admired both men, paints a convincing picture of the difficult relationship between the two.

needed to be protected."[47] Finally in August 1967 Gingras laid out his concerns for the archbishop. During the past year the direction of the Center had changed from a united parish-community effort to a less organized community action program. Its directors, he concluded, were unable to integrate their evolving program into the parish's long-range plans, nor had Dwan been able to interest the other priests or "more than a marginal number of parishioners" in this community-oriented approach. After long and fruitless discussions with all involved, including the Center's advisory board and the priests and parishioners, Gingras concluded that the increased involvement in the community envisioned by Dwan and Kate Trainor did not fit in with the united parish-neighborhood effort that the parish wanted and had long supported. While he had nothing but praise for Dwan, Gingras recommended that the assistant be transferred.[48]

O'Boyle agreed. Dwan was assigned to St. Teresa's in Anacostia, and the chancery assumed the cost of operating the Center while plans for its long-range future were considered. The archdiocese's St. Vincent de Paul Society hoped to acquire the building for its inner city hospice, but in the end Cardinal O'Boyle signed an agreement with the Presbytery of Washington City to transform the building into an ecumenical center under the joint sponsorship of the Presbyterians and Catholics.[49] Father Bouchard argued that the building should serve as a community center and insisted that the community be informed about the proposed change, but by 1969 the Vee Street Ecumenical Center was already in operation.[50] In addition to the familiar community activities, it housed the urban affairs offices of the two denominations as well as the Black Churchmen's Ecumenical Training Facility, SS. Paul and Augustine's Head Start, and the archbishop's Neighbor-

47. Author's intv. with Ralph Dwan.

48. Ltr., Gingras to O'Boyle, 22 Aug 1967, cy in SAA.

49. Ltr. O'Boyle to Richard Cooper, President, Central Council of the St. Vincent de Paul Society, 15 Jul 1967, cy in SAA. The Presbyterians assumed the cost of refurbishing the building, which thereafter operated with funds supplied by both denominations. The parish's last subsidy for the Center was a $2,900 payment made in fiscal year 1967. See "SS. Paul & Augustine Church Annual Statements" for 1966–1970 and Notitiae, same period. Patrick O'Boyle was elevated to the College of Cardinals in June 1967.

50. Parish Council Minutes (hereinafter PCM), 21 Oct 1968, SAA.

hood Youth Corps and adult education offices. Diocesan participation was directed by Father Ralph J. Kuehner operating out of the chancery. Although parish organizations continued to meet in the building, for all practical purposes the connection between the parish and the Center ceased.

News of Dwan's imminent departure sparked a protest among activists in the community. William Raspberry, the *Washington Post's* distinguished columnist, reported on a protest meeting attended by thirty-six Shaw residents at the W Street apartment of Thelma Johnson and her mother, Ann Jones. Although they admired Gingras and regretted the differences between the two priests, they were convinced that the cardinal remained unaware of the effectiveness of Dwan's community programs. Uninterested in distinctions between community-based versus parish-centered programs, they concluded that Dwan's "heart is with the people," and some decided to publicize their concern by picketing the cardinal's residence on behalf of the quiet, self-effacing priest, who was obviously embarrassed by all the fuss. When pressed on the subject, he replied simply: "The problem of the church is to get to the problems of the community—specially the youth. . . . Some people don't see it my way."[51]

In truth among those who did not agree with Dwan must be numbered many parishioners. Only three members of the congregation attended the protest meeting on W Street, underscoring Gingras's assertion that the Center's community-based activism had little support in the parish. Actually the congregation had always shown obvious pride in the work begun by Father Baroni, and their contributions over the past five years formed its single greatest source of support. Yet while the Parish Center and its activities had reawakened the congregation's historic interest in the welfare of its neighbors, its innovative programs were largely the work of scores of volunteers from around the city and community activists attracted by men like Baroni and Dwan. As the years went by, fewer and fewer parishioners could be counted among the participants. Most parishioners seemed more comfortable leaving such work to others while they concentrated on more traditional avenues of community support through their St. Vincent de Paul, Ladies

51. As quoted in *Washington Post*, 27 Aug 1967.

of Charity, and other parish-centered programs. In 1967, for example, the pastor allocated a substantial sum for Father Bouchard to begin a summer program for parish children in the parish school. Parishioners participated in the project with the clear understanding that aid to such children was a parish responsibility, not part of a wider community activity. In 1967 the parish's St. Vincent de Paul experienced a new burst of activity. Like the new summer school program, this increased charitable activity focused on the parish needy, especially the elderly. Father Dianda recalled officials of the St. Vincent de Paul complaining that he and Bouchard were spending too much of the society's funds on strangers in the community. When Father Raymond B. Kemp, a young activist sent to replace Dwan, began his ministry in the Shaw community, he easily enlisted the pastor's support, but received little help from parish leaders, who at that time according to Kemp "put up with our [Kemp and Bouchard's] militancy. They kind of tolerated it." When asked who did support them in those days, Kemp responded, "we weren't there yet."[52] Clearly, for many in the congregation the idea of community responsibility, exemplified by the work of those in the Parish Center and the young curates, still needed time to mature.

The Riot and Its Aftermath

This maturation would finally begin among a small group of parishioners in the wake of the urban violence that engulfed Washington following Dr. King's assassination in April 1968.[53] From their vantage point in the Shaw community, the priests and parishioners witnessed

52. See also author's intvs. with Fathers Dianda and Kemp (source of quote) and Ralph Dwan. In response to donations to the parish's St. Vincent de Paul fund from the cardinal and the society's affiliate at St. John Baptist de la Salle, Gingras, responded, "thanks, we can use it." See ltrs. O'Boyle to Gingras, 12 Jul 1967, and to Charles Steeg (St. John Baptist de la Salle), 7 Jul 1967, and Gingras to O'Boyle, 10 Jul 1967. Copies of all in SAA.

53. Disturbances of one magnitude or another occurred in at least 125 American cities, including Baltimore, Chicago, and Detroit. See Paul J. Scheips, "The Washington Riot of 1968" (unpublished manuscript, U.S. Army Center of Military History). Unless otherwise indicated, the following description of the King riot is based on this exhaustive study.

first-hand the arson and looting, the fires and clouds of tear gas, and troops patrolling their streets with bayonets at the ready—all elements of an event that would change the face of Washington forever. Memories seared by the sight of their community erupting in fury, frustration, and despair caused many people, black and white, to abandon the old neighborhood. In others the riot would test assumptions about the usefulness of community programs and produce in them a lasting indifference to the plight of those remaining behind. But to a determined few the riot represented a challenge and resulted in a commitment to fight for renewal. Out of this commitment would grow today's St. Augustine's.

The well-connected Father Baroni was first to hear the news at about 8 P.M. on April 4th.[54] Warned by the city's director of public safety, Patrick Murphy, Baroni ran to the corner of Fourteenth and U, gathering information and trying to console dismayed bystanders milling around the Poor People's Campaign headquarters. Soon, however, the crowd grew ugly, moving along Fourteenth and U Streets, smashing windows, blocking traffic, and urging others to join them. Baroni realized it was time to get out, and he hurried back to send workers and volunteers busy at the Parish Center home by safe routes. Father Kemp heard the news while visiting his family in Silver Spring. He immediately returned to the rectory, where he found the pastor trying to keep abreast of the situation on a police band radio. Eventually Kemp and Bouchard left the rectory to view the unrest. Previously free to walk in any street or alley in the neighborhood, they were now surprised to be met by two young parishioners, Darrell Stoutamire and Bobby Walker, who insisted that they return home, where they remained "protected" by two fifteen-year olds. Only at about three the next morning did they dare venture out.

Some neighborhood leaders sought to contain the crowd's anger. A vacillating Stokely Carmichael at one point successfully turned back some 500 protesters at T Street on their way down Fourteenth Street to the White House, looting and breaking things on the way. At the same time new groups continued to form along Fourteenth Street, especially

54. O'Rourke, *Geno*, pp. 54–59. The following information on the activities of the parish priests during the riot are based on this work and the author's interviews with Fathers Kemp and Dianda.

near the corner at Belmont and then at V Street. At about 8:30 P.M. the mayhem began anew. The Safeway and People's Drug Store were among the first to be hit. During the night more than 200 stores in the neighborhood had their windows smashed, 150 were looted, and seven serious fires burned out of control. The police, who had maintained a low profile in hope of avoiding an open riot, now launched a foray up Fourteenth Street. Using riot batons and tear gas, a 500-man force finally restored calm by 4 A.M.

Friday morning the city appeared normal, but by noon unrest had spread to the point that schools were closed, despite official efforts to keep the 150,000 students off the streets. The children in the parish school were also dismissed. An extraordinary effort was made by those in charge to see the students safely home. A chief concern at the rectory was the safety of the elderly in their apartments above the stores on Fourteenth Street. Father Kemp, clearly marked by his Roman collar, entered apartments north of Belmont Street to rescue some of those in danger. By afternoon the sidewalks were crowded from U Street north to Park Road, and soon the looting and burning began again. Crowds at the corners, especially at W Street, began overturning vehicles (even, in one instance, a police car), setting them afire. By this time, according to Kemp, "it wasn't worth a white man's life to be seen at Fourteenth and W." Rumors spread that Kemp himself had been stabbed. He met people on W Street surprised to find him walking around alive.

The rioting and more than 500 serious fires were concentrated in four sections of town on Friday, which also became known as "picnic day" as hordes of young rioters spent the afternoon looting many famous downtown stores before the arrival of the troops. With the police unable to control the situation, Mayor Walter Washington turned to President Johnson. At 4 P.M., after issuing the necessary warning to the rioters to cease and desist, Johnson ordered in federal troops and the D.C. National Guard. The first troops to get to Fourteenth Street through the traffic jams caused by anxious workers fleeing the center city were elements of the 503d Military Police Battalion. With one civilian policeman assigned to each of their vehicles, the soldiers began to saturate the area. Later a squadron of the 6th Armored Cavalry arrived from its staging area at Soldiers Home. Its men, combat-hardened veterans from Vietnam, began circulating in their armored personnel carriers. Finally, elements of the Army's 3d Infantry, the famed "Old Guard" regiment from Ft. Myer, entered the neighborhood along with national guardsmen assigned to protect the firemen. Despite this show of force, the Fourteenth Street corridor continued to burn, and the odor of tear gas wafted across the parish.[55] Standing on the lawn of the V Street Common that night with flames on the horizon and armed helicopters flying overhead, Baroni imagined himself in a war zone.

Baroni had had a busy day. By 6:30 Friday morning he had already completed arrangements for a food distribution service in the Parish Center. Anticipating trouble months before, he and fellow clergymen Newell and Wendt had won a promise from Joseph Danzansky, head of Giant Foods, to provide supplies for the needy in any future urban disturbance. By Friday afternoon many were desperate for food, and Danzansky stood ready to deliver, but city officials refused permission for the trucks to enter an area they still considered dangerous. By then plenty of tired and hungry neighbors were using the Center as a temporary shelter. Baroni had also spent part of Friday at the city's command headquarters with Cardinal O'Boyle. Officials wanted the city's leading churchmen to make a public appeal for calm. (Baroni dismissed this effort with the quip: "The rioters aren't watching TV, they're busy stealing TVs.") More important, officials looked to O'Boyle and the others to reason with the frightened business leaders, who were screaming for the soldiers to shoot to kill.

With more than 13,500 armed troops patrolling the city, an uneasy calm finally returned by Saturday morning. Soon, with the help of his fellow priests and especially Oblate Sisters Marcellina Brooks and Barbara Spears, Baroni had the food distribution operation going successfully in the parish and at other sites in the city. With the help of some parishioners he also later organized a clothing distribution center for the many who had been unable to return to their homes since Thursday. No one dwelt too long on the fact that some of the donated clothing looked as though it had just come from a store. (For years Father Kemp retained as a souvenir a pair of bright orange socks appropriated by some young rioter from D. J. Kaufmann's, a favorite Wash-

55. The parish buildings suffered four separate gas attacks aimed by soldiers at the crowds at Fourteenth and V Streets.

ington clothier, and donated to the clothing drive.) Sunday was Palm Sunday, and the priests were surprised by the number of parishioners who were able to attend that familiar service under the watchful eye of patrolling soldiers.

Although parishioners living in the neighborhood and the parish buildings survived the destruction unscathed, the riot affected everyone. Looking back years later, Father Kemp admitted that vivid memories of those days continued to haunt him. The riot opened his eyes to the fact that, with few exceptions, all those who lived north of Florida Avenue were strangers to the Church and that the parish had failed to touch those thousands living "on the other side of Cardozo," even though they were embraced by the parish's boundaries.[56] Those who knew Gingras well understood how deeply the riot had wounded him. The fact that he needed protection during those dark days led him to brood on the limits of his effectiveness as a pastor. Along with many of the distinguished African-American preachers in the region, he came to realize that their influence was severely limited and that they had come to be shunned by many whom they had dedicated their lives to serve.[57] Baroni reacted much the same way. As he told his biographer, "I knew immediately that the riot in Washington was not going to be forgotten quickly and that I was going to have to do things differently . . . . You could just feel that everything had changed."[58] Even he was no longer entirely comfortable walking the streets. In the months that followed, a depressed Baroni underwent several severe illnesses.

The impact on the laity took longer to register. Some frightened parishioners made the momentous decision to leave their old neighborhood, but their moving merely accelerated a trend noticeable since the merger of the two parishes. More ominous was the decrease in the number of nonresident parishioners now evident in the church. Whatever their sense of loyalty to SS. Paul and Augustine, their growing unease with the Shaw area led them to worship elsewhere. By 1969 Sunday attendance stood at 1,000, a 50 percent decline in six years. By 1972 it had fallen to 649, the rows of empty pews mute testimony to the

56. Author's intv. with Kemp.

57. In his intv. with the author, Father Dianda describes the lasting effect of the riot on Gingras's personality.

58. As quoted by O'Rourke in *Geno*, pp. 56 and 59.

power of local conditions to affect parish life. School enrollment, which stood at 349 the year before the riot, was down to 252 in 1972. The various parish organizations suffered similar losses with the once-flourishing Sodality counting just 180 members in 1972; the Holy Name was down to just 70.[59]

A profile of this reduced congregation revealed the same old social distinctions that had always been present at St. Augustine's, although the differences were now somewhat exaggerated by the departure of so many middle-class members.[60] Even before the riot the parish had watched the departure of many of its young, upwardly mobile professionals who would eventually enrich parish life at places like Nativity and St. Gabriel's. Fewer than two dozen white parishioners remained, a tiny remnant of the old St. Paul's congregation, along with a few non-residents of the area, like Joseph Belfiore, who were attracted to the parish by its progressive ways and open, welcoming air. Unlike Belfiore, few of these white parishioners actively participated in parish affairs.

Throughout the 1960s the most active element in the congregation continued to be representatives of a group of older, distinguished professionals, many with close ties to Dunbar High School, Howard University, and the D.C. Teacher's College. Although some were now settled in other areas of town, a surprising number remained in apartments along Sixteenth Street and New Hampshire Avenue and in homes along the northern edge of the parish. These were the heirs of the old aristocrats of color who had for many generations given St. Augustine's a special distinction among Washington's churches, and they remained fiercely loyal to their parish. Their college degrees and professional attainments and their highly refined social manners created a clear division between them and the always more numerous working-class families. Within this exclusive group might also be included a few families that traced their ancestry back to the "We Sorts," that

59. These statistics are based on the *Notitiae*, various years, and on a report prepared by the chairman of the budget and finance committee of the Parish Council (Joseph Belfiore) in 1970, cy in SAA.

60. This profile of the parish in the late 1960s is based on observations made to the author by Msgr. Hurley and Fathers Kemp and Dianda and Mrs. Pauline J. Jones.

proud and self-isolated band of immigrants from Maryland and Virginia of mixed Native-American and African-American ancestry.

These aristocrats continued to dominate the various parish organizations, including the parish council, which was initially an appointed body. Throughout the turbulent 1960s they continued to uphold the traditional way of doing things. These were the people, Father Kemp noted, who at best merely tolerated the increasingly radical community efforts he and Father Bouchard were trying to start. Many of them were descendants of converts who had been attracted to the church by the beauty and timelessness of its rituals. As to be expected, they were more comfortable with the old liturgy and old traditions. In the early 1960s, for example, under the leadership of Charles Whitby, one of their own, they helped revitalize the Confraternity of the Blessed Sacrament in the parish and sponsored a novena to coincide with the canonization of Martin de Porres, the parish's first patron. They also firmly backed the parish's musicians who carried on the great choral tradition of both St. Augustine's and St. Paul's. In distinction, they conspicuously failed to support the effort by Father Kemp and others to honor the slain Dr. King. Many were generally skeptical about the effectiveness of King's work, and they were not to be seen at the annual ecumenical service held in the church in his memory. By 1973 the *Washington Post* reported that only twenty parishioners had attended that year, quoting Father Bouchard's wry comment, "After only six years people sure have short memories."[61]

These lay leaders counted among their number several public school principals and retired teachers. They retained a somewhat jaundiced view of the scholastic potential of neighborhood children, who now accounted for a large part of the student body of the parochial school. When controversy erupted over educational policy at the end of the decade, they would provide firm support for the pastors against the principals.

While convenient, it would be incorrect to cast the parish's working-class members as in opposition to the aristocrats. Nor could the two groups be neatly divided between those eager to see the parish

61. *Washington Post*, 22 Jan 1973. On the Martin de Porres novena, see the *Post*, 22 Apr 1962. See also ltr., Whitby to Gingras, 5 Jan 1962, SAA.

embrace the neighborhood and those who wanted to protect the parish against what they believed was a hostile neighborhood. Nevertheless, just as social distinctions between the two elements were always clear, so too different opinions on the parish's future course were beginning to simmer beneath the surface. As denoted by their description, working-class parishioners were busy earning a living and had less time to devote to the direction of parish organizations. Still, Mae T. Brent, and members of the Joy and Jones families devoted precious leisure hours to help organize the parish council. Others were mainstays of parish organizations. Members of the Dines family, for example, gave vital support to the Credit Union, CYO, and choir. As a class, these parishioners could be included among those same office employees, government personnel, and blue-collar workers who formed the backbone of every congregation, black and white, in the city.

The parish also lost many of these busy people when they moved away from the troubled neighborhood, but still a significant number clung stubbornly to their homes, especially in the region between Eleventh and Seventeenth Streets in the southern section of the parish. Many could trace their Catholic heritage back to the early years of St. Augustine's, even if some of them could also remember a less than charitable welcome to the parish they now called their own. One working-class parishioner, for example, remembered as a young woman visiting the old downtown church with her mother only to be shunned by "fur-clad matrons with high society airs" who considered it more appropriate that people of her sort be accommodated in the decidedly *declassé* congregation at Holy Redeemer.[62] Nevertheless, many of these working-class parishioners were united with the aristocrats in their determination to preserve the parish's traditions and the time-tested way of dealing with things.

At the same time another, albeit smaller group of working-class parishioners was beginning to attract notice. This was the group that volunteered what time it could spare to the parish's community activities and formed the core of those demanding change. Its members served on the Parish Center Advisory Board and helped out in Father Dwan's community projects. They provided the manpower needed in

62. As quoted in author's intv. with Father Dianda.

the countless activities in the 1960s aimed at neighborhood involvement, supplying, for example, the scores of volunteers who worked with Vincent de Forest in his soap box derby project. As a group, these parishioners were also more likely to reject the deference traditionally bestowed on the clergy and to work for greater lay participation in the operation of the parish. For example, when Pauline J. Jones finally became prefect of the parish Sodality, she immediately stopped the time-honored practice of seating priests at a separate table during sodality functions, an arrangement, because of the color of the clergy, that lent an unhealthy racial tone to these parish activities. Henceforth, pastor Gingras and the rest would find a seat among the ladies. She was also an early advocate of a black history program in the parish, although to succeed she needed to overcome opposition from some of the traditionalists who charged that Jones and her friends "wanted to make too much of that black stuff."[63] Ardent civil rights supporters, Lozzie York, Anna Steen, and Pauline Jones among others took time off work to help organize the parish's part in the March on Washington.

It also followed that these parishioners tended to differ with the pastor and his allies among the retired principals and teachers in the congregation on matters involving the school. Where church officials traditionally saw parochial schools as an instrument for preserving and extending the faith, these hard-pressed parents viewed such institutions as a chance for academic excellence denied inner-city children elsewhere. They remained loyal to the teachers.

Members of the working class were also identified with efforts to make the liturgy more accessible to younger members.[64] Gingras carefully retained the early Sunday mass and the high mass with choir for the traditionalists in the congregation, but in keeping with changes springing from the Vatican II, he turned the 9:30 mass over to Kemp and Bouchard. There, with the help of Benedictine Sister Terence Fenlon and a group of teenagers from St. Anthony's in Brookland, along with guitar-playing deacon Carey Landry, they experimented with different types of music and accoutrements to the liturgy, innova-

63. As quoted in author's intv. with Pauline J. Jones. Jones would finally see the parish reestablish a Black History Week program in 1979.

64. For a detailed discussion of this subject, see following chapters and Appendix I.

tions that would lead directly to the transformation of parish worship in the decades to come.[65]

With such divergent currents running beneath the surface, some years would pass before the greatly reduced parish would finally chart a permanent new course for its future. Meanwhile, the last years of the turbulent 1960s played out in relative calm with the parish and neighborhood attempting to recover from the trauma of the riot. With the pastor's support Father Bouchard began operating a summer school program that soon rivaled the projects sponsored by the Parish Center in the past. Bouchard also won election as commissioner of Ward One in the Model Cities Program, which became a major source of support for the Harrison Community project. Operating out of the V Street Center and elsewhere, the Harrison project supplied educational, recreational, and nutritional services to the neighborhood. Using District funds channeled through the Neighborhood Planning Councils, Bouchard developed a community program with a budget that exceeded that of the parish school.[66] Father Kemp was kept busy with his neighborhood organizing efforts, running four community organizations within the parish boundaries (at old Garfield Hospital, near Seventeenth and Willard, Fourteenth and Fairmont, and Fourteenth and Corcoran Street). Altogether the two priests were managing a budget totaling more than $2.5 million of mostly government money each summer, a large part of which went as salaries for the teenagers employed by the various projects.

Typical of community activists of that period but unique among Washington priests, Kemp and Bouchard were arrested for their role in a welfare rights demonstration following the riot. That time their long-suffering pastor bailed them out, but, Kemp later admitted, what he and Bouchard were attempting in the neighborhood was not really much broader in scope than the projects started by Baroni earlier in the decade, "but was a lot wilder." Little of this activity was directly related to the parish or won the approval of the majority of parishioners, and Kemp soon came to realize that, without the support of

65. One leader of this group was John Butler, now president of John Carroll High School.

66. For details on these projects, see report by Joseph Belfiore, Chairman, Budget and Finance Committee, SS. Paul & Augustine Parish Council, n.d. (ca. 1970), SAA.

parishioners, he and Bouchard would never acquire a solid base for their community work. It also seemed obvious to them that unless the whole congregation put aside its emphasis on preserving old traditions and came to embrace the neighborhood, its future remained precarious. They decided, therefore, to concentrate on winning parishioners over to their way of thinking about the community and develop within the parish a new set of priorities to match the rapidly changing times.

Everybody agreed that after administrating the parish through twenty of its most turbulent years, Msgr. Gingras was rapidly approaching burnout. His confrontation with a school principal in 1970 provoked a situation that a younger, more vigorous Gingras might easily have avoided. In fact Gingras's decision to ask the Oblate's Mother General to replace Sister Majella Neale precipitated a controversy that would fall chiefly on his successor. Not long after school opened with a new principal in the fall of 1970, Cardinal O'Boyle decided that Gingras should be relieved of the cares of a parish in transition. In November he was assigned to the less demanding post of pastor of Our Lady of Lourdes in the Maryland suburbs. Meanwhile, O'Boyle brought back the young, energetic, and extremely likable Leonard Hurley to serve as sixth pastor of the venerable church. Father Hurley was expected to reverse the fading fortunes of what was now an inner city parish. On this subject his views were well known. With a strong respect for parish traditions, which he had learned as a young curate during his close association with Msgr. Olds, Hurley was determined to honor these traditions by administering the parish along the lines laid out by his two predecessors. Foremost on his mind were those faithful members who had formed the parish's principal support over the decades. They had overcome many obstacles since the war, and Hurley was determined that their hard work and sacrifices would not be forgotten as the church struggled with the larger problems of the community.

Such a program would attract many supporters, especially among those who remained in control of the parish's organizations. But it was also sure to generate opposition. Hurley's two assistants, who had by then sent roots deep into the local community, entertained very different ideas on how the parish should operate in the volatile 1970s, and their views were slowly gaining support among a small group of ac-

tivist parishioners. Until now largely inarticulate, these mostly younger members of the congregation were finally beginning to shed the deference traditionally shown the congregation's leaders and letting their
ideas be known. The stage was set for an exciting period of transition
during a time when the Church was undergoing changes in the way it
governed at the parish level and the city was adapting to a radically
different racial outlook following the turbulence of the 1960s.

TEN ❧ A PARISH COME ALIVE

*O*n December 12, 1971, Cardinal O'Boyle came to SS. Paul and Augustine to help celebrate the tenth anniversary of the merger of the two congregations. As it had so often over the decades, the parish pulled out all the stops to welcome its archbishop. Its musical forces joined in a liturgy that reunited the priests who had served under pastors Olds and Gingras as well as many former parishioners now scattered across the archdiocese. The reception that followed at the Statler Hotel allowed the congregation to meet the cardinal, socialize with old friends, and hear an address by District Supreme Court Judge Harry T. Alexander. Yet, in truth, beyond the pleasure of participating in a glittering occasion, the parish had little to celebrate.

Admittedly by now the mutual suspicion between blacks and whites in the congregation, which had so concerned Msgr. Gingras and at first imposed a somewhat artificial organization of parish functions, had faded, not so much because the races had learned to work together, but because so few of the old St. Paul's crowd remained. In fact the dramatic exodus from the neighborhood in recent years had also affected the strength of the St. Augustine segment. The drop in the number of African-American parishioners was especially evident in the years following the riot that saw the loss of some 10,000 housing units in the area. By the time of the cardinal's visit in 1971 many of the families long identified with old St. Augustine's had moved away, leaving a congregation numbering just 875 members and an average Sunday attendance of 755. (The nadir would finally be reached six years later when only 582 people on average could be counted at the parish's Sunday masses.)[1]

The fortunes of the parish school followed a parallel path. The 280 children enrolled at the time of the tenth anniversary constituted a student body that had decreased almost 50 percent in a decade. (In 1972, its low point, school attendance stood at 252.)[2] These losses occurred just as the number of lay teachers began to rise dramatically. By 1974 only four Oblate Sisters of Providence would remain in a school whose staff included seven lay teachers and a lay principal. Any sharp increase in tuition to cover these new expenses would only further reduce enrollment, since many students came from families already pressed to the limit. As in the past the congregation contributed generously to the school, but with such support running to one-fifth of parish revenues and promising to go much higher, clearly some other source must be tapped if the school was to continue.

Other inner-city parishes had faced similar crises because of dramatic demographic changes in the capital. Almost a generation earlier, St. Patrick's had seen its traditional congregation disappear, only to rebound with a new mission as the downtown church serving the business and government community. St. Dominic's, to cite one other, had survived the loss of its congregation during the lamentable reconstruction of southwest Washington. In its case, gentrification of the old neighborhood produced a radically different yet energetic parish, although at the cost of losing its school. SS. Paul and Augustine faced a greater challenge. Its largely middle-class congregation was still in the process of decline. Fear that the region was on the verge of another riot, a possibility seriously considered by city officials and anxiously discussed in the congregation, had largely disappeared by 1971, but multiple social problems in the poor and largely non-Catholic neighborhood had grown dramatically since 1968. With increased poverty and hopelessness came an even higher crime rate, which in turn tended to inhibit the activities of those Catholics who remained. In 1969

1. Ltr., Rev. Raymond Kemp to Parish, 11 Jan 1981. See also various parish reports, 1968–1975, and "Parish of Opposites," an article in the *Evening Star*, 1 Oct 1970. Cys. of all in SAA.

2. PCM, 17 Sep 1972, SAA.

the pastor had reported a drop in revenue, caused in part by "the inability to conduct more than a minimum of socials and benefits." By
1972 the parish bulletin published a request for volunteers for the
CCD program, citing a major need for male volunteers to provide security for the students.[3] Clearly, despite its proud history and close association with all phases of the growth of black Catholicism in the nation, there was no guarantee that the parish would survive such continuing losses in its new and threatening environment.

All sorts of proposals would be advanced to rescue the parish, and
during the next decade many initiatives would be set in motion to help
it "come alive," as the popular parish slogan put it. The forum where
these ideas were thrashed out and initiatives decided upon was the
parish council. There the heirs of the old aristocrats of color would exert their greatest influence on parish programs and newcomers to the
congregation would acquire the skills that allowed them later in the
decade to take the lead in a concerted campaign of evangelization and
parish activism. There also assertive parish leaders and a series of dynamic pastors would forge a unique partnership loosely based on
guidelines established by the Vatican Council in its Decree on the
Apostolate of the Laity. Although none could predict the outcome in
1971, it was obvious from the determination of the principals that a
hard-fought effort was underway to preserve this inner-city parish and
its racial heritage for future generations.

Organizing for Battle

Some of this determination could be detected in the early deliberations of the parish council. Since the days of William Lofton and
Thomas Turner, prominent members of the congregation had always
felt free to express strongly held views on the administration of the
parish. Many of the thirty-one volunteers who responded to Msgr. Gingras's invitation to form a parish council exhibited similar assertiveness. What might be described as the last generation of the old St. Augustine's aristocracy dominated the new council, which met for the

3. The possibility of another serious riot was discussed by the parish council in its
meeting on 21 Oct 1968. The quotation is from Gingras's 1969 Annual Report, SAA. See
also Parish Bulletin, 15 Oct 1972.

first time on December 11, 1967. Yet even in these early days the council included a small faction, harbingers of a later generation of parish leaders, less united by old associations but more questioning of the order of things. In its early years the council also included a significant minority of white members, some, like Ann Woodson, disciples of Geno Baroni associated with the V Street Center; a few, newcomers attracted to the parish by its welcoming spirit.[4]

Although council members were initially appointed by the pastor, by-laws were soon adopted that provided for elections. Eventually the council agreed that the pastor could appoint up to three members and the priests of the parish, superior of the convent, and school principal would participate as nonvoting, ex-officio members.[5] The council also organized standing committees to provide oversight and prepare individual budgets for various parish activities. In the early years the committees were four in number: worship and church, education, budget and finance, and hospitality. (At Father Bouchard's suggestion a parish and community committee was soon added to help coordinate the parish's increasing involvement in ecumenical and neighborhood initiatives.) To prioritize all these activities and set the agenda the council created a seven-member executive committee in 1970.[6]

From the start the council faced a formidable challenge in drumming up interest among members of a steadily diminishing congregation. Although a majority of members still lived in the neighborhood, considerable effort was made to attract those who had moved away but retained some allegiance to their old parish. (In fact the council's first president, Eula Trigg, then resided on the so-called Gold Coast off upper Sixteenth Street.) Many schemes were tried to publicize the council's work. It staged open meetings to which the whole parish was invited. To increase representation it invited each parish organization to

4. The original council also included a small group of white members selected by the pastor, who was anxious to show his regard for the remnant of the old St. Paul's group surviving in the neighborhood. See ltr., Gingras to Walter A. Jones, 7 Dec 1967, cy in SAA. For a listing of founding members of the parish council, see appendix, below.

5. PCM, 16 Oct 1971 and 20 Feb 1972.

6. All these organizational matters were discussed in various council meetings, 1968–1972. A nearly complete set of meeting minutes is on file in SAA.

appoint a member. It even nominated several young adults for membership in an effort to give that often ignored segment of the congregation a voice in parish deliberations. It also tried some self-discipline. Its haphazard schedule of meetings was soon regularized (three unexcused absences meant dismissal for elected members), and each standing committee was required to present a detailed report of its work at the regular monthly meeting.[7]

As to be expected in any new enterprise, the council endlessly debated the nature of its mission and the extent of its powers. Once, after several interminable sessions fruitlessly discussing changed mass schedules, refreshment rosters, and organizational minutiae, an exasperated Juanita Tolson put the question to the pastor: "Is this parish council an advisory council or only a rubber stamp?" Gingras, who on several occasions had publicly described the council as "a more effective means of expressing your [the congregation's] wishes," assured Tolson and her colleagues that that they were indeed advisors and an essential element of parish administration.[8] In fact even during its early, struggling years the council far exceeded the usual definition of an advisory body, and by the time of Gingras's departure in late 1970 had become an active participant in several important and long-range decisions.

The new pastor, Leonard Hurley, arrived in November 1970 with instructions, as he put it, "to put out the fire," that is, to solve the ongoing financial crisis and to settle mounting problems in the school.[9] It was a reasonable approach for him to take. A man of boundless energy (he always worked eighteen-hour days, during which he climbed the stairs two at a time, one associate noted), he was nevertheless overburdened. In addition to his full-time parish duties, he retained diocesan responsibilities, especially the time-consuming direction of the mass for shut-ins and his work with the Sodality Union. At the same time his

7. For discussion of these organizational matters, see, for example, PCM, 25 Jun 1969, 21 Jan 1972, and 16 Apr 1972. See also ltr., Carl Bransford, council president, to members, 29 Dec 1970, SAA.

8. PCM, 20 July 1970 {first quote} and Gingras, "1969 Annual Report to the Parish" {second quote}.

9. Author's intvs. with Hurley and Kemp. Unless otherwise indicated, the following sections of this chapter are based on these interviews.

two assistants were pre-occupied, far more than Father Hurley liked, in their community projects. The pastor later apologized to the council for failing to accomplish many things he had promised, admitting that its criticism was justified and that his extra-curricular duties had "spread me rather thin."[10] He promised to get out of his radio and TV chores, but in fact that never happened.

From the beginning Hurley made it clear that he wanted the council more actively involved in parish leadership. He had retained many friends in the parish from his days as a newly ordained priest, and he discovered in the council, especially among the parish aristocrats who dominated its deliberations, willing workers who strongly supported his ideas on how the parish should operate. They agreed that their primary mission was to guard the parish and its traditions against the changes in the neighborhood and changing attitudes among some of the younger laity in the congregation. Their first task was to staunch the hemorrhage of people and assets by downplaying some of the recent emphasis on social programs and restoring Msgr. Olds's vision of a complete parish, one that protected (and perhaps isolated) its members from problems in the neighborhood by serving them from cradle to grave in a respectable and caring community of believers. Hurley was convinced that the recent drop in church attendance was not so much because of changing demographics, but rather was traceable to the neglect of veteran parishioners and the new stress placed on the needs of largely non-Catholic neighbors. The hordes of converts of past decades, he concluded, had been attracted by the dignity and unchanging beauty of the liturgy, the excellence of the school, and the respectability of the congregation, not by social activism, and he wanted to restore the parish along the lines laid out by Olds a generation before. The dignified and articulate parish leaders of the council agreed, and they whole-heartedly cooperated with him. For his part Hurley endeared himself by reminding them that they had been his first parishioners and thus his principal teachers, who therefore must accept responsibility for how he had turned out. They were understandably proud when their charming young pastor was elevated to the rank of monsignor shortly after his return.

10. Ltr., Hurley to Belfiore and Parish Council, 10 Jan 1973, SAA.

From the beginning Hurley envisioned the council's mission as guiding and coordinating "the total thrust of parish life." He believed that this goal could be achieved when every parish organization participated as an integral working part of one or more of the major council committees.[11] Not surprising, he turned to these committees for assistance in dealing with his first priority, the financial crisis. Soon after arriving back in the parish he asked the council to help him draw up a revised budget.[12] In short order the budget committee submitted a statement that projected parish income for 1971 at slightly above the $111,000 collected in 1970, enough to cover expenses except for the projected sharp rise in school costs. The difference between school income and expenses in 1970 had totaled $29,000, which was covered out of parish funds. The subsidy projected for the coming year, however, was estimated at $40,000, a sum clearly beyond the parish's means. With school expenses now totaling almost $70,000 yearly and tuition bringing in less than half that amount, new sources of revenue must be found.

The council had been discussing the possibility of tuition increases for some time. Archdiocesan guidelines recommended fixing charges at what the majority of parents could afford, but in 1969 the council had discussed several possible alternatives, including dropping the upper grades to cut expenses and means-testing families to set tuition charges, a system strongly favored by Msgr. Gingras. No decision was reached, however, and members of the council tried to make do by recruiting parishioners to paint, repair, and clean the school and by conducting a raffle to pay for salary increases.[13] Now with a crisis looming, the education and budget committees got to work in earnest. Early in 1972 the council approved their recommendation to double tuition rates (to $223 per parish child and $273 for outsiders).[14]

11. Hurley, "A Possible Plan to Strengthen Parish Council Committees," 17 Mar 1973, SAA.

12. See discussion in PCM, 25 Apr 1971.

13. See PCM, 17 Jun and 15 Jul 1968, 25 Jan and 15 Mar 1969, and 25 Jul and 17 Aug 1970.

14. PCM, 20 Feb 1972. The 1970 rates had stood at $100 for parishioners and $150 for non-parishioners, with lower rates for a second child. See PCM, 17 Aug 1970.

Meanwhile, Hurley approached the cardinal for help. His predecessor had wheedled $33,000 from the chancery, in part to subsidize ordinary income and more than $6,000 to cover extraordinary school repairs. Hurley asked O'Boyle for $8,000 to cover costs in 1971, and in March 1972 he was back again seeking what he called "a welfare check." Knowing his superior's weakness for clearly drawn financial statements, he laid out parish expenses in great detail (including such minor items as $152 for cookies for the school and convent and $119.48 for the priests' laundry). He was asking only for another $8,000, he told O'Boyle, because the parish had made plans to raise part of the cost of school insurance and supplies, but, he went on to warn, he might well be back before year's end with another appeal. The parish got its $8,000 and later a second and even larger payment before the end of the year.[15] The archdiocese under O'Boyle and his successor would continue to subsidize the school until the sale of church property later in the decade canceled what had become a comfortable arrangement.

True to his word, Hurley, working with the various council committees, tapped other sources of income. With the fear of riots finally subsiding, the newly refurbished auditorium on Fifteenth Street once again became a money maker when rented out for dances and cabarets. (It brought in $4,200 in 1972 alone.) The parish also resorted to time-honored remedies, sponsoring countless candy sales, Vegas nights, pound parties, and the rest. A successful campaign was launched to solicit money from wealthier parishioners and friends of SS. Paul and Augustine for a scholarship fund for needy students.[16] All these sources, and a continuing rise in regular income despite falling attendance figures, allowed the parish to balance the books for the first time in many years and left the pastor and council free to concentrate on other pressing issues.

15. These financial matters were documented in PC Task Force cmte rpt, 17 Aug 1970; ltr., Hurley to O'Boyle, 15 Mar 1972; Parish Report, 1971; and undated PC Summary (ca. Jan 1973). All in SAA.

16. This fund would realize significant amounts over the years. See, for example, Parish Bulletin, 7 Jan 1973, and ltr., Rev. John J. Mudd to Msgr. Louis Quinn [pastor of St. Matthew's], 3 Aug 1987, cy in SAA.

The School Crisis

Of considerable import, the school, always a center of parish affairs, had become the focus of debate over the mission of black Catholic education. Despite a diminishing student body and deteriorating building, a series of postwar principals had managed to maintain standards while imparting to their charges some understanding of the history of black Catholics in the nation's capital. In 1968 the parish learned that Oblate Sister Marcellina Brooks, described simply by one priest as "a most excellent principal," was to be transferred.[17] Concerned about the loss of this valuable colleague, Father Bouchard wanted the parish council to quiz the Oblates' Mother General about the qualifications of any proposed replacement. Instead, the council prepared a request, signed by the pastor, asking the Oblates to extend Sister Marcellina's appointment. The request was denied, and in the fall the parish was introduced to Sister Reparata Clarke, O.S.P., its new principal.[18]

Although Sister Reparata reported to the parish council shortly after her arrival that she found little difference in the scholastic performance of children from parish families and those growing numbers of students from outside the parish, she faced falling test scores and began developing new approaches to handle weak students. She wanted the parish to limit the student body to 350 (a theoretical figure well above 1968 enrollment) with no more than 35 pupils accepted in any grade beyond the third. While declaring that the school's primary purpose was "to provide a Christian and moral education," she was obviously attuned to the growing self-awareness in African-American society and continued her predecessors' efforts to promote a knowledge of black achievements. Under her the school continued to celebrate black history week during which students and teachers produced mini-plays and school assemblies designed to illustrate historical and cultural events of special importance to African Americans.[19]

17. Both Fathers Dianda and Kemp were outspoken in their praise for Sister Marcellina's accomplishments. The quote is from author's intv. with Father Dianda.

18. PCM, 17 Jun and 21 Oct 1968.

19. PCM, 25 Jan 1969 (source of quote). See also notes on author's intv. with Sister M. Charlotte Marshall, O.S.P., 14 Aug 1997.

Unfortunately for the school's stability, Sister Reparata served only one year before the Oblates saw fit to replace her. The new principal, Sister Majella Neale, O.S.P., was a native of Maryland, but her teaching assignments had taken her to the deep South, and SS. Paul and Augustine's was her first assignment in the capital and her first exposure to the sophisticated urban Catholics who dominated the parish. A soft-spoken but determined woman, she too was concerned about academic scores, but she was also convinced that physical surroundings had considerable influence on performance and discipline. She wanted to refurbish the generally dilapidated interior of the school. After discussing the matter with the pastor, she appealed to the parents, who responded by donating paint and labor to brighten up the drab cafeteria. Although the record is unclear, this work was done apparently without reference to the parish council and its committees, and Sister Majella was surprised by the criticism she received from pastor and council for what was called a diversion of parish resources.[20] Even more insistent than her predecessors that students develop some appreciation of black culture, Sister Majella instituted extracurricular programs meant to highlight the attainments of African Americans since colonial times. Later in the year she closed the school for a day to lead the student body to the Shrine of the Immaculate Conception where students from schools throughout the region celebrated their racial solidarity. At a meeting of Catholic principals and diocesan educators, she gained some notoriety by offering her candid opinion on the racial situation in Catholic schools, thus stimulating a heated discussion.

However much these activities might have enriched the students, they did little to solve the school's academic and disciplinary problems, which particularly affected a small but noticeable minority of the student body. Nevertheless it came as a surprise to many in the parish when the council welcomed Sister Frances Aileen Holly, O.S.P., "our new school principal," to its membership in August 1970. After only one year on the job a principal had been asked to leave! The exact reason for this startling move and the roles of the parish council

20. Notes on author's telecon with Sister M. Majella Neale, O.S.P., 25 Apr 1997, SAA. According to Sister Majella, Msgr. Gingras accused her of "stealing money from poor parents."

and Msgr. Gingras in the affair will never be known for certain because Juanita Tolson's demand that the council's discussion of Sister Majella's "dismissal" be included in the minutes was rejected.[21] But the general causes of the dismissal are obvious. Sister Majella's approach was bound to have generated some criticism among the distinguished academicians on the council. These leaders, focused on scholastic achievement and discipline, had little sympathy for black awareness initiatives. For some, their experience in the public schools had left them with a poor opinion of the ability of the children of the working underclass, many of whom were now enrolling in the parish school. They questioned the suitability of including such marginal students in what had always been a solid academic program. For all his undoubted interest in civil rights, Msgr. Gingras had always been eager to uphold standards and protect the parish's academic reputation. He would have seen Tolson and her colleagues as allies in this case.

Sister Frances Aileen's brief tenure in the principal's office proved to be the stormiest in the school's history. It began promisingly enough. Like Sister Marcellina before her, Sister Frances Aileen was an active member of the parish council, keeping her colleagues informed about the school and its problems. Her aim, she told the council soon after her arrival, was to update the school and its equipment. To that end she worked with the council's education committee on developing plans to free the principal from teaching responsibilities and with the Home-School Association (the parish's name for its PTA) to explain testing standards and procedures and provide volunteer tutors. She also worked with diocesan officials to obtain furniture and textbooks found surplus to the needs of some suburban schools.[22] Using volunteers signed up through the Parish Come Alive program, she was able to form a roster of parents to perform custodial chores until the parish could afford a full-time janitor to replace the invaluable Gladstone Worrell.

Sister Frances Aileen was more aggressive than her predecessors in promoting black self-awareness, devoting considerable class time to these interests. Soon after his arrival in November, the new pastor let

21. PCM, 17 Aug 1970.

22. PCM, 12 Oct 1970. She was still looking for delivery of the furniture and books in the new year. See PCM, 11 Jan 71.

her know what he felt about what he considered an improper use of class time. He wanted the teachers to concentrate on academic subjects. "We had some real good fights," he later admitted.[23] But Hurley did more than argue. Like Gingras before him, he was determined to guard what he considered the traditional standards of the oldest school for black Catholics in the city, and he discussed his concerns with the parish council. He recommended that it appoint an ad hoc committee to study the matter. The council agreed, and three members, Juanita Tolson, Angela Bishop, and Eula Trigg, all retired professional educators with years of experience in District schools, reviewed student test scores over the past several years. They concluded that the school's standards had fallen off dramatically, a conclusion that the volatile Sister France Aileen rebutted in an impassioned and intemperate address to the council. Further irritating Hurley, she stirred up a public debate over the physical condition of the convent, blaming its "difficult, depressing and dangerous state" on the racial insensitivity of Church authorities.[24]

In a lengthy discussion of the school's future in January 1971, the parish council made it clear that the principal's fate had been sealed. Answering a question posed by Mrs. Tolson and speaking for the Oblates, Sister M. Magdalen Proctor, vicar general of the order and superior of the motherhouse convent, added that, although the need for a nonteaching principal "was not disputed," the recruitment of another nun was impossible. Lawrence C. Hill, chairman of the education committee and a public school principal, recommended that the position be filled by a lay person, and he made clear that the principal should be responsible to his committee. Father Kemp suggested that the council look for a strong administrator with progressive ideas about home, school, and parish and one who would find ways to obtain government funding. Sister Magdalen concluded with the observation that an innovator was needed to solve the school's problems. A profes-

23. Notes on author's intv. with Msgr. Hurley, which is source of quotations in the following paragraphs.

24. For Hurley's understanding of this complaint, see ltr., Hurley to O'Boyle, 19 Feb 1971, cy in SAA. The quotation is from Hurley's version of the conversation as reported in this letter.

sional approach, she predicted, would solve 80 percent of the trouble and win the enthusiastic help of the parents.[25]

The council agreed to fund a nonteaching principal position, but they wanted a religious. Father Hurley met with Mother Mary of Good Counsel, the head of the Oblates, who agreed to replace Sister Frances Eileen at the end of the school year. In June, however, the council learned that the Mother General had changed her mind. She would not supply another principal, although she would not object to her sisters remaining under the direction of a lay principal, a decision with which Sister Frances Aileen concurred. The council appointed a screening committee to select a suitable candidate, and in a short time the parish had a new principal, Charles E. Carter, a retired D.C. school administrator and a former colleague of several council members.[26] A parishioner at Nativity Church, Carter suffered heart problems, and a worried pastor fretted that the strain of the job might lead to a heart attack. After all, here was a lay person, a man to boot, placed in charge of a female faculty, including six nuns, and expected to reverse faltering scores in a student body increasingly deprived both economically and culturally. As it turned out, Carter did very well, with no apparent strain on his heart.

Meanwhile the transfer of a second black principal in a parish headed by a white pastor did not escape notice in the heightened racial sensitivity of the early 1970s. An unsigned broadside addressed to the "mentally dead black Catholics of Sts. Paul and Augustine" called on them to wake up and protest Father Hurley's "politics of genocide" against the Oblates. Inaccurate and inflammatory, the letter described the two dismissals as an attack on women of courage and stamina who sought to defend the rights and interests of black children. An organ of the Black Muslims, *Muhammad Speaks*, jumped into the fray, describing the nuns as being treated "as women in a harem of the white lord." It interviewed a small group, purportedly parishioners and parents, who accused the pastor of exerting "sinister pressure" upon black nuns and lay women to "keep them in their

25. PCM, 11 Jan 1971.
26. PCM, 20 Jun 1970.

place." The paper featured a picture showing picketers led by Gloria Thompson demonstrating before the church door in Hurley's presence.[27] While the specific charges were easily refuted, these critics undoubtedly struck a sympathetic chord that registered with a least a few parishioners. Pauline Jones, who was especially sensitive to the aims of the two principals, concluded from her position on the parish council that the dismissal of the two nuns was not so much over academic scores, but because of their insistence on "teaching children their culture." Others, like Father Kemp, saw in the public criticism an effort by some to apply national and even global concerns (the fight for racial justice) to a particular situation (a faltering school in crisis) when other factors complicated the picture.[28] Whatever the cause, the fact that the principals, staff, and students were African American and the pastor was white probably made confrontation inevitable at that time.

Despite the picketers and the more decorous complaints of a small parish minority, the school crisis faded. Charles Carter proved to be not only an effective educator but also a friendly, open person, always ready to listen to parents and treat their concerns with careful consideration, even when nothing could immediately be done to ameliorate them. This important element of a principal's job description had been somewhat neglected of late, and Carter, who also showed himself a stickler for the rules and a firm disciplinarian, quickly won the parents over. Soon student scores on standardized tests began to rise.[29] Carter also proved effective in dealing with the parish council. Despite a 12 percent drop in enrollment following the tuition increase in 1972, he successfully pushed for more equipment and supplies. During the 1972–73 school year the council provided Carter with funds for a staff of six Oblates and ten lay teachers.[30] For the first time pupils were offered the opportunity to study Spanish, and the school enjoyed a full-

27. "An Open Letter Re: Father Hurley's Destruction of Black Women (The Oblates of Providence)," unsigned and undated, [first two quotes] and *Muhammad Speaks* (Chicago, Illinois), 10 Sep 1971, [last three quotes]. Copies of both in SAA.

28. These views were expounded by Jones and Kemp in their intvs. with the author.

29. According to Hurley, Kemp, and Sister Charlotte. See author's intvs.

30. PCM, 17 Sep 1972.

time librarian, Sister Paschal Jackson, O.S.P. An additional faculty member, Sister Mary Quinn, a Dominican nun, was acquired to serve as eighth grade home room teacher, leaving the principal free to supervise the entire school. Carter was eager to discuss his ideas for improvements, and his infectious "can do" attitude clearly influenced the council's decisions and delighted the pastor.

One event that no doubt supported this optimism was the acquisition at last of the well-equipped school building next door to the rectory. Learning that Cathedral Latin School was about to vacate its building on California Street, Father Hurley asked Cardinal O'Boyle to relocate Mackin High and give its building to the parish. Adding that the Mackin teachers could also be comfortably housed on California Street, he went on to press for the return of Father Olds's old rectory down on Fifteenth Street, which now housed the Holy Cross Brothers who operated Mackin, for use as a new home for the Oblates. Hurley listed the immediate repairs needed on the school and convent and recommended that the diocese take them over, either leasing or selling them or refurbishing them for any one of a number of diocesan charities.[31] Although no decision was announced on the fate of the old buildings at that time, when Mackin vacated its premises on V Street in the summer of 1971, the archdiocese handed over to the parish the commodious building, built by St. Paul's to house its grade school in 1923.[32] Carter was anxious to take advantage of this good fortune. He proposed that grades six through eight immediately be relocated to the V Street building—dubbed for the interim the Community Education Center—where the older children might take advantage of its science lab and large gymnasium. The smaller children, along with a proposed day care center, would be left in the old school in the vain hope that the building would thereby become eligible for federal funding.[33] No decision was immediately forthcoming. Clearly the parish wanted to consider all the possibilities, and several years would pass before all elements of the school were finally united on V Street.

31. Ltr., Hurley to O'Boyle, 23 Feb 1971, cy in SAA.

32. The school was built by the Schneider Spleidt Co. for $170,224. Copies of the various deeds and contracts in SAA. Olds's rectory on Fifteenth Street was never returned to the parish, but remained under diocesan control into recent times.

33. PCM, 21 Oct 1971.

The Co-Pastor Experiment

In other areas of parish activity Msgr. Hurley tried to re-energize the policies of his predecessor. He worked hard to maintain the momentum of the Parish Come Alive campaign. Launched with great fanfare in the months before his arrival in 1970, the call for church volunteers had been designed to create a greater sense of common effort and mutual support in the parish. Hurley was particularly interested in its proposals to involve individual parishioners in ongoing operations, particularly the school.[34] Always supported by a majority of council members, many of whom were friends of long standing, he readily accepted their decisions while attempting to broaden their interests.[35] During his years as pastor the council fully shed the diffident attitude assumed under the august Msgr. Gingras to share in the direction of some parish affairs. Assured of its support, Hurley even agreed that a special committee be organized under Juanita Tolson and Father Kemp to establish guidelines under which the work of the parish priests, among others, would be evaluated by the council.[36]

In ways big and small, Hurley sought to protect parish traditions against radical change in what appeared to his friends and supporters as an increasingly hostile environment. He always went out of his way to highlight past achievements. In his first months on the job, for example, he had arranged for the parish to honor John J. O'Connor, the guiding light of the Catholic Interracial Council. Dr. Paul Cooke and all the old warriors from the church's fight for racial justice in Washington were on hand for the occasion.[37] A musician himself, Hurley actively supported the work of the choir, particularly the efforts of its director George Dines, Jr., to develop a large repertory of four-part masses. At the same time he was openly skeptical about suggestions that a choir whose reputation for excellence spanned a century of Washington's musical life should subordinate itself to experiments with gospel or contemporary sounds.

34. See, for example, ltr., Hurley to Parish, n.d. (ca. April 1972), SAA.

35. One tangible result of this firm support: Hurley's received a valuable grand piano, a surprise bequest from a wealthy parishioner.

36. PCM, n.d. (ca. June 1973).

37. *CS*, 31 Dec 1970.

In this as in other things the pastor found himself in serious disagreement with his two assistants. For the most part the three priests had gone their own ways. Although he wished otherwise, Hurley, frantically busy with parish affairs when he could spare the time away from his continuing diocesan obligations, tended to let Fathers Bouchard and Kemp concentrate on their special interests. As evidenced by a review of parish council minutes, both Bouchard and Kemp were conscientious participants in all parish deliberations, but they were also convinced—somewhat mistakenly, Kemp would later admit—that their duties exceeded the usual parish responsibilities.[38] Bouchard spent considerable time working as area representative in the Model Cities program, which included responsibility for the management of millions of dollars in federal funds. He also directed the summer school program begun by Father Dwan in the old parish Center and lately enlarged to include far-flung programs run out of various parish buildings with a budget exceeding that of the parish school. He tried to interest the council in community housing projects and succeeded in committing the parish to a joint housing venture with Augustana Lutheran. In October 1971 the council appointed a committee to explore the subject with the Lutherans under the guidance of housing experts. Within six months the two churches were sponsoring an independent service under the auspices of the New Inner City Community Organization-Economic Development Corporation (NICCO-EDC), the first, faltering step in what would later become a fruitful ecumenical effort to supply moderate and low income housing in the local community.[39]

Described as a militant in the fight for racial justice, Bouchard was fearless in criticizing what he saw as racism in the Church. In this regard he took on the diocese's CYO program. Under Gingras's direction the CYO had been thoroughly integrated in the 1960s, but some regulations remained in force that tended to limit the organization's effectiveness among African-American youth. At a meeting of the CYO's executive committee attended by Cardinal O'Boyle in 1971, Bouchard referred to these regulations, branding the board's reluctant commit-

38. These paragraphs are based in the main on author's intvs. with Kemp and Hurley.

39. NICCO also planned to sponsor job development programs. See PCM, 16 Oct and 21 Nov 1971, 16 Jan and 19 Mar 1972, and 29 Apr 1973.

ment to study the question of membership among inner-city children as "tokenism." He and other priests involved in black neighborhoods demanded that non-Catholics, who included the majority of young people in their parish areas, be made eligible for participation in CYO activities.[40] Frustrated in such diocesan fights, Bouchard succeeded in convincing the parish council to organize a social justice committee, through which the congregation would become involved in the ongoing crusade against what he saw as racism in church and state.[41]

In all this Bouchard had a ready ally in Raymond B. Kemp. Using the revered Chicago activist Saul Alinsky as his guide, Father Kemp had thrown himself into community organizing, devoting countless hours to his neighborhood centers. In the anxious weeks following the 1968 riot he pressed the parish council to fulfill what he called its responsibility to serve the people of the area. But at that time pastor Gingras put a damper on the discussion when he observed that "we moved out into the community, and unfortunately we left a number of our people behind."[42] By the early 1970s Kemp had decided that the attitude toward community activities exhibited by Gingras and his successor made the parish "an ever-dwindling place." He was convinced that, to survive, the parish must become a vital part of the community and serve all its people, and his work was intended to offset his superiors' restricted views. An immediate area of concern was the deteriorating condition of the public schools, and Kemp, the community activist, decided to become personally involved. Finding no suitable candidate available and urged on by his friends, the priest ran for the Ward One seat on the school board in 1971.

Cardinal O'Boyle publicly opposed the candidacy. Although the prelate admitted that things might have been different if the election were being held in his home town of Scranton, Pennsylvania, he was convinced that in Washington the largely non-Catholic and black voters "will kill you, they'll kill me, and they'll destroy the Church."[43] Kemp, defending his candidacy as a matter of conscience, ignored the archbishop's objections. After all, he reasoned, if O'Boyle was ada-

40. The meeting was reported in the *Michigan Catholic*, 14 Apr 1971.
41. PCM, 20 Oct 1973.
42. PCM, 17 Jun 1968.
43. As quoted by Kemp in his intv. with author.

mant, he could end the venture overnight by transferring him to any parish outside Ward One, thereby making him ineligible for the race. As it was, O'Boyle's opposition probably drew attention to Kemp's campaign in a seven-person field, and he won following a run-off election in which he out-polled his opponent by more than three to one.[44] In succeeding years as he became hopelessly bogged down in the morass of school board politics, Kemp came to appreciate the wisdom of the O'Boyle's comments. By the time he became co-pastor in 1974, he found himself in the thick of a fight with community activist Barbara Sizemore and her allies, and like Msgr. Hurley he suffered the unpleasant experience of being hounded by angry picketers.

Msgr. Hurley was considerably more comfortable with Father Kemp's methods than with Bouchard's more confrontational approach, which he considered counterproductive, given the opposition it raised among lay leaders. On Kemp's time-consuming work on the school board, for example, Hurley claimed that both he and his assistant were striving for the same goal but in different arenas. Nevertheless he continued to resent the younger priests' concentration on matters he believed extraneous to the parish's immediate concerns, and as the months went by tension in the rectory increased. For their part the two street-wise assistants found their charming, hard working pastor "smart in the old Church, but not in the inner city," a man out of joint with the times."[45] The riot and the subsequent intensification of racial sensitivities in the inner city made Msgr. Hurley's pastoral style (the well-meant, joking familiar who patted the men on the back and called the women "girls") that appealed to so many senior parishioners now appeared patronizing to some of the younger ones in the charged atmosphere of the mid-1970s. Bouchard and Kemp conceded that, had he lived in the parish during the riot and experienced first hand the impact of Stokely Carmichael and the black power movement on the neighborhood, Hurley would now be better equipped to engage the parish in the community—a necessary step, they were convinced, to

44. *CS*, 4 and 25 Nov 1971, and *Newark Advocate*, 25 Sep 1971.

45. A judgment made by Kemp in his intv. with author. See also Hurley's intv. It is fascinating to see how much these two men with such broad, philosophical differences agreed in their interpretation of this incident in their careers. The following paragraphs are based largely on these interviews.

survival. As it was, his emphasis on parish traditions and support for the conservative lay leaders in the parish council merely delayed changes that were imperative.

All these views were aired when a diocesan personnel committee visited the rectory during a survey of inner city parishes for the new archbishop, William W. Baum, in the summer of 1973. In an unusual move the two assistants recommended that Baum appoint Hurley to one of the new suburban parishes, where his energy and warmth should produce noteworthy results. For his part, Archbishop Baum recognized in Hurley a pastor devoted to the idea of the Christian family and a strong defender of the traditional parish with no pre-conceived agenda. He decided to assign Hurley to the daunting task of establishing a new parish in Maryland's rapidly growing upper Montgomery County.[46] In January 1974 Msgr. Hurley became the founding pastor of Mother Elizabeth Seton parish in Germantown.[47]

Both Kemp and Bouchard had been branded as mavericks by chancery officials. They had figured prominently in the priests association that had defied the papal encyclical on artificial birth control in 1968 and as a consequence had for a time been barred from hearing confessions (forcing Msgr. Gingras to press Msgrs. Armando Jimenez and Geno Baroni, both residents but unconnected to the parish, into service). Since then Kemp had publicly defied the archbishop by entering the school board race. But now a new archbishop seemed to be signaling the beginning of a new era in Washington. At first he indicated that he would name Kemp to replace Hurley, but Kemp begged off, citing his need to complete his time-consuming work on the school board and Bouchard's seniority in the parish. Kemp recommended instead that they be appointed co-pastors. Not yet tried in the Washington archdiocese, the concept of co-pastor had worked successfully in some other jurisdictions where particularly active parish councils and

46. Archbishop Baum succeeded Cardinal O'Boyle as archbishop of Washington in May, 1973. He expressed these views in an intr. in 1998.

47. Testifying to Hurley's success in Montgomery County (and obliquely to the wisdom of Baum's decision), the grateful congregation of Mother Seton parish later arranged for having a public thoroughfare, the frequently mentioned Father Hurley Boulevard, named in their beloved pastor's honor.

a team of parish administrators (the priests, sisters, and religious education directors) managed the parish. Baum agreed, and in January 1974, Fathers Bouchard and Kemp became the seventh pastors of SS. Paul and Augustine.[48]

In the end it proved easier to sell the archbishop on the idea of co-pastors than to convince the parish council of its merits. Some of its concerns were practical. "I called the rectory," one member joked, "and after fifteen rings I figured you two were sitting there trying to decide who was going to answer."[49] The old aristocrats on the council, still used to a father figure in charge, were anxious to learn who would be ultimately responsible for what. The co-pastors, on the other hand, wanted to convince the council that the team concept was a good idea because it would broaden the avenue of communication among the council (which, in their view, should set policy), the priests (who should execute that policy while remaining responsible to the archbishop), and the congregation, which elected the council. All these ideas were thrashed out in many council meetings and finally in a workshop held at the Washington Hilton in July 1974.

Council members were frankly skeptical about the extent of its powers. Could it overrule the priests, some wanted to know, even in questions involving marriages in the Church? It was obvious that members had by now come to regard the role of advisor as a meaningless sop; at the same time they were skeptical of just how far they could go in setting policy. The co-pastors sought to assure them, pointing out that the council had overruled the pastor on several occasions in the past and that it was free to make any decision "that will not violate those practices put down by Bishop [sic] Baum." The council and co-pastors continued to wrestle with these concepts for many months. Meanwhile, the priests encouraged the congregation to look on the council as their representatives. Calling on parishioners to participate wholeheartedly in the council elections in June 1974, they added, "the

48. *Washington Post*, 25 Jan 1974, and Parish Bulletin, 27 Jan 1974. Regarding the concept of co-pastors an anomaly in canon law, however, Archbishop Baum always considered Kemp sole pastor, and his chancery referred to Kemp in official communications.

49. Quoted in Kemp's intv. with author. See also, PCM, 16 Feb 1974.

council is the policy board for our parish and will be even more influential in setting goals and strategies for our family of faith than in the past."[50]

Bouchard and Kemp had to walk a fine line. They avoided all such talk of policy-making outside the parish because, as Kemp later explained quoting a fellow priest: "Bishops consider that their job."[51] But the two persisted in bolstering the role of the council, because, they were convinced, it was the key to the congregation's survival and the means by which the parish would finally come to embrace the community around it. To build this new congregation the parish must bear witness to any who would listen, a task that the class-conscious council leaders had so far been hesitant to undertake. The community activities that had preoccupied the two priests for so many years were undertaken in the name of the parish. Now they wanted this work placed front and center in the parish council. But in 1974 the council was still somewhat isolated. Its older members were frankly frightened by any talk of "black stuff," as they called it. They were the ones who objected to the gospel choirs—"all those people shaking their thing up there on the altar." Here then was the challenge for the co-pastors: they must convince the council that the key to the parish's survival was change, a change that only the council could direct. The parish must shake off its old isolation and come alive by becoming involved. It must experiment with new styles of worship to attract the young and alienated. It must show its compassion and concern for its neighbors by becoming more deeply involved in their problems. It must engage the interest of black Catholics throughout the city while attracting a new generation of faithful. They wanted the parish leaders to speak up, to take charge. They weren't disappointed. Slowly the council began to get things done. "They gave us a fit," Kemp later commented, "and it was wonderful."

During the ensuing months as the various council committees began slowly to assume greater responsibilities, regular parish business continued substantially as before. Because of his experience with administering large sums of money, Father Bouchard concentrated on parish finances. In November 1974 he was able to report that the V

50. "Notes Covering the Parish Council Workshop," n.d. (ca. 20 Jul 1974), SAA, (first quote) and Parish Bulletin, 2 Jun 1974 (second quote).

51. Author's intv. with Kemp. Kemp was quoting the late Msgr. George Ellis.

Street Center, which the diocese had returned to the parish, was now self-supporting. The various agencies that used the premises paid some $50,000 in annual rent, and the diocese promised to pay up to $12,000 to cover building expenses. The following month he persuaded the chancery to cancel some $8,500 in debts contracted by the parish in the late 1960s.[52] On the negative side the loss of two more sisters meant hiring more lay teachers and a corresponding increase in expenses. The council turned to the time-honored means of money raising. Pound parties for support of the convent, raffles, and "cursed bingo," as a frustrated Kemp put it, again became the order of the day.[53] Rescue finally came in the form of a deal Bouchard made with the chancery: the diocese would subsidize the school to the tune of $24,000 if the parish would cover the remaining $6,000 deficit.[54]

In fact in the last days of Charles Carter's tenure as principal, the school was showing signs of recovery. For the first time in a decade its enrollment topped 300 during the 1975 school year with classes divided between the old and new school houses. That fall the parish welcomed its new principal, Sister Barbara Spears, O.S.P., a popular educator who, to Bouchard and Kemp's high satisfaction, viewed the school as a base for community activities. By that time the council was developing plans to increase enrollment to 400 and operate two kindergartens and first grades. Beginning in the fall of 1976 tuition would rise to $440 for parishioners and $500 for non-Catholics.[55]

The expense of repairs and upkeep of the church itself sparked much debate in the council. Members agreed with the co-pastors that everything done must be first-class. Nothing tacky would be tolerated in a parish that had suffered so long from the racism of earlier times and the fiscal struggles of a recent past. In February 1974 the group decided to remodel the sanctuary, creating a Eucharistic altar and relocating the Sacred Heart statue, a beloved relic from the old down-

52. PCM, 16 Nov and 21 Dec 1974.

53. Rpt., Kemp to Chancery, "Parish Profile," n.d. (ca. June 1979).

54. PCM, 25 Sep 1974. The need to hire just two more lay teachers raised the per pupil cost from $303 in 1973 to $461 the following year.

55. These initiatives were approved by the council at its meeting on 17 Apr 1976, for which see minutes. The council had learned of Sister Barbara's appointment at its 15 Mar 1975 meeting.

town church. Various changes were routinely budgeted, including the addition of restrooms in 1975, but the $40,000 needed for repainting the interior in 1976 stumped the administration committee. A special fund drive netted only $14,000 in a year, but again the resourceful Bouchard came to the rescue by winning the chancery's promise to pay any amount outstanding after the parish had extended its fund drive for one more year.[56] By 1977 the council had approved other changes to improve the liturgical setting, including removal of altar rails and some pews and improved lighting throughout the church.[57]

During these months of co-pastorship the first tentative signs of outreach sought by Bouchard and Kemp appeared in the work of the council's social justice committee, which was beginning to involve the parish in new ways in community affairs.[58] In March 1974 it sponsored a meeting to discuss the Home Rule bill, and later in conjunction with other neighboring groups hosted a town hall meeting at the V Street Center to hear Sterling Tucker and Marion Crawford discuss home rule and the Urban Homestead program. It also sponsored a home rule information Sunday and offered strong support for the neighborhood advisory councils as a means of securing maximum citizen participation in District affairs. It held voter registration drives and sponsored voter forums where parishioners and their neighbors could meet and question Ward One candidates.[59]

Further initiatives included bringing Cesar Chavez and his United Farm Workers to the parish for a special Sunday mass and workshop to publicize their cause. In September 1974 the committee arranged for parish participation in a prayer vigil in front of the Soviet embassy on Sixteenth Street on behalf of Russian Jews.[60] In 1978 with council ap-

56. Ltr., PC president and co-pastors to parish, 28 Nov 1976, sub: Report on the Paint Project, SAA. In the end the parish and the chancery split the cost, each paying $18,000. See PCM, n.d. (ca. Jul 1979).

57. Vincent Brooks, "Update on Parish Council Activities," n.d. (ca. Jan 1977), SAA.

58. The committee was an offshoot of the council's old Parish and Community committee, its new name reflecting a broader view of its interests. See PCM, 25 Sep 1974.

59. See, for example, PCM, 17 Mar and 5 May 1974.

60. PCM, 14 Jul and 22 Sep 1974.

proval the parish contributed to an open letter to President Carter in the *Washington Post* protesting U.S. dealings with the Somoza regime in Nicaragua. Nor was the archdiocese exempt from criticism. In 1980 the social justice committee got the parish council to inform the archbishop of its displeasure over education director Leonard DeFiore's association with Ronald Reagan's presidential campaign and publicly rejected pleas for contributions to a southern Maryland parish because, it charged, such parishes only perpetuated segregation.[61] The committee also concerned itself with discrimination in local housing, employment, and retailing. In the first of what over the years became a regular service to the community, it sponsored a workshop in April 1975 where experts discussed problems in marketing and nutrition as applied to inner city neighborhoods. It also discussed Father Kemp's proposal that the parish play a part in the Community Release Organization. As a result parishioners were invited to volunteer to serve as alternatives to pre-trial detention (third-party custody of youth caught in the city's criminal justice system) or to help interview arrestees for the D.C. courts.[62]

As time passed the operation of the parish under two pastors became routine. Principal responsibility for getting things done fell to the implementers, the parish team. Bouchard generally handled the administrative chores, especially parish finances, while Kemp concentrated on parish programs, catechumens, council retreats, and community projects. The team approach was immeasurably strengthened by the executive ability of Sister Barbara, the school principal, (and in later years by Luis Grillo and John Butler in religious education and Leon Roberts, director of music). This executive team kept the lines of responsibility purposely hazy, in particular when dealing with the parish council, where, in the heady atmosphere created by their newly discovered prerogatives, some members campaigned for inappropriate and unwise causes. Typically the parish team would propose measures to the council, which, after hearing the views of its appropriate com-

61. The Somoza protest was originally proposed by Father Muffler, see PCM, 21 Oct 1978. On the DeFiore protest, see PCM, 18 Oct 1980 and St. Augustine's *Outlook* (Oct 1980).

62. PCM, 20 Jan 1974 and 15 Mar 1975.

SISTER BARBARA SPEARS, O.S.P., principal of St. Augustine's School and dynamic member of the parish team.

mittee, would pass them back, usually approved. While these idealistic young pastors were anxious to encourage participation, they understood that a fully democratic system was impossible and insisted that a member of the parish team be allowed to speak on any changes proposed by the council.

Looking back later, Kemp would judge the period of co-pastorship "pretty good times" during which he detected the beginning of the vital, enthusiastic congregation that was the necessary leaven for a reborn parish. Actually, those pretty good times proved too brief a period to produce any significant, enduring change. After just three years on the job the team was broken up when Father Bouchard was appointed pastor of Nativity parish. The chancery clearly considered the experiment a success, and Bouchard informed the council that Father Lewis Mangini, an Oblate of St. Francis de Sales who had been assisting in the parish, "can not yet be named as Co-Pastor but will function in that capacity."[63] But no one in the chancery or the parish appeared anxious to press for a continuation of the unique system, and in June 1977 Archbishop Baum appointed the thirty-six-year-old Raymond Kemp, who had spent almost his entire priestly life in the parish, sole pastor of SS. Paul and Augustine.

Other personnel changes followed. Father John P. Muffler, a young Washington native, succeeded Father Mangini as assistant in June 1978, and Father John J. Mudd, an activist strongly attracted by the parish's quest for social justice in its battered Washington neighborhood, volunteered to become a resident and provide part-time help. Although his job in the diocesan Office of Social Development curtailed his parish work ("Kemp was always trying to get me to do more, and I was always resisting," Mudd later recalled), he did join the parish council, where he was particularly active on its social justice committee, designing some of its important neighborhood housing initiatives. In December 1978 Mudd would leave his diocesan assignment to succeed Muffler as full-time associate, and in 1981, with strong support from the parish council, succeeded Kemp as pastor.[64] Meanwhile Muffler, freed of his associate's responsibilities, assumed the post of assistant principal in the school and began studies leading to an advanced degree in education.[65]

A Maturing Council

For a man who had successfully escaped the burden of administrative chores for so long, Kemp proved adept when it came to managing the parish's greatest financial undertaking, the sale of the Fifteenth

63. As quoted in PCM, 21 May 1977. See also ltr., Kemp to Parish Council Members, 23 May 1977, SAA.

64. PC Minutes, 16 Dec 1978. See also author's intv. with Father John J. Mudd, 17 Sep 1997.

65. To complete the circle, Muffler would serve as Mudd's assistant during the early 1980s. He received his doctorate in education from Columbia University's teachers college in 1989. His dissertation, "Thus Far By Faith: A History of St. Augustine's the Mother Church for Black Catholics in the Nation's Capital," has been frequently cited in this history and was among the first scholarly works to use the parish's noteworthy archives. For a discussion of Father Mudd's ideas on pastorship and parish governance, see chapter 11, below.

Street property. The return of the Mackin building to the parish in 1971 raised the possibility of giving up the old buildings, but even after the transfer of part of the parish school to V Street the co-pastors hesitated. Bouchard in particular harbored a vague hope that the buildings might be renovated and included in some kind of grand church-community educational institution. Besides, the parish had no assurance that the diocese would agree to sell or that the parish would profit from such a sale.

By 1977 Bouchard's dream had faded in light of financial realities. The school, after fifty years of hard use, was, in Kemp's words "the pits. Using V Street for sports was no worse than using the lousy school grounds on S Street. It was the only school in town situated in an alley." This assessment was underscored the following year when the primary grades were moved to the new school and pre-school classes transferred to temporary classrooms in the V Street Center. The convent, a graceful but aging building, was in such poor condition that the sisters were forced to take up residence with their Oblate friends at Holy Comforter–St. Cyprian's. The parish faced an expensive reconstruction of the convent or purchase of a new one. At the same time early signs of gentrification, a phenomenon with lasting social consequences for the western Shaw region, had appeared on Fifteenth Street. The influx of new, upwardly mobile owners caused a substantial increase in property values. Kemp decided that it was time to explore the possibility of a sale.

His first task was to sell the congregation on the idea. Many members retained a deep pride in the parish and still considered themselves exiles from their grand old downtown church. Some would never be happy in buildings associated with St. Paul's where they had once been treated so shabbily, and all knew how the financial sacrifices that had produced the old church and the buildings on downtown Fifteenth Street had been so cavalierly dismissed by authorities in the past. They were determined that their parish would not again be deprived of valuable holdings. As Kemp succinctly put it, "How do you get those folks to say o.k., unload the old buildings at Fifteenth Street and come up to V Street altogether?" He turned to the parish council for help, going over with its members in a series of meetings the pros and cons of the sale and the possibilities it opened to the parish. In the end the council agreed to his exploring the matter while they debated the uses of any income from such a deal.[66]

Following informal discussions in early 1978, the parish obtained the services of the chancery's legal and real estate advisors, who appraised the property and in short order obtained an offer from a local developer to purchase the convent and school-auditorium for $650,000. Kemp, appalled at such a low figure, promptly hired his own appraiser. Assured that the property was worth at least double that amount, he and Sister Barbara then discussed the matter with Cardinal Baum and his chancellor. They agreed to the parish's preliminary thinking about disposition of the property and assured the pastor that all moneys realized from the sale "would be used exclusively for the benefit of SS. Paul and Augustine."[67]

In November 1978 the council approved selling the property and published a set of guidelines for distributing the proceeds. It expected a substantial sum to remain after paying off parish debts (estimated at $60,000), purchasing a new convent, and making needed repairs to parish buildings. The surplus would be used to establish two endowments: one for the school, the other to help stabilize the neighborhood by assisting parishioners become home owners or secure decent rental housing.[68] In the hectic year that followed, the council and parish team thrashed out the specific proposals made in pursuit of these general guidelines. Deliberations intensified after receipt of the good news in May 1979 that the Urban Land Corporation had offered $1.4 million for the property, which it planned to convert into condominiums to be known as Bishop's Gate. In announcing the pending sale, the archdiocese's lawyer told Kemp that he hoped the matter would be settled soon "so that you can become a crusty old pastor, fat and independently wealthy."[69]

66. Author's intv. with Kemp (source of quote) and ltr., PC to Brothers and Sisters of the Community of SS. Paul and Augustine, n.d. (ca. 1 Nov 1978), SAA.

67. Ltr., Msgr John F. Donoghue [chancellor] to Kemp, 8 Nov 1978, SAA. On the various appraisals, see, for example, ltr., Richard O. Hasse, to Kemp, 8 May 1978 and sales contract, 17 Oct 1978, with att "rejected, R.B.K." Both in SAA.

68. Ltr., PC President to Brothers and Sisters of the Community of SS. Paul and Augustine, n.d. (ca. 1 Nov 1978), SAA.

69. Ltr., Paul F. Interdonato to Kemp, 17 May 1979, SAA. See also *Washington Post*, 7 Mar 1980 and 29 Jan 1983.

Unfortunately Kemp was not likely to become wealthy anytime soon, considering the extent of the parish's outstanding obligations. Immediately upon learning of the impending sale, the council agreed that the pastor should float a short-term loan to finance impending projects. It also agreed to purchase two houses owned by a parishioner on Fifteenth Street near the church. One, after extensive renovations, would become the convent; the other would serve as an investment to help pay for remodeling the convent.[70] Subsequent discussion led to the commitment of substantial sums to replace the deteriorating school windows in the new school building, to renovate its auditorium, re-named the St. Augustine Room, and to redecorate "1419," as the old V Street Center, now formally incorporated into the parish, was familiar-ly called. Consideration of these matters was enlivened by a debate in the council on the use of minority contractors to perform the work on V Street. Given the special expertise of the primary bidder and the fact that it employed many minority artisans, the Gibbons Company of Bal-timore was awarded the job.[71]

Much soul searching went into the discussions on where the re-maining money should be channeled "to best fill the needs of our com-munity of faith," as A. Anthony Bass, the council president put it. Members heard a presentation from Open Society, a corporation seek-ing a substantial investment from the parish to finance its revitaliza-tion of property in the Shaw area.[72] It also discussed various ways to create an endowment for the school. The enthusiasm with which it ap-proached these expensive undertakings and the efforts of its various committees to allocate large shares of the anticipated returns from the property sale prompted a worried Kemp to issue some prudent advice.

70. In the end the profits on the rental and eventual sale of this second house would be used to help reduce the loss suffered by the parish when the corporation that had been contracted to remodel the convent went bankrupt halfway through the job. Much correspondence and documents related to the purchase of these properties and the various deeds and bills of sale related to Bishop's Gate are on file in SAA.

71. PCM, 19 May, 17 Jul 1979, and n.d. (ca. Aug 1979). See also PC Administrative committee FY 1979 Report.

72. Ltr., Bass to Parishioners, 15 Oct 1979. See also ltr., Michael D. Mayer, Direc-tor, OPEN D.C. Program, to Kemp, 8 Aug 1980, and associated reports and analyses. All in SAA. The Open Society people made their presentation to the parish council on 18 Oct 1980.

In a detailed financial report entitled "Notes from a Tired Pastor on Your FY 82 Budget," Kemp warned that if the council continued to "talk big programs but does not raise big bucks," the parish faced bankruptcy in two years. Kemp was particularly proud of the congregation's generosity. (He once pointed out to the chancery that SS. Paul and Augustine received more per parishioner than any other parish in the archdiocese.) But now Kemp felt obliged to remind the council that, while further returns on the sale were expected, the parish was already spending itself into debt. As agreed, diocesan subsidies had ended at the time of the property sale. It was imperative, therefore, that a lean budget be adopted and ruthlessly adhered to despite the worthy appeals from the various committees. Ordinary expenses must be covered by ordinary income, he added, and capital investments so eagerly discussed in the council must be postponed until the money was in hand. The new council president, Michael A. Harris, took a similar tack when he proposed a revised budget that called for substantial cuts and some new and innovative approaches to money raising.[73]

It was timely advice. Shortly after Kemp's departure in 1981 the Urban Land Corporation, in financial difficulty, was forced to relinquish control of Bishop's Gate. Despite Father Mudd's continued dunning of the new directors, the final $285,000 payment was never collected. In the end the council was forced to settle for ten cents on the dollar, and the parish entered the 1980s debt free but faced with the formidable task of underwriting its regular expenses and its ever-growing outreach programs out of ordinary income.[74]

These protracted budget debates revealed a parish council, aided and abetted by the parish team, rapidly maturing into the policy-making instrument envisioned by Kemp and Bouchard. Increasingly jealous of its prerogatives and ready to question any decision affecting the

73. Kemp, "Notes From a Tired Pastor On Your FY 82 Church Budget" (source of quote) and "My final Presentation: A Balanced Budget," n.d. (both c. March 1981); memo, Harris to Parish Council, n.d., sub: budget FY 81–82. See also Kemp, "Parish Profile," n.d. (ca. Jun 1979). All in SAA.

74. On Mudd's effort to collect the final payment, see author's intv. and "Poverty, Drugs, Dispossession Occupy the Blocks Around the White House," an article by Arthur Jones in the *National Catholic Register*, 10 Dec 1982.

parish and propose any projects it deemed useful, the council had come to symbolize a generally rejuvenated congregation. This maturation coincided with a notable change in council membership. By 1980 over two-thirds of its members were newcomers either to the Church or to the parish in the past five years. Gone were the original leaders, representatives of the last generation of St. Augustine's old aristocrats of color, whose devotion to the parish was matched by an insistence on observing traditional social and ecclesial ways. In their place had risen a new group of leaders representing a different kind of aristocracy, the first generation to profit from the gains won during the civil rights revolution. The congregation had come to accept the outlook of these young, successful men and women, progressives determined to make the parish a major factor in a changing Church and changing society. Youthful both in age and outlook, they had grown up during the civil rights movement and learned its organizational and leadership styles during their college days and were able to apply them to their new parish. Included among these young Turks were Michael Harris, a Catholic from Chicago lately returned to the Church, who was an attorney associated with Howard University's general counsel; Ernest Withers, Jr., an official in President Jimmy Carter's political campaigns and a convert with a strong devotion to the cause of international justice; Bridgette Rouson, a Howard graduate and journalist and legal counsel for a trade association of newspaper publishers; Kenneth B. Winston, a management specialist who served as deputy clerk of the D.C. Superior Court; and Cecil Bushell, a Montgomery County housing official.[75]

Not all the activists on the council could claim such public achievement, but they too reflected the new spirit in the parish and its success in attracting a divergent and progressive congregation. Betty Washington, for example, who faced the daunting task of raising ten children alone, had moved from a position of anonymity in St. Luke's parish in far out southeast to become chair of the council's education committee and principal of the parish's venerable Sunday school. Cornelia Rajah, a convert who had grown up on nearby W Street, had,

75. A council nominee's qualifications were published before council elections or, in the case of appointees, were examined by the council. See, for example, PCM, 18 Oct 1980.

PAULINE J. JONES giving a history lesson to Mayor Marion Barry on the steps of St. Augustine's Church.

along with her sister, been attracted by the parish's outreach programs. Not only did she become a leader in the gospel choir, but in time served as president of the council. Vincent Brooks also served as council president during the very difficult time of transition. He was universally admired for his quiet dedication to the parish and was instrumental in establishing its athletic program and the awards program for young achievers. His pastoral sense showed clearly through the quiet aid and advice he gave to those in need. At his death in 1985 a grateful congregation established a Vincent Brooks Award to be bestowed annually on one who exhibited similar dedication to the parish.[76]

Essential to this change in outlook was the singular contribution of Pauline J. Jones. The young radical of the council's early years had

76. The conditions of the award, which is still given today, were discussed in the parish council. See PCM, 21 Dec 1985.

evolved into its wise tribal elder, the *grio* who imparted to its young leaders her sense of the parish's long history and the development of a black Catholic tradition even as she learned from them the vocabulary and techniques of a new generation of crusaders for racial justice. In reflecting on her importance to the development of an evangelization which underscored black Catholic traditions, Father Kemp observed that "here was a lay person wise enough to embrace a philosophy and theology that mixed religion, culture, and locale—the stuff of the life of the gospels."[77] Jones had a special gift for dealing with the parish's oldsters, visiting them regularly and keeping them alive to the exciting changes taking place. She would prove important in many areas of parish life, but her ability to synthesize religion with culture and lo-cale while imparting an understanding of history of African-American Catholics in Washington was her major contribution to the parish.

Such a change did not happen by chance, but was largely the fruit of the new programs devised by Kemp and the parish team. From his earliest days in the parish Kemp had been struck by the number of seniors who had been members of the congregation since the early years of the century and who could with ease trace their family roots to the parish's earliest decades. When he became pastor in 1977 he de-cided to honor these people who offered living proof that the Ameri-can church enjoyed a long black Catholic tradition. When a strict count was taken for the initial ceremony and those celebrations that followed in successive years, Kemp was surprised to find 160 parish-ioners who had worshipped at St. Augustine's for more than half a cen-tury, including 70—all over 80 years old—who had regularly attended Father Griffith's masses in the old church in the decades before World War I.[78] But while the parish rejoiced in the steadfast faith and physi-cal heartiness of nearly one-third of its active congregation, it was also left with the sobering thought that, as Kemp put it, "losing 60 or more

77. Author's intv. with Kemp.

78. As reported in the profile prepared in 1979, the parish census revealed that 225 members of its regular congregation of 650 were age 70 or above. On the parish celebrations honoring its seniors, see *CS*, 15 Jul 1978, and *Afro-American*, 10 Jul 1979. For discussion of the black Catholic tradition in Washington, see account of a memori-al mass celebrating the 150-year history of Mary Anne Jackson Cooke and her descen-dants in *CS*, 16 Sep 1976.

parishioners per year to the Lord indicates the need not only for a ministry to our aging but a major outreach program to recruit new parishioners."[79]

Formidable obstacles had to be overcome before any large-scale recruitment could succeed. Kemp and the parish council candidly outlined for the chancery in 1979 what they saw as the principal barriers to evangelization, some facing any parish, a few peculiar to SS. Paul and Augustine. In its neighborhood the parish confronted many divorced and remarried who lived in good faith and looked for acceptance in the Church. It also needed to devise an approach to a neighborhood where teenage and pre-marital pregnancies and unmarried and single-parent families predominated and where a growing acceptance of the homosexual lifestyle created a special pastoral challenge. Within the parish itself a general lack of familiarity with Scriptures and the teachings of Vatican II had led to a resistance, particularly among class-conscious, middle-aged congregants, to communal faith and to religious traditions associated with African-American culture (such as gospel music) whose adoption might go far in attracting new members. Beyond all these were those persistent problems that affected the whole American church: the gulf that existed between rich and poor parishes and black and white parishes.[80]

Important Initiatives

Over the years Kemp and his allies on the council developed a two-part strategy to build a large and vibrant congregation. For the first time the term "mother church" began to be employed to underscore the fact that so many of the black Catholics now scattered throughout the city and suburbs could trace their roots back to St. Augustine's. The parish decided to reach out to them, not so much to those comfortable in their new integrated parishes, but especially to the younger generation with no special connection to a parish or no longer practicing their religion. In Kemp's words:

79. Ltr., Kemp to Parish ["Greetings in the Lord"], 28 Aug 1978, cy in SAA.

80. Parish Profile, 1979, was drafted by Father Kemp and reviewed by the parish council.

We have sent children far afield. They have not been properly received by or have not sought out a Catholic church. Get the word out. We are an extended family. Cousins, get the word out. Find all those who had been alienated or estranged from the Church for whatever reason and bring them all home.[81]

The key to such an effort, Kemp was convinced, lay in a dynamic liturgy that respected and enhanced African-American traditions. At the same time the parish would appeal to its unchurched neighbors, those old clients of Father Baroni who had been through so much misery because of poverty, crime, and drugs. It would do this through a school that welcomed non-Catholic students and involved their parents; a restored catechumenate that used an entire congregation in spreading the Good News; and a parish council that was ready to respond to the needs and concerns of the local community. To continue this witness, the council would emphasize the virtue of hospitality as the focus of its social programs. Its doors would remain open, ready to welcome all comers.

One important initiative predated the appearance of the young progressives on the council. Kemp had long been convinced that any outreach program would benefit from the energy generated by gospel music. A liturgy incorporating the sounds and rhythms of this African-American art, he reasoned, would harmonize with the emerging self-awareness among black Catholics. Despite a marked reluctance on the part of the old leaders, the council went along with his suggestion. In January 1977 the parish bulletin announced the formation of a gospel choir under the direction of Earl Woodliff, who led a similar group at Holy Comforter–St. Cyprian's and had offered to get one started at SS. Paul and Augustine. Young and old were encouraged to consider joining what the parish team called a new ministry to the faith community. The team also appealed to the congregation's racial pride, reminding it that forming a gospel choir "is our way of keeping faith with Dr. Martin Luther King." Frequent notices followed as the choir recruited members, raised money for robes, and in April installed its first permanent director, Leon C. Roberts.[82]

81. Author's intv. with Kemp.
82. Parish Bulletins, various dates, Jan–Aug, 1977, SAA. The quotation is from the Bulletin of 14 Jan.

A professional musician, Roberts had learned from his training at West Chester State College and Howard University techniques that enabled him to incorporate the rich musical heritage of gospel music absorbed during his Pentecostal childhood into the Roman liturgy. His own popular masses and choral compositions would place him among that small, select group of artists who were creating a new movement in church music which blended the oldest of African-American traditions with ancient liturgical forms. After several years of hard work under his direction, the gospel choir emerged as a talented and disciplined musical group using forty singers and six instrumentalists who would make the liturgy at the 12:30 mass the trademark of the new St. Augustine's.[83] In 1979 Roberts assumed the post of parish music director, thereby uniting under one person both the gospel and traditional choirs. Now a member of the parish team, Roberts displayed an energy and spiritual force that contributed to transforming the outlook of the parish council. But not without grumbling from the old guard, which continued to complain about the new sounds. Like many in the American church, they believed art should come free, and questioned why the parish should pay instrumentalists, especially those who were parishioners. Complaints were also aired about the expense of robes for choir members who did not perform regularly.[84] More than a few traditionalists made their attitude toward gospel music known by their ostentatious shunning of the 12:30 mass. The pastor was obviously aware of this rearguard opposition and demanded a scrupulously even-handed treatment of the two choirs in both support and publicity.

In 1979 Kemp reported to the chancery that the gospel choir "has done much to bring the non-practicing Catholics back to the Church and interest non-Catholics in the Church."[85] If such a claim was slightly premature at that early date, it would be dead accurate in years to come. The innovative and spirit-filled liturgy, a crowded occasion of joyful celebration, proved especially stimulating for young

83. For a description of the choir's performance see, for example, *Washington Post*, 25 Dec 1981, and *CS*, 6 Oct 1984. For a detailed account of the organization of the choir and its work, see Appendix I, below.

84. PCM, 19 May 1979. The purpose of the parish's various choirs was discussed in the *SS. Paul & Augustine's Parish Profile, 1981–1982*.

85. Kemp, Parish Profile n.d. (ca. 1979), SAA.

black Catholics scattered throughout the capital area. Word spread quickly as the crowds grew: the 12:30 mass at SS. Paul and Augustine was the place to be on Sundays. Its liturgy was yet another reason to be proud of one's African-American Catholicism. In such a lively and open atmosphere many new friendships were formed and not a few romances begun. Somehow it seemed altogether fitting that the youthful Roberts, a man whose art would attract so many to Catholicism, was himself received into the Church in 1980.

Church membership and the number of visitors to the old parish now began to reverse recent trends. By 1982 Sunday attendance was again approaching the thousand mark, nearly doubling the number counted four years before. An unanticipated result of the new liturgy: the influx of new worshippers, many educated, middle-class Americans with no special social pretensions, finally put an end to the class-conscious attitude that lingered among the older lay leaders, an attitude that had bedeviled St. Augustine's since its early days.[86]

Among the newcomers to Sunday masses were many non-Catholic adults who expressed interest in joining the Church. St. Augustine's had always been noted for the number of its converts, and even in the turmoil of postwar Washington, Fathers Joyce and Benson had been forced to conduct back-to-back convert classes. The parish was among the very first to adopt the new catechumen program when it was introduced into the American church in 1974, and Catherine Mason (soon succeeded by John Butler) joined the parish team as a full-time coordinator for a program that replaced the old convert classes. It was no accident, therefore, that when the diocese took up the newly restored Rite of Christian Initiation for Adults (RCIA) in 1977, Cardinal Baum decided to conduct the first rite of enrollment, the initial phase of the new initiation ceremony, at SS. Paul and Augustine.[87] When the catechumens signed the book held on the cardinal's lap that day, they marked the completion of a process that had involved them for more than half a year in a rigorous program of prayer and study and progressive integration into the life of the parish. It also marked the close in-

86. In his intv. with the author, Father Mudd explored these benefits of the new gospel music that continued throughout his pastorate.

87. The ceremony on February 27, 1977, along with explanations of its significance, was carried both in the *Washington Post*, 4 Mar 1977, and the *CS*, 24 Feb 1977.

volvement of the congregation in that process. Some members served as instructors; others as godparents who accompanied the newcomer through each phase of the process; and still others who familiarized the catechumens with Catholic practices and the activities of the parish.

Father Kemp was particularly proud of the parish program, which he called a pioneer effort, a model for those seeking to rebuild a community in Christ's image and to join the fight for social justice.[88] His infectious enthusiasm spurred the congregation on. Its "Each One Reach One" campaign, its work in the school with the many non-Catholic parents, and its strong emphasis on hospitality at its popular Sunday liturgy produced a steady stream of candidates. In the 1977 rite Cardinal Baum enlisted 11 new members; 1981 saw 19 in the catechumen program; 31 converts joined the parish in 1984. (In its first six years the RCIA program added 120 new Catholics to the parish, not to mention the scores of lapsed Catholics who returned to the Sacraments under the influence of the parish's evangelization efforts.)[89] Perhaps even more important was the effect the program had on the congregation. In 1979 Kemp reported to the chancery his conviction that the catechumenate had focused the congregation on spreading the Good News and was one of the primary causes for the renewed sense of enthusiasm and identity among parish members.[90]

By 1981 the council, which by then included fifteen elected representatives along with the seven nonvoting members of the team, had achieved a dramatic reversal in the parish's fortunes. Once more a congregation of parishioners and visitors filled the pews at the principal masses, and the church's finances, although not freed from periodic crisis, were now established on a firmer and more disciplined footing. Related to these successes, the council had assumed responsibility for a number of innovative programs that thrust the congregation into the thick of neighborhood concerns and identified it as never be-

88. Ltr., Kemp to parishioners, 11 Jan 1981, SAA. Kemp has had extensive involvement with the catechumen program. See his *A Journey in Faith: An Experience of the Catechumenate* (New York: Sadler, Inc., 1997).

89. *SS Paul & Augustine Parish Profile, 1981–1982*. See also, PCM, 15 Dec 1984.

90. Kemp, Parish Profile, 1979. See also Kemp's ltr. to parishioners ("Greetings in the Lord"), 28 Aug 1978, both in SAA.

fore with the fight for racial justice both at home and abroad.[91] The hectic decade just past had wrought a fundamental change in the council's outlook and clearly demonstrated that Kemp and Bouchard were correct in turning to it to resuscitate a fading congregation. The parish council had come of age, and lest anyone mistake its intentions, a confident council president reminded his colleagues in 1980 that they "were not only a group of representatives but also a group of leaders."[92] He challenged them to devise programs that addressed both the spiritual and the socio-economic needs of the people, programs whose vitality and effectiveness would reflect the historical character of what was once again a dynamic parish.

91. These programs will be discussed in chapter 11, below.

92. Memo, Michael Harris to Council Committee Chairperson and Members, n.d. (ca. Aug 1980), sub: AGENDA '80–81, SAA.

ELEVEN ❧ BEACON FOR A
TROUBLED COMMUNITY

*I*t would be difficult to exaggerate the decline in the western Shaw region during the decade following the 1968 riot. Certainly poverty and its attendant social ills had marred the area in the days of Geno Baroni, but then enough of a coherent sense of neighborhood endured to give residents and urban reformers a measure of hope. The riot and the great exodus that followed changed all that. Some 10,000 housing units were lost and businesses big and small closed. Soon the major grocery chains and drug stores disappeared, and even Children's Hospital moved away. Boarded up buildings and weed-filled lots became commonplace. Crime, always a problem but held at bay in the postwar period, seemed to explode. Fourteenth and U Streets, for decades the bustling center of the neighborhood, abutted an open air drug market. A man was shotgunned in front of the rectory, and one of the eighty shootouts that occurred between police and area drug dealers in 1980 was witnessed by frightened parish children as they walked home from school.

Yet another threat loomed at the end of the decade as real estate speculators, attracted by the beauty of the old Victorian houses and apartments on tree-lined streets so convenient to downtown, began buying up the residences of the poor who remained. Housing costs rose accordingly, and tenants with little understanding of their rights or the power they might wield in a concerted action against landlords faced massive evictions. Along the southern and western edges of the neighborhood buildings like the old parish school and convent were being converted into luxury townhouses and condominium apartments. In a very real sense, gentrification, like poverty and crime, threatened the character of the neighborhood and its surviving churches.

During all this turmoil and change SS. Paul and Augustine had survived. Familiar landmarks had faded away, but the church and its school and community center endured on V Street, their doors opened and welcoming, a mark of concern for neighbors and a beacon of hope in a region filled with despair and helplessness. Symbolizing this concern, the parish, with its friends from Augustana Lutheran Church, conducted a special Stations of the Cross on Good Fridays. Then parishioners found memorials of Christ's journey to Calvary, not in the familiar renditions carved on church walls, but on the streets and vacant lots of their neighborhood. They carried their cross and recited prayers at locations associated with the continuing agony manifest in the battered lives of junkies, prostitutes, and the poor. Speaking for the marchers, Father Kemp emphasized that the Good Friday processions were not meant to place blame or win converts, but simply to recognize that poverty and misery existed in the area and that "we who are His people need to redeem this space, the neighborhood in which we live."[1]

The neighborhood Stations of the Cross was a sign of the congregation's intention, expressed by its parish council, to involve the church more closely in the delivery of social services and to organize the neighborhood so that its residents might play a greater role in the dramatic changes affecting the community. In their annual workshop/retreat in 1980, council members addressed the need to develop a master plan, a vision for the decade they called it, to channel the parish's energies in the fight for social justice. Traditional forms of charity and programs involving the parish's children as well as new initiatives aimed at community organization and housing relief were all carefully re-examined. Calling the parish "the anchor in a community of change," council president Michael Harris warned his colleagues that

1. As quoted in *Washington Post*, 4 Apr 1980. In later years the outdoor stations became a large, ecumenical affair with the first station marked in SS. Paul and Augustine and the fourteenth station at Augustana Lutheran. See, for example, *Washington Post*, 2 Apr 1988.

all the dynamic ministries they had fostered would be successful and grow "only if the parish keeps a strong presence in this community and pays attention to its needs, assets, and potential."[2] The council accepted the challenge implicit in these remarks, and during the 1980s led the congregation into an ever more intense involvement with community concerns. In its Christian witness during this era of neighborhood change, the parish would come alive as never before.

A Revitalized Social Ministry

Most of the parish's outreach programs devised in the mid-1970s could be ascribed to Raymond Kemp. During those years this forceful, charismatic pastor goaded an often timid parish council into initiating new courses of action, energized its leaders when interest flagged, and criticized himself and the council when goals went unmet. His successor faced an altogether different situation. In large part because of Kemp's efforts, the council by 1981 had evolved into a mature, policy-making body, insistent on its prerogatives and determined to control parish programs. When the new archbishop, James A. Hickey, appointed Kemp to his senior management team as full-time secretary of the newly created Office of Parish Life and Worship, both the council and parish staff met with the diocesan personnel committee to press their case for John Mudd as his successor. In June 1981 the thirty-seven-year-old Mudd, a native Washingtonian raised in Nativity parish, became the eighth pastor of SS. Paul and Augustine.[3]

A popular choice for the job, Mudd likes to describe himself as "a meek man." Right or wrong, this characterization seemed to appeal to the parish's lay leaders who, Mudd claimed, campaigned for his appointment because they assumed he would "go along with them or they

2. Memo, Harris to Executive Committee, n.d. (ca. Sep 1980), sub: Retreat/Workshop (first quote); Lorenz A. Wheatley, "Parish Council Takes Active Leadership Role," *St. Augustine Spirit* (Fall 1985), p. 3 (second quote).

3. The change of pastors received full coverage. See, for example, *Washington Star*, 28 May 1981. Mudd's installation, the first in the archdiocese's new rite of installation, was described in the *CS*, 15 Oct 1981, and *St. Augustine's Newsletter* (Summer 1981). Kemp continued to live in the parish, taking rooms and maintaining a small office at 1419 V Street.

STATIONS OF THE CROSS. Christian witness in a changing neighborhood under the auspices of St. Augustine's and Augustana Lutheran churches.

could push him around where a new man might tell them what to do and try to bring back the old ways."[4] In fact Mudd did promise to accept any council decision, unless it conflicted with Church doctrine—an error, he confidently added, the parish would never fall into. At the same time he promised that he would fight for his point of view. He had no intention of being dictated to, he warned, and meant to be involved in all decisions. By the same token Mudd pledged never to dictate to the council, which, he believed, should reflect the will of the congregation. All final decisions should be left to the people's representatives, he reasoned, because St. Augustine's had been founded by the people, who had sustained it during its many trials. On a practical level Mudd, like his predecessor, relied principally on the parish team to set the

4. Author's intv. with John Mudd. Unless otherwise noted, the following discussion on Mudd's philosophy of leadership is based on this source.

agenda, raise issues, and argue its position with the pertinent council committee. He was confident that he and the rest of the team had enough knowledge and information to influence the council and direct it toward good decisions. He was pleased, he noted, to find council members unfettered by a need to exert control and willing to let the Spirit move through the parish. The parish staff met frequently, he claimed, not to consolidate its control, but to learn "how its ministry might support and unify the active and spiritual life of the parish."[5]

Mudd understood that this democratic approach to setting directions and policy for the parish was charting a new course in the archdiocese. In preparing to welcome Bishop Eugene A. Marino on an inspection visit in 1984 he reminded the council that its performance on this occasion was important, for "we need to demonstrate to Bishop Marino that Parish councils can be effective, and we want to hold up ourselves as a model for other parishes in the Archdiocese."[6] Like any new approach, a decision-making council had its critics as well as champions. Some parishioners, and not just its senior citizens, were uncomfortable with an aggressive council and the changes it was enacting. Mudd admitted that the new permissiveness had facilitated the rise of political factions in the parish, each vying for power. But then, he argued, such factions existed in all communities, even in earliest Christian times as described in the Acts of the Apostles.[7] Some critics were concerned that the council-based activism was succeeding at the expense of explaining Catholicism's unique spiritual and moral values to newcomers. Pauline Jones, who would deny that the problem was connected with the new activism, nevertheless also decried the lack of understanding of basic Catholic beliefs among many in the congregation. "You can't just bring your Baptist beliefs into St. Augustine's," she scolded the newcomers, adding, "if this parish disappeared you'd still need to know what you believe."[8]

5. Mudd, "The Oldest Black Church in Washington, D.C.: A Parish Ministry Model," *Charities USA* (Jun 1984), p. 13. See also author's intv. with Leon C. Roberts, a member of Mudd's parish team.

6. Ltr., Mudd to Parish Council Members, 18 Jan 1984, SAA.

7. Mudd, "The Oldest Black Church in Washington, D.C."

8. From author's intv. with Pauline J. Jones, who also reflected on the complaints against the council and its programs.

Mudd admitted that many of the new parishioners had emerged from a catechumen program that had somewhat overemphasized what united Christians at the expense of a thorough grounding in Catholic doctrine. It was the result of a catechesis based on Scripture study, not on the old system of memorizing the virtues and vices. But if some questioned the knowledge of the newcomers, none criticized their devotion to their neighbors. From his retirement home Father Joyce, who had welcomed hundreds of converts at St. Augustine's, commended the activist council for its numerous outreach programs, which he saw as an attempt to follow the teachings of Vatican II.[9] Although commenting on an earlier period, Father Muffler's conclusion could also be applied to the parish in 1981:

these men and women were truly proud of what they and their forebears had accomplished at St. Augustine's. They felt a genuine sense of ownership, not of the buildings but of what they believed their parish stood for. Finally, though the people of St. Augustine's had no control over the institution itself, they could exercise control over the programs of the institution. They became, in essence, a church within a church—one where the pastor and priests were regarded as confreres, and the bishop seldom intruded.[10]

Little attention was paid to such concerns in a parish, as Raymond Kemp described it, "on the move, attempting to meet the demands of the Gospel and the need of our neighbors."[11] Central to such outreach was an expansion of the parish's social ministry. Traditional forms of charity were revitalized. The Ladies of Charity and members of a recharged parish Sodality continued, as of old, to provide short-term relief to the neighborhood needy, including supplying the food for the sizable sandwich distribution service operated by the priests out of the rectory kitchen. The women's work was underwritten by members' dues and special assistance from the diocesan office of the Ladies of Charity. To handle those cases of chronic need, traditionally the job of a now largely defunct St. Vincent de Paul Society, the parish council created an eight-member St. Martin de Porres committee, which investigated individual requests and distributed aid from an annual budget

9. Author's intv. with Father Joyce.
10. Muffler, "This Far By Faith," p. 155.
11. Ltr., Kemp to parishioners ["Greetings in the Lord,"], 28 Aug 1978, SAA.

of $7,500 financed in part through a monthly "Poor" collection at all masses. In time the council decided that the parish's charitable commitments were too broad and costly to be left to volunteers, and in 1979, in conjunction with the Ladies of Charity and the St. Martin de Porres committee, it hired Diane Williams, a social worker, as part-time coordinator of its social service ministries, later renamed the social services committee.[12]

The new director had plenty to do. In partnership with the Hunger Task Force of the city's Interfaith Committee, the parish had committed itself to providing a monthly meal, cooked, delivered, and served by parish volunteers to the homeless clients of So Others Might Eat (SOME). Williams coordinated this work as well as supervised the issuance of food certificates to the needy in a program the parish had negotiated with Safeway Stores. She and the members of the social service committee prepared Thanksgiving food baskets and served Thanksgiving dinner to neighborhood needy. In 1985, for example, some 350 families received holiday supplies; sixty volunteers cooked and served dinner to 80 needy guests in the school cafeteria and delivered dinners to 55 shut-ins. In later years the D.C. Department of Recreation and the alumni of Kappa Alpha Psi Fraternity assisted parishioners in delivering the baskets. One important task assigned the social service director was representing the parish in the Christian Communities Committed to Change, a so-called cluster program organized by six inner-city parishes in 1980. The CCCC generated more than $75,000 in funds to aid the city's elderly.[13] Nor did committee members eschew the difficult tasks associated with charity in a modern city. Beginning in February 1986 it assumed responsibility one night each month for manning both Christ House and Calvert Shelter, overnight havens for the homeless.

12. In later years the St. Martin de Porres committee was abolished and its work assumed by the Social Services committee. The Ladies of Charity, however, have endured. The Sodality did not sponsor a special ministry, but its members could be found in many of the ministries described in this chapter. (See the Sodality's Closing Report of the 1989–1991 Administration, 2 Jun 1991, SAA.) This brief summary of parish charities is based on the 1979 and 1981–82 parish profiles, the minutes of the parish council, 1977–89, and Mudd's "The Oldest Black Church in Washington, D.C.," pp. 12–13.

13. For a description of the organization and operation of the CCCC, see CS, 6 Mar 1980.

More publicized than most cases, but typical of the parish's response to the needs of its neighbors, was the outpouring of help when fire destroyed the apartment just beyond the church parking lot at 1444 W Street in the cold February of 1985. Some forty poor and uninsured families were left without clothing, furniture, or shelter. Even before the firemen completely extinguished the blaze, parishioners had sprung into action. The school's St. Augustine Room was turned into a temporary shelter, while volunteers began canvassing the neighborhood for blankets and clothing. The school soon became a relief center where tons of clothes piled in twelve-foot stacks awaited distribution. Sister Patricia Hamilton, Williams's successor as coordinator of social services, launched a donation drive that collected more than $46,000 from some 30 parishes and 25 Protestant and Jewish groups. The *Post*, citing its ties to old St. Augustine's, donated $5,000. Meanwhile the parish's social service committee helped arrange temporary housing for the 150 displaced persons, many of them Haitian and Salvadoran immigrants. The *Post* neatly tied the incident to the parish's central mission when, in a front page article on the rescue effort, it concluded that St. Augustine's "which began helping people more than a century ago was still at it yesterday."[14]

The presence of so many senior citizens in the congregation prompted the parish to develop a special ministry that transcended parish boundaries. It began with the Eucharistic ministers who regularly brought communion to sick and elderly shut-ins. These prayerful visits gave the ministers time to talk with the old folks and frequently to learn about their many physical and social needs. The ministers began meeting together to discuss what might be done to help. This in turn led the parish council to organize a new Health Ministry in 1979. Initially the Health Ministry employed twenty volunteers, whose regular visits to the sick and elderly included special assistance in the form of referrals to appropriate government agencies or one of the parish's other volunteer groups. Parishioners like Mayola McCrary, Jane Blaise, and Bob Roeder were closely identified with these efforts, which often centered around the need for adequate senior housing.

14. The fire and its aftermath were given considerable press coverage. See, for example, *Washington Post*, 5 and 7 [source of quote] Feb and 27 Jun 1985 and *CS*, 7 and 14 Feb and 21 Mar 1985.

Such cases were routinely referred to the parish's Housing Office, which would work on their behalf. At one time Diane Williams, with the help of Pauline Jones, was able to find new homes for many parish and neighborhood elderly in the brand-new Campbell Heights Apartments, the subsidized senior citizen center on the Fifteenth Street site of the old Dunbar Hotel.

By 1984 the Health Ministry had grown to some forty Eucharistic ministers and volunteers who regularly tended to the needs of 125 elderly homebound in addition to providing counseling to the neighborhood seniors on subjects of special interest like nutrition and hypertension. In 1985 the ministry sponsored an Adopt-A-Grandparent campaign whereby young volunteers pledged themselves to form a special relationship with an individual senior to provide companionship as well as a watchful eye.[15] Meanwhile the hardy senior citizens of the parish's Adult Adventures, successors to Beatrice Holton Stewart, Mary Johnson, and the rest of now-retired members in the Young at Heart Club, held their energetic meetings and pursued their special ministry.

Other social programs followed. For instance, the parish sponsored a counseling service in the early 1980s. Using the expertise of John Butler, the catechumenate director (and now president of John Carroll High School), who held a degree and certificate in counseling, this service addressed problems concerning troubled marriages and mental health questions and helped those students in the parish school with exceptional behavioral problems. Also in the early 1980s the council's social justice committee organized separate support groups for men and women. These support groups sponsored social affairs and hosted group discussions that treated family issues of pressing concern such as black male/female relationships, single parenting, problems of aging, and role models for the modern family.[16]

As time passed the focus of the support groups shifted away from marriage problems as they assumed greater responsibility for the parish's ministry to pregnant teenagers and the growing numbers of

15. See, for example, ltr., Father Michael J. Kelley to Helen McKiver, 11 Feb 1986, SAA.

16. James R. Henderson, chm., Social Justice committee, "Report, 19 Oct 1984," and SS. Paul & Augustine Parish Profile, 1981–82. Both in SAA.

unwed mothers in the community. Those interested in the triumphs and trials of the wedded state turned instead to St. Augustine's Marriage Encounter group, which was organized in 1985. Dedicated to making all marriages better, this national program, started in Spain and introduced in Washington in 1971, provided couples in both healthy and hurting unions the opportunity to experience a new awareness of their married role and to reflect on their relationship as it related to God. Father Michael Kelley, the parish's new associate pastor, was familiar with the movement and, as an experiment, arranged for six couples to attend an encounter weekend at a predominantly white parish in the suburbs.[17] Their enthusiastic reaction led the parish to form its own group. Encounter facilitators could have been brought in, but because it believed that many of the matters to be discussed had a racial dimension and that the special weaknesses and strengths peculiar to black marriages needed to be emphasized, the St. Augustine group decided to train its own African-American facilitators. Soon people like Peter and Linda Davidson, Thomas and Nancy Bailey, Oliver and Deborah Nophlin, and the Lawrence Blackwells had received leadership training, and some ninety couples had attended an Encounter weekend. By 1988 the St. Augustine's group, a pioneer in the black Marriage Encounter movement, had become the largest in the archdiocese and the largest group for African-American Catholics in the nation.[18] As in so many of these programs begun for parishioners, Marriage Encounter spread through the community. Fully 20 percent of the couples dancing the evening away at the group's Sweethearts Ball in 1990 were non-Catholics.

Like most parishes, SS. Paul and Augustine initiated many of its social programs to serve its own congregation, but, given the overwhelming needs of the local community, soon provided the services to the neighborhood generally. As in the case of the parish's traditional charitable works, these new community initiatives grew in size and complexity. In October 1983 the parish council decided the time had come to form a Community Outreach Advisory Board and hire a part-time di-

17. Author's intvs. with Linda Davidson, 30 Oct 1997, and Father Kelley, 31 Oct 1997. Kelley replaced Muffler, who left the active priesthood for work in education, in June 1982, after service at St. Thomas More and, during his deaconate, at St. Luke's.

18. PCM, 19 Nov 1988 and 17 Feb 1990.

rector. It chose Dominic Moulden, a young parishioner with advanced degrees in philosophy and theology, who quickly became involved not only in the parish's ongoing housing programs, but also in coordinating the efforts of all those parish volunteers involved in community activities.[19] The Parish Outreach Program, as it was called, combined evangelization with practical help for the needy and elderly. People like retirees Lozzie York and Josephine Chase volunteered countless hours attending tenant association and block meetings far into the night, providing advice and support to those trying to find or maintain affordable housing. In 1983, for example, parishioners helped secure safe housing for twenty-five needy families. They also sponsored a petition drive and gave testimony before District committees that ended in blocking the establishment of yet more liquor stores in the neighborhood. Volunteers brought together local merchants and the police to organize resistance to loitering, break-ins, and trash accumulation. They advised evicted tenants of their rights and represented the parish on important regional bodies such as the Third District Policy Community Advisory Council and the Fourteenth and U Streets Coalition.

This large volunteer effort was supported in part by a $10,000 grant from the Campaign for Human Development, the American church's national funding program for, as the bishops put it, "self-help projects of poor and low-income groups aimed at social change." In applying for this grant, the parish council prepared a statement that might well be used to convey the spirit of the parish in the 1980s:

The parishioners of St. Augustine Church have always understood their Christian obligation as extending beyond the sacramental and liturgical rites of Catholicism. Christian action in the area of social justice gives witness to the Gospel mandate that followers of Jesus feed the hungry, clothe the naked, shelter the homeless and visit the imprisoned.[20]

Sheltering the Homeless

It was well understood in the parish in those days that among this Gospel quartet of virtues, the need to provide decent housing in a safe

19. PCM, 15 Oct and 12 Nov 1983.
20. As quoted in *CS*, 3 Nov 1983.

environment for the less fortunate was primary. As Father Kemp observed in 1979, real estate speculation and condo conversion were radically changing the neighborhood. He warned that, with little subsidized housing available, the poor and lower-middle class would soon become a distinct minority in the neighborhood. For his part Father Mudd railed at the speculators. Among them he identified some prominent Catholics and publicly called on the archbishop to take a strong stand against the greed evidenced in the old Shaw region, "to confront the money interests in the city—especially the wealthy Catholics."[21] Later Mudd would ruefully observe, "In a way the prostitutes and junkies were our allies; they held the speculators at bay."[22]

While Mudd was inviting the archbishop to enter the fray, the parish was already fully absorbed in the battle for neighborhood housing. In 1975 it had participated with Augustana Lutheran in a project sponsored by a revitalized New Inner City Community Organization (NICCO) to build 160 housing units on Portner Place, across from the rectory and next to the senior citizen residence named in honor of Leroy Campbell. While this and the housing initiatives promoted by the parish's social justice committee continued, the council concluded that, to be more effective, it must educate the congregation and its neighbors about the rights of homeowners and renters and support individuals as well as groups who were struggling to remain in the Shaw area. It convened its first housing meeting in December 1977. During that and subsequent gatherings council members heard from experts like Father Baroni and D.C. Councilman Dave Clark on the subject. In April 1978 the parish council organized the Saints Paul and Augustine Neighborhood Housing Organization, Inc. (SPANHO), to share information and promote actions to slow rent increases and monitor land and building sales.[23]

21. As quoted in *National Catholic Reporter*, 4 Jul 1980. The Kemp warning appeared in the Parish Profile, 1979, SAA.

22. As quoted in author's intv with Mudd, .

23. Ltr., Kemp to parishioners ("Greetings in the Lord"), 28 Aug 1978, with attachments, SAA. The following brief account of SPANHO is based on this source and a summary of the history and work of this organization titled "Saints Paul and Augustine Neighborhood Housing Organization, Inc. and its Staffing Army: The Saints Paul and Augustine Housing Center," n.d. (ca. 1983), SAA.

SPANHO got an exceptional boost from Father Timothy Healy, S.J., the president of Georgetown University. Healy had become personally interested in the parish program and recruited a group of Georgetown students to help out. Through the auspices of Georgetown University's Community Action Coalition, student volunteers began researching neighborhood housing trends and the availability of subsidized housing in the area. When the council set up a hotline in the rectory basement to assist neighbors with housing-related problems ranging from evictions to lack of heat in apartments, these young Georgetown activists, along with others from George Washington University, manned the phones, providing information and referrals.[24] To channel the various activities of the new organization, the parish council created a Housing Information Center to serve as the operating arm of SPANHO. The center supported the efforts of the hotline workers and all those volunteers who were researching housing changes in the Shaw region, organizing tenants and homeowners, and disseminating housing information. In March 1980, for example, the Housing Center published *Housing Information*, a brochure that directed people to pertinent legal services, government agencies, community organizations, and emergency shelters. Funded by three of the Advisory Neighborhood commissions and Georgetown University, several editions of *Housing Information* and a bi-monthly newsletter, *Housing Voice*, spread the word about block clubs and tenant associations. By June 1980 the center's workload had grown beyond the point where volunteer help sufficed, and the council hired a full-time housing officer financed by the parish and an $8,000 grant from the Campaign for Human Development.[25]

Diane Williams, herself a Georgetown graduate, left her post in social services to take on the housing job. She had her work cut out for her. Along with the volunteers in SPANHO and Father Mudd, Williams and her staff organized tenant associations in five large

24. PCM, 27 Jan 1979.

25. Although the council had discussed the formation of a housing center as early as December 1978 (see Minutes, 16 Dec 1978), it was not always up-to-date on administrative details. As late as December 1980, when the new coordinator had been on the job six months, the council was still deliberating about her job description. Members were obviously pleased with Williams, whose performance, Administration committee chairman Jerry West reported, "continues to be exceptional." PCM, 18 Dec 1980.

apartment houses and helped residents of the complex at 1901–1907 Fifteenth Street purchase their buildings and convert them into cooperatives. The parish also co-sponsored the purchasers' applications for HUD mortgage insurance and Section 8 money, as HUD's rental subsidy program was familiarly known.[26] SPANHO and its housing center also supported local homeowners in their fight against higher tax assessments, frequently supplying experts to testify before the city council's revenue and finance committee and the Board of Equalization and Review.

The parish's housing center allied with other groups in the city to lobby the District government on behalf of tenants. In 1980 it joined the Emergency Committee to Save Rental Housing to fight for a continuation of rent controls and to regulate condominium conversions by making such moves subject to a vote by the tenants. In 1981 the center played a key role in organizing tenants at Hilltop House on Euclid Street in their successful effort to purchase the apartment complex. It also organized the 1500 T Street Block Council's united appeal of tax assessments.[27]

The parish's housing center played a key role in the success of one of the city's major neighborhood initiatives, the 14th and U Streets Coalition. The coalition grew out of a spontaneous citizen reaction to the local drug war. When the deadly confrontations between police and drug dealers climaxed in mid-May 1980 with a shooting watched by scores of school children, an angered Father Kemp decided to act. He got the parish council and local churches and schools to sponsor a meeting where 400 concerned neighbors committed themselves on the spot to launch a communal effort to deal not only with the drug scourge but also with the problem of redevelopment. They formed a coalition representing neighborhood organizations and housing associations and elected a board to deal with issues of special concern, including drug and crime prevention, housing, and neighborhood planning (i.e. monitoring proposals for Metro's Green Line). The parish made a major

26. The parish's contribution in this case received scant notice in the press, which emphasized instead the work of the Ministries United to Support Community Life Endeavors. See *Washington Post*, 3 Apr 1980.

27. *SS. Paul and Augustine Newsletter*, (Mar 1980) and (Summer 1981). See also *Washington Post*, 2 Apr 1981.

contribution to the new organization when it provided office space and arranged for its housing center director to serve as the coalition's only full-time worker.

In one of its first acts, the coalition organized a petition drive that demanded the District end the drug war in the neighborhood by providing increased police protection and more drug treatment centers. The city responded sympathetically, and meetings with the Inspector Reginald Catoe, Deputy Chief of the Third Police District, and other senior police officials resulted in a stepped-up police presence. Assessing progress on the coalition's first birthday, the *Washington Post* noted that arrests in the area were up and the drug market that had operated so brazenly on Fourteenth Street between U and V had closed down. The *Post* quoted Father Kemp's assessment that the extreme anxiety of the past year had disappeared.[28] Lest police vigilance be relaxed, however, witnesses also reported that the Mercedes and Cadillacs of the drug kingpins could still be seen patrolling the area of Fourteenth Steet below T. As for housing and redevelopment, the coalition was from the start determined to insure that the various arms of the community were "controllers and planners of change, rather than the victims."[29] To that end the coalition became a major sponsor of local block associations and tenants rights groups. In early 1981 it won a substantial Urban Development Act Grant from HUD which, with low-interest loans from two private-lending institutions, enabled the coalition to establish a $560,000 home improvement loan fund. Through it Shaw residents earning less than $30,000 per year could borrow money at below market rates to fix their property. The coalition also successfully persuaded some of the developers invading the area to adopt so-called mixed-use housing, whereby longtime residents would be retained in the remodeled complexes.[30]

The parish remained active in all these efforts. In addition to the contribution of its housing center personnel, parishioners routinely served on the coalition's board. In 1984, for example, Charlayne John-

28. *Washington Post*, 28 May 1981.

29. Quoted in *Saint Augustine Catholic Church Parish Ministries, 1985–86*, copy in SAA.

30. *SS. Paul and Augustine Newsletter* (Summer 1981). See also Parish Council Team Report, 15 Nov 1980 and unsigned, undated history of the coalition. Both in SAA.

son, Father Mudd, and James Henderson were elected members, Mudd serving as vice president. In applying for a grant from the bishops' Campaign for Human Development in 1988, Mudd explained the coalition's effort to organize area churches and community based groups to develop low cost housing in the Shaw area. Calling the coalition "the best known grass roots organization in the District," he went on to describe the fight for affordable housing without which many long-time residents, including many parishioners, were threatened with displacement.[31]

Mudd had recently been at the center of one of the coalition's major fights for affordable housing. From its inception the coalition had been especially concerned about the fate of Parcel 13, the large, mostly abandoned block in the center of the neighborhood bordered by Fourteenth Street and Portner Place between U and V. Even earlier, Father Kemp had discussed with the parish council ways in which it might promote Section 8 low-cost housing along the Fourteenth Street corridor and had walked with Mayor Marion Barry through the vacant lots across V Street from the church buildings discussing how the city should use this site for an apartment complex for the area's large families.[32] Father Mudd, who was also concerned about the loss of housing for large families in the neighborhood, wanted as a start to renovate the several abandoned row houses on the V Street side of the parcel into large units, as many as three to each building. The city had already donated property abutting the west end of the parcel along Portner Place to the National Housing Partnership, the same people who had built the Campbell Heights Apartments, for development as Section 8 low-cost housing. Working through the coalition, Mudd sought a similar disposition of the houses on V Street. The request was rejected by the city for reasons that quickly became known. In 1982 the Barry Administration announced plans for construction of a new municipal office building on Parcel 13. The houses in question were to be razed to make way for the entrance to the new building's underground garage.[33]

31. Ltr., Mudd to Joan Rosenhauer, Campaign for Human Development, 1 Feb 1988, cy in SAA.

32. PCM, 16 Dec 1978, and author's intv. with Kemp.

33. Anne Chase, "Community News New Area Housing," *St. Augustine Spirit* (Fall 1985), p. 7. The following account of the Baroni apartments is based on the Chase arti-

The coalition fought back, informing the District that it would never support a project that placed a garage entrance, and the heavy truck
traffic that entailed, on a residential street across from an elementary
school. It demanded that the building be redesigned to provide space
for housing along V Street. Father Mudd explored possible alternatives
to the city plan with Thomas Zuniga, the director of the District's
Housing Finance Agency. These discussions were going nowhere until
Michael Crescenzo, a young agency employee and, incidentally, a
member of the congregation, came up with the idea of replacing the
houses on V Street with a new apartment complex built atop the pad
(roof) of the underground garage whose entrance would be relocated.
Mayor Barry had promised Father Kemp that housing would be included on the site, but he needed reminding. Along with coalition representatives, Mudd and Zuniga discussed the proposal with Barry, who
agreed and ordered the municipal building redesigned.

Having won the battle with the city, the coalition now faced the
daunting task of securing financing. The coalition wanted the apartments reserved exclusively for low-income families, but help from the
federal government was no longer available now that HUD had ter-
minated its Section 8 rental subsidy program. After consulting with
his old friend, building contractor Joseph Horning, Father Mudd realized that any financial arrangement would necessitate renting a substantial number of apartments at regular market prices. Again Michael
Crescenzo came to the rescue by devising a so-called 80/20 option
that would mix moderate and low-income units in the project according to a strict ratio. The parish council agreed that, given the high cost
of building, Mudd should press for such a compromise solution.[34] Accordingly Tom Zuniga obtained an agreement whereby the District's
Housing Finance Agency put up $1.5 million, financed by tax-exempt
bonds. Another $500,000 in the form of low-interest loans from the
same agency and the District's community development department
was made available to supplement the low-income rentals. This
arrangement allowed nine of the building's thirty-two apartments to be
reserved for larger families at greatly reduced rates. In effect the rest

cle, the author's intv. with Father Mudd, and an article by Mary Ellen Webb in the *CS*,
11 Sep 1986.

34. Social Justice committee Rpt., 19 Oct 1984.

of the tenants subsidized their lower-income neighbors. The Horning Brother's Construction Company built the apartments, and the 14th and U Street Coalition, using money donated by St. Rose of Lima parish, set up an office to screen applicants.

Although Mudd concluded that, given the coalition's sponsorship of the project, the apartments should not be closely identified with the parish, the council believed otherwise. At Pauline Jones's suggestion, it recommended to the coalition that the building bear the name of Geno Baroni. The recently deceased Baroni was revered throughout the neighborhood, and the building was so dedicated on October 24, 1987, in the presence of the mayor and other local officials with special guests Senator Barbara Mikulski of Maryland and many friends and relatives of the beloved social activist.[35]

Even as the Baroni Apartments were being filled with its carefully screened tenants, the parish's social justice committee was experimenting with a new form of housing assistance in the neighborhood. In 1988 the city inaugurated the second phase of its Homestead Program, which was designed to transform multi-family buildings into co-ops where tenants could purchase their units for $250 and receive a $10,000 loan to redecorate. Not surprisingly, such laudable programs were frequently met with suspicion or open hostility by poor tenants who, above all, feared eviction and saw any change, no matter how much it promised to better their lives, as a threat to get rid of them. When the apartment complex at 1424 W Street was chosen for the Homestead Program, the parish decided to offer assistance.[36] Members of the social justice committee under the direction of the Outreach Program director, Dominic Moulden, spent countless hours with the residents, calming their fears about the change and instructing them in the intricacies of co-op housing and the joys and responsibilities of ownership. Moulden brought in lawyers, accountants, and architects who, in conjunction with the experts in the Washington Inner-city Self Help organization, volunteered their specialized assistance while city

35. Father Mudd later conceded that it was right to name the apartments after Baroni, even though he jokingly admitted he had at first pushed for an innocuous title, such as Capitol View or Mudd Flats. See author's intv. with Mudd.

36. Michael, Mayer, "Not Stoppin' Now," *Faith and Action, Newsletter of the Churches Conference on Shelter and Housing* (Fall 1990), pp. 2–3.

contractors carried out the extensive renovations. In less than two years a semi-derelict building was converted into a safe and comfortable home for its proud new owners. For the parish, the experiment opened yet another way to express its ongoing commitment to serve its powerless and forgotten neighbors.

Saving the Children

The third major thrust of the parish's renewed outreach program focused on the children. That St. Augustine's had been founded on the determination of Washington's black Catholics to provide an education for their children was evident. From the earliest days of the Republic, both African Americans and their masters had understood that education formed the most important dimension of liberation. That was why slaves were denied schooling and why freedmen and women grasped at instruction as the key to advancement. It also explained why for over a century the parish's leaders, both lay and cleric, had pushed education as essential to their crusade for civil rights and social justice. The modest school was at the heart of the little chapel built on Fifteenth Street just as education remained central to St. Augustine's mission nearly a century and a half later.

The parish school was also a powerful instrument of evangelizaton. As the parish council pointed out in 1985, St. Augustine's School not only stressed the legacy of black people as believers and survivors, it also by its very existence "stands as testimony to the values and ideals taught by the church." Educational experts agreed. As Vernon C. Polite pointed out, "A Catholic school in a plight-stricken community is more than a mere bright spot, it prepared its students by providing the tools needed to attack social injustices intellectually, economically, and spiritually."[37] These observations were particularly applicable to Washington, where once highly vaunted public schools, even in the days of segregation, produced some of the nation's most distinguished African-American leaders, providing them with a value-based educa-

37. Parish Council Education cmte, "Saint Augustine School and Study Plan," n.d. (ca. Summer, 1985) [first quote] and Vernon C. Polite, "Getting the Job Done Well: African American Students and Catholic Schools," *Journal of Negro Education*, 61, no. 2 (Spring 1992): 219 [second quote].

tion dedicated to community building and social action. By 1980, however, despite a population that boasted the highest percentage of black college graduates in the land, Washington's public schools were suffering from record numbers of dropouts and below-par academic performance. Black parents were aware of this, and in steadily increasing numbers were turning to Catholic schools. Ultimately the success of the schools attracted large numbers of these non-Catholics to the Church itself. The sacrifice made by the congregation to provide its neighbors one of society's most fundamental needs was leading many to seek full communion.[38]

At the beginning of the 1980 academic year almost 60 percent of the parish school's 280 students were non-Catholic, a percentage destined to rise in succeeding years as the school population reduced further.[39] The students, almost all African American, were then being taught by a faculty consisting of five Oblate Sisters and five lay teachers. These instructors were actively involved at that time in the self-evaluation program required for those seeking the coveted accreditation of the Middle States Association, a certificate the school received in 1983. In addition to their regular instruction, students were participating in a full range of extracurricular activities, including city-run enrichment programs meant to develop a sense of civic responsibility and increased pride in their African-American heritage. The principal, Sister Barbara Spears, had recently voiced her concern about a negative feeling toward school she detected in some of her charges, but, she reported to the council, such attitudes could be attributed to troubles in individual families and did not constitute a discipline problem.[40] In fact the only serious problem facing the school at the beginning of the decade was the perennial one of finance.

38. On evidence of the schools' role in recruiting new Catholics, see Diana T. Slaughter and Deborah J. Johnson, eds., *Visible Now: Blacks and Private Schools* (New York: Greenwood Press, 1988), p. 93. On the deterioration of Washington's schools, see Adele Logan Alexander's introduction to Fitzpatrick and Goodwin's *The Guide to Black Washington*, p. 24.

39. School population, which stood at 300 in 1978, had dropped to 240 by 1983, where it remained constant for the rest of the decade. See PCM, 15 Oct 1983 and 17 Oct 1987.

40. PCM, 27 Jan 1979.

The parish, lulled by years of diocesan subsidies, had failed to address the problem of constantly rising costs related to the need for more and higher-paid lay teachers. In presenting his FY 1981 budget, council president Michael Harris excoriated both the school board and his colleagues for failing to provide leadership in what he called the budget crisis in the school. He wanted the board reconstituted and called for greater interaction between the board and the teachers and parents.[41] That same year the school lost yet another sister, and although Father Muffler joined the staff as assistant principal, the school board was forced to hire another lay teacher, thereby adding to the budget crisis.

The council took Harris's criticism to heart. In 1981 it approved a substantial rise in tuition rates (to $700 per child, with significant discounts for larger families). To stimulate greater use of the St. Augustine Room by outside organizations for parties and receptions (all providing extra revenue for the school), the council renovated the school kitchen and launched an advertising campaign extolling the room's amenities. Extra money was also derived from an after-school program started and supervised by Sister Barbara, who used young adults supervised by the parish staff. Working parents paid a fee that allowed their youngsters to remain at school, involved in an array of enrichment programs, until they could be retrieved later in the day.[42]

Despite the severe budget problems, the parish council committed itself in 1981 to raising more than $7,000 to finance a neighborhood center for junior high students enrolled in the Higher Achievement Program (HAP). Originated in the mid-1970s at Gonzaga, HAP sought to take good students from the inner city and make them better. Over the years it proved dramatically effective in enhancing the academic skills and test scores of hundreds of the city's poorest and brightest public school students. Since many parish children were participating in the program at Gonzaga, Sister Barbara decided that the parish should get more closely involved. At her urging SS. Paul & Augustine

41. Memo, Harris to Parish Council, n.d. (ca. June 1981), sub: Budget FY 81–82, SAA.

42. All these programs were discussed in the parish council, for which see various meetings, 1979–1982. See also SS. Paul & Augustine Parish Profile, 1981–82.

agreed to sponsor a center for 120 students, who used the school during the summer and on school evenings for accelerated academic courses and some recreational activities. In time these classes, directed by an independent, non-profit agency, proved poorly supervised and the parish left the program, but not before demonstrating once again its determination to contribute to the needs of its neighbors in the community.[43]

It was during this period of intense activity, and just as the school had completed the Middle States visitation that would lead to its full accreditation in 1983 that the parish lost its dynamic principal. Although she continued to live in the parish convent and serve in many parish ministries, Sister Barbara accepted appointment as a teacher and administrator at Mackin High School. She was replaced by another Oblate, the soft spoken and much-loved Sister Ricardo Maddox.[44]

Meanwhile, the council continued to look for new ways to stabilize the school's finances. It had frequently considered the idea of endowments as a source of funding, and when Michael Harris died after a lingering illness, his friends and colleagues decided to create a scholarship fund in his memory.[45] This first, modest endowment was followed by several other small gifts and independent grants that supplemented the school budget in succeeding years. A 1983 archdiocesan grant, for example, was used to purchase computers for the school and send the faculty to a special workshop on computer education. Such efforts made a difference. After reviewing the school's books in December 1985 the council's administration committee reported that, to date, "income is ahead of target and expenditures are within approved guidelines."[46]

But the issue was not going to go away that easily. It was obvious that the problem fed on itself. The frequent need to increase the number of lay teachers and the constant pressure to pay them higher wages invariably led to periodic tuition increases, which further reduced the

43. SS. Paul & Augustine Parish Profile, 1981–82 and author's intv. with Father Mudd.

44. For an affectionate portrait of St. Augustine's convent and the five Oblates who lived there, see *Washington Post*, 20 Dec 1983.

45. PCM, 19 Nov 1985.

46. PCM, 21 Dec 1985.

CARDINAL JAMES A. HICKEY leaving St. Augustine's under the watchful eye of a phalanx from the Knights of Columbus.

school population, especially the poor neighborhood children most in need of such education. The drop in the number of students only added to the deficit. In preparing its part of a survey of diocesan schools during the summer of 1985, the parish council conducted yet another investigation of its school's chronic financial problems. Ways to avoid further tuition increases by reversing enrollment trends, attracting alumni and general parish support, and increasing volunteer help were discussed. Members were adamantly opposed to suggestions that the parish try to merge its school with those of nearby parishes. The education committee put it in the form of a resolution: "We will continue as an independent school, and we will not merge. If we have to, we will try to get other schools to merge *with us*."[47]

Bold words, but the specter of the deficits continued to haunt the parish council when the balance struck in 1985 proved short-lived. During the next three years the school deficit totaled $82,000. The council was forced in 1987 to authorize yet another tuition increase (to over $1,000 per child) despite the obvious threat that posed to enrollment figures. It also approved a second collection at all Sunday masses to supplement the parish subsidy to the school and placed all capital improvements, such as the much-desired air conditioning of the church, in abeyance. For his part Father Mudd continued to urge parishioners to consider tithing and pressed diocesan officials for financial assistance.[48] Calling a $3,500 grant from the central School Office "a drop in the bucket," he admitted to Archbishop Hickey his frustration over trying to meet diocesan assessments, like the annual subsidy for the *Catholic Standard*. He was particularly upset over assessments that failed to take into account parishes like St. Augustine's, which were trying to encourage tithing to support a school that served an important segment of the inner-city population. In that regard, Mudd also criticized diocesan guidelines on such matters as liability insurance, which would make a facility like the St. Augustine Room too expensive for renters. The result would be an annual loss of $25,000 in income for the strapped parish.[49]

47. PCM, 21 Dec 1985. Emphasis in the original. See also Education cmte, "Saint Augustine School Study Plan," n.d. (ca. Summer 1985), SAA.
48. Ltr. Mudd to Dear Parishioners, 30 Sep 1987, cy in SAA.
49. Ltrs., Mudd to Hickey, 30 Sep 1987 and to Dr. Jerome Parath, Schools Office,

Meanwhile the search went on for other sources of help. The parish council listened to proposals for expanding scholarship funds to assist low-income families in the neighborhood who could not otherwise afford the new tuition rates.[50] In keeping with a diocesan effort to link affluent parishes with those struggling to retain their schools, Father Mudd approached the pastor of nearby St. Matthew's for help. Msgr. Louis Quinn agreed to donate $5,000 annually to the scholarship fund. Generous donors from all over the capital region also joined in with significant contributions.[51] Meanwhile some parishioners assumed the onerous obligation of tithing, a form of generosity rarely seen in the Church, while many more participated in a wide variety of old-fashioned fund drives. They sold Christmas trees and sponsored fashion shows and ski trips. They earned money from nights at local dinner theaters, moonlight cruises, breakfast parties, and Lenten fish fries. A sale of arts and crafts kits by the school in 1987 netted more than $10,000![52] Still the deficit persisted, fueled by a 15 percent raise in lay teachers' salaries to bring them up to scale. In 1989 just three Oblates remained on the staff, and the motherhouse predicted the loss of yet another sister soon.[53] By then, despite the Christmas trees and other fundraisers bringing in $63,000, the council was obliged to authorize another $57,000 donation to the school, causing a parish deficit of $25,000 that year.[54] Faced with a seemingly endless series of deficits, the council decided on one all-out fund-raising drive, a so-called capital stewardship campaign, with the hope of creating a fund account capable of paying for needed improvements and establishing a permanent endowment for the school. It hired a fund-raising consultant, who

23 Sep 1987. On parish's assessment for the *Catholic Standard*, see ltr., Mudd to Father Donald S. Essex, 21 Aug 1987. Copies of all in SAA.

50. PCM, 12 Nov 1986.

51. Ltr., Mudd to Quinn, 3 Aug 1987. For an example of the parish's response to other donors, see ltr., Mudd to Richard H. Rubin, 4 Jan 1988. Copies of both in SAA.

52. On the variety and extent of these fund-raising events, see PCM, 22 Feb and 12 Nov 1986 and 17 Oct 1987.

53. PCM, 17 Feb 1990. The council discussed the number of Oblates necessary to retain the school's definition as an Oblate school.

54. Ltr., Mudd to Parishioners, 7 Oct 1990, cy in SAA. The total parish revenue for FY 1989 was $637,585, which included over $408,000 in regular offertory contributions and tithing commitments.

organized a canvas of the parish that garnered pledges amounting to more than $1 million. Most important, a gratifying number of these pledges were subsequently fulfilled. The money thus collected allowed the parish to establish an education fund for students from low-income families as well as air condition the church and contract major repairs to the roof.[55]

Despite these welcome acquisitions, it was obvious to all that the school would always present a financial challenge to the parish. Still, it would be a mistake to label this period of financial crisis one of doom and gloom. Rather, for a congregation convinced that education was central to its ministry, the effort to support a school for its children and those of its neighbors was an exhilarating crusade, one that placed them squarely in the tradition of the parish's founders and one entered into by the whole congregation with determination and optimism.

The Youth Ministry

This same sense of carrying on a sacred tradition undergirded the congregation's support of its Confraternity of Christian Doctrine. The Sunday school, as it was always called at St. Augustine's, also traced its roots back to the little chapel on Fifteenth Street, and over the decades thousands of children had depended on a long line of dedicated volunteer teachers, including many of the sisters, for their religious instruction. By 1972, reflecting the reduced size of the congregation, the Sunday school staff was greatly diminished, and despite the dedication of teachers like Charles Sords, who had proved especially effective in working with the children at Garfield Terrace, many parish children were going without proper religious training. Urged on by Monsignor Hurley, the parish council decided to reorganize the Sunday school. By the time classes met in September Sister Mary Bernard Hughes, a retired Notre Dame de Namur sister, was on the job, working with Father Kemp on devising a modern CCD curriculum and coordinating the training of new volunteer teachers, including fifteen young adults.[56]

55. Author's intv. with Father Mudd.

56. PCM, 16 Apr and 17 Sep 1972. The minutes for 16 April confuse Mary Hughes with Mary Houston.

Although still an assistant pastor, Kemp was already demonstrating the useful knack of recruiting dynamic personalities for what would become his parish team. For some time he had had his eye on Luis Grillo, a Carroll High graduate and Mount St. Mary's basketball star, who, in addition to his work for the Washington Urban coalition setting up recreation programs for inner-city youth, was serving as a volunteer coach for the parish's midget CYO team. Kemp arranged for Grillo to become coordinator of all sacramental programs in the parish school and Sunday school. Working with Sister Barnard and Charles Carter, the school principal at that time, Grillo launched a second CCD program for teenagers and young adults that quickly expanded to provide supplementary instruction for adult converts. The Sunday school also sponsored a bible school for neighborhood children. Most important, Grillo's personality drew many adults into a broad program that soon was engaging scores of parents in the religious education of their children.

Other changes came rapidly. Pastors and parish councils change Sunday mass schedules at their peril, and thus in October 1974 the new co-pastors went to great pains to justify dropping the 9:30 and 11:00 o'clock masses in favor of two masses at 10:00, one a mass for children and their parents in the Parish Center chapel. The more intimate chapel setting, they explained to the congregation, would allow the celebrant to interact more closely with the families and emphasize the instructional elements of the mass more effectively. Another important reason for the new schedule: it would provide a solid block of time before mass for CCD classes and a period after mass for parish organization meetings, sacramental preparation classes, and adult religious education for catechumens.[57]

Grillo, with the help of John Butler, then on the staff of Mackin High, also inaugurated a retreat program for the teenagers which incorporated a more sophisticated approach to religious experience. Grillo called it IMPAC (Improving My Personal Act with Christ). Here in a series of co-ed retreats away from the usual pressures and distractions, the young adults sought through a series of group rap sessions, self-searching exercises, and prayer, a new awareness of their feelings

57. Parish Bulletin, 21 Sep 1974. See also, PCM, 25 Sep 1974.

and beliefs. Butler and Ray Kemmerer at Mackin and Grillo and Sister Barbara on the parish team reworked the diocese's ECHO (Encountering Christ in Others) retreat program to infuse it with more African-American themes. Eventually IMPAC would be expanded to include semi-annual weekend retreats for catechumens, parishioners, and others. More than a thousand individuals have attended these retreats over the years, which remain today at the core of St. Augustine's spirituality process. Although continuing his involvement as a volunteer, Grillo retired as director in 1977 to direct various job programs in Washington and later to sign on as an NBA referee. In his place the parish hired Steve Hocker as part-time director and later Betty Washington, who has remained involved into recent times. With the help of one of the priests and a staff of lay teachers, all of whom had gone through the Vicariate training program, the Sunday school enrolled sixty-five elementary-school-aged children.[58] In 1979 Father Kemp predicted that the school would eventually enroll 150 students, a goal that was almost reached four years later when fifteen teachers and aides were instructing 135 pupils (a high point for the modern Sunday school).[59]

A logical outgrowth of the family mass and youth retreats was a separate family retreat program instituted in the parish later in the decade. It was suggested by three parishioners, Claudia Thorne, Cheryl Reynolds, and Maxine Le Gall, who had accepted an invitation from a suburban parish to attend one of its family retreats. Impressed by the enthusiasm and obvious spirituality they witnessed, the women became convinced that St. Augustine's families would also be strengthened by such an experience, and with Father Kelley's help they launched a similar program in the parish. In time large groups of

58. Father Mudd complained of what he saw as cultural and racial bias in the diocese's catechist formation program even as he promised to work with the diocese's Office of Religious Education to form catechists in the African-American community. See ltr., Mudd to Hickey, 4 Aug 1987, cy in SAA.

59. These developments in the Sunday school program were discussed in the parish council (see, for example, minutes, 24 Jul 1977) and in the two parish profiles, 1979 and 1981–82. By 1987 the Sunday school's student population had dropped to 87 pupils, not counting the number of teenagers who participated in the IMPAC program. See PCM, 17 Oct 1987.

families would retire to places like West Virginia's Coolfont Center for intensive 24-hour retreats that mixed sessions of spiritual contemplation and religious instruction with scheduled diversions ranging from T'ai Che exercises to all-night movie marathons for the youngsters.[60]

The parish's renewed dedication to its neighbors was clearly evident in its evolving ministry to young adults. That ministry had a long way to go. The council's initial effort in the early 1970s to include representatives of the congregation's youthful members had failed. As James McAdams, one of those early members, explained, after a few meetings at which they were ignored by their elders or their opinions dismissed as unqualified, they had drifted away. Father Kemp blamed the situation on a lack of communication caused by the fact that the greatly reduced congregation had so few middle-aged members who elsewhere bridged the gap between the young and the mostly elderly parish leaders. In 1972 the council invited a group of young men, including, in addition to McAdams, "Steve" Haines, John Hill, Donald Norris, and Braxton Wiggins, to discuss their complaints and suggest changes. These young men had gained attention for their effort to revitalize and expand the parish CYO from the tentative program they remembered from their own childhood days. Their comments emphasized the need for more church-sponsored activities, including an expanded sports program and social functions that would involve the high school students, who until then tended to drift off on their separate ways after graduating from the parish school.[61]

Although the council promised to promote a youth program and added several young adults to its membership, little came of its efforts. Asked in 1979 to identify the cause of alienation among the parish's teenagers, Father Kemp pointed to the strong sense shared by many young people that they could not belong to a congregation that showed no interest in them. In turn the new consciousness among young people of that time was especially suspect and misunderstood by their seniors. In fact the summer programs that Bouchard and Kemp had operated with public money in the late 1960s and early 1970s had all dried up and so had the teen programs. In a parish where so much at-

60. Author's intv. with Maxine Le Gall, 31 Oct 1997.
61. PCM, 16 Apr 1972,

tention was heaped on the Young at Hearts, Sodality socials, and adult support groups, youth activities were now pretty much limited to participation in the CYO basketball league, the Beltway football league, and the IMPAC retreats.

Such neglect was unacceptable to the young Turks who took over the council in the early 1980s. In organizing the 1981 council retreat, President Michael Harris posed a question: Are we adequately reaching our youth and, more specifically, do we encourage them to aspire to community service?[62] The answer was no, and in the ensuing months the council, despite its preoccupation with financial matters, launched several new youth programs. It organized an athletic association to enhance the parish sports activities, adding a tennis team to an enlarged schedule of football games and basketball tournaments for boys and girls. Describing a teen club as a serious attempt to develop a youth ministry that would involved young people in parish life, the council also sponsored an organization that offered programs of cultural and educational enrichment as well as "supervised, constructive recreational programs to the parish's high school students."[63] It can be assumed that the club also gave the kids time to have some fun, but all involved accented the serious purpose of a youth ministry. In 1984, for example, club members like Tom Venable, Rodney Day, and Richard Babb participated in a 24-hour fast during which they heard Peace Corps volunteers and others discuss the plight of the world's hungry and saw for themselves the impact of hunger in their own neighborhood by touring the Fourteenth Street drug district, where families of addicts subsisted on junk food and handouts. Their fast raised nearly $1,000 for SOME when sympathetic parishioners pledged money for all the hours the teenagers fasted.[64]

The parish opened a summer employment office in 1981 in which members of the parish team solicited local business owners for jobs for neighborhood teenagers. It proved a challenging task in an area with chronic low employment, but the parish persisted. In later years Linda Wallace directed the program, by then renamed the Job Seekers. In

62. Memo, Harris to Executive Committee, n.d. (ca. Dec 1981), sub: Retreat/Workshop, cy in SAA.
63. Quoted in SS. Paul & Augustine Parish Profile, 1981–82.
64. The Teen Club's fast was reported in the CS, 19 Apr 1984.

1985 the council organized a catechumen program for young people interested in learning about the Catholic Church as well as young parishioners who required instruction for confirmation. Alton Rhoe served as the first director of an effort that continued for years and attracted a gratifying number of youthful converts. For its part the parish council tried to work more young parishioners into the liturgy. The worship committee organized a training program for altar boys and girls. It also encouraged young adults to serve as ushers and even trained teenagers as lectors for Sunday masses.[65]

All the while these programs principally affecting young parishioners were receiving renewed attention, the council's social justice committee and the outreach director continued to enlarge the congregation's involvement in community youth affairs. On several occasions they sponsored forums where famed Chicago pastor and crusader on behalf of homeless children Father George Clements expounded to large audiences on the need for more African-American adoptions. He himself had adopted a son. Elaborating on a theme familiar in the parish, Clements spoke of his role "to make the Catholic Church make some sense to Black people."[66] He discussed with parishioners and community leaders alike the need to reconnect with their African heritage, especially as it related to family life and child rearing. On several occasions representatives of the National Black Child Development Institute were on hand to provide information on local adoption laws and how to go about finding a needy child.

The parish's concern also extended to those children already at risk and enmeshed in the criminal justice system. Cardinal Baum was especially interested in this problem, and in the late 1970s he had organized the archdiocese's Criminal Justice Task Force, which worked to improve the local prison system and to treat the special needs both of the incarcerated and those who worked with them. Several members of the parish served on this useful body. When Baum instituted Dismas Sunday, an annual day of prayer and reconciliation for those involved in the criminal justice system, the parish joined in. In January 1983, for example, the prominent activist Rev. Benjamin Chavis spoke

65. Worship cmte. rpt., 13 Mar 1989, SAA.

66. As quoted in the *CS*, 10 Sep 1981. Clements's visits received considerable press coverage, including the in-depth survey of his crusade in this *Standard* article.

at the Dismas Sunday mass on the urgent need to reform the District system and proposed an ecumenical coalition to deal with the escalating problems facing African-American youth.[67]

The parish council welcomed such proposals even as it continued its own specialized efforts on behalf of young offenders. Although discussion of a third-party custody program for young men who had run afoul of the law had yet to bear fruit, the parish contributed significantly to the efforts of the archdiocese's Office of Social Development to improve the District's criminal justice system, and in a sort of test case it successfully placed three youths in the Montgomery County Alternative Community Services Program for First Offenders. St. Augustine's Community Outreach volunteers also inaugurated a unit of After School Kids (ASK) in the parish. ASK offered counseling and tutoring service for neighborhood youth convicted of drug-related offenses. In conjunction with D.C. Superior Court and Georgetown University, ASK enrolled offenders who opted to join this program on probation in lieu of detention at Oak Hill or Cedar Knoll. Keith Crawford, Dominic Moulden, and a group of volunteers worked with the young people during a nine-month course that stressed values, education, and respect for African-American traditions. Although not specifically religious in nature, the program embraced spirituality. Crawford and the others helped the youngsters meditate on racism and the disadvantage it had placed on black youth. They taught that survival consisted of recognizing obstacles, bonding, and above all, taking responsibility for one's life. The school basement was a lively place on Tuesday and Wednesday nights as young offenders and their volunteer counselors met to discuss alternatives to the drug culture and to seek a healthier structure for these teenage lives. By 1990 over 170 boys had graduated from the program, which, supported by District funds supplemented by donations from the parish, claimed a 60 percent success rate.[68]

Unlike the other participants in the ASK program, St. Augustine's

67. Henderson, Social Justice cmte. rpt., 1984. Celebration of Dismas Sunday was suspended in the parish for several years in the mid-1980s because it conflicted with programs associated with Black History Month. It was resumed in 1989. See PCM, 2 May 1988. See also SS. Paul & Augustine Parish Profile, 1981–82.

68. Author's intrv. with Dominic Moulden, 30 Oct 1997. See also, *Washington Post*, 9 Feb 1990.

enrolled youth living in city-controlled shelters away from their unstable families and used volunteers from Howard University, along with parishioners, to teach them. For administrative reasons, Georgetown University, the ASK sponsor, could not supervise such an arrangement, and Crawford, himself a Howard professor and biomedical specialist at the National Institutes of Health, formed an independent program in the parish. Dubbed Kujichaculia (a Swahili word meaning self-determination), the St. Augustine program employed the workshop technique to teach African history and culture and entrepreneurship and the need for self-improvement. Volunteers emphasized setting personal goals and networking with those in the community who could provide effective support. Actually, the youth from the city's shelters were, on average, older and more disciplined and therefore added an element of stability to St. Augustine's program lacking in the ASK program generally.

Meanwhile Moulden and some of the volunteers in the Community Outreach Program were especially anxious to reach neighborhood children who were not yet in trouble with the law, but whose attitudes were being shaped by the twin pressures of poverty and racism. Learning of the findings of famed social psychologist Kenneth B. Clark and other African-American scholars through the writings of journalist Courtland Milloy, Moulden came to understand how a destructive psychology, the heritage of slavery and racism, had seriously disadvantaged some black children and how it was imperative that it be replaced with a positive psychology that stressed self-awareness, self-esteem, and self-confidence. A positive attitude, the psychologists concluded, was the key to empowerment for these young people and the surest way to arm them against the dangers of their environment. Already their ideas were being put into action. Groups like Washington's Concerned Black Men organization were going into local schools and churches to talk with kids about their roots and to serve as role models.[69] Moulden had a more specific aim. He wanted to expose local black children to the culture, aesthetic values, and accomplishments of African Americans through study and observation, so that they were made aware of and could take pride in their cultural heritage. In Octo-

69. See Courtland Milloy's article in the *Washington Post*, 4 May 1986.

ber 1987 the parish council authorized him to explore the possibility of sponsoring an organization dedicated to this purpose.[70] With the help of Dena Grant, Maxine Le Gall, and others he responded by founding Aesop Nia (combining the name of the famous Greek slave with the Swahili word for purpose). Aesop Nia targeted children in the immediate neighborhood (i.e. those living in the Portner Place housing, Baroni apartments, and on nearby W Street). Volunteers like Gillian Pratt helped recruit students at Howard University and others with special skills to organize a program of classes, cultural activities, and adult-supervised entertainment. In succeeding years hundreds of children met in the school one evening a week for basic instruction in role playing, public speaking, story telling, and other esteem-building exercises. On Saturday mornings the kids and their tutors would take field trips to museums and attend cultural events.

By the end of the decade the list of ministries supported by parishioners numbered some forty-two separate organizations, ranging from the credit union founded by Msgr. Gingras to a speech club, from the venerable Sodality and a Boy Scout troop to a new program to welcome returning Catholics to the sacraments. The incredible variety and complexity of these many activities—a parish directory of the time bears more than a passing resemblance to the Yellow Pages of a small town—led the parish council to restructure itself. Now, under the pastor/president and council chairperson and facilitated by a salaried parish team, five committees and the youth and family ministries assumed responsibility for the direction and budgeting of all its volunteer operations.[71]

Ironically, when the complexity and sophistication of twentieth-century urban society is stripped away, little had actually changed at St. Augustine's since its founders so many years before assumed responsibility for welcoming the newly freed men and women, sheltering black orphans, and supporting the city's indigent. The hallmark of the continuum that united the tiny band of African-American Catholics in

70. PCM, 17 Oct 1987. These paragraphs on Aesop Nia are based on author's intvs. with Dominic Moulden and Maxine Le Gall, 31 Oct 1987.

71. See undated (ca. 1988) parish organization chart and directory, SAA. Some of the groups included in this list will be discussed in Chapter 12, below.

Civil War Washington with today's sophisticated congregation with its
$600,000 annual budget and myriad social and cultural interests is
the willingness shown in every era to accept responsibility for the
needs of neighbors and a determination to serve as an instrument of
social justice. All those ministries of the 1980s represented a stagger-
ing amount of volunteer giving and personal sacrifice, and the dedication of lay and cleric leaders aside, it was the congregation's understanding of this continuum, the pride it felt in its heritage of social activism, that animated all its good works.

TWELVE ❦ A PARISH FOR THE
POST-INTEGRATION ERA

*T*he crusade for racial justice, a cause as old as the Republic, has evolved through several distinct phases. One of its most profound changes began in the mid-1960s as the fight for civil rights organized by W. E. B. DuBois and his allies at the beginning of the century gave way to a new, broader battle for equal treatment and opportunity, fueled by a spirit of self-determination and racial exclusiveness based on a new self-confidence and renewed racial pride among young African Americans. The new crusade manifested itself in every area of life, even reaching into the councils of the Church when African-American priests and lay persons began to defend their interests and express their aspirations openly. Echoes of this new militancy could be heard in any parish with a racially mixed congregation, but nowhere more loudly than at St. Augustine's, whose roots, its articulate leaders were quick to point out, were so closely identified with the struggle for equality in church and state.

The Quest for Racial Justice, 1965–1980

By the mid-1960s the crusade for racial justice had abandoned the tactics if not the goals of past decades. By then the moderate civil rights organizations and their allies in the liberal white community had, under the influence of such groups as the NAACP and leaders like Martin Luther King, Jr., broken down the legal and administrative barriers to full citizenship based on race. With the passage of the great civil rights legislation in 1964 and 1965, these moderates won over the last branch of the national government to their cause, ending the 100-year struggle to guarantee, as President Johnson said in his celebrated address to Howard University's 1965 graduates, "the black man's right to vote, to hold a job, to enter a public place, to go to school . . . to be treated in every part of our national life as a person equal in dignity and promise to all others."[1]

The president's message that June day, and his subsequent pledge to make fulfillment of these guarantees the chief goal of his administration, marked the apex of what historian C. Vann Woodward called the Second Reconstruction. Although Johnson warned on the occasion of his signing the Voting Rights Act on August 6 that many difficulties were still to be overcome before rights now "woven into law are also woven into the fabric of the nation," neither he nor anyone else seemed prepared for the wave of violence that crashed upon urban America, beginning just five days later in the Watts section of Los Angeles. Watts would come to typify to a greater or lesser degree the serious race riots and hundreds of minor disturbances that occurred during the next four years and ended the era of nonviolent protest.

A primary cause of the abrupt change was the shift in focus of America's race problems to the north and west. Fully half the black population lived in northern and western cities by the mid-sixties, many in ghettos where patterns of a *de facto* segregated social and economic order rivaled the *de jure* segregation suffered by their brothers and sisters in the Old South. The great civil rights legislation of the period was aimed primarily at *de jure* segregation, and the enthusiasm of northern African Americans quickly waned as they came to realize that the victories won by freedom marches and court battles would have little practical effect on life in the ghetto. With their expectations raised and patience gone, some blacks outside the South, especially the have-nots, began to heed the importuning of a radical element, which claimed that civil disorder alone would win concessions. The dozens of riots and racial disturbances in various parts of the country

1. "To Fulfill These Rights," Commencement Address at Howard University, 4 Jun 1965, *Public Papers of the Presidents, 1965*, vol. II (Washington: GPO, 1966), pp. 635–40.

in the next years clearly mirrored the built-up frustration and desperation of the ghetto as young people expressed their fury over unsatisfied
demands concerning employment, housing, and police brutality.

Martin Luther King tried to regain the loyalty of this large group
for the moderate civil rights organizations and his nonviolent philosophy. In the summer of 1966 he took his crusade north, but his month-
long series of marches and demonstrations in Chicago came to naught.
Although King would retain his personal popularity among all classes
of African Americans until his death, his leadership of the civil rights
movement generally went into eclipse after Chicago. New leaders now
took the stage, ready to propose radical solutions to the problems of
urban America. Their philosophy was best expressed in the black
power movement. Although several have been credited with originat-
ing the provocative phrase, it was Stokely Carmichael, the young militant leader of SNCC and a neighbor well known to those in the Parish
Center on V Street, who popularized it when he reminded his audience: "From now on when they ask you what you want, you know what
to tell them. Black Power!"[2] The phrase swept the community, its
vague connotations of seizing control proving irresistible to thousands
of young people, particularly among the extremely disadvantaged.
Events would prove that Carmichael and other radicals had chosen
their audience shrewdly, for just as the civil right movement of the previous generation was centered in the middle class, the new black power crusade quickly gained prominence by offering a simplistic but easily grasped connection between political and economic powerlessness
and conditions in the ghetto.

Carmichael and his followers in SNCC and the Congress of Racial
Equality (CORE) reasoned that the black community should seize
upon the resurgent pride and ambition of its young to project itself as
an equal in a pluralistic society. Too long, they pointed out, had
African Americans watched only a few—those middle-class brothers
and sisters acceptable and useful to white society—escape into the
mainstream; too long had the vast majority been debilitated by poor
self-image and the inability to overcome the role assigned by a complacent white majority. Their answer was a form of ethnic identification, a

2. As quoted in August Meier and Elliott Rudwick, *Black Protest in the Sixties*
(Chicago: Quadrangle Books, 1970), p. 19.

heightened sense of race consciousness and community loyalty, of black pride and black brotherhood. They saw this racial unity as a necessary prelude to the essential task of gaining control over the black community, over those political, social, and economic aspects of society that had the greatest impact on black lives, i.e., housing, education, social services, churches, and local businesses. Finally, armed with self-pride and political and the economic power that came with community control, black could then enter into an equal partnership with white America.

Probably the mildest form of the separatism that rose in the 1970, certainly the most frequently discussed and immediately noticeable to the public at large, was the manifestation of cultural nationalism that sprang up among the urban young. Dismissed as fads by some of their elders, the new symbols of black pride and cohesion were derived in part from a heightened interest in emerging nationhood in black Africa. Blacks began to demand the formation of black studies programs and African language courses in schools.[3] Americans whose ancestors had been brought from Africa centuries before began to adopt African names and experiment in African cultural forms. A significant market sprang up for African-inspired clothing and jewelry, and even more widespread, black Americans adopted the Afro and other natural hairstyles. A campaign to extol the concept of "black is beautiful" found a receptive audience through the press and the world of entertainment. Another innovation introduced by young African-Americans loosely related to the new cultural nationalism was the elaborately choreographed handshake, known as the "dap," and other methods of greeting, including the notorious raised fist of the black power salute that attracted world attention when used by some American athletes at the 1968 Olympic games.

The success of the black power leaders presaged the more radical efforts of an extremist fringe, which demanded a separate black state within the Union. Prominent among the separatists were the Black Muslims led by Elijah Muhammad. Although no strangers to violence, most Muslims scorned the aims of Carmichael and his allies. Not so

3. On the connection between the black student movement and cultural nationalism, see *Campus Unrest: The Report of the President's Commission on Campus Unrest*, 26 Sep 70 (The Scranton Report), Chap. III.

their most famous son, Malcolm X, who split with Elijah Muhammad to become the spiritual leader of the black power movement, the one to whom in later years all types of radicals paid homage. Ironically, at the time of his assassination in 1965, Malcolm X had begun to turn away from black nationalism and redefine his revolutionary goals. It was only later that the moderates came to realize the potential for racial harmony that had been lost at Malcolm X's death.

The most publicized black nationalist group was the Black Panthers. Led by Huey P. Newton, Eldridge Cleaver, and Bobby Seale, the Panthers openly called for armed confrontation and were subsequently convicted of numerous acts of violence. Alienated by their extremism from their black power base, hounded as no other group by the authorities, their leaders in jail or exile, the organization quietly faded away. In fact, the black power organizations in general, riddled by internal division and pressed for funds and members, followed the Panthers into oblivion in the 1970s.

Yet if many of the black nationalist organizations and their symbols proved ephemeral, they also marked a change in the nature and character of the crusade for racial justice. They instilled in a multitude of young African Americans a new sense of self-respect and self-reliance. To some extent they redefined the concept of blackness for a new generation, stressing its positive aspects and using it to unite the African-American community under a mantle of brotherhood. As historian Benjamin Muse put it, "They helped increasingly to stimulate interest in Negro history and culture, and a healthy pride in *negritude*."[4] Lacking leaders and an organizational base, the black power movement was left in the end with little more than a provocative phrase, but that phrase became a potent rallying cry for a whole new generation of crusaders who would boldly fight for redress of economic and social grievances.

True, integration, as well as opposition to violent solutions to race problems, continued to receive overwhelming support.[5] Yet succeeding decades would also witness an accommodation by moderate civil

4. Benjamin Muse, *The American Negro Revolution: From Nonviolence to Black Power, 1963–1967* (Bloomington: University of Indiana Press, 1968), p. 245.

5. For a contemporary discussion of this support, see Louis Harris polls in "Black America 1970," *Time* (6 Apr 1970), pp. 28–29.

rights forces to the philosophy of self-determination implicit in the black power movement. Increasingly, the moderates came to question some of their previous assumptions. Given the fact that African Americans were only a tenth of the population, for example, how would their values and culture be preserved under integration? Given problems in the quality of public education and social services, areas of special concern to urban blacks, was integration necessarily the best solution? In fact, given the persistence of white flight in the face of any black advances, was integration an answer to anything at all? Finally, with the rise of new ethnic minorities, each advancing its particular claims on government, did not consolidation of political power in the black community make sense?

In addressing such questions in terms of black community and black interests, moderates unconsciously revealed the persistence of the separatist idea that stretched back in American history at least to Marcus Garvey. Such aspirations would gain new allure when Louis Farrakhan and his Nation of Islam began to attract legions of followers. Actually, as the 1970s wore on, tensions in the African-American community clearly began to ease, and the political differences between moderate and black nationalist strategies for achieving racial progress began to narrow as both pressed for programs that stressed self-determination and affirmative action. It remained to be seen how such a synthesis would play out in the Catholic Church.

The American church was itself undergoing profound change in the wake of Vatican II, as Catholics renewed what historian Martin Marty called their sense of peoplehood. To a great extent they repudiated both assimilation—the idea fostered for so long by leaders like Cardinal Gibbons that Catholics were a group of Americans like any other—and consensus—the idea fostered by Cardinal Spellman and others in later times that Catholics speak with one voice. Now ethnic and cultural diversity was again valued and national subgroups that had always been part of American Catholicism reemerged.[6]

Prominent among these subgroups of Catholics were the African Americans. Their numbers had grown considerably since World War II, nearly tripling by 1968 to almost 800,000, making them the fourth

6. Marty, *Pilgrims in Their Own Land*, p. 464, and Hennesey, *American Catholics*, p. 324.

largest religious organization among African Americans (after the two Baptist conventions and the African Methodist Episcopal Church). Although pitifully small in number because of past discrimination and lack of educational opportunity, black priests had also registered impressive gains, from six priests in 1935 to 171 in 1968, including the first African Americans in the hierarchy.[7] Many of these Catholics were converts who, according to black sociologist E. Franklin Frazier, were attracted to the Church by its doctrine of universal acceptance, its advocacy of racial justice, and its concern for the educational and social needs of the black community.

Ironically, the growing appreciation of the Church in the larger black community paralleled a renewed criticism of Church practices among black Catholics. This time black clergymen formulated the charges. This "historic milestone," as Father Cyprian Davis described it, was reached a week after Martin Luther King's assassination as priests gathered in Chicago for the Catholic Clergy Conference on the Interracial Apostolate. Shocked by the brutal reaction of local authorities to the rioters, the secretary of the conference, Father Herman Porter, invited all the nation's black priests to attend a special caucus preceding the conference sessions. More than sixty responded. Their meeting, the first such gathering of Catholic clergy in American history, was a prolonged and frequently heated affair, as each member examined his twin identities as priest and African American. The immediate result was the preparation of a letter to the hierarchy in which they baldly stated their belief that "The Catholic Church in the United States, primarily a white racist institution, has addressed itself primarily to white society and is definitely a part of that society."[8]

The caucus warned that the Church's recent gains among African Americans were endangered by the indifference of the hierarchy to the black community's new self-awareness. They called on the bishops to listen to the militancy that had emerged in response to the black

7. Statistics as presented by Lamanna, "The Catholic Church and the Negro," pp. 169–74.

8. As quoted by Davis, *Black Catholics in the United States*, p. 259. Davis, who was present at the caucus, summarized its deliberations on which these paragraphs are based. See also Conley, "'All One in Christ': Patrick Cardinal O'Boyle, the Church in Washington and the Struggle for Racial Justice," pp. 165–66.

power movement and insisted that the Church recognize the moral justification for such militancy. They wanted African Americans to exercise control of Catholic institutions in their community, and to that end listed some specific demands. Included among these they wanted more leadership positions opened to black priests, and, a century after Archbishop Spalding had made a similar appeal at the Second Plenary Council, they called for a separate episcopal vicar to represent African Americans in the hierarchy. Specifically reflecting the popular desire for self-determination, they demanded that a department for African-American affairs be created in the U.S. Catholic Conference (the national body of bishops). They also called for a greater effort by the bishops to recruit black priests and permanent deacons and to let black priests and sympathetic white priests concentrate their ministry in the black community.

Considering the caucus' heated rhetoric and unprecedented demands, the response of the hierarchy was surprisingly cordial and positive. Bishop John Wright, chairman of the bishops' committee on social development and peace, met with caucus leaders to develop a comprehensive plan that addressed their concerns. As a result the bishops in November 1969 established the National Office of Black Catholics within the U.S. Conference and allocated $500,000 to fund its work. The money was rejected by spokesmen for the black clergy, and when the new office opened in July 1970 under its first director, Marianist Brother Joseph Davis, it was largely funded by donations collected from black parishes. Over the years St. Augustine's contributed to its support through special collections.[9]

Manifestations of this new spirit of self-determination among black Catholics quickly followed in Washington when two groups, the Black Catholic Clergy and Religious of Washington and the Black Lay Caucus, were established with the proclaimed purpose of informing the hierarchy about the needs and aspirations of the black community and helping the local church plan its programs for black Catholics.[10] At the time of their appearance Cardinal O'Boyle, a leader of the postwar fight for integration in the Church, was under increasing attack from

9. See, for example, PCM, 25 Sep and 6 Oct 1974.

10. The following paragraphs are based primarily on Father Conley's survey in 'All One in Christ'," pp. 167–83.

extremists. The SNCC-inspired Black United Front was demanding millions of dollars in reparations from the Church for what the Front called its racism. Meanwhile militant whites, allied with those dissident priests fighting over the papal encyclical on contraception, attacked the archdiocese on a wide front, including the treatment of African Americans. A self-styled Center for Christian Renewal, some of the dissenting priests, and the Washington Lay Association combined to issue demands through the press, sponsored guerrilla theater with actors portraying priests dressed in KKK outfits, and conducted teach-ins that interrupted services at St. Matthew's and elsewhere. Some of their demands had merit, but their inflammatory rhetoric and obvious ulterior motives left them with few allies. Unfortunately, the radicalism of all these groups caused some of the moderate white Catholics who had so strongly supported the Interracial Council in the past to abandon the fight for racial justice and turn instead to anti-Vietnam war protest and other causes.

While O'Boyle could dismiss the radical publicity seekers, he recognized in the newly formed Black Lay Caucus a legitimate voice for the concerns of African-American Catholics and agreed to preside over the mass that opened their convention in August 1970. The Washington group respected O'Boyle for his work in integrating the diocese, but it echoed many of the complaints and demands made by the Black Clergy Caucus in previous years. For his part the cardinal clearly acknowledged that the Church must grant some degree of self-determination to its African-American minority, but, given his strong respect for authority and sense of loyalty, any such independence accepted by him would be carefully circumscribed within standing ecclesiastical structures.

In time, as the group's demands escalated, including its insistence on the right to name pastors for black churches, O'Boyle dropped all connection with the Lay Caucus, branding its members "radicals," a particularly strong condemnation in his lexicon. Yet the caucus's demand for self-determination did not go unheeded. A committee appointed by Cardinal O'Boyle to evaluate diocesan programs recommended in July 1972 the formation of a secretariat for black Catholics, an agency to be staffed by African Americans to investigate racial discrimination in the diocese and elsewhere, develop leadership among the diocese's black Catholics, and promote vocations in the black community. This new approach in the diocese's effort to include black Catholics in the decision-making councils of the Church was well received, and many African Americans waited anxiously to learn what Archbishop Baum, who succeeded O'Boyle in May 1973, would do about the secretariat, which some black leaders predicted would be "the real test of sincerity" for the new Ordinary.[11]

By then black Catholics of all stripes had come to accept the need for an authentic African-American voice in the higher councils of the American Church. Even St. Augustine's William N. and Mary C. Butler, founding members of the Catholic Interracial Council and stalwarts of the crusade for integration, admitted that organizations like theirs had always ended up dominated by its white members. They welcomed the idea of a black secretariat and its promise of self-determination as a fulfillment of Thomas Turner's efforts in the Federation of Colored Catholics so long ago.[12] They did not have long to wait. Within months of his installation Baum approved the concept, and even before the new office became official, St. Augustine's parish council was asked to appoint a representative. Charles Carter, the school principal, accepted the assignment and was closely involved in the organization of the secretariat and the election of its board of directors (later the Council of Black Catholics), which included eighteen lay members. Black parishes in the various sections of the diocese nominated two additional members each.[13]

The secretariat assumed greater responsibility as it evolved in succeeding years. When the new archbishop, James A. Hickey, reorganized his chancery in 1981, the executive director of the secretariat became a member of the archbishop's staff. Jacqueline Wilson later outlined the purpose of her office, which went some way toward addressing the issues raised at the Black Clergy Caucus in 1968. Washington's Office of Black Catholics participated in diocesan planning and decisions; its director served on the various executive committees in the chancery. It also kept the Archbishop and his staff informed

11. "Who is William Wakefield Baum and When is He Going to Do It?" *Washington Magazine*, n.d. (ca. Apr 1974): 126.

12. Nickels' intv. with William and Mary Buckner.

13. PCM, 17 Feb 1973 and 16 Feb and 23 Jun 1974.

about the needs and concerns of African Americans and insured black input in all decisions of interest. The director maintained the diocese's contact with African-American organizations throughout the country.[14]

The passions and controversies that had characterized race relations in church and state since the turbulent 1960s had cooled considerably by 1983. In the Catholic Church the spirit of confrontation between black priests and laity and Church leaders had been replaced by one of cooperation. Yet when the African-American bishops (now ten in number) issued a pastoral letter on evangelization in 1984, they too were concerned about empowerment. In "What We Have Seen and Heard," they insisted that the unique heritage of African-American Catholics must be carefully preserved as a distinct experience and shared not only with people of color but with all their fellow Catholics. The Church was universal, but universality, they pointed out, did not mean uniformity, and the gifts of all those who belong should become the common heritage of the whole Church. Of those special gifts that derived from the peculiar experience of their race in American history, they singled out a black spirituality that was uniquely contemplative, joyful, and community-focused; the notion of liberation and reconciliation that was at the heart of black religious experience since slave times; and a specially strong sense of family. Finding ways to explain the unique contribution of the black religious experience to the American church was a major theme explored by the 1,200 delegates at the 1987 National Black Catholic Congress. This gathering was the first of its kind since Daniel Rudd had organized his Colored Catholic Congresses a century before, beginning in 1889 at St. Augustine's.[15] The major work of the Congress, to develop a national program for evangelization in black communities, led directly to the plan adopted by the American bishops in 1989.[16]

14. Office of Black Catholics, News Release, Sep 1989, cy in SAA.

15. Another indication of the growth of black Catholics: the 1987 delegates to the 1987 congress represented some 1.2 million Catholics in more than 160 dioceses. In addition to a number of observers, St. Augustine's was represented by four official delegates: Tillie Gibson, Catherine Mason, Rachel J. Newman, and Matilde Springer. The congress was given extensive coverage in the *Washington Post*, 23 May 1987.

16. The congress also led to the Washington archdiocese's pastoral plan for evangelization, "Many Gifts, But the Same Spirit," drawn up by delegates to the national meeting.

The determination of African-American Catholics to preserve their heritage was eloquently summarized by Biloxi's Bishop Joseph L. Howze when he addressed Pope John Paul II during the pontiff's visit to New Orleans in 1987. The expression "being black and Catholic," he explained, did not denote a sense of separation, but rather was meant to identify those gifts and talents that integrated the faith and culture of African Americans into the common heritage of the Church. These gifts contributed to the building of the whole Church, he claimed, and their sharing was a confirmation of the expression "authentically Black and truly Catholic." It was the responsibility of the Church to admit African Americans to its leadership; it was the responsibility of black Catholics to remain faithful to both their Roman Catholic heritage and their African-American heritage.[17]

The quest for empowerment outlined by the black bishops required patience on the part of African Americans and a commitment by the hierarchy to act decisively. On the other hand, those whose memory of racism in the Church ran deep were convinced that empowerment was possible only through autonomy. They wanted their unique Catholic heritage preserved in a separate African-American rite controlled by a separate African-American ecclesiastical authority. They found their spokesman and leader in a young, charismatic priest of the Washington archdiocese, George A. Stallings.

As pastor of St. Teresa's, Stallings had turned a faltering Anacostia parish into one of the diocese's largest and most vibrant congregations. Leaving there in 1988 to work exclusively in evangelization, Stallings had taken up residence at St. Augustine's, where his monthly masses and periodic revivals electrified the congregation. The repeated call for complete autonomy and self-determination that ran through all his evangelism in 1989, however, prompted Cardinal Hickey to act.[18] Citing the overarching requirement of unity of faith even while recognizing the importance of cultural differences, Hickey suspended Stallings's privilege of saying public masses. Stallings reacted by announcing that a public mass in a new African-American rite would be celebrated in the chapel of Howard University's law school on July 2.

17. "Presentation of Bishop Joseph Lawson Howze to His Holiness Pope John Paul II on his pastoral visit to the Archdiocese of New Orleans," 12 Sep 1987, cy in SAA.

18. Hickey was elevated to the College of Cardinals in 1988.

That service, attended by more than 1,000 people including Catholics, Protestants, and Muslims, retained little of the ritual familiar to Catholics, as Stallings proclaimed the African-American's right to religious, liturgical, and theological self-determination. One guest, a representative of Minister Farrakhan's Nation of Islam, predicted that the movement begun by Stallings "will sweep the world."[19]

The celebration at Howard marked the birth of the Imani Temple (variously translated from the Swahili as "faith" or "peace"). In succeeding weeks ever greater crowds attended; within the month some 2,300 were numbered in a congregation, which included a large contingent from St. Teresa's as well as significant groups from St. Augustine's and other parishes around the city. As might be expected, the Imani Temple and Stallings's confrontational approach—he rejected a plea from the nation's black bishops for reconciliation by branding their request "predictable"—attracted much media coverage. Father Russell L. Dillard, the young African-American pastor of Washington's St. Martin's parish, found himself matched against Stallings in a forum on the Oprah Winfrey Show, while the reactions of all of Washington's black priests were anxiously solicited and aired in the press.[20] For his part Stallings announced that a second priest, Salvatorian Father Bruce Greening, had joined his independent congregation.

Nor could the popularity of Stallings's message be judged by the attendance figures at his temple. As one black lay leader put it, "There are a lot of people who can identify with what George is feeling. But most of them will not identify with the action he's taken."[21] Many would also agree with the conclusions of the National Black Catholic Clergy Caucus which admitted that, in spite of recent reforms, the American church "remained primarily a white racist institution." Speaking for the nation's thirteen black bishops in November 1989, Bishop John Ricard of Baltimore pointed out that their evangelization program, endorsed by all the bishops, was meant to change the per-

19. As quoted in *National Catholic Register*, 16 Jul 1989. The Imani Temple attracted wide press coverage, much of it contained in a special Stallings collection in SAA.

20. See, for example, *Washington Post*, 8 Aug 1989.

21. Herbert Johnson, president of the National Association of Black Catholic Administrators, as quoted in *Our Sunday Visitor*, 6 Aug 1989.

ception that the Church was a white institution. Ricard explained to those who would treat black Catholics as a monolithic group that individual black Catholics were attracted to many different expressions of their faith, "including the more quiet European one."[22]

Such analyses by church leaders tended to obscure the very real turmoil suffered by those who were strongly attracted to the spirit-filled celebrations at Imani Temple with its promise of black empowerment but remained full of love for the Church and loyal to its teachings. St. Augustine's parish council discussed the Stallings case (the pastor wisely abstained from expressing an opinion), and no one in the congregation was berated for attending the new temple.[23] The press routinely featured stories about those who found their loyalties torn, but these stories often noted that churches like St. Augustine's, with its gospel choir and vibrant liturgy, made the decision to remain true to the Church easier.[24]

On February 1, 1990, Stallings formally withdrew from the Church to organize a separate denomination, the African-American Catholic Congregation, and a week later he and his followers were excommunicated. With lines so clearly drawn, members of the Imani congregation had to choose. Father Greening and 300 members of his temple (by then the movement supported three houses of worship and averaged 1,300 attendees on Sundays) declared their intention to return to the Church, where they would continue to press for an autonomous African-American rite.[25] Others, disturbed by Stallings's pronouncements on abortion and women priests, and his independent canonization of Martin Luther King, also quietly returned to their old parishes. Eugene Marino, now the archbishop of Atlanta, finally broke his silence and spoke out to those who had left the Church. Breaking away, he claimed, was "divisive and regressive" and no answer to the needs and challenges of African-American Catholics. "We need one another more today than ever before," he concluded. "We must at all costs

22. The clergy caucus as quoted in *BCR*, 9 Aug 1989 (first quote) and Ricard as quoted in *Washington Times*, 9 Nov 1989.

23. Author's intv. with Father Mudd.

24. See, for example, article in *Washington Post*, 3 Aug 1989, which featured members of St. Augustine's congregation.

25. *Washington Post*, 12 Feb 1989. Only some in his group eventually returned.

maintain that unity which has the Spirit as its source and peace as its fruit."[26] Most black Catholics made the decision to stick with the arch-diocese. But lest any see this as some sort of victory, they saw the Imani Temple continue to thrive, a constant reminder that the quest for empowerment and respect for African-American religious traditions that it represented were not going away.

A Renewal of Racial Self-Awareness

The new racial currents flowing through American society were also felt at St. Augustine's. Considerations of empowerment and pre-servation of African-American heritage were especially appealing to young lay leaders like Michael Harris and Ernest Withers, Jr. They and their colleagues in the congregation had come of age during the black power movement and experienced the ferment on their college cam-puses. As Father Mudd observed, the black consciousness movement was taking root at that time, and these young leaders, just beginning their careers, were anxious to articulate a vision of black America as it related to black institutions. And St. Augustine's was one of those black institutions.[27] It was only logical for them to attempt to translate the aims expressed by the Black Clergy Caucus and black bishops into a plan of action for a historic black parish. As president of the parish council in 1981, Harris concluded his vision statement with the follow-ing declaration: "Certainly we do not intend to return to an earlier, un-conscionable practice of discriminating against people of specific racial origins. However, one who would choose to attend must realize and accept the fact that Saint Augustine is a parish with a Black cul-tural heritage and Black leadership."[28] The 1984 Vision statement was even more specific when it stated prominently among the parish's aims:

1. Remain a black Church, overcoming the challenge of changing demographics in order to hold onto our legacy of a Black Church.

2. The ministry and leadership of the Church remain with the laity.

26. As quoted in *Washington Post*, 26 Feb 1990.
27. Author's intv. with Mudd.
28. Memo, Harris to executive committee, n.d. (ca. Dec 1981), sub: Retreat/Work-shop 81: A Vision for the 80's, SAA.

3. The music and liturgy reflect the cross section of our culture.

4. Pass on our legacy as Black people and continue to be a haven for all people.[29]

During the 1980s the congregation would direct its considerable energies to fulfilling the vision it proclaimed (and still proclaims every Sunday) in the parish mission statement:

As the Mother Church of Black Catholics, Saint Augustine Church continues in the tradition in which it was founded, namely as a strong Black Catholic institution which witnesses in faith to the Living God, His Son, and the Holy Spirit. Saint Augustine will continue to be a center which recognizes, proclaims, and preserves our Black Roman Catholic heritage.

Long before the black power movement made explicit the connection between black history and empowerment, Pauline Jones had been active in the preservation and promotion of the history of St. Augustine's. She had grown up among parishioners whose memories extended back to the building of the old church in the 1870s and as a young women had enjoyed their accounts of the trials and triumphs of the old days. The merger of the parish with St. Paul's in 1961 and the very real danger that this rich heritage might be forgotten inspired her to began a systematic collection of documents and pictures pertaining to parish life.[30] She always presented the history of the parish to the catechumens early on in their process to make them aware of the commitment they were about to make. Her collections of documents and artifacts were frequently used in the parish school, where the idea of setting aside a week each February to investigate and extol African-American history was encouraged by Sister Marcellina and her successors.

The parish joined the rest of the country in the renewed interest in African-American history during the 1970s. Considerable effort was made to devise programs that helped parishioners learn more about their roots. As Father Kemp noted, few Catholics realized that a black Catholic tradition could be traced back to the days of Maryland's foundation, and St. Augustine's had been a major component of that evolv-

29. "Vision of Saint Augustine Parish," Parish Council Retreat September 14/15, 1984, cy in SAA.

30. *CS*, 27 Feb 1986. See also author's intv. with Jones.

CRUSADERS. Members of a rejuvenated parish council and leaders in St. Augustine's fight for social justice in recent times (clockwise from above): Michael Harris, Ruby Ellis Robertson, and Ernest Withers, Jr.

ing tradition.[31] It followed then that when the National Office of Black Catholics sponsored a city-wide celebration of Black History Month in 1978, the ceremonies which united black Catholics from around the diocese opened with mass at SS. Paul and Augustine with Bishop Marino and Howard University's Gospel Choir participating. The large audience heard Father Giles Conwill, the national director for black vocations, link African-American Catholics in a common heritage that could be traced to great theologians from Africa like Origen, Cyprian, and Augustine.

By 1980 the parish was sponsoring weekly seminars during Black History Month (February), which featured nationally recognized scholars and lay leaders who discussed the legal, cultural, and religious history of black people under the rubric "A People's Heritage is their Most Priceless Possession."[32] The following year the parish council formed a special committee under Ernest Withers to organize, with the help of 120 volunteers, a Black History celebration. It attracted more than 3,000 from the community to lectures, art exhibits, and ethnic food offerings.[33] The elaborate program received much press publicity, and for the first time the lectures were aired by local radio stations. The programs were also videotaped and arrangements made for parish and community groups to use them in future programs. The idea of making the study of black history a year-round occurrence prompted the parish council to institute its Black Coffee series. Organized by Brigette Rouson and Ernest Withers, the coffees, in reality a series of conversations on the state of African Americans in the Church and society, featured experts like Grambling University's chaplain, Father Edward Branch, Father Rollins Lambert from the National Catholic Conference's Africa office, and Dr. Ivan Van Sertima, an Africa studies scholar from Rutgers University.[34] The parish's celebration of Black History Month evolved in succeeding years. Its structured programs

31. Ltr., Kemp to Parishioners, 11 Jan 1981, SAA.

32. For a list of subjects and lecturers, see *Baltimore Afro-American*, 16 Feb 1980.

33. Other committee members included Esther Robinson, Jerry West, and Mary Jo Pauyo. See PCM, 28 Mar 1983, with att. SS. Paul & Augustine Black History Month Observance 1981, Final Report.

34. SS. Paul & Augustine *Newsletter*, Summer 1981. For report on a later celebration, see *Washington Afro-American*, 26 Feb 1983.

featured lectures by nationally recognized experts on African-American traditions and culture and presentations by African musicians, artists, and storytellers.[35]

The focus of Black History Month in the parish was not always so world-encompassing. Programs devised for the school children, for example, often emphasized personal family history. In announcing upcoming programs in 1985, Mary Garnes reported to the council that the future lectures would seek to profile individual parishioners and their recollections of parish life in earlier times.[36] Such programs complemented a research project inaugurated by the Office of Black Catholics that year to prepare educational materials on the African-American heritage. The project anticipated a comprehensive history of black Catholics in the archdiocese. Coordinated by Nevill R. Waters, the diocesan project planned to organize an archives and oral history program that would capture the rich history of the area's black Catholics for future generations.[37]

The new interest in parish archives stimulated by the diocesan project led St. Augustine's to reconsider its own collection. Unorganized and largely unused, this treasure of local African-American history needed professional attention. In early 1985 the council hired Howard University's Dr. Barbara Flint to head an archives and parish history project. During the next year, with the help of university student researchers and parish volunteers, the first steps were taken to create a professional collection, an exhibition service, and an oral history program, all in anticipation of a parish history.[38] Each step forward in this project, however, added to everyone's understanding of

35. See, for example, the four-week program organized for the 1987 celebration that featured the KanKouran (African Drummers and Dancers) and speakers including Philip F. Lee of the Tuskegee Airmen, Calvin Rolark, founder of United Black Fund, and A. Michael Auld, Jamaican storyteller, cy in SAA.

36. PCM, 21 Dec 1985.

37. Archdiocese of Washington, Black Catholic History Research Project, Sep 1985, cy in SAA.

38. PCM, 21 Dec 1985. See also Flint, "The Black Catholic Presence in the Nation's Capital, St. Augustine's Catholic Church History/Archival Project," May 1985, and memo, Barbara Flint to archives/history cmte, 11 Jun 1986, sub: Activities Report. Both in SAA.

the long-term and expensive obligation involved in organizing an archives that properly collected and maintained documentation pertaining to the parish's long history. Yet there was no question that the task might be abandoned. Proud of its heritage as one of the nation's first black Catholic congregations, the parish had always been historically aware. Moreover, its young leaders agreed with historian Dr. John H. Clarke when he told an audience at Howard University that "We suffer because African people did not keep records. . . . For the last five hundred years we have looked at the world through the lens of a European camera. We must now focus *our* lens on the world."[39] Cardinal Hickey obliquely referred to these sentiments when he commented on "that deep sense of pride which the parishioners of Saint Augustine take in their history. Elderly parishioners share with younger parishioners the story of the founding of Saint Augustine Parish and its pivotal role in our community and in our Church." This pride and the enthusiasm it engendered, he added, motivated parishioners of all ages to devote themselves to the many activities and ministries that are part of parish life.[40]

By the simple act of restoring its name. Hickey himself had done much to insure that the history and traditions of the parish would endure. Placing the merged parishes under the combined care of St. Paul and St. Augustine may have made sense in 1961 when the congregations and assets of the two were more equally balanced, but, as council president Michael Harris pointed out, where once two parishes and two distinct traditions existed, only one had survived.[41] Pauline Jones had first been stirred to action when she heard little children shortening the awkward combined name as people tended to do. When asked where they went to school, they would answer "St. Paul's." It suddenly occurred to her, she later recalled, that a whole generation of children and converts had known the parish only under the double name, and she feared that the spirit and traditions of St. Augustine's as well as the story of its long struggle for survival were endangered, not only by the

39. Clarke, Address at Howard University, 17 Sep 1988, cy in SAA.

40. Ltr., Hickey to Mudd, 22 Mar 1990, SAA.

41. Memo, Harris to executive committee, n.d. (ca. Dec 1981), sub: Retreat/Workshop 81: A Vision for the 80's, SAA.

tide of gentrification that was washing through the neighborhood, but because an historically black church that had lost its name was also losing its memory.

Father Mudd also appreciated what's in a name. He had seen in the case of some of the mergers and changes in Catholic institutions in southern Maryland the rich history of black Catholics lost. This parish was demonstrably among the few where young African-American newcomers felt at home. The name of the great African saint and his mother were familiar to them, since so many black churches around the country bore those names. That they now attended the oldest of them all, the mother church with its long tradition, gave them an incentive to join even as it sent a message to their folks back home: our children in the big city are remaining loyal to our roots and traditions.[42]

The parish leaders had another reason for proposing the change. They saw in the escalating gentrification of the neighborhood yet another threat to the parish's black traditions. Restoring its historic name, they reasoned, also in effect restored its former status as a "national" church serving African Americans throughout the city. St. Augustine's had enjoyed such status until the 1961 merger restricted its area of responsibility to a geographically defined portion of the city. Restoring the old name, the parish council believed, would go far toward renewing the parish's old suzerainty. In making their request, the pastor and parish council reminded the archbishop that as things had evolved, "Saints Paul and Augustine is actually St. Augustine's congregation housed in St. Paul's facilities." It was the spirit and faith born at St. Augustine's that fortified them all, they concluded, yet the parish's combined name threatened to rewrite history by submerging "the story of the faith and sacrifice of our ancestors."[43]

After discussing the proposal with his consultors, Hickey agreed, and on November 12, 1982, he announced that henceforth the parish would be called St. Augustine's. He asked that the change be made tactfully, so as not to offend any of St. Paul's old parishioners and ordered that a plaque honoring the devotion of the priests and people of

42. Author's intv. with Mudd.

43. Ltr., Michael Harris, Ruby Ellis and John Mudd to Hickey, 12 Jul 1982, cy in SAA.

St. Paul's be erected in the church and that the artifacts pertaining to the old congregation be sent to the diocesan archives. The petitioners had made no mention of their desire for a renewal of national parish status, and the archbishop's decree that changed the name repeated the 1961 definition of the parish's geographical boundaries.[44] Celebration of the event, scheduled to coincide with the close of Black History Month in February, was a grand affair. Billed as a homecoming mass, the liturgy presided over by the archbishop drew more than 2,000 parishioners and former parishioners, relatives, and friends from all over the diocese. In sharing the good news with the parishioners, Father Mudd called the renaming a great compliment to the people who struggled to build the parish as well as "a challenge to all of us to remain faithful to the task of building up a Catholic community which will reflect our Afro-American culture."[45]

In an effort to reinforce the congregation's understanding of its past and to remind the city of St. Augustine's prominence in the history of the capital, Fathers Mudd and Muffler approached officials of the *Washington Post* in 1983 with the request that the church that once stood on the *Post* site be memorialized. During those times everyone, it seemed, was erecting plaques on buildings marking some important historical event in the city's history. Why not, they asked, install a plaque at the *Post* to remind the community of the significance of this site, not only as the home of one of the nation's most important newspapers, but as the first home of one of the nation's oldest black churches, one of special significance in the development of the Catholic Church in America. Dr. Vincent Reed, the *Post's* vice president for communications, asked the priests to document the church's connection with the land and received, in addition, a number of testimonials from the congregation's oldest parishioners. Underscoring the neglect of black citizens in the pages of the local press (for many years most metropolitan papers routinely omitted obituaries for African Americans) eighty-three-year-old Beatrice Holton Stewart provided Reed

44. Ltr., Hickey to Mudd, 12 Nov 1982 with att Decree, SAA. See also ltrs., Mudd to Hickey, 18 Jan 1983, and to fellow pastors, 31 Jan 1983. Cys of all in SAA.

45. As quoted in *CS*, 10 Feb 1983. See also *CS*, 3 Mar 1983, and *Washington Afro-American*, 26 Feb 1983.

AT THE WASHINGTON POST. Festivities marking the installation of a memorial plaque on the site of the original St. Augustine's Church and commemorating the ongoing ties between parish and newspaper.

with a detailed account of her family's century-long connection with St. Augustine's that, by inference, demonstrated the importance of the old church to the faith of thousands of African Americans.[46]

In the end the *Post* agreed not only to install a plaque but also to host a dedication ceremony and treat its guests to an elaborate reception. Figuring he was on a roll, Mudd also pressed the *Post* for a contribution to the parish's scholarship fund. Although the paper politely declined at the time, it later established a scholarship fund "in further recognition of its role as neighbor, friend, and supporter of quality education."[47] The installation took place on Trinity Sunday, 1984, the

46. Ltr., Stewart to Reed, 19 Sep 1983, cy in SAA. See also, for example, ltr., Susie Lemmon to Reed, same date. On the installation of the plaque, see author's intv. with Father Mudd.

47. As quoted in *Shoptalk*, a weekly publication of the *Post*'s Public Relations Department, 14 Jun 1990, p. 3.

118th anniversary of the opening of the Blessed Martin de Porres chapel on the site. Mayor Barry issued a proclamation declaring June 17 Saint Augustine Catholic Church Day in the city, and a large crowd of parishioners and friends paraded down Fifteenth Street in the bright spring sunshine to witness a ceremony presided over by Bishop Marino and officials of the newspaper. Members of the Taylor family, who represented four generations of worshippers at St. Augustine's, unveiled the plaque that can be seen today at the entrance to the building.[48]

Another important element in the parish's journey to self-awareness, one with strong echoes of the black power crusade, was its identification with the African liberation movement. Beginning in 1977 the parish council sponsored a series of workshops and lectures, usually during Black History Month, that emphasized the ties binding black Catholics in America to their brothers and sisters in the lands of their ancestors. In January 1979, for example, the parish held a Zimbabwe Sunday, which featured an address by Sister Janice McLaughlin, who had recently been expelled from Southern Rhodesia. In 1982 the congregation welcomed Bishop Kaseba, then president of the Zairian conference of bishops, who reported on conditions in his country.[49] Such activities, Father Kemp once pointed out, "led us as a parish to the conclusion that we are not free as long as fellow Catholics and humans are denied their rightful dignity."[50] This awareness in turn led to the planting of a sign on the church lawn. In rude letters the parish spelled out its demand: "Free South Africa."[51] A small but heartfelt token, the sign proved to be a mighty symbol that spoke to a whole generation of African Americans. As Father Kemp noted at the time, the sign was a public statement of the congregation's link with the peo-

48. *Washington Afro-American*, 23 Jun 1984. The city recognized the parish with similar declarations on Trinity Sunday for several years. See, for example, D.C. Resolutions (D.C. Register #5-683, 15 Jun 1984; #6-156, 26 Jun 1985; and #6-716, 11 Jul 1986).

49. PCM, 27 Jan 1979, and Africa and diaspora cmte, "Proposal to the Parish Council for a Sister Parish Program," 19 Jan 1985.

50. Ltr., Kemp to parishioners ("Greetings in the Lord"), 28 Aug 1978, SAA.

51. In one of its several manifestations the sign read "Free Southern Africa" in keeping with the crusade to liberate all European-controlled colonies in the region.

ple of Africa, the link of sons and daughters to a mother. It was a relationship, he insisted, that transcended racial identity and was built on
the catholicity of the Church.[52]

In fact the sign proved a potent force in the evangelization of young
African Americans. Kemp knew that many newcomers to the parish,
both lapsed Catholics like Michael Harris and numerous converts, had
first been attracted by the sign, which to them signified a social consciousness they had never before ascribed to the Church. As to be expected, the sign also attracted criticism. In 1980 an elder of the Fifteenth Street Baptist Church demanded that the parish remove what
was considered a provocative message. His request was rejected. On
several occasions the sign was defaced, and in 1985 it was stolen, only
to be restored immediately. The parish council was adamant; the sign
would remain as a public symbol of St. Augustine's commitment to
black solidarity in the fight against apartheid.[53]

Even as Kemp was exalting the sign and its symbolism, he was
chiding the congregation for doing so little at a time when official
Washington needed to be reminded that some Americans at least were
vitally concerned about U.S. policy toward Africa. He wanted the
parish council to form a special committee to concentrate on such issues. He also wanted the parish to evangelize among the many
unchurched Africans living in Washington and to incorporate African
parishioners more fully into the life of the parish.[54] The council responded by organizing its Africa and diaspora committee (from the
Greek meaning scattered colonies of people). Chaired by Ernest Withers, it sponsored projects aimed at improving the social and economic
conditions of Africans, both in their homeland and in the Caribbean
and the United States. Among the committee's early projects was a let-
ter-writing campaign directed at officials of the South African government demanding freedom for Father Smangaliso Patrick Mkhashwa. A
grateful Father Mkhashwa later appeared at St. Augustine's before a
large audience that included many national leaders of the anti-
apartheid movement, where he credited the parish with obtaining his

52. Ltr., Kemp to Parishioners, 11 Jan 1981, SAA.
53. PCM, 14 Jun 1980 and 21 Dec 1985.
54. Ltr., Kemp to Parishioners, 11 Jan 1981, SAA.

release. Committee members were also upset with news that the pope had granted the South African prime minister an audience. They fired off a letter to the pontiff outlining their concerns and requesting that, to counterbalance the propaganda of the South African government, the pope grant an audience to Father Mkhashwa, who had recently been elevated to the post of general secretary of the South African Bishops Conference.[55]

By 1984 the committee had become more aggressive in its protests. It sponsored a mass on December 9, designated as Bishop Desmond Tutu Sunday, at which Washington's Bishop Marino praised the work of the African prelate who had just been awarded the Nobel Peace Prize. After mass St. Augustine's sent two busloads of people to a prayer vigil near the South African embassy. There guests, including Father Stallings, then still pastor of St. Teresa's, and Twiggs Xiphu, a member of a South African students' committee, spoke to the crowd that included hundreds of demonstrators from area churches. Ernest Withers, speaking for the St. Augustine group that organized the rally, promised yet another demonstration later that week.[56] As promised, an interfaith demonstration was staged near the South African embassy as one of the events planned for Human Rights Week. It coincided with the publication of Archbishop Hickey's condemnation of apartheid as both "racist and unjust." Father Kemp read parts of the archbishop's statement at a press conference held during a demonstration that was enhanced by the presence of many area clergymen, Georgetown students, Gray Panthers, and even Larry Holmes, the boxing champion. Three of the ministers were arrested.[57]

Capping off a month of protests, seventeen members of St. Augustine's congregation, along with their pastor, Father Mudd, and Sister Barbara Spears were arrested while demonstrating against apartheid near the South African embassy. None of them had been involved in civil disobedience before, but now, Father Kelley reported, their awareness of the injustices suffered in Africa and their sense of soli-

55. Social justice cmte rpt., 19 Oct 1984, SAA.

56. For full coverage of the vigil, see *CS*, 13 Dec 1984.

57. Hickey's statement, as well as a full account of the demonstration, was carried by the *CS*, 20 Dec 1984.

darity with their brothers and sisters overseas had led to their willingness to be arrested.[58] Although arrests and jailings for civil disobedience had become commonplace by 1984, Father Mudd reported that his mother was definitely not pleased to learn that her son had been booked by the D.C. police.

Ever since its formation, the Africa and diaspora committee had been discussing ways to stimulate the congregation's personal involvement with individual South African Catholics. The idea of adopting a sister parish to establish a dialogue and person-to-person exchange was considered, but not until Ernest Withers visited Regina Mundi (Our Lady Queen of the World) parish in the heart of Soweto in May 1984 did the idea take definite shape. With its 5,000 Catholics, Regina Mundi was one of the centers of anti-apartheid activity, and in approving the new connection the St. Augustine's parish council noted the need to demonstrate the congregation's "solidarity with the people of Africa for independence, freedom, economic development, and Christian faith."[59] The relationship between the two congregations proved satisfyingly intimate. Dr. Deborah Nolphin, who coordinated the sister parish project, described the many activities involved: pen pals were found, parish organizations shared plans and discussed programs with their counterparts, care packages in the form of choir albums, bulletins, and videotapes were exchanged. In November 1987 the parishes were linked telephonically to celebrate Regina Mundi's twenty-fifth anniversary. Pastor, parish council chairmen, sodalities, and even teen clubs exchanged greetings and information.[60]

Given their efforts on behalf of African liberation, St. Augustine's parishioners had earned the right to join in the celebration when recently freed Nelson Mandela made his triumphal visit to Washington in June 1990. Father Mudd called the day, which saw 150 parishioners serve as organizers and marshals of the giant rally, "a fitting conclusion to our long effort." Mandela's release was known at St. Augus-

58. *National Catholic Reporter*, 25 Jan 1985. See also *Washington Post*, 12 Jan 1985.

59. Africa and diaspora cmte, "A Proposal to the Parish Council for a Sister Parish Program in Africa," 19 Jan 1985, SAA.

60. PCM, 21 Dec 1985 and 17 Oct 1987. See also *CS*, 8 Sep 1988, and *Community News* (Howard University), 29 Oct 1987.

tine's just minutes after the event, when members of Regina Mundi's parish council passed the news on to their Washington counterparts. Fikile Miotshwe and Joseph Contres, neighbors of the Mandela's, had called, they told Ernest Withers, to reaffirm Regina Mundi's unity with St. Augustine's and to share this great moment with their American brothers and sisters.[61]

African-American Traditions and Culture in Catholic Worship

The recent history of St. Augustine's has centered on the effort of its leaders to broadcast the Good News in symbols and liturgical practices that reflected the congregation's African-American heritage. Those leaders might attest to the validity of Bishop Ricard's observation that black Catholics did not constitute a monolithic society. Some in the congregation, for example, could trace their Catholic roots back to the foundations of Maryland and had reason to cherish the Western European form of Catholicism embraced by their ancestors. Others, recent converts deeply imbued with the Southern Protestant traditions of their childhood, looked with nostalgia on those more emotional forms of worship. Still others were Africans or Caribbean islanders, some unchurched, all heirs of very different cultures and religious practices. Nevertheless parish council leaders like John Butler, Dominic Mouldin, and Brigette Rouson also agreed with those scholars who had defined a distinct African-American spirituality and believed that it should be reflected in the liturgy at St. Augustine's. Like Father Cyprian Davis they believed that having ethnic traditions in the liturgy was important because the liturgy should be an expression of people's culture as well as a vehicle for worship. As Davis put it: "The expression of our worship should not be foreign to the culture in which we live much of our lives."[62]

Scholars like Father Giles Conwill had studied those elements of

61. *CS*, 15 Feb 1990 and 5 July 1990 (source of quote).

62. As quoted in a Catholic News Service article by Katharine Bird, which appeared in several Catholic newspapers. See, for example, "How Liturgy Reflects Culture," *Georgia Bulletin*, 26 Apr 1990. The following paragraphs are based on Bird's article and on Brigette Rouson's "Bridge," an editorial in the *CS, 13 Dec 1990*, and Giles Conwill's "Black and Catholic," *America*, 29 Mar 1980, pp. 265–67.

black culture that influenced liturgy. Based on expressive oral tradition, that culture had led to a more dynamic approach to religion featuring passionate sermons, lively exchanges between preacher and
congregation, high energy singing, loud voices, and dance-like movement. It was a Christianity that downplayed the European emphasis on
the kingship of Christ and a courtly liturgy to extol instead the brotherhood of Christ. Speaking as an African-American priest, Conwill explained black Catholic feeling: "The Lord is my brother. Let's celebrate the redemption wrought by my brother Jesus; let's let my hands
clap, my voice shout, let's let even my feet be happy."

It followed that the liturgy as performed by African Americans
would exhibit certain characteristics. First it would be hospitable, emphasizing warmth, friendliness, and a welcoming informality with the
kiss of peace and the final benediction becoming an extended party
among God's children. Second it would be holistic, that is, it appealed
not just to the intellect but to the emotions with tears and laughter,
with heartfelt amens and joyful clapping. It would also emphasize
preaching that related Scriptures especially to the liberation stories
and the experiences of the congregation in a race-conscious society. It
would feature music based on the stories of the Gospels and sung by
people swaying to African rhythms and instruments, the kind of
sounds that African Americans traditionally heard when they gathered
together. Finally, the environment and vestments would be decked out
in those swirls of colors and designs familiar in black artistic expression. John Butler summed up the conclusion of the experts that black
Catholics had much to contribute to the Church. They can remind people, he noted, "that it's o.k. to express joy at the realization that we
have been saved."

Father Clarence J. Rivers is frequently cited for his tireless effort
in exhorting black Catholics to think of their special sense of spirituality as a gift for the whole Church and to fashion from it an effective and
authentic form of American worship. Like a latter-day apostle Paul,
Rivers traveled tirelessly around the country trying to infuse the liturgy of American parishes with the sounds and emotions that made
black churches such joy-filled places. He appeared several times at
St. Augustine's. During the Trinity Sunday celebration in 1987, for example, he called on the congregation to make the liturgy "an effective

channel of the Spirit." A man of great humor, Rivers measured the progress of gospel music in Catholic churches by 1986: "Some did well, others not, but the fact that we were doing anything at all should evoke the sentiment that 'thank God we aint what we was.'"[63]

Another influential apostle of black spirituality was the Franciscan Sister Thea Bowman. A convert from rural Mississippi and granddaughter of a slave, Sister Thea worked effectively to raise awareness and appreciation of black Catholic culture. Her lectures, storytelling, and especially her singing performances electrified audiences across the country. Her appearances in the pulpit of St. Augustine's marked some of the most dramatic and emotional moments in the long history of the church.[64]

As he had in so many other areas of parish life, Father Kemp challenged the congregation; this time he wanted them to consider its African-American heritage when designing an environment that would "bring our worshipping community into the action of the mass and into interaction with one another."[65] He was aware of the pitfalls facing anyone who would tamper with a church's furnishings, but he addressed the fears of those who believed that any alterations might destroy the appearance of one of the city's most beautiful gothic churches. Working together through the parish council, he claimed, they would respect the design of the church while making it more functional and meaningful for the congregation. During the 1980s the building saw considerable modification, as Father Mudd and the parish council prepared the interior for use in the post-Vatican II era.

In 1982 after lengthy consultation in the council's worship and church committee, the front pews were removed and the sanctuary extend outward to make the altar and pulpit more visible and provide

63. Rivers, "'Thank God We Aint What We Was': The State of the Liturgy in the Black Catholic Community," *U.S. Catholic Historian* 5 (1986): 81–89. On Rivers and St. Augustine's, see also Tracey Moses, "Rivers Uses Music, Drama in Worship," *The Community News* (Howard University), 18 Jun 1987, and *Washington Afro-American*, 13 Jun 1987 and *Washington Times*, 15 Jun 1987.

64. Sister Thea, who earned her doctorate in rhetoric and literature from Catholic University, died of cancer just as she was being honored by Notre Dame University with its prestigious Laetare Medal. Of the many articles on this nun, see, for example, *Washington Afro-American*, 7 Apr 1990.

65. Ltr., Kemp to Parishioners, 11 Jan 1981, SAA.

space for the choirs and cantors and their instruments. The pews in the upper side aisles were reset at a 90-degree angle, bringing people into visual contact and thus adding to the sense of community. One specially symbolic touch: the strait-back pews once used by St. Paul's black parishioners segregated in the back of the church were refurbished and set in the place of honor in front of the sanctuary. At the same time the replaced pews, with a patina developed over many generations, were refabricated as the new Eucharistic altar. The old pulpit, a reminder of the long history of the parish, was repositioned to indicate the prominent place of the Word in the revised liturgy. Both altar and pulpit were bedecked in linens of African design that complimented the banners and quilts and hangings that used the vibrant, patterned Kente cloth.[66] The parish's new electronic organ was added to the sanctuary, replacing the pipe organ in congregational singing. Despite the efforts of the former parish organist and master technician Ray Brubacher, the valuable Moeller organ, one of the few of its kind in the city, was slowly shutting down rank by rank. The congregation's steadfast commitment to Catholic education meant that many worthwhile projects had to depend on special fund drives. The parish council organized an organ fund campaign, and over $20,000 was collected before the project was incorporated along with other causes into the Stewardship Campaign.[67]

Construction of a baptismal pool was yet another of the major renovations made to the church interior. The fathers of the Vatican Council had urged consideration of the ancient rite of immersion as an optional form of baptism in the Western Church. A few churches around the country were offering such an option by 1985, and the parish council noted that several of the adults preparing to receive the sacrament, including those whose Baptist heritage led them to consider immersion especially appropriate, had expressed interest in being baptized in

66. For a comprehensive description of the modifications of the interior of the church, see "Renovations at St. Augustine's 1982", a pamphlet prepared by the worship cmte, cy in SAA.

67. The organ stands mute today, awaiting the more than $150,000 needed for overhaul. See ltr., Brubacher to Mudd, 18 Feb 1986, Rpt of organ fund steering committee, 28 Apr 1986, and PCM, 2 May 1988 and 13 Mar 1989. All in SAA. For more on the organ, see appendix I, below.

this way. In January 1985 the worship and church committee organized a presentation by several liturgical experts that led to serious discussion of a baptismal pool at St. Augustine's. The archbishop approved the idea, with the proviso that it be presented as an option in no way superior to the traditional form and that nothing be said to offend those who shunned it.[68] In 1986, while Father Mudd negotiated the final design of a nine-by-eight-foot pool, which included as its centerpiece the font used in the baptism of so many generations of St. Augustine's parishioners, the parish council allocated $30,000 for its construction. The pool was ready for the baptism of fifteen adults during the 1987 Easter Vigil and twenty-five children in succeeding weeks. Alluding to the usual tension that met any change in parish practices, Father Kelley noted that "even people who thought we were a little nuts for doing it have been pleased." Kelley described the pool as a new focal point in the everyday life of the parish. The soothing sounds of its running water, he added, reminded the people that they had reclaimed a portion of Catholic history.[69]

All these changes were welcomed by the congregation, but the parish council remained unsatisfied with efforts to introduce what it called "artistic representations of St. Augustine's Afro-American heritage." Admitting that this heritage was reflected in the congregation's "style of worship," the worship and church committee nevertheless called for more visible manifestations in the church's art and artifacts. Earlier efforts to introduce such changes through exhibitions and performances sponsored by a parish art and culture committee came to little, but in September 1988 parish council president Cecil G. Bushell charged the worship committee with developing an acquisition program for Afro-centric art and iconography.[70]

The committee's interests immediately focused on the church's windows, especially the one along the north wall of the nave depicting Saints Augustine and Monica with Caucasian features, a relic of an age when their African heritage was given scant recognition. The window inspired the committee to search for a suitable alternative. They

68. PCM, 15 Dec 1984 and 9 Nov 1985.

69. As quoted in *Washington Post*, 16 May 1987. See also PCM, 2 Dec 1985.

70. Worship and church cmte minutes, 2 Aug 1988 (source of quote), PCM, Sep 1988, and "An Odyssey: Images, Words, Music," 7 Mar 1982. All in SAA.

found their artist in Akili R. Anderson, a local craftsman experienced in designing, fabricating, and installing stained glass. Although the usual budget constraints precluded action in 1988, the committee recommended allocating $14,000 for the project in the following year.[71] At that time the noted Washington arts organizer and commentator Peggy Cooper Cafritz offered to donate a window as a memorial to her mother, Gladys Mouton Cooper. Unaware of the committee's earlier discussions, Cafritz also recommended Anderson for the work. After considerable discussion over theme and design, the work, with its vibrant colors typical of African visual art, was completed in time for the celebration of the church's patron in August 1990, with formal dedication ceremonies following in December.[72]

These artistic and environmental changes created an apt setting for a liturgy that fused Catholic ritual and African-American spirituality as promoted by Father Rivers and the other reformers. John Butler, director of the parish's catechumenate program, sounded the keynote of St. Augustine's liturgical renewal of the 1980s: "evangelize and celebrate in joy and gladness." Referring to George Stallings's comment that many Christians left church looking like they had just sucked a lemon, Butler called on black Catholics to commit themselves to a more expressive liturgy that freed them "to express ourselves in body and voice." Above all, the liturgy should promote community. "Be a healing community," he added, "we are gathered broken—only in community do we find wholeness."[73]

Adding immeasurably to St. Augustine's joyful and expressive liturgy was its gospel choir, which, reminiscent of its nineteenth-century counterpart, was bringing fame and national attention to the parish.[74] One reporter commented on the choir's participation one warm September Sunday:

71. Worship and church cmte minutes, 13 Mar 1989.

72. "Dedication and Blessing of the Saints Augustine and Monica Window," 16 Dec 1990, and Nora Hamerman, "New Stained Glass Image of St. Augustine Recalls African's Contribution to World Culture." Cys of both in SAA.

73. As quoted in *Catholic Key* (Kansas City, MO), 13 May 1990.

74. A bibliographical essay could be prepared on the many articles and reports written on the choir during the 1980s. See, for example, *Washington Post*, 25 Dec 1981, and *Washington Times*, 13 Jun 1987. On its national notice, see, for example, ltr., Rev.

The music for the feast brings both freshness and sensitivity to the occasion with sounds alternately soothing, spirit-stirring, and, yes, flat-out rollicking enough to produce shivers of excitement despite the heat.

Another witness came away with a similar impression:

The walls of the inner-city church seemed to tremble with joy as the parish's 50-voice choir led the congregation in exuberant singing. With arms raising, voices praising, hands clapping and toes tapping, the people seemed to really know how to *celebrate* the Eucharist.[75]

No room here for hiding behind missalettes or indulging in rapt contemplation. Instead, an overwhelming sense of community demanded that all participate in a liturgy that served as an example for the American church, as one participant put it, "of a worshipping community that *has* found its gifts—of song and celebration—and is unafraid to sing out its thanks to God."[76] In such a setting, clapping and swaying seemed the obvious and appropriate response to the sheer emotional power of the ritual.

This sense of community was nowhere more evident then during the kiss of peace when the church erupted in a spontaneous outpouring of comforting sociability; every hand, it seemed, was shaken a hundred times, people wandered the aisles, exchanging hugs and greetings. The communion procession was another time of intense interaction. A somewhat anxious pastor and worship committee once discussed ways of abbreviating these portions of the liturgy, but finally decided to do nothing, figuring that the choir's adherence to the flow of the ritual was sufficient. One newcomer reported that the gospel mass was one of the "messiest" she had ever witnessed. It was also, she added, "without a doubt one of the most inspired. And I left it feeling very much touched by God's spirit at work."[77]

Jack Meehan, pastor of All Saints parish, New York, to Mudd, 28 Mar 1988, SAA. For an extended account of the choir's activities, see appendix I, below.

75. Kaki Roberts, "Hallelujah! Gospel Sound is vivacious, Spirited, Liberated, Inviting," *CS*, 6 Oct 1987 (first quote), and Mark Zimmerman, "Special Treatment?," *CS*, 11 Jun 1987.

76. Corine Erlandson, "A Taste of the Spirit," *National Catholic Reporter*, 6 Apr 1986.

77. Erlandson, "A Taste of the Spirit." See also worship and church cmte minutes, 9 Mar 1987.

Again calling to mind Bishop Ricard's observation that black Catholics were not a monolithic group, it comes as no surprise that the new Afro-centric liturgy had its critics in the parish. As Pauline Jones noted, "not everybody has been for the new ways. And not only the old folks are in opposition. Some of the young people don't like the window and pool and gospel mass."[78] Some black scholars like Bishop James Lyke and Father Giles Conwill, for example, dismissed such opposition as a subconscious expression of a persisting self-hatred and "ashamed-of-my-blackness."[79] But such explanations appear a little glib in the case of those St. Augustine parishioners with deep roots in the American Catholic Church. Mary Cooke Buckner spoke for those who cherished the familiar Catholic mass which, she remembered, had sustained them through the dark days of segregation and racism. Along with those remnants of the old black aristocracy that had dominated St. Augustine's for so long, many of the hard-working, middle-class Catholics who had formed the backbone of the parish and were the main support of its many organizations took great comfort from the familiar liturgy and the music that accompanied it.[80] Some of the newcomers to the parish too were unmoved by the high emotionalism of the gospel mass, which reminded them of an alien or recently shunned fundamentalist Protestant service.

The tensions that arose from these different attitudes might easily be exaggerated, even though Father Muffler reported that in its early days the gospel mass was one of the most divisive issues to face the parish in modern times.[81] Parish leaders fully supported a traditional liturgy, including a special mass for families and a high mass accompanied by a chorale of genuine artistic merit. At the same time they continued to explore the full dynamics of a gospel mass infused with African-American music, dance, and storytelling. By the end of the decade St. Augustine's had achieved a modus operandi that seemed to satisfy the disparate elements of a congregation that, throughout its long history, had learned to tolerate all sorts of religious and social

78. Author's intv. with Pauline J. Jones.

79. Lyke's comments were quoted in *Wall Street Journal*, 5 Nov 1985. See also Conwill's "Black and Catholic," p. 266.

80. Nickels' intv. with William and Mary Buckner.

81. Muffler, "This Far By Faith," p. 168.

viewpoints. Commenting on the gamut of spirituality that existed in the parish, which ran from those comfortable with traditional expressions of Catholicism to those "who are into a higher-energy kind of approach to worship," a future pastor of St. Augustine's marveled that "all these types of faith expressions are found in this one parish—not vying against each other, but in a loving co-existence."[82]

The parish also had the satisfaction during the 1980s of seeing its example followed in many other parishes with the approval and active support of important church leaders. It followed that the parish played a major role in the influential Rejoice conferences on black liturgy and evangelization inaugurated in 1983 by the diocese's Office of Black Catholics. Acting on the premise that the liturgy was the principal means of evangelization in the African-American community—an idea articulated by St. Augustine's pastor and parish council a decade before—these conferences discussed the various ways in which black culture could contribute to the Roman rite. Black Catholics gathered annually for these meetings, which featured workshops dealing with African contributions to the origins of Christianity, church history from a black perspective, and liturgical innovations in the gospel mass. The 1986 conference, for example, found some 400 delegates gathered for the closing gospel mass concelebrated by Archbishop Hickey and Bishop Marino and to hear Jacqueline Wilson, the Rejoice coordinator, sound the purpose for these annual events: to teach black lay Catholics how to become involved in "building Church while preserving their heritage."[83] This premise was further explored when the Rejoice conference convened in Rome in 1989. There more than 100 delegates, including Thomascena Nelson and Jerry Vorbach from St. Augustine's, spoke to the pope and other church officials about the history and culture of African-American Catholics.[84]

So far these activities had centered on the idea of an African-American rite as a unique order of service within the regular parish structure. At the same time, prompted by the Black Clergy Caucus and the headline-grabbing demands of Father Stallings, church officials

82. Russell L. Dillard, as quoted in CS, 31 Jan 1991.

83. As quoted in the CS, 19 Jun 1986. See also Our Sunday Visitor, 6 Aug 1989.

84. For an account of the Rome conference, see Catholic News Service, 4 Aug 1989, and CS, 30 Nov 1989.

had opened discussions about an African-American rite in the sense of a body in full communion with Rome but otherwise autonomous, with a separate hierarchy and clergy responsible for its own institutional structures. In July 1989 Bishop John Ricard of Baltimore, chairman of the U.S. Bishop's Committee on Black Catholics, announced that his group had begun "very preliminary" study of an independent rite. Ricard promised to find out if a consensus existed among black Catholics for such a separation, even though he remained convinced that the demands made by Stallings and others did not have a large audience.[85] Just as in other areas of life, African-American Catholics were being asked to draw a fine line between self-determination and separatism.

An African-American Pastor

The parish's final step in its journey to self-awareness began with the acquisition of an African-American pastor. Although Father Mudd was the unanimous choice of parish leaders in 1981, they had informed the archbishop's representatives at that time of their "strong desire" to have a black pastor in the "nearest future" and asked that the archbishop seriously consider appointing a black priest as Father Mudd's assistant. In considering these matters the parish council made its motives clear. In addition to the obvious and important symbolism of having an African American in charge of the oldest black parish in the diocese, a black man sensitive to and a strong advocate for the aspirations of black Catholics would help preserve the membership and heritage of a parish threatened by demographic change.[86] At its 1984 re-

85. Ricard was quoted extensively on this subject in the *Washington Post*, 26 Jul 1989. For a discussion of such a rite and its relationship to the newly granted Roman rite for Zaire, see the *Washington Times*, 28 Jul 1989. For a broader discussion of separate rites and the appropriateness of a special rite for African Americans, see Memo, Dr. Leona L. Hayes to Paulette [*sic*] Jones, 19 Aug 1989, sub: Paper-African-American Rite, cy in SAA.

86. Minutes of an emergency meeting of the parish council, 6 Jun 1981. See also memo, Ernest Withers, Jr., to Cornelia Rajah [pc president], 19 May 1986, sub: Correction of Council Minutes of April 19, 1986. Both in SAA.

treat, council members linked the recruitment of a black pastor to their effort to overcome the threat of gentrification and retain the parish's African-American legacy.[87]

Throughout these discussions Pauline Jones cautioned against precipitate action. Having an African-American pastor, she warned, did not necessarily assure the parish of a leader who understood its feelings or shared its goals. Nevertheless the council took up the question in earnest in 1986, when the assignment of a white deacon to the parish underscored the racial distinction between rectory and congregation. Members agreed that Fathers Mudd and Kelley, always sympathetic to the aspirations of the congregation, had worked closely with them in fulfilling the parish's goals, but Ernest Withers cautioned against being "too negative" in considering the pressing need for black leadership. At the very least, he pointed out, the council should recognize the parish as an ideal training ground for black clergy and that the presence of a young African-American assistant might encourage vocations among parish youth.[88] Following this discussion the council organized a committee on the Future of the Pastorate, which met from time to time to explore the subject further.

Three years would pass before the parish received its first black priest. As an Augustinian seminarian, John Payne had served his deaconate year at St. Augustine's, and his ordination by Bishop Ricard in November 1989 marked the first such ceremony ever held in the parish. Through a special arrangement with the Augustinian provincial, Cardinal Hickey assigned the young priest as an associate pastor. He quickly became immersed in many parish ministries, including membership on the council's future of the pastorate committee. Like other black priests at that time Father Payne was pressed by journalists to comment on issues raised by the Stallings case. He was committed, he told them, to expanding the African-American tradition in Catholicism, but within the institution. Why, he asked, "should I leave something my grandfathers and grandmothers died for?"[89]

Discussions of an African-American pastor began in earnest in

87. PC, "Vision of Saint Augustine Parish," 14/15 Sep 1984, SAA.
88. Memo, Withers to Rajah, 19 May 1986, sub: Correction of Council Minutes.
89. As quoted in *Washington Times*, 24 Nov 1989.

February 1990 when Father Mudd announced his attention to step
down. On a personal level, Mudd explained how after fourteen years in
the parish he believed it time to leave while still young and energetic
enough to give a new community the commitment he had given St. Augustine's. More to the point, he told Cardinal Hickey that he was convinced the time had come when the parish needed a black pastor. Nor,
he added, given parish sentiments, the reaction to the Imani Temple,
and the cardinal's stated position on the importance of black leaders,
did he think the decision could be delayed much longer.[90] To the congregation Mudd put it more bluntly: "Contributing to my decision was
a growing realization that it is not right for black institutions or
churches to have white leaders and pastors."[91] In his request for reassignment Mudd also informed the cardinal of Father Kelley's willingness to remain to help the new pastor become acclimated. He also expressed the wish to continue to serve the black community and reiterated his commitment to Catholic education for African Americans by
offering to devote a year to fundraising for the parish school, a task he
had always considered central to his administration. His subsequent
assignment as director of development and fundraising at the predom-
inately African-American John Carroll High School would seem to
have fulfilled his wishes.

Although any decision on a replacement was likely to take many
months, the parish council lost no time in working on its arguments
and recommendations for a black pastor. Following lengthy discussion, chairman Horatio Lanier informed Cardinal Hickey that the
parish would like to retain Father Mudd as pastor for at least another
year to conclude several ongoing projects. At the same time he passed
on for the cardinal's consideration the parish council's criteria for a
new pastor: he should be an African American, committed to the system of parish management developed over the years at St. Augustine's;
a man sensitive to the history of the parish and its heritage, culture,
and purposes as outlined in the parish's mission statement; and, above
all, a man able to deliver the Word "in a manner which will address

90. Mudd's account of his letter to the cardinal is summarized in ltr., Mudd to Ray
Lanier, 2 Mar 1990, cy in SAA.

91. Mudd, Homily delivered on 28 Oct 1990 ["Last Mass at Saint Augustine"], cy
in SAA. See also PCM, 17 Feb 1990.

RUSSELL L. DILLARD is installed as the first African-American pastor of St. Augustine's by Bishop Leonard J. Olivier.

the unique needs of people of African descent living in these United States."[92] Calling this letter "a nice beginning" to the process, the cardinal advised Lanier that he would nevertheless respect Father Mudd's judgment on the timing of his reassignment. He was fully aware of the parish's desire for an African-American pastor, he added, and in keeping with recently instituted procedures, the congregation would be invited to discuss the matter with diocesan officials when the

92. Ltr., Lanier to Cardinal Hickey, 21 May 1990. The contents of this letter were, in the main, circulated to parishioners in "Statement on the Occasion of the Announced Departure of Our Pastor. . . ," 29 Sep 1990. The parish council recommendations were summarized in memo, Ruth Palmer, Laila Araya, and Dominic Moulden, to Cmte on the Pastorate, 3 Apr 1990. Both in SAA.

director of priest personnel met with members of the parish staff and council.[93]

Parishioners had their say, and in October, after several months of anxious waiting, they learned the cardinal's decision: Russell L. Dillard, native Washingtonian, Baptist convert, graduate of Cathedral Latin School, St. Mary's Seminary, and Washington Theological College, former chaplain at Howard University, and pastor of St. Martin of Tours parish, would be the ninth pastor of St. Augustine's. In the presence of 2,000 parishioners and friends singing the familiar words of the old hymn "We've Come this Far by Faith," the slim, 42-year-old African American made his way into the sanctuary on January 28, 1991, for his formal installation by Bishop Leonard Olivier. In a moment rich with symbolism, Olivier handed over the keys of the church to the new pastor, reminding him of his responsibility "as preacher, teacher, sanctifier and leader" of one of the most historic faith communities in American Catholicism. Having had a church of its own since Civil War days, it now had a pastor of its own.

93. Ltr., Hickey to Lanier, 7 Jun 1990, SAA.

✦ EPILOGUE

*I*f the history of St. Augustine's parish has an overarching theme, it is the unstinting determination with which a community of African-American Catholics has pursued its special Christian mission in the face of formidable challenges. Expression of this unique mission has varied as racial and socio-economic conditions have evolved in the nation's capital since Civil War times, but its essential character has remained unchanged. Russell Dillard's definition in 1991 might well have applied to the little congregation that opened a modest chapel and school on Fifteenth Street in 1866:

The Church generally has a mission to bring the word of God to the community. An African-American Catholic church has the mission to bring that word in a way that liberates people, frees them from all kinds of bondage, gives them a sense of self worth. It lifts people not only spiritually, but with the power of knowledge and of self-empowerment.[1]

For fourteen decades the priests and people of St. Augustine's have worked diligently and sacrificed much in pursuit of spirituality, knowledge, and self-empowerment, each generation emphasizing a variety of techniques, sometimes startlingly innovative, always deeply committed to succeed.

1. Extract from a homily addressed to St. Augustine's congregation on 24 June 1991 as quoted in Cliff Peale's "Washington Reporting," cy in SAA.

For the founding generation the goals and challenges were unambiguous. Free and relatively prosperous Washingtonians, many of them heirs of a religious tradition that stretched back to the earliest days of colonial America, these black Catholics wanted a place to worship free from the racial inequities that infected the American Church of those times and a school for their children in a city that shunned their educational needs. Their success was spectacular. In the face of formidable financial hardship they sponsored a flourishing parochial school and Sunday school and built one of the city's most imposing churches, where the beauty of the liturgy attracted distinguished visitors of all races and religions and a steady stream of converts from among the African Americans who had come to live in Washington.

Among these newcomers were large numbers of the so-called aristocrats of color, accomplished educators, many associated with Howard University and leaders in the city's public school system, along with some of the physicians, government employees, and successful entrepreneurs who had made Washington a mecca for black talent and influence in that era. These articulate leaders increasingly came to resist restrictions imposed by law and custom on the rights of African Americans as citizens and as Catholics. Their leadership in organizations ranging from the venerable Congress of Colored Catholics, the NAACP, the Federation of Colored Catholics, and in later times the Catholic Interracial Council thrust St. Augustine's into the forefront of the fight for racial justice in the capital. Their heirs who joined in the March on Washington in 1963 were only continuing a parish tradition that predated America's civil rights movement.

Every achievement, it seems, grew out of a sustained determination to overcome a serious challenge. For example, the financial dislocations of the Great Depression combined with demographic changes in wartime Washington to force a greatly reduced congregation to give up its beloved church in 1947. The survivors responded with a revived commitment to social activism, which not only proved fruitful in spreading the Good News, but also made a congregation, once again growing in size, "Come Alive" (as the slogan put it) to a renewed sense of unity, vitality, and commitment. In fact the willingness on the part of each generation to assume responsibility for the needs of its neighbors—in Msgr. Dillard's words, "freeing them from all kinds of bondage"—was another continuum linking the parish's founders to their sophisticated twentieth-century heirs. Despite the complexity of today's urban problems, parish efforts in recent times to work on behalf of the dispossessed and downtrodden clearly echo the work of earlier generations to welcome newly freed men and women, educate their children, shelter their orphans, and support their indigent.

Ironically, the latest challenge to face St. Augustine's grew out of the successful effort of Washington's archbishops to enforce racial justice in the local church. The decision of Archbishop Spalding in 1867 to dedicate the parish to the exclusive care of the city's black Catholics—a situation analogous to the so-called national or ethnic parishes being created at that time for the newly arriving immigrant groups—marked an accommodation to the realities of race relations in post–Civil War America. Racially separated parishes were preserved and enhanced by his successors during the long reign of Jim Crow. Yet if a racially separated St. Augustine's would be viewed by progressives as a lapse in the Church's commitment to the Gospel, it also must be admitted such detachment encouraged the development of a vibrant, cohesive congregation that realized the many spiritual, cultural, and social achievements celebrated in this history.

The reforms of Cardinal O'Boyle and his successors integrated the diocese's congregations and encouraged Catholics to attend and support their local parish. In keeping with these policies, St. Augustine's became a territorial parish in 1961 with responsibility for all Catholics in the western Shaw region of the city. The implications of this change were muted at first. When the definition of parish membership relaxed in the days following Vatican II, the soul-satisfying liturgy, the evidence of a rich African-American heritage, and the exciting commitment to social activism drew increasing numbers of black Catholics from all over the area to worship regularly at what was popularly called "The Mother Church of Black Catholics." In effect, Archbishop Spalding's idea of a national black parish was now accepted by progressive voices as a tradition worthy of preservation.

At the same time St. Augustine's exciting liturgy and commitment to social activism was also bound to attract many progressive white Catholics to the parish, some of whom quickly indicated their determination to join the congregation. This attraction coincided with a pro-

found change in the local neighborhood. The so-called gentrification of
the old streets introduced many new white Catholic residents to the
area, even as the Latino population of the Mt. Pleasant region, including many Catholics, began to spread across the parish's northern and
western boundaries. Some of these new neighbors began to look to
their local parish for sustenance. Clearly, a culturally diverse congregation, the goal of generations of crusaders for racial justice, also
posed a serious challenge to those seeking to preserve the parish's
African-American culture and traditions. Parish leaders of the 1980s
were of one mind. St. Augustine's must remain true to its tradition as a
parish ready to welcome all comers. At the same time the notion of
cultural diversity, of being all things to all people, must be rejected.
They made their intentions explicit in a mission statement published
in 1988 and still embraced today:

> . . . St. Augustine's Church continues in the tradition in which it was
> founded, namely as a strong Black Catholic institution which witnesses in
> faith to the Living God, His Son, and the Holy Spirit. St. Augustine's will con-
> tinue to be a center which recognizes, proclaims, and preserves our Black Ro-
> man Catholic heritage . . .

Each generation of parishioners has faced its challenges. To preserve its mission of evangelization, education, and social activism, to
lift its people spiritually "with the power of knowledge and self-empowerment," to open its doors to all comers—to do all this while preserving its essential charism as a black Catholic institution—is the
daunting challenge facing today's priests and people.

APPENDIX I ❧ THE GIFTS OF MUSIC

Music has played an essential role in the history of St. Augustine's. Across the decades scores of talented parishioners have raised their voices in praise of God, fully conscious that their art served other causes as well. From the first the quality of sacred music in the church not only enhanced the meaning of the liturgy, but also attracted a large audience of visitors, black and white, Catholic and non-Catholic. Music has been a major factor in the decision of many white Catholics to become parishioners in all but name. Martin Luther King Jr.'s observation that Sunday mornings were the most segregated time in America did not apply to St. Augustine's, whose congregation at Sunday masses and vespers was fully integrated during the long reign of Jim Crow in Washington. This contribution to the advance of race relations in the capital deserves to be celebrated.

Music also served the cause of evangelization. Ironically, at different times in its history the parish seemed to attract converts and lapsed Catholics precisely because its art ran contrary to popular conceptions. In early decades the grandeur of European masterworks performed by African Americans accompanied by a regal pipe organ occasionally supplemented by full orchestra drew people who had come to disdain the unsophisticated services of their fundamentalist Protestant churches. In recent times, the rhythms and harmonies of gospel music have attracted many newcomers hungry for worship that exploited this unique African-American art form in a fusion with the soul-satisfying Roman ritual. In every era racial pride and racial self-awareness have played a role. Parishioners have always taken great satisfaction from the fact that in times of both triumph and trial their choirs have been recognized as important repositories of culture in the capital. They could not help but be pleased when a vespers service in their church in the early days of Emancipation prompted Frederick Douglass to remark, "St. Augustine's is the colored people's pride."[1] Judging by frequent notice in both the secular and religious press, the parish's senior choir in the nineteenth century, its sanctuary choir of men and boys in the World War I era, and the gospel choir of recent times, have led the area's professional musicians and critics to conclude that St. Augustine's possessed special abilities, which contributed greatly to the musical life of the city.

Not to be overlooked, these musical forces also contributed significantly to the material well-being of the parish. In testament to the ability of these musicians, audiences across the decades have paid money to hear them perform. On several occasions the ability to earn money through its music rescued a parish in financial crisis. Nor have performances been limited to churches and concert halls of Washington. Once they toured nearby East Coast cities; in recent times St. Augustine's singers have sung at the Kennedy Center, appeared on national television, and jetted to Rome. Longtime parishioner Mary C. Buckner summed up the feelings of those who had endured the dreary decades of economic struggle. "It's important to remember," she once told a pastor trying to resolve the competing needs of the parish's ministries, "that the choir sustained us through the hard times and everything must be done to preserve its excellence, because it will be there to save us when hard times come again."[2] Buckner, whose roots can be traced to the founders of the parish, knew whereof she spoke.

The Esputa Era

It is not known whether St. Matthew's ever availed itself of the musical talents of its African-American parishioners before the Civil War, but while that conflict still raged a small group of black singers staged a benefit performance to raise money for the school and chapel planned for Fifteenth Street. Shortly after the chapel opened its doors in February 1866, its congregation organized a 14-voice choir under the direction of William T. Benjamin and accompanied by Mary T. Smith on a small reed organ. (The following year Henry Jackson replaced Benjamin as director, while Katie Jackson assumed the duties of organist.)[3] None of these musicians were pro-

1. Quoted in an intv. with J. H. Beadle printed in the *Yenowine's Illustrated News* [Milwaukee, WI], 10 May 1894, repr in *St. Joseph's Advocate* 3, no. 1 (Jul 1894): 601–2.

2. Buckner's remarks as recalled by Father Raymond Kemp in intv. with author, 13 May 1997.

3. *The New Century*, 21 Feb 1903. Members of the parish's first choir included: Agnes Gray, Magdaline Coakley, Caroline Jones and Victoria Queen, sopranos; Mary

fessionally trained, nor was much available to them in the way of hymnals
and sheet music. Nevertheless, considering the number of those who would
later go on to local prominence as performers in the St. Augustine choir and
the Colored American Opera Troupe, the group must have possessed singers
with impressive natural talent ready for molding into a first-rate professional ensemble.

Their chance came when John Esputa became director in 1868.[4] This
experienced teacher immediately recruited more members and thoroughly
rehearsed the four sections in the classics of sacred music. The soloists—
sopranos Jane Smallwood and Lena Miller, altos Mary Coakley and Mrs.
William Smith, tenor Frank Soevyn, and basses William Benjamin and
Thomas H. Williams—received individual coaching and were encouraged
to enlarge their repertoires to included popular operetta literature. Soon the
rare opportunity to hear the masses and motets of Haydn, Mozart, and other
European masters was attracting overflow congregations to the tiny chapel.
On Easter Sunday in 1873, for example, the choir performed Haydn's
Solemn Mass in Honor of the Blessed Virgin and Antonio Diabelli's *Gaudea-
mus* accompanied by a small orchestra of trumpets, horns, and strings. By
October it had mastered Mozart's *Holy Trinity Mass* and a trio by Mer-
cadante, the latter first sung at a Sunday vespers service.[5] Even after discounting the hyperbole in local reportage of those days, it is difficult to ignore the regular attendance of some of Washington's most distinguished music lovers in the little chapel or the frequent discussion in the press about
the cultural contributions being made by this young group.

One review of the 1873 Easter services noted that "members of the celebrated colored opera troupe" formed part of the chorus in the Haydn Mass.
As mentioned elsewhere in this history, the Colored American Opera
Troupe, organized by William Benjamin and T. Harry Donahue and trained
by Professor Esputa, began in 1873 performing operettas in Washington and
on "tour to the North" as one news account put it. The first operatic organization "in the history of the country . . . composed entirely of colored ladies
and gentlemen," raised substantial sums for the parish. Nor was the fact
that such a culturally ambitious enterprise been undertaken in Washington

---

Coakley, Margaret Gray, Katie Howard, and Mrs. George Thomas, altos; James Neuby,
Francis Jones, and Augustus Myers, tenors; and James Bowman, Gabriel Coakley, and
William Benjamin, bassos.

4. On Esputa's work at St. Augustine's, see chapter 2, above.

5. *CM*, 19 Apr and 11 Oct 1873. The *Mirror* gave frequent notice to the choir, both
its programs and personnel. See, for example, *CM*, 24 Feb 1872, 4 Jan and 12 Jul
1873.

less than a decade after emancipation lost on the press. Reporters congratulated the performers for demonstrating the "remarkable musical abilities" of
African Americans and advised those readers interested in fine music to attend the final performances for 1873, which were presented in the city's
large and well-equipped Wall's Opera House.[6] In fact the company's first
presentation at the smaller Lincoln Hall had drawn an audience of 1,500,
about one-third white. Typical of nineteenth-century music reviews, the patrons received as much attention as the performers. The *Evening Star* reported on the "large and fashionable audience, including those lovers of
music in the city who patronize the Italian and French opera," and whose
enthusiasm "was aroused to a high pitch by the ringing choruses" of the
troupe.[7] Some accounts mentioned the performers' lack of acting experience, but the music critic of the *National Republican* singled out Jane
Smallwood and T. H. Williams for both their singing and acting while noting
that Richard Tompkins and William Benjamin "added materially by their
conception of the play to the success of the evening."[8]

The consecration of the new church on Trinity Sunday 1876 included a
music presentation described as "perhaps the grandest ever heard in Washington."[9] Director Esputa's forces included an orchestra of 18 brass and
string instruments and a 30-voice chorus supplementing the parish choir.
Soloists for the occasion included Jane Smallwood, Mary Coakley, Henry
Grant, and William Benjamin. Vespers that evening featured the U.S. Marine Corps Band playing LeJeal's *Solemn Vespers* orchestrated by John
Philip Sousa. The dedication marked the first of several occasions when
the famous American composer would perform at St. Augustine's. During
the next decade the choir would sing other compositions orchestrated especially for it by the music world's march king and Esputa's best-known student.[10]

Concert performances by the opera troupe with the parish choir in those
times were the first of many efforts on behalf of the building fund. During
the years of economic depression in the 1870s the group staged several con-

6. *National Republican*, Jan 1873, as quoted in *CM*, 1 Feb 1873. See also *Evening Star*, 23 May 1873.

7. *Evening Star*, 13 May 1873. See also the *Star*, 10 May 1873.

8. *National Republican*, Jan 1873, as quoted in *CM*, 1 Feb 1873.

9. Major Edmond Mallet, "St. Augustine's Church," *The Fair Gazette*, 13 Feb 1882.

10. See *CM*, 17 Jun 1876, for a description of the dedication ceremony along with the names of the choir members at that time. Sousa's contribution to the parish's music program is reported in *CM*, 1 and 7 Apr 1888. A careful search of St. Augustine's archives has failed to uncover a trace of Sousa's orchestrations, and they must unfortunately be considered lost.

certs that raised money to buy materials and pay the workers raising the walls of the new church. Small wonder that these parishioners, abetted by their pastor, Father Barotti, pressed for the installation of a first-class organ in the new building despite the archbishop's call for a moratorium on nonessential spending. The $14,000 instrument, built by the Baltimore firm of Heiler and Schumekleer, contained 34 speaking stops arranged on 2 manuals. Although the organ would be considerably enlarged in later years, its exterior casing of walnut and oak with its sixteen-foot gilt pipes framing the rose window remained unchanged until the church's razing in 1948.[11] The parish hired "Professor" Charles Thierbach to play the instrument and no doubt recruited boys to work the pump that supplied the wind chests in the days before electric motors.

Like many artists, director Esputa seemed to pay scant notice to minor details like money. Despite the parish's crushing debt, he employed "a powerful chorus" to assist the choir in a performance of Millard's *Vespers* on Easter Sunday 1877, and three months later assembled the orchestral forces needed to present Haydn's *Imperial Mass* to mark the golden Jubilee of Pope Pius IX. By November an augmented choir was rehearsing for a Christmas performance of Paolo Giorza's *Mass* with orchestration by Sousa.[12]

The relative immaturity of the choir in those days adds to the amazement, when one considers the number of new and difficult masterworks it added to its repertoire each year. At a vespers service in February 1878 it sang Mozart's *Magnificat* with its demanding parts for solo quartet just hours after performing one of Haydn's grand masses. That day produced a review by the correspondent of an Ohio newspaper that typified the frequently voiced opinion of local critics. Exhibiting the racially insensitive attitudes of the day, he began by discussing the difficulty and culturally significant compositions being performed, adding "I mention these facts to impress you with the idea these are *negroes!*" But the power of the performance seemed to overwhelm prejudice:

Under the leadership of Professor John Esputa's, whose name and fame as musician is of the first order and stands no. 1 in Washington City, add to this a chorus of forty-two well-trained voices, an organ of 24 stops played by Professor Thierbach, who in his beautiful combination of flute and violincellos, blended with the bourdon, followed by the reed stops, the sixteenths, and this with the swell

11. For a full description of the organ's specifications, see *CM*, 20 May 1876.

12. *CM*, 7 Apr, 9 Jun, and 17 Nov 1877. Giorza's *Mass* was first sung by the choir at the opening of the first Colored Catholic Congress the previous January. See *CM*, 5 Jan 1889.

organ coupled with choir organ, all concluding with the metallic clash of the double gamba, overpowered by the immense choral wave, and you will have some idea of St. Augustine's choir.

Adding that foreign ministers, members of Congress, and the aristocracy in general were frequently seen in the church, the correspondent concluded that "the elite and upper citizens generally consider it their special privilege to be present." [13]

These performances marked the climax of Esputa's career. Sometime in 1878 illness forced him to seek recuperation in sunny Florida. Expecting his early return the parish arranged for the temporary services of Leonard Glannon, a noted singer and director of both St. Matthew's and St. Aloysius' choirs and, at his departure, Professor Basildi, a well-known Washington musician. Basildi led the now 40-voice choir when it sang a *Requiem* composed by John Esputa at Father Barotti's funeral in 1881. He also conducted the choir in a "grand concert" at Lincoln Hall when a large Washington audience paid fifty cents each to hear popular and religious selections, all for the benefit of the church's debt association. [14]

Only after Esputa's death in 1882 did the parish decide on a new director. With the 1882–83 music season in full swing, Charles Thierbach, the organist, assumed control of a choir dubbed by one New York critic as "second to none at the national capital." [15] Thierbach appeared determined to carry on in the grand tradition of his predecessor. On St. Augustine's feast day in 1883 he led the choir, accompanied by a full orchestra, in Carl Maria von Weber's *Missa Sancta*, and in succeeding months the congregation heard Mozart's *Twelfth Mass* with chorus and orchestra, and the first performance of Weber's *Mass in C* in Washington. This outpouring of new and difficult music fulfilled the *Catholic Mirror's* prediction that under its new leader the reputation of the choir "would suffer no diminution." [16] Although William Benjamin's bass would continue to ring through the church for many years, the rest of the early soloists were gradually replaced. By 1883 Martina Irving had begun her many years as the choir's principal soprano, to be joined in succeeding seasons by alto Lavinia Dey (later the wife of Dr. William Lofton) and tenor Ignatius Jackson. In 1886 Dey organized a 25-voice children's choir recruited from among the Sunday school students. This group, which Dey directed from the organ, sang at the parish's chil-

13. Quoted in *CM*, 2 Feb 1878.

14. *CM*, 28 Oct 1882. See also *The Fair Gazette*, 10 Feb 1882.

15. Quoted in *CM*, 28 Oct 1882.

16. *CM*, 8 Jul 1883. The *Mirror* kept its readers fully informed of the choir's programs through these years. See various issues, 1883–88.

dren's mass every Sunday and proved a source of talent for the senior choir, who recruited youthful members after their graduation.

Illness forced Thierbach to arrange for substitutes for increasing periods during 1887; when he retired the following year, one of them, George Isemann, was appointed director. Isemann was probably the best-trained musician to lead the choir. A graduate of Leipzig University's prestigious conservatory, he was a pupil of Franz Liszt and had served as professor of music at the Washington Conservatory and Georgetown College. For both directing and accompanying the choir, this skilled musician received an annual salary of $400.[17] During Cardinal Gibbons's visit to the parish in November 1888, Isemann led the choir and Shroeder's orchestra (a professional ensemble well known to Washington audiences) in music by Mozart and Handel. Obviously moved by the performance, the cardinal declared it the best he had heard in his archdiocese, diplomatically adding "outside the Cathedral at Baltimore." Others made no such subtle distinctions. The popular national journalist Frank Carpenter reported that so famous had St. Augustine's choir become that "many strangers include a service [at the church] in their sight-seeing program."[18] In fact, during Isemann's brief tenure, the choir gained a reputation for professionalism that appeared to set the standard for Catholic church music in Washington.[19]

The records fail to explain why Isemann left after just four years, but his departure introduced a period of rapid and unsettled change. Anton Gloetzner, another European-trained musician who had served with several Washington churches, led the choir for several months before the parish hired a 28-year old member of the Marine Corps Band, Arthur Tregina, as

17. The parish's expenditures for music in addition to Isemann's stipend in 1888 included $120 for junior choir organist and $47 for music. See parish financial report, reprinted in *CM*, 19 Jan 1889. See also *CM*, 18 Mar and 7 Oct 1888, and *CN*, 10 Jul 1887, on change in directors.

18. *Carp's Washington*, p. 239. Carpenter's observation was made ca. 1885. The cardinal's comment was reported in *CM*, 1 Dec 1888. See also *CN*, 2 Dec 1888,

19. Members of this famous group in the 1880s and early 1890s included (among others): Martina Irving, Anna E. Swann, Blanche Ferguson, Anna Dey, Mary Simms, Annie Johnson, Clara Wheeler, Susie B. Green, Lulu Prater, Mary Martin, Gertrude Smith, Flora Cole, Julia Johnson, Mary E. Weldon, Carrie Hawkins, sopranos; Lavinia Lofton, Carrie Johnson, Marie C. James, Agnes Robinson, Ada Jackson, Hannah Johnson, Lulu Hamilton, Julia Johnson, Phoebe Broughton, altos; John Ignatius Jackson, James A. Simms, Vincent Duvall, William Goodrich, Frank M. Parkham, George A. Lemon, Dr. A. T. Augusta, William J. Smith, John B. Kelly, F. Dionysius Jackson, tenors; and William Benjamin, John F. Cole, W. T. Benjamin, Jr., Nace Jackson, A. Waldron, Arthur Chesley, and Harry Radcliffe, J. E. Battly, Dr. Radley, and Richard Spriggs, basses.

director and William Braxton as organist. Tregina lasted just two years before Gloetzner returned, promising to reorganize the group.[20] Actually, under Gloetzner the choir continued to add to its classic repertoire. On Trinity
Sunday 1896 the congregation heard Beethovan's *Mass in C* for the first
time. Important compositions by Hummel and Wagner were also introduced.
Yet for reasons unexplained, membership in the choir began to shrink, and
in October 1899 Madame J. Esputa-Daly, daughter of the first director, assumed command with Jennie Glennon as organist. Esputa-Daly promised to
reorganize the choir, which the *Church News* noted, had retained its enviable reputation "in spite of its deterioration in recent years."[21]

Although Esputa-Daly's three years with the choir did not allow for significant additions to the choir's repertoire, it was unlikely that she would
have contemplated any change from the grandiose presentations in the Esputa tradition that had become the choir's hallmark. Her first priority
seemed to be enlarging her musical forces to better execute the old, large-
scale works. The size of the choir was expanded, and the pastor was pressed
to enlarge and modernize the organ. Father Griffith, who had inaugurated
the annual pastor's dinner for the choir (a tradition of good food and music
that would continue unbroken for decades), always seemed prepared to support the parish's musical aspirations. In 1901 he signed a contract with the
Adam Stein Company of Baltimore to rebuild the organ, paying $5,080 to
install a 3-manual, 54-stop instrument with a crescendo pedal operating all
speaking stops. The dedication of this musical monster, held in April 1903,
featured several of the area's prominent organists showing the instrument's
capabilities with music by Mendelssohn, Wagner, Saint-Saens, and Dubois
while the choir sang works of Haydn and Wagner's mighty chorus from
Tannhauser.[22]

The dedication recital included a violin solo by Anton Kasper, the new
director of the choir. The European-trained Kasper, with Mary Mullaly serving as organist, continued to polish the 35-voice choir that now boasted ten
principal singers (the indefatigable William Benjamin completing his thir-
ty-sixth year as bass soloist). Although it is unlikely that Kasper introduced
the choir to any new music, he obviously maintained its high standard of
performance. The disciplined singing, often accompanied by his violin, con-

20. *CN*, 12 Oct 1895.

21. *CN*, 7 Oct 1899. See also, same publication, 20 Jan 1900. Glennon would later
gain notice as director of St. Patrick's choir.

22. The speaker at the dedication was the noted orator Rev. Dr. Denis Stafford,
pastor of St. Patrick's. For documents related to the purchase of the organ, its
specifications and its dedication, see organ file, SAA.

tinued to attract a large audience. In an appreciative article in 1905, the *Washington Post* called St. Augustine's "a mecca for lovers of sacred music" where whites as well as blacks "throng" to its services. Another paper of the times marveled at the general mixing of the races at mass, calling it "a condition [that] will scarcely be found in any other southern city." It attributed this phenomenon mainly to the fact that the parish "had reached a high place in the esteem of local music lovers, particularly those who have a penchant for sacred music."[23]

The Sanctuary Choir

Ironically, the elevated reputation of the parish choir coincided with a move by the Vatican to curtail the use of polyphonic music in the liturgy. The theatrical presentations at St. Augustine's were mirrored in many other large parishes, where corps of earnest sopranos and altos formed the major resource of the choirs. Few American parishes were prepared for the changes now demanded of them. In 1903 Pope Pius X issued a *motu proprio* that called for the elimination of female voices and modern harmonies from the liturgy and the reinstatement of Gregorian chant as the norm in western church music. This decree, scheduled to go into effect in six years, imposed an impossible burden on American parishes, where the European tradition of training boys in the choral arts was unknown and the expertise and money to support such an effort nonexistent. Cardinal Gibbons tried to soften the blow. He noted that few churches were ready at once to follow the pope's "advice" concerning female voices and that "some time must elapse before the full letter of the instructions can be carried out."[24] Meanwhile, he appointed a commission to propose a suitable diocesan response. Although St. Augustine's, like other large choirs in the city, continued to perform the polyphonic masterpieces that had made it famous, some accommodation was made to the pope's wishes when the parish organized a sanctuary choir of men and boys.

Thanks to the efforts of Lavinia Dey Lofton and public school music teacher Annie Savoy and others, many parish children already had some idea of music performance. The junior choir continued to sing in church, and throughout the 1890s large groups of young singers had been recruited to perform at parish functions. In 1891, for example, fifty youngsters presented the Washington premier of *Messiah*, a cantata composed by the Jesuit Fa-

23. *Washington Post*, 20 May 1905 (first quote); *Evening Star*, n.d. (ca Sep 1905) (other quotes).

24. As quoted in the *Washington Post*, 5 Mar 1904.

ther Healy. One music critic singled out Bessie Cole for her performance in the role of the Virgin Mary. In 1895 the junior choir staged an operetta, and three years later their performance in the cantata *The Berry Pickers* was the highlight of a financially successful parish May festival.[25]

As early as 1908 Sunday school teacher John F. Cole, himself a violinist and singer, was promoting the idea of training young voices in Gregorian chant. Only in 1912, however, was such a program finally organized: Father Olds, then an assistant priest, persuaded his brother, musician Leo F. Olds, to take on the task of training young school boys to participate in a new choir of men and boys which, suitably robed, would participate in the liturgy from its designated space in the sanctuary.[26] It was a daunting assignment. Most of the members, especially the boys, had no knowledge of Latin and little vocal training. Nevertheless with a strenuous effort a sanctuary choir of fifty men and boys had learned enough chant to assist in Holy Week services in 1912. The choir made rapid progress, quickly acquiring the characteristic and immensely satisfying timbre associated with the famed English choristers. Soon the beauty of the Divine Office chanted by these young male voices became a regular feature of Sunday vespers service. In November 1913 the apostolic delegate, Archbishop John Bonzano, was on hand to hear the men and boys, decked out in cassocks and surplices, intone for the first time the responses and Gregorian Proper of the liturgy while the senior choir performed a Haydn mass.[27]

Until then the new choir had limited itself to chant, but in 1914 it began to experiment with polyphony, performing a harmonized version of the vespers service for the first time. Good Friday 1914 marked its first performance of Theodore Dubois's *The Seven Last Words of Christ*, an enormously popular cantata designed to accompany prayers and meditations suitable to that feast. Father James O'Connor, an associate pastor at that time, was heard in the solo baritone parts of a work that became an annual presentation of the choir until its dissolution. (The Dubois cantata would later be taken up by the senior choir, which continued to perform the work into recent decades.)

Nor did Leo Olds restrict his talented group to church music. Beginning in June 1913 it staged an annual performance of an operetta whose music was appropriated from popular songs of the day but with a book written ex-

25. All these performances gained generous notice in the diocesan paper. See, for example, *CM*, 10 Jan 1891; 28 Dec 1895, and 28 May and 4 Jun 1898.

26. A detailed account of the organization of the new choir was published by Father Olds in the *BCR*, 4 Apr 1925, and is the basis for the following paragraphs.

27. *BCR*, 29 Nov 1913.

SANCTUARY CHOIR OF MEN AND BOYS introduced the parish to the rich tradition of Gregorian chant in the post-World War I era.

pressly for the occasion by its multi-talented director. Large, paying crowds gathered for evenings of musical comedy with titles like *The Pretender, The Mummy Princess,* and *A Romance of Old Japan,* in which nine- and ten-year-old boys acted and sang both male and female parts in two-hour, costumed performances. Father Olds later recalled perennial stars of the shows like the "rotund" Leo Spriggs and the "diminutive" Cardinal Carter, who enthralled audiences with their comedic acting and beautiful voices.[28]

The choir suffered a serious blow when Leo Olds died in 1917. Although George H. Wells and Charles Plummer tried to keep it going, little was achieved until 1920 when Father Olds, now pastor and determined to carry

28. Other members of the original choir included John Jones, James Plummer, Charles Miles, Milton Dorsey, George Quander, Leo Holton, Eugene Butler, and Romeo and Russell Bowser. For a more comprehensive list of choristers, see programs of annual plays and concerts, SAA.

on his brother's work, hired Henry T. (Harry) Hall as director. Hall had already demonstrated his expertise in training young male voices at St. Patrick's. In succeeding years he increased the proficiency of St. Augustine's choristers and enlarged their repertoire. In addition to providing the chant responses during the liturgy, the busy group prepared for performance such major oratorios as Gounod's *Gallia* and Stainer's *Crucifixion*. Hall also kept up the tradition of an annual musical comedy for a while, producing a reprieve of *The Starry Flag* for the benefit of the parish debt fund.[29] Under Hall, the sanctuary choir began to make appearances throughout the city. At the invitation of the Cuban ambassador it sang at a benefit for Cuban orphanages in Carroll Hall in 1924. The following year a standing-room only crowd filled Howard Theater to hear the choir sing a benefit concert for the Holy Name Guild. In 1925 the men and boys traveled to Baltimore for another benefit. These later concerts highlighted the performance of the choir's most famous singer, twelve-year-old boy soprano Ira Merriwether.[30]

Father Olds was especially proud of the sanctuary choir. In 1926 he had a fully-equipped practice room built for it in the church basement. He had just received permission from Archbishop Curley to stage the choir's concerts in the church itself. The persnickety Curley set conditions: the music must be "altogether" sacred; the Blessed Sacrament must be removed and, if possible, the altar screened from sight; and applause "of any kind whatsoever" was forbidden.[31] An obedient pastor duly inserted a stern warning across the program of the first concert held that May: "By the order of his Grace the Archbishop of Baltimore, DO NOT APPLAUD after the various numbers."

This concert was especially notable because, as nearly as can be ascertained, it marked the first time a St. Augustine choir performed works that reflected the African-American heritage of the congregation. Harmonized renditions of *Sweet and Low* and *Deep River* took their place in a program that also included works by Haydn, Mendelssohn, and Weber. First brought to the attention of the music public before the turn of the century by the Fisk Jubilee Singers and other groups, the so-called Negro Spirituals—actually the sacred folk songs of a people in bondage—were by 1925 being

29. Interestingly, this patriotic musical was first performed during the war in the period after Leo Olds's death, a time, according to Father Olds, when the group was foundering. See *BCR*, 1 Jun 1918.

30. Merriwether was the recipient of much newspaper notice. See, for example, *BCR*, 18 Dec 1921 and 18 Apr 1925.

31. Ltr., Curley to Olds, 13 Feb 1926, O-951, Curley Papers, AAB. On cost of the practice room, see *Notitae*, 1926.

sung in choir lofts and concert halls across the country in arrangements made by scholars like Harry T. Burleigh, James Weldon, and Howard University's William L. Dawson.[32] Judging by their programs, St. Augustine's musicians appeared little interested in such music, even though in succeeding years many parishioners could be found in the large audiences attending concerts of spirituals and gospel music by the Roland Hayes Choir and other artists. One possible explanation for their seeming indifference was the fact that Catholic choirs were caught up in discussions of acceptable music in church. They listened, for example, to visitors like Father J. Leo Barley, the director of the diocesan music committee, who defined what constituted music "proper" to a Catholic service.[33] His warning about appropriate musical decorum in the house of God and emphasis on the necessary subservience of music clearly demonstrated that, in those pre–Vatican II days, such experts did not fully appreciate the varied role music could play in the liturgy.

For all the attention paid young singers in the previous decade, the sanctuary choir slowly faded into obscurity after Henry Hall assumed responsibility for the senior choir in the late 1920s. Some of its members joined the senior choir, but the chant so ardently championed by musical purists gradually ceased being heard in the parish except at tenebrae services during Holy Week. Even that was short-lived. By 1937 tenebrae was being chanted by the Hermits of St. Augustine, as the Augustinian Friars were then called. In succeeding years the parish made do with the services of Augustinian seminarians or students from one of the other houses of study at Catholic University for this beautiful Holy Week service.[34] In fact the sanctuary choir, like most such American groups, had only a limited amount of plainsong available to them and quickly came to compete with the polyphonic renditions of the senior choir. Only after World War II and the work done by the Benedictines at Solesmes in France did the world gain access to and a renewed appreciation for the vast literature of Gregorian music.

Other outlets opened for the musically talented youngsters in the congregation. The junior choir continued to function during the 1930s under

32. "A Historical Account of the Negro Spiritual," *Songs of Zion*, J. Jefferson Cleveland, ed. (Nashville: Abingdon Press, 1981), pp. 73ff.

33. On Barley's talk at St. Augustine's, see *BCR*, 24 Jan 1930. The subject was also discussed in the parish magazine. See C. A. Benson, "The Choir and the Congregation," *St. Augustine's Parish Review*, Feb 1932, and Barley, "An Observation," same source, Mar 1932, copies in SAA.

34. Notice of the Hermits appeared in the *St. Augustine's Parish Review*, 1937, cy in SAA.

the direction of Dr. Euphemia Haynes.[35] The musical and acting abilities of St. Augustine's youth were also exposed to an appreciative public in a series of operettas produced by the parish's Junior Activities Committee and directed by Lillian Clarke, a librarian in the public schools. Scores of young people, including several who would go on to impressive careers and leadership roles in the parish, sang and danced their way through productions of Gilbert and Sullivan's *Mikado* and *H.M.S. Pinafore* and dramatic crowd-pleasers like *Lelawala, the Maid of Niagara* and *The Sunbonnet Girl* before large audiences in the new auditorium on upper Fifteenth Street.[36]

Maintaining Musical Traditions

The senior choir inherited by Professor Hall in the mid-1920s had undergone considerable change in the preceding decade. Three directors, Mary Mullaly, Leo Stock (with the help of organist Agnes Dowling), and Margaret Walsh, had followed Anton Kasper in rapid succession. All well known from their work in local Catholic churches, they nevertheless found it difficult to maintain the choir's strength. Finally, just before Hall took over in 1920, director Walsh had launched a well-publicized membership drive that resulted in bringing the choir up to forty voices. (In succeeding years the choir would slowly shrink to thirty members, a number it would retain until 1979.)[37] A strong quartet of soloists, including the by-then legendary voices of Martina Irving and Ignatius Jackson, allowed the group to continue the noteworthy presentation of the large works of Haydn and Gounod, and the complicated psalm renditions of Johann Weiland. Several of the names associated with the parish's music program in later decades first appeared in the 1920s, including Martina Irving's daughters (one of whom, Katherine Dean, would remain a member until 1975!). During the 1920s Annie and Octavia Tillman joined, and at the end of the decade Eunice Quander (Taylor), then a junior high school student, successfully auditioned before Harry Hall for a place among the sopranos. Bernard Cole was

35. Dr. Haynes' work with the junior choir was reviewed in the *BCR*, 22 Mar 1924. Haynes was the daughter of the early civil rights leader Dr. William S. Lofton and Lavinia Day Lofton, her predecessor in the choir.

36. Among the stars of these productions were Juanita Smackum (Tolson), Bernard Cole, Charles Carter, Carlton Smith, Joseph Cole, Theodore Smith, Agnes Plummer, Eunice Quander, Joseph Johnson, and William Taylor. See programs for various productions, SAA. The *St. Augustine's Parish Review*, Feb 1932, advertised for cast members of that year's production of *Mikado*.

37. Notice of the membership campaign appeared in the *BCR*, 22 Mar 1924.

another long-time member first trained by Professor Hall during that period.[38]

Hall remained in charge until 1936. Although boasting a group of exceptionally fine voices and its professionalism underscored by the fact that its members could readily absorb the demanding scores assigned their sections, the choir would find it necessary to forego the extravagant presentations of earlier times. Severe budget constraints during the Depression precluded hiring orchestras and even the purchase of new music. When Marie Quander replaced the elderly Hall, her hard work and youthful enthusiasm seemed to overcome the disappointment the choir and congregation must have felt at the scaled-back program. The appointment of Quander marked several firsts for St. Augustine's: she was the first African American to hold the post, the first from Howard University's school of music, and the first to have been a member of the congregation. No doubt these assets helped her when, a very young professional in her first job, she faced her highly skilled group, many of whom had been singing together for years.

Quander would lead the choir through the dark days of World War II. When she left to work in other churches, she was succeeded by another trained musician, her cousin (Marian) Ophelia Quander. Ophelia was also a graduate of Howard University and had earned a Master's degree in music from New York University. She taught music in the D.C. public schools, which explained why her sister and choir member, Eunice, was frequently called on to substitute as organist at weddings and funerals. In many ways, Ophelia Quander must have felt the most frustration of any of St. Augustine's musical directors. It was she who turned the great pipe organ off for the last time on Christmas Day in 1946 before moving to the new church/auditorium with its tiny reed pump organ and makeshift space for the choir in a corner outside the altar rail. Everything of necessity became small scale. Inevitably tensions developed between the music director and the rectory and between a youthful Quander and some of her senior choristers over the scope and objectives of the music program. In such a setting, for example, a boys' choir performing simple hymns and chants would have been appropriate, but Quander's effort to organize a group failed. She remained in charge for several years, leading the choir through a reduced schedule, before finally leaving in 1950 to work with larger forces elsewhere.

After a brief period of uncertainty, the parish accepted the offer of one of the basses, George A. (Gus) Jackson, to take charge. Jackson was not a

38. Intv., author with Eunice Q. Taylor, 13 Dec 1997, and with Bernard and Julia Cole, 18 Dec 1997, copies in SAA. Unless otherwise indicated the following paragraphs are based on these interviews and one with George Dines, Jr., 30 Nov 1997.

THE SENIOR CHOIR on the eve of a recruitment campaign in 1919 under director Margaret Walsh (center). The fine attire of the musicians provides some indication of the social and economic standing of the congregation at the time.

trained musician, but he possessed two assets essential to a successful
leader: a sensitive musical ear and close rapport with his choir. Jackson was
a strict disciplinarian, well liked by his singers. Under his direction, music
suitable to the modest setting was introduced. A scaled-down version of
Gounod's *St. Cecilia's Mass* became part of the repertoire. Large new works
like Pergolesi's *Stabat Mater* were reserved for concert performances, where
the choir combined forces with its counterpart from nearby Holy Redeemer.
One member later recalled how this combination served both parishes well,
since it occurred at a time when St. Augustine's tenor section was especially
strong and its altos under strength, while Holy Redeemer possessed a strong
alto section but weak tenors. Jackson also introduced an important innova-

tion in a choir largely focused on masses and hymns sung in Latin. During what was then called Negro History Week, he led St. Augustine's musicians in their first performances of classic pieces from the Negro Spiritual litera- ture, including the haunting *My Lord What a Morning*.

Jackson enjoyed the confidence of Father Gingras, the new parish ad- ministrator. Gingras proved supportive so long as the director, who was paid $50 a month (a fee he was expected to share with the organist), did not threaten the parish's precariously balanced budget with outsized demands. In fact, Gingras personally led a fund drive that succeeded in raising enough money to purchase a small Baldwin electronic organ (with partial pedal board) to replace the old-fashioned reed instrument. (Early on, Jackson had prevailed upon Nancy A. Dines, a recent convert and wife of chorister George Dines, Sr., to serve as organist, a post she held with some interrup- tions until the parish's merger with St. Paul's in 1961.) Grateful for the parish's generosity, Jackson promised that, since the congregation at every mass had responded to Gingras's plea for the organ fund, the congregation at every mass would have music, either the choir itself or simply an organ ac- companiment for hymn singing.[39]

For a decade the congregation could watch the diminutive Jackson, just visible from his perch atop a high podium, leading the parish's musicians. His sudden death on New Year's Day 1961 forced the choir to find yet anoth- er leader. Again the musicians turned to one of their own, George Dines, Jr. Dines had been a full-time member for just three years, joining on his re- turn to Washington from prep school and college. In his words, he "just drifted into the job," accepting the assignment on a temporary basis before being appointed permanently. Dines, who had been raised in the parish and whose parents were long associated with the choir, had studied music theo- ry in college. Although one of the group's youngest members, he was re- spected for his musicianship, a respect shown him in later years by his col- leagues on the archdiocese's music commission.[40] Just weeks after taking charge, he led the choir in a series of concerts in Baltimore and Washington in memory of Gus Jackson and in honor of the Oblate Sisters of Providence.

The merger of SS. Paul and Augustine in September 1961 suddenly opened all sorts of musical possibilities. Dines assumed directorship of the combined group, although the already-reduced strength of old St. Paul's choir would quickly dwindle to a hearty few. More important, the music pro- gram once again enjoyed the support of a magnificent, albeit aging, pipe or-

39. Ltr., Jackson to Gingras, n.d. (ca 1957), SAA.

40. Intv., author with Father Paul F. Liston, 9 Dec 1997. Liston was the director of the music commission in the 1970s. See also author's intv. with George Dines, Jr.

gan. Leroy Merring, the St. Paul's organist, remained at his post with the combined choir. (A medical student, Merring was succeeded by his talented wife, Mildred, during his medical internship.) Some indication of the relative wealth of the two parishes at that time: St. Paul's paid its organist $350 per month; St. Augustine's choir director was still sharing his $50 per month stipend with his organist. Father Gingras questioned the inequity, but prudently decided that, since Dines was employed full-time elsewhere and Merring was a struggling student, they would retain their separate pay rates. (Dines would still be receiving $50 a month in 1977, when an embarrassed Father Kemp arranged for a modest raise.) During Dines's stewardship the parish employed seven organists. After the Merrings' departure in 1963, Ray Brubacher began his eleven-year stint. Brubacher had grown up in St. Paul's and had been playing its Moeller since his teen years. Even after he left to become the associate organist at St. Matthew's Cathedral, Brubacher spent countless hours performing temporary repairs to the Moeller organ in a losing struggle to keep the unique instrument going without resorting to the costly overhaul still beyond the parish's slender resources. He was followed by Richard Metcalfe and Jeff Tacy for intermittent tenures and then by Cathy Bounds. During Dines's directorship Joicey White played regularly at the 12:30 mass and filled in whenever needed at other services.

Maintaining the large pipe organ and a competent instrumentalist was important to Dines's philosophy as director. Although anxious to carry on the parish's traditional performance of classical church music, he had neither the money nor the desire to emulate his more flamboyant predecessors. When he introduced new masterworks like Faure's *Requiem* and new compositions, including the masses of Washington composer Reginald Bailey, they were presented with simple organ accompaniment. Enthusiasm for the lengthy masses of the great composers had cooled, and the call for the reform of church music had led to simpler liturgies. Large works like the Faure and Pergolesi were reserved for special occasions and presented in concert form. It was also at this time that St. Augustine's routinely joined forces with the choir from Augustana Lutheran Church, beginning with an annual ecumenical service on Thanksgiving Day.

Although Dines would occasionally introduce a modern composition, the choir for the most part continued to sing music with which it was comfortable, that is, the standard hymns and cantatas, usually in Latin and familiar to most accomplished Catholic choirs across the country. The idea of performing music derived from the congregation's African-American heritage never arose. Dines concentrated on improving the quality of performance—never an easy task, especially in a volunteer group with a high quotient of senior citizens. (At least four members were in the age eighty-and-

over group celebrated by Father Kemp and the parish in 1974.) On one occasion an exasperated director reported that only five members had shown
up for practice just one month before Holy Week. Reminding his singers of
his determination to maintain a strict schedule, he warned the choir that
members must attend two rehearsals a week until Easter, "at which time we
will evaluate the change."[41] The director's rehearsal problem stemmed in
part from his humane personnel policy. Dines figured that, in a volunteer organization where people had given so much for so long, they should be retained as long as they liked, even if they no longer contributed. His oldsters
included a few disoriented souls, but even here, Dines discovered, several
still sang well, and one such old timer was the mainstay of the alto section
with her strong and true voice.

Dines would remain in charge until 1979, his eighteen-year tenure the
longest in the choir's history. Although he would continue to involve himself
in the parish's musical life (he still leads the music at the 8 o'clock mass), he
agreed to make way for Leon Roberts. Father Kemp had requested the
change for two reasons. On the practical level, he needed to build up
Roberts's responsibilities in addition to his work in the gospel choir and the
parish school in order to justify a full-time, living wage. But most of all
Kemp hoped that unifying the choirs under one director would neutralize the
tension and rivalry between the two groups—natural enough perhaps among
supporters of the two musical styles, but detrimental to a unified parish on
the move.

The Gospel Choir and Chorale

Actually Leon Roberts was closely associated with the parish for more
than two years before he assumed the post of music director in the fall of
1979.[42] St. Augustine's, like most Catholic parishes in those post–Vatican II
years, had gone through its folk-music phase in the 1970s, although its amateur guitar-accompanied hymnody had for the most part been limited to the
9:30 Sunday mass. During those years the chapel at 1419 V Street had hosted a gathering of Hispanic Catholics, whose Sunday liturgy featured the exciting rhythms and tempos of their Latin American heritage. That group
quickly outgrew the chapel and moved elsewhere, but its example was not
lost on the parish. Father Kemp, for one, was anxious to exploit the similar-

41. Ltr., Dines to choir members, 4 Mar 1969, cy in SAA.

42. Author's intv. with Roberts, 12 Jan 1998. Unless otherwise noted the following
section is based on this extensive interview and the author's interviews with George
Dines, Fathers Kemp and Mudd, and Pauline J. Jones.

ly exciting and attractive gospel music that had made black Protestant
church services so appealing and which was finally coming to the attention
of the Catholic Church through the efforts of Father Clarence Rivers,
Grayson Warren Brown, and other pioneer liturgists. Holy Comforter–St.
Cyprian's and St. Benedict the Moor already had gospel choirs. In December 1976 at the suggestion of Cathy Bounds, the parish organist and a member of the Howard University gospel and concert choirs, Kemp asked
Roberts to lead the gospel choir at SS. Paul and Augustine. It was a shrewd
choice. Roberts's work with the Howard choirs and with Roberts Revival, a
small ensemble of gospel singers he organized during his student days, had
marked him as a young professional of exceptional musical and organizational talents.

Roberts had at first refused. He was already busy directing the choir at
Mount Zion Baptist Church in northwest Washington, and his strict Pentecostal rearing had left him, he later admitted, ignorant of and prejudiced
against the Catholic Church. But Kemp persisted. He knew that the
arrangement with Earl Woodliff to organize a gospel group was a temporary
solution because of that musician's commitment to Holy Comforter–St.
Cyprian's, so he was back a month later renewing the offer to Roberts. This
time Roberts agreed to meet with the parish team, which included, in addition to co-pastors Kemp and Bouchard, Sister Barbara Spears, the first
Catholic nun Roberts had ever encountered. "It was just very different for
me to deal with," Roberts later admitted. "I didn't know what I was walking
into." Nevertheless the team members convinced Roberts that they understood the nature and purpose of the gospel idiom and what it would mean for
the liturgy at their parish. He temporized, suggesting that he share the job
with Kirk Hams, a musician friend. But the team was adamant: they wanted
him and him alone. Finally, after prayer and consultation with friends and
despite his family's continued opposition—"you can't do this, we raised you
better than this," his mother told him—he accepted the position. (Later the
Roberts family would become firm friends of St. Augustine's, an early example of the choir's evangelizing powers.)

In preparation for the new group's debut in April 1977, Roberts started
working with its original thirteen members weeks earlier. He faced a formidable challenge. It quickly became apparent that the group knew nothing
about gospel music, its performance style or the discipline required to express its message musically. Nor could the co-pastors supply the Protestant
newcomer with any detailed manual outlining the requirements of the
Catholic liturgy. Kemp's advice was to the point: "Just so long as you have
an entrance song, offertory and communion hymns, and a closing hymn,

you'll be all right. Just start there." Which is exactly what the choir did. Roberts began with simple but effective gospel music like the *Alleluia* attributed to Andre Crouch and a few old spirituals like *Let Us Break Bread Together* that seemed appropriate to the sections of the mass. The early repertoire was limited in part because the director was pressed to find pieces that were authentic gospel music and not simply jazzed-up hymns. While scouring for appropriate music, Roberts achieved an early breakthrough when he successfully recruited a small number of new members from Howard University, some lapsed Catholics and all knowledgeable singers. (These were the first of the many lapsed Catholics who would return to the Church under the influence of the music.) These newcomers formed the nucleus of the choir's various sections, insuring that the four sections could maintain their parts. Tenor Bill Tucker was the mainstay of these newcomers, who also included Ruth (Claire) Gidney, Darleen Cockfield, and bass Richard Magruder.

The choir's initial performance practices and the congregation's reaction to gospel music offered a marked contrast to the triumphant experiences of later times. The little group sang from their assigned places in the church's first two pews, only occasionally at Roberts's direction turning to face a silent congregation. The singers were accompanied on a battered piano that was rolled in on its old iron castors for the 12:30 mass. With the help of several fund raisers, the parish purchased choir robes. Concerned that they be liturgically correct, Kemp and Roberts visited a Boston monastery to examine appropriate fabrics and styles. In the end the choir was decked out in robes similar to the albs worn by the priests and deacons.[43]

White robes were appropriate, considering the frosty reception the group received from the people. Participation of the congregation was central to gospel singing, but the few people who attended the 12:30 mass were not only reserved and restrained in their reaction to the music but markedly cool to Roberts's efforts. "If looks could kill," he recalled, "I would be dead." There was little appreciation for the choir and its music, and a discouraged director would quickly and quietly leave the church after mass—"I'd just get out of there."

Despite the poor reception, Roberts persisted. Although most gospel choristers do not read music, the new director was first and foremost an educator, who wanted his singers to be well-rounded musicians. He started classes in theory, sight reading, and ear training to build up the choir's skills, and in 1983 made sight-reading a membership requirement. His

43. In later years choir members purchased their own robes, for which they received a refund upon their departure. See PCM, 9 Nov 1987,

classes had a strong spiritual emphasis, and all sessions began with long and heartfelt prayer. At the same time he was a strict disciplinarian, who roundly chided the absentees and latecomers for their sins and demanded that rehearsals be serious musical occasions, not social gatherings. The parish council also issued periodic calls for a more disciplined choir at mass and in rehearsals.[44] In time these efforts paid off. By 1979 the parish could take satisfaction in a carefully trained gospel choir of nearly forty voices. It was accompanied, in addition to the piano, by a bass guitar (played initially by Father Kemp's brother Paul) and drums, first by Hannibal Taylor and then by Sherman Blair, an instrumental soloist with whom the congregation would come to enjoy a close affinity. These were the first of what would eventually become six instrumentalists accompanying the choir's performance. To the chagrin of some of the parish's old guard, these instrumentalists received a modest stipend. For all his work, Roberts was paid $225 per month.

By 1979 also the congregation at the 12:30 mass had begun its spectacular growth. Led for the most part by the parish's younger contingent and increasing numbers of visitors, the crowd began to assume a more active role in the liturgy. The key to this change was the presence of a strong cantor. After Roberts got his musical forces trained to an acceptable level, he acquired John Butler, an active member of the parish team and a compelling leader, as cantor. Roberts alluded to the vital role of the cantor in gospel-based liturgy in the introduction to his *Mass of St. Augustine:* "In addition to the classical choral part writing, the congregation must provide a basic foundation for the effective performance of the mass."[45] Under Butler's direction the congregation soon became an active participant, and the old church began to vibrate with the new sounds and lively rhythms.

The growing popularity of the gospel choir only served to accentuate the division in the parish over the role of the church in post-riot Washington. Many questioned whether gospel songs were a valid form of musical expression in a Catholic Church. It had never been difficult to justify what the traditional choir did, because it did what choirs had always done in church, and its performances had won St. Augustine's fame in the past. But some still clung to the idea that gospel music in a Catholic setting was outrageous, that rocking and clapping and shouting out loud in church was

44. Memo, Roberts to Gospel Choir Members, n.d. (ca Sep 1983), sub: Review and Direction, SAA. At one time the parish's Worship and Church committee asked Father Kelley and Gail Jackson to address the gospel choir on proper conduct in the sanctuary. See PCM, 9 Nov 1987.

45. *Mass of St. Augustine*, Chicago: Gregorian Institute of America, 1978.

wrong. Somehow the conflict over the music program came to symbolize for both factions the conflicting viewpoints over the parish's future. Those dedicated to maintaining the status quo, to protecting St. Augustine's traditional middle-class values and respectability in an era of upheaval, clung to the old choir, now inelegantly designated "the 10 o'clock choir," as the symbol of their dedication to the Church's traditional liturgy and the parish's past glories. The progressives, generally younger and newer members of the congregation, embraced the gospel choir, not only for the new meaning it gave the liturgy, but because the fellowship it engendered symbolized the social activism they espoused.

Anxious to bridge the gulf between the two factions, Father Kemp turned to the musicians to lead the way. He convinced the parish council that the solution to the dangerous division should start with the choirs. In 1979 he appointed Leon Roberts Director of Liturgical Music, with full control of both choirs and with a charter to unify the music ministry. Roberts was also expected to begin a children's choir and teach music in the school. This multiplicity of assignments meant that Roberts would be working full time for the parish directing, teaching, and composing. It also justified the council's paying him a living wage.[46] Roberts realized that each Sunday liturgy appealed to a specific audience, each with a unique mindset and a pronounced preference in church music. The disunity arising from these differences had been exacerbated by the individual and often competing styles of the various directors and cantors. His major challenge was to devise a way to get everyone to celebrate together. This was particularly true during the year's major feasts, when all elements of the divided parish came together for mass. He wanted to devise a unifying concept, using music found acceptable and satisfying to all factions. That meant developing a common appreciation for the emerging body of church music composed or arranged by African-American composers while maintaining respect for parish traditions. The need for music that transcended modern gospel music and the hymnody of the traditional Catholic choir inspired Roberts to begin his own successful career as a composer.

Before these serious matters could be dealt with, the new director faced an immediate crisis in the choir loft. His first meetings with the 10 o'clock choir—which he renamed the "Chorale," to more accurately describe the weighty purpose and style of the group—were, in his word, "awkward." In fact the choir was in near rebellion. Some members objected to what they

46. Added to Roberts's compensation was his job as director of the Mackin High School Chorus and his rent-free quarters and office space at 1419 V Street. Roberts would receive substantial raises in 1987 and 1988. See PCM, 2 May 1988.

considered Roberts's evangelical emphasis on the Spirit. Like many traditional Catholics they were uncomfortable with his insistence that practice
begin with spontaneous prayer. Some questioned the wisdom of appointing a
young man as director of a group whose members had been singing the masterworks of choral literature for decades, overlooking the fact that he had
been trained as a classical choral conductor in Howard's prestigious musical department. Above all, most feared that he intended to transform them
into some kind of gospel choir, "to whoop and holler," as one member joked
about the new sounds in the church. Such misgivings prompted many members to retire, leaving Roberts with the task of building a whole new choir.
He turned first to the gospel choir for help. Six members who could read
music volunteered to sing in both groups (thereby imitating Ralph Biscoe, a
longtime member and chairman of the Chorale, who had also sung in the
gospel choir since its early days and remained a valued member of both).
Roberts also brought in James Jones, a gifted keyboard artist from Howard
University and a member of Roberts Revival, to replace the departing organist, Richard Metcalfe. (The peripatetic Metcalfe would return to the
parish for a third and last time in the early 1980s to replace Jones.)

After several years of arduous work the Chorale was reconstituted as a
30-voice ensemble. It continued to perform the familiar masterpieces, although Roberts insisted that the still-popular but artistically suspect *Seven
Last Words* be scrapped. Instead, new composers were heard and the use of
soloists became common. Roberts had always been concerned about the
placement of the choirs. After some early experimentation, the gospel choir
had taken up its highly visible position above and behind the altar facing
the congregation. Now several years later he decided it was time to get the
Chorale out of the organ loft, which he considered a place for singers in the
"performance mode," and into the sanctuary, a place for a choir in the "music ministry mode" ordained by Vatican II reforms. In 1983 the Chorale,
clad for the first time in choir robes, took its "rightful place," as the parish
council reported, in front of the congregation. At the same time Father
Mudd, the pastor, announced that the council had authorized spending
$17,000 for the purchase of a large electronic organ to support congregation-
al singing and to accompany the chorale in the sanctuary. In time the parish
council would inaugurate a special organ fund to solicit the large sums
needed to restore the pipe organ, a goal still to be realized.[47]

47. PCM, 13 Oct 1983. The parish council appointed an organ committee (including Roberts, Dines, Metcalfe, and Eileen Gunther, organist at Foundry United
Methodist and noted radio personality) to explore the possibility of restoration. The
committee raised more than $20,000 in pledges, nowhere near the hundreds of thou-

From the start Roberts's aim was fusion of the parish's musical forces into a single choir capable of expert performances in both classical and gospel idioms. An early step in this process was his decision to stage a performance of Handel's *Messiah* employing all three choirs with full orchestra. The gospel group opposed the idea, some complaining that "we don't do that kind of music." Even his colleagues around town thought Roberts was kidding when he announced the event, but he persisted, and eventually the gospel singers came around. They learned the difficult music and participated with the Chorale and the school choir in successful presentations of its exacting choruses in two consecutive holiday seasons. Later the combined group would perform excerpts from Verdi's *Aida* with the D.C. Youth Orchestra in Constitution Hall. Ironically, the experience of singing Handel and Verdi with the Chorale and full orchestra changed the gospel choir's sound. In Roberts's estimation, the tone became more refined, tighter, and musically more appealing. Others seemed to agree. It was after these performances that the congregation at the 12:30 mass registered another sharp increase in size. Now worshippers packed the pews, filled the aisles, and crowded the loft.

On the other hand, efforts to move the Chorale toward a closer association with the gospel sound was more difficult, because serious composers were only then beginning to write music in the African-American tradition suitable for the Catholic liturgy. As a composer Roberts differed with famous precursors like Father Rivers and Sister Thea, who wanted to create a soul mass (or soulful mass as they sometimes called it) that fused gospel music with the liturgy. Roberts adopted a different approach, which began by examining the meaning of the words in the mass and then trying to express them in musical terms appropriate to the gospel music idiom.[48] This was the way his first important liturgical composition, *The Mass of St. Augustine*, had been conceived in 1978. Roberts later described that moment of inspiration:

I remember one day going into the empty church. I was frustrated because I really wanted this to work, and I wanted people to feel good about it. So I prayed and sat at the piano. All of a sudden the sun hit the rose window at the back of the church, and the light came straight through to me. Suddenly I started playing as the tears began running down my cheeks. All the parts of the mass started coming out of me: the "Lord Have Mercy," "Gloria," the Responsoral Psalm,

---

sands needed for restoration. See PCM, 2 May 1988 and 13 Mar 1989, and rpt of Organ Fund Steering committee, 28 Apr 1986. All in SAA.

48. For further discussion of these different approaches, see *Baltimore Afro-American*, 15 Aug 1981, and *Washington Times*, 13 Jun 1987.

and the setting for the eucharistic acclamation. I knew that God intended for me to do that because that was the first time in my life anything like it had happened. And it hasn't happened like that since!

Roberts knew he must not stop with this one liturgical composition what with his choirs hungry for more mass settings. He continued writing, eventually producing among others the *Mass of St. Martin de Porres* and *Deliver the Word!*, a collection of original compositions and musical settings of Scripture for choir. He was inclined to such titles, he explained, because he wanted the music fused with both the parish's spirituality and its history.[49] Both choirs would perform these masses and sing these hymns at major feasts that brought the whole congregation together. The less demanding passages were also employed by the cantors at regular Sunday masses.

Despite the efforts of the parish to blunt the rivalry between the two choirs, tension persisted well into the 1980s, tension that caused the music director to precede with great care. Roberts concluded that it was up to him to smooth things out, and much of his time was spent reaching out to people, telling all who would listen that "it's ok, we're all part of the same family, there's nothing negative going to happen here. It's all part of God's program." On a practical level he began conducting well-attended workshops in 1982 on the nature of gospel music to demonstrate just how the synthesis of West African and African-American music was a celebration of the Christian experience of salvation and hope and a declaration of black selfhood. (These workshops evolved into the popular annual Rejoice! conferences that brought musicians together from all around the country.) Roberts constantly exhorted the congregation to participate actively in the mass, extolled those who made "a joyful noise," and pleaded with the judgmental for more understanding for those who in increasing numbers were finding so much satisfaction in this lively expression of the Spirit.[50] His education program required persistence. As late as 1986 members of the parish council were still noting "different perceptions and attitudes about the 12:30 mass," and calling for forums and workshops "to bring about a better understanding over the differing dynamics in worship."[51]

At the same time Roberts pushed the gospel crowd to support the Chorale and chided those musicians who had failed to attend the concerts sponsored by the traditional choir.[52] His concern may have been misdirect-

49. *CS*, 29 Oct 1981.
50. Memo, Roberts to PC, Staff, and worship and church committee, 23 Mar 1982, sub: A Statement on Gospel Music in the Parish of SS. Paul and Augustine, SAA.
51. PCM, 12 Nov 1986.
52. Memo, Roberts to Gospel Choir Members, n.d. (ca. Sep 1983).

ed. In later years he would report to members of the council that that
Chorale habitually received greater support from its congregation than did
the gospel choir. He concluded that more praise—"stroking," he called it—
might strengthen the ministry of the younger group.[53] Actually, for the
gospel choir the decade of the 1980s was one of increasing fame and fortune. Even more than their nineteenth-century forebears, these musicians
concertised extensively, all in the name of evangelization, ecumenicism,
and fundraising. In 1981 the prestigious music publisher, the Gregorian Institute of America, released a recording of the *Mass of St. Augustine* as sung
by the gospel choir. Four years later the parish council sponsored production of an album of music from Roberts's *Deliver the Word* popularized by
the choir at the 12:30 mass. The album was designed as a major outreach to
the local community, and cuts from the record were heard regularly on
Washington's radio stations. Yet the recording's premier, celebrated at the
choir's eighth anniversary concert in Howard University's Cramton Auditorium, underscored another mission. The evening's program netted $2,900
for the music ministry, and two years later the parish council could report
that the recording itself had become profitable.[54]

The choir's frequent performance for fees necessitated the appointment
of a business manager. In 1990 an anxious parish council, leery about the
choir's affairs, decided to form a steering committee composed of choir representatives and members of the council to provide advice and logistical
support for the musicians.[55] For several years the parish's concert series was
an important source of revenue. The Chorale had sponsored a formal series
beginning in 1983, and in 1988 the parish council agreed to underwrite a St.
Augustine Concert Series to include guest artists of national reputation like
the immensely popular Sweet Honey and the Rock and large groups like the
Howard University Choir. The major event of the series was always the annual Christmas concert that combined the musical forces of the parish in a
unified performance.

Meanwhile the gospel choir continued to concertize widely in keeping
with its evangelical and ecumenical missions. Crowds at places like the Old
Post Office Pavilion, Constitution Hall, the Kennedy Center, and the National (Episcopal) Cathedral experienced the same Spirit-filled performanc-

53. Worship and church committee minutes, 9 Mar 1987.

54. PCM, 21 Dec 1985 and 9 Nov 1987. See also Monica Barron's article on the
gospel choir in *St. Augustine Newsletter* (Fall 1985).

55. PCM, 9 Mar, 17 Oct, and 9 Nov 1987. See also, memo, Melvin J. Gipson, pres.,
St. Augustine Gospel Choir, to worship and church cmte, 9 Oct 1990, sub: St. Augustine Gospel Choir Activities, SAA.

AN APPRECIATIVE AUDIENCE. Pope John Paul II receives members of the Gospel choir (director Leon Roberts at the Pope's right) after attending their concert at the Vatican in 1990.

es as members of Alcoholics Anonymous, prisoners at Lorton, or poor neighbors during impromptu concerts in Fourteenth Street alleys. (Roberts later confessed that the reaction of the Lorton inmates to the choir's message of hope and understanding gave him the most joy in his ministry.) The choir also appeared regularly in area churches, sometimes in joint performances with other Christian groups, continuing the tradition begun with the musicians at Augustana Lutheran. The faith sharing and communal prayer that accompanied such music making in many Protestant churches like Foundry United Methodist, Roberts pointed out, helped strengthen the musicians spiritually while showing their Christian brothers and sisters how the beauty of the Catholic ritual combined with the cultural dynamics of the "Black Experience."[56]

The announcement of one of these ecumenical performances caused a

56. Memo, Roberts to Gospel Choir Members, n.d. (ca Sept 1983).

great ruckus that shoved a reluctant Father Mudd into the limelight. In 1983 the choir made a verbal commitment to perform in a fundraiser for the Metropolitan Community Church, a local church catering to the needs of homosexual Christians. St. Augustine counted a number of gay Catholics in its congregation and had always, as Father Kemp noted, shown "a sensitive ministry to persons who are homosexual." Mudd elaborated on this point, explaining that the parish "has been very open to all . . . struggling to do what God wants and to understand how he wants us to live. We try not to be judgmental of anyone." Nevertheless, after the implications of such a joint concert were discussed, Mudd decided to cancel the choir's participation, touching off a bruhaha in the press.[57] More important, the incident caused some anxious times for some choir members, who needed to reconcile the explicit teachings of the Church with the spirit that undergird their ministry. In the end, despite an embarrassed pastor, who said he had found himself coming across like a fundamentalist preacher, the issue quietly died down.

Throughout his years in the parish Roberts continued to pursue his goal of bridging the gap between the two choirs so that all the musical forces of the parish would be known simply as St. Augustine's choir. He was spurred on by the thought of one group able to sing a choral masterwork with precision and beauty a minute before turning to a rousing gospel piece with the spontaneity and joy that could move a congregation to swaying and clapping, to shedding tears and embracing neighbors. He thought his goal nearly realized in the wake of the music ministry's involvement in the *Lead Me, Guide Me* hymnal project, the first comprehensive collection of music reflecting both the African-American heritage and faith of black Catholics.[58] The compilation, performance, and eventual recording of this music involved all three choirs (including the school children) singing sacred music in all styles. Even then, however, some continued to resist. People from both choral traditions would question one piece or another, asking "why do we have to sing together?" Roberts's stock answer was a blunt and pointed plea for tolerance: "We are a family, and when we die we're bound for the same place."

His efforts to bring the choirs together peaked during 1990–91, around the time of the gospel choir's international tour. Successful appearances in cities like New York and Philadelphia in the late 1980s had preceded its

57. See, for example, *National Catholic Reporter*, 13 May 1983, and *CS*, 28 Apr 1983 (source of quotes).

58. *Lead Me, Guide Me* (Chicago: G.I.A. Publications, Inc., 1987). Roberts was an important contributor to this project which was directed by a group of black Catholic bishops and the National Black Catholic Clergy Caucus.

first international trip in 1990. Some of the singers, as members of Roberts Revival, had already participated in a sold-out tour of Japan sponsored by parishioner Albert Nellum, president of the Black Business Council, and the Arita family of Japan. (The Aritas initiated the project after attending a gospel mass at St. Augustine's during a tour of the United States.) This tour served as a prelude for a nine-day tour of Italy by the whole gospel choir, now 80-voices strong, during which it sang before audiences in Florence, Assisi, and during High Mass in St. Peter's in Rome, where members also enjoyed an audience with Pope John Paul II.[59]

Looking back at all the successes of the 1980s, a thoughtful director concluded that "the growing popularity of the liturgy at 12:30 mass revived St. Augustine's. As for developments during the time I was there, only God could have achieved something like that." It was not the gospel choir itself that deserved the praise, Roberts pointed out; rather it was the spirit of the people and the power of God working through the people. It was, in fact, music's ultimate gift to St. Augustine's, a parish that since its foundation many decades before had emphasized the power of music in the worship of God.

59. Both tours received extensive press coverage. See, for example, *Washington Post*, 14 Oct and 24 Dec 1990.

Pastors

Felix Barotti	1867–1881
Michael J. Walsh, S.S.J.	1881–1892
Paul Griffith	1892–1919
Alonzo J. Olds	1919–1957
George L. Gingras	1957–1970
Leonard F. Hurley	1970–1974
Raymond B. Kemp	1974–1981

(Andre Bouchard co-pastor until 1977)

John J. Mudd	1981–1990
Russell L. Dillard	1990–

Assistant Priests and Associate Pastors

Bartolomeo Sanmartino	1872–1875
Peter B. Tarro	1876–1881
Sebastian Rabbia	18??–18??
William Hooman, S.S.J.	1881, 1888–1892
Gerardus Wiersma, S.S.J.	1881–1883
Francis P. Kervick, S.S.J.	1881–1883
Cornelius Hurley, S.S.J.	1882–1887
Denis F. Hurley, S.S.J.	1883
John A. de Ruyter, S.S.J.	1883–1887
Richard T. Burke, S.S.J.	1885–1892

Patrick J. Fahey, S.S.J.	1890
George A. Dougherty	1892–1904
Francis X. Bischoff	1894–1907
Olonzo J. Olds	1904–1919
William A. Cahill	1905
Peter L. Ireton	1906–1907
James J. O'Connor	1907–1923
Nicholas Jaselli	1908–1912
William McVeigh	1912–1918
Andrew H. Mihm	1919–1922
Joseph J. Deppe	1921–1925
Robert J. Froehlich	1923–1930
James F. King	1925–1936
George M. Rankin	1930–1940
John E. Hamilton	1936–1946
Terence J. Evans	1936–1945
Francis P. Wagner	1940–1943
John P. Menash	1943–1945
A J. Mendelis	1945–1947
George V. Joyce	1946–1957
Joseph Scannell	1946–1948
John D. Benson	1947–1950
Harold F. Trehey	1951–1952
Anthony Bouvier	1953–1954
Charles Wilk	1954–1958
Roger P. Gallagher	1957–1964
Leonard F. Hurley	1958–1964
Bernardine Patterson, O.S.B.	1958–1959
Vincent P. Cieri	1961–1962
Geno C. Baroni	1962–1965
Carl F. Dianda	1964–1967
Ralph H. Dwan	1965–1967
Andre Bouchard	1965–1974
Paul P. Norton	1967
Raymond B. Kemp	1967–1974
Lewis Mangini, O.S.A.F.	1977
John P. Muffler	1978–1982
John J. Mudd	1977–1981
Michael J. Kelley	1982–1992
Edward Branch	1989
John Payne, O.S.A.	1990–1996

George W. Wilson	1992–1996
A Gregory Butta	1996–1998
Charles Green	1996–

Principals of St. Augustine's School

Mary T. Smith	1866–1867
(Girls division)	
Ambrose Queen	1866–1867
(Boys division)	
Sister Seraphina Noel, O.S.P.	1867–1875
(Girls division)	
John McCosker (& two unknown laymen)	1867–1875
(Boys division)	
Sister M. Angelica Holton, C.S.C.	1875–1885*
Sister M. Euphemia McConvery, C.S.C.	1877–1889
Sister M. Emerita Kelly, C.S.C.	1885–1888
Sister M. Scholastica Humphrey, C.S.C.	1885–1895
Sister M. Englebert Purcell, C.S.C.	1890–1895
Sister M. Eugracia Donahue, C.S.C.	1890–1895

(*Dates for the Holy Cross Sisters represent years at the school. The exact periods each served as principal are unknown.)

Sister M. Luke Russell, O.S.P.	1908–1916
Mother Mary Teresa Shockley, O.S.P.	1916–1924
Mother Rita Barrett, O.S.P.	1927–1930
Mother Dominica Saunders, O.S.P.	1930–1931
Mother M. Luke Russell, O.S.P.	1931–1934
Mother Dominica Saunders, O.S.P.	1934–1939
Mother Praxedes Stewart, O.S.P.	1939–1944
Mother M. Angela Wade, O.S.P.	1944–1955
Sister M. Consolata Gibson, O.S.P.	1955–1958
Mother M. Claude Hudlin, O.S.P.	1958–1966
Sister Marcellina Brooks, O.S.P.	1966–1968
Sister M. Reperata Clarke, O.S.P.	1968–1969
Sister Majella Neale, O.S.P.	1969–1970
Sister Frances Aileen Holly, O.S.P.	1970–1971
Charles E. Carter	1971–1974
Sister Barbara Spears, O.S.P.	1975–1983
Sister Ricardo Maddox, O.S.P.	1983–1989
Adela Acosta	1989–1994
Shelor Williams	1994–

Founding Members of the Congregation

[Note: the following roster was derived from available parish documents as well as early press notices, principally the lists compiled for the *St. Augustine's Gazette*, 2 February 1882, and *The New Century*, 21 February 1903. As far as can be determined, the definition of founding member in these sources included parishioners in the congregation before Father Barotti's arrival in 1867.]

Cecilia Ann Bean
Susan H. Bean
William Bell
William T. Benjamin
Mrs. John Bowie
Thomas Bowie
Louisa Bowser
John H. Butler
Samuel Butler
Victoria Byrne
Abraham Clark
Gabriel Coakley &
family
Magdaline Coakley
Phillips Coakley
Eliza Ann Cook
Grace Delaney
Grace Dyson
Gustavus Fluger
Ellen Freeman
Patrick Garner
Harriet Gay
Anna Gillen
Agnes Gray
Louisa Gray
Margaret Gray
William Green
Henry Grinnell
Eliza Hall
Jane Hall
John Hamilton

Annie Harrison
Mary A. Harrison
Francis Hawkins
Harriet Hunter
Basil Jackson
Daniel Jackson
Henry Jackson &
family
Mr. & Mrs. James F.
Jackson
Charles Johnson
Mr. & Mrs. Jones
Mr. & Mrs. Isaac
Landic
Mr. & Mrs. Vincent
Lemon
Eugene R. Lewis
Jeremiah Lowe
Mrs. Frances Madison
Bazil Mullen
Mr. & Mrs. Henry
Neal
Mary Parker
Mr. & Mrs. James
Penny
William Pinnion
Elizabeth Pullerson
Ambrose Queen
Victoria Queen
Lucy Ross
Mary Simms

Jane Smallwood
Mary T. Smith
Sarah Ann Smith
Mr. & Mrs. Thomas
Smith
Mr. & Mrs. William
H. Smith
Charity Solomon
Sarah Solomon
Henry Stephenson
Harriet Teagle
Jane Teagle
Alexander Thomas
George Thomas
Henry Thomas
Katie Thomas
Annie Turner
Elizabeth Turner
Mary Clara Turner
Mr. & Mrs. Henry
Warren
Nellie Warren
Romulus Warren
Nancy Weldon
John West
Marcellus West
William H. Wheeler
Mr. & Mrs. Paul
Wilson
Willis Young

Founding Members of the Parish Council

Gwendolyn Adams
Joseph Belfiore
Angela Bishop
Carl Bransford
Mae T. Brent
Mary C. Buckner
John L. Clark
Dr. Pinyon Cornish
Fred Correy
Belford Fisher
Mary L. Gardner

Lawrence C. Hill
Charles Holloway
Mary Houston
Walter A. Jones
Pauline J. Jones
Natalie Joy
Raymond Lucas
Blanche R. Lucas
Catherine McKillip
Frederick Maples
Albert Noppenberger

Irene Powell
Helen Reed
Esther A. Robinson
Clifton Spriggs
Ann Thomas
Juanita Tolson
Eula Trigg
Eugene Wingert
Ann Woodson

❦ BIBLIOGRAPHY

Abbreviations

AAB	Archives of the Archdiocese of Baltimore
AAW	Archives of the Archdiocese of Washington
ASSJ	Archives of the Society of St. Joseph (The Josephites)
BCR	*Baltimore Catholic Review*
CM	*Catholic Mirror*
CN	*Church News*
CS	*Catholic Standard*
DCPL	Public Library of the District of Columbia (Washingtoniana Collection)
HUA	Moorland-Spingarn Archives, Howard University
LC	Library of Congress
NARA	National Archives and Records Administration
OR	*War of the Rebellion: A Compilation of Official Records of the Union and Confederate Armies* (Washington)
PCM	Minutes of St. Augustine Parish Council
RCHS	*Records of the Columbia Historical Society*
SAA	St. Augustine's Parish Archives
SAB	Sulpician Archives, Baltimore

Manuscript and Archival Material

St. Augustine's parish has preserved an unusually rich collection of materials—manuscripts, correspondence, legal documents, and photographs—pertaining to its nineteenth- and early twentieth-century history.

Although the record of the post-World War II period during the later years of Msgr. Olds's pastorate is less complete, the comprehensiveness of the collection covering recent decades, especially since the formation of the parish council in 1967, must rival any parish archives in the archdiocese. This important collection is complimented by the holdings of the Archives of the Archdiocese of Baltimore. There, papers of archbishops from Spalding to Curley, parish *notitiae*, the chancery collection of documents pertaining to selected Washington parishes (largely the work of chancellors like Msgr. Nelligan and Bishop Corrigan), and the diocesan necrology file contain scores of documents that help detail the evolution of the parish during its first eighty years. The Archives of the Archdiocese of Washington also contains some items of importance for a parish history. The Josephite Archives not only has on file hundreds of documents relating to the parish during the eleven years that the Mill Hill Fathers served at St. Augustine's, but, thanks to the indefatigable labors of archivist Father Peter E. Hogan and his able assistants, it possesses a unique and comprehensive collection of materials relating to the whole history of African-American Catholicism.

Other archives are important to any account of specific events in the history of the parish. The Grimke, Turner, and Cole collections in the Moorland-Spingarn Archives at Howard University, for example, shed considerable light on The Federation of Colored Catholics and the NAACP in Washington and the connection of these organizations to the parish. The Archives of the District of Columbia has a number of documents of importance to the parish history, especially the materials collected by Dorothy Provine on the free black families of Washington before the Civil War.

Interviews

In the course of his research the author interviewed the following people with special knowledge of the parish. Notes on these conversations—in some cases full transcripts of the interview—have been deposited in the parish archives.

Msgr. John D. Benson	Vincent DeForest	Esther H. Jackson
Dr. Loretta Butler	Rev. Carl F. Dianda	Rev. Mr. Bernard C.
Sister Mary Alice	George Dines, Jr.	Johnson
Chineworth, O.S.P.	Ralph H. Dwan	Pauline J. Jones
Bernard and Julia Cole	Archbishop Philip	Rev. George V. Joyce
Dr. Paul F. Cooke	M. Hannan	Rev. Michael J. Kelley
Dr. Paul F. Cornely	Msgr. Leonard F.	Rev. Raymond B.
Linda Davidson	Hurley	Kemp

Maxine Le Gall	Rev. John J. Mudd	Mr. and Mrs. Charles
Sister Charlotte	Sister Majella Neale,	Stewart
Marshall, O.S.P.	O.S.P.	Eunice Q. Taylor
Dominic Moulden	Elizabeth Pohlhaus	John T. Taylor
William Moore	Leon C. Roberts	Willis Thomas

In addition the author received permission from Marilyn W. Nickels to quote from her interviews with Dr. Thomas W. Turner, William and Mary C. Buckner, and Horace McKenna, S.J., conducted in 1973 and 1974 in preparation for her work on the Federation of Colored Catholics. Copies of these interviews are also on file in the parish archives.

Newspapers and Bulletins

The author systematically screened the following Washington newspapers: *Evening Star* and *Sunday Star*, *The Bee*, and the *Catholic Standard*. Also consulted were the *Post, Times-Herald, National Intelligencer, National Republican, Metropolitan*, and *Washington African-American*. Four other Catholic newspapers (including two published in Baltimore) were systematically screened: the *Catholic Mirror, New Century, Church News*, and *Baltimore Catholic Review*. Especially valuable for some aspects of the nineteenth-century story are three Josephite publications: *The American Supplement to St. Joseph's Foreign Mission Advocate, St. Joseph's Advocate*, and *The Colored Harvest*. The parish archives contains a complete run of parish bulletins from the mid-1960s to the present, along with a scattering of issues (with various names) from earlier decades.

Secondary Materials

Abell, William S., ed. *Patrick Cardinal O'Boyle as His Friends Knew Him.* Washington, 1986.

Anderson, George M. "The Civil War Diary of John Abell Morgan, S.J., A Jesuit Scholastic of the Maryland Province." *Records of the American Catholic Historical Society of Philadelphia.* 101 (Fall 1990): 33–54.

Billon, Merton L. *Benjamin Lundy and the Struggle for Negro Freedom.* Urbana: University of Illinois Press, 1966.

Borchert, James. *Alley Life in Washington: Family, Community, Religion, and Folklife in the City, 1850–1970.* Urbana: University of Illinois Press, 1980.

Brown, Letitia W. *Free Negroes in the District of Columbia, 1790–1846.* New York: Oxford University Press, 1972.

_____. "Residence Patterns of Negroes in the District of Columbia, 1800–1860." *RCHS* 69–70 (1969–70): 66–79.

Bryan, Wilhelmus B. *A History of the National Capital.* 2 vols. New York: Macmillan, 1914–16.

Carpenter, Frank G. *Carp's Washington.* New York: McGraw-Hill, Co., 1960.

Clark-Lewis, Elizabeth. "From Servant to 'Day Worker': A Study of Selected Household Service Workers in Washington, D.C., 1900–1926." Ph.D. dissertation, University of Maryland, 1983.

Congress of Colored Catholics of the United States. *Three Catholic Afro-American Congresses.* Cincinnati: The American Catholic Tribune, 1893; repr. Arno Press, New York, 1978.

Conley, Rory T. "'All One in Christ' Patrick Cardinal O'Boyle, the Church of Washington and the Struggle for Racial Justice, 1948–1973." Master's thesis, The Catholic University of America, 1992.

Conwill, Giles. "Black and Catholic." *America* (29 Mar 1980): 265–67.

Corrigan, Mary Beth. "The Ties That Bind: The Pursuit of Community and Freedom Among Slaves and Free Blacks in the District of Columbia, 1800–1860." In *Southern City, National Ambition: The Growth of Early Washington.* Ed. Howard Gillette. Washington: George Washington University Center for Washington Area Studies and the American Institute of Architects, 1995.

Corrigan, Owen B. *The Catholic Schools of the Archdiocese of Baltimore: A Study in Diocesan History.* Baltimore, 1924.

Cromwell, John. "First Negro Churches of Washington," *Journal of Negro History.* 7, no. 1 (Jan 1922): 65–106.

Dabney, Lillian. *The History of Schools for Negroes in the District of Columbia, 1807–1947.* Washington: The Catholic University of America Press, 1949.

Davis, Cyprian. *The History of Black Catholics in the United States.* New York: Crossroads Publ. Co., 1991.

_____. "The Holy See and American Black Catholics." *U.S. Catholic Historian* 7 (1988): 157–79.

Dolan, Jay. *The American Catholic Experience: A History from Colonial Times to the Present.* New York: Doubleday, 1985.

Duncan, Richard R. "Catholics and the Church in the Antebellum Upper South." In *Catholics in the Old South: Essays on Church and Culture.* Ed. Randall M. Miller and Jon L. Wakelyn. Macon, GA: Mercer University Press, 1983.

Ellis, John Tracy. *Documents of American Catholic History.* Milwaukee: Bruce Publ., 1956.

————. The *Life of James Cardinal Gibbons, Archbishop of Baltimore, 1834–1921*. 2 vols. Milwaukee: Bruce Publ., 1952.

Fitzpatrick, Sandra, and Maria R. Goodwin. *The Guide to Black Washington: Places and Events of Historical and Cultural Significance in the Nation's Capital*. New York: Hippocrene Books, 1990.

Foley, Albert S. "The Catholic Church and the Washington Negro." Ph.D. dissertation, University of North Carolina, 1950.

Gatewood, Willard B. *Aristocrats of Color: The Black Elite, 1880–1920*. Bloomington: Indiana University Press, 1990.

Gemmill, Jane W. *Notes on Washington, or Six Years at the National Capital*. Washington: Brentano Bros., 1883.

Gillard, John T. *The Catholic Church and the Negro*. Baltimore, 1928.

Green, Constance McLaughlin. *The Secret City: A History of Race Relations in the Nation's Capital*. Princeton: Princeton University Press, 1967.

————. *Washington: A History of the Capital, 1800–1950*. 2 vols. Princeton: Princeton University Press, 1976.

Hennesey, James. *American Catholics: A History of the Roman Catholic Community in the United States*. New York: Oxford University Press, 1981.

Hines, Christian. *Early Recollections of Washington City*. Washington, 1866, repr. Junior League of Washington, 1981.

Hogan, Peter E. "Archbishop Curley and the Blacks." *The Catholic Historical Society of Washington Newsletter* 4, no. 1 (Jan–Mar 1996): 2–16.

————. "Catholic Missionary Efforts for the Negro Before the Coming of the Josephites." Paper delivered at The Catholic University of America, 1947.

————. "Josephite History: Origins of the American Josephites." *The Josephite Harvest*. 95, no. 3 (Autumn 1992): 1–14.

Johnson, Lorenzo D. *The Churches and Pastors of Washington, D.C.* New York: Dodd, 1857.

Johnson, Thomas R. "The City on the Hill: Race Relations in Washington, D.C., 1865–1885." Ph.D. dissertation, University of Maryland, 1975.

Kemp. Raymond B. *A Journey in Faith: An Experience of the Catechumenate*. New York: Sadler, Inc., 1979.

Kirrane, John P. "The Establishment of Negro Parishes and the Coming of the Josephites, 1863–1871." Master's thesis, The Catholic University of America, 1932.

Kuhn, Sister M. Campion. "The Sisters Go East—And Stay." Paper delivered at Congregation of the Sisters of the Holy Cross Annual Historical Conference, 1983.

Lackner, Joseph H. "Dan A. Rudd, Editor of the *American Catholic Tribune*

From Bardstown to Cincinnati." *Catholic Historical Review* 80 (Apr 1994): 258–81.

LaFarge, John. *The Manner Is Ordinary.* New York: Harcourt, Brace, 1954.

Lamanna, Richard A., and Jay J. Coakley. "The Catholic Church and the Negro." In *Contemporary Catholicism in the United States.* Ed. Philip Gleason. Notre Dame: University of Notre Dame Press, 1969.

Leech, Margaret. *Reveille in Washington, 1861–1865.* New York: Harper & Bros., 1941.

McColgan, Daniel T. *A Century of Charity: The First One Hundred Years of St. Vincent de Paul in the United States.* 2 vols. Milwaukee: Bruce Publ., 1951.

McGreevy, John T. *Parish Boundaries: The Catholic Encounter with Race in the Twentieth-Century Urban North.* Chicago: University of Chicago Press, 1996.

McMurray, Gerald R. "Remembering Geno Baroni." *America* 151 (22 Sep 1984): 145–48.

McNally, Arthur. "Green Pastures in a Black Ghetto." *Sign* 45 (Jan 1966): 18–27.

Marchell, John P. "Patrick Francis Kenrick, 1851–1863: The Baltimore Years." Ph.D. dissertation, The Catholic University of America, 1965.

Marty, Martin E. *Pilgrims in Their Own Land: Five Hundred Years of Religion in America.* Boston: Little Brown, 1984.

Miller, Randall M. "The Failed Mission: The Catholic Church and Black Catholics in the Old South." In *Catholics in the Old South: Essays on Church and Culture.* Ed. Randall M. Miller and Jon L. Wakelyn. Macon, GA: Mercer University Press, 1983.

Misch, Edward J. "The American Bishops and the Negro from the Civil War to the Third Plenary Council of Baltimore (1865–1884)." Ph.D. dissertation, Pontifical Gregorian University, 1968.

Mudd, John J. "The Oldest Black Church in Washington, D.C.: A Parish Ministry Model." *Charities USA* (June 1984).

Muffler, John P. "This Far By Faith: A History of St. Augustine's The Mother Church for Black Catholics in the Nation's Capital." Ed.D. dissertation, Teachers College, Columbia University, 1989.

Murphy, D. I. "Lincoln, Foe of Bigotry." *America* (11 Feb 1928): 432–33.

Neary, Timothy B. "Creating a City of God in the Nation's Capital: The Work of Saint Augustine Parish School." Senior American Studies thesis, Georgetown University, 1993.

Nickels, Marilyn W. *Black Catholic Protest and the Federated Colored Catholics 1917–1933: Three Perspectives.* New York: Garland Pub., 1988.

_____. "The Federated Colored Catholics: A Study of Three Variant Perspectives on Racial Justice as Perceived by John LaFarge, William Markoe, and Thomas Turner." Ph.D. dissertation, The Catholic University of America, 1975.

Ochs, Stephen J. *Desegregating the Altar: The Josephites and the Struggle for Black Priests, 1871–1960.* Baton Rouge: Louisiana State University Press, 1990.

O'Connor, John J. "A Man's A Man for A' That." *Interracial Review* 20, no. 6 (June 1947): 86–89.

O'Neil, Robert. *Cardinal Herbert Vaughan, Archbishop of Westminster, Bishop of Salford, Founder of the Mill Hill Missionaries.* Tunbridge Wells, Kent: Burns & Oates, 1995.

O'Rourke, Lawrence M. *Geno, The Life and Mission of Geno Baroni.* New York: The Paulist Press, 1991.

Osborne, William. "Slavery's Sequel: A Freeman's Odyssey," *Jubilee* 3 (Sep 1955): 10–23.

Philibert, Helene, Estelle, and Imogene. *Saint Matthew's of Washington, 1840–1940.* Baltimore: A. Hoen and Co., 1940.

Polite, Vernon C. "Getting the Job Done Well: African American Students and Catholic Schools." *Journal of Negro Education* 61 (Spring 1992): 211–22.

Powell, Francis J. "A Study of the Structure of the Freed Black Family in Washington, D.C., 1850–1880." Ars.D. dissertation, The Catholic University of America, 1980.

Procter, John Clagett, ed. *Washington Past and Present: A History.* New York: Lewis History Publ., 1930.

Provine, Dorothy S., compl. and ed. *District of Columbia Free Negro Registrars, 1821–1861.* 2 vols. Bowie, MD: Heritage Books, 1996.

Reynolds, Edward. *Jesuits for the Negro.* New York: The America Press, 1949.

Rivers, Clarence J. "'Thank God We Aint What We Was': The State of the Liturgy in the Black Catholic Community." *U.S. Catholic Historian* 5 (1986): 81–89.

Rouse, Michael Francis. "A Study of the Development of Negro Education Under Catholic Auspices in Maryland and the District of Columbia." *The Johns Hopkins University Studies in Education,* 22. Baltimore: The Johns Hopkins Press, 1935.

Scheips, Paul J. "The Washington Riot of 1968." U.S. Army Center of Military History, 1992.

Seale, William. *President's House: A History.* 2 vols. Washington: White House Historical Association, 1986.

Spalding, Thomas W. *Martin John Spalding: American Churchman.* Washington: The Catholic University of America Press, 1973.

_____. *The Premier See: A History of the Archdiocese of Baltimore. 1789–1989.* Baltimore: The Johns Hopkins University Press, 1989.

_____. "The Negro Catholic Congresses, 1889–1894." *Catholic Historical Review* 55 (Oct 1969): 337–57.

Tenth/Two Hundredth Anniversary of the Church of SS. Paul and Augustine, Sunday, December 12, 1971. Ed. Charles Whitby, Jr., and Gladys Scott Roberts. Washington, 1971.

Wade, Richard C. *Slavery in the Cities: The South, 1820–1860.* New York: Oxford University Press, 1964.

Warnagiris, Sister M. Clare. "Maria Becraft and Black Catholic Education, 1827–1832." Paper presented to Professor Benjamin Quarles, Morgan State College, 1974.

U.S. Office of Education. *Special Report of the Commissioner of Education on the Improvement of Public Schools in the District of Columbia, 1871.* Washington: Government Printing Office, 1871; repr. in part by Arno Press and the New York Times, 1969, as *History of Schools for the Colored Population.*

Weitzman, Louis G. *One Hundred Years of Catholic Charities in the District of Columbia.* Washington: The Catholic University of America, 1931.

Whitby, Charles, et al., eds. *Monsignor Alonzo J. Olds: Golden Jubilee of the Priesthood, 1903–1953.* Washington, 1953.

Williams, George Washington. *A History of the Negro Troops in the War of the Rebellion, 1861–1865.* New York: Negro University Press, 1969. Repr. of Harper Bro. Edition, 1888.

Williams, Melvin R. "Blacks in Washington, D.C., 1860–1870." Ph.D. dissertation, The Johns Hopkins University, 1975.

_____. "Blueprint for Change." *RCHS* 48 (1971–1972): 359–93.

INDEX

The Emergence of a Black Catholic Community: St. Augustine's in Washington was designed and composed in Bodoni Book by Kachergis Book Design, Pittsboro, North Carolina; printed on 60-pound Glatfelter Natural Smooth and bound by Braun-Brumfield, Inc., Ann Arbor, Michigan.